Y0-BQN-834

ANTITRUST POLICIES

VOLUME I

THE TWENTIETH CENTURY FUND, founded in 1919 by the late Edward A. Filene, is a nonprofit, philanthropic foundation conducting research and public education on economic and social problems. The Fund's income, administered as a public trust by a Board of Trustees, is devoted to its own research and educational activities. The Trustees choose subjects for research studies and vote the appropriation to cover the expenses of each project. The Trustees, however, assume no responsibility for the facts and opinions contained in research reports.

COMMITTEE ON ANTITRUST POLICY. The special committee listed below was appointed by the Fund to advise and comment on this project, without, however, assuming responsibility for the author's findings of fact or his analysis of them.

ANTITRUST POLICIES

AMERICAN EXPERIENCE IN TWENTY INDUSTRIES

BY SIMON N. WHITNEY

NEW YORK 1958

THE TWENTIETH CENTURY FUND

Library of Congress Catalog Card Number: 58-9954

Printed in the United States of America by
Wm. F. Fell Company, Philadelphia, Pennsylvania

FOREWORD

The Twentieth Century Fund has a long record of interest in the forms, organization and significance of "big business." During the thirties a special research staff was appointed to study the role of the giant corporation in the American economy. Two volumes — *Big Business: Its Growth and Its Place* and *How Profitable Is Big Business?* — subsequently incorporated the main results of its work. The second world war, inevitably pushing competitive factors into the background, diverted this line of inquiry; but after 1944 the Fund returned to this fundamental concern, adapting its approach to the changed conditions of the world. A research team headed by George W. Stocking and Myron W. Watkins produced three major studies dealing with international cartels and domestic monopolies.

The emphasis of these scholarly works and committee reports was on the need for preserving competition. "The trend toward concerted action or collective controls in economic affairs, with or without government sanction or direction, is unmistakable," wrote Professors Stocking and Watkins. "But it is not, in our view, inevitable." It seemed to the Trustees of the Fund that work still remained to be done in ascertaining the actual results of policies adopted by the United States in this field. How effective had the antitrust acts actually been in curbing monopolies and restoring the conditions of competition?

The present study, by Simon N. Whitney, was undertaken to explore this question. Neither the Fund nor the author has supposed that complete or final answers were to be found. They offer this work in the belief that only as students venture into this field can a reliable evaluation of our competitive policy ever be made. Dr. Whitney's method has been to take the situation as it presents itself in various industries showing how a multiplicity of factors has been responsible for the degree of competition or of monopoly which prevails. The antitrust laws have been, of course, a significant and shaping influence in the total scheme; but Dr. Whitney, who adds the skepticism of the historian to the trained analysis of the economist, avoids suggesting that any single cause is determining. The structure of American business is what it is because of a complicated interaction of events and circumstances. Law can affect, but it cannot totally direct the result.

Dr. Whitney was Associate Economist of the Fund when this work was begun, and later became Chief of the Research Department. An opportunity to serve as Chief Economist and Director of the Bureau of Economics of the Federal Trade Commission was subsequently offered him, and in 1956 he accepted the post, which challenged him to submit many of his ideas to the test of action. The change necessarily delayed completion of the study, but the Fund is grateful for the way Dr. Whitney cooperated with the Fund's staff in carrying it through its last, difficult stages despite his duties in Washington. On behalf of the Fund I would like to thank also the members of the Committee on Antitrust Policy for the advice and aid they gave in the course of the study.

AUGUST HECKSCHER, *Director*
The Twentieth Century Fund

41 East 70th Street, New York
April 1958

ACKNOWLEDGMENTS

The Trustees of the Twentieth Century Fund suggested the subject of this study in 1950 and sketched the general plan it should follow. Their original appropriation and their continuing interest and encouragement are gratefully acknowledged. I am appreciative also of the Trustees' willingness to increase the number of case studies from twelve or less as originally planned to twenty, and to continue their support of the project over a considerably longer period of time than had originally been contemplated.

Several persons deserve credit for their able assistance in the early stages of this work. Research assistance was received for nearly a year and a half from Marvin Levine, then Instructor in the Department of Economics, School of Commerce, Accounts and Finance, New York University, and now Lecturer in Economics at Brooklyn College. Thereafter Jerome C. Strong, now with the Department of Economics, Princeton University, put in two and a half years at the task. Irwin M. Stelzer, while a graduate student in economics at New York University and Cornell University successively, prepared first drafts of the chapters on aluminum, cement, chemical manufactures, corn refining, cotton textiles and insurance. He is not responsible, however, for opinions expressed in these chapters as printed. Jane Earle Henderson, formerly with the Princeton Film Center and now teaching at the Lawrence School in Hewlett, Long Island, gathered materials on motion pictures. Benjamin M. Slatin of the Econometric Institute, New York City, now its Director of Industrial Studies, did the same for the paper chapter.

Valuable help was obtained from a leading corporation in each of three industries. Swift & Company included me in its Summer Program for Economists in 1953. Similar opportunities to observe operations and confer with officers of United States Steel Corporation in 1952 and Hercules Powder Company in 1954 were made possible by the Fellowships in Business program of the Foundation for Economic Education of Irvington-on-Hudson.

I found interviews, both with members of the twenty industries studied and with university economists, government officials, private attorneys and other authorities, the most fruitful source in preparing these chapters. The risks in relying so heavily on interviews are obvious. Not all informants remember accurately, some may wish to mislead, and some may contradict each other. Whenever a fact could be verified and documented from a written source, this was done even though the information had been disclosed originally in interviews or private correspondence. In recognition of the time given me by the several hundred persons interviewed, I can do no more than offer a general expression of gratitude.

Copies of each case study, in preliminary form, were sent for comment to between ten and twenty-five persons. Besides representatives of big and little business in the industries concerned, these readers included customers, trade association and labor union officials, lawyers, government employees and scholars who had made special studies of the industries. The list of those who responded with comments and suggestions runs to over one hundred; again I can only express general appreciation. An exception must be made for Herbert C. Morse of Swift & Company, who reviewed each draft of the meat packing chapter with painstaking care. Goldthwaite H. Dorr contributed a similar intensive review of the preliminary draft of the bituminous coal, cotton textile and petroleum chapters, and the other members of the Fund's special Committee on Antitrust Policy helped with comments and ideas privately or at the three meetings of the Committee. Each chapter was reviewed by at least one lawyer, but I am aware that some legal errors have probably slipped by and that some of my legal terminology is unorthodox.

A word of public thanks should be added to my private expressions of gratitude to the forty-one persons who reviewed the case studies in final draft and contributed the critiques which appear in the Appendix.

The Fund's staff, including several who left it during the course of the study, gave three sorts of essential help: typing and other physical preparation of the manuscript, editorial advice, and impartial judgment on many disputed points.

At the beginning of 1956, when the manuscript was complete but responses from readers of the case studies were still coming in, I resigned my position on the staff of the Twentieth Century Fund and from the faculty of the University College of Arts and Science at New York University to take a position with the Federal Trade Commission—an association which I welcomed because of my belief in the broad value of the antitrust laws to the American economy and society. Revision based on the readers' suggestions continued, and some materials published in 1956 were drawn upon, but new antitrust developments were ignored. Neither the content nor the emphasis of the manuscript, therefore, was affected by my connection with an antitrust enforcement agency. Nothing said in the book is to be taken as reflecting opinions of the Federal Trade Commission.

SIMON N. WHITNEY

CONTENTS

VOLUME I

TABLES

VOLUME I

MAJOR INDUSTRIES

Meat Packing

Petroleum

Chemical Manufactures

Bituminous Coal

Automobiles

Cotton Textiles

VOLUME II

FAMOUS ANTITRUST CASES

Cast Iron Pipe

Tobacco Products

Anthracite

Aluminum

Shoe Machinery

Motion Pictures

Tin Cans

Farm Machinery

Corn Refining

Cement

Pullman Cars

Insurance

THE SUMMING UP

Summary of the Case Studies

INTRODUCTION

CHAPTER 1

Introduction

When President Benjamin Harrison signed the Sherman Antitrust Act on July 2, 1890, he could hardly have envisioned the immense number of court decisions which would be needed to interpret that statute, or the dominating position it would come to occupy in the regulation of the American economy. For today antitrust legislation clearly ranks in importance with legislation on public utilities and transportation, on currency and banking, corporate finance, taxation, labor relations, agriculture or foreign trade. It may be said to have a central significance, since it sets the rules within which most business is conducted and most Americans earn their living.

An increasing volume of scholarly and popular literature has discussed the antitrust laws directly or, by analyzing the considerations affecting the price and production decisions of business firms, has evaluated the legislation implicitly. As a contemporary writer observes, "One shudders to think of what the position of an editor of an economic or legal journal in search of manuscripts must have been before the passage of the Sherman law." [1] Before presenting the case for another volume on the subject, it will be well to sketch briefly the history of antitrust policy.

Background of the Antitrust Laws

The antitrust policy of the United States has until recent years been almost unique. It is still looked upon as a strange phenomenon by many foreign observers, although some countries finally paid it the tribute of imitation. The Canadian law is perhaps the most effective,

1. Edward S. Mason, "Market Power and Business Conduct: Some Comments," *American Economic Review*, May 1956, p. 471.

but it lacks our prohibition of monopoly. No country has adopted so thorough a system of laws against combinations and restraints of trade in industry.

The precedents for this remarkable body of legislation go far back in English history: to the medieval regulations against acts considered monopolistic ("forestalling," "regrating," "engrossing"); to the rule enforced by the courts as early as the fifteenth century that a person who sold out his business and agreed not to re-enter it was not bound by the contract, since it deprived him of his best means of livelihood and the public of his services; to the Case of the Monopolies in 1602 and the Statute of Monopolies in 1623, both of which attacked royal monopoly grants; and to the common-law rule which emerged in the eighteenth century that agreements among sellers to limit output, divide markets or fix prices were conspiracies in restraint of trade for which injured parties could claim damages.

The rule against trade conspiracies was enforced in the nineteenth century in American courts, although a minority of courts permitted such agreements when their terms seemed reasonable in the light of industry conditions. But it was only after the rise of big business, beginning with the Civil War, that the monopoly problem emerged in its modern form. Between 1859 and 1889, with the burgeoning of modern industrialism, the number of wage earners in manufacturing increased more than threefold and the value added by manufacture almost fivefold — without dilution by any rise in the general price level.[2] An increasing proportion of the output came into the hands of the big new manufacturing consolidations. When the Standard Oil Company of Ohio adopted the legal trust form in 1879 and the sugar, whiskey and several other combinations later imitated it, all the giant business firms began to be known as "trusts." The name stuck, even after the trust device as such — whereby the stockholders surrendered their shares and voting power to managing trustees in return for dividend-paying trust certificates — was abandoned as a means of operating large corporations.

Passage of the Sherman Act

Opposition to monopolies became an important economic issue in the politics of the late 1880s, rivaling the demand for more currency,

2. U.S. Census Bureau, *Historical Statistics of the United States, 1789–1945*, pp. 179, 234.

and in 1890 Senator John Sherman gave his name to an important statute in each field. In his autobiography he called the Silver Purchase Act the real Sherman law,[3] but the country soon learned otherwise.

The Antitrust Act, drafted in the Senate Judiciary Committee, contained two fundamental substantive provisions, which still form the core of our antitrust laws: Section 1 forbade contracts, combinations and conspiracies in restraint of trade; and Section 2 forbade monopolizing and attempting to monopolize. The prohibition of trade restraints codified the earlier common-law rule, but added two essentials: a means of enforcement (action by the Department of Justice) and a penalty (fine or imprisonment). The prohibition of monopolizing was in the spirit of an old Anglo-Saxon tradition, but went beyond the common-law precedents. The statute was intended especially to destroy great combinations of capital which might monopolize necessities of life. Senator George F. Edmunds (who, as chairman of the Judiciary Committee, was in fact the law's chief draftsman) denied its application to a person who obtained all the orders in an industry by means of superior skill.[4]

Big business in 1890, most writers agree, considered the Sherman Act "impractical and unenforceable and hence innocuous." [5] This attitude might account in part for the lack of opposition in a Congress elected on the Republican high-tariff platform. The statute was passed with but one dissenting vote in the Senate and went through the House of Representatives by 152 to 72 at the first vote and by 240 to 0 in final form.

Landmarks in Antitrust History

The beginnings of enforcement, 1890–1904. For several years the attitude of the Department of Justice and the courts seemed to confirm the optimism of trust leaders. Few cases were instituted, and in 1895 the Supreme Court ruled that the American Sugar Refining Company's almost complete monopoly in manufacture was untouched by this

3. *John Sherman's Recollections of Forty Years in the House, Senate and Cabinet: An Autobiography*, Werner Co., Chicago, 1895, Vol. 2, pp. 1061–71, cited in Hans B. Thorelli, *The Federal Antitrust Policy: Origination of an American Tradition*, Johns Hopkins Press, Baltimore, 1955, p. 167, note 10, and p. 625.

4. Oswald Whitman Knauth, *The Policy of the United States towards Industrial Monopoly*, Longmans, Green, New York, 1914, p. 30, note 3, and p. 33.

5. Thorelli, *The Federal Antitrust Policy*, p. 221.

statute dealing with "commerce." [6] In the atmosphere created by this decision, by the conservative Republican political victory in 1896 and by recovery from the long business depression of 1893–97, the greatest merger movement in American history began in 1898. Between 1890 and 1897 there were 84 new combinations, according to one list, with total authorized stock capital of $1.0 billion; but between 1898 and 1902 there were 189 combinations, with capital of $4.0 billion.[7] Many of the earlier consolidations were now absorbed into larger ones. The government's victories in the Supreme Court after 1897,[8] which outlawed as being in restraint of trade all agreements among competitors on prices and production, had the effect of encouraging combinations as the legal route to agreement.

Finally, after the big merger movement had faded for lack of new fields to conquer and inability to discover continued sources of financing, the Supreme Court in 1904 ordered its first dissolution of a monopoly under the Sherman Act. This *Northern Securities* decision [9] split up the Great Northern–Northern Pacific railroad combination of Edward H. Harriman, James J. Hill and J. P. Morgan.

The antitrust crusade of the Progressive era, 1904–15. The first big antitrust "crusade" was launched by President Theodore Roosevelt, to be taken up even more vigorously by the otherwise conservative and cautious President Taft. Trusts were viewed almost as "public enemies" in the Progressive era, and many of the best-known were challenged by the Department of Justice's Antitrust Division, established in 1903. The climax came in May 1911, when the Supreme Court ordered dissolution of two of the most famous combinations — the Standard Oil and the American Tobacco companies.[10]

But these decisions marked the limits as well as the climax of this crusade. Chief Justice White declared that the Court would thereafter apply a "rule of reason" under which only "unreasonable" restraints of trade would be unlawful. Enthusiasts for militant action were aroused by this proposition, and all three major political parties

6. *U.S. v. E. C. Knight Co.*, 156 U.S. 1 (1895).

7. Thorelli, *The Federal Antitrust Policy*, pp. 294–303.

8. *U.S. v. Trans-Missouri Freight Ass'n.*, 166 U.S. 290 (1897); *U.S. v. Joint Traffic Ass'n.*, 171 U.S. 505 (1898); *Addyston Pipe and Steel Co. v. U.S.*, 175 U.S. 211 (1899).

9. *Northern Securities Co. v. U.S.*, 193 U.S. 197 (1904).

10. *Standard Oil Company of N.J. v. U.S.*, 221 U.S. 1 (1911); *U.S. v. American Tobacco Co.*, 221 U.S. 106 (1911).

promised in the 1912 campaign to take vigorous measures against monopolies. The outcome was the passage of two new antitrust statutes in 1914 — the Federal Trade Commission Act and the Clayton Act. The former created an administrative body of five members, whose most important function would be to prevent unfair competition. This term was intended to cover both unethical and deceptive practices and those which were unfair because they were likely to exclude competitors or achieve a monopoly. The Clayton Act forbade several specific monopolistic practices, on the theory, emphasized by President Wilson and by some economists,[11] that trusts gained their supremacy through unfair practices and could be forestalled by attacking these. The same statute in broad language exempted labor and farm organizations from the antitrust laws — the first of a series of legislative exemptions.

Stabilized enforcement and suspension, 1915–35. The passage of these two statutes was, surprisingly, to be followed by a long period of less active antitrust enforcement. The Federal Trade Commission gradually built up its power to enjoin unfair methods of competition through successful proceedings against such practices as misbranding,[12] falsely claiming to manufacture the goods sold,[13] and selling through lotteries.[14] The drive against combinations by the Department of Justice, however, was brought almost to a halt by the Supreme Court's 1920 decision that the biggest trust of all, United States Steel Corporation, was lawful in the absence of proof that it had abused its power.[15] Many of the big trusts had by now been subjected to some form of remedial decree or cleared by the courts, and the Department of Justice turned to attacks on collusive agreements and trade association activities. Its suits were still numerous, but they were less important individually. Significant Supreme Court decisions included two in 1925 which declared that trade association activities not involving outright agreement on prices or output were legal,[16] and one in 1927 which ruled that price agreements were illegal "*per se*" wherever found and no

11. Compare William H. S. Stevens, *Unfair Competition*, University of Chicago Press, Chicago, 1917, pp. 219–20.

12. *FTC v. Winsted Hosiery Co.*, 258 U.S. 483 (1922); *FTC v. Algoma Lumber Co.*, 291 U.S. 67 (1934).

13. *FTC v. Royal Milling Co.*, 288 U.S. 212 (1933).

14. *FTC v. R. F. Keppel & Bros., Inc.*, 291 U.S. 304 (1934).

15. *U.S. v. U.S. Steel Corp.*, 251 U.S. 417 (1920).

16. *Maple Flooring Manufacturers Ass'n. v. U.S.*, 268 U.S. 563 (1925); *Cement Manufacturers Protective Ass'n. v. U.S.*, 268 U.S. 588 (1925).

matter how reasonable the prices set might be.[17] The same decade was marked by a second merger movement — though a much less striking one than that of the 1890s.

This period culminated in the great depression, and in a growing feeling among businessmen that unrestricted competition was driving down prices, wages and employment. The National Industrial Recovery Act of June 1933 suspended the antitrust laws for any industry that devised a code of fair competition which met with the President's approval. This experiment, which marked the historic low point in antitrust popularity and enforcement, ended with the Supreme Court declaration that the NRA was unconstitutional,[18] just when the controls upon which it relied were already making the "Blue Eagle" an unpopular bird.

Renewed vigorous enforcement since 1935. The revival of the antitrust laws which began in 1935 has continued to date. In 1936 the Robinson-Patman Act strengthened the Clayton law by tightening the definition of price discrimination. In 1938 the Wheeler-Lea Act strengthened the enforcement powers of the Federal Trade Commission. The activity of the Department of Justice was suddenly stepped up in 1938 with the advent of Thurman W. Arnold as Assistant Attorney General — though he was previously known in this field chiefly for his witty comments on "entirely futile but enormously picturesque" antitrust "crusades." [19] The hearings and monographs of the Temporary National Economic Committee, set up by Congress in 1938 when President Franklin Roosevelt warned of the dangers of industrial concentration, also signaled the return to antitrust principles. In the first forty-eight years of Sherman Act history 433 suits had been filed, an average of 9 each year, but from July 1938 to June 1943, 347 were filed, or 69 each year.[20] Federal Trade Commission complaints were also stepped up sharply beginning in 1935.

Among the landmarks of this period have been the *Alcoa* decision that monopoly is unlawful even if not accompanied by abuses; [21] the

17. *U.S. v. Trenton Potteries Co.*, 273 U.S. 392 (1927).

18. *Schechter Poultry Corp. v. U.S.*, 295 U.S. 495 (1935).

19. Thurman W. Arnold, *The Folklore of Capitalism*, Yale University Press, New Haven, 1937, p. 217.

20. Commerce Clearing House, *The Federal Antitrust Laws with Summary of Cases Instituted by the U.S., 1890–1951*, Chicago, 1952.

21. *U.S. v. Aluminum Company of America*, 148 F. 2d 416 (2d Cir. 1945).

American Tobacco and *Paramount* decisions, which gave the Department of Justice legal triumphs over "oligopolies" of a few large companies; [22] the *Cement Institute* case,[23] in which the Federal Trade Commission finally secured the abolition of the "basing point" system of pricing twenty-four years after the Commission's first order on the subject; and several decisions which sharply limited the previously accepted rights of a patent holder.[24] Paradoxically, this period of vigorous enforcement has seen an increase in the number of legislative exemptions — including those for the oil producing industry and bituminous coal in 1935 (the latter expiring in 1943); the Miller-Tydings Act of 1937, reinforced by the McGuire Act of 1952, which sanctioned resale price fixing as demanded by retailers; and the exemptions of insurance in 1945 and of railroad rate-setting associations in 1948. [In December 1950, however, the antitrust laws were strongly buttressed by the addition of the Celler-Kefauver amendment to Section 7, the anti-merger clause of the Clayton Act.]

Varying Opinions on the Antitrust Laws

Even after more than six decades of enforcement, there is nothing like unanimity of opinion among students of antitrust policy as to the wisdom and significance of these laws. Their attitudes may be summarized for the reader's convenience under four general viewpoints, though this oversimplifies the variety of opinions and ignores the fact that some writers are on the borderline between two of the categories or combine thoughts from more than one.[25]

Most students support the antitrust principle, even if they do not wholly approve of each successive and changing application of the laws. Some would like enforcement relaxed in certain directions and intensified in others. But supporters of antitrust policy can be divided broadly into two groups: those who feel that it is working well and either needs no change or at most relaxation in certain details, and those who feel that it is not effective and should be applied much more

22. *American Tobacco Co. v. U.S.*, 328 U.S. 781 (1946); *U.S. v. Paramount Pictures, Inc.*, 334 U.S. 131 (1948).

23. *FTC v. Cement Institute*, 333 U.S. 683 (1948).

24. *Hartford-Empire Co. v. U.S.*, 323 U.S. 386 (1945), and several other cases.

25. Compare Fritz Machlup, *The Political Economy of Monopoly: Business, Labor and Government Policies*, Johns Hopkins Press, Baltimore, 1952, pp. 226–28; and Marshall Edward Dimock, *Business and Government*, Henry Holt, New York, revised edition, 1953, p. 175.

drastically. As one moves from the middle ground toward the extremes of these two viewpoints, the clash between them becomes sharp. The first position was that of the majority (mostly private lawyers) and the second that of a few members (especially three economists and two law professors) of the fifty-seven-man Attorney General's National Committee to Study the Antitrust Laws, which reported in 1955. The majority stand was just the opposite in a symposium in 1949. Then three private lawyers and one economist upheld the first position while nine economists, a law professor and two former antitrust officials took the view that the antitrust laws had accomplished "relatively little since 1890." [26]

Of the two generally favorable positions, the first inclines toward less insistence by the antitrust agencies and the courts that specific business practices be declared illegal *per se* and more reliance on the "rule of reason." [27] The second looks toward dissolution of giant corporations,[28] or stripping them of any advantages they may have in ownership of raw materials, patents, distribution facilities and so on.[29] Both groups agree on two fundamental propositions: that competition between sellers is essential to the healthy functioning of a free enterprise economy, and that government watchfulness is essential to preserve competition. Their clash arises over the question whether this watchfulness has in practice been successful in preserving the kind of competition a successful economy needs.

In their common support of the antitrust principle these two groups are undoubtedly in harmony with the overwhelming opinion of the voters of the country. The unwavering support given the antitrust laws by all factions in Congress and every four years by the platforms of both major parties leaves little doubt how the voters stand. The third and fourth categories of writers on antitrust policy take issue with this popular majority, and are skeptical of the whole antitrust principle.

The handful of students in the third group holds that the antitrust laws either are injurious or would be if they were forcefully applied,

26. Dexter Merriam Keezer, ed., "The Effectiveness of the Antitrust Laws: A Symposium," *American Economic Review*, June 1949, pp. 689–724.

27. See S. Chesterfield Oppenheim, later co-chairman of Attorney General's National Committee to Study the Antitrust Laws, "Federal Antitrust Legislation: Guideposts to a Revised National Antitrust Policy," *Michigan Law Review*, June 1952, pp. 1139–1244.

28. Vernon A. Mund, *Government and Business*, Harper, New York, 1950, pp. 181–87.

29. Henry A. Wells, *Monopoly and Social Control*, Public Affairs Press, Washington, 1952, pp. 82–83. (The name is a pseudonym.)

because they stand in the way of the corporate bigness and intercorporate agreements which these students believe to be necessary under today's technological conditions.[30] Members of this group differ in the degree to which they would keep competition as the guiding principle of the economy. Some, and perhaps most, believe that competition would be maintained by market or technological forces without antitrust laws.[31]

The fourth viewpoint is that of students who consider any turn in the direction of uncontrolled *laissez faire* to be the equivalent of inviting enslavement to monopolies and cartels, but have no faith in such mild measures of control as the antitrust laws. Socialist writers want outright nationalization of the large industries. More conservative students prefer regulation of price and production policies by government commissions.[32] A few writers are prepared for such regulation for certain monopolistic industries, but believe that others can still be redeemed by more adequate antitrust enforcement.[33]

One difference of opinion which cuts across these several viewpoints is in the attitude toward the "behavior" or "workable competition" or "public interest" test — that is, whether satisfactory economic performance should be a permissible defense against an antitrust action, especially one seeking dissolution of a big corporation. This test is suggested by some representatives of each of the first three viewpoints discussed: those who otherwise approve of our antitrust policy,[34] those who want more drastic enforcement,[35] and those who want less stringent policies.[36] This emphasis on performance, which appears to

30. David E. Lilienthal, *Big Business: A New Era*, Harper, New York, 1953; compare John Kenneth Galbraith, *American Capitalism: The Concept of Countervailing Power*, Houghton Mifflin, Boston, 1952, pp. 53–65, 89–99.

31. Lilienthal, *Big Business: A New Era*, pp. 56–57; Harold Fleming, *Ten Thousand Commandments: A Story of the Antitrust Laws*, Prentice-Hall, New York, 1951, pp. 87–92.

32. Arthur Robert Burns, *The Decline of Competition*, McGraw-Hill, New York, 1936, Chaps. 11 and 12.

33. Walton H. Hamilton, *The Pattern of Competition*, Columbia University Press, New York, 1940, pp. 83–99.

34. Clare E. Griffin, *An Economic Approach to Antitrust Problems*, American Enterprise Association, New York, 1951.

35. Report of Twentieth Century Fund Committee on Cartels and Monopoly, Chap. 16 of George W. Stocking and Myron W. Watkins, *Monopoly and Free Enterprise*, Twentieth Century Fund, 1951, pp. 563–64; Louis B. Schwartz, "The Complete Dissenting Opinion of Prof. Louis B. Schwartz" (originally written for Attorney General's National Committee to Study the Antitrust Laws), *Antitrust Bulletin*, April 1955, p. 43.

36. Lilienthal, *Big Business: A New Era*, pp. 184–88.

be growing, recently drew a rebuttal from two economists who argue for traditional standards, more strictly enforced than in the past.[37]

Plan of the Book

The purpose of this book is to throw some light on the relative merits of these varying points of view by analyzing the effects of the antitrust laws. A great deal has been written on legal interpretations and on the economic theories involved in antitrust policy, but relatively little on the impact upon business of the existence and application of this whole body of legislation. To appraise this impact one must examine the concrete results and the subtler consequences of legal proceedings, as well as the business behavior encouraged or forestalled by the laws. Ideally, such a study would encompass the entire economy, but the approach of this book is to investigate the experience of representative industries. This case study method has limitations, it will be seen at once, not least of which is the practical impossibility of devoting sufficient attention to each industry if the sample is to be large enough to be representative. Yet this approach has the advantage of setting forth the facts in orderly fashion and, it is hoped, clarifying the important issues even if not resolving all of them.

The industries were selected in ways which were intended to ensure an unbiased sample. Eight were chosen by taking the two largest mineral industries — bituminous coal and petroleum — and the industry with the largest sales in each of six broad classes into which the Census of Manufactures could logically be divided.[38] These were: meat packing, from the food and tobacco group; cotton textiles, from the textile and apparel group; paper, from the forest products group; chemical manufactures, from the chemical, rubber and leather products group; steel, from the metals group; and automobiles, from the machinery and equipment group.

The same outline was adopted for discussion of each of the eight industries: a brief description, a section on specific antitrust suits, one on the competitive status of the industry, and a summary. The third section, "Competitive Status," was included to show the effects of the antitrust laws as reflected, not in the traceable consequences of par-

37. Joel B. Dirlam and Alfred E. Kahn, *Fair Competition: The Law and Economics of Antitrust Policy*, Cornell University Press, Ithaca, 1954.

38. *Statistical Abstract of the United States*, 1950, pp. 759, 771–74.

ticular suits, but in the whole structure and behavior of the industry. For each industry as it stands is in part the resultant of the manner in which the antitrust laws have been applied, as it is of all other factors which have shaped the American economy.

In order to obtain a broader sample on which to rest conclusions, an analysis of "famous antitrust suits" in twelve industries was added to the eight "major" studies. These twelve were: cast iron pipe, tobacco products, anthracite, aluminum, shoe machinery, motion pictures, tin cans, farm machinery, corn refining, cement, Pullman cars and insurance. Since it proved unduly restrictive to study one suit alone in each industry, the whole history and structure of these industries too were taken into account, though the formal chapter division of "Antitrust Suits" and "Competitive Status" was dropped. Each of the two groups is presented in approximately the order in which an important antitrust case in the industry first reached the stage of court decision — from the meat packing decree of 1903 to the automobile finance decrees of 1938 (there was no important case in cotton textiles); and from the Supreme Court's 1899 decision in cast iron pipe to its 1944 decision revolutionizing the regulation of insurance.

The limitation to twenty industries, which many readers may still consider too small a sample for generalization, meant that important cases arising elsewhere had to be ignored. It is hoped that the General Electric Company, the Great Atlantic and Pacific Tea Company, and many other large corporations that have participated in epoch-making antitrust cases, as well as smaller firms in the lumber, linseed oil, maple flooring and other businesses which have had the same experience, will not feel slighted by the omission. More seriously, it is hoped that the treatment of cases industry by industry, rather than chronologically or topically, will not give too confused an impression, or leave too many gaps.

This approach necessarily excluded consideration of many related topics — for example, exemptions from the antitrust laws, changes in public attitudes toward the laws, policies and methods of enforcement, and comparisons with the economic policies, structure and performance of other countries.

Thus confined and focused, this is obviously not a theoretical study of monopoly or competition. It is a practical study of industry and national policy in action. Though it is a study by an economist of an issue which is both economic and legal, care has been taken to avoid the technical language of both economics and the law, and to explain terms that might not be familiar to all readers.

Definition of Terms

It may nevertheless be helpful to some readers to define at this point a few terms often used by economists in discussing competition and monopoly:

Pure competition: a situation in which there are so many producers of an identical article that none can have any influence on the price, the result being that each will produce up to the point where his cost exceeds the going price, and will offer for sale his entire production.

Perfect competition: pure competition plus complete knowledge of all the facts of supply and demand and complete mobility of capital and labor into and out of the industry. Both of these concepts are of theoretical value only.

Workable competition: the kind of competition that does as satisfactory a job for the consumer as could reasonably be expected under the conditions of the real world.

Monopoly: control of the supply of a product by a single firm. Complete monopoly is rare except in local markets.

Monopolistic: any tendency toward monopoly (admittedly a broad use of the word, not necessarily connoting illegality).

Oligopoly: an industry with so few producers that each must think very seriously before taking any competitive action which will cut into the sales of his rivals and bring retaliation. The word is much disliked by businessmen, but does refer to a real situation.

Dominant firm: one so strong that smaller firms in the industry fear to take independent action on matters of trade policy.

Vertical integration: combination in one firm of two or more production stages — e.g., mining and manufacturing, or manufacturing and distribution.

Horizontal combination: union of two or more competing plants in a single firm.

Cartel: an agreement among firms to set prices, divide markets, limit production, or share technical knowledge on a broad but exclusive basis. The term is usually reserved for the legalized cartels which exist in some European countries, or for international cartels between firms in different countries.

The Basic Antitrust Statutes

A summary of those provisions of the three fundamental antitrust laws which will come under discussion in this book may also be helpful to some readers.

The Sherman Act, 1890. The heart of the antitrust legislation ever since 1890 has been the first two sections of "an act to protect trade and commerce against unlawful restraints and monopolies," as the Sherman law was entitled. These sections read, in part:

> Sec. 1. Every contract, combination in the form of trust or otherwise, or conspiracy, in restraint of trade or commerce among the several States, or with foreign nations, is hereby declared to be illegal . . .
>
> Sec. 2. Every person who shall monopolize, or attempt to monopolize, or combine or conspire with any person or persons, to monopolize any part of the trade or commerce among the several States, or with foreign nations, shall be deemed guilty of a misdemeanor . . .

Both sections provided fines for violation up to a $5,000 maximum (changed in 1955 to $50,000) and prison terms up to one year. Section 4 instructed the Attorney General to bring civil proceedings in the federal circuit courts (which after 1911 became the district courts) to restrain violations. Section 7 allowed persons injured by violations to sue for three times the damages they had suffered, plus a reasonable attorney's fee. Section 8 made it clear that "person" included "corporations and associations."

The Federal Trade Commission Act, 1914. By this statute, the Federal Trade Commission replaced the Bureau of Corporations, which had been established in the Department of Commerce in 1903, and took over its work of economic investigation. The chief substantive provision of the law is Section 5, which originally read:

> The commission is hereby empowered and directed to prevent persons, partnerships, or corporations, except banks, and common carriers subject to the Acts to regulate commerce, from using unfair methods of competition in commerce.

Subsequent amendments excluded first livestock and meat companies and then airlines, and, in 1938, supplemented the prohibition of "unfair methods of competition" with one of "unfair or deceptive acts or practices." Thus the unfair practices to be prevented, originally limited to those which injured competitors, were extended to include those which simply injured customers. Section 5 is enforced against acts which are unfair ethically and also those which are unfair merely because they are monopolistic. Agreements in restraint of trade can be prosecuted either by the Department of Justice under Section 1 of the Sherman Act or as unfair competition under the Federal Trade Commission Act.

Many activities of the Commission will receive little or no mention in this book; for example, prosecution of false and misleading advertising and other deceptive acts in commerce, trade practice conferences after which the Commission drafts lists of practices considered unfair in the particular industry, supervision of export trade associations, and enforcement of honest labeling in the wool and fur trades.

The Clayton Act (1914) as amended by the Robinson-Patman Act (1936). The Department of Justice and the Federal Trade Commission were given concurrent power to enforce the Clayton Act, but the Commission has generally assumed primary jurisdiction. The Clayton Act, besides its procedural provisions and exemptions, forbade certain specific anti-competitive practices.

Section 2 prohibited price discrimination between purchasers "where the effect of such discrimination may be to substantially lessen competition or tend to create a monopoly in any line of commerce." It provided, however, for defenses based on quantity sold, cost of selling or transportation, and price cuts to meet competition "in good faith," and these weakened the prohibition. After an extensive investigation of chain stores disclosed their competitive advantage due to mass purchasing of goods,[39] the Robinson-Patman Act was passed in 1936 to amend Section 2 of the Clayton Act. The new legislation

(1) added to substantial lessening of competition a criterion of unlawfulness easier to prove: that the discrimination "injure, destroy, or prevent competition with any person who either grants or knowingly receives the benefit of such discrimination, or with customers of either of them";

(2) tightened the justification of price differences "on account of" quantity sold or that make "only due allowance for difference in the cost of selling or transportation" to a requirement that they "make only due allowance for differences in the cost of manufacture, sale, or delivery resulting from the differing methods or quantities";

39. See FTC, *Final Report on the Chain-Store Investigation,* S. Doc. 4, 74th Cong., 1st sess., 1934. There were 33 earlier pamphlet reports in this study.

(3) in determining whether a price difference was lawful, put the burden of proof on the person charged;

(4) denied the defense that the discount had been given to meet competition in good faith if the price set was lower than the competitor's.

The rest of the Robinson-Patman Act — on brokerage, advertising allowances, liability of a purchaser who knew he had received a price discrimination, and a new right of the Federal Trade Commission (never made effective) to fix maximum quantity discounts if necessary to prevent monopoly — will not be discussed in this book.

Section 3 of the Clayton Act forbade tying contracts (refusal to sell or lease one product unless another is taken with it) and exclusive dealing arrangements, where the effect might be substantial lessening of competition or a tendency toward monopoly.

Section 7 forbade the purchase of stock by one corporation in another if the result would substantially lessen competition between the two or tend toward monopoly. Evasion became possible through purchase of assets instead of stock, or by purchasing all the stock of the smaller corporation and then dissolving it before the Commission could take action. The Celler-Kefauver amendment of 1950, therefore, altered this section to prohibit mergers through purchase either of stock or assets if they tended "in any line of commerce in any section of the country" to lessen competition substantially or create a monopoly.

Section 8 forbade interlocking directorates between any two corporations either of which had a net worth of over $1 million, when elimination of competition between the two would violate any of the antitrust laws.

Other legislation. Although the three acts just reviewed constitute the principal antitrust legislation, one compilation (not a complete list) includes passages from twenty-seven other laws which deal with the subject.[40] Some are procedural; others (like the Federal Power Act, the Civil Aeronautics Act, and the Packers and Stockyards Act) are laws on specific situations which contain antitrust provisions; and a good many give outright exemptions to favored groups or regulated industries. The forty state antitrust laws — eighteen of which were passed between 1889 and 1891 — also have some significance, but on the whole their role has been a minor one. Because their use to control the

40. Commerce Clearing House, *The Federal Antitrust Laws*, pp. 5–6.

operations of large corporations would interfere with the federal power to regulate interstate commerce, they can restrain such corporations only with pinpricks. And because punitive action might merely drive plants away, to the detriment of workers and consumers within the state, the laws are not always invoked against local manufacturing firms. Other local businessmen, such as building contractors and owners of service establishments, may have political influence which helps protect them from attack.[41]

Enforcing the Sherman Act

The Antitrust Division of the Department of Justice receives a thousand-odd complaints each year, a few from other government agencies but most of them from competitors or customers of the firms complained against. On rare occasions Sherman Act suits originate in news items or known facts about an industrial situation which arouse the Division's suspicions, in studies by the Division of a whole industry or type of business practice designed to start a series of suits, or even in consultations with businessmen who present a plan which the Division then or later concludes is illegal (in which case it never employs criminal action).

The lawyer who conducts the investigation has a considerable influence on whether a suit should be filed; the Assistant Attorney General must approve it and often decides it; and the Attorney General may at times exert his authority. There is likely to be time or money only for the important suits, or for those in which the Division has the best evidence, or perhaps for a few which dramatize some policy of the Administration.

When the Division discovers what it considers an outright ("hard-core") violation of the statute, it brings criminal proceedings. It may do so in less flagrant cases too, since a federal grand jury can then subpoena the defendants' records; but many civil defendants permit the government full access to their files. Civil proceedings have advantages in that the Division need have only a preponderance of the evidence rather than prove its case beyond a reasonable doubt, it can appeal an adverse verdict, and the court can order positive measures of "relief" designed to cure the specific monopolistic situation. Under Thurman Arnold the Division experimented with simultaneous

41. See William F. Brown and Ralph Cassady, Jr., "Guild Pricing in the Service Trades," *Quarterly Journal of Economics*, February 1947, pp. 311–38.

criminal and civil proceedings. It sometimes brings criminal proceedings and then drops them when it has gathered the evidence and the defendants have agreed to a consent decree.

Consent decrees, not mentioned in the Sherman Act, have concluded an increasing proportion of the government's civil antitrust victories since their first use in 1906. The government may win more drastic remedies by this route — even "the enjoining of otherwise lawful acts" in order to "dissipate the effects of the unlawful conduct" [42] — because the defendants will make sacrifices to save trial costs. Also, a consent decree, unlike a court verdict, does not provide *prima facie* evidence for a private plaintiff in a treble damage suit. The same considerations often influence defendants to plead *nolo contendere* ("I do not wish to contest") instead of standing a criminal trial, for, although the penalties are the same as with a verdict of guilty, a *nolo* plea neither admits nor implies guilt in the eyes of the law and it saves trial costs and makes treble damage action harder.

The criminal trials are held before a jury in one of the ninety federal district courts. The government cannot appeal an acquittal, but the defendant can appeal conviction to the appropriate one of the eleven circuit courts of appeal. If the conviction is sustained there, the defendant can request the Supreme Court for a writ of certiorari to hear the case. The writ is granted only when the Court considers the case important. In a civil case, either party can appeal directly from the district court to the Supreme Court, provided the latter grants the necessary writ.

No businessman outside the "racketeer" class has ever been sent to jail under the Sherman Act, although suspended prison sentences have been given on rare occasions. Fines are imposed on directors and officers of corporations if they are made defendants along with their companies and plead *nolo contendere* or are found guilty. It may be supposed that their fines are paid by the corporation.

Federal Trade Commission Procedure

The Federal Trade Commission is one of several independent, bipartisan, quasi-judicial, government agencies (by their initials: ICC, FPC, SEC, FCC, NLRB and CAB). Its chairman and four other members are presidential appointees, but the Commission is respon-

42. Herbert A. Bergson, "Enforcing Antitrust," *Fortune*, August 1949, p. 117.

sible to Congress. Its procedure, after some changes in details, is now standardized as follows:

1. The Commission's Bureau of Investigation follows up complaints of violation of Section 5 of the Federal Trade Commission Act or Sections 2, 3, 7 or 8 of the Clayton Act. The Commission itself decides, upon reviewing the facts, whether there is enough evidence to issue a formal complaint.

2. The "respondent" in a complaint may accept a "cease and desist order" without admission of guilt, or may have a hearing before one of the Commission's staff of independent trial examiners. Here the Commission is represented by attorneys of its Bureau of Litigation. The examiner gives his decision in a written opinion, which becomes final if not appealed.

3. Either the respondent or the Commission's counsel (known formally as "counsel supporting the complaint") is likely to appeal to the Commission itself. The full Commission, which has had nothing to do with the case from the time it issued the complaint on *prima facie* evidence, now sits as a court of appeal and makes its decision. Although its dual role of accuser and judge has often been criticized, the Commission has dismissed many complaints after the full evidence was before it. Between 1915 and 1948 it issued 3,964 cease and desist orders and dismissed 1,009 complaints. In 25 per cent of the actions, in other words, the Commission decided that its original *prima facie* evidence would not stand up on fuller exposure of the facts. For 1950–55, figures on anti-monopoly complaints alone, excluding anti-deceptive practices complaints, show that 127 orders were issued and 54 complaints were dismissed or closed for other reasons (such as discontinuance of the practice or the business).[43]

4. Dismissal by the Commission is final, but the respondent may appeal a cease and desist order to the appropriate federal circuit court of appeal. The court gives the case priority over other pending suits. Either party may appeal the circuit court's verdict to the Supreme Court by asking for a writ of certiorari.

5. When an order under the Federal Trade Commission Act becomes final through non-appeal or court decision, proven violation is punishable by a fine of not more than $5,000 for each violation. The Department of Justice prosecutes violators. There is an extra step in

43. FTC, Annual Report, 1948, p. 51; 1951, p. 35; 1952, p. 27; 1953, p. 11; 1954, p. 28; 1955, p. 33.

Clayton Act orders: when a violation occurs, the Commission may secure an injunction against repetition, and then undertake contempt proceedings if the injunction in turn is violated.

The Commission has a special standing before the courts by virtue of the expert status conferred upon it by Congress in 1914. Under Section 5(c) of the Federal Trade Commission Act, "the findings of the Commission as to the facts, if supported by evidence, shall be conclusive," and Section 11 of the Clayton Act has a similar clause. Evidence which the court itself might not consider sufficient thus becomes acceptable.

Private Damage Suits

The right of persons injured by antitrust violations to sue for recovery of three times their losses was originally expected to be a major weapon of law enforcement. As it turned out, potential plaintiffs were deterred by the costs of suing and the difficulty of procuring evidence without governmental authority. They usually wait until the government has won an antitrust suit, so as to rely on the court verdict for their own *prima facie* evidence. Most damage suits have been dismissed, or settled for sums much smaller than those claimed. It was reported in 1938 that only 13 of the 175 private actions brought since 1890 had been successful.[44]

Since the end of World War II the number of treble damage actions and the percentage of decisions for the plaintiff have increased very sharply. There is little question today that the danger of being forced to pay a huge award as a result of such action is an ever-present and powerful influence on the competitive practices of large corporations, and that it makes them more willing to settle their cases with the Department of Justice rather than risk an adverse verdict which private plaintiffs could then use as evidence.

Problems of Antitrust Enforcement

Antitrust enforcement certainly does not present a simple and clear-cut picture. Businessmen object to the duplication of powers between the Department of Justice and the Federal Trade Commission. Other government agencies (such as the Department of Agriculture for meat packing and the Federal Communications Commission for companies

44. Annual Report of the Attorney General, 1938, p. 233.

operating in its field of jurisdiction) have separate enforcement powers. Moreover, many economic groups — labor unions, the shipping industry and the railroads, for example — have been given exemptions, the exact scope of which has been gradually defined by litigation in the courts. In practice, neither the expense of duplicating enforcement nor the peril of double jeopardy has been very serious. Instances of intervention by both the Federal Trade Commission and the Department of Justice in the same case have been extremely rare.

Some writers believe these two agencies have been so starved for funds that enforcement has never really been attempted.[45] Thus the Antitrust Division never spent as much as $300,000 a year or had more than twenty-five lawyers before 1935. Its expenditures finally passed the million-dollar mark in 1940 and were $3 million in 1955, and the number of lawyers on its staff was about 200 in each of those years. The Federal Trade Commission has usually spent about a million dollars more a year than the Antitrust Division; it spent $1 million in 1920, $2.3 million in 1940, and $4.1 million in 1955. One former official of both agencies has said that even quadrupling their staffs would be insufficient.[46] Comparisons are sometimes made with the much larger sums which antitrust defendants can afford: perhaps as much as $2 million was spent by the defense in the Mid-Continent gasoline case of 1936–40 [47] and still more has been spent by the du Pont Company in antitrust suits since 1947. However, the scale of legal fees is higher in private practice than in the government, and any suggestion that the defendants are fortunate in being able to spend larger sums than the government on these cases might be greeted with a wry smile.

Despite the various handicaps under which the enforcement agencies labor,[48] the balance of victories is heavily on their side. Between 1895 and 1953, for example, the Department of Justice won 69 of the 99 Supreme Court decisions on Sherman and Clayton Act cases.[49] The Federal Trade Commission, between 1915 and 1948, won 200 cases in

45. Mund, *Government and Business*, pp. 194–97; Walton Hamilton and Irene Till, *Antitrust in Action*, TNEC Monograph 16, 1941, pp. 23–26.

46. Corwin D. Edwards, *Maintaining Competition*, McGraw-Hill, New York, 1949, p. 298.

47. TNEC Monograph 16, p. 80, note 11, referring to *U.S. v. Socony-Vacuum Corp.*, 315 U.S. 150 (1940).

48. See TNEC Monograph 16; Edwards, *Maintaining Competition*, pp. 287–318.

49. Victor H. Kramer, "The Antitrust Division and the Supreme Court: 1890–1953," *Virginia Law Review*, May 1954, p. 433.

the circuit courts and lost 103, but the number lost falls to 52 when separate company docket numbers in the same case are combined. In the Supreme Court the Commission won 31 appeals and lost 15, a record which is improved by taking into consideration the 48 denials of writs of certiorari to respondents as against the 9 denials of writs to the Commission.[50]

If we consider the problems of antitrust enforcement as having three aspects — deciding what business practices should be proceeded against, securing a court verdict, and ensuring that the resulting "relief" answers the need — it is the first and third which have caused most difficulty and to whose solution the case studies following are intended to contribute.

50. FTC, Annual Report, 1948, p. 51.

MAJOR INDUSTRIES

MEAT PACKING

PETROLEUM

CHEMICAL MANUFACTURES

STEEL

PAPER

BITUMINOUS COAL

AUTOMOBILES

COTTON TEXTILES

CHAPTER 2

Meat Packing

In the colonial period, when pickled meat was "packed" in barrels for shipment south or overseas, the commercial slaughtering and processing of livestock became known as meat packing. Meat packing and prepared meats — an associated industry which buys fresh and cured meats from slaughterers for canning and other processing — added $1.7 billion in value to the $8.5 billion paid to farmers, according to the Census of Manufactures for 1954. Although the value added by manufacture was greater in both beverages and bakery products, in net value of final shipments meat packing, with $8.2 billion, and prepared meats, with $1.4 billion, led the food manufacturing group by a wide margin.

The Livestock and Meat Industries

Over 90 per cent of the meat animals raised on six million farms are sold; slaughter for home consumption also contributes to the national meat supply. Cattle frequently go through the hands of two, or even three, farm owners, since most young steers and many sheep are sold by western ranchers to specialized "feeders" who "finish" them for the market on corn and prepared feeds. In 1955 almost three times as many hogs were slaughtered as cattle, but the weight of beef produced exceeded that of pork by nearly a third. Veal and lamb together accounted for less than 10 per cent of the total meat supply. (See Table 1.)

Packing houses buy either "direct" or on public stockyards. Direct buying is largely at the plant or at a local "buying station," but is carried on increasingly at auctions. Stockyards are public service agencies supported by rental of facilities and sale of feed, where com-

TABLE I

MEAT PACKING: LIVESTOCK SLAUGHTER AND MEAT PRODUCTION, 1955

Livestock Slaughter			Meat Production		
Type	Commercial	Farm	Type	Commercial	Farm
	(Million Head)			*(Billion Pounds)*	
Total	128.5	8.5	Total	25.5	1.5
Cattle	25.7	.9	Beef	13.2	.4
Calves	12.4	.5	Veal	1.5	.1
Sheep and lambs	16.2	.3	Lamb and mutton	.7	a
Hogs	74.2	6.8	Pork (excluding lard)	10.1	1.0

Source: U.S. Department of Agriculture, Agricultural Marketing Service, *The Livestock and Meat Situation,* March 2, 1956, p. 27; July 9, 1956, pp. 23–26.

a. 11 million pounds only.

mission agents who represent the livestock owners make sales to packers, dealers, or feeders or their representatives.

The slaughtering process is highly efficient, even though variations in animal carcasses limit the use of precision instruments.[1] Much of the work consists of a series of hand operations performed by specialized operators, especially with hogs — the chief item on the famous "disassembly" line. Lambs and calves are usually shipped to distributors as dressed carcasses, beef often in sides and quarters. Plants that sell in interstate commerce or to the federal government operate under the constant supervision of agents of the Department of Agriculture, who stamp each approved carcass "U.S. INSP'D & P'S'D." On the average, lamb and mutton constitute less than 50 per cent, and beef, pork and veal less than 60 per cent, of live animal weight.[2] "Edible" by-products include heart, liver, lard and many more; the "inedible" class includes hides, wool, animal feed made from blood and bones, and others. The largest packers also sell "sidelines," or products developed out of the meat business directly or indirectly — such as dairy and poultry products, cottonseed oil and shortening, and mineral fertilizer.

About two thirds of the livestock is raised west of the Mississippi River, about two thirds of the consumers live east of it, and slaughter-

1. Stanley Vance, *American Industries*, Prentice-Hall, New York, 1955, p. 581.

2. Calculated from U.S. Department of Agriculture, Statistical Bulletin 162, *Livestock Market News Statistics and Related Data*, 1954, pp. 18–19, 51–54.

TABLE 2

MEAT PACKING: SALES OF TEN LEADING PRODUCERS, YEAR ENDING OCTOBER 31, 1955

Firm	Amount	Per Cent
	(Millions)	
Industry total	$10,800.0	100.0
Ten leading companies	6,870.9	63.6
1. Swift & Co.	2,404.1	22.3
2. Armour & Co.	1,967.7	18.2
3. Wilson & Co.	650.5	6.0
4. George A. Hormel & Co.	336.6	3.1
5. John Morrell & Co.	336.1	3.1
6. Hygrade Food Products Corp.	334.3	3.1
7. Cudahy Packing Co.	308.1	2.9
8. Rath Packing Co.	254.0	2.4
9. Oscar Mayer & Co.	220.2	2.0
10. Tobin Packing Co.	59.3	.5

Sources: Company figures from Moody's *Industrials;* industry total estimated in George M. Lewis and J. Russell Ives, *Financial Results of the Meat Packing Industry,* 1955, American Meat Institute, Chicago, p. 3. The eleventh firm in size, Cudahy Brothers, does not publish figures. Sales, especially for the large packers, include varying amounts of nonmeat products.

ing has most of its chief centers in the Mississippi Valley. In 1955 Chicago was surpassed for the first time by Omaha as the largest livestock market. Iowa, Illinois and Minnesota, with 11, 10 and 9 per cent of value added by manufacture in 1954, respectively, lead in wholesale meat packing, but all states contain packing plants.

National and Local Packers

Swift & Company and Armour & Company have been the two giants of the meat packing industry since the late nineteenth century. Wilson & Company and the Cudahy Packing Company have been coupled with them for thirty years as "the big four" or "the national packers"; but these labels are obsolete, for in 1955 Cudahy closed unprofitable plants and dropped to seventh place, while many medium-sized companies also sell on a national scale. In 1955 the ten largest producers had 64 per cent of estimated industry sales. (See Table 2.)

In 1954 there were 455 slaughtering plants under federal inspection. These competed with meat produced by 952 wholesale and 1,810 local packing plants mostly under state or city inspection,[3] and by perhaps 8,000 retail butchers. The federally inspected plants accounted for about 78 per cent of commercial production (measured in live weight) in 1954, other plants with 300,000 pounds a year output for 19 per cent, and butchers for 3 per cent.[4] Another important branch of the meat industry is the prepared meats division, consisting in 1954 of nearly a thousand companies having 1,316 establishments, less than half of which were federally inspected. The large meat packers participate in this field as well.

Distribution

Most meat, except pork destined for cold storage or curing, goes out immediately by refrigerated freight car or truck for quick sale to the consumer. In 1939 the Department of Agriculture estimated the sales by packing plants as follows: 44 per cent direct to retailers; 30 per cent to the larger packers' "branch houses," which resell chiefly to retailers; 16 per cent by smaller packers to wholesalers; 9 per cent to institutional users or for export; and only one per cent to consumers through packer-owned stores.[5] Branch houses are much less important today, since supermarkets have taken over some of their functions. Brokers, and the hotel and restaurant supply houses, are employed in some transactions. According to the 1954 Census of Business, there were 279,440 stores selling meat.

Although packers prefer to sell under their own grades and brands, the Department of Agriculture grades beef, lamb and veal carcasses when either packer or buyer will pay the cost. Between 40 and 50 per cent of beef is thus graded; beginning with top-quality beef for the best hotels and on through beef for upper and then lower income localities down to ready-to-serve items and hamburger, the grades are prime ("U.S. prime"), choice, good, standard, commercial, utility, cutter and canner. In January 1956 prime steers at Chicago averaged $22.05 per 100 pounds live weight, while canner and cutter cows averaged only $9.58.[6]

3. U.S. Department of Agriculture, Agricultural Marketing Service, *The Livestock and Meat Situation*, July 8, 1955, p. 23.

4. *Ibid.*, p. 22.

5. E. B. Alderfer and H. E. Michl, *Economics of American Industry*, McGraw-Hill, New York, 2d edition, 1950, p. 578.

6. *The Livestock and Meat Situation*, March 2, 1956, p. 38.

Antitrust Suits

The importance of livestock to the farmer and of meat to the consumer has long made the packing industry an object of public interest and even of suspicion. Its antitrust history has thus been a stormy one.

The Beef Pools, 1885–1902

In 1890 a Senate committee, completing a two-year investigation, unanimously reported that five large packers (S. W. Allerton, Armour, Hammond & Company, Morris & Company and Swift) had been for about five years in an agreement to fix prices and divide markets for beef.[7] Although the disclosure of this "Allerton pool" is said to have contributed to the passage of the Sherman Act,[8] it continued in operation (with Allerton acquired by Morris) and in 1893 was extended to include Cudahy and the St. Louis Dressed Beef & Provision Company. For three years (according to testimony of the pool's secretary twenty years later) weekly meetings assigned quotas for shipment into each of several eastern territories. A packer exceeding his quota paid into the pool 40 cents per 100 pounds — a significant penalty in terms of unit profits then prevailing. When the price in a market fell, quotas were reduced. A uniform system of accounts was established, by which it was hoped "to make the margin of profit identical" among the packers.[9] In 1896 competition from an outside firm, Schwarzschild & Sulzberger, disrupted the pool's operations, and cooperative activities were reduced to mere interchange of data on margins and shipments. Early in 1898 the competing firm entered the pool, which operated again until 1902.

It is unlikely that the pool raised average prices, since the packers did not reduce over-all supply by refusing to purchase all livestock offered or by destroying meat. One aim was certainly to steady the prices of meat in the different sections of the country by reducing local gluts and shortages, and perhaps this was accomplished. Packers try

7. *Report of the Select Committee on the Transportation and Sale of Meat Products*, S. Rept. 829, 51st Cong., 1st sess., p. 446, cited in FTC, *Food Investigation: Report on the Meat-Packing Industry*, Part 2, 1918, p. 13.

8. Charles B. Kuhlmann, "The Processing of Agricultural Products after 1860," in Harold F. Williamson, ed., *The Growth of the American Economy*, Prentice-Hall, New York, 1944, p. 438.

9. FTC, *Meat-Packing* Report, Part 2, p. 16.

to do this by independent action today. Long-distance telephones, better market reports, and better transportation and storage make it much easier than in the past, and the temptation to use a pool is correspondingly weaker.

The quotas and penalties suggest that another aim of the pool was to reduce the incentive to push sales into any market at the expense of competitors. This illustrates the abuses inherent in the old, now unlawful, pool method of doing business.

First Antitrust Suits

In 1895 and again in 1896 federal grand juries refused to indict the pool participants, whose actions were in accord with current business philosophy.[10] The first antitrust suits in either the livestock or the meat industry were brought in 1896 and 1897 against two "exchanges," one an association of commission firms and the other of dealers, operating at the Kansas City stockyards. The Department of Justice argued that rules like those fixing fees for members, and forbidding them to have certain kinds of dealings except with other members, restrained trade. Overruling the lower courts,[11] the Supreme Court held by a 7–1 vote that stockyard transactions were not in interstate commerce [12] and that rules "entered into with the object of properly and fairly regulating the transaction of the business" did not restrain trade.[13] Justice Peckham delivered both opinions, and Justice Harlan dissented without giving reasons. The exemption from commerce is obsolete, but the defense of the rules themselves anticipated Justice Brandeis' famous *Chicago Board of Trade* opinion, which stated that some exchange rules were legal as being intended to regulate and thereby perhaps promote competition.[14] Rules governing stockyard transactions today are under the regulation of the Department of Agriculture.

In April 1902, as a result of agitation in the press and in Congress and a Department of Justice investigation, the packers abolished their

10. "The Significant Sixty: A Historical Report on the Progress and Development of the Meat Packing Industry, 1891–1951," *National Provisioner*, January 28, 1956, Section 2, p. 79.

11. *U.S. v. Hopkins*, 82 Fed. 529 (D. Kan. 1897), Department of Justice, *Decrees and Judgments in Federal Antitrust Cases*, 1918, pp. 41–43, 45–46.

12. *Hopkins v. U.S.*, 171 U.S. 578 (1898).

13. *Anderson v. U.S.*, 171 U.S. 604, 615 (1898).

14. *Chicago Board of Trade v. U.S.*, 246 U.S. 231 (1918).

formal pool and destroyed its records. In May the U.S. District Court in Chicago issued a temporary injunction prohibiting them from violating Section 1 of the Sherman Act by collusion in either buying or selling and Section 2 by demanding discriminatory rebates from railroads.[15] The injunction was made permanent in April 1903 and affirmed by the Supreme Court in 1905 in an opinion by Justice Holmes.[16] There was no trial on the merits.

Meanwhile the big packers had been fined $5,000 each in 1904 for violating the Missouri antitrust law.[17] This was "a sum rather less to them than five cents to the average citizen," and, besides, a price increase at Kansas City the day after the fines were announced recouped the amount and gave the defendants "quite an agreeable profit in addition." [18] Another inconclusive proceeding consisted of eleven indictments by a federal grand jury in New Orleans of railroad officers for "granting rebates and special privileges" to big packers.[19] These indictments were never brought to trial.

The National Packing Company Episode

Within ten days after the 1902 injunction J. Ogden Armour, Gustavus F. Swift and Edward Morris signed a contract to merge their companies, and if possible other meat packers, into a single unit. This huge project — no more than had just been accomplished in tin cans and steel — strongly suggests that the packers had valued the pool as a means of harmonizing their policies. Borrowing money from the banks, the three big packers acquired thirteen other firms, among them Hammond, the fourth largest. (The thirteen acquisitions gave the three large companies 36 per cent of total meat sales, as of 1909, as against their own 29 per cent.[20]) Cudahy and Schwarzschild, fifth and sixth in size, agreed to go in. The grand merger was not achieved, however, since money stringency on Wall Street late in 1902 caused Kuhn, Loeb & Company to withdraw its offer of financing, and the participants lost their courage in the face of mounting criticism.[21]

15. *Decrees and Judgments*, pp. 61–65.

16. *U.S. v. Swift & Co.*, 122 Fed. 529 (N.D. Ill. 1903), 196 U.S. 375 (1905).

17. *State v. Armour Packing Co.*, 173 Mo. 356, 73 S.W. 645 (1903).

18. Charles Edward Russell, *The Greatest Trust in the World*, Ridgeway-Thayer Co., New York, 1905, pp. 17, 202.

19. *Ibid.*, p. 202.

20. *State v. Armour Packing Co.*, 265 Mo. 121, 176 S.W. 382, 393 (1915).

21. *National Provisioner*, January 28, 1956, p. 87.

The net result was that the three big packers organized the National Packing Company in March 1903 to take over their acquisitions. Swift received 46.70 per cent, Armour 40.11 per cent, and Morris 13.19 per cent of the stock. The twelve original directors were, with one addition, the same men who had been meeting to run the pool, and they even met in the same office as before. Apparently they continued to regulate shipments in the same way the pool had done. There is evidence that meetings of the same sort had been held at the residences of the men concerned.[22] Wherever the meetings occurred, they could easily have had a purpose explicitly permitted by the decree: "curtailing the quantity of meats shipped to a given market where the purpose of such arrangement in good faith is to prevent the overaccumulation of meats as perishable articles in such markets." [23] The antitrust laws as interpreted today would never permit cooperation even for this purpose.

A second antitrust complaint was filed against the packers in 1905, on the basis of evidence collected by the Commissioner of Corporations.[24] The defendants argued that information given to the Commissioner, acting in his public fact-finding capacity, could not be used against them in court, and in March 1906 the District Court sustained this contention as to the individual defendants.[25] This ruling drew much public criticism as being an "immunity bath." [26] The government was unwilling to press, and finally dismissed, the case against the corporate defendants alone.

In 1910 the government returned to the attack with civil and criminal suits against the National Packing Company, and indictments of its ten directors and of five other corporations.[27] The *National Packing* suits were eventually dismissed (in 1913 and 1915), but the other indictment came to trial in 1912. The charges included buying livestock in agreement, figuring list selling prices by a uniform system

22. Complaint in *U.S. v. Armour & Co.*, Civil 48 C 1351 (N.D. Ill. 1948), paragraph 27.

23. *Decrees and Judgments*, p. 65.

24. *Report of the Commissioner of Corporations on the Beef Industry*, 58th Cong., 3d sess., H. Doc. 382, 1905.

25. *U.S. v. Armour & Co.*, 142 Fed. 808 (N.D. Ill. 1906).

26. Criticism cited in Deane W. Malott and Boyce F. Martin, *The Agricultural Industries*, McGraw-Hill, New York, 1939, p. 101.

27. *U.S. v. National Packing Co.*, Cr. 4384 (N.D. Ill. 1910), *Decrees and Judgments*, p. 749 and Civil 29953, *Decrees and Judgments*, p. 241; *U.S. v. Cudahy Packing Co.*, Cr. 520 (S.D. Ga. 1910), *Decrees and Judgments*, p. 750; *U.S. v. Louis F. Swift*, 186 Fed. 1002 and 188 Fed. 92 (N.D. Ill. 1911), *Decrees and Judgments*, p. 752.

of accounting, and keeping quotas for sales of each firm in different markets. After the government had offered its evidence, the defendants stood on the record and won an acquittal.

The big packers were not happy with the situation, less because the two *National Packing* suits were still pending or because of an indictment in Missouri (which was to bring a $25,000 fine for each packer in 1915 [28]) than because the tripartite control of National Packing Company was clearly inefficient. They followed their legal victory in 1912 at once by winding up the company's affairs and dividing its assets according to their stock ownership. This left each packer correspondingly larger than before 1902, but it did sever their indirect ties through this subsidiary. An obstacle to free competition in the industry was thus removed.

The Muckrakers

In 1904 and 1905 the "muckraking" journalist, Charles Edward Russell, published a series of articles in *Everybody's Magazine* which denounced the packing industry as a "greedy monopoly" and "rotten business." The articles alleged that the Commissioner of Corporations had been so handsomely entertained at the Saddle and Sirloin Club in the Chicago stockyard that his 1905 report failed to discover excessive profits.[29] J. Ogden Armour replied at once in the *Saturday Evening Post*.[30]

A much more effective piece of muckraking was Upton Sinclair's novel of 1906, *The Jungle*,[31] which aroused the country with its bitter denunciation of labor and sanitary conditions in the Chicago plants. Although two technical officials and the solicitor of the Department of Agriculture, who were sent immediately to study conditions, pronounced the novel "intentionally misleading and false from beginning to end," [32] public opinion insisted on sanitary legislation. The Pure Food and Drug Act, and a Meat Inspection Act which vastly strengthened the federal inspection begun in 1890, were passed in 1906.

28. 265 Mo. 121, 176 S.W. 382.

29. Russell, *The Greatest Trust in the World*, p. 144.

30. J. Ogden Armour, *The Packers, the Private Car Lines, and the People*, Henry Altemus, Philadelphia, 1906.

31. Reprinted by Vanguard Press, New York, 1916.

32. *National Provisioner*, January 28, 1956, p. 91.

The Federal Trade Commission Investigation

In 1910 a Senate committee concluded after lengthy study that a recent rise in meat prices had natural causes.[33] The inflation of World War I produced a much greater rise, which the public viewed as "profiteering." In February 1917 President Wilson directed the Federal Trade Commission to investigate monopoly in food processing. Although the Commission studied flour and canned goods as well, it paid most attention to the "big five" packers — Armour, Cudahy, Morris, Swift, and a new firm, Wilson & Company, which had taken over the assets of Schwarzschild & Sulzberger in 1916. The report concluded:

> The power of the Big Five in the United States has been and is being unfairly and illegally used to — manipulate livestock markets; restrict interstate and international supplies of foods; control the prices of dressed meats and other foods; defraud both the producers of food and consumers; crush effective competition; secure special privileges from railroads, stockyard companies, and municipalities; and profiteer.[34]

To indicate the scope of their power, the Commission noted that the five packers (1) slaughtered 61.2 per cent of federally inspected hogs and 82 per cent of cattle; (2) were "rapidly extending their control over all possible substitutes for meat — fish, poultry, eggs, milk, butter, cheese, and all kinds of vegetable oil products"; (3) had expanded into the distribution of fruit, vegetables and staple groceries; and (4) were important producers of fertilizer, hides, leather and wool.[35]

As "instruments of control and monopoly" the Commission named: (1) their control of stockyards handling 57 per cent of total livestock received at terminal markets, and their interest in yards handling 28 per cent, as well as control of terminal railroads, of cattle-loan banks, and (through either ownership, loans or subsidies) of market newspapers; (2) their ownership of refrigerator cars, for whose use the railroads paid them rentals which the Commission viewed as equivalent to rebates; (3) their control of 45 per cent of the country's cold-storage capacity; (4) their complex distribution systems built around the branch house; and (5) their affiliation with many banks through common officers or directors.[36]

33. *Ibid.*, p. 98.
34. FTC, *Meat-Packing* Report, Summary and Part 1, pp. 32–33.
35. *Ibid.*, pp. 33–38.
36. *Ibid.*, pp. 38–45; Part 3, p. 26; Part 4, p. 88.

The Commission also charged the packers with (1) "well-known methods of unfair competition" such as "bogus independents, local price discriminations, short weighting, acquiring stock in competing companies, shutting competitors out of livestock markets" and "a vicious system of rotation in price cutting"; (2) collusion in the purchase of livestock; and (3) jointly financed attempts to influence government action and public opinion.[37]

The remedy urged was government ownership of (1) all rolling stock used for livestock or meat; (2) all "principal and necessary" stockyards; and (3) enough branch houses, cold-storage plants and warehouses to create competition in marketing and in storage at the "principal centers of distribution." [38]

From the Investigation to the 1920 Consent Decree

The packers replied that the Commission's report was inaccurate and unfair.[39] It was certainly *ex parte* since the packers were neither invited nor permitted to introduce evidence or cross-examine witnesses, and some disinterested students considered it biased.[40] Nevertheless, this comprehensive and searching report did reveal evils which the packers' rebuttals failed to touch, and it had a more lasting influence than previous investigations and legal attacks. The author of a book whose content reveals sponsorship by one large packer has written: "In many respects the Federal Trade Commission investigation had exerted a constructive influence on the packing industry." [41] Although this evidently referred merely to greater cooperation in the livestock and meat industry and a new public relations program, the latter would have to rest on defensible industry practices. A representative of small packing companies reports today that they gained greatly from the changed attitude of their big rivals following the Commission's report.

Meanwhile the investigation had stimulated important direct action by law enforcement agencies and Congress. In December 1919 the

37. *Ibid.*, Summary and Part 1, pp. 64–74.

38. *Ibid.*, pp. 76–78.

39. Swift & Co. published five replies to different parts of the Commission's report, the longest being *Swift & Company's Analysis and Criticism of Part II of the Report of the Federal Trade Commission on the Meat Packing Industry of November 25, 1918*, Chicago, April 5, 1919.

40. The word "biased" appears both in Malott and Martin, *The Agricultural Industries*, p. 102, and in lecture notes, graduate school course in American economic history, Harvard University, 1938–39.

41. Bertram B. Fowler, *Men, Meat and Miracles*, Julian Messner, New York, 1952, p. 131.

Federal Trade Commission filed a formal complaint against the five packers, charging violation of the Clayton Act through purchase and control of thirty-one competitors. At the same time the Department of Justice prepared a suit under the Sherman Act. Although the packers felt that their legal position was "unassailable," they decided to "bend the knee to public opinion" [42] and accepted a consent decree in February 1920.[43]

The decree, which ran against both individual officers and corporate defendants, still stands as the leading example of antitrust action in the meat packing industry and as perhaps the most famous of all antitrust consent decrees.[44] The five packers agreed to (1) sell their holdings in public stockyard companies, in public cold-storage plants except where specially exempted, in stockyard terminal railroads and in market newspapers; (2) cease to handle, or to let others use their facilities to handle, 114 nonmeat products (such as fish, vegetables, fruit, specified canned goods and cereals); (3) cease to handle fresh milk or cream except for sale in processed form; and (4) operate no retail meat markets in the United States. They agreed also not to enter any conspiracies, attempts to monopolize, or "illegal trade practices of any nature whatsoever." The decree required the defendants to open on written demand from the Attorney General such records and correspondence as might relate to violations of the decree alleged in "reasonably specific terms." Like other consent decrees, this one stated that its acceptance "shall not constitute or be considered an adjudication that the defendants or any of them have in fact violated any law of the United States."

The Packers and Stockyards Act of 1921

A second result of the Federal Trade Commission's investigation was the passage in 1921 of the Packers and Stockyards Act. This forbade meat packers ("any person . . . manufacturing or preparing meats") to discriminate, to apportion territories, or to control prices; and it put stockyards of more than 20,000 square feet, and market

42. *National Provisioner*, January 28, 1956, p. 110.

43. *U.S. v. Swift & Co.*, Eq. 37623 (Sup. Ct. D.C. 1920).

44. William D. Kilgore, Jr., "Antitrust Judgments and Their Enforcement," in Section of Antitrust Law, American Bar Ass'n., Proceedings of Spring Meeting, 1954, Chicago, p. 104, note 1.

agencies and dealers operating on them, under the regulation of the Secretary of Agriculture. One reason for selection of this official is said to have been opposition of the big packers to vesting jurisdiction in the Federal Trade Commission.[45]

The chief activity of the Department of Agriculture's Packers and Stockyards Branch (called "Division" until 1954) is control of the public markets. As of July 1, 1955, its regulations covered 335 "posted" (i.e., regulated) stockyards, about 270 auctions of significant size, 3,723 dealers, 1,652 market agencies, 1,308 poultry dealers and agencies, and 1,915 meat packers.[46] Yardage fees have been set so as to yield a "fair return" on stockyard investment.[47] Fees of commission men have been set to cover "all reasonable expenses and a reasonable profit to all those firms which handle a reasonable volume of business in a reasonably efficient manner." For example, rates for Omaha in 1926 were set according to five classes of expense on sale of a carload of cattle: yardmen's salary, other salaries and promotional expenses, interest, exchange dues, and $5 for "salesmanship" — or $13.25 in all. In February 1930 the Supreme Court, in an opinion by Justice Brandeis, unanimously upheld the Secretary's power to set such rates,[48] thus establishing the legality of this somewhat rough-and-ready evaluation of personal services in contrast to the usual basing of public utility rates on capital investment.[49] Since the Omaha Livestock Exchange had fixed its members' fees previously, it was not competitive rates which were being displaced by government regulation. Eventually a more effective and less costly method of control had to be found than handling such cases one at a time. Exchanges and commission agents now file schedules of their expenses regularly, and by reference to these the Branch judges whether rates are too low or too high.

To cite one example of rate fixing, the fee for selling cattle at Chicago averaged 90 cents a head in 1921 when regulation began and

45. Testimony of C. B. Heinemann, in *Utilization of Farm Crops: Meat Products*, Hearings before a Subcommittee of the Senate Agriculture and Forestry Committee, 81st Cong., 2d sess., 1951, Part 5, p. 2539.

46. Letter from Chief, Packers and Stockyards Branch, Livestock Division, Agricultural Marketing Service, U.S. Department of Agriculture.

47. For one example see Howard Douglas Dozier, "The Nashville Stockyards Case," *Journal of Land and Public Utility Economics*, February 1930, pp. 102–04.

48. *Tagg Brothers & Moorhead v. U.S.*, 29 F. 2d 750 (D. Neb. 1928), 280 U.S. 420 (1930).

49. G. N. Dagger and Howard Douglas Dozier, "Reasonable Livestock Commission Rates," *Journal of Land and Public Utility Economics*, February 1931, pp. 45–51.

had come down to 67 cents in 1933. By 1953 it had increased only to $1.05, or 15 cents more than in 1921, although cattle prices had trebled. Between 1933 and 1953 the number of active commission firms involved declined from 105 to 100, but it was the fall in Chicago's volume of federally inspected slaughter from 15 to 7 per cent of the total,[50] rather than the decline in fees, which accounted for this. For all posted stockyards in 1953, the average yardage plus commission on cattle was $2.10 per head, or about 1.5 per cent of average selling price.

There is an important difference between the stockyards and the typical regulated public utility. No one stockyard possesses monopolistic power, except possibly over a mere handful of farmers who might have no alternative outlet. Many shippers, and certainly nearly all the large ones, have their choice of two or more markets as well as the choice of selling at one or more country buying stations or auction markets. Thus in 1950, 25 per cent of cattle and 60 per cent of hogs slaughtered under federal inspection were not bought on federally regulated stockyards.[51] A market or a commission firm that consistently overcharged would soon lose its largest patrons. Nor is there any suggestion that widespread collusion among markets has been or could be tried. Consequently, although regulation has indeed operated to keep rates down, competition would probably have done this in any event.

Enforcing Fair Competition at the Stockyards

The Branch has worked to make the public stockyards free and efficient markets, holding that this is their best defense against the inroads of direct buying — a practice which the Branch has not favored, in view of the concept of public markets as institutions important to the nation's welfare on which the 1921 act was based. When the Branch found a yard on which there were too few buyers, it persuaded others to come into the market. It punished false weighing. It ferreted out certain racketeers who entered the packing industry merely to exploit commission agents or farmers. Having found that buyers were not always taking due account of quality in making bids, it has tried to educate them to this factor's importance. At some yards

50. *Business Week*, August 27, 1955, p. 73.

51. U.S. Department of Agriculture, *Yearbook of Agriculture*, 1954, p. 489.

it has eliminated instances of collusion among buyers — as when packers agreed in the morning to purchase a certain quantity of livestock later in the day from speculators at an agreed price, or from dealers at an agreed margin over their buying price, or from commission men at "the established price." [52]

For some years the Branch has been fighting the "order" or "turn" system which occasionally appears at stockyards. When livestock shipments are low, commission men are pressed by a number of buyers for the first chance to bid, and sometimes a formal system of rotation is set up under which each "regular" buyer bids first on successive days. Because of the implied exclusion of "visiting" or irregular buyers (often stock feeders), the Branch has required the elimination of this system on a number of stockyards. One system which involves no favoritism, and is used on practically all markets, is for two or more buyers who want to purchase at the same time from a single seller to toss a coin for the first bid. Whether "coin flipping" prevented sellers from getting the advantages of buyer competition was one question at issue in a case involving the Union Stock Yards at Omaha which the Branch brought at the end of 1955.[53]

The Act and the Meat Packers

Contrary to a misconception occasionally held, the statute does not regulate output or prices of meat packers. The Branch has handled two big cases relating to the packers. The first, in 1923, resulted from Armour's purchase of Morris, which had suffered heavy losses in the 1921 price collapse and which bankers believed could be saved by this merger. This reduced the "big five" to four and for the moment increased Armour's share of total inspected slaughter from 17.4 to 23.5 per cent, almost equal to Swift's 24.2 per cent for the year ending June 30, 1924.[54] Secretary of Agriculture Henry Wallace, Sr., filed a complaint against Armour under Section 202 of the statute, forbidding acts designed to, or likely to, control prices or create a monopoly. From April 1923 to October 1924, 300 witnesses testified, and the

52. Compare Report of the Administrator, Production and Marketing Administration, U.S. Department of Agriculture, 1949, pp. 47–48.

53. U.S. Department of Agriculture, Packers and Stockyards Docket 2165, December 1955; *Business Week*, January 28, 1956, p. 109.

54. FTC, *Packer Consent Decree*, S. Doc. 219, 68th Cong., 2d sess., 1925, p. 20.

record grew to 12,265 pages plus exhibits. In 1925 the new Secretary, William M. Jardine, ruled as follows:

> The overwhelming weight of the testimony is in favor of the view that competition has not been materially lessened by reason thereof, either in the buying of livestock or the sale of the meat or meat products thereof.[55]

The Federal Trade Commission still considered the acquisition a violation of the consent decree.[56] However, buyers who had previously given part of their business to Armour and part to Morris now decided to avoid undue dependence on one source, and began buying from others. Within a few years Armour had lost all its market gain. The facts thus showed that no government action to protect competition from this merger was needed. Its chief legacy to Armour was a heavy bonded debt.

The second case resulted from a complaint filed by the Secretary against the large packers in 1937, charging manipulation of prices paid for livestock and elimination of competition in its purchase. Hearings were held in 1938, after which the defendants were directed by the Secretary to "show cause" why an order should not be issued against them. In December 1940, the Secretary decided that there was nothing conclusive in his vast accumulation of records. Although only the charges relating to turkey purchases were dismissed,[57] leaving the meat packers to assume that the other charges were still pending,[58] the whole case was in fact abandoned.

The Branch has also cooperated with the Federal Trade Commission in correcting exaggerated claims made in advertising, and in investigating complaints of short weight and of unfair or fraudulent practices in general. The courts (under the Fourth Amendment to the Constitution) have protected the packers' books of account against inspection except as warranted by specific complaints of violation of the act.[59] The Branch chief stated that this prevented the agency's studying in detail the costs of distributing meat or taking any action

55. *Secretary of Agriculture v. Armour & Co.*, Docket 19, Conclusion and Order of the Secretary of Agriculture, September 14, 1925.

56. FTC, *Packer Consent Decree*, pp. 16–17.

57. Packers and Stockyards Docket 909, January 1941.

58. Salomon Bros. & Hutzler, debenture prospectus for Swift & Co., New York, April 28, 1948, p. 18.

59. *Cudahy Packing Co. v. U.S.*, 15 F. 2d 133 (7th Cir. 1926).

which might be suggested by such a study.[60] Recently, however, it has issued a set of regulations which asserts its right to inspect books of account, and has inspected them in several cases without running into a court test.

In the first ten years (1922–31) of the Packers and Stockyards Act the Secretary of Agriculture issued only one order against a meat packer prohibiting unfair practices, in the next ten years 17 orders, and in the third ten years 6 orders. The meat packers profess satisfaction with the operation of the act and the standards of fair competition it maintains. They believe it is more expertly and fairly handled than if it were not in the hands of specialists in the livestock and meat industries. The possibility that meat distributors might gain the same exemption as meat packers from direct Federal Trade Commission supervision was opened up by a court ruling in 1940 that a distributor that had purchased 20 per cent of the stock of two meat canners came under the Secretary of Agriculture's jurisdiction rather than the Commission's.[61]

History of the Consent Decree after 1920

It was only very slowly that the big packers disposed of all their outside interests as required by the consent decree. By 1924 they had sold their holdings in livestock newspapers and public cold-storage warehouses.[62] They had also turned over their shares in the public stockyards to trustees, though they were unable to sell them owing to lack of investor interest in the shares of regulated stockyard companies.[63] The General Stockyards Corporation bought Armour's interests in various yards in 1928, and in 1937 was merged into the United Stockyards Corporation, which had bought Swift's interest in 1936. This company now operates twelve stockyards.[64]

Legal proceedings delayed the enforcement of the entire decree until 1929. The California Cooperative Canneries, which had made a ten-year contract with Armour in May 1919 to distribute its canned

60. Testimony of M. J. Cook, chief of Packers and Stockyards Division, U.S. Department of Agriculture, in *Utilization of Farm Crops*, Senate Hearings, p. 2471.

61. *United Corp. v. FTC*, 110 F. 2d 473 (4th Cir. 1940).

62. FTC, *Packer Consent Decree*, p. 10.

63. Brief of Swift and Armour in Support of their Petitions for Modification of Packers' Consent Decree, *U.S. v. Swift & Co.*, Supreme Court, District of Columbia, Eq. 37623 (1931), 179–82.

64. Moody's *Industrials*.

fruit, moved in April 1922 to enjoin the decree insofar as it prevented Armour from fulfilling this engagement. This claim was sustained by the trial court, but the Supreme Court (with two justices not sitting) declared the decree valid in 1928 and overruled the intervention in 1929.[65] Justice Brandeis, who delivered both opinions, held that even if the terms of the decree covered some transactions "wholly intrastate," so that the court had "erred," the defendants had "waived such error by their consent" in 1920. In short: "The power to enjoin includes the power to enjoin too much."[66]

In August 1929 and April 1930 Armour and Swift petitioned to vacate the decree on the ground that conditions had changed.[67] They cited four instances: the rise of grocery chains, which could legally pack their own meat although the big packers could not sell groceries, and which bought from small packers because they did not need the warehouse facilities of the big ones; the recent rise of independent packers; the semi-depressed state of the whole industry; and the regulation by the Secretary of Agriculture. The national farm organizations, previously hostile to the packers, supported the petition. They hoped now to expand the market for farm products by letting them operate retail stores and sell unrelated products.

The Supreme Court Affirms the Decree

Justice Jennings Bailey of the District of Columbia Supreme Court found in January 1931 that the competitive situation in meat packing had been much improved since 1920.[68] (1) The big packers' sales and earnings had declined compared with those of competitors favored by truck transportation. (2) The rise of chain stores and new food processors had deprived the big packers of any opportunity of winning a food monopoly. (3) There was no proof that the "sporadic examples" of unfair practices and price fixing by both big and small packers had been authorized by their executive officers. (4) Not only had a number of small packers testified that neither monopoly nor unfair advantages existed, but the Department of Justice had signed a stipulation to the

65. *Swift & Co. v. U.S.*, 276 U.S. 311 (1928); *U.S. v. California Cooperative Canneries*, 279 U.S. 553 (1929).

66. 276 U.S., at 331.

67. See J. Donald Fewster, "The Packers' Consent Decree," *Harvard Business Review*, April 1930, pp. 350–51.

68. This opinion is not officially reported.

effect that the meat packers were "in active competition with each other in the purchase of livestock and in the sales of their products." Justice Bailey concluded that the big packers should be allowed to distribute "unrelated" food products at wholesale, but not to enter retailing or to own stockyards and terminal railroads (where they might obtain secret preferences).

A 4–2 vote of the United States Supreme Court in 1932 reversed this decision and finally affirmed the original consent decree.[69] Although Justice Cardozo, in his opinion, granted that "the meat monopoly has been broken, for the members now compete with one another,"[70] he held that the two reasons given by the government for the original decree were still as valid as in 1920:

1. The packers had a competitive advantage in distribution of groceries because they could use distributing facilities they already owned.

> When they add groceries to meats, they will do so, they assure us, with substantially no increase of the existing overhead. Thus in the race of competition they will be able by their own admission to lay a handicap on rivals overweighted at the start. The opportunity will be theirs to renew the war of extermination that they waged in years gone by.[71]

2. The packers would "certainly have the temptation to resume" the practice of "fixing prices for groceries so low over temporary periods of time as to eliminate competition."[72] Here Justice Cardozo made some significant remarks which opened a breach in the Supreme Court's *U.S. Steel* decision of 1920:

> Their low overhead and their gigantic size, even when they are viewed as separate units, would still put them in a position to starve out weaker rivals. Mere size, according to the holding of this court, is not an offense against the Sherman Act unless magnified to the point at which it amounts to a monopoly, but size carries with it an opportunity for abuse that is not to be ignored when the opportunity is proved to have been utilized in the past.[73]

69. *U.S. v. Swift & Co.*, 286 U.S. 106 (1932).
70. *Ibid.*, at 117.
71. *Ibid.*, at 118.
72. *Ibid.*, at 116.
73. *Loc. cit.*

The dissenting opinion of Justice Butler, emphasizing the growth of competition in both the meat and grocery trades, focused on the interest of the consumer rather than that of the competitor:

> Defendants should be permitted more efficiently to use their help and equipment to lessen their operating expenses. That makes for lower prices, and so is in the public interest.[74]

Several economic commentators agreed that the packers' possession, through their meat business, of facilities usable for other foods was an economic, rather than an unfair, advantage.[75]

Economic Consequences of the Decree

The disposal of the big packers' holdings in stockyards, terminal railroads, market newspapers and public cold-storage plants undoubtedly relieved their smaller competitors of the danger that these agencies might be used as weapons of unfair competition. Many examples of actual misuse of stockyard control had been listed by the Federal Trade Commission.[76] Thus, rendering companies affiliated with the big packers received monopolies of the business of processing animals that died in transit or in the pens. Small packers were unable to get permission to construct lanes, chutes, spur tracks and gates which they needed — at least until they sold out to the big packers — and met delays in weighing livestock. Commission men, being dependent on the stockyards for their existence, faced the temptation of partiality to the big packers' interests. Outside observers feel that the decree removed danger of this sort of discrimination, while the big packers say they are glad to be rid of the "headaches" that ownership of the stockyards involved. The widespread suspicion and occasional complaints to the Department of Justice [77] that the big packers still control the stockyards are unfounded.

74. *Ibid.*, at 122.

75. Harold Paul Alspaugh, *Marketing of Meat and Meat Products*, unpublished doctoral thesis, Ohio State University, Columbus, 1936, pp. 61, 368; A. C. Hoffman, *Large-Scale Organization in the Food Industries*, TNEC Monograph 35, 1941, p. 23; Myron W. Watkins, "Meat Packing and Slaughtering: Social Aspects," *Encyclopaedia of the Social Sciences*, Vol. 10, p. 260. Both economic and unfair advantages are implied in FTC, *Packer Consent Decree*, p. 31.

76. FTC, *Meat-Packing* Report, Part 3, pp. 61–105.

77. Complaints in files of Antitrust Division, summaries of which were shown to the writer by a small packer to whom they had been "leaked."

Control of market newspapers also created danger of abuse, although these journals were already relying by 1920 on the Department of Agriculture's reporting services for the figures they published. The prohibition of ownership of public cold-storage warehouses had little significance, for the big packers were still allowed to operate as public warehousemen in the seasons when they had empty space available.

Disposal of the "Unrelated Food" Business

The order to dispose of business in "unrelated" foods was complied with gradually, as the packers found purchasers for their wholesaling subsidiaries. Swift did not sell its 74 per cent ownership in Libby, McNeill & Libby (one of the country's biggest fruit and vegetable canners) until 1941, but it had put its stocks into the hands of voting trustees after the Supreme Court's 1932 decision. The effects of the decree in this regard may be summarized as follows:

1. *Independent food distributors* were spared the threat of competition from the big packers. There would in all probability have been some further expansion of these "unrelated" activities of the packers had it not been for the decree. However, the law of increasing costs with expanding operations would undoubtedly have prevented the big packers from achieving dominance in the wholesale grocery trade.

2. *Consumers* would presumably have gained from the decree if the Federal Trade Commission had been correct in its view that the packers had distributed unrelated foods in order to tighten their control over meat consumers by supplying their other needs as well.[78] There was no direct evidence of this, however, and the aim was more likely to make fuller use of facilities for buying from farmers, of space in refrigerator cars,[79] of space in cooling facilities in branch houses, and of salesmen's time by giving them a full line of products to handle.[80] Hence, the decree may have tended to keep packers' costs higher, besides reducing competition in other foods. These effects are not great, however: space is not always available for nonmeat products, and meat is a large-volume item which can occupy a salesman's time reasonably well on most of his visits.

78. FTC, *Meat-Packing* Report, Part 4, p. 14.

79. President John Holmes, in report of Annual Meeting, Swift & Co. shareholders, January 20, 1944, pp. 6 ff.

80. TNEC Monograph 35, p. 23.

3. *Farmers,* according to some of their representatives, suffered from the decree's refusal to let the packers compete with established distributors in handling their products. It is doubtful that this was significant in practice.

4. *The packers themselves* state that they have been blocked repeatedly from handling foods (such as salad dressing) which would have been suggested by their raw materials or methods of marketing, but for a long time they seemed to view these difficulties as pinpricks. This restriction made little difference to them competitively, since the smaller packers, although not restricted, had not entered the general grocery business aside from a few instances like Hygrade's brand of coffee. One big packer has viewed its inability to enter the Los Angeles market — because it is not allowed to load fruit and vegetables for the return truck trip — as the consumer's worry, not its own. In recent years, however, the packers have felt increasingly that their lack of a full line to sell to chain and supermarket customers is a serious obstacle to their expansion. They are resentful of the restrictions imposed by a decree more than thirty-five years old, whether or not its absence would significantly change their operations.

The prohibition of retailing by the big packers is of minor significance in view of the practical difficulties in combining packing with retailing.[81] Aside from the antagonism this would arouse among retailers,[82] retailing is a specialty quite different from packing. Thus Swift's Canadian affiliate did operate retail stores, but dropped them as unprofitable more than two decades ago; and the smaller packers do little retailing. When Armour and Swift asked permission to resume meat retailing in the United States in 1929, it may have been partly with the idea of gaining a bargaining weapon against the chain stores. Later the chains, which had been buying from small packers, changed their policy to spread their purchases among large and small alike, and also disposed of some of the packing plants they had opened. The chains and supermarkets, however, prefer to buy and sell their beef, lamb and veal on the basis of government grades rather than packer brands. The increasing proportion of their output sold under grades may give the packers a new motive for seeking to establish at least a few stores to promote their own brands.

81. Alspaugh thesis, pp. 61–62, based partly on interviews with packers and chain stores.

82. Argument of government counsel, cited in Brief of Swift and Armour, Eq. 37623 (1931), pp. 154, 160.

Recent Opinions on the Decree

In 1945 and 1947 the Department of Justice investigated complaints of competitors that the packers were violating the consent decree.[83] These investigations "failed to obtain evidence which would stand up in a court of law."

In 1950 the Department reviewed its files on this subject and concluded that, despite occasional complaints, there was insufficient evidence to justify a demand to search the packers' records. It was admitted that there were two possible views of each of the "suspicious" circumstances: (1) Frederick H. Prince, a big stockholder and director of Armour, was also the dominating figure in the Union Stockyards of Chicago; but in a 1948 rate dispute he had defended the Stockyards' interest against Armour's. (2) The packers had ceased giving discounts to hotel and restaurant supply houses and were selling direct to hotels; but this was probably a "wholesale" business permitted by the decree. (3) Former officers of Swift had become officials of the United Stockyards Corporation and of Libby, McNeill & Libby; but it was not proved that Swift dictated their actions. (4) Members of the Cudahy family, named in the 1920 consent decree, owned over 50 per cent of the stock in Red Wing Company, maker of grape products; but no single family member owned the prohibited 50 per cent.

The late C. B. Heinemann, leading trade association representative of the smaller packers, stated to the writer in 1951 that the consent decree was working well on the whole. He complained only that the big packers were increasing their business in poultry and dairy products to an alarming extent. He had asked the Department of Justice to bring proceedings to add these to the lines of business forbidden to them (but not, of course, to small packers) in the decree. No such proceedings have been brought.

Railroad Relationships

The big packing companies had been among the many corporations that received rebates from the railroads before the Elkins Act of 1903 outlawed them. According to the Interstate Commerce Commission, the result was that smaller competitors had "in the main ceased to exist."[84]

83. These paragraphs are based on Department of Justice memoranda, which were shown the writer by a small packer.

84. ICC, 15th Annual Report, January 17, 1902, p. 11.

The failure of the consent decree to order the big packers to sell their refrigerator cars was considered by the Federal Trade Commission its chief weakness. Although one reason the packers owned them was that the railroads had refused to take the risk of building such bulky, top-heavy cars,[85] the Commission believed them to be a source of monopolistic power and of illegal rebates through the rental paid by the railroads for their use.[86] (The shippers pay the regular rates on the meat and other articles sent in them.) If these rentals were excessive, they would indeed constitute a rebate; but they are regulated, and there have been few if any complaints in recent years.

The Federal Trade Commission also charged that the large packers received preferential treatment on their cars, including prompter return of empties than was given the small packers (who owned less than 10 per cent of private cars).[87] One smaller firm, however, had objected to the Commission's plan of pooled ownership, on the ground that having its own cars assured it of good service.[88]

In 1930 and 1931 Swift sold its 6,000 or so refrigerator cars and tank cars (used for fats and oils) to the General American Transportation Company, from which it now leases them.[89] Armour sold its 461 tank cars in 1932, but kept its refrigerator cars, and Cudahy and Wilson also still own such cars. Swift's action throws doubt on the view that ownership by packers was a significant source of monopolistic profit.

One abuse of intercorporate connections in this general area was illustrated by Federal Trade Commission orders in 1931 and 1932 against two small railroad equipment manufacturers, controlled by officers with big-packer connections.[90] The officers were charged with threatening to have meat traffic withdrawn from certain railroads unless these were willing to buy minor items of railroad equipment from them. These intercorporate connections no longer exist.

85. Lawrence Oakley Cheever, *The House of Morrell*, Torch Press, Cedar Rapids (Iowa), 1948, p. 27; Kuhlmann, "The Processing of Agricultural Products after 1860," p. 435.

86. FTC, *Packer Consent Decree*, pp. 30–34.

87. FTC, *Meat-Packing* Report, Summary and Part 1, p. 41.

88. Cheever, *The House of Morrell*, pp. 175–78.

89. Moody's *Industrials;* Ralph C. Epstein, *GATX: A History of General American Transportation Corporation, 1893–1948*, North River Press, New York, 1948, p. 95.

90. *Waugh Equipment Co.*, Docket 1779, 15 FTC 232 (1931); *Mechanical Manufacturing Co.*, Docket 1727, 16 FTC 67 (1932); Arthur Robert Burns, *The Decline of Competition*, McGraw-Hill, New York, 1936, p. 173.

Merger Sleight-of-Hand

A way around the legal barrier to mergers was opened by Supreme Court decisions in 1926 and 1934. In 1916 the Western Meat Company (a California packer controlled by Swift) purchased the stock of a Nevada competitor; in 1917 Swift purchased the stock of one competitor in Alabama and another in Georgia; and in 1919 the Thatcher Manufacturing Company, the largest producer of milk bottles, bought the stock of four others. Federal Trade Commission orders, based principally on Section 7 of the Clayton Act, reached the Circuit Courts of Appeal in 1924 and 1925; they were overruled on the real issue of the *Western Meat* case, but sustained in the other two.[91] The Supreme Court reversed all three decisions. In the *Swift* and *Thatcher* cases, Justice McReynolds spoke for a 5–4 majority in holding that the voting of the purchased stock to acquire the assets of the company before the Commission filed its complaint neutralized Section 7, the purpose of which was merely "to prevent continued holding of stock and the peculiar evils incident thereto." [92] Justice Brandeis, in a one-paragraph dissent, objected to these words and quoted Section 11, which called for action when anyone "*has violated*" any earlier section.[93] The Western Meat Company, which did not acquire the Nevada firm's assets until after the Commission's complaint, was pursued by the courts and eventually, in 1930, was forced to sell them.[94]

By the first two of these decisions, reinforced by another in 1934,[95] the Supreme Court opened a loophole in Section 7 and left the government (as Justice McReynolds pointed out [96]) to its Sherman Act remedy. In December 1950 Congress closed this loophole with the Celler-Kefauver Anti-Merger Act.

The Antitrust Drive of 1941

In 1928 two of the medium-sized packers, Hormel and Rath, were indicted for allegedly restraining trade by not bidding for hogs in

91. *Western Meat Co. v. FTC*, 1 F. 2d 95 (9th Cir. 1924), 4 F. 2d 223 (9th Cir. 1925); *Swift & Co. v. FTC*, 8 F. 2d 595 (7th Cir. 1925); *FTC v. Thatcher Manufacturing Co.*, 5 F. 2d 615 (3d Cir. 1925).

92. *FTC v. Western Meat Co., Thatcher Manufacturing Co. v. FTC, Swift & Co. v. FTC*, 272 U.S. 554, 561 (1926).

93. *Ibid.*, at 564.

94. *Western Meat Co. v. FTC*, 33 F. 2d 824 (9th Cir. 1929); FTC, Annual Report, 1930, pp. 89–91.

95. *Arrow-Hart & Hegeman Electric Co. v. FTC*, 291 U.S. 587 (1934).

96. 272 U.S., at 561.

each other's territory, but were acquitted.[97] The next antitrust actions were eleven criminal proceedings brought between June 1941 and October 1942.

The "fat lamb" and "Easter ham" cases. Three big packers and the Denver stockyard and commission firms were indicted in the "fat lamb" case for conspiring to eliminate all interior (country) purchases of fat lambs in this area and to compel shippers to sell at Denver. Cynics say that the case was inspired by the Washington representative of the sheepmen, who, anxious to show some "results" to his constituents, "camped on the doorstep" of the Antitrust Division until the suit was brought.

The District Court dismissed the first indictment as merely alleging an agreement to centralize purchases on one of the stockyards regulated by the government for the farmer's benefit, and as showing no influence on the price of lambs.[98] After the Supreme Court had voted 5 to 3 not to hear an appeal,[99] the government specified the "turn" system used from 1935 to 1940 as being in restraint of trade. This system had been set up to correct the situation at a time when drought conditions caused buyers to go to homes of commission men at early morning hours to get the first chance to bid. Tossing a coin for the first bid next morning seemed at least preferable to this. The coin-tossing vanished when receipts returned to normal. The District Court expressed doubt about the legality of such a system, if it existed, and therefore overruled a demurrer.[100] Nevertheless, the government asked for a dismissal early in 1944, saying that the purchasing system used "has not for the past two years actually operated to the detriment of the producers," and that even as to 1935–1940 "the evidence . . . was incomplete and . . . erroneous conclusions had been drawn."

In accepting dismissal, Judge John Foster Symes reminded the government attorneys of the stigma and expense inflicted on the defendants thus "unjustly accused" and admonished them against using criminal proceedings in such cases. To this the attorney present in court "fully" agreed.[101]

97. *National Provisioner*, February 25, 1928, p. 21; May 12, 1928, p. 24.

98. *U.S. v. Swift & Co.*, 46 F. Supp. 848 (D. Colo. 1942).

99. *Ibid.*, 318 U.S. 442 (1943); also 135 F. 2d 745 (D. Colo. 1943).

100. *Ibid.*, 52 F. Supp. 476 (D. Colo. 1943).

101. *Ibid.*, Commerce Clearing House, *1944–1945 Trade Cases*, No. 57249, p. 57365.

In the "Easter ham" case, eighty-one packers, who sold 80 per cent of the output of ham, were indicted for allegedly agreeing since 1936 not to quote prices on hams for Easter delivery until the four weeks just preceding.[102] The government stated that wholesalers and retailers thus had to pay higher prices than those which had prevailed in January and February. "As an integral part of the scheme," the packers advertised the idea of "Easter hams" in national magazines under a plan sponsored by the American Meat Institute. The packers replied that they were attempting to cope with refusal of retailers to honor their long-term contracts for Easter hams when the prices fell after the contracts had been placed (sometimes six months ahead). Their point of view was expressed as follows:

> They claim that the closest they came to conspiring was to read trade-paper editorials — and listen to industry convention orators damning the forward-contract practice, while government men sat in the meetings and joined in the applause.[103]

The "government men" were from the Department of Agriculture, representing the interests of the hog raisers.

One defendant was willing to pay a fifth of the maximum fine to get out of the courts, for he pleaded *nolo contendere* a year after the suit was brought and paid $1,000.[104] As to the others, the government asked first for a continuance, and then in 1949 for a dismissal.

In the "fat lamb" case the government "got as far as first base" in the courts but no further; in the "Easter ham" case it scared one out of eighty-one defendants into yielding. In the other nine proceedings it was to get nowhere.

Acquittals. Three indictments for collusion in purchase of hogs resulted in jury trials and acquittals. One charged Armour and Swift with holding Saturday hog prices at the St. Joseph livestock market at the same level as on Friday, inducing other packers to discontinue country purchase of hogs in order to concentrate transactions at St. Joseph, and sharing by agreement the hog receipts there.[105] During six of the preceding nine years, the purchases of Armour and Swift had

102. *U.S. v. Cudahy Packing Co.*, Cr. 32839 (N.D. Ill. 1941).

103. *Business Week*, January 10, 1942, p. 24.

104. Commerce Clearing House, *The Federal Antitrust Laws with Summary of Cases Instituted by the United States, 1890–1951*, Chicago, 1952, No. 634.

105. *U.S. v. St. Joseph Stock Yards Co.*, 44 F. Supp. 31 (W.D. Mo. 1942).

been approximately equal. This lent plausibility to a "revelation" to the grand jury by a buyer that there had been a 50–50 agreement; but in court he confessed with much embarrassment that he had been exaggerating. The defense impressed the jury with some of its "character witnesses" — farmers who sold at St. Joseph because they considered it their best market.

The next case to be decided did not involve the four largest packers. The Indianapolis Live Stock Exchange and three medium-sized firms that bought 90 per cent of the livestock there were charged with (1) fixing hog prices by *collective* bargaining with commission sellers; (2) arranging for the latter to refuse to sell late-arrival hogs to others until they had been given first chance; and (3) rotation of the right to bid first on successive trading days.[106] After two witnesses had been called, the judge declared the evidence not pertinent, and the jury returned a verdict of not guilty.[107]

Armour and Wilson were indicted for collusion in hog purchases at Oklahoma City, where year after year their annual purchases had been almost exactly equal. The defendants replied that their plants had been built with the same capacity, and pointed out that during the alleged conspiracy their combined share of total purchases had dropped from 89 to 77 per cent. The government also charged that the defendants had agreed that only one of the two should bid on any given Saturday, had boycotted commission men who sold to others, had exchanged full information on hog purchases, and on one occasion had agreed on a common bid equal to the Kansas City price less 15 cents. After a procedural appeal had been overruled,[108] the case was tried in 1947. The Court heard the government's evidence and then directed a verdict of not guilty, on the ground that no actual influence on prices had been proved — in the absence of which there was no right to infer a conspiracy to affect prices.

Cases dismissed without trial. The six remaining cases were dismissed before trial. One charged a medium-sized packer and three large ones with allocating buying points in Nebraska and Iowa so as to avoid competition.[109] The second accused three big packers of dividing pur-

106. *U.S. v. Kingan & Co.*, Cr. 7451 (S.D. Ind. 1942).

107. *National Provisioner*, December 5, 1942, p. 22.

108. *U.S. v. Armour & Co.*, 48 F. Supp. 801 (W.D. Okla. 1943), 137 F. 2d 269 (10th Cir. 1943).

109. *U.S. v. John Morrell & Co.*, Cr. 8807 (D. Neb. 1941).

chase of hogs at Sioux City on a 40–40–20 basis.[110] The defendants were said to be enforcing these percentages by exchanging full information and by occasional withdrawals from the market to allow laggards to catch up. The government later asked a dismissal because it had failed to put women on the grand jury panel! Next, a charge that Armour and Swift divided hog and sheep purchases at Fort Worth equally, using the same methods as at Sioux City,[111] was dismissed "for want of prosecution."

The last three cases were not dismissed until 1949, after their substance had been incorporated into a civil suit filed against all four big packers in 1948. In one, the American Meat Institute and fifteen members had been indicted for allegedly attempting to prevent price cutting.[112] Two methods were said to be in use: formulation of "cutting tests" which suggested standardized "slaughtering, cutting, processing, boxing and selling expenses"; and distribution to salesmen for small packers of *Meat Trade Topics*, an Institute publication which often advised against shading the list price unless the meat was in danger of spoiling. The Institute now ceased to circulate the cutting tests, which showed the different cuts that normally are produced from various species of animal and how to translate prices for each cut into an over-all value for the live animal, but the *National Provisioner* took them up.

In Chicago, Armour, Swift and Wilson were indicted for allegedly agreeing on their offering prices and on hours their buyers would appear in the market.[113] The reply made was that the charges really involved activities of the "Chicago Subcommittee of the Joint Marketing Improvement Committee, Sheep Section," which had been organized in 1939 by packers, stock growers and commission firms to foster marketing of animals through central stockyards — an aim which lower prices of sheep at stockyards would hamper.[114]

Finally, the "Hog Section" of the same committee was charged with fixing the price of hogs at direct buying points at a specific differential

110. *U.S. v. Floyd M. Sherwood*, Cr. 3923 (N.D. Iowa 1942); *National Provisioner*, June 6, 1942, p. 17.

111. *U.S. v. Swift & Co.*, Cr. 7890, and *U.S. v. Armour & Co.*, Cr. 7891 (N.D. Tex. 1942).

112. *U.S. v. Swift & Co.*, Cr. 33033 (N.D. Ill. 1941); *Business Week*, December 6, 1941, pp. 83–84.

113. *U.S. v. American Meat Institute*, Cr. 32776 (N.D. Ill. 1941).

114. *Business Week*, June 28, 1941, p. 24.

below the Chicago price, thus preventing competition with the Chicago market.[115] The defendants replied that Department of Agriculture studies had never found a fixed difference between public markets and interior points, and that price movements in fact started now at one, now at the other.[116] Dismissal of this case in 1949 completed the 99.9 per cent failure (one small fine had been collected) of this series of prosecutions.

The Dissolution Suit of 1948

One of the most ambitious dissolution suits in the history of the Sherman Act was filed against Armour, Cudahy, Swift and Wilson in September 1948.[117] The government saw more hope in winning a civil suit than the pending criminal proceedings, and the Attorney General announced (in the midst of an election campaign in which control of the cost of living was an issue) that the suit would help "prevent the basic necessities of life such as food from falling into the hands of monopolistic groups." [118] The complaint charged that the four defendants and predecessor companies had been conspiring to restrain trade and monopolize the industry since about the year 1893. At first, it was alleged, they had done this through formal meetings in pools and via the National Packing Company, but "By about 1920, the executives of each concern had become so habituated to the use of these identical methods and policies, that they were expert in conducting the operations of their respective companies along parallel noncompetitive lines that achieved the objectives of the said conspiracy." [119]

The following *buying offenses* were charged: (1) agreeing to keep percentages purchased at each public market constant year by year, and facilitating this by exchanging figures on purchase totals; (2) avoiding competition by putting direct buying stations at different locations; (3) depressing livestock prices by "laying back" and refusing to bid until late in the day when sellers had become desperate; and (4) "paying substantially identical prices for livestock of similar species, grade, and weight." [120]

115. *U.S. v. Wilson & Co.*, Cr. 32801 (N.D. Ill. 1941).
116. *National Provisioner*, July 12, 1941, p. 12.
117. Complaint in *U.S. v. Armour* (1948).
118. Department of Justice press release, September 15, 1948.
119. Complaint in *U.S. v. Armour* (1948), paragraph 52.
120. *Ibid.*, paragraph 21.

On the *selling* side, the collusive practices charged were: (1) imposing on customers identical discounts and times for paying bills, and quoting delivered rather than f.o.b. prices; (2) conspiring with the American Meat Institute in using test cost formulas to achieve identical prices of meat, in urging salesmen not to cut prices, and in limiting allowances made to buyers for shrinkage; (3) selling stable proportions of meat in the several markets year by year; and (4) "selling meat and meat products at substantially identical prices in the same sales area." [121]

As to *relations with independents*, the defendants were said to have (1) tried to persuade them to follow their own purchasing, cost-finding and selling policies; (2) resisted any expansion in their buying percentages on the public stockyards by outbidding any who started to expand; and (3) acquired some independents outright in order to obtain their buying positions, and then kept these buying positions even when, as often happened, they shut down the acquired plants.

The complaint demanded that Armour and Swift be broken up into five companies each, and Cudahy and Wilson into two each. The reason for this demand was expressed as follows:

> They possess such tremendous power to suppress competition and the systematic use of that power is so deeply imbedded in their whole method of doing business, that nothing less than destruction of that power can provide an opportunity for any real or effective competition in the sale of meat and the purchase of livestock.[122]

The specific plants to be included in each new company were chosen on the general principle of giving each firm as wide a geographical spread as possible. Thus one successor to Cudahy was to own the plants in Sioux City, St. Paul, Wichita, Phoenix, Fresno and Los Angeles; and the other those in Jersey City, Albany (Ga.), Kansas City (Kan.), Omaha, Salt Lake City, Denver and San Diego. It may be observed that each new company would remain as important *at each particular stockyard* as its predecessor had been; and thus collusion in purchasing livestock which might have existed at any given stockyard would not be affected.

Some attorneys in the Antitrust Division never favored the suit. Their doubts were confirmed when, in November 1949, the U.S.

121. *Ibid.*

122. Department of Justice press release, September 15, 1948.

District Court for Northern Illinois ruled that no actions prior to 1930 could be received in evidence. The government (in March 1954!) decided that this was a fatal bar to success of the suit, which it dropped with the remark that it would insist on obedience to the consent decrees of 1903 and 1920.[123]

Certain Specific Effects of the Antitrust Laws

Several specific effects of the antitrust prosecutions may be noted. One is abandonment by many livestock buyers and meat salesmen of any discussion or interchange of price information with each other. Formerly they would "pass the time of day" by asking, "What are you paying for hogs?" or "What are you asking for chucks?" No doubt such conversations, which are not illegal in themselves but could serve as supporting evidence of collusion, have not entirely disappeared, despite prohibitions from the head office. In their absence, livestock buyers have to get their information from sellers, and salesmen from customers. In either case, the information is still obtained — as it must be if business is not to be done clumsily in the dark.

The large packers used to collect, partly from each other, figures on livestock purchases by firms at the different markets. They abandoned this practice around 1940 as a result of the government's criticism, and now rely on published data.[124]

One company has, since 1903, required all salesmen, auditors, plant managers, and higher officers including directors, to sign once each year and place on file at the head office individual pledges to comply fully with all federal and state antitrust laws. The pledge in its present form concludes as follows:

> You are *never* to enter into *any* arrangement or combination, either personally or for Swift & Company, or any of its associated companies, either written or verbal, which would in any manner violate the foregoing.

Under this rule, it is said, a salesman was once dismissed for exchanging price lists with a competitor, even though this in itself was not a violation of the antitrust law.

Finally, it is possible that the big producers have been deterred by the antitrust threat from an aggressive campaign to capture a larger

123. *Ibid.*, March 17, 1954.

124. See Answer of Armour in *U.S. v. Armour* (1948), February 1, 1950, paragraph 34.

share of the market at the expense of their competitors. Their attitude was expressed thus by an economist of Swift & Company:

> Purely as a matter of self-interest, no intelligent and successful business man wants to destroy his competitors. He knows that he himself may not survive the competitive struggle. Or if he should survive that struggle and become a monopolist, he knows that private monopoly, in these days of democratic government, will invite public ill-will and destructive legislation.[125]

Whether or not this disclaimer of intent to monopolize was sincerely meant thirty years ago, later developments were to prove that ease of entry into meat packing is great enough that no plan of monopolization was ever likely to succeed. The small packers, nevertheless, say they are glad to be able to rely on the antitrust laws in case of need.

Competitive Status

Until very recent times the impossibility of preserving fresh meat during transportation made most slaughtering a local, small-scale enterprise. This was still true in 1850, although hundreds of firms were "packing" salt pork for shipment from Cincinnati and other western towns. The opening of the prairie states to livestock raising through railway construction caused the center of pork packing, and of cattle purchasing for shipment east alive, to move to Chicago after the Civil War.

Rise of the Chicago Packers

The modern meat packing industry grew up in the 1870s. Philip D. Armour, George H. Hammond, Nelson Morris and Gustavus F. Swift were leaders who established successful businesses at Chicago. The chief technical and commercial developments on which their success rested were: (1) refrigerated packing houses, cold storage and the refrigerator car, which made it possible to produce fresh meat at a large central plant, winter and summer alike, and ship it to distant points; (2) reduction of costs through the conveyor technique, invention of special processing tools and machines, and careful utilization of by-products; and (3) creation of a wide and efficient system of distribution.

Retail butchers were now forced to compete against fresh meat coming in by train. State laws keeping out "foreign" meat were found

125. See George E. Putnam, *Supplying Britain's Meat*, George G. Harrop, London, 1923, p. 125.

unconstitutional by the courts, and signs saying "No Chicago beef sold here" were gradually taken down as the consumer's preference became clear.[126] Armour and Morris set up branch houses to distribute their meat; Swift sold through partnerships with local men. The former method proved superior, and Swift, too, adopted it in most areas. By the late 1880s the Chicago firms were truly "national packers," and there was increasing talk of a "meat trust." The whole development is, however, a clear example of how improved transportation increases competition at the point of consumption, despite the concentration of manufacturing necessarily involved.

Decentralization after 1920

The geographical concentration of the industry eventually reversed itself. After World War I the packing industry, especially hog slaughter, began drifting away from the big midwestern cities.[127] Two of the principal causes were the westward extension of corn cultivation and hog raising, and better highways, which made truck shipments possible. Packers found that by operating close to the stock raiser they could accomplish several things: (1) offer the grower a delivered price, which spared him the risk of weight shrinkage, casualties and price decline during transit, and at the same time reduce freight costs and save stockyard charges because the packer either shipped dressed meat rather than livestock to the cities or sold his whole product by truck locally; (2) avoid higher manufacturing costs characteristic of big cities and take advantage of the presumption that "country boys are more efficient meat packers than city lads"; [128] and (3) sometimes achieve economies of product concentration by packing only the predominant local type of livestock. Between 1920 and 1945 the proportion of federally inspected hog slaughter which took place in Iowa, Minnesota, Nebraska and the Dakotas increased from 39.0 to 66.6 per cent, and much of this was at small towns rather than major markets.[129]

126. *National Provisioner*, January 28, 1956, p. 73.

127. See "The Name is HOR-mel," *Fortune*, October 1937, p. 129; Edward A. Duddy and David A. Revzan, "The Changing Relative Importance of the Central Livestock Market," *Journal of Business of the University of Chicago*, July 1938, Part 2.

128. James D. Cooney, president of Wilson & Co., quoted in J. Richard Elliott, Jr., "Bringing Home the Bacon," *Barron's*, January 9, 1956, p. 31.

129. W. E. Hoadley, Jr., E. Baughman and W. P. Mors, *A Financial and Economic Survey of the Meat Packing Industry*, Research Department, Federal Reserve Bank of Chicago, 1946, p. 11.

At first the central-market packers met this threat by increasing their purchase of animals at country points and continuing to ship them to terminal plants for slaughter. After 1928 they built or bought "interior" plants in an effort to compete on an equal basis.

Fluctuations in Corporate Concentration

The trend of concentration in this industry is usually measured by the share of the four (previously five) largest packers. The Federal Trade Commission used the figures for federally inspected slaughter only, on the following ground:

> The fact that the farmer has an opportunity to raise and slaughter cattle for his own use or for the local use of an adjacent town or village has little bearing on the question of the monopolistic position of the big packers as regards their control of the prices which the great majority of the urban population must pay for meats.[130]

The opposite position may be similarly phrased:

> The fact that the local slaughterer escapes the burden of federal inspection does not mean that the national packer does not have to meet his competition everywhere, and control of all federally inspected slaughter might be offset by consumer preference for freshly slaughtered local meat.

There are thus three possible bases of measurement — federally inspected slaughter, total slaughter, or, between the two, total commercial slaughter excluding farm slaughter. Each is relevant in some respects.

Some of the earliest estimates for the industry refer to cattle slaughter alone. In 1900 Swift, Armour and Morris accounted for 27.8 per cent, and in 1903 for 29.3 per cent, of the national total.[131] The 1903 figure for the five biggest packers and their affiliates was 45 per cent.[132] Some felt that this 45 per cent was an underestimate; [133] but the 1908 figure seems to have been lower still. For 1908 to 1935 the Federal Trade Commission has estimated percentages of interstate slaughter

130. FTC, *Meat-Packing* Report, Summary and Part 1, p. 118.

131. *Ibid.*, p. 127, and U.S. Census Bureau, *Historical Statistics of the United States, 1789–1945*, p. 102.

132. *Report of the Commissioner of Corporations on the Beef Industry*, pp. 57, 58, 66.

133. Russell, *The Greatest Trust in the World*, pp. 144–56.

for cattle, calves, sheep and hogs; and these can be converted, despite some loss in accuracy, into approximate percentages of total slaughter. They show a rise in the share of the big companies between 1908 and 1919 (from 35.8 to 45.7 per cent, in pounds), but by 1935 a loss of over half the previous gains (back to 39.6 per cent). (See Table 3.)

TABLE 3

MEAT PACKING: PROPORTIONS OF LIVESTOCK SLAUGHTERED AND MEAT PRODUCED BY FIVE LARGEST COMPANIES, 1908–19, AND FOUR LARGEST, 1924–35

(Per Cent)

Year	Total		Cattle	Calves	Sheep and Goats	Hogs
	Number[a]	Pounds[b]				
			Interstate or Federally Inspected Slaughter[c]			
1908[d]	59.7		74.9	63.0	71.6	53.2
1916	70.5		82.2	76.6	86.4	61.2
1919	69.3		78.5	77.3	86.8	61.8
1924	60.6		73.2	72.9	83.2	52.7
1929	58.7		69.5	70.9	85.8	47.9
1935	66.2		67.1	71.0	85.3	51.9
			Total Slaughter			
1908[e]	35.3	35.8	40.6	19.3	52.5	31.7
1916	44.2	44.0	49.5	27.4	68.1	39.3
1919	45.7	45.7	52.7	37.4	69.8	39.3
1924	41.4	41.7	47.6	36.7	64.0	36.3
1929	40.9	40.3	48.1	43.0	68.8	32.7
1935	42.4	39.6	44.5	42.2	68.4	29.4

Sources: Top half of table from FTC, *Agricultural Income Inquiry*, Part 1, "Principal Farm Products," 1937, p. 198. Figures in U.S. Census Bureau, *Historical Statistics of the United States, 1789–1945*, p. 102, permit conversion from interstate and federally inspected to total slaughter (figures for which are less accurate), as well as to meat production by pounds.

a. This first column is heavily influenced by hogs, whose share in total slaughter declined from 66 per cent in 1929 to 49 per cent in 1935. This shift accounts for most of the rise of the big packers' share in total animals slaughtered from 58.7 per cent in 1929 to 66.2 per cent in 1935, since these packers slaughtered a larger percentage of cattle than of hogs.

b. This second column assumes that the big packers produced the same percentages of beef, veal, lamb and pork that they slaughtered of cattle, calves, sheep and hogs. The source does not give federally inspected meat production by pounds.

c. The 1908 and 1916 percentages in the top half of the table apply to "interstate slaughterers," the later percentages to federally inspected slaughterers.

d. 1908 is for the fiscal year ending June 30, and includes National Packing Co. figures.

e. Total slaughter figures used for 1908 are the mean of the 1907 and 1908 figures.

TABLE 4

MEAT PACKING: SHARE OF FOUR LARGEST COMPANIES IN DOLLAR SALES AT WHOLESALE, 1929–55

Year	Number of Packers Reporting	Total Sales	Share of Four Largest
		(Millions)	*(Per Cent)*
1929	587	$ 3,848	64.4
1935	614	2,785	66.6
1947	680	9,425	58.5
1948		10,270	54.8
1951		11,550	53.7
1954		10,975	52.0
1955		10,800	49.4[a]

Sources: Reports of regulated packers to Packers and Stockyards Division, U.S. Department of Agriculture, as tabulated and continued on total industry basis since 1948 in George M. Lewis and J. Russell Ives, *Financial Results of the Meat Packing Industry,* 1955, American Meat Institute, Chicago, p. 21; percentages based on sales of four largest packers as given in Moody's *Industrials.*

a. Cudahy Packing Company is still included, although no longer fourth largest in 1955.

Trends since the 1920s

The livestock figures have not been published again, but there are three fragmentary sources for more recent trends.

1. The Packers and Stockyards Branch published for 1925–47 total sales of packers reporting to it, and the American Meat Institute has made annual estimates of wholesale meat industry sales since then. The share of Swift, Armour, Wilson and Cudahy Packing Company was 64.4 per cent in 1929, 66.6 per cent in 1935, and between 1947 and 1955 declined from 58.5 to 49.4 per cent. Only limited reliance can be placed on the trend down to 1947, since the number of packers reporting increased by about 10 per cent. On the other hand, if these were *new* firms, it would not distort the trend of the four companies' share of total industry sales. (See Table 4.) Besides the fluctuation in number of packers reporting, which caused the abandonment of this tabulation after 1947, the series suffers from inclusion of the large packers' nonmeat "sidelines" (which in Swift's case amounted to 26 per cent of 1947 sales [134]), from the omission of unregulated slaughterers, and from the possibility of a bias if little packers did not report as regularly (especially in unprofitable years) as big ones.

134. Debenture prospectus for Swift & Co., 1948, p. 6.

2. In apparent contrast to the decline in concentration just shown between 1947 and 1955, the Census Bureau has estimated the wholesale meat packing "concentration ratio" (share of the four largest firms) at 41.3 per cent of *value added by manufacture* in 1947 and at 46 per cent of *employment* in 1951.[135] The writer has found no one in the packing industry who believes that concentration increased between 1947 and 1951, and the explanation undoubtedly lies in a larger ratio of employment to value added on the part of larger packers. Figures supplied by one of the latter, based in part on Department of Labor data, show a 46–47 per cent employment concentration ratio in 1947 as well. The 1947 Census also showed the prepared meat industry to have a concentration ratio for the four largest of 29.5 per cent of *value added* compared with a median for 452 industries of 36.4 (as against meat packing's 41.3). It is interesting that the fifty largest meat packers accounted for only 68.3 per cent of *value added*, as against a median of 90.5 per cent for the largest in other industries (nearly all of which were measured according to *shipments*). Evidently small firms have a very much larger share of the meat market than the fringe of smaller firms in other industries. (See Table 5.) These figures omit the chief sidelines (such as dairy products, poultry and fertilizer), since these are produced in plants not counted by the Census as meat packing establishments. This omission accounts for the "national-packer" percentages being in the 40s instead of the 50s as in Table 4. However, they include a few nonmeat items such as margarine and, like the Packers and Stockyards series, they exclude retail and farm slaughter (which in 1954 and 1955 represented 11 per cent of total livestock slaughter [136]).

3. Swift has estimated its share of the weight of meat and lard produced, including farm slaughter, since 1900.[137] By decades, beginning with 1900–09, this has moved from about 11 per cent (or 13 if one allows for Swift's ownership in National Packing Company) to 13, 14, 16, 14½ and (for 1950–51) 13½ per cent. Armour has published its share of livestock slaughtered in 1948 as 11 per cent of calves, cattle

135. The 1951 figure is a Census estimate, with standard error of 3 per cent (two chances in three that the true figure is within 3 points of that shown), in *Statistical Abstract of the United States*, 1955, p. 801.

136. George M. Lewis and J. Russell Ives, *Financial Results of the Meat Packing Industry*, 1955, American Meat Institute, Chicago, p. 2.

137. Figures from Swift & Co. See chart in *Utilization of Farm Crops*, Senate Hearings, p. 2530.

TABLE 5

MEAT PACKING: PERCENTAGE OF VALUE ADDED BY MANUFACTURE, LARGEST 4, 8, 20 AND 50 COMPANIES, 1947

Number of Companies	Wholesale Meat Packing	Prepared Meats	Median of 452 Manufacturing Industries[a]
Largest 4	41.3	29.5	36.35
Largest 8	53.6	39.6	50.95
Largest 20	62.5	49.6	71.7
Largest 50	68.8	62.5	90.1
Total number[b]	1,999	941	
Rank in 452 manufacturing industries, based on 4-company ratio	192	279	

Source: U.S. Census data, in *Study of Monopoly Power*, Hearings before Subcommittee on Study of Monopoly Power, House Judiciary Committee, 81st Cong., 1st sess., 1950, Serial 14, Part 2-B, pp. 1446–53.

a. For all but 12 of the 452, value of shipments is used instead of value added (*ibid.*, p. 1445). This column was calculated for the present study.

b. These 1,999 wholesale meat packers exclude as too small many of the 3,463 plants slaughtering annually over 300,000 lbs., live weight, as reported in Bureau of Agricultural Economics, U.S. Department of Agriculture, *Livestock Slaughter by States*, November 28, 1952, p. 9. The number of prepared meat companies in 1947 was later stated by a special Census Bureau tabulation to be 942, rather than 941.

and hogs and 21 per cent of sheep,[138] or about 12 per cent of meat on a weight basis. Using the 1948 weights, Swift and Armour had about 26 per cent, and, based on dollar sales of Wilson and Cudahy, the four might have had 34 per cent of total meat production. This would indicate a decline of 6 or 8 points since the 1920s and 1930s, and information from the industry indicates that since 1948 there has been a continuing and significant decline. With their branded meats and their by-products, however, the four appear to have a larger share of value added than of pounds of livestock processed.

Swift states that its aim today is not specifically to gain or hold a percentage of the market, but to keep at least its present physical volume, to grow with the country as far as it can, and to make as much profit as possible out of its operations — with 7 per cent on total capital considered a practical goal.[139]

138. Answer of Armour in *U.S. v. Armour* (1948), paragraph 21.

139. Compare "Swift & Co.: Profits the Hard Way," *Fortune*, September 1952, p. 183.

Stability but No Rigidity

The lack of rigidity in market positions of the principal packers is illustrated by the following increases in sales between 1931 and 1955 of the ten largest firms as of 1931: Swift, 239 per cent; Armour, 195 per cent; Wilson, 207 per cent; Cudahy, 70 per cent; Morrell, 394 per cent; Kingan, merged with Hygrade; Hygrade (including Kingan), 298 per cent; Hormel, 987 per cent; Rath, 877 per cent; Oscar Mayer, 1,275 per cent.[140] In spite of the wide range of these increases (in a period during which livestock prices trebled, so that a 200 per cent increase would not really show any physical growth), all these companies kept their original rank except Cudahy and Hormel, which exchanged places. Swift consolidated its leather subsidiary between 1931 and 1955, whereas Armour and Wilson ceased consolidating their foreign operations, so the greater advance of Swift is at least in part deceptive.

Any trend toward concentration in meat packing will always be at least partially offset by the ease of entry. The trade saying is that "a rope and a knife are all you need to go into this business." Such equipment may not do a finished or an efficient job; but it sufficed for Gustavus F. Swift in 1855, and not much more was needed by some of the many black-market slaughterers who undermined the price-control efforts of the Office of Price Administration during and just after World War II. The increase in wholesale packing establishments, reported by the Census, from 1,392 in 1939 to 2,153 in 1947 and 2,367 in 1954 represents principally new companies. Between 1939 and 1955 the number of meat plants owned by Swift, Armour, Wilson and Cudahy increased only from 93 to 97. The number of meat packing corporations filing income tax returns is reported to have increased from 910 in 1939 to 1,392 in 1952.[141]

The difficulties faced by the larger packers, which had based their distributing operations on the branch house almost since they became sellers on a national scale, are illustrated by the figures of the Census of Business. The number of branch houses, and the share of branch houses in total wholesale sales of meat, declined steadily from 1929 to 1954, while the number and sales of wholesale establishments not controlled by packers were increasing just as steadily.

140. Moody's *Industrials*.

141. *Wall Street Journal*, April 17, 1956, p. 28. That there were 1,392 corporations in 1952 and 1,392 establishments in 1939 is just a coincidence.

Possible Causes of Concentration: Unfair Advantages and Mergers

In its 1918 report the Federal Trade Commission emphasized various unfair practices and artificial reasons to explain the growth of concentration in meat packing. Among these were manipulation of stockyards, refrigerator cars and cold-storage warehouses, and aid from banks and railroads with which the big packers had connections.[142] The ability of the big packers to maintain their position after many of these connections had been severed indicates that these were probably not basic elements in their success.

Mergers have furthered the expansion of the big packers. According to the antitrust complaint in 1948, Swift acquired 32 independent companies between 1927 and 1947, Armour 21, Wilson 7, and Cudahy 4.[143] However, it is reported that some of these acquisitions were mere formal mergers with formerly affiliated companies; and between 1929 and 1947 the share of these four in total meat sales declined sharply (see Table 4). In 1948 Swift and Cudahy each acquired a very small packer. If there were later mergers by the "big four" through July 1954, they were too small to be reported in the financial services.[144]

A recent study of the relative growth of large corporations by mergers and by internal growth showed that the median firm out of 74 drawn from many industries had effected 14.25 per cent of its growth (from the earliest date assets of the companies were published) by means of acquisitions, while the percentages for Armour, Wilson, Swift and Cudahy were 44.3, 11.8, 7.6 and −11.5 per cent, respectively (indicating, in the last case, a net divestment rather than acquisition).[145] Armour's figure is dominated by its unprofitable purchase of Morris in 1923.

A Department of Agriculture economist concluded in 1941 that "in many instances, if not in most," the motive of packing-house mergers was to achieve economies of production and distribution.[146] It must be granted that a large merger always reduces by at least one the sources of supply available to some or many customers, but the instances in

142. FTC, *Meat-Packing* Report, Summary and Part 1, pp. 38–45.

143. Complaint in *U.S. v. Armour* (1948), Exhibit D.

144. *Corporate and Bank Mergers*, Interim Report of Antitrust Subcommittee of House Judiciary Committee, 84th Cong., 1st sess., 1955, pp. 48–57.

145. J. Fred Weston, *The Role of Mergers in the Growth of Large Firms*, University of California Press, Berkeley, 1953, pp. 143–44.

146. TNEC Monograph 35, p. 23.

which a buyer of fresh meat no longer had a choice of several suppliers must have been few in number.

Functions of Large Packers

Not monopolistic practices or mergers but certain economic functions of large packers offer the basic explanation both of their origin and their continued existence.[147] These advantages may be summarized in two broad categories:

1. Although small as well as large companies can now make use of the conveyor system in cutting, of refrigerated cars and trucks, and of other cost-saving devices, the big companies can still finance research more easily, utilize by-products more intensively, and hire more highly trained specialists.

2. By their wide distribution systems, the big packers can sell a full line of meats, carry stocks over to times of shortage, and shift meat constantly from surplus to deficit areas — just as they originally came into the industry by carrying the surplus meat from the Middle West to the East. The "loading table," where the different departments of a big packer coordinate orders from various regions with the available capacity of various plants and transportation facilities, is an illustration of the distribution function. Theoretically, brokers and jobbers working independently could transfer the meat, but opinion in the industry is that they could not do it with the same promptness and smooth coordination as the integrated company.

Advantages of Small Packers

The data on comparative profits of large and small packers are subject to various weaknesses, such as irregularity of reporting, varying valuations of "net worth" and differences in inventory accounting. On the basis of available figures, it appears that medium-sized and large packers did better in the depression years 1930–34 than the smaller ones, but that over a long period the smallest companies did best and the largest ones worst. The fact that the next-to-largest group did better than the next-to-smallest in 1929–45 and 1949–54 is a statistical irregularity which weakens the conclusions. (See Table 6.)

147. See Donald R. G. Cowan, "Meat and Related Products," Chap. 9 in Richard M. Clewett, ed., *Marketing Channels for Manufactured Products*, Irwin, Homewood (Ill.), 1954, pp. 232–33.

TABLE 6

MEAT PACKING: EARNINGS BY SIZE GROUPS, 1929–47 AND 1949–54

(*Percentage Return on Net Worth: Average of Annual Figures*)

Net Worth	1929–45	1930–34	1946–47	Sales Volume	Number of Companies in 1954[a]	1949–54
(*Millions*)				(*Millions*)		
Under $1	6.0	.7	29.6	Under $1.5	18	8.6
$1–$4	4.4	.9	19.8	$1.5–$3	10	6.9
$4–$20	5.5	2.9	15.6	$3–$15	27	8.3
Over $20	4.3	2.0	12.8	Over $15	26	4.9

Sources: 1929–47 from figures collected by Packers and Stockyards Division, U.S. Department of Agriculture, grouped in W. E. Hoadley, Jr., E. Baughman and W. P. Mors, *A Financial and Economic Survey of the Meat Packing Industry*, Research Department, Federal Reserve Bank of Chicago, 1946, p. 19, and *ibid.*, Supplement, 1948, p. 8; 1949–54 calculated from packers' financial statements tabulated in George M. Lewis and J. Russell Ives, *Financial Results of the Meat Packing Industry*, 1954, American Meat Institute, Chicago, p. 29.

a. According to the source, "Number of companies varied slightly between the years, but this difference does not materially affect the comparisons."

The deduction from such figures that their size makes large packers less efficient [148] is undermined by certain of the reasons for the profits of their small rivals:

1. Those small enough to sell within one state are subject to the normally less stringent state or local inspection, and sometimes to no inspection at all. It is interesting that packers not federally inspected had a higher average return on net worth than the federally inspected group in every year between 1929 and 1945 except 1932–34.[149]

2. The medium-sized and smaller packers, being in most cases newer to the industry than the largest companies, often have more modern plants, in better locations. This is strikingly illustrated by the superannuation of facilities of Swift, Armour and Wilson at Chicago, where modern meat packing for a national market began. By 1950 these plants were obsolete, heavily taxed and subject to high labor cost, and their central rail location was neutralized by the rise of the

148. Harry L. Purdy, Martin L. Lindahl and William A. Carter, *Corporate Concentration and Public Policy*, Prentice-Hall, New York, 2d edition, 1950, pp. 559–60.

149. Hoadley, Baughman and Mors, *A Financial and Economic Survey of the Meat Packing Industry*, p. 46.

motor truck. Swift abandoned the slaughtering of hogs at Chicago in 1952, though continuing to process carcasses shipped there from the interior, and rehabilitated its other facilities. Armour completed a two-year reconstruction program in 1955, having abandoned no fewer than fifty buildings. In the same year Wilson dropped its Chicago meat operations and sold all its facilities except those used to make nonfood products. Cudahy, not a Chicago packer but an old and large one, closed four meat plants, twenty-six wholesale branches, and six egg and poultry plants between 1952 and 1955, and even sold its Old Dutch Cleanser. The seven packing plants it retained were just the number the dissolution suit brought by the Department of Justice in 1948 would have permitted it to keep. Cudahy had fewer products to sell after 1955, but it began to earn money.

3. Many small packers find economies in specialization. Thus 25 of the 56 firms with net worth between $1 and $4 million in 1945 were pork packers. It is suggestive that these 25 earned an average of 6.0 per cent from 1929 to 1945 as against only 4.4 per cent for the general packers of the same size; but the force of this comparison is weakened by the fact that pork profits were unusually high in the war years and that in the size group below $1 million net worth the general packers did as well as those that specialized.[150] A comparison of 1949–54 earnings shows 44 general packers lagging behind 20 pork packers in all six years and behind 17 beef packers in five of these years; but the factor of size is not "controlled" in this comparison. When earnings are related to net sales rather than to net worth, the ratios tend to come together.[151] This seems to indicate a need for larger investment per dollar of sales to do a general packing business than a specialized business.

4. There remains the very important group of advantages which inhere in local operation — the ability to buy livestock raised close to the plant, to buy only as much as will be profitable, to ship expeditiously and cheaply by truck, and to cater to local tastes and needs like those for fresh meat, particular cuts and quick service. These are real profit advantages of a small company — or of a plant owned by a large company but operating on a local basis. They are tied in, however,

150. *Ibid.*, pp. 46–47.

151. Lewis and Ives, *Financial Results of the Meat Packing Industry*, 1954, p. 28. This source classed as pork or beef packers those with 66 per cent by live weight in the category; but abandoned the whole classification in 1955 as not being rigorous enough.

with nonperformance of certain high-cost distribution functions. In the words of one student:

> The overhead cost of distribution by national packers is high when compared with the costs of the small packers, but it is the author's belief that it is low when compared with the would-be costs if the small packers were to attempt to sell on a nationwide basis.[152]

Thus the basic services of the large packers — to see that all livestock shipments find a market, to ensure that the fluctuating supplies of all kinds of meat are kept moving into consumption, and to equalize supplies between one place and another and from peaks in slaughter to other seasons of the year — are the ones that inevitably involve high costs in terms of market risks, carrying charges and maintenance of many outlets. The large packers admit that they regularly lose money in some areas because of transportation costs or sparsity of population.[153] If the big companies were to be broken up into smaller firms and these in turn were to attempt a national distribution (without which they would not be in competition with each other), the same problems would arise:

> A multiplicity of sales organizations would mean more overlapping of territories and more duplication of sales effort than already exists, which in turn would increase costs to consumers.[154]

Interlocking Directorates

In 1918 the Federal Trade Commission found a large number of intercorporate connections among the five big packers.[155] Interlocking directorates with scores of banks, stockyards, supply companies and the like were involved.

Three decades later it appeared that many of these connections had been dissolved. For 1946 the Commission found only the following interlocking directorates: (1) directors of Armour and Wilson met on the board of the Hat Corporation of America; (2) directors of Armour and Cudahy met on the board of the Continental Illinois Bank of

152. Alspaugh thesis, p. 80.

153. Herrymon Maurer, *Great Enterprise: Growth and Behavior of the Big Corporation*, Macmillan, New York, 1955, p. 175.

154. Alspaugh thesis, p. 80.

155. FTC, *Meat-Packing* Report, Summary and Part 1, chart facing p. 46.

Chicago; (3) directors of Armour and Borden — "potentially, if not actually, competitors in sales of evaporated milk, butter and dog food" — were on the board of the American Telephone and Telegraph Company; and (4) the chairmen of both Wilson and Rath were on the board of the Illinois Central Railroad.[156]

The same report found that three of the four big concerns had an indirect interlock with a baking company through joint membership on the boards of a bank or an industrial company. The Commission felt that these interlocks "may have operated to reduce the sales opportunities of smaller manufacturers of cooking fats and oils." [157] There were other interlocks with producers of cream separators, freight cars, refrigerants and refrigeration equipment.

The Commission's findings for 1946 are more interesting as evidence of the decline in such connections since its 1919 report than for the connections actually disclosed. It is hard to imagine the directors of Armour and Borden, for instance, using the monthly meeting of the American Telephone and Telegraph Company either to fix the price of butter or to agree not to make dog food.

Trade Associations

In 1906, the year of the muckrakers, the American Meat Packers Association was organized. In 1919, the year the Federal Trade Commission's big report was completed, it was replaced by the Institute of American Meat Packers. This in turn gave way in 1940 to the present American Meat Institute. The Institute has about four hundred members who conduct meat processing operations of one kind or another, and they handle 80 per cent of the total slaughter. Its chief activities have to do with public relations, cooperative advertising, research consultation, reporting of statistical information to members on livestock production and supply trends, and aid to members with operating and management problems in such varied fields as ham curing, sewage disposal and accounting. Two of the reactions of the Institute to the antitrust laws and the antitrust history of the industry are (1) never to discuss prices, and (2) to consult with its attorneys before starting a project like collection of retail prices, a discussion of ideal package sizes, or a survey of profits.

156. FTC, *Report on Interlocking Directorates*, 1951, p. 44.
157. *Ibid.*, p. 46.

In July 1942 a number of the one-plant packers felt that their interests diverged from those of the large ones with regard to Office of Price Administration regulations. Aware that the Institute could champion only those causes common to the whole industry, they founded the National Independent Meat Packers Association. Its 650 members sell in local or regional markets, chiefly in the East; the majority of them belong to the Institute as well. The Western Meat Packers Association, with about 400 members, also represents the interests of small packers.

Economic Characteristics of Meat Packing

Several product characteristics of meat strongly influence pricing and competitive methods of the packers.[158] (1) The packers have no control over the current supply of livestock, for this depends on the decisions of thousands of farmers and ranchers whose shipments are subject to unpredictable fluctuations depending on weather, prices of feed and many other factors. (2) Packers cannot determine, except to a modest degree by varying cutting methods and cold-storage operations, the quantities of various products they will put on the market. They do not assemble products as they choose but disassemble the raw material in the forms that its nature permits. (3) This means also that all their hundreds of products and by-products are manufactured under conditions of joint cost. Cost, therefore, can be only a limited guide in pricing any one of them. (4) Cuts of beef or pork from different animals are not precisely standardized or homogeneous, and the accepted cuts often differ with the region. (5) Fresh meat does not lend itself easily to company branding which will distinguish it in the eyes of consumers, although some packers are increasing their experiments with branded, prepackaged, frozen table cuts. Most sales are made to retailers, who are more interested in price than in the company name, and the meat is sold in carcasses, sides, quarters and wholesale cuts. Few cuts of fresh meat at retail carry the packer's name. (6) Fresh meat is perishable: the trade cliché is "Sell it or smell it." Freezing reduces the sale value, and facilities to store much meat in this form are lacking. (7) Finally, demand is determined by such factors as consumer incomes, the weather, and the supply and price of competing foods. Advertising has evinced little power to affect it.

158. This analysis relies in part on suggestions by Henry B. Arthur, Economist of Swift & Co.

The resulting position of the industry is described by a leading investment advisory service in the following terms:

> This dependence upon uncontrollable factors differentiates the trade from most other lines of activity and renders operations highly speculative.
>
> The inherent uncertainties of the industry, together with substantial capital leverage and narrow margins, make the shares of the meat packing companies highly speculative.[159]

Competition in Selling

Because of the economic factors, fresh meat products have to be sold at a price that will keep the supplies moving; in other words, for "what the traffic will bear." [160] Price reductions come quickly when inventories rise, whether because of increase in supplies or decrease in demand. When demand falls off in a locality, the price may be dropped, or shipments to that place reduced. When demand rises, so many wholesalers and retailers insist on increasing their orders that it is only by raising the price that supply and demand can be equalized until more meat can be shipped in.

A retailer usually likes to be on the calling routes of several salesmen. Interviews with 257 retail operators by one student brought out that "delivery service, friendship with salesmen, reciprocity buying, customer preferences, reputation of the packers, patronage of home industry whenever possible, and dealer services" played some part in determining which packer's meat would be bought, but that price was "the most important factor." Dealers were often found to shift their purchases for a difference of 1/8 to 1/4 cent a pound.[161] Quality is important to the retailer, but he has come to expect satisfactory quality from all established packers. *Fortune* has described the effect on packing companies as follows:

> The big packers . . . know they are in as rugged a competitive scramble as there is in business. They fight one another for pennies, day in and day out.[162]

159. Standard & Poor's Corp., *Industry Surveys*, "Meats and Dairy Products," Basic Analysis, May 10, 1956, pp. M 68, M 73.

160. See comment by Senator Guy M. Gillette of Iowa in *Utilization of Farm Crops*, Senate Hearings, p. 2398.

161. Alspaugh thesis, pp. 294–95, 311.

162. "One Man's Meat," *Fortune*, May 1946, p. 97.

The way profits are made is enterprise capitalism in its most exacting and varied form.[163]

The Department of Justice has looked at the facts more suspiciously. Noting that salesmen of the packing houses learn from retailers — not always accurately, as it happens — what prices their competitors are quoting, it comments:

> When differences are found in the prices of defendants, the salesmen telephone this information to the branch house managers, who then revise their own selling prices so as substantially to conform them to the level of prices being charged by other defendants.[164]

Making the assumption that Armour's price was found to be 50–52 cents for top-grade "rounds" and Swift's price 49–51 cents, the question arises which of the two will "conform" its price to the other. Usually the wrong price — that is, the one which did not meet the needs of the market — will be conformed to the right one. Swift will raise its price to 50–52 cents if it finds demand high and supply in the area relatively low, for it will decide there is no danger of being left with unsold meat. If demand is low and the supply of meat relatively high, Armour will soon find that it must lower its price to 49–51 cents in order to dispose of current supplies. If all national packers together should put the price higher than supply and demand justify, local slaughterers would undersell them.

In spite of these tendencies toward uniformity, Office of Price Administration records, the range of prices in Department of Agriculture quotations, and private studies made by the big packing companies suggest that price differences frequently occur. In addition to quality and service differences, sheer mechanics make it impossible to meet competitors' prices perfectly. Thus, if retailers shopping at competing branch houses are quoted different prices, the high-priced house may not learn of its mistake until after it has lost sales.

Charges of Manipulation

Charges of restraints in selling markets have at times been brought against the large packers. Thus the Federal Trade Commission argued in 1918 that they manipulated local meat prices by reshipping from

163. *Fortune*, September 1952, p. 102.

164. Complaint in *U.S. v. Armour* (1948), paragraph 47.

one area to another, by freezing meat to hold it over for higher prices, and by sale to other packers.[165] A Department of Agriculture economist has commented on this as follows:

> It is a little difficult to see how these things in themselves could result in a permanent or widespread enhancement of dressed meat prices. Meat not sold in one area must be sold in another, and the freezing of meat obviously results only in changing the time of sale.[166]

Some critics hold that much stability exists in the shares of the different packers in specific markets, and tend to suspect collusion as in the days of the pool.[167] Any such stability — which in any case does not prevent short-run fluctuations in volume among the packers for individual products and cuts — is more likely the result of independent attempts by packers to maintain their market positions.[168] If, for example, packer A ships more meat into a territory in order to expand his sales there, packer B will find his sales declining. He may respond by continuing his regular shipments, or his branch house may continue its regular orders, but he will make every effort to restore sales by price cutting or aggressive promotion. Packer A is thus unable to dispose of his additional quantity except at prices which are low compared to those in other markets. He is likely to conclude that his effort was a mistake.

The comment has been made that such marketing practices imply "that meat may be distributed on the basis of local price discrimination." [169] Granting the truth of this, it is hard to see how a meat producer could stay in business permanently, or avoid considerable waste of meat, if he sold at the same price (after allowing for transportation costs) in all markets without any regard for the local supply and demand.

Are Livestock Prices Fixed?

In charging the four largest packers with collusion in fixing prices to be paid for livestock, the Department of Justice stated that the

165. FTC, *Meat-Packing* Report, Part 2, pp. 108–31.

166. TNEC Monograph 35, p. 110.

167. Complaint in *U.S. v. Armour* (1948), paragraphs 45 and 46.

168. See Alspaugh thesis, pp. 143–44.

169. William H. Nicholls, "Market-Sharing in the Packing Industry," *Journal of Farm Economics*, February 1940, p. 234.

employees who do the actual buying on the stockyards learn each other's prices (usually in the morning) either by exchanging information or by asking commission men what the others are offering. This claim is subject to several qualifications: Much of the information received may be inaccurate; government and other market reports are used to supplement buyers' reports; much information relates to completed transactions rather than to current offerings; and, above all, many and possibly most individual buyers do not exchange price information. Assuming that competitive prices are learned, the following process occurs, according to the Department of Justice:

> The buyers then call their central offices and inform them of the prices being paid or offered by other defendants and other buyers. The central office considers these reports and, when differences exist, modifies its paying prices for livestock so that they are substantially identical with those of other defendants.[170]

The context in which this statement appears suggests that the "central office" referred to is that of the company; but it is only on rare occasions (e.g., purchase of livestock for shipment to a second plant of the same company) that the company's central office would be informed at all. Even the central office of the plant is often not informed of rumors that a buyer picks up, or of guesses that he makes as to what a competitor may have paid for a particular lot of steers, sheep or hogs. There is often great uncertainty about details of transactions between particular sellers and particular buyers.

To the extent that prices are made "substantially identical" as the quotation asserts, it does not necessarily follow that prices are reduced. Cudahy may be offering $22.00 for a certain quality of prime steers, find that Wilson is buying at $22.25, and have to raise its price to that figure in order to get any steers. It must be granted that Wilson, learning that Cudahy was offering less, might regret having paid so much and proceed to lower its own bid. With only two buyers, there might well be identity at a lower level than is warranted by supply and demand; but there are in fact many buyers at all important stockyards. If prices at one stockyard are successfully kept lower than those elsewhere, (1) farmers will switch their shipments, (2) out-of-town packers will put in bids, and (3) local packing plants will soon have to lay off their workers. The mere fact that two prices are identical

170. Complaint in *U.S. v. Armour* (1948), paragraph 43.

does not prove collusion; it may be an instance of the familiar economic principle that there is only one price in an open competitive market at any one time. Finally, a trip to a stockyard will show that prices being paid by different buyers are by no means always identical. Indeed, observers from the Packers and Stockyards Branch who have accompanied buyers of the big packers on several markets say they "compete like cats and dogs."

Stability of Livestock Buying Percentages

One of the main charges brought by the Federal Trade Commission in 1919 was that the big packers had divided their livestock purchases at the different public markets according to agreed percentages, probably since 1902.[171] This was also a principal accusation of the Department of Justice in its proceedings brought in 1941–42 and 1948, all of which resulted in dismissals or verdicts of acquittal. William H. Nicholls, the most widely quoted academic critic of the industry, has emphasized the same point.[172] It may be illustrated by purchases of hogs at Denver and Oklahoma City and of cattle at Fort Worth. At Fort Worth, for example, Armour accounted for 47.9 to 50.1 per cent of the cattle bought by Swift and itself (excluding consideration of cattle bought by others) in each year between 1913 and 1917, and for 49.8 to 52.2 per cent in each year between 1934 and 1945. (See Table 7.)

In support of the view that such constant percentages must be due to deliberate market sharing, two types of arguments are advanced: (1) that if decisions were made independently, changes in the relations of plants to each other, both as to demand for their products and as to the personnel in charge, would be bound to lead to greater variation in the percentages;[173] and (2) that several letters and statements of the packers and their employees have seemed to refer to deliberate market sharing.

Evidence of this latter sort has caused at least one writer, who does not assert that there is outright collusion in livestock buying today, to

171. FTC, *Meat-Packing* Report, Part 1, pp. 49–51, Part 2, pp. 28–99.

172. William H. Nicholls, *Imperfect Competition within Agricultural Industries*, Iowa State College Press, Ames, 1941, *passim*, and *idem*, "Market-Sharing in the Packing Industry," pp. 225–40. See also Clair Wilcox, *Competition and Monopoly in American Industry*, TNEC Monograph 21, 1941, pp. 184–85.

173. Burns, *The Decline of Competition*, pp. 163–64; TNEC Monograph 35, p. 108.

TABLE 7

MEAT PACKING: ARMOUR'S PROPORTION OF LIVESTOCK PURCHASES OF TWO LARGE PACKERS AT THREE MARKETS, 1913–17 AND 1934–45

(*Per Cent*)

Year	Denver, Hogs	Fort Worth, Cattle	Oklahoma City, Hogs
1913	48.9	50.0	50.0
1914	49.9	47.9	50.1
1915	47.7	50.1	51.0
1916	48.5	50.0	52.1
1917	49.9	49.8	49.8
1934	49.4	50.4	50.2
1935	49.1	49.8	50.0
1936	47.4	50.1	50.0
1937	49.4	50.0	50.0
1938	50.1	50.0	50.0
1939	49.5	49.8	50.5
1940	50.0	50.4	50.1
1941	[a]	49.8	49.9
1942	50.0	50.6	50.0
1943	50.1[b]	52.2	50.1
1944	50.6	51.0	50.0
1945	49.3	51.0	50.1

Sources: FTC, *Food Investigation: Report on the Meat-Packing Industry*, Part 2, 1918, pp. 73, 75; government complaint in *U.S. v. Armour*, Civil 48 C 1351 (N.D. Ill. 1948), Exhibits B-4, B-5-b, B-12. (Figures rounded.) The second big packer at Denver and Fort Worth was Swift; at Oklahoma City, Schwarzchild & Sulzberger in the earlier period and Wilson in the later. The 1913–17 figures for Armour at Oklahoma City are those for Morris, which it later absorbed. Cudahy is a third large packer buying hogs at Denver.

a. Not available.

b. One of the packers has figures showing a sharper rise and fall in the 1943–45 Denver percentages. There are several sources for such figures (stockyard records, packer records and, occasionally, others), and they are not always consistent.

hold that the packers did originally engage in collusive buying.[174] Two examples of such statements were produced from a letter of Philip D. Armour written from Denver in 1916: "As you know, everything here is done on a 50–50 basis"; and a telegram sent by Alden B. Swift from St. Joseph in 1913: "Hammond unable to buy their proportion." [175]

174. Nicholls, *Imperfect Competition within Agricultural Industries*, p. 5.

175. FTC, *Meat-Packing* Report, Summary and Part 1, p. 53; Part 2, p. 60.

One packer explained the crucial phrases, respectively, as follows:

> . . . each plant aims to buy at least 50 per cent of the receipts at that market, and . . . neither wishes to see the other packer become the larger factor.
>
> . . . the word "share" . . . does not mean an agreed upon percentage, but merely the share or proportion that each packer has been accustomed to purchase or that we think such packer ought to purchase in order to do his part in supporting the market.[176]

These explanations would imply that, even without a deliberate agreement, a percentage division of the market may develop as a trade custom and be accepted as such. This could be called an indication of tacit agreement or, in the words of Swift & Company in 1919,

> of the close watch that each packer keeps on the others. . . . each packer keeps a record from week to week of the percentages of total receipts at the various markets purchased by himself and by each of the other packers. Swift & Company is jealous of its position and does not intend to let the other packers gain in their proportion of the total by so much as a fraction of one per cent.[177]

Since 1919, however, Swift at least has changed its policy and now neither keeps these detailed records of other packers' purchases nor admits to any effort to hold a specific percentage.

Before commenting further on this phenomenon, it is worth remarking that the constancy of percentage is not as great on a week-by-week or day-by-day basis as on an annual basis. It would be impossible to keep percentages constant over such short periods; those who suspect market sharing merely claim that a deviation from normal will be reversed within a few weeks.[178] Nor was the constancy necessarily as great on the markets not named by the Department of Justice.

Discussion of "Laying Back" and Constant Percentages

The charge that packers "lay back" when purchasing livestock need not imply collusion, but can be discussed along with market sharing. What would happen if a big packer reduced its purchases in order to bring prices down at a certain market? Sellers would have to lower their asking prices in order to dispose of their stock, and competing

176. *Swift & Company's Analysis and Criticism*, 1919, pp. 38, 32.

177. *Ibid.*, p. 27.

178. Burns, *The Decline of Competition*, p. 159, note 3.

buyers would thus get the benefit of the lower prices. No processing company wants to let its competitors gain a buying advantage in this way. Smaller packers, order buyers for out-of-town packers, dealers who resell to feedlot owners or packers, and speculators would also benefit at the expense of any big packer that "lay back" until late in the day as charged by the government's 1948 complaint — unless the big packer's judgment was commercially sound. Packers do "lay back" when they consider the price too high, but if they made this a regular practice they could only lose by forfeiting their freedom of action and letting others always know their plans.

A local manager will also have difficulty in increasing his share of the market. He may know that by slaughtering more animals he can bring down his unit cost, but the only way to obtain his supply is by outbidding competitors. In order to keep their own costs down and their labor force at work, these in turn will raise their bids, for no manager wants to report to the head office that he has lost his place in the market or to lay off workers for lack of raw material. The net result will be higher prices to all and no gain to any packer.

This means simply that no packer wants to start a price war. What a packing-industry economist wrote as far back as 1923, in defense of the constant percentages, still holds true:

> In the case of Swift and Company it is an individual, common-sense policy, arrived at independently, not to invite retaliation and trade wars by using over-aggressive tactics. The company has deliberately tried to avoid cutthroat competition wherever it was legally possible to do so.[179]

In other words, constant percentages emerge because large buyers at each market are few in number. A market with hundreds of very small buyers would show no such stability among them, since each would feel that it could increase its demand when it wished, without having enough influence on the market as a whole to invite retaliation. William Nicholls, in an article pointing this out, referred to the history of Jacob Dold, a small packer who entered the Omaha market after World War I.[180] The weekly fluctuations of Dold's purchases, very great at first, died down by 1936, when he had grown to be as big in that market as Swift. His importance as a buyer had created stability in his share. (In 1938 he sold his plant to Wilson.)

179. Putnam, *Supplying Britain's Meat,* p. 125.
180. Nicholls, "Market-Sharing in the Packing Industry," pp. 229–30.

Paradoxes in Buying Percentages

In view of the charges made against constant percentages since 1919, some may wonder why the packers have made no effort to eliminate them. The most practical way might have been by agreement with each other to alter the percentages now and then. Paradoxically, therefore, fluctuations rather than constancy of percentages might have proved the existence of collusion.

One critic of constant buying percentages argues that they reflect "imperfect" competition, "presumably with ill effects on prices to farmer and consumer." [181] If there are such "ill effects," it must be by contrast with some other possible system, but, as he recognizes, it is quite another matter to prove that a more serviceable system can be set up and made to function successfully. The most obvious remedy would be to reduce the size of the plants buying on each stockyard to the point where none would any longer be a significant factor in the market and each would, therefore, engage in price competition. But the creation of more buying firms would add a burden of overhead and excessive personnel on the markets from which the livestock raisers themselves would suffer. A plant large enough to be technologically efficient is probably going to be represented by buyers who play a major role on the local livestock market. Nor would there really be much gain to sellers in eliminating constant percentages in favor of spasms of cutthroat competition.

Recent information from the industry is that the constancy of buying percentages has declined a little in recent years, under the influence of the growth of medium-sized packers and the competition of direct buying of livestock.

Buying Policy off the Principal Markets

When the declining receipts of hogs at terminal markets caused the Chicago packers to set up direct buying stations in the interior, they were found to have put at least some of them close to the interior packers' plants. It was suspected that the purpose might be "not so much to get cheap hogs as to keep their competitors (the interior packers) from getting cheap hogs." [182] The distinction between getting

181. *Ibid.*, p. 240.

182. Geoffrey S. Shepherd and Norman V. Strand, *Local Hog Marketing Practices in Iowa*, Agricultural Experiment Station, Research Bulletin 262, Ames, 1939, p. 179.

cheap hogs and preventing competitors from getting cheaper hogs is, however, an artificial one. The big packers were simply trying to maintain their competitive positions by getting livestock as cheaply as their competitors. They certainly would not have chosen locations which were unattractive from the point of view of supply of hogs raised locally or railroad facilities, merely because interior packers were already (hypothetically) at such unattractive locations.

A second criticism is that the big packers never placed their direct buying stations at the same point — with the sole exception of Mankato, Minnesota! [183] A packer tries to set up a plant where there will be an adequate supply of hogs to justify his facilities, and if a big competitor is already there, the supply may not be enough for both. He may be glad to stay away from a competitor, but this does not mean a loss to farmers. While some farmers are regretting that their existing local market was not broadened, others are pleased that a new buying station has been put closer to them.

A third suspicion, frequently voiced, is that the price at terminal markets, especially Chicago, is kept under control by the national packers, and that the price paid the farmer at smaller markets or when buying direct is kept below it by a fixed differential equal to transportation cost. Both parts of this charge are unfounded. There are too many farmers who have a choice of selling direct to local packers, and too many competing buyers at terminal markets, to permit such terminal market control. As to the facts, study has shown that there is no fixed differential "and that a change in hog prices, for instance, often emerges first at interior markets." [184]

Charges are rarely heard that prices are fixed on the auction markets which in recent years have taken so much of the trade from both central markets and buying stations.

Do the Big Packers Dominate the Small Ones?

Accusations that the large packers used threats and manipulations to prevent small competitors from enlarging their business were an old story, even before the Federal Trade Commission report of 1919 gave what a Department of Agriculture economist called "plenty" of evi-

183. Complaint in *U.S. v. Armour* (1948), Exhibit C.

184. *The Direct Marketing of Hogs*, U.S. Department of Agriculture Miscellaneous Publication 222, 1935, pp. 176–77.

dence.[185] Representatives of the big packers themselves admit, without specifying the practices, that their companies did things then that they would not defend today, and add that this rise in business standards is typical of other companies and industries as well as their own.

In recent years these complaints have been much fewer. Occasionally champions of small business will argue that a big packer could slash meat prices in order to ruin some small competitor, while making its own profit in other markets or on by-products.[186] The big packer puts it another way: sometimes competition in beef is so strong that he cannot make money except by efficiency in utilizing by-products.[187] Similarly, a small packer will in one letter warn that the "big four" can cut meat prices by making their profit on poultry, ice cream or sporting goods, and will demand "divorcement" from these lines; and in the next letter he will point with pride to the rise of the small firms and warn that the big packer "must decentralize if he is to continue to compete." Again, four packers who complained to the Department of Justice in 1947 against the big companies' threat to their existence [188] told the writer five years later that allegations of unfair practices generally turn out to be misunderstandings and that they themselves are quite able to compete. This suggests that the big packers may have some justification for their suspicion that their competitors occasionally use complaints to the government as competitive weapons, for instance to "scare off" the big one from encroaching on their market.

Small packers told *Fortune* in 1952 that they were not afraid of the big packers or of their advantages in the utilization of by-products.[189] The farthest any went in talking to the present writer was to say that the big ones keep a close watch, and that a small packer putting on a vigorous sales drive in a particular market is likely to meet retaliation. It was conceded that the same situation — quick retaliation to avoid loss of a market — prevailed among big packers themselves and among small ones.

185. TNEC Monograph 35, p. 109.

186. Wilbur LaRoe, in *National Provisioner*, April 26, 1947, p. 42; E. F. Forbes, in *Meat Magazine*, March 1950, p. 57; speech by Senator Joseph C. O'Mahoney of Wyoming, reported in *National Provisioner*, February 21, 1948, p. 44.

187. Testimony of T. R. St. John, assistant manager, Beef, Veal & Lamb Division, Armour & Co., in *Utilization of Farm Crops*, Senate Hearings, p. 2414.

188. Complaints in files of the Antitrust Division, shown to the writer by a small packer.

189. *Fortune*, September 1952, p. 183.

The increasing dominance of supermarkets in meat merchandising is one development which has helped independent packers on net balance. The preference of supermarkets for selling under their own brands or under government grades deprives the large packers of an advantage that big concerns have in other industries: possession of a national brand which commands consumer patronage. The national packers are striving by product and package improvements and by advertising to increase their business in branded meats, which of course carry a wider profit margin.

Interindustry Competition

Wholesale meat packers compete not only with each other but with retail slaughterers, including many of the country's several thousand locker plants. Nor can packers ignore the fact that, if either farmers or chain stores think packing profits are too large, some of them may arrange to slaughter for themselves.

Meat is often spoken of as a necessity of life, but its near absence from the diet of many poorer countries almost warrants its being called a luxury. Even in the United States it is not an absolute "necessity," since it must compete with other proteins, especially fish, poultry, eggs and cheese. Prices of these substitutes tend to vary with those of meat except as diverse supply influences may be at work. Consumer substitution occurs when price ratios get out of line,[190] although attempts to prove these relations statistically have not succeeded. The big packers, with their poultry and dairy products, have some protection against shifts in consumer demands.

Although a family is likely to increase its purchases of meat when its income rises, this does not mean that meat consumption fluctuates with national income. As a matter of fact, the share of personal disposable income going for meat has ranged from 3.7 to 6.7 per cent in the last thirty-three years.[191] It shows no correlation with times of prosperity or depression. Nor does the per capita consumption of meat, which fluctuates with livestock slaughter, show such correlation.[192] The percentage of income spent on meat appears to be determined by the volume of slaughter and by prices of meat and of sub-

190. Hoadley, Baughman and Mors, *A Financial and Economic Survey of the Meat Packing Industry*, p. 8.

191. *The Livestock and Meat Situation*, March 2, 1956, p. 35.

192. *Ibid.*, p. 26.

stitutes (interpreted broadly to include any food a family might want to buy in its stead when the price of meat is exceptionally high).

A recent statistical analysis of meat demand made an "important finding" (known previously, but never proved as completely) that "when the price level is rising, if meat prices only keep pace with the average price level of all consumer's goods, consumers will demand an increased amount of meat. Consequently . . . meat prices . . . will rise more rapidly than the general level of commodity prices." [193] In other words, when incomes rise, meat is among the first items for which consumers increase their expenditures. Thus, given the nature of the livestock industry—which does not ship immature animals to market in great numbers just because prices are high, and may even hold more of them back for breeding than usual—it is their own increased income which, by causing general inflation, also causes the special rise in meat prices against which consumers or their spokesmen complain.

Performance and Popularity of the Industry

Meat packing has long ranked among the American industries with a world-wide reputation for mass production methods and efficient utilization of all parts of the raw material ("all of the hog but the squeal"). Henry Ford is said to have planned his automobile assembly line after watching the operation of an Armour conveyor.[194] Although later technological achievements have not been so spectacular, there have been continuing improvements in methods and in utilization of products.[195] Some of these, like quicker curing of ham, smoking of bacon and chilling of carcasses, have resulted in considerable savings in costs.[196] The extent of the industry's achievement in one of its sidelines is suggested by a professor at a medical school who says, "I think first of medical advance when I hear the name Armour." The British "Productivity Team" studying the industry a few years ago was amazed at the care with which animal glands were preserved in order "to further medical research." [197]

193. Elmer J. Working, *Demand for Meat*, University of Chicago Press, Chicago, 1954, p. xi.

194. "Armour & Co.," *Fortune*, June 1934, p. 60.

195. Vernon W. Ruttan, *Technological Progress in the Meatpacking Industry*, Marketing Research Report 59, U.S. Department of Agriculture, January 1954, p. ii.

196. *Wall Street Journal*, November 23, 1954, p. 19.

197. Anglo-American Council on Productivity, *Meat Packaging and Processing*, London, 1951, p. 11.

The low points of the meat packers' popularity were reached in the first two decades of the century, at the time of the "muckraking" books and the Federal Trade Commission's investigation. Since 1920 public relations have improved, as a result of efforts of the American Meat Institute and others. According to public opinion polls taken in recent years, some of the old-time hostility has remained.[198] There was a flare-up during the World War II and Korean War price-control periods, when meat shortages, high prices and black markets were common subjects of complaint. Although packers conducting legal operations were squeezed between higher prices for their raw material and ceiling prices on meat, to the point where the government had to pay them heavy subsidies during World War II, they drew at least as much public denunciation as cattle ranchers and hog raisers who were really profiting.

The sequence of events in 1954–56 illustrates a recurring situation. In 1954 the packers, to keep their plants operating at capacity, bid more for hogs than was warranted by consumer demand, and would have gone into the red except for their beef and miscellaneous operations. In 1955 farmers shipped nearly 10 million more hogs to market, and hog quotations declined much further than the more sluggish prices of pork products (bolstered by an $85 million government pork purchase program). Packers' profits, which in 1954 had been lower than at any time since the late 1930s, doubled in 1955, a recovery to which the drop in hog prices in the autumn made a major contribution. There followed not only congressional demands for an investigation,[199] but a warning to the packers from the Republican Secretary of Agriculture to "keep your profits and margins in line" and not to "take advantage of the American farmer." [200] The statisticians of the Department attributed the widening of packers' pork margins in 1955 to natural causes.[201]

Two Contrasting Judgments

Meat packing has always been noted for its very low percentage of profit per dollar of sales. In 1954 and 1955 this figure was 0.4 and 0.8

198. Public opinion polls taken for American Meat Institute.

199. *New York Times*, January 20, 1956, p. 8; *Journal of Commerce*, April 26, 1956, p. 4.

200. Speech of Ezra Taft Benson, reported in *New York Times*, February 1, 1956, p. 17.

201. *Pork Marketing Margins and Costs*, U.S. Department of Agriculture Miscellaneous Publication 711, 1956, pp. 3–4.

per cent, respectively, for 14 packers, as against 5.9 and 6.7 per cent for 1,765 manufacturing corporations whose earnings were tabulated by the First National City Bank of New York. The return on net assets was 3.3 and 6.7 per cent in meat packing as against 12.3 and 15.0 per cent in all manufacturing. In margin on sales, meat packing ranked lowest; in 1955 return on net assets, sugar, brewing and distilling alone were slightly lower out of forty industries listed.[202] The fact that the packer's raw material and supplies cost him between 70 and 80 per cent of his receipts may help to explain why his margin on sales is lower than that of the typical manufacturing industry, whose material cost (including also fuel and purchased energy) has regularly ranged between 54 and 60 per cent.[203] But such a consistently low return on net worth can only be explained by the "intense competition" noted by the British Productivity Team.[204] It is reflected in the price lag of meat packing stocks behind the market averages. Thus between the year 1929 and March 1956 the Standard & Poor's Corporation index of meat stocks advanced about 30 per cent while the average advance of 420 industrial stocks was about 150 per cent.

Contrasting judgments of the industry come from a bank and a labor union. In 1946 the National City Bank, always a champion of American industry but with no special commitment to meat packing, published the following tribute:

> The record of American meat packing in mass production and distribution, maintenance of quality standards, recovery of byproducts, and low cost to the public is probably unexcelled by any industry in any society, whether capitalist, socialist, or communist.[205]

A recent book written with the cooperation of the Amalgamated Meat Cutters & Butcher Workmen, AFL, found that the antitrust laws had failed to improve the industry's unsatisfactory performance and called for dissolution of the four biggest packers and operation of the fragments by separate government corporations under a Public Meat Authority.[206] The other principal labor union — which is plan-

202. First National City Bank of New York, Monthly Letter, April 1956, p. 43.

203. 1919–39 figures, calculated from *Statistical Abstract of the United States*, 1948, p. 825.

204. Anglo-American Council on Productivity, *Meat Packaging and Processing*, p. 53.

205. National City Bank of New York, Monthly Letter, May 1946, p. 53.

206. Lewis Corey, *Meat and Man: A Study of Monopoly, Unionism and Food Policy*, Viking Press, New York, 1950, especially pp. 234–42.

TABLE 8

MEAT PACKING: CHANGES IN POSITION OF PACKERS, LIVESTOCK GROWERS AND WORKERS, 1939–41 TO 1953–55

Group	Annual Average 1939–41	Annual Average 1953–55	Increase (*Per Cent*)
Meat packers			
Net earnings (*millions*)	$48.0	$76.7	59
Livestock growers			
Cash receipts from meat animals (*millions*)	$2,632	$8,572	226
Share of retail price (*per cent*)	51.5	56.4	10
Production and related workers in meat products			
Employment of production and related workers (*thousands*)	179.0	254.7	42
Weekly earnings	$28.27[a]	$78.10	176
Calculated weekly payroll (*thousands*)	$5,060	$19,892	273

Sources: Net earnings from George M. Lewis and J. Russell Ives, *Financial Results of the Meat Packing Industry*, 1955, American Meat Institute, Chicago, p. 21 (drawing on Packers and Stockyards Division reports from packers for 1939–41 net earnings); farm income from U.S. Department of Agriculture, Agricultural Marketing Service, *The Livestock and Meat Situation*, and farmer's share of price from *idem*, *The Marketing and Transportation Situation;* employment and earnings from *Survey of Current Business;* payroll is the product of employment and earnings.

a. 1939–41 earnings are for "slaughtering and meat packing." The figures are approximately 1.3 per cent above those for "meat products" in both 1947 and 1948 (years in which both are given).

ning, as this is written, to unite with the Amalgamated — commented in 1951 on the technical advance "during recent years":

> . . . wages and salaries together account for 10 per cent or less of the sales dollar . . . and in a situation where charging what the traffic will bear is pervasive, . . . packing companies and chain stores have been the real beneficiaries of this higher level of productivity.[207]

It would be more accurate to say that packers, their employees, livestock raisers and, presumably, distributors have all benefited. Between 1939–41 and 1953–55, the net earnings of all reporting meat packers increased by 59 per cent, the cash income of livestock raisers

207. Statement submitted by United Packinghouse Workers of America, CIO, in *Utilization of Farm Crops*, Senate Hearings, pp. 2492, 2493. Neither union accepted a request to comment on the present chapter.

by 226 per cent (while their share of the retail price went up from 51.5 to 56.4 per cent), and earnings of packing-house labor by 273 per cent — this being a composite of a 42 per cent increase in employment and one of 176 per cent in wages. (See Table 8.) Consumers also gained, since in 1939–41 they consumed 138 pounds of meat per capita at a cost equal to 5.2 per cent of disposable income and in 1953–55, 156 pounds at a cost of 5.3 per cent [208] — thus adding 13 per cent to consumption for only 2 per cent more of their income.

SUMMARY

1. The *so-called "national" meat packers*, Swift, Armour, Wilson and Cudahy (which dropped to seventh place in 1955), accounted in 1955 for approximately 50 per cent of the dollar sales of the wholesale meat packing industry. After eliminating their "sidelines" (such as dairy and poultry products and fertilizer), and adding to the total the sales of retail slaughterers, the big packers' share of meat sales, by weight, is probably less than 35 per cent. Measured in dollars, it may be nearly 40 per cent. Their competitors consist of about 1,400 wholesale packers (some of them also "national" packers long rivaling the smaller of the "big four" in size), perhaps 1,800 local packers, and thousands of retail butchers and locker plants.

2. Antitrust investigation in 1902 was instrumental in causing the packers to drop their *beef pool*. Lacking control over either demand or the cattle supply, the pool had probably never affected the average price level even though it alleviated local gluts and shortages and thus affected local prices. Faster communication permits individual firms to do this today without the need of resorting to pooling methods which are open to abuse.

3. After the attempt to form a giant trust in 1902 failed owing to financial difficulties, the *National Packing Company* emerged as a creation of Swift, Armour and Morris. Its dissolution in 1912 was probably due more to its inefficient three-headed structure than to antitrust prosecution, but its continuance would have created a standing danger of collusion.

4. The *Federal Trade Commission reports of 1918–19*, with their severe criticisms of the big packers' operations, were an important influence toward improvement of their practices. In weighing this influence, it must be remembered that many actions which were accepted as normal before World War I have since been condemned by public and business opinion, and discarded in other industries as well.

208. *The Livestock and Meat Situation*, March 2, 1956, pp. 26, 35.

5. The *consent decree of 1920*, which still controls the activities of Swift, Armour, Wilson and Cudahy, protected the independents by cutting the ties between big packers and the stockyards and terminal railroads. The decree's prohibition of the wholesaling of "unrelated" food products by the large packers aided the wholesale grocers, but the fear that the defendants would eventually monopolize wholesale food distribution was a phantom. Nor would the packers ever have diffused their efforts by retailing meat on a large scale, even without the decree. The Federal Trade Commission's demand that the packers dispose of their refrigerator cars was not accepted by the decree, but Swift has sold its cars as a purely business transaction. In 1930, in connection with a request by two defendants for relief from the decree, the Department of Justice agreed to a stipulation that competition existed in the industry; and in the late 1940s its investigations turned up no evidence of violations. In the 1950s the big packers were increasingly restive under the restrictions of an old decree which could not be adjusted to changing market conditions.

6. The *Packers and Stockyards Act* of 1921 is both a kind of public utility act regulating stockyards and a special antitrust law applying to meat packing. Although fees charged by stockyards and commission agents are probably lower than they would be without the law, they would in any case be governed mainly by competition among the stockyards and between them and local livestock markets. The act has had little or no influence on prices, output or the structure of the packing industry itself. It is a healthy thing, however, to have fair trading on the public yards and in the meat industry supervised by an impartial government agency.

7. In its *merger decision in 1926*, the Supreme Court affirmed the right of Swift to acquire competitors by stock purchase, since it had consolidated the assets before a complaint was brought. This opened a gap in Section 7 of the Clayton Act which was not closed until 1950.

8. *Eleven Sherman Act indictments brought in 1941–42* charged collusion in the purchase of livestock on public stockyards and in certain other respects. Three cases resulted in acquittals by juries, and eight were dismissed at the government's own request. The statement of one judge that the Department of Justice ought not to have imposed the stigma of criminal proceedings on the defendants without better evidence seems justified.

9. The *Sherman Act dissolution proceeding filed in 1948* recited the charges made in 1941–42 and claimed that the four largest packers and their predecessor corporations had been in collusion to control competition since 1893. The remedy sought, breakup of the four companies into fourteen, was unrelated to the government's chief item of evidence — the constancy of buying percentages at stockyards caused allegedly by collusion of the two or three largest buyers at each — for it would have left the same number of companies operating at each location. The suit, brought during a national election cam-

paign with the claim that it would keep food prices down, was dropped six years later on the ground that the government could not be expected to prove its case without going back beyond 1930 for evidence, as it was prohibited from doing. Within two years of the dismissal of this suit, market forces had compelled Cudahy to make as drastic a reduction in the number of its packing plants as the government had asked.

10. The *antitrust laws* have discouraged communication between representatives of rival companies, but this is hardly an important matter. The laws have some influence in giving increased confidence to small packers that their big rivals will not attempt to drive them out of business. Such confidence, however, rests very much more on their assurance that they can compete economically on even terms.

11. The chief *trends in concentration* in the packing industry have been the following: (1) a great rise in the share of the market controlled by the Chicago packers in the last third of the nineteenth century as a consequence of improvements in production, transportation and storage — but with the effect of increasing competition in the meat trade in every area in the country; (2) a continued growth of the then five largest packers in the first two decades of the twentieth century; (3) a decline in their share in the early 1920s when increasing use of motor trucks and other factors permitted new firms to open successful plants in the livestock-raising districts; (4) a stabilization of shares as the big packers set up interior plants and increased their direct buying; and (5) a significant further decline in the big packers' share since 1935.

12. *Entry* into the packing industry is relatively easy and is a powerful force making for competition.

13. *Mergers* have not accounted for a substantial part of the growth of the large packers. Even in the case of Armour, which absorbed Morris in 1923 over strong opposition by the Secretary of Agriculture, the expansion was in plant and other facilities, but not more than temporarily in sales. Many meat packing mergers have been motivated by the desire for operating economies.

14. Both *large and small packers* have special advantages of their own in competition. A small company slaughtering a single type of livestock bought from nearby farmers for local sale has operating economies which are likely to give it a higher rate of profit than a national packer whose local operations of the same type must be averaged with its other operations. National packers, in turn, are needed to carry storable products over from times of surplus to those of shortage, to handle the full line of beef, lamb, pork, veal and by-products, to move meat from surplus to deficit areas, and to clear the markets in case livestock shipments are unusually heavy. Such functions require large investment in operating facilities and hence large capital.

15. *Interlocking directorates* and similar connections were important at the time of the Federal Trade Commission investigation in 1918, but were no longer so when it analyzed the situation as of 1946.

16. Charges once made by the Department of Justice that *trade association activity* in the industry tended to suppress competition were not proved.

17. Competition in the *sale of meat* is dominated by the necessity of moving available supplies before they spoil. The fact that retailers will shift their patronage because of a difference as slight as ⅛ to ¼ cent a pound means that all sellers in a given market have to follow closely price changes of competitors insofar as these correctly reflect current supply and demand. In situations where shares of the different packers in specific markets are found to be stable, it is probably because an attempt by one packer to increase his sales aggressively stimulates self-defensive moves by the rest.

18. A tendency toward uniformity of buying prices for livestock is evidence of competition rather than of collusion. Available statistics at the principal stockyards on the *relative percentages of different types of livestock bought by the leading packers* usually show little change from year to year. Such stability may have been caused by collusion at some times or places. It can also be explained by the fact that each large buyer realized that an attempt to increase his percentage would merely prompt competitors to meet his higher bids in order to maintain their relative position in the market. It has never been proved to be harmful to the livestock raiser, and it cannot be eliminated, for a packing plant of efficient size is almost sure to be a major buyer on the local stockyard.

19. The *direct buying* policies of the big packers indicate, as would be expected, that they are interested in obtaining livestock at least as cheaply as their smaller competitors. The charge that they control the prices at interior markets through manipulation of prices at Chicago is not supportable either by logic or by evidence.

20. *Small packers* at one time may have feared elimination at the hands of the national packers; but this fear hardly exists today — owing both to the antitrust laws and, even more, to the competitive advantages of small operations. Recent complaints that the big packer can make his money on by-products and conduct cutthroat competition in the meat markets have been unconvincing, in view of the declining trend of concentration.

21. *Interindustry competition* exists for wholesale meat packers in that they must compete, not only with other packers, but also with various sorts of retail slaughterers, with substitute foods, and indirectly with all other demands on income which may cause consumers to economize on this particular high-priced food. When the income of consumers increases, they tend to buy more meat and thus to push up its price relative to other foods. Complaints against the high price of meat generally follow, and the industry gets its full share of the blame.

22. The industry has an excellent *performance record* from the standpoint of cost reduction and avoidance of waste. To the extent that economies have tended to offset the rising operating and distribution costs of the modern American economy, they have been of benefit to livestock growers. Workers also have shared in the gains of the industry in recent years. Profits are low as a result of keen competition.

In brief, the packing industry, as an official of the Department of Agriculture puts it, appears to be soundly and efficiently established and adequately competitive. A number of factors, especially the nature and wide spread of supply of and demand for the product, the ease of entry, and the fact that both national and local operation offer their own special economies, are the real reasons for the state of competition; but antitrust investigations and suits have played a role in discouraging collusive and coercive practices. Even the numerous unnecessary suits have had such an effect — a fact which is not suggested as justification for them.

CHAPTER 3

Petroleum

The size of the petroleum industry is impressive on any count except perhaps employment, which is low in relation to dollar sales. Petroleum is a major product of both mining and manufacturing. The crude oil produced in the United States in 1955 was worth about $7.0 billion,[1] three times as much as its nearest rival in the mineral field — bituminous coal. Oil refining ranks high among manufacturing industries in value added, with $1.9 billion at the time of the 1954 Census.

Production, Transportation and Refining

In 1950, according to one estimate, at least fifty-four companies operated in all four fields of petroleum activity [2] — production, transportation, refining and marketing. A few hundred more are integrated into either two or three fields. At the end of 1955 thirty-four leading oil companies had a gross investment of $18.0 billion in production facilities, $3.4 billion in transportation, $7.3 billion in refining, $3.9 billion in marketing, and $0.5 billion in other interests.[3]

Production, which includes exploration, drilling, operation of wells, and storage in the oil fields, occupied approximately 12,000 firms in 1949. (See Table 9.) In 1955 half a million wells were producing oil, with Texas accounting for 43 per cent of output and California,

1. See figures in *National Petroleum News*, Factbook issue, Mid-May 1956, pp. 192, 208.

2. John G. McLean and Robert Wm. Haigh, *The Growth of Integrated Oil Companies*, Division of Research, Graduate School of Business Administration, Harvard University, Boston, 1954, p. 50.

3. Frederick G. Coqueron, *Annual Financial Analysis of the Petroleum Industry*, 1955, Chase Manhattan Bank, New York, p. 37.

TABLE 9

PETROLEUM: NUMBER OF ENTERPRISES, 1949

Operation	Number of Firms
Production	12,010
Oil and gas production	7,182
Drilling and other contract services	4,828
Transportation	1,378
Pipeline	54
Tank ship	42
Tank car	45
Barge line	174
Tank truck	1,063
Refining	513
Petroleum refining	270[a]
Lubricants and greases not made in petroleum refineries	243
Wholesale marketing	28,174
Bulk stations and terminals	14,047
Fuel oil	11,127
LP-gas (liquefied petroleum gas)	3,000
Retail outlets of all sorts (reported by 91 refiners, 1956)	374,495
Service stations (1954 Census)	181,734

Sources: Retail outlets from *National Petroleum News*, Factbook issue, Mid-May 1956, pp. 175, 204; other figures from Harold Fleming, *The American Oil Industry — A Forty-odd Thousand Company Enterprise*, Oil Industry Background Information Bulletin 4, Oil Industry Information Committee, American Petroleum Institute, New York, 1953, p. 10. Production and refining enterprises and the first two wholesale marketing groups are from the Bureau of Old-Age and Survivors Insurance of the U.S. Social Security Administration; others are from miscellaneous sources.

a. Other estimates of the number of refiners run as low as 225.

Louisiana and Oklahoma together for 33 per cent.[4] Arizona became the thirtieth producing state in that year. Despite the reliance of would-be producers on geologists, geophysicists and other scientists, the element of chance remains strong. Even "development" wells (drilled in established fields) often prove dry, and a recent study of 20,478 wildcat explorations (in new territory) showed only one in fifteen striking oil and only one in forty-three finding the minimum (a million-barrel field) for economic production.[5] Once a well is flowing, its rate of output is controlled in most states by public authorities, under a system of proration.

4. *Statistical Abstract of the United States*, 1956, p. 741.

5. Frederic H. Lahee, consulting geologist, cited in *Business Week*, September 8, 1956, p. 198.

Crude oil from established fields moves through small pipelines called gathering lines to local refineries or to long-distance transportation facilities. About three quarters of the crude going to distant refineries travels by pipeline, and nearly all the rest by tanker or barge. In 1956 there were reported to be 431 oceangoing tankers serving the United States, 2,225 inland barges and tankers, over 140,000 miles of pipelines for crude oil, and some 28,000 miles for refined products.[6] There are also about 100,000 railroad oil cars and 150,000 oil trucks.[7] Nearly 1,400 firms were engaged in petroleum transportation in 1949, over a thousand of them truck carriers for hire (Table 9).

Crude oil has to be refined, to separate the various compounds of carbon and hydrogen. The simplest method is by distillation through heat, called "topping" or "skimming." Thermal "cracking," which relies on pressure as well as heat and breaks down the heavier hydrocarbons into lighter ones so as to get more gasoline and less low-grade fuel oil out of a barrel of crude oil, came into use after 1913. Such complex methods as catalytic cracking, catalytic reforming, polymerization, alkylation and hydrogenation followed, and refineries that use these have a big advantage in achieving the products they want. At the beginning of 1956 there were 294 operating refineries, with Texas leading in numbers, followed by California.[8] Nearly all the one-plant refining companies have always been located close to oil fields, while the integrated concerns have built some of their large refineries near consuming markets or ports like Chicago, Philadelphia and New York. Besides the refiners, a count in 1949 showed 243 firms making lubricating oils and grease (Table 9).

Majors and Independents

Before its dissolution in 1911, the old Standard Oil "trust" divided the industry with the "independents." Afterward distinction was made between the Standard "successor companies" and the independents, and later between "majors" and independents — the majors being

6. Standard & Poor's Corp., *Industry Surveys*, "Oil," Basic Analysis, June 14, 1956, p. O 37. Compare U.S. Petroleum Administration for Defense, *Transportation of Oil*, December 1951, pp. 17, 18, 22, 23, 43, insert facing 86, and 97, for authoritative figures at that time.

7. Sun Oil Co., *Competition in the Oil Industry*, pamphlet issued by Industrial Relations Research Center, University of Chicago, Chicago, 1954, p. 22.

8. U.S. Bureau of Mines, *Petroleum Refineries, Including Cracking Plants*, 1956.

TABLE 10

PETROLEUM: REVENUES AND PRODUCTION OF MAJOR COMPANIES, 1955

Firm[a]	Gross Operating Revenue	Per Cent of Total Domestic Net Crude Oil Production[b]	Per Cent of Total Domestic Refinery Crude Runs[b]	Domestic Production of Crude Oil as Per Cent of Refinery Intake
	(Millions)			
Twenty major companies	$23,332	47.6	82.7	52.4
1. *Standard Oil Co. (New Jersey)*	6,270	6.1	10.5	52.8
2. Gulf Oil Corp.	1,896	3.4	7.0	43.8
3. *Standard Oil Co. (Indiana)*	1,781	3.5	7.7	41.8
4. Texas Co.	1,767	4.9	7.7	58.5
5. *Socony Mobil Oil Co.*	1,721	3.4	7.2	42.2
6. Shell Oil Co.	1,484	4.0	6.2	59.6
7. *Standard Oil Company of California*	1,278	4.0	6.0	59.5
8. Sinclair Oil Corp.[c]	1,110	2.0	5.6	32.6
9. Cities Service Co.[c]	923	1.7	3.5	43.1
10. Phillips Petroleum Co.	913	1.8	3.1	54.8
11. Sun Oil Co.	660	1.7	3.0	49.8
12. *Continental Oil Co.*	529	2.0	1.9	97.0
13. *Atlantic Refining Co.*	513	1.3	2.6	45.3
14. Pure Oil Co.	485	1.0	2.0	43.6
15. *Tide Water Associated Oil Co.*[d]	479	1.3	2.2	53.6
16. Union Oil Company of California	368	1.5	2.1	64.7
17. *Standard Oil Company of Ohio*	367	.4	1.7	23.4
18. Sunray-Mid-Continent Petroleum Co.[e]	298	1.2	1.3	80.6
19. *Ohio Oil Co.*	257	1.4	.6	228.6
20. Skelly Oil Co.[d]	232	1.0	.6	145.6

Source: Calculated from *National Petroleum News*, Factbook issue, Mid-May 1956, pp. 98, 99 and 208.

a. Successor companies of the Standard Oil Company of N.J., dissolved in 1911, are given in italics. Continental Oil Co. is a merger of a successor company with a larger independent (Marland Oil Co.).

b. Crude production abroad of fifteen of the companies, and foreign refinery runs of seven, are omitted.

c. Cities Service and Sinclair also own 30 per cent each of the stock of Richfield Oil Corp., whose size and (on the whole) separate management give it the right to rank as a major, though the source used here, like most others, omits it.

d. Tide Water and Skelly are controlled by the same holding company (the Mission Corp.). Only 33 per cent of Tide Water's stock had been held by the "trust" in 1911.

e. This company was formed in May 1955 by a merger of the smallest major with one of the largest independents (Sunray).

generally counted as the twenty largest integrated companies, eleven of which had been originally classed as independents. The twenty so-called majors — of which Standard Oil Company of New Jersey is by far the largest — accounted for 47.6 per cent of the crude and 82.7 per cent of the refined production in 1955. The typical major produced about half and purchased about half of its refinery run, although two of the smallest sold crude oil on net balance. (See Table 10.)

In this chapter the traditional division between majors and independents will be followed — but without implying that there is a necessary conflict or even a clear dividing line between the two types.

Refined Products and Their Distribution

There are said to be over 1,200 useful products of petroleum.[9] Eighty-seven per cent of 1955 output, measured in quantity, was accounted for by four groups: gasoline, 46.6 per cent; distillate fuel oil (home heating and light diesel fuel), 21.1 per cent; residual fuel oil (for industry use), 14.7 per cent; and kerosene, 4.1 per cent.[10] Lubricants, although only 2.0 per cent in quantity, rank much higher in value.

Storage tanks situated in or near practically every town in the country, and known as "bulk stations," hold the oil products shipped in bulk before they are divided into smaller lots for sale to retailers. Gasoline is distributed at wholesale either by (1) the sales departments of the refiners, (2) "consignees" or "commission agents" acting for them, or (3) independent jobbers. "Branded" jobbers, often called "distributors," are those who ally themselves with a particular refiner and handle his products almost exclusively. "Unbranded" jobbers are independent and use their own brand names. Recently there were estimated to be about 14,000 petroleum jobbers, 11,000 fuel oil dealers, and 3,000 LP-gas (liquefied petroleum gas or "bottled" gas) dealers (Table 9).

Sales by the refinery to its marketing subsidiary, to jobbers or to commercial customers make up the "refinery wholesale market" or "tank car market." Sales to retailers, whether made by the majors and their agents or by competing jobbers, constitute the "tank wagon market."

Almost all gasoline is marketed to consumers under a brand name, whether of a major or an independent. Makers of advertised brands

9. Benedict Saurino, "Petroleum Products," Chap. 11 in Richard M. Clewett, ed., *Marketing Channels for Manufactured Products*, Irwin, Homewood (Ill.), 1954, p. 283.

10. *Statistical Abstract of the United States*, 1956, p. 740.

sell large quantities to independent marketers for private brand ("off brand") resale. In 1939 only one refiner marketed in all the states,[11] and this was still true in 1956. In the latter year, a group of ninety-four "important oil companies" marketed their products in nine states each, on the average, and every state was in the territory of at least twelve of these firms.[12]

At the time of the 1954 Census of Business, there were 61,000 one-man service stations, 121,000 service stations with employees,[13] and perhaps 200,000 garages and other retail outlets for gasoline. Probably less than 2 per cent of service stations are owned and operated by integrated refiners,[14] but nearly half are leased by their operators from refining companies that own or have leased the site. A substantial part of the average station's gross income comes from motor oil, from tires, batteries and accessories (universally called "TBA"), and from lubricating, washing and other services. Jobbers own some of the stations, and also sell the bulk of the home heating oil. Many important oil products are sold direct to industrial users.

Antitrust Suits

A recent chief of the Antitrust Division has declared that "its major battles historically and daily have been against the oil industry." [15] Fifty-seven formal complaints had been filed by the Federal Trade Commission before 1950, exclusive of false advertising proceedings.[16] In that year the Commission, in reference to its own twelve economic investigations down to 1936 and fourteen congressional studies of petroleum since 1945, asked for an appropriation for another study "filling in gaps." [17] Published material on monopoly and competition in petroleum probably exceeds that on any other industry.

11. Roy C. Cook, *Control of the Petroleum Industry by Major Oil Companies*, TNEC Monograph 39, 1941, pp. 88–89.

12. Calculated from *National Petroleum News*, Factbook issue, Mid-May 1956, pp. 170–73.

13. *Ibid.*, p. 204.

14. *Ibid.*, p. 175.

15. Assistant Attorney General H. Graham Morrison, in *Interstate Oil and Gas Compact*, Hearings before House Interstate and Foreign Commerce Committee, 82d Cong., 1st sess., 1951, p. 95.

16. Commissioner John Carson, in *Petroleum Study*, Hearings before a Subcommittee of the House Interstate and Foreign Commerce Committee, 81st Cong., 2d sess., 1950, p. 251.

17. Letter of Acting Chairman Lowell B. Mason, *ibid.*, pp. 315–16.

The First "Trust"

The Standard Oil Company of Ohio was incorporated in 1870, eleven years after Colonel Drake's historic oil strike in western Pennsylvania. Standard emerged triumphant from the competitive battles of the next decade, both through skilled management by John D. Rockefeller and his associates and through sharp competitive practices, including collection of rebates from the railroads.[18] It produced very little crude, for it was unwilling to risk much capital in this speculative business, but was dominant in transportation and refining. In 1879 the shares of several Standard companies were transferred to the management of a small group of trustees in return for dividend-paying trust certificates, and it was this expedient that gave the name "trust" in popular parlance to any big combination or even big corporation.

Public feeling against the oil monopoly was an important factor in causing passage of the Sherman Antitrust Act in 1890. The first legal blow was struck two years later, but by the state of Ohio. A common-law suit sought to revoke the charter of the Standard Oil Company of Ohio on the twofold ground that (1) it had acted illegally in turning over its control to the trustees, and (2) its possession of 90 per cent of the country's refining capacity constituted a monopoly contrary to public policy. The result was a court order to the defendant to terminate its connection with the trust,[19] which was thereupon dissolved. The individual operating companies continued to operate under a "community of interest arrangement," until this too was assailed in Ohio as illegal.[20] In 1899, therefore, the group created a more formal and a legal pattern by establishing the Standard Oil Company of New Jersey to hold the shares of these enterprises (as well as several refineries directly).

Standard Oil under Public Attack

More serious difficulty was foreshadowed by the great public interest in Ida M. Tarbell's *The History of the Standard Oil Company*, a thoroughly documented attack on the company which appeared in

18. Compare Ralph W. and Muriel E. Hidy, *Pioneering in Big Business, 1882–1911* (History of Standard Oil Company of N.J., Vol. 1), Harper, New York, 1955, pp. 24, 34–35, 650–51.

19. *State v. Standard Oil Co.*, 49 Ohio St. 137, 30 N.E. 279 (1892).

20. Eliot Jones, *The Trust Problem in the United States*, Macmillan, New York, 1921, p. 56.

McClure's Magazine in 1902–04 and then at once in book form.[21] Impressed by this outstanding example of "muckraking" journalism, Congress asked the Bureau of Corporations to study Standard Oil. Commissioner James R. Garfield, perhaps mindful of the criticism of his "beef trust" report as "wishy-washy," made a comprehensive and critical investigation.[22] His first report appeared in May 1906, and reports by his successor, Herbert Knox Smith, in May and August 1907.[23] The flow of state antitrust suits against Standard Oil and its subsidiaries, which began with a Texas action "ousting" one unit from the state in 1900 and continued with three more suits in 1904 and four in 1905, produced no less than fourteen in 1906 (although only eleven states participated in these twenty-one cases).[24] There were some defense victories, but elsewhere fines were imposed or subsidiaries temporarily ousted. In Missouri Attorney General Hadley brought a successful ouster suit in 1905,[25] which the state's Supreme Court reaffirmed on appeal as late as 1913. But with Standard Oil (Indiana) about to vacate its big refinery at Sugar Creek, the community made known its resentment (with the support of ex-Governor Hadley among others). A majority of the Court, saying little more than that it was "now fully advised," quickly changed its mind [26] — an action which the dissenting judge characterized as assumption of the power to pardon.

The greatest publicity attended a $29,240,000 fine imposed by Judge Kenesaw Mountain Landis on Standard in 1907 for shipping 1,462 cars of petroleum products from its Whiting (Indiana) refinery at less than the regular railroad tariff — the penalty being $20,000 for each violation of the Elkins Act of 1903 against rebates.[27] A Circuit Court of Appeals reversed the verdict a year later, with Judge Peter S. Grosscup taking the view that there were only thirty-six offenses, since he counted them by shipments and not by single cars, and holding,

21. Reissued by Macmillan, New York, 1925.

22. Hidy and Hidy, *Pioneering in Big Business*, p. 677.

23. *Report of the Commissioner of Corporations on the Transportation of Petroleum*, 1906; *Report of the Commissioner of Corporations on the Petroleum Industry*, Part 1, "Position of the Standard Oil Company in the Petroleum Industry," Part 2, "Prices and Profits," 1907.

24. Hidy and Hidy, *Pioneering in Big Business*, p. 683.

25. *State v. Standard Oil Co.*, 218 Mo. 1, 116 S.W. 902 (1909).

26. *Ibid.*, 158 S.W. 601, 602 (Mo. Sup. Ct. 1913); Paul H. Giddens, *Standard Oil Company (Indiana): Oil Pioneer of the Middle West*, Appleton-Century-Crofts, New York, 1955, pp. 89–97, 138–39.

27. *U.S. v. Standard Oil Co. (Ind.)*, 155 Fed. 305 (N.D. Ill. 1907).

further, that there was no official rate on petroleum and its products, but only a rate derived informally from several different classifications.[28] Despite this reversal, Judge Landis' fame, thus initiated, was to win him later the post of first Commissioner of organized baseball.

The Dissolution of the Trust

The decisive court test grew out of a Department of Justice suit filed in Missouri in November 1906, resting largely on Bureau of Corporations findings. The main charges were that Standard Oil of New Jersey (1) controlled over 75 per cent of the refining and marketing of petroleum products; and (2) had gained its position by such unfair practices as obtaining rebates from railroads, cutting prices in local areas to eliminate independent competitors, using bogus independent companies for price competition in order to deceive customers, bribing employees to obtain data on other companies' transactions, and excluding competitors' oil from its pipelines.

The government won the verdict in the trial court, which paid little attention to the alleged unfair practices but emphasized monopoly and the intent to monopolize.[29] The defendants appealed to the Supreme Court. Here Chief Justice White enunciated in May 1911 the celebrated "rule of reason," under which only "unreasonable" restraints of trade were to be considered violations of the Sherman Act.[30] He rested his position on the principle that words in a statute must be presumed in the absence of contrary evidence to have the meaning already attached to them by the common law, and on those common-law precedents which gave validity to "reasonable" restraints of trade. Justice Harlan, dissenting, pointed to former decisions barring any rule of reason [31] (to which Justice White had dissented), to the trouble the courts would have in deciding which contracts were reasonable, and to the fact that the word "reasonable" did not appear in the Sherman Act.

The entire Court agreed, nevertheless, that Standard Oil's monopolistic intent and unfair practices excluded it from the benefit of the rule of reason. The combination was ordered dissolved, and Standard of

28. *Standard Oil Co. (Ind.) v. U.S.*, 164 Fed. 376 (7th Cir. 1908).

29. *U.S. v. Standard Oil Company of N.J.*, 173 Fed. 177 (E.D. Mo. 1909).

30. *Standard Oil Company of N.J. v. U.S.*, 221 U.S. 1 (1911).

31. *U.S. v. Trans-Missouri Freight Ass'n.*, 166 U.S. 290 (1897); *U.S. v. Joint Traffic Ass'n.*, 171 U.S. 505 (1898).

New Jersey was obliged, therefore, to distribute to its stockholders its controlling shares in its thirty-three subsidiaries. Recombination of any of the corporate units to create a new monopoly was forbidden.

It is reported that the financial markets "stood still" for months awaiting this decision. When it was announced, the defeat to Standard Oil was considered less important than the implication in the rule of reason that organization of industry by large corporations was fundamentally sound. The stock market rose in response.[32] This was true of Standard Oil stock among others, although owners of one share found themselves with inconveniently small holdings in thirty-four firms, whose value ran as low as 10 cents in the case of Swan & Finch Company and 7 cents in that of Washington Oil Company.[33] Ex-President Theodore Roosevelt, who had brought the suit originally, remarked in 1915 that "not one particle of good resulted to anybody and a number of worthy citizens of small means were appreciably injured," and, commenting, with his usual outspokenness, on two cases still pending in court, said the results would probably be the same if United States Steel Corporation and International Harvester Company were dissolved.[34]

Competition among Successor Companies

When, between July and December 1915, the retail price of gasoline increased sharply — 47 per cent for an average of nine states — the newly created Federal Trade Commission added a study of this rise to the thorough investigation of the oil industry which had been one of its first tasks.[35] Although an estimated 74 per cent increase in automobile use of gasoline and a 51 per cent increase in exports, between 1914 and 1915 (while crude production was up only one per cent), might have explained this phenomenon in conjunction with speculative market movements, the Commission considered lack of competition among the Standard successor companies to be one cause. Controlling stock interests, it contended, were still in the hands of members of the

32. Giddens, *Standard Oil Company* (*Indiana*), p. 126.

33. *Ibid.*, p. 131.

34. *Ibid.*, pp. 137–38.

35. FTC, *Report on the Price of Gasoline in 1915*, 1917, especially pp. 16, 17, 21, 29, 33, 48, 146–50, 184. See summary and analysis by Lewis H. Haney (a principal author of the FTC report), "Gasoline Prices as Affected by Interlocking Stockownership and Joint Cost," *Quarterly Journal of Economics*, August 1917, pp. 635–55.

group that had managed the trust, and each Standard company still sold within the same marketing territories as before.

Although the Commission merely took for granted that a monopolistic group would exploit a rise in demand and shortage of supply more quickly than a competitive industry, and although no heed was paid to its recommendations that control through common stockholdings be curbed by law and that pipelines be made independent companies, the lack of competition among the successor companies could not be denied. Soon, however, both conditions which served to prevent competition changed. Some of the dominant stockholders died; others turned over large blocks of shares to philanthropic organizations that took no part in control of the companies.[36] Some of the successor companies, finding themselves handicapped in competition because they operated in only one or two branches of the industry, tried to round out their operations by mergers. When they acquired firms that were already in competition with other Standard companies, successor companies came into direct competition. Other successors began selling to jobbers, who in turn resold in the territories of other Standard companies.[37]

The first successor to enter the territory of another for direct marketing was the Atlantic Refining Company, which between 1916 and 1918 moved from its own territory, Delaware, New Jersey and Pennsylvania, into the area of the Standard Oil Company of New York. Others spread out later, perhaps motivated in part by fear that expansion in their original territories would lead to a charge of monopoly.[38] The Standard Oil Company of New York (today Socony Mobil Oil Company) had 92 per cent of the New York–New England gasoline market in 1909, 55–60 per cent in 1918, 46 per cent in 1926, less than 35 per cent in 1929, 24 per cent in 1939, and 19 per cent in 1952;[39] but it was steadily expanding in states farther west. By 1927 the Federal Trade Commission found that "a considerable degree of competi-

36. FTC, *Petroleum Industry: Prices, Profits and Competition*, S. Doc. 61, 70th Cong., 1st sess., 1928, p. xviii.

37. *Ibid.*, p. 55.

38. Warren C. Platt, "40 Great Years — The Story of Oil's Competition," *National Petroleum News*, March 9, 1949, p. 46.

39. U.S. Interior Department, *Final Report of the Marketing Division, Petroleum Administrative Board*, 1936, pp. 7–8; Herbert Willetts, vice president of Socony-Vacuum Oil Co., in *Petroleum Study (Gasoline and Oil Price Increases)*, Hearings before House Interstate and Foreign Commerce Committee, 83d Cong., 1st sess., 1953, p. 226.

tion" had developed among the former Standard units.[40] By 1955 at least three successor companies were selling in each state.[41] One obstacle had been that in each state only one company could use the Standard Oil trademark. "Esso," for instance, was excluded by court order from Standard of Indiana's territory. This obstacle was overcome by establishment of new trademarks (like Mobilgas) and purchase of companies with their own trademark (like Amoco).

Rise of Independents

Even before the Supreme Court decision of 1911, the independents had been making great inroads into Standard Oil's monopoly. They whittled down its share of total refining from 90 per cent in 1899 to 80 in 1911, and that of the successor companies to 65 per cent in 1915, 49 in 1919 and 43 in 1927.[42] Several factors contributed to this trend.

The immense development of new oil fields in the Gulf and Mid-Continent districts, beginning with the famous Spindletop well of January 1901 in Texas, transferred the center of production westward from the territory dominated by Standard Oil. Output of crude petroleum quadrupled between 1899 and 1911, and local refineries had to be built to prevent oil from running to waste.[43] Independent crude producers like the Mellon family (Gulf Oil Corporation) determined to integrate so as to stay free of Standard Oil control.[44] In short, it would have required an empire-building campaign as strenuous as John D. Rockefeller's original fight in the 1870s for the Standard companies to have kept their control of the industry during such a rapid expansion in new areas.[45]

Second, the emergence of the automobile made gasoline a more important outlet than kerosene, and new companies were quicker than Standard Oil to take advantage of the new opportunities in refining

40. FTC 1928 Report, p. 264.

41. *National Petroleum News*, Factbook issue, Mid-May 1955, pp. 200–03.

42. Arthur Robert Burns, *The Decline of Competition*, McGraw-Hill, New York, 1936, pp. 103–04.

43. See FTC 1928 Report, p. 262; Carl Coke Rister, *Oil! Titan of the Southwest*, University of Oklahoma Press, Norman, 1949, p. 64 and p. 70, note 6.

44. McLean and Haigh, *The Growth of Integrated Oil Companies*, pp. 77, 95.

45. See Hidy and Hidy, *Pioneering in Big Business*, pp. 408, 477; George Ward Stocking, *The Oil Industry and the Competitive System*, Houghton Mifflin, Boston, 1925, p. 62.

and distribution.[46] One authority holds that this would have put the independents "pretty close to where they are today," even without the antitrust decree.[47]

Another authority holds [48] — although there is dissent [49] — that the monopoly position of the Standard group had produced inertia, which was bound to be reflected in a decline in its share of the market. The directors had failed to train a younger management group to replace them. The "trust's" policy of wide margins and high unit profits invited competition to enter. New ideas — e.g., the use of tank cars and tank trucks — were being pioneered by independents. The freeing of research, which could now be launched in competition by many different units, has been called by some the chief result of the decree. The principal example was the research of William Burton and Robert Humphries into the "cracking" of petroleum molecules to convert more of them into light hydrocarbon compounds. Only after the 1911 decision removed what seemed an antitrust threat to the stability of investments, and power came into the hands of local directors of Standard of Indiana, who knew Burton personally, was a large appropriation to build stills secured.[50] The resulting process practically doubled the output of gasoline from a given amount of crude oil.

It can be argued that the condemnation of unfair practices in Chief Justice White's decision gave independent firms greater confidence in their ability to develop.[51] Little fear, however, had been shown by new entrants from 1901 to 1911, and the Clayton and Federal Trade Commission acts were to forbid unfair competition in 1914 in any event.

Possibly the Standard group itself profited financially in the end from the dissolution.[52] Certainly many of the successor companies eventually became larger than the original trust had been. Govern-

46. Robert S. Eckley, *The United States Petroleum Industry in Transition, 1910–1920*, unpublished doctoral thesis, Harvard University, Cambridge, 1949, p. 83.

47. Fayette B. Dow, in *The Independent Petroleum Company*, Hearings before Special Senate Committee Investigating Petroleum Resources, 79th Cong., 2d sess., 1946, pp. 191-92.

48. Platt, "40 Great Years," p. 45.

49. Herrymon Maurer, *Great Enterprise: Growth and Behavior of the Big Corporation*, Macmillan, New York, 1955, p. 52.

50. Giddens, *Standard Oil Company (Indiana)*, p. 149; Robert E. Wilson, *Oil Competition in the Midwest: A Case History*, National Petroleum Ass'n., Washington, 1950, pp. 6–8.

51. FTC 1928 Report, p. 264; Joe S. Bain, *The Economics of the Pacific Coast Petroleum Industry*, University of California Press, Berkeley, 1944–1947, Part 3, "Public Policy toward Competition and Pricing," p. 69.

52. Platt, "40 Great Years," p. 34.

ment enforcement officers have sometimes cited this fact to "cheer up" businessmen who were under antitrust investigation.

The Equipment-Leasing Cases

Soon after service stations first appeared, the oil companies began offering to lease pumps and underground tanks, free or for a nominal consideration, to retailers who would promise to use this equipment only for the lessor's branded gasoline. Beginning in 1919, the Federal Trade Commission issued twenty-seven cease and desist orders against this practice.[53] The charge was violation of Section 3 of the Clayton Act and Section 5 of the Federal Trade Commission Act, by barring the retailers concerned from purchasing gasoline of other suppliers.

The Commission's orders were enjoined in four Circuit Courts of Appeal, and in 1923 were finally vacated by the Supreme Court's unanimous decision for the company in the *Sinclair* case.[54] The opinion, by Justice McReynolds, denied that the leases tended to foreclose the market. It held that the operator was free to terminate the lease on short notice and to purchase or lease other tanks or pumps with little cash outlay, if he wished to change his gasoline. Nor did it concede that a type of action engaged in openly, and which helped the customer know that the product was the same as that advertised on the pump, was "unfair." Finally, it noted that the leasing practice enabled many men without capital to enter the filling station business, and thus added to competition there.

The decision had several significant consequences: (1) Competition in service stations was fostered — to the point of overexpansion, in fact. (2) Many service stations could operate with better and newer equipment than they would otherwise have had. (3) Larger refiners and jobbers were given some advantage, since they could more easily carry the capital cost of a great many tanks and pumps thus leased out. (4) Retail dealers were tied more effectively to individual suppliers, and this contributed to an effective, if loose, form of integration.

In June 1928 the American Petroleum Institute initiated a campaign which led to the promulgation by the Federal Trade Commission a year later of a code of fair trade practices for marketing of refined petroleum products. The provision most emphasized was perhaps the

53. Myron W. Watkins, *Public Regulation of Competitive Practices,* National Industrial Conference Board, New York, 2d edition, 1929, p. 205, note 2.

54. *FTC v. Sinclair Refining Co.*, 261 U.S. 463 (1923).

outlawing of tank and pump leasing. Although 15,800 marketing firms signed the code, "the whole thing fizzled out with the coming of the depression." [55] The code, which had meanwhile served as a model for the marketing section of the National Recovery Administration code of fair competition,[56] was rescinded in September 1937. Leasing decreased in the 1930s owing to the refiners' lack of cash to make the necessary investment in equipment,[57] but even today about 90 per cent of all pumps and a somewhat smaller percentage of tanks are said to be owned by the suppliers. The station owner usually pays a small rental for them.

Mergers by the Successor Companies

The 1911 dissolution left nearly all the Standard successor companies operating in only one branch of the industry, and thus placed them at a disadvantage as against firms like Texas Company and Gulf which had integrated as part of the competitive battle against the trust. Partly by reinvestment of earnings and partly by mergers, the successor companies proceeded to round out their operations and put themselves into a stronger position. The Federal Trade Commission later commented on two of these groups of mergers:

> These acquisitions greatly strengthened the Standard of New York as an individual unit of the industry and changed it from practically only a marketing company to a completely integrated organization.[58]

> These companies, therefore, were competitors to some extent, although not great, in the purchase of crude, and were in a position to be strong competitors for new leases in at least three states. On the other hand, most of the operations of the Producers & Refiners were complementary to those of the Prairie and the effect of the consolidation of these interests may have been to give to an active competitor of other Standard and independent companies stronger financial backing in the refining and marketing fields.[59]

In March 1930 the Attorney General asked the federal court in Missouri which had jurisdiction over the 1911 decree to halt the proposed merger of the Standard Oil Company of New York and another

55. Giddens, *Standard Oil Company (Indiana)*, p. 326.

56. Myron W. Watkins, *Oil: Stabilization or Conservation?*, Harper, New York, 1937, p. 46.

57. Sidney A. Swensrud, "Economics of Domestic Marketing," *Transactions of the American Institute of Mechanical Engineers*, 1932, p. 90.

58. FTC 1928 Report, p. 93.

59. *Ibid.*, p. 91.

successor firm, the Vacuum Oil Company. A three-judge court ruled in April 1931 in favor of the companies,[60] and no appeal was taken. With Judge Kimbrough Stone as spokesman, the court held that the main business of Vacuum Oil Company was in lubricating oil, two thirds of it for sale to foreign countries, while Standard Oil of New York was strong in crude production and gasoline sales, four fifths being domestic. Thus there was too little competition between the companies to bring their merger within the prohibition contained in the 1911 decree, and an integrated company whose competitive position would be stronger than that of either member alone was the real outcome of the merger. The Vacuum Oil Company had in fact been hampered in competition by the relative inefficiency of selling lubricating oil without gasoline — for example, its salesmen visited retailers once in several months instead of daily — and found it desirable to "get on the stream of motor fuel and ride down with the current." [61]

Oligopoly in Petroleum

Encouraged by this decision, the merger trend continued, even though some proposals, like the one to merge Standard of New Jersey with Standard of California,[62] fell through — perhaps fortunately in this instance, because of the huge consolidation that would have resulted. Thus, Socony-Vacuum Corporation (renamed Socony-Vacuum Oil Company, Inc., in 1934 and Socony Mobil Oil Company in 1955) proceeded to purchase firms of medium size in Illinois, Kentucky, Michigan and Wisconsin, in order to get their refining facilities and marketing organizations in states in which its predecessor companies had not been active. The original thirty-four Standard companies were gradually reduced by merger to nineteen.

Petroleum has illustrated what might be called the normal oligopolistic structure of major American industries — neither a single dominating concern nor a mass of little competitors, but a moderate number of larger corporations plus many small firms. Under this structure, the large companies are usually well-rounded — technically, operationally, geographically, and from the standpoint of product. The public must rely on their energy to replace the automatic pressures, like the

60. *U.S. v. Standard Oil Company of N.J.*, 47 F. 2d 288 (E.D. Mo. 1931).

61. Platt, "40 Great Years," p. 46.

62. Standard Oil Company of N.J., *The Lamp* (house organ), October 1931.

threat of bankruptcy, which are counted on to operate in an industry of small firms.

Had the courts not permitted these mergers, some companies that outlived the depression because of their financial strength might have succumbed. No major oil company has been close to failing except Richfield Oil Corporation, which was thereupon bought jointly by Sinclair Oil Corporation and Cities Service Company, after each had tried to buy it separately for its outlets on the Pacific Coast. A stronger unit was thus put into competition in California, reinforcing the view that petroleum mergers, by affording financial strength and economic and product diversification, have been "a device for withstanding economic shock." [63] The struggle to get into the majors' ranks by this route still influences "semi-major" companies.[64]

The Cracking Patents Pool

Standard of Indiana's monopoly on the cracking process, through which it secured large royalties from competitors after 1914, was broken by substitute processes patented around 1920 by competitors. Several infringement suits which ensued appeared to jeopardize the very business of the firms involved.[65] Negotiations followed, and in September and October 1923 the complicated situation was settled by creation of what some called the "Patent Club," a pool consisting of the Standard companies of Indiana and New Jersey, the Texas Company and the Gasoline Products Company. Terms were fixed for cross licensing of the various patents.

In March 1923, Senator Robert M. LaFollette's subcommittee of the Senate Committee on Manufactures had declared that gasoline production was "greatly limited" by patents "largely controlled by Standard Oil Companies." [66] In June 1924 the Department of Justice charged that the cross-licensing agreement was a monopolistic restraint of trade, and in 1929 it won its case in the District Court.[67] The Supreme Court, however, reversed this decision unanimously (with

63. Irene Till, "Gasoline — the Competition of Big Business," Sec. 4 of Walton H. Hamilton and associates, *Price and Price Policies*, McGraw-Hill, New York, 1938, p. 134.

64. J. Howard Marshall, book review, *Yale Law Journal*, July 1948, p. 1326.

65. Giddens, *Standard Oil Company* (*Indiana*), p. 264.

66. *High Cost of Gasoline and Other Petroleum Products*, S. Rept. 1263, Subcommittee of Senate Committee on Manufactures, 67th Cong., 4th sess., 1923, p. 69.

67. *U.S. v. Standard Oil Co.* (*Ind.*), 33 F. 2d 617 (N.D. Ill. 1929).

two justices not sitting) in April 1931.[68] The opinion, by Justice Brandeis, emphasized that this patent pool covered only 55 per cent of total cracking capacity, the rest being divided among twenty-one independently owned cracking processes, and that cracked gasoline formed only 26 per cent of total production. The Court considered a cross-licensing agreement to be a natural and legitimate way of meeting the conflicting claims of the various patent holders, and it noted that the pool had not been restrictive or exclusionary in its tactics.

One legal authority argues that a breakup of the pool and resumption of patent litigation among the major holders might have led to some or all of the patents being declared invalid and thus available to anyone, or might have led to additional competitive research or to independent competitive licensing — alternatives preferable, in his opinion, to approval of a patent pool shared by only a few large companies.[69] The majority view of legal experts, however, supports the Court's decision;[70] and one writer argues for it that "it is unlikely that any small producer would venture into the field until the giants had resolved their conflicts" through such an agreement.[71] A penalty on licensing of inventions, even in the form of cross licensing, might also have encouraged originating firms to monopolize their discoveries.[72]

In January and February 1931, even before the Supreme Court's decision, seven of the large refiners purchased the Universal Oil Products Company, a research organization that held other important patents related to cracking. This facilitated further research — still, of course, in the hands of the large companies — with greater security against litigation.[73] During World War II congressional committees and the Department of Justice again intervened, and under threat of a suit against control of this important research enterprise by a few firms, the owners of Universal Oil Products Company gave their

68. *Standard Oil Co. (Ind.) v. U.S.*, 283 U.S. 163 (1931).

69. *Report of the Attorney General's National Committee to Study the Antitrust Laws*, 1955, dissent of Louis B. Schwartz, p. 247.

70. *Ibid.*, pp. 242–45.

71. Bartholemew Diggins, "The Patent-Antitrust Problem," *Michigan Law Review*, June 1955, p. 1108.

72. Henry R. Seager and Charles A. Gulick, Jr., *Trust and Corporation Problems*, Harper, New York, 1929, p. 146.

73. Giddens, *Standard Oil Company (Indiana)*, pp. 453–56.

shares to the American Chemical Society. By 1956 the company was believed to be worth $50 million.[74]

Besides those mentioned, there have been other patent pools and arrangements among the majors.[75]

Cooperative Programs on the Pacific Coast

Discovery of new oil fields in California in the 1920s led to price instability there. In 1928 a cooperative plan was set up, called the "Long pool" after its manager, who negotiated the regular purchase of "distress gasoline" by the West Coast majors from independent refiners. Jobbers and retailers who had formerly handled this gasoline complained to Washington, and in February 1930 the Department of Justice charged nineteen oil companies with purchase of distress gasoline, agreements on prices, terms and conditions of sale, and boycotting retailers who refused to sell to consumers at fixed prices. Just before the case was to come up for trial, in September 1930, the defendants accepted a consent decree enjoining these practices.[76]

A series of price wars in the early 1930s developed out of flush production and reduced demand. Several temporary stabilization measures in states like Oklahoma led to the Petroleum Code of Fair Competition under the National Recovery Administration, with a Supplementary Agreement for the Pacific Coast. Although its quotas and penalties for the major companies had been approved by the Secretary of the Interior, the Attorney General quickly sought indictments against the participating West Coast majors for violation of the 1930 consent decree.[77] Cooperation then ceased, and tank wagon prices sank to 5 cents a gallon. The indictments were dismissed, and in June 1934 a new "Pacific Coast Petroleum Agreement" was recognized as a valid NRA Supplementary Code. This differed from the first one in not specifying quotas or price differentials, but it provided for the purchase of distress gasoline. Taking advantage of the guaranteed market, about fifteen new small refiners appeared in California in 1934–35.[78]

74. *New York Times*, September 14, 1956, p. 10.

75. Compare William J. Kemnitzer, *Rebirth of Monopoly*, Harper, New York, 1938, chart on p. 173.

76. *U.S. v. Standard Oil Company of California*, Eq. 2542–S (N.D. Calif. 1930).

77. Bain, *The Economics of the Pacific Coast Petroleum Industry*, Part 2, "Price Behavior and Competition," p. 264.

78. *Ibid.*, p. 268.

For several years after the NRA expired, more than half the output of the California independents was being bought by the majors under this program.[79] In November 1939 the Department of Justice once again charged existence of a buying pool for distress gasoline, elimination of price competition in gasoline enforced by periodic inspection of prices, and boycotting of retailers who did not abide by the resale price-fixing provisions.[80] The case against three defendants was dismissed in 1940, but thirty-eight others changed their original pleas of not guilty to *nolo contendere* and paid fines.

Although one company alone will rarely assume the burden of trying to stabilize the whole market, it is logical to think purchases of distress gasoline may still be made by individual majors.[81] By definition an independent refiner lacks assured marketing outlets, so that purchases by a major refiner may easily be necessary to his continued operation. Undoubtedly the improved condition of the gasoline market, due to the general prosperity which has prevailed since 1940, has very much reduced the need for special stabilization methods. However, the government alleged in 1950 that cooperative stabilization had continued in California, under new methods.[82]

The Tank Steamer Pool and the Madison Trial

In 1932 tanker rates fell so low that a "Tank Steamer Pool" was set up to include all the tankers of the participating independent owners and an equal number owned by the majors (amounting to 16 per cent of their own ships).[83] Part of the pool's profits were to be paid to owners of surplus tankers in return for laying them up, with the object of causing rates to rise. Independent oil shippers secured a Department of Justice investigation, upon which the plan was dropped. This tanker pool was suggested again under the NRA code, but was not adopted.

A more important attempt at stabilization was aimed at the chaotic marketing situation in the Mid-Continent area that resulted chiefly

79. *Ibid.*, p. 272.

80. *U.S. v. General Petroleum Corporation of Calif.*, 33 F. Supp. 95 (S.D. Calif. 1940).

81. Bain, *The Economics of the Pacific Coast Petroleum Industry*, Part 1, "Market Structure," p. 156.

82. *U.S. v. Standard Oil Company of Calif.*, Civil 11584–C (S.D. Calif. 1950).

83. Louis J. Walsh, TNEC Hearings, Part 14, pp. 7334–35, 7574; TNEC Monograph 39, pp. 26–27; Standard Oil Company of N.J. and Sun Oil Co., TNEC Monograph 39–A (a reply to No. 39), p. 38; Gilbert Burck, "The Jersey Company," *Fortune*, October 1951, p. 193.

from the discovery in October 1930 of the East Texas field, the largest ever found in the United States. Many refineries were set up to skim this crude, and, since they lacked regular market outlets, their products were dumped on the market for what they would bring. General price demoralization followed, with which the NRA attempted to cope through "buying programs" authorized by the Petroleum Code of Fair Competition in April 1934. Each large refiner was to purchase the surplus gasoline of a particular independent (called its "dancing partner"). When the NRA was declared unconstitutional in May 1935, the refiners' committee decided to continue the program, which it considered legitimate and desirable.

Hundreds of complaints were received by the Department of Justice in 1935 and 1936 from both branded and unbranded distributors. The margin of the former had been reduced one half cent to one cent a gallon late in 1935, and the latter had flourished on the distress gasoline against which the buying program was aimed. In May 1936 a grand jury was convened at Madison, Wisconsin, and in July eighteen big companies, fifty-four officers, and four representatives of the *Chicago Journal of Commerce*, the *National Petroleum News* and the Western Petroleum Refiners Association were indicted under Section 2 of the Sherman Act for participation in or aid to the buying program. For three months in late 1937 the presence of so many executives on trial made Madison almost the "oil capital" of the nation. The journals were quickly cleared of all suspicion, but most of the corporations and a number of their executives were convicted by the jury in January 1938. The verdict was upheld as to twelve corporations and five officers by the District Court,[84] then reversed by a unanimous Circuit Court in 1939,[85] and finally reinstated by a 5–2 vote of the Supreme Court in May 1940.[86]

After the jury trial, the defendants against whom the government was pressing a second indictment [87] — for agreeing upon margins and other contract provisions of branded distributors — thought better of having to stand trial, pleaded *nolo contendere* and paid fines. The fines of $437,500, or a total of $543,000 for both cases, were the largest in Sherman Act history.

84. *U.S. v. Socony-Vacuum Oil Co.*, 23 F. Supp. 937, 24 F. Supp. 575 (W.D. Wis. 1938).
85. *Ibid.*, 105 F. 2d 809 (7th Cir. 1939).
86. *Ibid.*, 310 U.S. 150 (1940).
87. *Ibid.*, Cr. 11364 (W.D. Wis. 1936).

Significance of the Socony-Vacuum Decision

The basic principle which governed this *Socony-Vacuum* decision of the Supreme Court, that price fixing is illegal *per se,* had been established in the *Trenton Potteries* case of 1927.[88] The 1940 decision was significant chiefly in showing that this ruling had not been seriously modified by the Supreme Court's *Appalachian Coals* opinion of 1933,[89] which permitted cooperation by a limited segment of a distressed industry but which the 1940 opinion of Justice Douglas distinguished on the ground that coal prices had not been fixed or affected. Two justices who had sat in the *Appalachian Coals* case dissented in the *Socony-Vacuum* case, with Justice Roberts drawing the analogy between the two situations. It should be noted that there had not been outright price fixing in gasoline, but merely support at varying prices. Justice Douglas made an extension of the law when he declared that any concerted action "for the purpose and with the effect" of influencing prices was unlawful.[90]

The defendants might have been cleared by a liberal interpretation of the rule of reason. Not only had the buying program been launched with Interior Department approval under the NRA, and the Department's Petroleum Administrative Board been kept informed of its operations, but the Board had recommended a similar plan for Pennsylvania and Secretary Ickes had expressed gratification to Congress over the very plan which was to come under attack. One post-trial episode relevant to reasonableness was a stockholder's suit charging the directors of Socony-Vacuum with personal liability in the affair — to which a New York court replied that the directors "did not know or believe or have reason to believe that their participation in the buying program was prohibited by the Sherman Act." [91] More than forty treble damage suits are said to have been launched by firms claiming injury by the support program,[92] but none of these was successful in the courts.

The position of the small East Texas refiners first became precarious after 1933 when governmental control cut down the flow of cheap

88. *U.S. v. Trenton Potteries Co.*, 273 U.S. 392 (1927).

89. *Appalachian Coals, Inc. v. U.S.*, 288 U.S. 344 (1933).

90. 310 U.S., at 223.

91. *Simon v. Socony-Vacuum Oil Co.*, 179 Misc. 202, 38 N.Y.S. 2d 270, 274 (1942); affirmed without opinion, 267 App. Div. 89 (1942).

92. *Variety*, January 5, 1955, p. 59.

crude oil from this field; and remained so because of the technical inadequacy of these refineries, the surplus capacity (since about one hundred of them had been built), and their failure to build up assured marketing outlets.[93] As long as their "dancing partners" bought much (sometimes most) of the output of these independents, distributors became accustomed to purchasing from the large refiners. When the support program was halted in 1936, scores of the small refineries shut down; the total number in operation dropped from 76 at the beginning of 1936 to 14 at the beginning of 1940. Independent producers of crude blamed the disappearance of these customers of theirs on the Madison proceeding, but this affected the timing, not the fact, of their eventual disappearance.

The *Socony-Vacuum* case, with its long trial far from their homes, influenced that generation of oil executives for many years. The residue it left is said to have been a sense of antagonism toward the Department of Justice, a resolution to avoid anything which might be interpreted as price fixing, and reluctance to attempt any form of cooperation, no matter how constructive it might promise to be. However, in World War II and the Korean War the companies did not wait for every "i" to be dotted before agreeing to cooperative action as urged by the government. The full influence of the case on the industry will not be revealed unless similar conditions should arise to suggest a similar stabilization plan.

The "Ethyl" Licensing System

In December 1921 Thomas Midgley, Jr., working with C. F. Kettering on a General Motors Research Corporation study of the removal of the "knock" from gasoline, discovered that a small addition of tetraethyl lead would have that effect.[94] Not being equipped to manufacture a chemical of this type, General Motors licensed the du Pont Company to make it on a fee basis. Early in 1923 Standard Oil of New Jersey patented a manufacturing process which used chlorine, an abundant chemical, instead of bromine, a scarce one. Since it was blocked from making the product, and General Motors from using this process, the two corporations in August 1924 organized

93. McLean and Haigh, *The Growth of Integrated Oil Companies*, pp. 587–99.

94. Sources used include *U.S. v. E. I. du Pont de Nemours & Co.*, 126 F. Supp. 235, 301–13 (N.D. Ill. 1954), and Plaintiff's Pre-Trial Brief, same case, October 15, 1952, pp. 77–105.

as a joint subsidiary the Ethyl Gasoline Corporation (later called Ethyl Corporation).

Before production could really get under way, Standard Oil's attempt to make some of the output itself despite its lack of experience with this type of chemical manufacturing cost five lives and resulted in a one-year withdrawal of the product. Even the Dow Chemical Company now declined to enter the business. The du Pont Company, which had designed new equipment, became the sole maker at its Deepwater, New Jersey, plant, on license from the Ethyl Corporation. Du Pont's profit proved to be about half of Ethyl Corporation's at the rates which were set, and in addition, as owner of about 23 per cent of the stock of General Motors, it received indirectly a share of Ethyl Corporation's own profit and of patent royalties.

The "ethyl" fluid itself was distributed by Ethyl Corporation to all interested oil refiners, who treated their premium or "Ethyl" gasoline with it, and after 1933, in smaller amounts, their regular gasoline. In 1937 Ethyl Corporation, not wanting to be forced out of business by its licensee when the patents should expire, opened its own tetraethyl lead plant at Baton Rouge, a plant which du Pont had designed at its request. Ethyl Corporation built another large plant in 1952 at Houston, and now makes over half of the total supply.

The Licensing System Outlawed

In February 1937 the Department of Justice sued to enjoin Ethyl Corporation's jobber licensing system as a violation of Section 1 of the Sherman Act. The District Court's decision for the government was affirmed unanimously in 1940 by the Supreme Court, with two justices not sitting. Justice Stone's opinion found Ethyl Corporation's jobber licensing system illegal. First, it had permitted its refiner customers to sell treated gasoline only to consumers, retailers or other refiners, or to jobbers whom the Corporation itself licensed (numbering about 11,000 out of the nation's total of 12,000). Second, it had supported resale price maintenance by refusing to license jobbers who "cut prices or refuse to conform to the marketing policies and posted prices of the major refineries or the market leaders among them." [95]

This was the first of several decisions in the 1940s which in effect have outlawed any effort of a patentee to use his patent rights to fix

95. *U.S. v. Ethyl Gasoline Corp.*, 27 F. Supp. 959 (S.D. N.Y. 1939); *Ethyl Gasoline Corp. v. U.S.*, 309 U.S. 436, 450 (1940).

resale prices. The practical consequence in this instance was to condemn the whole jobber licensing system for ethyl fluid and thus the requirement of a premium price (usually 3 cents a gallon) formerly imposed upon distributors. Although the courts gave this aspect little attention, it had been Ethyl Corporation's own interest in the resale price structure: it wanted to get a premium price for a premium product. Most outlets continued, however, to charge the premium, which was as much, or more, to their benefit as to Ethyl Corporation's.[96] The licensing system was dropped after the District Court decision, and by the end of 1939 all "cut-price marketers" covered in one survey were selling gasoline treated with tetraethyl lead.[97]

When the last of four basic patents expired at the end of 1947, du Pont began to sell its antiknock fluid on its own account, although without the "Ethyl" trademark. It was reported that du Pont wanted to make the money directly rather than wait for dividends from General Motors.[98] In 1951 it built a new, large, continuous-process unit at Deepwater. Even in the absence of the antitrust decision, this competition would eventually have prevented any boycotting of customers engaging in gasoline price cutting — a phenomenon to which du Pont would be indifferent.

The Pipeline Antitrust Problem

In the nature of things, pipelines had to be built by large oil companies. The huge investment required would rarely be risked by a company that did not plan to ship enough of its own crude oil or products to keep the pipeline occupied, and that was not big enough to stand the loss if the oil field on which a pipeline depended should dry up.[99] Twenty majors controlled 57.4 per cent of gathering-line mileage in July 1936 and, in January 1938, 89.0 per cent of crude oil trunk line mileage and 96.1 per cent of gasoline line mileage.[100]

The 1906 Hepburn Amendment to the Interstate Commerce Act itself carried an "oil amendment" moved by Senator Lodge, conserva-

96. Eugene V. Rostow, *A National Policy for the Oil Industry*, Yale University Press, New Haven, 1947, p. 86.

97. McLean and Haigh, *The Growth of Integrated Oil Companies*, p. 219.

98. *Business Week*, October 12, 1946, p. 19.

99. Fayette B. Dow, "The Issue of Pipe Line Divorcement," TNEC Hearings, Part 15, pp. 8720–30; McLean and Haigh, *The Growth of Integrated Oil Companies*, pp. 190–91; George S. Wolbert, Jr., *American Pipe Lines: Their Industrial Structure, Economic Status and Legal Implications*, University of Oklahoma Press, Norman, 1951, pp. 9–11.

100. TNEC Hearings, Part 14-A, pp. 7720, 7723, 7729.

tive Republican, who had Standard Oil specifically in mind.[101] As later interpreted by the Supreme Court, this brought under ICC regulation interstate pipelines which either shipped oil for others or bought their oil for shipment,[102] or over which others even "sought" to ship.[103] The Hepburn Act in turn brought into effect the Elkins Amendment of 1903, which forbade a common carrier to give a rebate to any shipper, including the owner of the carrier itself. Independent oil men argued that the high profits made by the owners of pipelines — never below 20 per cent on investment in regulated pipelines between 1922 and 1940 — amounted to rebates on their own shipments of oil. A second complaint was that pipelines refused to accept oil for shipment unless "tendered" in excessively large quantities, the minimum frequently being 100,000 barrels.

Thus independent producers, facing the prospect of paying high rates and unable to store up the minimum tender requirement anyhow, were under pressure to sell their crude to the companies owning the pipelines. Small refiners could escape paying the high rates on the crude they bought only by setting up near an oil field, on whose continuance their operation would thus depend, rather than near consuming markets where they might have a longer future. Granting that the issue was academic to those small producers and refiners who would not have wanted their capital tied up in oil in transit,[104] it was not so to others. It is not surprising that bills to prohibit refineries from owning pipelines were introduced in every Congress but one between 1931 and 1949.[105] Another approach favored thoroughgoing regulation of the pipelines as public utilities.[106]

The Pipeline Consent Decree

In September 1940 the Department of Justice charged several pipelines with paying disguised rebates to their owners in the form of

101. Leslie Cookenboo, Jr., *Crude Oil Pipe Lines and Competition in the Oil Industry*, Harvard University Press, Cambridge, 1955, p. 3.

102. *The Pipe Line Cases*, 234 U.S. 548 (1914).

103. *Champlin Refining Co. v. U.S.*, 329 U.S. 29 (1946); *U.S. v. Champlin Refining Co.*, 341 U.S. 290 (1951).

104. Wolbert, *American Pipe Lines*, pp. 45–48.

105. *Ibid.*, p. 4, note 4.

106. William Beard, *Regulation of Pipe Lines as Common Carriers*, Columbia University Press, New York, 1941, pp. 169–73; Roy A. Prewitt, "The Operation and Regulation of Crude Oil and Gasoline Pipe Lines," *Quarterly Journal of Economics*, February 1942, pp. 210–11.

excessive profits.[107] The Department would probably have demanded divorcement of pipelines and oil companies had not the National Defense Commission warned that this would interfere with war preparations.[108] In December 1941, while these suits were still pending, all the majors and fifty-six affiliated pipelines accepted a consent decree.[109] They agreed to limit dividend payments by common-carrier pipelines to 7 per cent of their valuation as found by the Interstate Commerce Commission. Extra profits could be made, but had to be reinvested in equipment, in working capital, or to retire debt, and could not be counted in the base against which future dividends would be calculated. The refiners accepted all of this rather than contest the case and run the risk of having to pay huge sums in treble damages if the courts should accept the Department of Justice's interpretation of the meaning of "rebates."

The financial effects of the decree can only be guessed. There are, it is true, figures on revenues for all pipelines reporting to the ICC, including up to twenty that had not been included in the consent decree. Their trunk line revenue per thousand barrel-miles declined from an average of 55.0 cents in 1940–41 to an average of 47.5 cents in 1942–43, and continued in the range between 44 and 54 cents through 1953 despite a general wholesale price increase and a sharp increase in the price of oil and refined products. Return on investment declined from 20 per cent in 1940–41 to 12 per cent in 1942–43 and held at around 7 or 8 per cent after 1947. (See Table 11.) However, the author of a recent study of the pipelines believes that several other factors, including an ICC order in 1940 which reduced tender requirements to 10,000 barrels and directed that rates should not yield over 8 per cent on pipeline valuation, were more influential than the consent decree.[110]

Recent Pipeline Developments

Typical complaints against pipelines in recent years have stressed their failure to extend gathering lines to all wells newly opened by

107. *U.S. v. Phillips Petroleum Co. and Phillips Pipe Line Co.*, Civil 182 (D. Del. 1940); *U.S. v. Standard Oil Co. (Ind.)*, Civil 201 (N.D. Ind. 1940); *U.S. v. Great Lakes Pipe Line Co.*, Civil 183 (D. Del. 1940).

108. "Sun Oil," *Fortune*, February 1941, p. 116.

109. *U.S. v. Atlantic Refining Co.*, Civil 14060 (D. D.C. 1941).

110. Wolbert, *American Pipe Lines*, pp. 15–16, 24–25, 136–37, 159–60, 163.

TABLE II

PETROLEUM: REVENUE AND PROFIT
OF REPORTING CRUDE AND PRODUCT PIPELINES, 1937–53

Year	Depreciated Investment	Barrel-Miles Carried	Trunk Line Revenue per 1,000 Barrel-Miles	Ratio of Net Earnings after Taxes to Depreciated Investment
	(Millions)	*(Billions)*	*(Cents)*	*(Per Cent)*
1937	$ 389	303	61.4	26.4
1938	375	287	61.4	24.7
1939	384	290	56.6	21.0
1940	384	306	56.1	20.8
1941	417	351	53.9	19.1
1942	467	384	48.0	12.2
1943	490	454	46.9	12.5
1944	500	509	47.0	13.1
1945	515	495	46.9	12.8
1946	555	488	44.9	10.1
1947	651	537	44.6	8.2
1948	781	599	45.7	7.3
1949	874	590	47.4	6.6
1950	1,001	684	48.1	8.1
1951	1,124	817	48.3	7.3
1952	1,329	857	53.8	7.3
1953	1,565	917	52.8	7.0

Source: Interstate Commerce Commission, Bureau of Transport Economics and Statistics, *Statistics of Oil Pipe Line Companies*, as tabulated in Leslie Cookenboo, Jr., *Crude Oil Pipe Lines and Competition in the Oil Industry*, Harvard University Press, Cambridge, 1955, pp. 98, 101. The number of reporting pipelines varied; for example, there were 58 in 1937, 71 in 1941, 76 in 1951.

independent producers, and the failure of the refining companies owning the pipelines to purchase all the crude oil tendered to them. These allegations, which appear to call for a considerable extension of the pipeline utility concept, are now more often heard than the old complaints about rates and service. An increased use of the lines by nonowners noted in the postwar period [111] might also be interpreted as indicating a more satisfactory situation. The pipeline requirements dealing with identity and quality of the product shipped are now considered fair and nonrestrictive,[112] even though independent shippers

111. See *ibid.*, p. 44.

112. See *ibid.*, p. 39; compare Eugene V. Rostow and Arthur S. Sachs, "Entry into the Oil Refining Business: Vertical Integration Re-examined," *Yale Law Journal*, June-July 1952, p. 885.

will comment privately that a pipeline owner naturally may sometimes give itself the benefit of the doubt when its interests clash with those of an independent shipper. Once again, ICC regulation is probably the most significant cause of the improvement. According to a recent student, the consent decree has made pipeline operation unnecessarily hazardous because of ambiguities in its drafting, the danger of treble damage suits against an owner who violates it, and the fact that it regulates earnings rather than rates. He recommends that the decree be lifted and that regulation be turned back entirely to the ICC.[113]

The days of big pipeline profits appear to be past. An industry source reports that "most pipe lines today are actively fighting for business from non-owner shippers, and . . . earn substantially less than the rate allowed by the ICC." [114] It is also noticeable that — owing in part to the required reduction in profits while the capital risks were as big as ever [115] — most big recent lines have been built as joint ventures rather than by a single company. Although continued expansion of the pipeline system can be interpreted to mean that current regulation permits a high enough return to induce new investment, it may also mean that a line is usually built not as a means of earning money directly, but as a unit in an integrated petroleum structure. In fact, pipelines were never built as common-carrier transportation agencies until after World War II.[116]

In the last few years, it is true, the Buckeye Pipe Line Company (formerly Standard-owned) has vastly expanded its mileage as an independent, while at least five small independent lines have been laid down. Although not subject to the consent decree, these are regulated by the ICC. Like one larger line which was not in fact carried through,[117] they met the risk problem by selling long-term space contracts. The purchasers, had space become tight, would thus have received the same type of favored position as if they themselves had built the lines.

113. Wolbert, *American Pipe Lines*, pp. 159–60.

114. John W. Boatwright, *Petroleum and Economic Progress*, Oil Industry Background Information Bulletin No. 8, American Petroleum Institute, New York, 1954, p. 4.

115. McLean and Haigh, *The Growth of Integrated Oil Companies*, p. 509.

116. Ralph C. Heath, *The Development of Petroleum Pipe Lines in the United States*, unpublished doctoral thesis, Indiana University School of Business, Bloomington, 1953, p. 116; Wolbert, *American Pipe Lines*, p. 102; *Journal of Commerce*, February 1, 1952, pp. 1, 11.

117. Rostow and Sachs, "Entry into the Oil Refining Business," pp. 906–11.

The I.G. Farben–Standard of New Jersey Agreements

The first international cartel agreement relating to oil to reach the courts on an antitrust issue was that between the German chemical trust, I.G. Farben, A.G. (Interessengemeinschaft Farbenindustrie Aktiengesellschaft), and Standard Oil of New Jersey. In 1927 Standard began to prepare against disappearance of new crude oil sources by exchanging more than $30 million of its stock for rights in the hydrogenation process of synthesizing oil from coal developed by I.G. Farben. Two years later the two corporations entered into detailed patent and process agreements under which they were to share their technological developments and to pool royalties — generally on the basis that Standard would have control (except in Germany) of developments in oil and I.G. Farben in chemicals. During World War II the Bone, Kilgore and Truman committees of the Senate brought out the agreement's defects — among which were the slowness with which I.G. Farben turned over the know-how of its Buna synthetic rubber process and Standard's slowness in licensing American rubber companies in this field.[118] Some writers have pointed out that there were offsetting gains in the form of productive petroleum research in America based on the hydrogenation process thus secured.[119]

After Pearl Harbor, the Department of Justice intervened, and Standard, unwilling to fight such a case during the war, signed consent decrees in March 1942 and April 1943.[120] These provided for the licensing free during the war and on reasonable royalties thereafter of the patents relating to synthetic gasoline, synthetic rubber production and catalytic refining.

The antitrust laws did not have a major practical influence in this case, since World War II had ended the agreements. Even without a decree, the important patents would certainly have been made available during the war. The judicial proceeding did not fully clarify the type of agreement which would be permissible with foreign companies

118. See Joseph Borkin and Charles A. Welsh, *Germany's Master Plan*, Duell, Sloan & Pearce, New York, 1943, pp. 189–98; George W. Stocking and Myron W. Watkins, *Cartels in Action*, Twentieth Century Fund, 1946, pp. 87–117.

119. Charles R. Whittlesey, *National Interest and International Cartels*, Macmillan, New York, 1946, p. 42; "Creating Tomorrow's Oil," *Fortune*, November 1951, pp. 144, 146.

120. *U.S. v. Standard Oil Co. (N.J.)*, Complaint and Consent Decree, Civil 2091 (D. N.J. 1942), Supplemental Judgment (D. N.J. 1943); *Standard Oil Co. (N.J.) v. Markham*, 64 F. Supp. 656 (S.D. N.Y. 1945).

in peacetime; but the strong reaction of public opinion has had a lasting influence.

Service Stations: The Iowa Plan

During the 1920s the major oil companies expanded their direct operation of service stations; but retail price cutting after 1929 began to reveal weaknesses in this policy.[121] Independent stations took business away from company stations because they could cut prices on shorter notice, with less risk of ill will, and without violating the Clayton Act or one-price laws in a number of states. Between 1933 and 1934 the number of stations owned by eighteen majors was reduced from 125,327 to 98,246, and by 1935 it was only 75,547.[122] The new factor which became effective in 1935 was Iowa's severe tax on chain stores, including stations. Standard of Indiana at once leased out to their operators all its stations in the state, and this "Iowa plan" quickly spread to other refiners and other territories. Besides escaping the chain store tax, which seven states had adopted at the end of 1939, the refiners were glad to be relieved of responsibility for service station employees, who were now being organized into unions and covered by social security and wage and hour legislation.

The number of refiner-operated stations continued to decline, amounting to only about 3,000 in 1956.[123] Although some majors still keep a core of salaried dealers, most of them have retained only a few selected locations to use as models or experimental and training plants, and for the profit of their concentrated, high-volume sales.[124] Their attitude was in general that of the president of Standard of Indiana, who found the Iowa chain store law and the resulting change in company policy to have proved a "decided blessing." [125] A deterioration in station cleanliness and operation was soon noticed, however, and Standard was obliged to launch an educational campaign in sales and maintenance for the independent dealers who distributed its gasoline.[126] Today most majors have representatives who tour their brand outlets

121. McLean and Haigh, *The Growth of Integrated Oil Companies*, pp. 289–94, 300–01.

122. TNEC Monograph 39, p. 90.

123. *National Petroleum News*, Factbook issue, Mid-May 1956, p. 175.

124. *Fuel Investigation — Petroleum Prices and Profits*, Progress Report of House Interstate and Foreign Commerce Committee, 80th Cong., 2d sess., 1948, answers of oil companies to question 13, at pp. 20–21, 25, etc.

125. Giddens, *Standard Oil Company (Indiana)*, p. 552.

126. *Ibid.*, p. 553.

and try to keep them up to a certain standard of maintenance and operation.

Service stations today may be divided into five groups and the number in each roughly estimated as follows: [127] (1) over 3,000 owned by suppliers and run by salaried managers; (2) about 8,000 of the new and rapidly growing "commission-type" stations run as independent businesses except that they buy their gasoline on consignment, thus giving the supplier control over prices; (3) some 90,000, more or less, which are leased by the supplier — usually a refiner, but often a jobber and occasionally the owner of a chain of stations — to the operator, subject to cancellation for unsatisfactory performance; (4) perhaps 15,000 or 20,000 leased by the dealer from a third party; and (5) the remaining 60,000 or so which are on land and premises owned by the dealer himself. Types (4) and (5) are the "independent" or "contract" stations whose operators merely buy their gasoline, and usually other products, on contract from their suppliers. As to the most important single group, which sells much more gasoline per station than the contract type [128] — those leased by refiners to dealers — it can reasonably be said that the refiner keeps much of the control that he had before 1935 but without the disadvantages of ownership.[129] In other words, the refiners have made the best compromise they could find between ownership and arm's-length contracting.

The Standard Stations Suit

The Department of Justice's attitude had been one of the reasons for the adoption of the Iowa plan, since it had (by advance warnings) killed an agency plan and a lease-and-license plan which the industry had worked out between 1930 and 1935. In 1947 the Department filed several suits to determine the legality of exclusive dealing practices, commencing with what is called the *Standard Stations* suit against Standard Oil of California. This refiner operated perhaps one sixth of

127. Figures based on estimates in *National Petroleum News*, Factbook issue, Mid-May 1956, p. 175, July 1956, p. 93; and in E. I. du Pont de Nemours & Co., Petroleum Chemicals Division, *The Service Station Operator*, Wilmington, 1955, 4th report, p. 9. Other estimates would undoubtedly differ.

128. Calculated from *Gasoline Price War in New Jersey*, Report of Senate Small Business Committee, S. Rept. 2810, 84th Cong., 2d sess., 1956, p. 10.

129. Compare Louis B. Schwartz, "Potential Impairment of Competition — The Impact of *Standard Oil Company of California v. United States* on the Standard of Legality under the Clayton Act," *University of Pennsylvania Law Review*, November 1949, p. 16.

its own stations: these were the "Standard stations," but the case, despite the title given it, did not deal with them. What it did attack was an arrangement whereby Standard lent money at very low rates, or gave equipment, to the independently owned and managed "Chevron stations," whose operators agreed to buy their entire "requirements" of petroleum products and tires, batteries and accessories (TBA) from their sponsor. In June 1948 the trial court held that these exclusive agreements restrained trade under the Sherman Act and were also illegal under Section 3 of the Clayton Act.[130]

A year later the Supreme Court by a 5–4 vote sustained this decision, although it did not discuss the Sherman Act count.[131] The key to Justice Frankfurter's opinion for the majority was the fact that the company sold a substantial quantity of merchandise through such contracts — $57 million a year of gasoline and $8 million of other products through 6,000 service stations. Since Standard's contracts prevented competitors from bidding for this much of the trade, the opinion interpreted the arrangement to be a "substantial lessening" of competition within the meaning of the Clayton Act.

Three members of the Court denied, through an opinion of Justice Jackson, that requirements contracts which affected only 6.7 per cent of West Coast gasoline would necessarily lessen competition substantially. They asked to see further evidence. This is sometimes called the qualitative view of competition as opposed to Justice Frankfurter's quantitative view. Decisions since 1949 seem on the whole to have retreated from quantitative substantiality.[132]

A separate dissent by Justice Douglas argued that if majors were refused the right to make these contracts with independent dealers, they would be driven either to ownership of filling stations or to making stations their agents handling gasoline on consignment, thus "increasing the monopoly of the oil companies over the retail field." [133]

Standard of California did not in fact attempt to convert its lessees to employees. It wrote them in May 1950 to say that exclusive dealing contracts had been invalidated, but that it still insisted on the right to

130. *U.S. v. Standard Oil Company of Calif. and Standard Stations, Inc.*, 78 F. Supp. 850 (S.D. Calif. 1948).

131. *Standard Oil Company of Calif. and Standard Stations, Inc. v. U.S.*, 337 U.S. 293 (1949).

132. *Report of the Attorney General's National Committee to Study the Antitrust Laws*, p. 142.

133. 337 U.S., at 320.

control the use of tanks and pumps which it owned.[134] This insistence was in full accord with the trial court's judgment, which guarded against deception of the public by providing that Standard could ensure that substitute gasolines not be used in tanks and pumps marked with its name. In 1953 Standard gave some of its employee-operated stations more independence by putting them on a consignment basis.[135]

Other Exclusive Dealing Cases

District Judge Leon R. Yankwich tried both the *Standard Stations* case and the companion suit against the Richfield Oil Corporation. His decision against Richfield in July 1951[136] was sustained on the precedent of the *Standard Stations* case by a 7–0 vote of the Supreme Court in April 1952.[137] The four *Standard Stations* dissenters could have used this chance to reverse the rule of that case, but refrained, "evidently in deference to the absent two Justices." [138]

Judge Yankwich found no substantial difference between the Standard and Richfield patterns. He held that (1) Richfield's exclusive agreement with the 45 per cent of its stations which were "leased out" deprived other suppliers of the opportunity to deal with operators whom he considered (contrary to the defendant's contention) to be "independent"; and that (2) Richfield's "maximum-minimum" contracts with its other stations (whose alleged independence he denied because of details of their contracts with Richfield), under which they agreed to accept a stated minimum amount of gasoline monthly but could not demand more than a stated maximum, were no different from the Standard requirements contracts. Richfield proceeded to cancel its existing leases and offer new contracts which included (1) a 30-day instead of a 24-hour cancellation clause; (2) an increase in station rentals paid by the dealers from one cent to 2.25 cents a gallon on all gasoline sold, to compensate for the value to Richfield of the exclusive dealing arrangement it lost; and (3) a reduction in tank wagon prices on all Richfield products. Dealers would

134. *National Petroleum News*, June 7, 1950, pp. 17–18.

135. *Business Week*, November 14, 1953, pp. 55–56.

136. *U.S. v. Richfield Oil Corp.*, 99 F. Supp. 280 (S.D. Calif. 1951).

137. *Richfield Oil Corp. v. U.S.*, 343 U.S. 922 (1952).

138. *Report of the Attorney General's National Committee to Study the Antitrust Laws*, p. 142, note 51.

thus be kept loyal, because the higher rental rate applied to all gasoline handled, while the compensating lower purchase prices applied only to Richfield products.[139] The Department of Justice did not consider this adequate compliance.[140]

At least two further exclusive dealing cases have been brought. In October 1952 the Federal Trade Commission charged Shell Oil Company with insisting that its dealers (1) handle only Shell fuel oil, (2) use the Shell color scheme and name on delivery trucks, and (3) buy from Shell an amount equal to the total bought from all sources in the previous year. Shell neither admitted nor denied the practices, but accepted the Commission's order in March 1953.[141] A Department of Justice suit filed in January 1950 against Sun Oil Company's maximum-minimum contracts was still pending in 1956.[142]

A Federal Trade Commission complaint of a somewhat similar nature was filed in July 1950 against five Standard companies and the Atlas Supply Company, which the five had created in 1929 as a mechanism for making money on the TBA business. Atlas bought TBA articles at discounts from their manufacturers and resold them to dealers. Most of the other majors and some minor companies and jobbers used a different pattern to obtain profits on the TBA business: they agreed to represent specific tire and other manufacturers in selling to their dealers, in return for an over-all commission. The Atlas group was enjoined in July 1951 from violating the Robinson-Patman Act by using its combined buying power to obtain a better price than competing buyers.[143] The order was not appealed, and the respondents stated that it would not hurt them.[144] Each of the five firms now makes its own purchases of Atlas-brand products.[145] Meanwhile, the over-all commission plan of the other oil firms has been under investigation.

Improvement Noticed

Although the *Standard Stations* and *Richfield* cases dealt primarily with exclusive dealing in gasoline, there is in fact little future in the attempt

139. *National Petroleum News*, September 17, 1952, p. 36.
140. *Ibid.*, December 10, 1952, p. 29.
141. *Shell Oil Co.*, Docket 6051, 49 FTC 1182 (1953).
142. *U.S. v. Sun Oil Co.*, Civil 10483 (E.D. Pa. 1950).
143. *Atlas Supply Co.*, Docket 5794, 48 FTC 53 (1951).
144. *National Petroleum News*, June 20, 1951, p. 26.
145. *Ibid.*, Factbook issue, Mid-May 1956, p. 146.

to have stations handle more than one brand. "Split pump stations," as they were called, were formerly quite common, but defects of the system caused most of them to disappear. As early as 1931 two surveys showed 85 and 95 per cent of motorists expressing themselves as opposed to it, primarily out of fear that the dealer would substitute the second brand for the desired one.[146] Not only did dealers find that handling one brand required less investment and less bookkeeping, but six out of seven felt that it actually increased sales.[147] As to suppliers, they naturally dislike operating through dealers whose lack of special enthusiasm for their own brand is obvious to the customer.

In bringing the *Standard Stations* suit, the Department of Justice probably had in mind elimination of exclusive dealing in motor oil and TBA as much as or more than in gasoline. In 1951 it was reported that manufacturers of Pennsylvania-grade lubricating oil — which has always kept an outstanding reputation for quality and performance — had found the decision of assistance in getting their product into service stations affiliated with the majors.[148] In 1955, however, officials of the Pennzoil Company of California complained that the improvement had been only temporary, except in the Chevron and Richfield stations themselves.[149] The same impression — of a mere temporary improvement — is held by the general counsel of the National Congress of Petroleum Retailers.[150]

Further evidence appeared in the responses to a questionnaire sent out to ten Pennsylvania-grade oil refiners at the end of 1955, as part of the present study. Of the eight that answered, two had noticed a considerable improvement in the reception of their product in major-affiliated stations since the *Standard Stations* and *Richfield* decisions, and two a mild improvement. The other four said they sold mainly or entirely in the East, and neither had expected to see nor saw any effect of these decisions originating in California.

146. *Ibid.*, February 4, 1931, p. 83.

147. *Ibid.*, pp. 83–84.

148. Two interviews mentioned in Marshall C. Howard, *The Marketing of Petroleum Products: A Study in the Relations between Large and Small Business*, unpublished doctoral thesis, Cornell University, Ithaca, 1951, p. 242.

149. Leland F. Johnson, in *Distribution Problems*, Hearings before Subcommittee No. 5 of House Small Business Committee, 84th Cong., 1st sess., 1955 (hereafter called Roosevelt Hearings), Part 1, p. 810; John B. Beman, Jr., *ibid.*, p. 819.

150. William D. Snow, *ibid.*, p. 465.

Exclusive Dealing Not Yet Abolished

Impressive evidence appeared in 1955 that local representatives of the suppliers still threatened dealers with cancellation of their contracts or denial of benefits (such as repainting of stations or resurfacing of driveways) unless they would handle only the company-approved motor oil and TBA. Dealer after dealer testified to this effect before a subcommittee of the House Small Business Committee.[151] It is true that every official of a refining company who appeared denied that exclusive dealing was company policy or that any reprisals were authorized.[152] However, a dealer who sold competitive products would hardly be considered the most valued type of representative for a refiner. A spokesman for Esso Standard Oil Company, whose contracts contain no exclusive dealing provisions of any sort, could have been speaking for many others when he said: "We certainly would not have our money tied up indefinitely with some one who elected to not push the sale of our products." [153]

Exclusive dealing is not a moral issue, as dealers and independent manufacturers would naturally think, but an economic and human relations issue. A corporation commits no immoral act when it builds a service station, finds a tenant, and arranges for him to carry only its products. Nor does this prevent competition among the products of the majors or with those of independents sold through independent stations. The court-developed rule that no large (substantial) refiner shall do this is defensible, however, in that it aids the independent motor oil or TBA manufacturer to stay in the market despite the major's natural advantages of size — and without seriously impairing the economic contribution that size can make. Admittedly many dealers will prefer to handle only their supplier's products — whether for convenience and economy or through loyalty or timidity — but there will always be some dealers willing to take on the motor oil or TBA of the independent manufacturer if coercion by the majors is banned, even if the ban cannot be fully enforced. Even complete divorcement of majors from their service stations would not give the independent manufacturer as much to offer the dealer as the major has.

151. *Alleged Coercive and Discriminatory Practices against Retail Gasoline Operators by Oil Company Suppliers*, H. Rept. 1423, Interim Report of same subcommittee, 1955, pp. 8–10.

152. *Ibid.*, p. 7.

153. H. G. Burks, Jr., executive vice president of Esso Standard Oil Company of N.J., in *Petroleum Study* (*Gasoline and Oil Price Increases*), House Hearings, p. 403.

The Detroit Price Discrimination Case

The leading case on the clause in Section 2(b) of the Clayton Act (as amended by the Robinson-Patman Act in 1936) which makes good-faith meeting of competition a defense against a charge of price discrimination has been the so-called *Standard Oil* suit. Begun in 1940 and still alive in 1956, it has been one of the most durable of all antitrust cases.

In the late 1930s Detroit was one of the retail gasoline markets most subject to price cutting, partly because refining capacity in Michigan more than doubled from 1935 to 1940.[154] A state fair trade act was passed, applying to oil and bakery products only, which forbade sale below cost for the purpose of injuring the business of (taking business from?) a competitor. Although general cost surveys were made competent evidence of an individual firm's costs, it was not possible to enforce this law effectively. From 1937 to 1940 there were never less than 79 filling stations selling below the prevailing price, out of more than 2,000.

One source of price cutting was traced to jobbers, and those of Standard of Indiana drew the most attention since it was the biggest supplier in the market. From 1937 to 1940 it supplied between 16 and 17 per cent of Detroit's gasoline through about 350 stations to which it sold direct, and between 3 and 4 per cent through its four bulk plant customers. One of these, Ned's Auto Supply Company, sold almost entirely through its own stations; the others, Citrin-Kolb Oil Company, Wayne Oil Company and Stikeman Oil Company, almost entirely at wholesale. Ned's had a regular policy of cutting prices, Citrin-Kolb cut prices selectively, and Wayne is assumed to have cut prices since its gallonage increased while total Detroit consumption was decreasing. In other words, three of Standard's jobbers passed on to their own customers, whether retailers or motorists, part of what they saved from being able to purchase at the tank car price (usually 1.5 cents a gallon lower than the tank wagon price paid by dealers). Although the four jobbers' share of the market did not change strikingly (in the five years from 1936 through 1940 it was 2.2, 3.4, 4.1, 3.3 and 3.0 per cent), their price advantage became a main object of

154. These paragraphs rely on John S. McGee, "Price Discrimination and Competitive Effects: The Standard Oil of Indiana Case," *University of Chicago Law Review*, Spring 1956, pp. 398–473, especially pp. 409, 437–43, 466–73.

criticism by dealers who had to compete with their retail outlets or their customers.

The Detroit Case in the Federal Trade Commission

As a result of this situation, Standard of Indiana was first charged with violating the state's fair trade law, but after a hearing the Wayne County Recorder's Court dismissed the complaint.[155] The Retail Gasoline Dealers Association of Michigan tried in vain to interest the Department of Justice, and then found a better reception at the Federal Trade Commission. In November 1940 the Commission charged Standard with violating Section 2 of the Clayton Act by discriminating in price in favor of the four jobbers. The legally necessary lessening of competition was found in use of these discounts "to divert large amounts of business from other retailers of gasoline, including customers of the respondent, with resultant injury to them and to their ability to continue in business and successfully compete." [156] The Commission also investigated Gulf, Shell and Texas, but by mutual agreement Standard's case was made the test for all.

Standard's attempt to prove the lower cost of selling to firms with bulk storage facilities was disallowed by the Commission for lack of convincing itemized proof. The Commission thus implicitly held that a trade discount to jobbers must be fully justified by the reduced cost to the supplier. Standard also argued that it was merely meeting competition in good faith, since it had lost three other jobbers to competing refiners whose price offers it failed to meet and since it had given these four the tank wagon price only after they had threatened to find other suppliers. The Commission, however, considered the argument irrelevant, as long as competition was actually damaged by Standard's policy.

After a delay due to the war, the Commission ruled against Standard in October 1945. A modified order in August 1946 directed Standard to cease giving discounts to any jobber who either (1) sold at retail, or (2) resold to dealers at a tank wagon price below that charged by Standard itself.[157] Lowell B. Mason, who had been appointed to the Commission in October 1945 as its first new member in ten years, dissented. It became known in February 1949 that the three remaining

155. Giddens, *Standard Oil Company (Indiana)*, pp. 576–77.

156. *Standard Oil Co.*, Docket 4389, 41 FTC 263, 276 (1945).

157. *Ibid.*; also 43 FTC 56 (1946).

members of the 1945 and 1946 Commission majority believed that Standard's position should be made lawful by interpretation or amendment, since "the policy of the law should not discourage active competition by preventing the meeting of competition in good faith." [158]

The Detroit Case in the Courts

In March 1949, just after the Commissioners' private opinions were disclosed, the Seventh Circuit Court of Appeals ruled in favor of their official stand in the litigation. The opinion, by Judge Minton, granted that Standard's low prices had been offered in good faith to meet competition, but cited the Chairman of the House conferees on the Robinson-Patman Act to the effect that letting good faith be "an absolute bar to liability" would "nullify the act entirely." [159]

That the Department of Justice disagreed with the Commission's proceeding was suspected when the Solicitor General left to the Commission's General Counsel the responsibility of arguing the Supreme Court appeal. The Court heard the case argued twice and then, in January 1951, voted 5 to 3 to reverse the Circuit Court.[160] Justice Burton, speaking for the majority, refused to read the Robinson-Patman Act as requiring a seller who faced a price raid by a competitor to choose between stepping out of competition at this point and ruinously reducing prices to all his customers. The case was remanded to the Commission with instructions to rule, as it had failed to do previously, whether Standard was acting in good faith — and if so to release it.

Justice Reed, for the minority, objected that this interpretation amounted to saying that this clause of the Clayton Act had been left unchanged by the Robinson-Patman Act. In the minority view, good-faith meeting of competition merely rebutted the *prima facie* case that a price difference among customers was illegal and did not bar the Commission from proving that it did in fact tend to injure competition. Under this view, good faith is a temporary procedural defense, rather than a substantive and conclusive one.

The Commission, resuming the case, ruled in 1952 and repeated in 1953 that Standard had not in fact acted in good faith. Its reasons

158. Letter of Ewin L. Davis, *Competitive Absorption of Transportation Costs*, Hearings before a Subcommittee of the Senate Interstate and Foreign Commerce Committee, 81st Cong., 1st sess., 1949, p. 275.

159. *Standard Oil Co. v. FTC*, 173 F. 2d 210, 215 (7th Cir. 1949).

160. *Ibid.*, 340 U.S. 231 (1951).

were that the corporation's pricing structure was an old one rather than one set up to meet an emergency, and that the latest competitor who had bid for the trade of Ned's was one selling unbranded gasoline, which the Commission deemed to be noncompetitive with Standard's Red Crown. On appeal from this order, Standard secured a reversal in the Circuit Court.[161] The opinion, by Judge Major, rejected the Commission's interpretation of the facts, emphasizing that Standard had bargained hard with its four jobber-customers and had given Ned's, in particular, the lower price only when faced with certain loss of its trade.

The Detroit Case and Dual Distribution

The facts on which the *Standard Oil* case was based no longer prevail in Detroit. Ned's has given up its retail chain, and both it and the other jobbers now operate service stations only when they cannot find a satisfactory lessee. Price cutting is less prevalent. Independent gasoline, however, still has its place in the market.[162]

Despite Standard's legal victory to date, some other majors may have read the case as a warning of legal dangers arising from dual distribution (sale both to jobbers and to dealers in the same territory). If required to take a choice, most majors would probably continue their direct selling and eliminate jobbers — and it was no doubt in fear of such an outcome that jobber organizations supported Standard's appeal to the Supreme Court.[163] An alternative for a refiner might be to sell at the same price to jobbers and dealers, but this also would put the jobber out of business. Under the Commission's order, a refiner could also have insisted that gasoline bought from it at the tank car price be resold at wholesale only and at a price not below its own tank wagon price — thus requiring a resale price maintenance policy otherwise frowned on by the antitrust laws.[164] Although the courts might condemn such action through fair trade contracts as constituting price fixing between a company and its competitors (for the jobbers would be competitors when they sold at wholesale), they

161. *Ibid.*, 233 F. 2d 649 (7th Cir. 1956).

162. McGee, "Price Discrimination and Competitive Effects," p. 463.

163. Brief Amicus Curiae of Empire State Petroleum Ass'n. et al. in the Supreme Court, *Standard Oil Co. v. FTC*, Twentieth Century Press, Chicago, 1950, pp. 1–2.

164. See M. A. Adelman, "Antitrust Upside-Down Cake and Eat It Too," *Fortune*, March 1950, pp. 57–58.

might also approve it on the ground that it was required by court interpretation of the Clayton Act. If so, a principal effect of such an order as the Supreme Court rejected would have been to prevent jobbers, or retailers who were in process of becoming jobbers (as they often do [165]), from expanding their markets by price cutting. This would tend toward "a rigid stratification of functions in distribution." [166]

Two lengthy law review articles on the case, one at Harvard and the other at Chicago, have reached similar conclusions. The Harvard study concludes that reduction of jobber discounts to those justifiable by cost might not prevent the price cutting to which dealers were objecting — since an efficient jobber-retailer could perhaps draw on other savings to cut prices — but might well injure the efficiency of the distributive system. It urges a full analysis of probable effects before a suit is brought, even if there is a "threat to competition." [167] The University of Chicago study agrees with the Commission's first proceeding and the Supreme Court minority on the proper interpretation of the Robinson-Patman Act, but maintains that jobber discounts neither reduced competition in Detroit nor are likely to do so elsewhere.[168]

In general, there can hardly be a solution of the good-faith issue which will work in every situation without threatening injury to some legitimate interest. The Supreme Court's 1951 decision, for example, is adverse to dealers who have no ambition to become jobbers. Nor is there any ideal solution of another conflict which was not stressed in the Detroit case — that between a national and a local refiner or other type of manufacturer. The Supreme Court's interpretation of good faith would make it hard for a local refiner to win customers from a national one, since the latter could reduce prices to these customers alone while making its usual profit on sales to others. The opposite interpretation, which would make the major a "sitting duck" unable to resist raids by little competitors unless it were to cut prices to far more customers than the small refiner could approach, missed becoming law in 1956; it died in committee in the Senate after passing the House by 393 to 3.

165. *National Petroleum News*, November 11, 1953, p. 22.

166. Clair Wilcox, *Public Policies toward Business*, Irwin, Homewood (Ill.), 1955, p. 197.

167. Norman M. Gold and Richard McGrath, "Functional Discounts under the Robinson-Patman Act: The Standard Oil Litigation," *Harvard Law Review*, December 1953, p. 317.

168. McGee, "Price Discrimination and Competitive Effects," pp. 452, 462–63, 465.

Buying Stock in a Customer

In April 1947 a federal grand jury in Chicago brought Sherman Act indictments against the National City Lines Company, which managed local bus systems in forty-five cities, and several of its suppliers, including Phillips Petroleum Company, Standard Oil of California, General Motors and others. The bus company, having found that the public was not receptive to new issues of transit securities in 1938 except at a prohibitively low price, had asked these suppliers to buy its preferred stock and they had agreed to do so (after discussion with each other) in return for contracts to supply its gasoline, vehicles and other supplies. Such buying of stock in customers has had a long and often successful history [169] — e.g., financing of cotton mills by machinery manufacturers [170] — but this evidence was excluded in court as equivalent to the plea that "lots of people break the law, so why shouldn't I?"

In 1951 the Seventh Circuit Court affirmed the conviction of the defendants [171] while a civil suit remained in the courts. The fact that the purchaser was a regulated public utility company did not enter into the case. In this decision Judge Lindley relied on the *Yellow Cab* case [172] to hold that exclusive contracts to supply the bus company's petroleum products, tires and vehicles monopolized a "substantial segment of interstate commerce" — i.e., the custom of this one large purchasing company.

One outcome of the case was that National City Lines bought in at a bargain some of the preferred stock its suppliers were directed to sell. It remained a stable and prosperous company [173] — an unusual phenomenon in the city transit field. It continued to buy its equipment from General Motors, and is noted for efficient use of first-rate equipment.[174] Even if one may guess that the company had never been victimized by its co-defendants in the antitrust suit, the precedent against foreclosure of a market (especially of a public utility) in this

169. Testimony of Neil Jacoby (Brief for Defendant-Appellants, 7th Cir., Nos. 9943–9953, 1950).

170. J. T. Lincoln, "The Cotton Textile Machinery Industry," *Harvard Business Review*, July 1933, at p. 96.

171. *U.S. v. National City Lines, Inc.*, 186 F. 2d 562 (7th Cir. 1951), certiorari denied 341 U.S. 916 (1951).

172. *U.S. v. Yellow Cab Co.*, 332 U.S. 218 (1947).

173. Moody's *Transportation Manual*, 1955, p. 1439.

174. *Wall Street Journal*, July 6, 1955, p. 6.

way is a sound one from the standpoint of open competition. There should, however, be a rule of reason in such cases, under which the courts would have decided whether ten-year exclusive contracts were justifiable as a reward for helping finance a company unable to raise capital otherwise.

State and Private Antitrust Suits

State investigations at times of price increases are frequent, and many state suits have been brought against large petroleum companies, but almost never successfully. The Attorney General of North Carolina asserts that enforcement of the state law against interstate oil companies has been "impossible." [175] Texas in 1952 fined two companies $25,000 for exclusive dealing.[176] In July 1955 it lost a more ambitious suit, which it had filed against the ten largest oil companies in the state five years earlier. This had alleged a conspiracy, the proof consisting of (1) identical tank wagon prices and price increases, (2) identical business practices, (3) cooperation with the American Petroleum Institute, (4) exchanges of gasoline, (5) standardization of three grades of gasoline, (6) higher gasoline prices by fractions of a cent than in states with fewer refineries, (7) control of 80 per cent of gasoline marketing in Texas, and even (8) cooperation in pricing under the Office of Price Administration. Many of these proofs were being used in the simultaneous federal suit against the seven largest West Coast producers. The Texas Supreme Court ruled them out on various grounds — for example, that the state could make the percentage of the market controlled as high as it wished by simply choosing any given number of defendants, that obedience to government price ceilings could not be made a charge against a company even if it did provide good practice in price cooperation, that the government had offered no proof that the identical prices were not the result of competition or that the lower prices in other states were not the result of their own supply and demand conditions, and that standardization and trade association activity were normal business practices.[177]

At least one dealer association, which had fixed retail prices said to have been obeyed by 90 per cent of the members and by 55 per cent

175. *National Petroleum News*, August 1, 1951, p. 27.

176. *Journal of Commerce*, May 7, 1952, p. 1.

177. *Arkansas Fuel Oil Co. v. Texas*, No. A-4758, Texas Supreme Court (1955), Commerce Clearing House, *1955 Trade Cases*, No. 68070.

of nonmembers who received its bulletins, was prosecuted by its state, fined $2,000 and ordered dissolved.[178]

Treble damage suits have not been important in petroleum. Paul Hadlick's book on such suits, published in 1940, mentions only two.[179] The suits which followed the Madison case were all dismissed. A recent suit by the Meriden Retail Gas Dealers Association against the Sun Oil Company and four Sunoco dealers, charging that their price cuts of 4 cents a gallon to meet a Shell price cut tended to destroy competition, was dismissed on several grounds — among others that the plaintiffs themselves were members of a retailers' association that fixed prices.[180]

The West Coast Divorcement Suit

As this is written, the oil industry is as usual under antitrust attack. One proceeding is an outcome of the all-encompassing or so-called "Mother Hubbard" suit filed in September 1940, which charged the American Petroleum Institute, 22 major companies and 344 subsidiaries or secondary companies with generally controlling the industry.[181] Deciding later that it would be easier to prove this type of charge in a single region, the Department of Justice filed a broad suit in May 1950 against the seven majors operating on the West Coast and against the Conservation Committee of California,[182] and in January 1951 formally dropped the Mother Hubbard case.

This West Coast suit, called by its first prosecutor "the biggest case that the government has ever brought in the antitrust field," [183] warrants a fuller explanation. The seven majors (only two of which were primarily West Coast companies) produced 50 per cent of the California crude oil, purchased 44 per cent of the oil sold by independent producers, owned all the tankers, 97 per cent of the crude trunk pipelines and 77 per cent of the gathering lines, possessed 85 per cent of the refining capacity, and sold 90 per cent of the gasoline used, through 86 per cent of the retail outlets. Besides pointing to this degree of concen-

178. *State v. Retail Gasoline Dealers Association of Milwaukee, Inc.*, 256 Wis. 537, 41 N.W. 2d 637 (1950).

179. Paul E. Hadlick, *Treble Damages under the Antitrust Laws*, Ransdell, Inc., Washington, 1940, pp. 243–45, 414, citing *Ballard Oil Terminal Corp. v. Mexican Petroleum Corp.*, 22 F. 2d 434 (E.D. Mass. 1927), and 28 F. 2d 91 (E.D. Mass. 1928), and *Lipson v. Socony-Vacuum Corp.*, 7 F. Supp. 961 (D. Mass. 1934), 76 F. 2d 213 (1st Cir. 1935), 87 F. 2d 265 (1st Cir. 1937), appeal dismissed 301 U.S. 711 (1937).

180. *Spencer v. Sun Oil Co.*, 94 F. Supp. 408 (D. Conn. 1950).

181. *U.S. v. American Petroleum Institute*, Civil 8524 (D. D.C. 1940).

182. *U.S. v. Standard Oil Company of Calif.*, Civil 11584–C (S.D. Calif. 1950).

183. William C. Dixon, Roosevelt Hearings, p. 298.

tration as constituting monopolization, the government made certain specific charges which it claimed added up to a picture of unified action and illegal domination of the West Coast oil industry:

(1) *Proration* or production control in California was administered by the majors to support oil prices and to discriminate in quotas against independent crude producers. (2) *Prices* were fixed in various ways, including refusal to sell to price cutters and a developed system of price leadership by "a designated defendant." (3) Independents were refused access to the majors' *transportation* facilities on the terms granted to other majors. (4) *Exchanges* of crude oil and oil products were made among the majors, with grades standardized to facilitate exchanges, but were refused to independents. (5) Crude producers were kept in line by long-term *purchase contracts.* (6) Independent refiners were controlled by "*throughput*" *contracts*, under which either a major refined the independent's oil when more elaborate refining was required, or the independent refined oil for a major whose facilities were fully occupied. (7) The majors were gradually extinguishing competition through *mergers* with independents and occasional "*squeezes*" which raised the price of crude oil while holding down product prices. (8) *Jobbers and retailers* were controlled through refusal to sell to price cutters and through tying clauses.

The relief demanded by the Department of Justice on these counts, in order, was as follows: (1) abolition of privately operated proration, (2) abolition of price fixing and of public posting by refiners of crude oil prices they would pay, (3) a common carrier status for the majors' land and water transportation and terminal facilities, (4) nondiscriminatory exchanges of oil and products, (5) no contracts for the purchase of crude oil running beyond one year, (6) abolition of throughput contracts, (7) no purchase of independent refineries by a major unless approved by the Department of Justice, and (8) complete divorcement of all marketing facilities owned by the majors and elimination of any contractual or other control over independent jobbers or retailers.

The "International Petroleum Cartel"

In July 1952 a study by the staff of the Federal Trade Commission entitled *The International Petroleum Cartel*[184] was made public by a

184. FTC Staff Report, *The International Petroleum Cartel*, issued by Subcommittee on Monopoly, Senate Small Business Committee, 82d Cong., 2d sess., 1952.

Senate committee. The Department of Justice, using the same material, opened in August a grand jury investigation of the control of foreign oil production. In January 1953 the National Security Council warned that this proceeding was endangering the oil concessions themselves and therefore American national security.[185] In April it was replaced by a civil suit under the Sherman Act and the Wilson Tariff Act, charging five leading American corporations whose subsidiaries were engaged in foreign oil production with close agreements, on a market-sharing basis, plus monopoly of oil production abroad and of world trade and transportation in oil.[186] (The big British and Anglo-Dutch companies had been investigated, but were not included in the suit.) Another suit which made use of some of the same facts had been filed by the Mutual Security Agency to recover alleged overpayments for oil bought for European countries under the foreign aid program. The propriety of charging a Texas port quotation plus transportation for Middle Eastern oil was challenged.

Oil companies do not deny that the structure and practices of the industry in the Middle East differ from those in a domestic industry operating under the antitrust laws. One legal authority concludes from the government's own evidence (which, as he points out, he accepts in advance of trial only for purposes of discussion) — and especially from allegations concerning an "As Is Agreement" of 1928 by which oil companies agreed not to invade one another's international markets — that the oil industry conducted "the most successful experiment in economic world government thus far achieved in the twentieth century." [187] Briefs of the defendant companies make less extensive claims, but do insist that such agreements (not renewed since World War II) were justified under prewar conditions of intergovernmental oil rivalry and overproduction.[188]

Whether the antitrust laws apply could depend on (1) whether practices forbidden at home may become "reasonable" under the different conditions abroad, and (2) the degree to which the Sherman Antitrust Act can legally, or should politically, be made to apply to operations

185. *New York Times*, April 10, 1953, pp. 1, 12.

186. *U.S. v. Standard Oil Co.* (*N.J.*), Civil 1779–53 (D. D.C. 1953).

187. Adolf A. Berle, Jr., *The 20th Century Capitalist Revolution*, Harcourt, Brace, New York, 1954, p. 147.

188. Based on Socony-Vacuum Oil Co. "Answer," in Civil 86–27, September 1, 1953, paragraph 105.

outside the United States. A leading organ of British opinion, commenting on an order of the Minister of Fuel and Power to the Anglo-Iranian Oil Company not to produce the documents demanded by the grand jury in the District of Columbia (including the company's entire correspondence with all "sovereign governments"), called "alarming" this extension of American criminal law to acts carried out abroad which were legal in the jurisdictions where they occurred.[189]

Industry Opinion on the Antitrust Laws

Representatives of the various branches of the industry say they are satisfied with at least most of the effects of the antitrust laws. Many jobbers feel that if the antitrust laws were removed from the statute books the major oil companies would soon own the entire industry, but their general counsel considers this fear exaggerated.[190] One jobber complains that the majors, guided by skilled antitrust lawyers, have learned how to push their competition to a point just short of illegality.[191] Other jobbers stress the aid received from congressional investigating committees in procuring supplies during times of shortage. Officers of the largest major are quoted as saying in private that the law "keeps them concerned with balancing what they rightfully owe to their owners, their employees, their customers, and the national interest." [192]

Some groups in the industry are of the opinion that, along with the good it does, the antitrust legislation produces some regrettable results. It has been alleged to take a national emergency for the Attorney General to permit the big oil companies to gather certain information under government auspices, or approve the setting up of machinery to meet possible shortages of oil; and even then he is said to be likely to slow the formation of such a plan and to speed its abandonment.[193] Agreements among oil companies to help out a foundering small firm, to attack unfair practices, to stabilize tanker rates in order to prevent wild fluctuations with variations in tanker space, or to

189. "Comity and the Oil Companies," *The Economist* (London), November 22, 1952, pp. 556–57.

190. *National Petroleum News*, June 6, 1951, p. 42.

191. James E. Stevens, executive secretary of Pennsylvania Petroleum Ass'n., *ibid.*, July 25, 1951, p. 27.

192. Burck, "The Jersey Company," p. 200.

193. *Journal of Commerce*, February 18, 1953, p. 12, February 21, 1953, p. 1; *The Economist*, June 16, 1951, p. 1465; *Business Week*, February 18, 1956, p. 145.

eliminate cross hauling, they say, will always be under suspicion and may be blocked altogether.[194] The industry, it is said, must operate on rumor rather than fact, since some sellers fear antitrust actions if they inform their competitors of prices or engage in discussion of certain mutual industry problems (quite apart from any agreement).[195]

Since such agreements and discussions can easily shift from the constructive to the restrictive, the antitrust authorities cannot give them a free rein. The responsible critics merely claim that the rein is held too tight through bureaucratic caution.

Competitive Status

Trend of Concentration

The fierce competitive battles of the early petroleum industry had ended by 1879, when Standard Oil did 90 per cent of the refining, owned 80 per cent of the pipelines, and "dominated the field of marketing." [196] By 1911 Standard's share of refining was down to 80 per cent, and by 1926 the successor companies had only 43 per cent. Meanwhile the share of the Standard group in crude production was increasing; from 17 per cent of the nation's total in 1906 it advanced to 21 per cent in 1919 and 29 per cent in 1926.[197]

By the mid-1920s the key group had become the majors. From 1926 to 1937 twenty majors increased their share of oil refined from 71.2 to 82.6 per cent, a figure which was practically unchanged at 82.7 in 1955. In production, their share increased from 46.3 per cent in 1926 to 52.5 in 1937, and went back to 47.6 per cent in 1955.[198] This decline may be explained by the fact that under proration the little "stripper wells," more of which in proportion are owned by small independent operators, are allowed their full production.

A tabulation from Bureau of Mines data revealed that between 1920 and 1950 the majors' share of refining *capacity* increased from 52.9 to 78.6 per cent, with the bulk of the gain occurring in the 1920s. The

194. Dwight T. Colley, vice president of Atlantic Refining Co., *Journal of Commerce*, November 10, 1952, p. 23.

195. *Idem*, in *Gasoline Price War in New Jersey*, Hearings before Subcommittee of Senate Small Business Committee, 84th Cong., 1st and 2d sess., 1956, Part 3, pp. 339–40.

196. George W. Stocking, "Oil," *Encyclopaedia of the Social Sciences*, Vol. 11, p. 442.

197. Burns, *The Decline of Competition*, pp. 103–04.

198. 1926 and 1937 figures in TNEC Monograph 39, pp. 67, 76.

refining capacity of the independents increased in each decade and doubled in the period as a whole; but the majors did so much building and bought so many independents that their total capacity increased more than sixfold. (See Table 12.) In one product, lubricating oil, the majors were believed to have 80 per cent of total capacity at the end of 1951.[199]

In the expansion program launched with government encouragement during the Korean War, small refiners were expected to enlarge their share of capacity fractionally.[200] At the end of 1955, however, the twenty majors had 78.9 per cent of refining capacity, or 80.4 per cent if Richfield is included.[201] Ten per cent of the independent capacity was obsolete and kept in a shut-down condition, as against only one per cent of the major capacity.

One of the large oil companies keeps figures which throw some light on the degree of concentration in the gasoline market *by states* in 1950. In more than half the states the leading refiner had less than 20 per cent of the market, and in every state it had less than 35 per cent.[202]

Size as a Factor in the Oil Industry

In each branch of the industry there are distinct advantages of large size. Examples are: *production* — a large company can offset the losses on dry wells against the profits on successful ones; *transportation* — only a large company can achieve the tremendous operating economies accruing from the ownership of an expensive tanker fleet or pipeline system; *refining* — large refineries have lower investment costs for a corresponding amount of capacity and lower unit operating costs.[203] Although recent improvements have enabled smaller refineries than formerly to use catalytic cracking and other modern methods,[204] it remains "indisputable that the trend is toward larger plant size." [205]

199. Calculated from National Petroleum Association estimates of plant capacity, *Journal of Commerce*, April 22, 1952, p. 16.

200. *Journal of Commerce*, February 21, 1952, p. 11.

201. Calculated from J. G. Kirby, *Petroleum Refineries, Including Cracking Plants in the United States, January 1, 1956*, U.S. Bureau of Mines Information Circular 7761.

202. Ralph Cassady, Jr., *Price Making and Price Behavior in the Petroleum Industry*, Yale University Press, New Haven, 1954, p. 339, note 13.

203. McLean and Haigh, *The Growth of Integrated Oil Companies*, p. 585.

204. *National Petroleum News*, August 12, 1953, p. 18; *Business Week*, October 2, 1954, p. 133.

205. Joel B. Dirlam, "The Petroleum Industry," Chap. 8 of Walter Adams, ed., *The Structure of American Industry*, Macmillan, New York, revised edition, 1954, p. 245.

TABLE 12

PETROLEUM: REFINING CAPACITY OF MAJORS AND INDEPENDENTS, 1920–50[a]

(*Thousand Barrels per Day*)

	1920	1930	1940	1950	Total Change, 1920–50
Twenty majors	810	2,711	3,365	5,262	4,452
Independents	721	1,055	1,264	1,434	713
Majors as per cent of total	52.9	72.0	72.7	78.6	
Twenty majors, net change during decade preceding		1,901	654	1,897	4,452
Purchased from independents		475	196	98	769
Added to existing plants		878	463	1,779	3,120
Construction of new plants		663	241	298	1,202
Plants sold or dismantled		–115	–246	–278	–639
Independents, net change during decade preceding		334	209	170	713
Total added		809	405	268	1,482
Sold to majors		–475	–196	– 98	–769
Number of majors	16	20	20	20	
Number of independents, including "inactive"	258	230	363	203	

Source: U.S. Bureau of Mines, *Petroleum Refineries, Including Cracking Plants*, annual, tabulated in *Growth and Structure of U.S. Refining Industry, 1920–1950*, Coordination and Economics Department, Standard Oil Company of N.J., New York, mimeographed, 1951, pp. 2, 9.

a. As of January 1.

About half the country's refining capacity is in plants so large that a year's purchases of crude oil would cost over $100 million. The cost even of a "conventional" refinery of a given size increased by a full 450 per cent between 1910 and 1950,[206] while the general price level was rising less than 150 per cent. As to *marketing*, establishment of wide consumer acceptance through an efficient distribution system and national advertising of a brand name is possible only for a company with large financial resources.

Small firms have offsetting advantages deriving from their flexibility of operation. Many new pools are brought in by small wildcatters, and they can sometimes operate smaller wells at a greater profit than the majors, since they have lower overhead cost and can give them

206. McLean and Haigh, *The Growth of Integrated Oil Companies*, pp. 553–54.

personal attention. An operator with a few trucks and low overhead costs can often transport refined products most efficiently. A one-plant refiner producing for a local market can escape many of the selling and other costs that national distribution requires. The independence, energy and pride associated with proprietorship, along with freedom from some legal regulations which apply only to interstate business, have given individuals a strong place in wholesaling and a still stronger one in retailing.

A comparison recently made between the average rate of return on net worth of eighteen majors and of nineteen large, but not major, refiners showed that the former earned more money in the depression years 1930–35, while returns were approximately equal in 1929, 1949 and 1950, and the non-majors did better in all other years.[207] Success in the market is continually determining which firms are too big and which too small. The industry thus reaches for an equilibrium in which large and small fill their own niches.[208] The economies of size are sufficient for the big companies to do the bulk of the business, but the little companies fill the interstices, and serve as suppliers and customers of the big ones.

The large and small companies differ in their social and political as well as their economic functions. The large companies now offer service to the public and security to their employees far beyond what was known in earlier years. In 1951 *Fortune* selected the largest petroleum company to illustrate the thesis that "the large corporation is becoming one of free society's major instruments of economic justice," [209] and declared that this company was becoming "well-known, even famous, for its enlightened policies and practices." [210] On the other hand, a proliferation of small firms gives more men the chance to develop qualities of self-reliance, independence and responsibility — along with, regrettably but inevitably, insecurity.

Advantages of Integration

Considerable light has been shed on the issue of integration in petroleum by McLean and Haigh's recent massive study of *The*

207. Cassady, *Price Making and Price Behavior in the Petroleum Industry*, pp. 326–30.

208. Ronald B. Shuman, *The Petroleum Industry: An Economic Survey*, University of Oklahoma Press, Norman, 1940, p. 12; McLean and Haigh, *The Growth of Integrated Oil Companies*, p. 659.

209. Burck, "The Jersey Company," p. 98.

210. *Ibid.*, p. 99.

Growth of Integrated Oil Companies. This work points out that integration in petroleum has succeeded because it has offered solutions to practical problems facing investors and managements in various branches of the industry. When disintegration seemed to offer a better solution to a given problem, it in turn was adopted; [211] and it is only because integration has proved itself by a process of trial and error that it has become the dominant form. The book summarizes its advantages in three general categories: [212]

1. The continual change in profit margins in the different branches of the industry encourages companies to achieve stability by participating in more than one branch. It also enables them to increase their profits, if they can successfully change their operating policies to take advantage of the "ebb and flow of profit opportunities" in one branch after another.

2. The costliness of physical installations makes it difficult to attract adequate capital unless some protection is given against the danger of a decline in volume. The desirability of controlling crude production and marketing facilities in order to assure refinery operations is an example, and one which is recognized by government agencies and independent oil men as well as by majors.[213]

3. The management of an integrated operation finds it much easier to plan capital investments, and to adjust operations to changing conditions in the market. For example,

> Investments in producing, transportation, refining, and marketing facilities can have their maximum economic and business utility only if they are properly correlated time-wise, place-wise, and size-wise with respect to one another . . . By the strategic use of seasonal inventories to obtain more uniform refinery runs, refinery yields, and transportation requirements, an integrated company can often secure important savings in investment and operating costs.[214]

Critics of Integration

Contrary to these views, three scholars who have written since World War II find little good in integration to offset the danger of its

211. McLean and Haigh, *The Growth of Integrated Oil Companies,* p. 289.

212. *Ibid.,* "Abstract" (leaflet enclosed in book).

213. FTC 1928 Report, p. 183; Henry Brown, in *Oil Marketing Divorcement,* Hearings before Subcommittee No. 3 of House Judiciary Committee, 76th Cong., 1st sess., 1939, pp. 48–50.

214. McLean and Haigh, *The Growth of Integrated Oil Companies,* p. 326.

use as a means of achieving monopoly power. Joe S. Bain holds that "market considerations rather than considerations of technical efficiency have ordinarily prompted integration in the petroleum industry." [215] Although there are "some," but not "very great," economies in the elimination of buying and selling activities and in "better coordination of operations at successive stages," there is also "such managerial inefficiency as results from attempting to coordinate the varied activities of a large integrated firm." He adds: ". . . the processes are spatially isolated and technologically distinct, and there is apparent no technical complementarity of processes which would allow savings through integration." In short, "the total impact of the system on technical efficiency seems approximately neutral." [216]

Eugene V. Rostow illustrates this same "technical neutrality" of integration by saying: "There is no apparent reason, for example, why a refinery should distill gasoline at a lower unit cost, because it is owned by a corporation which also owns tankers, filling stations and pipe lines." [217] He and a collaborator find that the reason independents try by integration to assure their own supplies and markets is that the majors have already "foreclosed" so much of the available supply and so many markets by their own integration.[218] They see no better reason for refiners to own wells or pipelines than for automobile assemblers to own parts factories or railroad lines.[219] Finally, Rostow argues that the "effective pressure of independent companies in every phase of the industry, and the elaborateness of the major companies' efforts to contain and offset them, seems to belie the contention that there are substantial economies of integration in the sense of cost advantages." [220]

Joel B. Dirlam argues that "neither assurance of supply or market can be said to contribute to the economy of the industry as a whole" and that independent refineries that are able to operate today without ownership of pipelines and tankers could surely be even more effective if the ownership of these were equally shared.[221] He finds that research and capital expenditures are somewhat favored by large size, and

215. Bain, *The Economics of the Pacific Coast Petroleum Industry*, Part 3, p. 17.

216. *Ibid.*, p. 18.

217. Rostow, *A National Policy for the Oil Industry*, p. 143.

218. Rostow and Sachs, "Entry into the Oil Refining Business: Vertical Integration Re-examined," pp. 900, 914.

219. *Ibid.*, p. 901.

220. Rostow, *A National Policy for the Oil Industry*, p. 143.

221. Dirlam, "The Petroleum Industry," p. 268.

perhaps by integration, but feels that a moderate program of horizontal and vertical disintegration would do more good than harm. He advocates various sorts of government action, including recurrent studies of pricing by congressional committees, to protect small firms against the giants.[222]

The Criticisms Analyzed

It is true that market considerations were influential in motivating integration, but this does not mean that integration cannot have technical advantages as well. Nor does the fact that processes are "spatially isolated" mean there can be no economy in combining them: a warship is a separate physical unit, but a fleet is more efficient than several warships without a common command. The same applies to the criticism that the operations are "technologically distinct": two or more types of technology are often combined successfully. If a refinery runs at a more even rate because of a steadier supply from an affiliated producing subsidiary than could be assured by purchasing in the open market, gasoline will be distilled more cheaply. "Technical complementarity of processes" *does* exist if "technical" is defined to include the concept of lowering overhead cost by constant operation. The argument that automobile assemblers do not require control of their parts manufacture is weakened by the recent difficulties of the least integrated assemblers and the efforts of Ford and Chrysler to match the integration of General Motors.

In addition to managerial advantages arising from ability to plan efficiently and coordinate processes, there are certainly strategic advantages of integration, as its critics have pointed out. Granted that there are still thousands of independent producers and jobbers, a refining company may nevertheless want to be sure that it does not lose to some competitor the ones on which it depends. It may be concerned about having to buy crude at the relatively rigid price brought about by the proration system, while selling products in a competitive market — and may integrate in order to get its crude at actual cost. On the other hand, integration was well advanced before the onset of proration, and during the first sixteen years of proration the average price of refined products yielded a 48 per cent "mark-up" over the Mid-Continent crude price as against a 40 per cent mark-up in the

222. *Ibid.*, pp. 269–72.

thirteen previous years.[223] In times of shortage, a refiner may fear that he will incur dangerously high costs by bidding in the open market, and in times of surplus he may want to sell without making the deep price cuts that a competitive market might require.

In an ideal economic world, abstractly conceived, the strategic advantages of integration might not be needed. Such an economy would have to have hundreds of competitors in production, in transportation, in refining and in marketing, to make a "perfect" market in each — even at the sacrifice of the economies of large-scale operation. Cycles of shortage or surplus arising either from oil production or from trends in consuming industries would have to be wished away, unless recurring company failures were to be accepted as part of the utopia. In the real world, however, investors are more likely to risk their money in the oil industry if they are offered some security by vertical integration and, for that matter, by large-scale organization.

Rostow's argument that the majors admit their inferior efficiency when they try to "contain and offset" the "effective pressure" of the independents evidently refers to (1) patent control by the big companies, (2) exclusive arrangements with marketers, and (3) "pools" like those in the California and Madison antitrust cases of the 1930s.[224] However, (1) patents are usually found by major research and licensed on liberal terms;[225] (2) exclusive arrangements with jobbers and retailers are even more a weapon of competition between majors than of competition against the independents; and (3) the pools were not intended to contain and offset the successful competition of the independent refiners so much as to keep the market from collapsing under desperate price cutting by independent refiners whose position had become precarious.

Dirlam's point that independent firms that have operated without owning pipelines or tankers would surely do even better if these were more equally shared could even be interpreted as an argument for integration, since integration permits a company to build or buy just those facilities which it needs for most efficient operation. Conversely, the primary argument against legally ordained disintegration is that it

223. Calculated from data collected since 1920 by a large midwestern company, as reported in Cassady, *Price Making and Price Behavior in the Petroleum Industry*, p. 137.

224. Rostow, *A National Policy for the Oil Industry*, pp. 68, 72–76, 76–84.

225. Platt, "40 Great Years," pp. 55–57; Till, "Gasoline — the Competition of Big Business," p. 143, note 2.

would confine the possibilities of innovation and cost reduction within a rigid framework set by government decree.

Interest Groups and Interlocking Directorates

Many people believe the big petroleum companies are in reality one gigantic monopoly — a suspicion which may arise in part from memories of the old Standard Oil combination and from the retention of the Standard name by so many successors.[226] This view has received some support from two government reports.

In 1939 a report of the National Resources Committee contended that six majors were controlled by "the Rockefeller interests," since this family and the philanthropic institutions it had endowed held 7 to 24 per cent of the companies' shares.[227] The Chase National Bank of New York was said to be an organ of control used by these interests. This analysis is at variance with the opinion of investment analysts that each Standard company is controlled by its executive officers. The Rockefeller family and endowments have probably long given their proxies to the officers as a matter of course; the famous Standard of Indiana proxy contest in 1929 cited in the National Resources Committee report was probably unique.

The Federal Trade Commission called attention to interconnections between oil companies in its report on interlocking directorates. The only direct connections it found for 1946 were those which reflected the joint control of Richfield by Sinclair and Cities Service, and three other interlocks of large companies with small ones which had disappeared by 1949.[228] Indirect interlocks connected nearly all the majors through the boards of banks or other corporations; for example, four directors of the Chase National Bank were directors, respectively, of three "Rockefeller" companies and one "Mellon" company. Concerning the two biggest majors (Standard of New Jersey and Socony-Vacuum), whose absence from this group of interlocks "made the chain conspicuously incomplete," [229] the Commission could report only their role as joint participants in Middle Eastern oil development

226. Analysis of public opinion polls, by W. M. Jablonski, *Journal of Commerce*, October 25, 1951, p. 6.

227. Paul M. Sweezy, "Interest Groupings in the American Economy," Appendix 13, of Part 1, "Basic Characteristics," in National Resources Committee, *The Structure of the American Economy*, 1939, p. 311.

228. FTC, *Report on Interlocking Directorates*, 1951, pp. 360; 363, note 27; 364, note 31.

229. *Ibid.*, p. 365.

and their joint construction of domestic pipelines. Certainly the oil companies have these types of interconnection, but it is certain too that a sound business reason (aside from conspiracy) can be found for each one.

Trade Associations

The American Petroleum Institute is the all-embracing trade organization. It works in such fields as public relations, fundamental technical research, industry statistics, and standardization of oil equipment. The Independent Petroleum Association of America represents domestic producers and is interested in preventing imports, maintaining proration, etc. The producers are often organized in local associations as well. There are refiners' associations in several areas, usually including both independents and majors: thus the National Petroleum Association represents primarily the Pennsylvania lubricating oil refiners. Most jobbers are represented by the National Oil Jobbers Council, although a few unbranded jobbers belong to the more belligerent National Oil Marketers Association.

Trade associations have been involved in two antitrust cases. Officers of the Western Petroleum Refiners Association were indicted, but not convicted, in the Madison case of 1936.[230] The American Petroleum Institute was called a mechanism of industry domination in the Mother Hubbard civil suit of 1940. The government alleged that the Institute not only collected production statistics on crude oil and refining but also made suggestions, which its members accepted, as to the amounts of oil to be produced and refined.[231] The case was later dropped, and this charge has not been repeated.

In the period 1928–30, sixteen of the largest companies formed a registered export trade association under the Webb-Pomerene Act, but they abandoned it when the Federal Trade Commission criticized its practice of fixing export quotas and prices for its members.[232]

Does Competition Exist in Oil?

Conflicting popular opinions on the existence of competition in petroleum were shown by a public opinion poll in 1949, which re-

230. *U.S. v. Standard Oil Co. (Ind.)*, Cr. 11365 (W.D. Wis. 1936), tried as *U.S. v. Socony-Vacuum Oil Co.*

231. *U.S. v. American Petroleum Institute*, Civil 8524 (D. D.C. 1940), paragraph 28.

232. Mentioned in *U.S. v. Standard Oil Co. (N.J.)*, Civil 1779–53 (D. D.C. 1953), paragraph 9(c).

vealed 57 per cent of respondents believing that "the oil companies get together and set the prices" as against 31 per cent holding that prices were set individually "to meet competition" and 12 per cent giving qualified answers or none.[233] By 1954 (in a poll taken by Standard of California in seven western states) the vote was only 49 per cent that prices were fixed against 39 per cent that they were not.[234]

Among closer observers one can find many opinions more favorable to the industry. At a meeting sponsored by the National Advisory Committee for Aeronautics in June 1940, for example, the government representatives, "on the grounds of previous experience with the intense competitiveness of the oil industry, doubted that industry representatives could work effectively with the government and each other." [235] Similarly, one independent refiner testified before Congress: "I used to think it was a controlled industry and the prices were fixed . . . but, having gotten into the thing, and realizing the competitive forces that are always present, my ideas have changed because I know that what I used to know was not so." [236] A tribute from an impartial source is the statement in Justice William O. Douglas' dissenting opinion in the *Standard Stations* case that "Today there is vigorous competition between the oil companies for the market." [237]

One evidence of competition is the continual shifting in the percentages of the market held by the various sellers. Thus in Ohio the majors had 71 per cent of the gasoline market in 1926 and 70 per cent in 1951, but six companies shared the 71 and eleven companies the 70. Figures at five-year intervals show repeated fluctuations in the shares of most of these majors. (See Table 13.)

Forms of Nonprice Competition

Two types of sellers operate in the refined products market. In the first group are the majors and other firms that are ambitious to have an established trade reputation as sellers of quality products. They do

233. Opinion Research Corporation poll, quoted from *National Petroleum News*, October 19, 1949, pp. 46–49, by Cassady, *Price Making and Price Behavior in the Petroleum Industry*, p. 338, note 11.

234. *National Petroleum News*, June 1955, p. 125.

235. S. D. Heron, "Development of Aviation Fuels," in Robert Schlaifer and S. D. Heron, *Development of Aircraft Engines and Fuels*, Division of Research, Graduate School of Business Administration, Harvard University, Boston, 1950, p. 632.

236. Roland V. Rodman, in *Petroleum Study* (*Gasoline and Oil Price Increases*), House Hearings, p. 462.

237. *Standard Oil Company of Calif. v. U.S.*, 337 U.S. 293, 320 (1949).

TABLE 13

PETROLEUM: PER CENT OF GASOLINE SOLD IN OHIO BY PRINCIPAL MARKETERS, 1926–51

Firm	1926	1931	1936	1941	1946	1951
Standard Oil Co. (Ohio)	37.6	28.6	21.4	26.5	28.8	28.4
Shell Oil Co.	13.0	4.9	5.2	5.7	5.5	5.6
Sinclair Oil Corp.	7.7	5.2	4.6	3.7	3.5	4.1
Atlantic Refining Co.	6.1			1.0		
Pure Oil Co.	5.6	6.2	5.0	4.6	4.2	3.8
Texas Co.	1.0				3.6	3.3
Cities Service Oil Co.		4.2	3.7	1.3	2.1	2.2
Gulf Oil Corp.		4.2	5.7	9.7	7.2	7.2
Sun Oil Co.		4.2	7.1	7.8	7.3	8.9
Socony-Vacuum Oil Co.			2.7	1.9	4.4	2.7
Ohio Oil Co.			2.0		2.8	3.1
American Oil Co.[a]					.8	1.0
Independents	29.0	42.5	42.6	37.8	29.8	29.7

Source: 1926 from FTC, *Petroleum Industry, Prices, Profits, and Competition,* S. Doc. 61, 70th Cong., 1st sess., 1928, p. 225; 1931 from Ohio Petroleum Marketers Ass'n., and 1936–51 from Standard Oil Co. (Ohio) records — all as cited in John G. McLean and Robert Wm. Haigh, *The Growth of Integrated Oil Companies,* Division of Research, Graduate School of Business Administration, Harvard University, Boston, 1954, pp. 106–07. Blank spaces indicate either absence from the market or lack of data.

a. Subsidiary of Standard Oil Co. (Ind.)

not compete in price but emphasize quality and service, in which their large resources have given them the biggest advantage; when forced into price competition, they confine it to as small a territory as possible. In other words, they try to dispose of excess gasoline or other products in a particular locality or without using their own brand names, so as to keep the price cut from spreading.[238]

The second group of producers and distributors sells unbranded products or little-known brands. Without price cutting, these could find no market; and they can cut prices with greater safety than large companies whose place in the market is so important that they know any price cut will bring retaliation.[239]

Nonprice competition in petroleum emphasizes (1) product improvement, well illustrated by the steady lifting of the octane rating of gasoline year after year; (2) advertising and selling, which in gasoline merely redistributes the sales rather than increases the demand for

238. Joel B. Dirlam and Alfred E. Kahn, "Leadership and Conflict in the Pricing of Gasoline," *Yale Law Journal,* June–July 1952, pp. 831–33.

239. Ralph Cassady, Jr., and Wylie L. Jones, *The Nature of Competition in Gasoline Distribution at the Retail Level,* University of California Press, Berkeley, 1951, p. 95.

the product but in heating oil is of value in the contest with coal and natural gas; and (3) the offer of convenience and service to the buyer.

An example of nonprice competition obvious to all is the effort of each major to put its gasoline on sale to the public at a great many desirable locations and to make these outlets known for service as well as quality. The gradual change in name from "filling" station to "service" station is significant and deliberate. If surveys of customers may be trusted, the emphasis put on service shows a true understanding of consumer desires. A study made in 1954 found that 66 per cent of motorists patronized the same station as a general rule, and, of these, approximately 40 per cent named service among reasons for such patronage, 30 per cent named location, 25 per cent mentioned a liking for the dealer and 25 per cent preference for the brand, while hardly more than 5 per cent mentioned price.[240] A more recent poll of 1,046 midwestern motorists disclosed that "dealer characteristics" (no doubt including service) and then "convenience" (presumably location) were the most important determinants of station choice. Brand preference ran a "poor third," and price was somewhere further down.[241]

Are There Too Many Service Stations?

The competition of the majors in service stations is frequently criticized as wasteful of capital, labor and choice commercial sites. In the 1930s, when the number of stations doubled and their average sales declined by 20 per cent, this criticism seems to have been justified — even granting that this trade represented a form of unemployment relief for men who entered it for lack of other job opportunities. Between 1939 and 1948, however, the number of stations decreased by a quarter, and sales per station trebled. It was principally the little one-pump and crossroads stations that disappeared. At the time of the 1954 Census the number of stations had hardly changed, but sales had increased by 65 per cent. On the assumption that gasoline constituted 75 per cent of the typical station's business in 1929 and 1939 and 70 per cent in 1948 and 1954,[242] and that all of it was sold at the average

240. Du Pont Co., *The Service Station Operator*, 2d report, p. 19.

241. University of Michigan Survey Research Center poll, *National Petroleum News*, July 1956, p. 106.

242. Calculated from *Census of Distribution*, 1929, *Census of Business*, 1939 and 1948, and Marketing Research Committee, Division of Marketing, American Petroleum Institute, *Urban Consumer Expenditures for Transportation*, New York, 1955, pp. 16, 44.

TABLE 14

PETROLEUM: NUMBER OF GASOLINE SERVICE STATIONS AND THEIR SALES, 1929–54

	1929	1939	1948	1954
Number of stations (*thousands*)	121.5	241.9	179.6	181.7
Total receipts (*millions*)	$1,787.4	$2,822.5	$6,470.2	$10,780.1
Year's receipts per station[a]	$14,710	$11,670	$36,022	$59,322
Average price of gasoline (*cents per gallon*)	21.42	18.75	25.88	29.04
Estimated monthly gasoline sales per station (*gallons*)	4,300	3,900	8,100	11,900[b]

Sources: Station numbers and total receipts from Census of Business, the 1929 and 1939 data being reported in *Statistical Abstract of the United States*, 1952, p. 896; 1948 and 1954 from U.S. Census Bureau; price from 50-city series compiled by Texas Co.; monthly sales estimated on assumption that gasoline constituted 75 per cent of total sales in 1929 and 1939 and 70 per cent in 1948 and 1954, and that price was as given.

a. Calculated from figures above, but using all their digits.

b. By way of comparison, another estimate of monthly gasoline sales per station in 1954 is 16,533 gallons (*National Petroleum News*, Factbook issue, Mid-May 1956, p. 205).

price for fifty cities compiled by the Texas Company, gasoline sales per station may be estimated roughly at 4,300 gallons a month in 1929, nearly twice as much in 1948 and nearly three times as much in 1954. (See Table 14.) The gain for gallonage per pump would be less, since the average number of pumps per station has increased.

On the basis of these figures and assumptions, it would appear that the trade is at least less overcrowded than before the war, and that service stations are doing a much better business and probably making a better return. This conclusion is supported by figures for the gross monthly profit on gasoline sales of one refiner's dealers: it increased from $281 in 1936–39 to $1,133 in 1953–54.[243]

Two other surveys are of interest, although they lack a prewar base for comparison. A study of 398 dealers made by Dun & Bradstreet in 1951 showed the average owner receiving a compensation of $3,900 for his services plus 11.1 per cent on the net worth of his $10,800 investment.[244] A du Pont study of a representative sample of stations in 1954 showed 22 per cent earning less than $3,000, 11 per cent earning more than $7,500, and the median earning $4,160.[245] If we ascribe $3,900 to owner's personal compensation, the return on investment would be

243. S. H. Elliott, vice president of Standard Oil Company of Ohio, Roosevelt Hearings, p. 580.

244. Calculated from report of Elmer T. Sivertsen, *ibid.*, p. 192.

245. Du Pont Co., *The Service Station Operator*, 4th report, p. 19.

2.4, 5.2 or 8.7 per cent depending on whether we assume that investment was $10,800 as in the Dun & Bradstreet study or $5,000 or $3,000 as estimated by a congressional committee.[246] The $3,900 compensation is low for a 72-hour work week.[247] Ease of entry, favored by competition among refiners to market their products widely and by their willingness to finance newcomers in the business, is probably responsible for this low level. In this sense, the business is still overcrowded.

Price versus Convenience

Gasoline could be sold on a lower margin if there were fewer stations in operation to share the existing volume — although there would be correspondingly less competition to compel the passing on of much of the saving to motorists. However, the overexpansion is much less marked than superficial observation would indicate. Shifts in population, traffic and the character of neighborhoods are bound to stimulate construction of new stations while old ones continue for a while to operate at obsolete sites.[248]

More important, the typical American motorist wants convenience and speed in securing his gasoline or service even if he pays a high price. He neither wants to wait in line at a station nor to cross traffic to reach one. Much clustering of stations is explained by the tendency of motorists to plan to buy gasoline where there is little danger of delay. One critic of overexpansion speaks of the "grotesque extremes" in building stations "at every conceivable corner where traffic might pass in sufficient volume";[249] but the last phrase is the key to choice of locations. Few stations are built today without a careful analysis of the traffic, which generally eventuates in profitable operation.[250]

In short, although the price of gasoline might be reduced by a more efficient pattern of station location, this could only be accomplished by suppressing the right of free entry into the industry and by forcing on motorists nuisances most of them are willing to pay to avoid.[251]

246. *Alleged Coercive and Discriminatory Practices against Retail Gasoline Operators by Oil Company Suppliers*, House Report, p. 6.

247. Du Pont Co., *The Service Station Operator*, 1st report, p. 12.

248. Sidney A. Swensrud, TNEC Hearings, Part 15, p. 8416.

249. Rostow, *A National Policy for the Oil Industry*, p. 76.

250. Information from John W. Boatwright, manager of Distribution Economics Department, Standard Oil Co. (Ind.).

251. See Richard D. Lundy, "How Many Service Stations Are 'Too Many'?," Chap. 20 of Reavis Cox and Wroe Alderson, eds., *Theory in Marketing*, Irwin, Homewood (Ill.), 1950, pp. 321–33.

Retail Prices of Major Brands of Gasoline

The fact that posted gasoline prices of the major brands are generally the same or about the same has frequently aroused public suspicion that a price agreement is at work. At times it doubtless is. "Oil men's luncheons" of Texas marketers are rumored to have reduced the number of price wars.[252] Retailers probably agree on prices upon occasion, forgetting the antitrust laws or assuming that they will not be enforced against small businessmen.[253] In 1955 the Department of Justice filed a suit against a group of New Jersey retailers for agreeing on a 6.7-cent mark-up (calculated as true cost by Dun & Bradstreet [254]) and for blocking the driveways of nonconformers.[255] Retailers have also contributed to price fixing indirectly by obtaining state legislation to prevent price cutting or by getting the thirty-odd state unfair practices acts (which forbid sales below cost for the purpose of destroying competition) applied to gasoline.[256]

Despite these overt acts and agreements, most cases of retail price uniformity appear to result from a combination of two forces: fewness of sellers and competition. Each one of a half dozen or dozen dealers thinks, and the supplier, whose advice on prices the dealer usually follows, also thinks, that any price reduction will bring retaliation. On the other hand, none dares hold his price above the rest, for fear of losing sales by "ceasing to be competitive." The more keenly consumers are interested in price, the more likely are prices to be identical.

Nevertheless, prices were identical in very few of the local retail market areas observed by the writer in the course of this study. In the five towns (in three separate states) checked most recently the posted prices of "regular" gasoline of major brands at stations along a three-block section of the main street ran as follows (in cents per gallon): (1) 30.3, 30.3, 31.0, 31.0, 31.5, 31.5; (2) 30.0, 30.5, 31.8, 32.0; (3) 29.9, 29.9, 30.2, 30.9, 31.9; (4) 30.9, 30.9, 30.9, 30.9, 31.5; and (5) 30.9, 30.9, 30.9, 30.9, 30.9, 31.6, 31.9. A recent study of four Texas cities, with a total of 530 stations, disclosed that 96, 75, 59 and 56 per

252. *National Petroleum News*, October 1955, p. 153.

253. Cassady, *Price Making and Price Behavior in the Petroleum Industry*, p. 246.

254. H. Bradford Graeff, in *Gasoline Price War in New Jersey*, Senate Hearings, Part 1, p. 12.

255. Department of Justice press release, May 25, 1955.

256. Cassady, *Price Making and Price Behavior in the Petroleum Industry*, pp. 248–51.

cent of the stations, respectively, sold at the most typical ("modal") price.[257]

Higher-priced dealers sometimes remark: "What if another station is underselling us? He can't fill everyone's tank." They rely on the customer's inertia and on loyalty of regular patrons to sell in spite of higher prices. In a recent poll of motorists which revealed that 85 per cent wrongly supposed that local gasoline prices are "uniform," one interesting reason given by those who liked such uniformity was that it saved them the nuisance of bargain hunting.[258] In many towns bargain hunters can in fact get major brands at prices at least a cent below the typical price, by driving one block off on a side street. Still farther from the main street, however, isolated stations charge higher prices again.

Unbranded or Off-Brand Gasoline

These retail price differences among major brands may be welcomed by the minority of consumers keenly interested in "pinching pennies," but they are too small and too spasmodic to be of very much help. Where consumers can really gain is at stations offering little service and selling an unbranded or private-brand (not nationally advertised) gasoline, for these sell typically and rather consistently at two, three or even four cents a gallon below the major brands. Apparently in some parts of the country one differential is necessary to divide customers in stable proportions between unadvertised and advertised gasoline, in other parts of the country another. The exact amount depends also on whether prosperity or depression prevails. Two cents is the most common figure.[259]

The industry's service to the public would be improved if such brands were available at more places, since it would then be adapting its offers more completely to consumers' desires. One estimate puts the ratio of off-brand to branded stations at only one in twenty.[260] In some communities the prevailing economic standard may be too high to provide enough business for an unbranded station. Elsewhere private

257. Vernon T. Clover, "Price Influence of Unbranded Gasoline," *Journal of Marketing*, April 1953, p. 392, note 3.

258. Opinion Research Corporation poll, reported in *National Petroleum News*, March 1956, p. 48.

259. Cassady, *Price Making and Price Behavior in the Petroleum Industry*, p. 278.

260. Clarence Dority, executive secretary of North Carolina Service Station Ass'n., Roosevelt Hearings, p. 371.

brands are reported to account for 25 to 45 per cent of total sales — as in Los Angeles, Chicago, Indianapolis, Milwaukee, St. Louis, Minneapolis-St. Paul and Houston.[261] In most areas there are too few independent refineries left to support any large number of off-brand stations, and major-brand gasoline is available to such stations on an unbranded (or "rebranded") basis only at times of surplus.

Retail Price Wars

Despite both natural motives and concerted efforts in favor of stabilization, retail price wars are "perhaps more common in gasoline distribution than in any other distributive trade." [262] They have raged in as many as thirteen important cities at once,[263] though in most areas they rarely or never occur.

Price wars may result from efforts of suppliers to unload surplus gasoline, endeavors of new and aggressive station operators to break into a market by price cutting, or attempts of operators in an area with too many stations to boost an unprofitably low volume of sales — a situation which may have come about through an excessive margin between the tank wagon and the retail price.[264] In other words, they reflect a surplus of gasoline or of filling station capacity. The most famous series of price wars, which continued in New Jersey for six years beginning in 1950, began with price cutting of 22-pump and 24-pump semi-self-service stations selling gasoline obtained cheaply from a subsidiary of Standard Oil of California, which was trying in this way to establish a market in a new state.[265] Price wars end when the weakest competitors are eliminated or when the aggressive ones decide to "cease fire."

Dealers forced into price wars appeal to their suppliers for a lower tank wagon price. When the price cuts become deep enough to threaten the existence of their dealers and thus the outlets for their

261. J. G. Jordan, vice president of Shell Oil Co., *ibid.*, p. 761.

262. Cassady, *Price Making and Price Behavior in the Petroleum Industry*, p. 262.

263. *The Gasoline Retailer*, February 15, 1950, cited in Sun Oil Co., *Competition Makes Gasoline Prices*, pamphlet, Philadelphia, 1950, p. 9.

264. Cassady, *Price Making and Price Behavior in the Petroleum Industry*, pp. 266–75; *National Petroleum News*, August 22, 1951, pp. 23–24, September 12, 1951, pp. 29–30.

265. Willard W. Wright, general sales manager of Sun Oil Co., *Gasoline Price War in New Jersey*, Senate Hearings, Part 3, pp. 358–60; statement by Sun Oil Co., *ibid.*, p. 580; *Gasoline Price War in New Jersey*, Senate Report, pp. 17–19.

gasoline, refiners give an allowance to the dealers involved — although it is usually less than the full amount of the price cut. Thus:

> Price wars are often started by dealers and are maintained by support from suppliers. They begin like snowball fights among children. The fight gets rougher until a father comes out of the house. Then other fathers come out, and the simple fight turns into a riot.[266]

At this point the law now intervenes. One refiner has been held (by the trial court, at least) liable for treble damages under the Clayton Act because it refused this allowance to a dealer who would not cut his own price — in this case because he sold to motorists just off the parkway who were happily unaware that they were driving toward a price war. The defense of "good-faith meeting of competition" was disallowed because the competition met was with the refiner's customers rather than itself.[267] There have been Sherman Act prosecutions of such allowances on the ground that they involve retail price fixing by the supplier.[268] They are also threatened by state legislation.[269]

If these allowances could be abolished, and a "sink or swim" policy applied to dealers, it was the opinion of both an official New Jersey commission and a Senate investigating committee that price wars would be over more quickly and that the outcome in terms of dealers able to stand on their own feet would be healthier.[270] No refiner, however, wants his dealers to disappear, and his own sales with them, just because they may be less efficient or pay more for gasoline than their price-cutting rivals.

Among the suggested remedies for price wars are control of production to avoid surpluses,[271] resale price maintenance and state price-fixing legislation. Production control is difficult to achieve in an industry where each refiner decides for himself how much to produce and each wants to increase his share in the market. Resale price maintenance was installed in New Jersey in 1956, probably inspired by the Senate investigation of 1955, and brought this price war to a close.

266. Dwight T. Colley, *National Petroleum News*, March 1956, p. 35.

267. *Enterprise Industries, Inc. v. Texas Co.*, 136 F. Supp. 420 (D. Conn. 1955).

268. *National Petroleum News*, Factbook issue, Mid-May 1956, p. 145; *Journal of Commerce*, June 29, 1956, p. 6.

269. Herbert Willetts, *Gasoline Price War in New Jersey*, Senate Hearings, Part 3, p. 400.

270. *Gasoline Price War in New Jersey*, Senate Report, p. 21.

271. *Ibid.*, p. 17; Senator Hubert H. Humphrey, interview in *National Petroleum News*, June 1956, p. 97.

Elsewhere, however, "fair trading" has raised serious enforcement problems in gasoline as in other commodities. State price-fixing laws exist in Massachusetts and Michigan, and in modified form elsewhere, but enforcement is by no means smooth.[272] Above all, any price-fixing remedy will have the regrettable consequences of (1) preventing efficient retailers from passing on to consumers any of their reduced costs, and (2) eliminating the one real value in price wars: that the fear of an outbreak prevents refiners and dealers from setting the retail margin too high.

Uniformity in Crude Oil and Refined Product Prices

The various wholesale petroleum prices tend toward uniformity. Refiners "post" (publish) the prices they are offering for each type of crude oil, with differentials according to quality and exact location. A producer must either sell his crude locally, or, if there is a common-carrier pipeline available, to a distant refinery. Posted prices are almost always uniform among the buyers. No producer will sell to a refiner whose posted price is lower than another refiner's unless he has a long-term contract with him or the other's facilities are fully occupied. If his facilities are occupied, a refiner is likely eventually to reduce the price he is paying to the level posted by his rivals.

The fact that the big refiners take the initiative in posting prices for crude oil sometimes makes them targets of criticism when producers of crude dislike a reduction or consumers or the government dislike an increase. As buyers of crude on balance, the majors would be more likely to want its price low than high, even though a few would receive a net gain by having more of their income receive the special depletion allowance given to crude production by the income tax. Whatever they might wish, the majors could not control the price of crude without collective action, and collective action has never been proved.

Some of the factors bearing on price uniformity among sellers on the wholesale markets for petroleum products are illustrated by a study of New York City prices for heavy and light fuel oil and gasoline in 1947 and 1948.[273] When supplies were ample and demand was low, asking prices tended to come together, for sellers had to meet their rivals'

272. Compare A. A. Stambaugh, *Below Cost Selling of Petroleum Products*, pamphlet, Standard Oil Company of Ohio, Cleveland, 1951, pp. 10–12.

273. Quotations in *Journal of Commerce*, analyzed in Raymond Rodgers and H. E. Luedicke, "Dynamic Competition," *Harvard Business Review*, March 1949, pp. 237–49.

quotations if they were to remain in the market. When supplies were tight and demand high, a wide gap appeared between the high and low prices asked by sellers — the low prices being perhaps those of firms with a deliberate policy of price stabilization. In other words, uniformity existed when competition among the sellers was keen, and it disappeared when the high demand (i.e., competition among buyers) put each seller in the same sort of privileged position one associates with monopoly. This study was based on a short and unusual period,[274] and uniformity of price quotations is probably more frequent than it showed. On the other hand, identity of quotations is often deceptive because of special concessions and arrangements.[275]

Price Leadership

In each district in the oil industry, as in some other industries, one company has often made the first official announcement of a price increase or price cut and others have followed. The leaders have normally been Standard successor companies, because of their size, their coverage of the whole country, and above all, perhaps, because of historical tradition.[276] Thus, in the Los Angeles area, 25 of the 40 gasoline price increases and 16 of the 42 decreases between 1923 and 1949 were first announced by Standard of California, and the rest largely by other majors. However, the compilers of these figures believe that "in most instances" (especially on price cuts) the so-called leader had merely recognized informal price changes by other sellers already in effect.[277]

It seems probable that price leadership is less prevalent now than before World War II. The five increases in the posted crude price in 1946–47 were initiated by four separate refiners (the small major, Sun Oil Company, led twice).[278] Standard Oil of Indiana maintains that it long since abdicated price leadership in its territories, having found that this merely gave its competitors the chance to underbid it for a time after it had raised its prices, and to undercut informally when the

274. Cassady, *Price Making and Price Behavior in the Petroleum Industry*, p. 155, note 31.

275. *Ibid.*, p. 91.

276. Shuman, *The Petroleum Industry*, pp. 130–31. Compare Burns, *The Decline of Competition*, pp. 93–109.

277. Cassady and Jones, *The Nature of Competition in Gasoline Distribution at the Retail Level*, pp. 177–78.

278. Congressman John W. Heselton of Massachusetts, in *Petroleum Study* (*Gasoline and Oil Price Increases*), House Hearings, p. 665.

market was weak, before its own formal action.[279] Recently half of the price advances in the East were led by companies other than the traditional leaders.[280]

Some contracts between refiners and jobbers fix a price a certain distance below "the" tank wagon price, which may be defined as that appearing in a recognized publication. In the absence of a commodity exchange on which oil is traded — which experience has shown is impractical on any large scale — some such point of reference serves a purpose in protecting those who have committed themselves to receive or deliver oil products on contract.

Observers generally agree that the price leader is not followed unless competitors are convinced he has understood the true demand and supply situation. His public announcement sometimes merely reflects the fact that premiums are being demanded or discounts offered without publicity by smaller companies.[281] In other words, petroleum price leaders are "barometric" rather than "dominant" firms.[282] As long ago as 1928 the Federal Trade Commission wrote:

> If price cutting occurs in a sufficient number of localities, the Standard Oil Company affected reduces its general price level throughout its territory, or, in some cases, throughout the state where price cutting has become general. In some cases the initiative in making a price reduction is taken by a large independent.[283]

Examples of Attempted Price Leadership

A glance at several well-publicized failures from the field of price leadership will serve to remove any idea that the phenomenon works automatically or smoothly.

In July 1947 the Esso Standard Oil Company — big operating subsidiary of Standard of New Jersey and traditional price leader in New Jersey and states to the south — announced that it would not advance prices in spite of the tremendous current demand. It wanted to contribute to the fight against inflation and gain a reputation for dependability as contrasted with profiteering. This action drew a

279. Wilson, *Oil Competition in the Midwest*, pp. 26–27.

280. Harold Fleming, *Oil Prices and Competition*, American Petroleum Institute, 1953, p. 56; compare *Business Week*, June 2, 1956, p. 146.

281. McLean and Haigh, *The Growth of Integrated Oil Companies*, p. 158.

282. Cassady, *Price Making and Price Behavior in the Petroleum Industry*, p. 87.

283. FTC 1928 Report, p. 241.

congratulatory telegram from the White House, but resulted in price distortions within the industry. Other sellers took over the leadership for the time being.[284]

The Standard Oil Company of Ohio is the price leader in its state; but its many competitors sometimes ignore its increases, thus forcing it to reverse its position, and its reductions often merely constitute public recognition of cuts made informally by rivals. The company has found that, if economic conditions are right, it can lead the market up, but that, in view of the political influence of independent gasoline dealers, it is not prudent to lead the market down.[285]

In September 1948 Phillips Petroleum Company raised its posted price from $2.65 to $3.00, and Sinclair soon followed — but in December both dropped the price again because other companies were still able to get all the crude oil they needed without paying so much. The net result was that Phillips had "paid out a lot of extra money," although it had also gained new "crude connections." [286]

An increase in the tank wagon price of gasoline was announced by the traditional New York leader when Office of Price Stabilization ceilings were lifted in February 1953. After only one week, it collapsed "in the face of competition from several major suppliers who had refused to go along." [287] In June the increase was successfully made, because the price of crude had risen 25 cents a barrel on June 15. Investigations by a congressional committee [288] and the Department of Justice followed; but no action proved to be warranted.

Proration

One of the fundamental determinants of petroleum prices is the proration program. In the early decades of the industry there was great waste of both oil and the natural gas which is associated with it underground. After various futile attempts at organized conservation, effective national action began in 1933, when the flush production of

284. Harry L. Hansen and Powell Niland, "Esso Standard: A Case Study in Pricing," *Harvard Business Review*, May–June 1952, pp. 114–32.

285. Edmund P. Learned, "Pricing of Gasoline: A Case Study," *ibid.*, November 1948, pp. 723–56.

286. Platt, "40 Great Years," p. 57; W. W. Keeler, vice president of Phillips Petroleum Co., in *Petroleum Study (Gasoline and Price Increases)*, House Hearings, p. 92.

287. *Journal of Commerce*, March 6, 1953, p. 1.

288. *Petroleum Study (Gasoline and Oil Price Increases)*, House Hearings, p. 1, and statement of Herbert Willetts beginning at p. 195.

the East Texas field coincided with a drop in demand to force crude oil prices to a record low level. Control of output was made part of a code of fair competition under the National Recovery Administration. This was followed in 1935 by the Interstate Oil Compact approved by act of Congress, along with the Connally "Hot Oil" Act which forbade interstate transportation of oil produced in violation of state laws. All the important oil-producing states except Illinois (which has less than 3 per cent of production) now limit monthly output to "allowable" amounts, either through a public commission or, less effectively in California, through a committee of producers. These authorities have as guides a monthly estimate of the Bureau of Mines concerning the prospective demand for crude oil produced in each state, estimates presented by oil companies and much other statistical data; but they make up their own minds — except as the lead of the Texas Railroad Commission is likely to carry weight with the rest.

The proration program has unquestionably conserved oil and gas. Wasteful gushers and flaring of gas have been abolished, and engineers employed by the commissions or trained by them have encouraged proper spacing of wells and the best modern methods of preserving the pressure on which full recovery of underground reserves depends. Moreover, the prevention of excessive production has tended to prevent waste above ground — both physical waste and low-value uses which would have ensued from very low prices.

Proration and Prices

It is evident that proration has both a conservation and a price-supporting aspect, although congressmen were able to question the chairman of the Texas Railroad Commission for hours without drawing an admission that maintenance of prices was in any way a purpose of proration.[289] The statutes in states with 72 per cent of 1955 output [290] limit supply to "maximum efficiency rates" (the highest rates consistent with maintenance of pressure) or "market demand," whichever is lower. Repeatedly in recent years large output and mounting inventories have posed a threat to prices, only to have the authorities order a reduction in "allowables," whereupon inventories would decline and the threat to prices vanish. Although, of course, allowables are raised

289. Ernest O. Thompson, *ibid.*, pp. 608–69, especially 619–20 and 648–49.

290. *Report of the Attorney General Pursuant to Section 2 of the Joint Resolution of July 28, 1955, Consenting to an Interstate Compact to Conserve Oil and Gas*, September 1, 1956, p. 93.

when stocks are low, the average crude price tends to be higher than it would be without proration — as a recent writer sympathetic to the industry has mentioned.[291] One reviewer of his book, claiming that this admission "misses the main point," calls proration "the most significant single fact in determining the domestic price structure." [292]

It should not be assumed that the result of proration will necessarily prove in the end to be a very much higher long-run average price. An unrestrained flow of oil might so reduce prices as to drive enough producers out of business to create a shortage later — especially if irreplaceable oil had been wasted on uneconomic uses just because it was cheap. Moreover, as oil gradually becomes scarcer, its price would in any case rise faster if proration were not postponing use of some of the supply.[293] However, the current price-maintenance aspect of proration is conceded even by those observers who believe that "as a conservation authority the [Texas] commission deserves the highest praise." [294] Strict physical controls, to prevent drilling of wells too close together and to keep the rate of production from exceeding the level most favorable to maximum long-run output of a field, would suffice to prevent most physical waste, and would tend to keep prices more stable than before proration, without need for a formally stated goal of meeting market demand.[295] They would leave only the lesser physical waste due to excess storage and evaporation above ground, and such economic waste as would result from oil being cheaper now than the prospect of eventual shortage would justify. Since there would still be difficulties as to equitable allocation of output among producers, it is clear that there is no ideal solution of the problem.[296]

Similar in its price-stabilizing effect is the action of the big oil companies with sources of supply in the Middle East and Venezuela in restricting imports into the United States to planned amounts. These

291. Cassady, *Price Making and Price Behavior in the Petroleum Industry*, pp. 113–14.

292. George W. Stocking, book review, *American Economic Review*, September 1954, pp. 694–95. Compare Watkins, *Oil: Stabilization or Conservation?*, pp. 138, 252; and Standard & Poor's Corp., *Industry Surveys*, "Oil," Basic Analysis, June 16, 1955, p. O 2–8.

293. Dirlam, "The Petroleum Industry," p. 263.

294. "Conserving Oil at a Price," *The Economist*, February 12, 1955, p. 544; also Max W. Ball, Jr., *This Fascinating Oil Business*, Bobbs-Merrill, Indianapolis, 1940, p. 269.

295. Cassady, *Price Making and Price Behavior in the Petroleum Industry*, pp. 113–14, note 11.

296. See Hines H. Baker, president of Humble Oil and Refining Co., "Achievements and Unsolved Problems in Oil and Gas Conservation," reprinted in *Price Increases in Petroleum Products*, Hearings before a Subcommittee of the Senate Banking and Currency Committee, 81st Cong., 1st sess., 1949, pp. 44–47.

amounts are far smaller than relative costs of production would dictate, and doubtless less than the firms would prefer to import even taking full account of the desirability of keeping their domestic crude oil connections. This policy, adopted individually and not by agreement, is forced on the companies by the political influence of the domestic oil producers (represented by groups like the Independent Petroleum Association of America and the Texas Independent Producers and Royalty Owners Association), and is the only means by which they can escape or minimize a political struggle and possibly the imposition of a quota on imports (especially of residual fuel oil) by act of Congress.

Proration and the Antitrust Laws

The proration system is made possible by an actual, though unstated, exemption from the antitrust laws under the Interstate Oil Compact and the Connally Act. It is in conformity with these laws that the Interior Department requires applicants for public land leases to obey proration orders. Moreover, the head of the Antitrust Division declared in 1951 that the Division had found "no information or evidence" that the Compact had been used to violate the antitrust laws.[297] This view presumably rests on the position that Article 5 of the Compact, which states that the plan is not to be used "for the purpose of stabilizing or fixing the price," should be interpreted as meaning that the plan is not to be used solely or primarily for stabilizing prices.

Another issue related to the antitrust laws is whether proration gives the majors an advantage. It did originally give them an advantage over smaller refiners, since these were able to flourish on the excess flow of oil before proration, and in many cases lost their sources of supply when the plan came in — or, specifically, when the Connally Act made it illegal to handle oil produced beyond a well's allowable figure. Proration does not give them as producers any advantage over the smaller producers. The majors produce only half of their crude oil requirements domestically and are on net balance buyers rather than sellers of crude. Although the majors are glad of the market stability created by proration, the small producers are fully as much the beneficiaries. The number of Texas producers increased from 4,000 to

297. H. Graham Morison, in *Interstate Oil and Gas Compact*, House Hearings, p. 96.

13,000 between 1932 and 1953.[298] The Independent Petroleum Association of America is accordingly the program's warmest champion. Under the rule that little wells are allowed their full production, the majors are likely to have somewhat less of their capacity translated into current production than are many independents.

In California, the government's current antitrust suit charges that proration by the Conservation Committee, which represents producers rather than the state, is one means by which the majors take advantage of the independents. According to one authority, writing in 1945, "the merits of this issue defy analysis." [299] The government has been understood to believe that, if the California plan can be enjoined, the state may adopt a proration law; but referenda on compulsory proration were defeated in 1932, 1939 and 1956 on the slogan that "the big corporations want it." The fact that in the 1953 recession California continued a high rate of output while commissions were ordering a reduction in the other important producing states [300] was interpreted by some as a consequence of the government's pending antitrust suit.

Conservation and the Antitrust Laws

The antitrust laws and their enforcement touch in several ways on the question of conservation of oil. First, we have seen that exemption of the proration plan from the Sherman Act permits a degree of conservation.

A further approach to conservation is offered by "unitization," or unified development of oil pools with the land royalties divided on an agreed basis. In its absence, only state well-spacing laws, which are not universal and are a crude instrument at best, prevent the oil and gas from being drained inefficiently by an excessive number of poorly placed wells. A landowner who does not drill near his property line would otherwise find his neighbor's wells sucking up his reserves. Unitization is especially important for "repressurizing" an oil field. Its use has been increasing; but the number of persons and interests concerned usually makes the necessary agreement impossible. It was

298. Ernest O. Thompson, in *Petroleum Study (Gasoline and Oil Price Increases)*, House Hearings, p. 662.

299. Bain, *The Economics of the Pacific Coast Petroleum Industry*, Part 2, p. 75.

300. "The Petroleum Industry on the Pacific Coast and Recent World Oil Developments," Supplement to *Monthly Review*, March 1954, Federal Reserve Bank of San Francisco, p. 15.

recently reported that only twelve out of 550 California fields were completely unitized, and that ultimate recovery in these twelve would be 41.7 per cent of all the oil as against only 23.4 per cent without unitization.[301]

The legal status of unitization is gradually being clarified. In 1947 the Department of Justice filed a Sherman Act suit against one plan, conceding that joint production was legal but not joint action in refining and selling.[302] Such joint action, however, is common in unitization plans.[303] The case was dismissed because it rested on Federal Bureau of Investigation documents which could not be made public in court. In April 1951 dissenting leaseholders sued the California Conservation Commission, claiming refusal to let them develop their leases independently when the Coalinga Nose pool had been unitized ten years before.[304] Nevertheless, there has been no holding that unitization is illegal, and legal opinion is tending toward the view that it is perfectly safe under the law.[305] Mere lawfulness of unitization, or even compulsory unitization if desired by leaseholders of 75 or perhaps 51 per cent of acreage involved, is a long way from the compulsory unitization of all fields advocated by some as the best approach of all to conservation.[306]

The interpretations of the antitrust laws which have permitted the growth of the majors have been favorable to conservation, since this is more likely to be achieved when producers are big than when they are small. The majors feel they are in business permanently, and they have transportation and refining facilities which require a continuing flow of crude oil; hence they cannot afford the short-term attitude of "getting out the oil for the most immediate profit." In addition, their financial resources make it easier for them to use the most modern methods of production as well as to weather periods of drastic curtailment, and their small number makes it easier also to enforce compliance with conservation regulations.

301. *Business Week*, February 11, 1956, p. 134.

302. *U.S. v. Cotton Valley Operators Committee*, Civil 2209 (W.D. La. 1947); John C. Jacobs, "Unit Operation of Oil and Gas Fields," *Yale Law Journal*, June 1948, pp. 1207–28.

303. *Oil and Gas Journal*, July 21, 1949, p. 52.

304. *Ibid.*, April 26, 1951, p. 80.

305. Rostow and Sachs, "Entry into the Oil Refining Business," p. 858, note 4; Robert E. Hardwicke, *Antitrust Laws et al. v. Unit Operation of Oil and Gas Pools*, American Institute of Mining and Metallurgical Engineers, New York, 1948, p. 175.

306. Rostow, *A National Policy for the Oil Industry*, pp. 119–22; Joe S. Bain, "Rostow's Proposals for Petroleum Policy," *Journal of Political Economy*, February 1949, p. 56.

Domination of Refining by the Majors

Some issues concerning domination of the industry by the majors have been raised by the Mother Hubbard and West Coast divorcement suits brought by the government and by recent discussion in industry circles and before committees of Congress.

In the area of refining, the smaller firms have always been dependent to some extent on the good will of the majors. Majors handle distribution for some of the independents. With some others, according to men in the industry, there is an unspoken understanding that the independent will operate in certain areas and not infringe on the territory of a particular major, which in turn will apply the principle of "live and let live." Elsewhere there is competition with no holds barred.

In the California suit, the government has charged that the growth of the majors and the relative decline of the independents have been due to oppressive practices.[307] A brief discussion of three of the practices cited will show that they may have natural causes.

Mergers. Although many independent refiners have disappeared through merger, the merger has been more often a consequence of fundamental trends than an original cause. As McLean and Haigh point out in writing of petroleum integration, independent refiners have suffered from three serious difficulties: (1) lack of ready access to large capital with which to finance the installation of expensive modern equipment; (2) elimination under the proration system of the type of flush new oil field on which independents formerly drew for their crude; and (3) the technical superiority which integration provides in dealing with the particular economic risks of this industry.[308] Under these conditions, an independent refiner is strongly tempted to sell out if he sees the opportunity.

Transportation cost squeeze. The accusation that the majors "squeeze" independent refiners through charges for the use of tankers and pipelines is perhaps another way of saying that an integrated organization can make efficient use of such facilities that a nonintegrated one cannot match. To "squeeze" was not the intention when pipelines and tankers were built: they were in every case built for actual use. If

307. *U.S. v. Standard Oil Company of Calif.*, Civil 11584-C (S.D. Calif. 1950), paragraph 70.

308. John G. McLean and Robert M. Haigh, "How Business Corporations Grow," *Harvard Business Review*, November–December 1954, pp. 90–91.

independents are squeezed, it is unlikely that it is through having to pay higher rates than they had *expected* when they began to produce or refine oil, since pipeline rates declined from 1938 to 1946 and since then have increased much more slowly than the prices of crude and refined oil. They are also lower than the rail rates which had been or would be the alternative, and, of course, much cheaper to the small refiner than construction of his own pipelines would be. As for tanker rates, they fluctuate sharply with supply and demand of tanker space.

Exchanges of oil products. Failure of the majors to exchange crude oil and products with the independents as often as with each other is one charge by the Department of Justice and has often been a subject of complaint to the Federal Trade Commission.[309] The purpose of such exchanges is to avoid transportation, however, and it is unusual for a one-plant refinery, using a topping process and selling in a local market, to be in a position to make a helpful exchange with a multi-plant company.[310]

Bureau of Mines data on number and size of refineries illustrate both the decline in number of independents and the trend toward larger capacities than an ill-financed independent can match. The only break in both these trends was during the 1930s, when the flush oil from East Texas and other fields encouraged the building of many small refineries which made a quick profit, then shut down, and later were abandoned. The size of shut-down refineries has been consistently less than that of refineries still able to operate successfully. (See Table 15.) The increasing need for efficiency in refining operations is illustrated by the Census figures on value added by manufacture in relation to value of product shipped. This ratio, which represents the refiner's margin, averaged 17.8 per cent for 1899, 1904 and 1909, when the Standard Oil trust was the principal refiner. In the next thirteen Census years, down through 1947, it ranged from 17.9 to 23.6 per cent (in 1914 and 1919, respectively) and averaged 20.7 per cent. The six annual figures from 1949 through 1954 showed a sharp reduction, the range being 15.8 to 17.3 per cent with an average of 16.5 per cent.[311]

309. FTC Commissioner John Carson, in *Petroleum Study*, House Hearings, p. 257.

310. McLean and Haigh, *The Growth of Integrated Oil Companies*, pp. 437–38. Compare Cassady, *Price Making and Price Behavior in the Petroleum Industry*, pp. 55–56, numbers 5 and 8.

311. Census of Manufactures data through 1947 tabulated in American Petroleum Institute, *Petroleum Facts and Figures*, 9th edition, 1950, p. 216; 1949–54 from U.S. Census Bureau.

TABLE 15

PETROLEUM: NUMBER AND AVERAGE CAPACITY OF REFINERIES, 1921–56

Year	Number of Refineries		Average Daily Capacity	
	Operating	Shut-Down	Operating	Shut-Down
			(Thousand Barrels)	
1921	350	65	5,127	1,452
1926	352	158	7,279	1,839
1931	346	89	10,713	2,653
1936	422	210	8,885	1,749
1941	420	136	9,954	3,959
1946	364	29	13,973	7,920
1951	325	32	20,621	8,182
1956	294	24	28,506	10,483

Source: Calculated from U.S. Bureau of Mines, *Petroleum Refineries, Including Cracking Plants,* annual (figures before 1951 collected in American Petroleum Institute, *Petroleum Facts and Figures,* New York, 9th edition, 1950, p. 256).

The Position of the Jobber

The method of wholesaling chosen by refiners in various territories may be dictated by the type of distribution channels available. If there is ample choice, the method they select will depend on whether they believe that use of their own salaried employees, commission agents, branded distributors or unbranded jobbers will yield them the most profit. A study of seven major companies brings out that they prefer to operate their own bulk plants where the volume of business is largest, use commission agents in intermediate situations, and rely on branded jobbers in areas where markets are thin. They use unbranded jobbers "only as a last resort or as a temporary expedient." [312] Some companies, on the other hand, place substantial reliance on jobbers. Only Standard Oil of Ohio, which sells Sohio gasoline in a single state and tries to exploit it fully, has no independent distributors at all.[313]

The unbranded jobbers buy from independent oil refiners and from majors with an excess of refining capacity over marketing connections. Their numbers have shrunk with the decline of the independent refiner and with the progress of the majors' programs for doing their own marketing. According to their National Oil Marketers Association, the decline was 40 per cent from 1932 to 1952. On the other hand, the

312. McLean and Haigh, *The Growth of Integrated Oil Companies,* p. 473.

313. *National Petroleum News,* August 1956, p. 94.

branded jobbers, according to a 1952 statement of the chairman of their National Oil Jobbers Council, have for forty years "consistently walked off with an ever increasing share of the business." [314]

Census figures suggest that the independent jobbers, branded and unbranded combined, have fully held their own since 1939. Between 1939 and 1948 their share of total wholesale trade in petroleum products increased from 16.5 to 17.1 per cent, and between 1948 and 1954 their share plus that of cooperative bulk stations increased from 18.7 to 30.1 per cent. Although some doubt is thrown on this 1948–54 increase by a change in Census categories, it would seem hardly in doubt that jobber sales have increased substantially. Nevertheless, officers of jobber associations insist that they have been hurt by the increase in sales at refinery terminals. Certainly the bypassing of bulk stations by direct shipments from refinery terminal to retail dealers or to industrial users is an important current trend, motivated by the desire to reduce distribution costs. The figures indicate, however, that it has been entirely at the expense of the refiner's own bulk stations, whether these had been operated on a salary or a commission basis, or a combination of both. (See Table 16.)

Jobber representatives insist also that no figures are significant in the absence of a breakdown among types of petroleum product. That jobbers have made a better showing in distribution of home fuel oil than in gasoline appears from the fact that between 1936 and 1950 their sales of distillate fuel and gasoline increased by 78 and 28 per cent, respectively, while total United States sales were increasing by 70 and 39 per cent.[315] A cost survey of twenty-one jobbers in 1955 showed them earning 1.00 cent per dollar of gasoline sales and 3.17 cents per dollar of fuel oil sales; [316] but there are no figures on investment.

Grievances of Jobbers

The jobbers' associations are engaged in continual controversy with the big refiners. It was said in 1949 that jobbers had been behind nearly every complaint against the majors in the past,[317] and in 1951

314. *Ibid.*, May 28, 1952, p. 22.

315. *Ibid.*, April 2, 1952, p. 34; James S. Cross, "Vertical Integration in the Oil Industry," *Harvard Business Review*, July–August 1953, at p. 75.

316. National Oil Jobbers Council survey, *National Petroleum News*, Factbook issue, Mid-May 1956, p. 176.

317. Platt, "40 Great Years," p. 53.

TABLE 16

PETROLEUM: BULK STATIONS AND TERMINALS, 1939, 1948 AND 1954

Type of Wholesale Operation	Number of Establishments			Per Cent of Total Sales		
	1939	1948	1954	1939	1948	1954
Total terminals and bulk stations	30,825	29,451	29,189	100.0	100.0	100.0
Refinery						
Distributing terminals	220	744	1,241	8.5	23.1	36.0
Bulk plants						
Salary and salary-commission	6,053	3,937	1,288	45.7	34.0	10.3
Commission stations	17,530	16,292	15,298	28.4	24.2	22.1
Other bulk plants	7,022	8,478	10,482	17.5	18.7	30.1
Independent bulk stations	6,357	7,417	[a]	16.5	17.1	[a]
Cooperative bulk stations	665	1,061	[a]	1.0	1.6	[a]
L-P gas wholesale facilities	[a]	317[b]	870	[a]	.8[b]	1.4

Source: Census of Distribution, 1939, and Census of Business, 1948, reported in *Statistical Abstract of the United States*, 1948, p. 955, and 1952, p. 884; 1954 calculated from data of Census of Business.

a. Not available.
b. Included in other categories also.

that antagonism had been undergoing a "slow but gradual increase." [318] Some of the principal complaints of recent years are that suppliers are cut off in times of shortage, that the jobber is bypassed, that his margin is inadequate, and that the integrated companies subsidize their marketing.

Cutting off of supply. In times of shortage, a jobber may find himself cut off by his supplier. One remedy is to get help by appeal to congressional committees, several of which intervened during or after the cold winter of 1947–48 when high demand for fuel oil caused a shortage.[319] Another is to maintain a "historical position" with a refiner which will at least assure some quota during a shortage — an aim which inevitably weakens the jobber's independence.

Bypassing. A jobber naturally objects when his refiner begins selling direct to customers in his territory. The most common example is sale

318. *National Petroleum News,* October 17, 1951, p. 40.

319. *Oil Supply and Distribution Problems,* title of Hearings of Senate Committee on Problems of American Small Business, 80th Cong., 1st and 2d sess., 1948, and of S. Rept. 25, 81st Cong., 1st sess., 1949; *Oil Shortage,* Hearings before a Subcommittee of the Senate Interstate and Foreign Commerce Committee, 80th Cong., 2d sess., 1948; *Investigation and Study of Monopolistic Practices in the Petroleum Industries,* Hearings before House Small Business Committee, 80th Cong., 2d sess., 1948.

to "commercial accounts" such as bus and truck lines and manufacturing corporations. The refiner's best defense is that refusal to sell to these large buyers may not help his jobbers, but merely give the accounts to other refiners.[320]

Inadequate margin. The jobber's operating margin, which for gasoline corresponds roughly to the difference between the tank car and tank wagon prices, is fixed by the majors in the sense that they sell both to jobbers and dealers. Forty-five per cent of jobbers answering a 1951 questionnaire put a higher margin as their principal need in their relationship with their suppliers.[321] In 1952 a survey by the National Oil Jobbers Council found that the gross profit of 450 jobbers per gallon of gasoline sold had increased only from 2.53 to 2.56 cents between 1939 and 1950 [322] — while the average selling price, exclusive of taxes, had increased from 9.58 to 15.10 cents.[323] By 1955, however, gross profit (of 21 jobbers) was 3.48 cents per gallon, while net profit before taxes (of 96 jobbers) was 3.37 per cent of sales [324] as against the 4.51 per cent in 1946 and 3.15 per cent in 1950 which had been found in the earlier study. That study had shown profit after taxes as 12.2 per cent of net worth in 1946 and 10.4 per cent in 1950. The same studies showed the jobber's margin on fuel oil to be wider than that on gasoline. Dun & Bradstreet surveys of gasoline and lubricating oil wholesalers with a tangible net worth over $50,000 disclosed an average return (evidently before taxes) of 2.09 per cent on sales in 1939, 3.50 per cent in 1950, and 2.28 for the whole 1936–50 period. The return on net worth was 6.00 per cent in 1936–40, 9.70 per cent in 1941–45, and 13.87 per cent in 1946–50.[325] Dun & Bradstreet found that profits were a higher percentage of sales in six other lines of wholesaling, and lower in fourteen lines.

Subsidized marketing by integrated companies. The complaint of a low operating margin shades into one that the integrated companies take a loss on their marketing operations in order to win customers from jobbers or even to drive the latter out of business. This, again, is hard to document in figures. The profitability of marketing fluctuates as

320. Compare McLean and Haigh, *The Growth of Integrated Oil Companies*, pp. 278–79.
321. *National Petroleum News*, September 26, 1951, p. 25.
322. *Ibid.*, April 2, 1952, pp. 33–34.
323. *Petroleum Facts and Figures*, 1950, p. 367.
324. *National Petroleum News*, Factbook issue, Mid-May 1956, p. 176.
325. Cross, "Vertical Integration in the Oil Industry," p. 72.

does that of producing and refining, but over-all returns for 1920–52 show that companies engaged only in marketing (such as Standard Oil of Kentucky) did better in net return on investment than integrated companies.[326] This would imply that the marketing departments of integrated companies were also profitable. It is true, however, than when competition is especially keen in marketing the integrated refiner will accept a lower margin at this point while getting his normal profit or more elsewhere.[327] A jobber cannot do this. He also knows that his refiner may be tempted to replace him with direct distribution when the business in his area has grown to a large volume. The way out is frequently a profitable merger with the refiner.[328]

The National Oil Jobbers Council has not supported the legislation requiring refiners to do their selling at the refinery gate or port, but this threat is held in reserve. Although the divorce of refining and marketing would solve some problems, it would probably increase the marketing margin and thus consumer prices by preventing the contributions which vertical integration can make to reduced marketing costs [329] and by eliminating refiner-jobber competition.[330]

Domination of Dealers

Discussion of the relations of refiners and retailers, which will be confined here to service stations, must begin with recognition of the dealer's inferior bargaining power. Refiners who allow general dissatisfaction among their dealers, however, will face heavy costs of turnover.

Dealer satisfaction is, of course, difficult to measure quantitatively. The du Pont survey in 1954 found over 80 per cent satisfied with their relations with their suppliers, and the only suggestions for improvement which drew more than a 5 per cent vote were that suppliers should spend more money on improving the station's appearance and that they should improve their advertising.[331] The average turnover of

326. McLean and Haigh, *The Growth of Integrated Oil Companies*, pp. 145–46.

327. Alfred E. Kahn, "Standards for Antitrust Policy," *Harvard Law Review*, November 1953, p. 46.

328. Marshall C. Howard, "Interfirm Relations in Oil Products Markets," *Journal of Marketing*, April 1956, p. 358.

329. Cross, "Vertical Integration in the Oil Industry," p. 79.

330. Dirlam and Kahn, "Leadership and Conflict in the Pricing of Gasoline," pp. 851–52.

331. Du Pont Co., *The Service Station Operator*, 4th report, p. 11; 3d report, p. 7.

this group of dealers might be interpreted as 16 per cent a year, since the average respondent had been in charge of his station for 6.2 years.[332] The turnover in New Jersey, measured by cancellation of state dealer licenses, was successively 16.2, 16.4, 14.7, 16.1, 14.1, 13.8, 13.6, 13.0, 12.7 and 13.2 per cent from 1945–46 to 1954–55. The governor interpreted the figures as showing that cancellations were "definitely on the increase." [333] Turnover of dealers of three majors in 1954 was 14, 19.8 and 13 or 14 per cent, respectively, but refiners believe that very few of these changes reflect either supplier-dealer conflict or dealer failure.[334] Department of Commerce figures indicate that annual discontinuances of filling station firms in 1949 and 1950 averaged 6.8 per cent of the number in operation, while transfers to new ownership averaged 26.6 per cent. The total figure, 33.4 per cent, may be compared with 33.3 per cent for eating and drinking places and 22.0 for all retail establishments.[335] The 33.4 per cent figure is larger than those given by the companies, since it includes all forms of transfer, even leases of new stations to successful dealers.[336]

Presumably the dealer-supplier relationship is normally beneficial to both. Suppliers often compete vigorously for contracts with efficient dealers.[337] The Department of Commerce has advised prospective dealers to tie up with refiners and jobbers, for they "have wide experience in the operation of their own service stations, and will have an understanding of the independent operator's problems." [338] Without supplier influence, the standards of many stations would probably deteriorate. In Great Britain, oil companies recently undertook a program of financing the cleaning up and improvement of retail establishments, in return for exclusive dealing arrangements.[339]

Despite the advantages of a dealer-refiner tie-in, the hearings before a subcommittee of the House Small Business Committee in 1955,

332. *Ibid.*, 4th report, p. 8.

333. Governor Robert B. Meyner, *Gasoline Price War in New Jersey*, Senate Hearings, Part 2, p. 75.

334. S. H. Elliott, Roosevelt Hearings, pp. 580, 592; James W. Ross, sales department of Standard Oil Co. (Ind.), *ibid.*, p. 723; J. G. Jordan, *ibid.*, pp. 762–63.

335. Calculated from *Statistical Abstract of the United States*, 1955, p. 489.

336. Herbert Willetts, Roosevelt Hearings, pp. 661–62.

337. Statement of "a typical oil jobber in the Southwest," *National Petroleum News*, July 1955, p. 43.

338. U.S. Department of Commerce, *Establishing and Operating a Service Station*, Industrial (Small Business) Series No. 22, 1945, pp. 21–22.

339. *Wall Street Journal*, October 1, 1951, p. 1.

under the chairmanship of James Roosevelt, received testimony from dealer after dealer as to dictation by suppliers, price wars, squeezing of the dealer's margin to the minimum, cancellation on short notice resulting in loss of investment, and other problems. In the end the subcommittee recommended that suppliers give all dealers three-year leases after their first year of operation, that Congress pass a stronger law against price discrimination, and that the Committee continue studying the desirability of placing this and similar industries under "an administrative agency." [340]

It was clear that the petroleum industry was facing at the very least a serious human relations problem which had to be solved if it wanted to avoid legislative action. This was so whether the injured and complaining dealers were a majority, a minority, or even a small minority.

Intercommodity Competition

The demand for gasoline is relatively inelastic. Not only is there no available substitute for its principal uses (unless one so considers the higher-priced and less efficient alcohol sometimes used in Europe and Asia), but the cost of gasoline is low enough compared to that of the vehicle to make the consumer relatively indifferent to its price. The competition of gasoline with diesel oil and LP-gas in the truck, tractor and bus markets is competition within the petroleum industry. Lubricants are an even more essential use of petroleum than gasoline, since substitutes cannot perform many of their functions no matter what the cost.

All producers of crude, nearly all refiners and many marketers must rely for their profits on other petroleum products besides gasoline and lubricants. In some of these, competition with the products of other industries is severe. This is notably true of distillate and residual fuel oils, each of which constitutes about one seventh of the total output of refined products by volume. The former competes with coal and gas in home heating, the latter with electric power and bituminous coal in powering industry and transportation. Many consuming companies can and do convert back and forth between fuel oil and coal according to their relative prices. A statistical analysis

340. *Alleged Coercive and Discriminatory Practices against Retail Gasoline Operators by Oil Company Suppliers*, House Report, p. 3.

covering the years 1926–51 showed a "close relationship" between the prices of coal and residual fuel oil in Boston, New York and Baltimore.[341]

In this competition with other fuel industries, petroleum has been notably successful. One comparison will be sufficient proof: between 1899 and 1955 the proportion of total energy production attributable to petroleum increased from 4.7 to 37.0 per cent.[342]

Performance of the Industry

The record of performance of the petroleum industry has been striking. Particularly worth noting are prices, quality, technology, wages and ease of entry.

Prices. Between 1918 and 1955 the average retail price of gasoline, after deducting federal, state and local sales taxes, declined from 25.1 to 21.4 cents a gallon. Inclusive of sales taxes, the price increased from 25.1 to 29.1 cents, or by 16 per cent, while the average of all cost-of-living items included in the Bureau of Labor Statistics index was increasing by 78 per cent.[343]

Quality. A study by the Ethyl Corporation showed that between 1925 and 1950 improvements both in gasoline and automobile engines resulted in a 50 per cent better performance in miles per gallon and in acceleration, and in ton-mile consumption of gasoline by trucks.[344] A similar improvement has occurred in other petroleum products.

Technology. The $150 million which a recent estimate indicated the oil industry was spending on research annually [345] is reflected in its rapid technological progress. Thus between 1901 and 1951 output per man-hour in a typical refinery increased a little more than eight times over.[346]

Wages. Refining wages in recent years have usually been the highest of any manufacturing industry.[347]

341. National Petroleum Council study, summarized in *Journal of Commerce*, January 20, 1953, pp. 2, 11.

342. National Coal Ass'n., *Bituminous Coal Trends*, 1956, Washington, pp. 26–27.

343. *Petroleum Facts and Figures*, 1950, p. 367; Standard & Poor's Corp., "Oil," June 14, 1956, p. O 45; *Survey of Current Business*.

344. *National Petroleum News*, September 20, 1950, p. 29.

345. Dirlam, "The Petroleum Industry," p. 269.

346. Robert G. Dunlop, president of Sun Oil Co., *Journal of Commerce*, November 5, 1951, p. 14.

347. *Survey of Current Business*.

Entry. Despite the dominance of large concerns in the industry, the little businessman still finds many opportunities.[348] The service station operator and the jobber are obvious examples. Other openings are in specialties like seismic consulting (100 firms) and various sorts of equipment. The Texas Company was recently making purchases from 10,000 firms, of which 3,000 had a financial rating below $20,000. Production, long the most profitable branch of the industry, is thronged with small operators. For example, when the Scurry County field in Texas opened in 1949, the majors soon had 27,420 acres under lease, and one hundred small producers had the remaining 30,980 acres.

One of the most influential critics of the position of the majors in the oil industry concludes a recent analysis with a compliment both to the industry and to the antitrust laws — plus a call for more antitrust action (divorcement of pipelines):

> All things considered, the oil industry is one of the most striking instances in our history of the success of the antitrust laws, and of the driving force, creativeness and vitality of American business. . . . It is turbulent, active, and aggressive, with a good deal of room for change and growth.
>
> That the industry is more competitive than it was is not evidence that it is yet as competitive as it could be or should be, given the broad purposes of the Sherman Act.[349]

Profits

The profits of the petroleum industry have regularly formed a substantial fraction of those of American industry as a whole. In 1955 five of the ten industrial corporations with earnings over $200 million were in petroleum, while 92 oil companies accounted for 22.4 per cent of the earnings of 1,765 manufacturing companies. While it is true that petroleum net book assets were 23.6 per cent of the total for manufacturing, and that the average 1937–55 return on such assets was 11.5 per cent for large oil companies as against 12.1 for all manufacturing,[350] comparisons based on these asset figures are deceptive. Many companies capitalize into assets the expected future return from producing

348. This paragraph is based on Delbert J. Duncan, Ralph S. Alexander, James W. Partner, Charles I. Gregg and Leon A. Bosch, *An Economic Appraisal of Vertical Integration and Proposed Involuntary Divorcement of the Major Functional Activities of Integrated Companies in the Petroleum Industry*, Texas Co., New York, mimeographed, 1950, pp. 45–46, 60, 63.

349. Rostow and Sachs, "Entry into the Oil Refining Business," pp. 911–12.

350. First National Bank of New York, Monthly Letter, April issues.

lands, thus pulling the industry's published rate of return down toward normal levels.[351]

The largest oil profits in recent years have been in crude production.[352] They have been supported both by proration and by the special income tax allowance for depletion of up to 27½ per cent of gross, or 50 per cent of net, income from crude oil and gas. The purpose of this allowance is to stimulate exploration and drilling, on the theory — certainly a debatable one as applied to a wasting resource — that we need a profitable producing industry able to finance continuing exploration for new domestic reserves rather than oil in the ground in case war should cut off imports. In other words, it is specifically intended to make the profits in oil production higher than those in the average industry. The independents, it may be recalled, have a much larger share of domestic crude production than of refining. The few majors engaged in Middle Eastern production have a corresponding bonanza there — not without a political risk attached.

SUMMARY

1. The twenty largest integrated petroleum companies, often called the *majors*, accounted in 1955 for 47.6 per cent of domestic crude oil produced and 82.7 per cent of that refined, and owned over 80 per cent of two basic transportation facilities, ocean tankers and pipelines. The largest company had 6.1 per cent of crude production and 10.5 per cent of the refined output. The line between majors and large independents is an arbitrary one.

2. *Dissolution of the old Standard Oil Company of New Jersey* by antitrust action in 1911 broke up a corporation which at that time refined 80 per cent of the country's oil output. Chief Justice White's Supreme Court opinion established the lawfulness of big industrial corporations under the "rule of reason," but found Standard Oil's own restraints unreasonable. Within a few years Standard successor companies were making inroads on one another's territories. Competition was also stimulated by developments unconnected with the dissolution: discovery of crude oil in Texas and the Mid-Continent region beginning in 1901, and the rapid increase in gasoline demand from automobile users. A decline in the share of refining done by Standard Oil even before 1911, and a continued decline of successor companies as a group, indicate that the decree merely supported current trends.

351. Dirlam, "The Petroleum Industry," p. 263, note 57.

352. Compare McLean and Haigh, *The Growth of Integrated Oil Companies*, p. 146.

3. In 1923 the Supreme Court overruled the Federal Trade Commission's orders against *free leasing of tanks and pumps* to service stations conditioned on their use for the supplier's gasoline. This turn of events stimulated overexpansion of service stations, led to improvement of their physical equipment on average, gave a competitive advantage to large suppliers, and strengthened the connections between suppliers and dealers.

4. The present structure of the oil industry has been influenced by the attitude of the courts toward *mergers*, as exemplified by approval in 1931 of the Socony-Vacuum merger on the ground that the two corporations were complementary rather than competing. Most majors have developed in considerable part from such mergers of complementary units — especially Standard successor companies, which had first suffered in competition owing to their individual lack of a well-rounded position.

5. In the *cracking patents* case of 1931, the Supreme Court permitted four big companies to cross-license their patents as a legitimate way of settling conflicting claims, and as nonmonopolistic since only 26 per cent of gasoline output was covered. This encouraged the spread of technical information, although it also strengthened the position of the majors.

6. The flush production of California in the 1920s and Texas in the 1930s led to price cutting on gasoline by independent refineries built to process this abundant crude oil. Private *programs to stabilize gasoline prices* were set up in California and the Mid-Continent region and received the blessing of the National Recovery Administration in 1934. They rested on purchase of "distress gasoline" from the independents by the majors and on agreements as to selling contracts and practices. Through antitrust suits filed in California in 1930 and 1939 and in Wisconsin in 1936, these plans were outlawed. The Supreme Court decision in 1940 on the Madison case affirmed the illegality of all concerted activities affecting price, regardless of any state of distress in the industry involved. A large number of independent refineries whose existence had been threatened by the restrictions on crude oil production after 1933 finally closed down after the Mid-Continent buying program was halted in 1936; but economic forces would have caused their disappearance eventually in any case.

7. In the *Ethyl Corporation* case of 1940, the use of patent licenses to set resale prices was condemned by the Supreme Court, and jobbers not previously licensed were given access to ethyl fluid. Perhaps equally important to consumers was du Pont's entry as an independent producer after the basic patents expired.

8. Because of the huge investment and risk involved in constructing *pipelines*, nearly all the large ones have been built by the majors. Their efficiency as specialized transport agencies resulted in large profits for their owners until 1940, when the Interstate Commerce Commission ordered rates reduced to

yield not more than 8 per cent, and a consent decree restricted dividend payments to 7 per cent, of their valuation. Ensuing rate cuts, attributed by one authority chiefly to the ICC order, brought the average revenue per barrel-mile down by 14 per cent between 1940–41 and 1942–43 and tended to keep it from rising during the postwar inflation. Complaints of independent shippers against their treatment by major-owned pipelines have changed to complaints that pipeline owners do not buy all the independent's crude. The pipelines have not all found it easy to earn the 7 per cent return allowed them by law, but they are still built as units in integrated operations, and sometimes as independent firms relying on long-term space contracts with shippers.

9. Participation by oil companies in *international cartel arrangements* has led to antitrust action on two occasions. In 1942 a consent decree formalized the wartime dissolution of the patents agreement between Standard of New Jersey and I.G. Farben, the German chemical combine. The agreement apparently had mixed effects on technological progress in the United States. In 1952 an antitrust action was begun against five companies engaged in production abroad, charging that their agreements were beyond the bounds allowed by the Sherman Act. This raised the questions how far foreign conditions justified such agreements and how far the Sherman Act governed actions outside the country.

10. After 1935 nearly all the majors disposed of most of their directly operated service stations, but usually kept formal or informal *exclusive dealing* arrangements with their new dealer representatives. The Supreme Court held in 1949 that such contracts prevented other companies from competing for the stations' trade and were illegal if they covered a "substantial amount" of business. Most stations prefer in fact to handle only one brand of gasoline, and these decisions have not prevented many station owners from continued exclusive dealing in lubricating oil, tires, batteries and accessories to please suppliers or in fear of reprisals. It appears impossible to assure complete equality in access by A and B to C if A financed C's entry into business in the first place and regularly supplies his chief product. A (the major) cannot be forced to do business with C (the dealer) if C does not sell a satisfactory amount of A's products.

11. In the Supreme Court decision in 1951 on the Detroit *price discrimination* case, Standard of Indiana's price differential between retailers and jobbers was upheld against a Clayton Act charge, even though the jobbers used their advantage to cut prices through their own retail outlets in competition with other retailers. The Court accepted Standard's defense that good-faith meeting of competitive prices (those offered by competing refiners to its jobbers) was legal despite injury to competition (i.e., to the other dealers). The opposite decision would have been a blow to jobbers and would have made it hard for successful dealers to develop into jobbers in time-honored fashion, but

would have helped regular dealers. There is no ideal solution of the good-faith issue which will work in every situation.

12. The *National City Lines* decision of 1951 disallowed long-term contracts to purchase from supply firms that had helped the purchaser raise needed capital by subscribing to its preferred stock. The fact that a regulated public utility was the buyer tends to support the wisdom of the rule against monopolizing a market as applied in this case.

13. The frequent *state antitrust suits* going back to 1892 have not had a significant effect on the petroleum industry — some probably because they lacked merit, others certainly because the industry is an interstate one.

14. *Industry opinion on the antitrust laws* is on the whole favorable, but there is some complaint that they hamper constructive as well as restrictive cooperative action.

15. A decline in concentration in the petroleum industry preceded and followed the dissolution of Standard Oil in 1911, culminating in the present structure of majors and independents. Between 1926 and 1937 there was a *renewed trend toward concentration*, which then leveled off. No refiner controls as much as 35 per cent of the business in any state.

16. There are distinct *advantages of large-size operations and integration* in oil production, transportation, refining and wholesale marketing. Some writers, in stressing the important strategic advantages of integration, have slighted its definite contributions to efficiency. Small firms have held their own in many areas where prompt action and knowledge of local conditions are important; but, on the whole, big business is dominant in petroleum.

17. *Intercorporate connections* restricting competition in oil have been charged in two government reports which assailed, respectively, (1) "interest groups" said to control many oil companies and (2) interlocking directorates through banks, supply firms and industrial customers. The first charge seems no longer to fit the situation, however, and the two biggest companies are missing from the list of interlocks.

18. *Trade associations* in oil conduct the normal type of activity and are not directly concerned with price and competition. Charges of restraint of trade made by the government against the associations were not proved.

19. Despite much public suspicion, *competition* in the oil industry is vigorous in the opinion of close observers. However, the majors, with the reputations of their well-known brands to protect, are more interested in product and service competition and in selling drives than in foredoomed attempts to sell at a price differential below their large competitors. Thus price competition is very much subdued.

20. *Overexpansion in service stations* was apparent in the 1930s, but great numbers of little stations with low gallonage had disappeared by 1948. Monetary returns are still low, however, owing to ease of entry. If there were

fewer stations today, the lower overhead cost per unit would permit sale of gasoline more cheaply — provided dealers did not capitalize on their greater degree of local monopoly to keep prices up. It is doubtful that any gain to the average motorist here would seem to him to compensate for the resulting inconvenience in buying gasoline.

21. *Retail gasoline prices* of major brands are not absolutely uniform in all markets, since differences of a cent or less per gallon do not often induce enough consumer switching to make uniformity necessary. Some areas are fortunate in having off-brand gasoline on sale at two or three cents below the standard brands. Price stability is occasionally broken by retail price wars due to efforts to utilize idle filling station capacity, or to invasion of the market by new cut-rate retailers, or to shipments of surplus gasoline by a supplier. These are too spasmodic, and too destructive to small enterprises, to constitute a desirable form of competition; but at least their threat does have a tendency to prevent the retail price margin from being set and kept too high. The usual remedies — resale price fixing, concerted dealer action or state legislation — eliminate this good in price wars along with the harm.

22. *Prices of crude, and of refined products at wholesale,* tend to be uniform as a result of competition, except as there may be secret concessions and allowances. Each refiner fears being outbid in buying crude or undersold on products. There has long been a generally recognized "price leader" in each area, but a leader cannot make its price increases stick unless the rest of the industry believes it has assessed the situation correctly, and its reductions often represent merely recognition that the formal quotation is obsolete because of the prevalence of discounts.

23. *Proration,* based on an exemption from the Sherman Act given by the Interstate Oil Compact, is the program under which state regulatory commissions set the monthly allowable production of oil wells. It is intended primarily to conserve oil. It is also a strong price-supporting factor in crude oil, although production quotas are increased when inventories decline, thus giving prices a ceiling as well. One effect of early proration in the 1930s was to limit the unrestrained flow of crude oil on which some independent refiners depended, whereupon a number of them disappeared. Today, however, proration is favorable, if anything, to the competitive position of the small producers.

24. The purpose of *conservation* could probably be achieved in large part without the laws and regulations which now, under proration, limit production to "market demand." Physical conservation would itself be a price-supporting factor. One of the best approaches toward conservation is through unified development of oil pools, and this is becoming recognized as lawful in most circumstances under the Sherman Act. It is, however, usually blocked by unwillingness of some leaseholders to cooperate. Conservation is probably

well served by the fact that half the crude is produced by a handful of large firms that must make long-range plans.

25. The *decline of the independent refiner*, whose numbers have decreased sharply since the 1930s, has been due in part to the cutting off of the free flow of oil as a result of proration, but mainly to the advantages of size and integration in coping with the increasingly complex refining processes. Disappearance of independents through merger has not represented monopolizing tactics by the majors so much as it has the seeking of a refuge by the independents.

26. Although *jobbers* have apparently improved their share of the wholesaling of oil products since 1939, they lost in the gasoline market from 1936 to 1950, making it up in fuel oil. Independent jobbers have tended to give way increasingly to branded distributors who represent a single refiner and are thus assured of at least some supply in a time of shortage. Although there is no proof that the jobbers as a group have not made good money, they face handicaps in competition with the marketing departments of majors in having no backlog of profits from other departments to fall back on when competition in marketing is severe. Also, the more successful they are, the more profitable it is for the major to take over their territory — normally by buying them out.

27. In the nature of things, the *individual dealer* is more dependent on his supplier than the supplier is dependent on him. This has an advantage for the public, since high standards of retail operation are more likely to be imposed by the supplier than adopted individually by thousands of retail operators. It does mean that leases may sometimes be canceled without just cause; but a jobber or refiner will himself lose if he cancels a representative for other reasons than poor performance. The suppliers must find ways of making dealers feel that they are being treated justly, or face a solution imposed by legislation.

28. The petroleum industry has succeeded notably in its *competition with other fuels*. This competition is a factor which tends to control the prices of heating and fuel oils, though it scarcely touches gasoline or lubricants.

29. The *record of the industry* has been an outstanding one in expansion of production, reduction of price, advance in technology, level of wages and ease of entry into some branches. The reward of success, and of the tax subsidy given to oil production, has been reaped in the form of high profits.

In brief, the antitrust laws, by breaking up the old monopoly and forbidding price agreements, while permitting free leasing of equipment, pooling of patents, and rounding out of integrated companies through mergers, have helped shape the structure and behavior of this outstandingly successful industry.

CHAPTER 4

Chemical Manufactures

The American chemical industry had its real start around 1900, and by 1950 *Fortune* could call it the successor to automobiles as "the premier industry of the U.S."[1] In 1953 two far-ranging writers named it the world leader in both output and technical knowledge.[2] In 1955 "chemicals and allied products" had sales of $23.0 billion and an average of 813,000 employees during the year.[3]

Chemical Products and Processes

Less than half of the value added by manufacture in this field (which amounted to $9 billion in 1954) is in chemicals proper, such as acids, dyes, pigments or solvents. The larger part is in "chemical process" industries, which use these products to change the molecular structure of their raw materials. Although such process industries include glass, paper, rayon, sugar and many more, the Census classes as chemical "allied products" only drugs and medicines, paints, soap and some smaller industries. (See Table 17.) This chapter will deal with these allied products so far as companies producing chemicals have extended their operations into them, which is a good deal more in some products than in others.

The familiar classification of chemicals into inorganic and organic is based on the presence in the latter of the carbon atom. A second customary division is into "heavy" and "fine" chemicals. The former are produced in amounts of at least half a million tons a year and sold

1. "The Chemical Century," *Fortune*, March 1950, p. 69.

2. W. S. and E. S. Woytinsky, *World Population and Production*, Twentieth Century Fund, 1953, p. 1178.

3. Estimates by U.S. Departments of Commerce and Labor.

TABLE 17

CHEMICALS: VALUE ADDED BY MANUFACTURE, 1954

(*Millions*)

Product	Value Added by Manufacture
Total	$9,149
Industrial inorganic chemicals	1,235
Industrial organic chemicals (synthetic fibers, plastic materials, synthetic rubber and other)	3,166
Drugs and medicines	1,335
Soaps and related products	817
Paints and allied products	786
Gum and wood chemicals	67
Fertilizers	234
Vegetable and animal oils	395
Miscellaneous (toilet preparations, compressed and liquefied gases, and other)	1,114

Source: Advance reports, *Census of Manufactures*, 1954, covering "Chemicals and allied products."

in bulk at a low price. These are chiefly inorganic (examples are sulfuric acid, caustic soda, chlorine and synthetic ammonia), but a few organic chemicals (benzene, ethyl alcohol, methanol) are now "heavy." Fine chemicals, like drugs and dyestuffs, have a high unit value and are sold in small quantities. A third, or "vertical," classification yields the following:

(1) Basic chemicals — acids, alkalies, salts, tonnage organic chemicals, etc.

(2) Chemical products to be used in further manufacturing — synthetic fibers, plastic materials, solvents, colors and pigments, etc.

(3) Finished chemical products ready for consumption — drugs, cosmetics, paints, detergents, fertilizers, etc.[4]

The industry is producing its many thousands of products from relatively few materials. In 1945 it was reported that either water or air, or both, served as a material for nearly 100 of the 150 most important chemicals, with coal, sulfur, salt and limestone next in importance, all being used in 63 or more.[5] Mines, farms and forests all produce important materials. The original "batch" process of preparing the material, bringing about the desired chemical reactions, re-

4. *The Chemical Industry: Facts Book*, 1955, Manufacturing Chemists Ass'n., Washington, p. 13.

5. R. Norris Shreve, *The Chemical Process Industries*, McGraw-Hill, New York, 1945, p. 6.

covering the products and purifying them to meet specifications is being replaced increasingly by continuous flow methods under automatic controls. However, many synthetic organic chemicals are still made by a series of separate operations supervised by highly skilled labor.

The industry is widely dispersed, since it is tied more closely to markets than to materials. In 1953 only New Jersey accounted for over 10 per cent of the value added by manufacture; twenty-one other states accounted for at least one per cent each.[6]

The Big Chemical Companies

The giant of the industry has long been E. I. du Pont de Nemours & Company, and Union Carbide and Carbon Company is now the unchallenged second. Fifteen big corporations classifiable as chemical companies had sales and other operating revenues as of 1955 approximating $150 million a year or more; their combined total revenues amounted to $7.6 billion. (See Table 18.) Omitting soap and oils, since companies like Proctor & Gamble and Archer-Daniels-Midland are not in the list, the grand total of chemical industry sales can be estimated at roughly $20 billion in 1955. Of this aggregate, du Pont would have about 10 per cent, the four largest 22 per cent, and the fifteen largest (exclusive of estimated non-chemical revenues of several of the companies) perhaps 35 per cent. This is a moderate degree of concentration as manufacturing industries go.

Within subindustries — the manufacture of closely related groups of chemicals or products — concentration is necessarily greater. Thus, in 1947, four companies accounted for 75 per cent or more of the shipments of each of the following: cyclic (coal-tar) crudes (90.6 per cent), carbon and graphite products, compressed and liquefied gases, explosives, soap and glycerin, synthetic fibers, carbon black and synthetic rubber.[7]

Such concentration as exists in chemical manufacture is partially explained by the fact that the industry requires a huge investment of capital, both for research and manufacture. Corporate capital investment per production worker for 1951 was estimated at $22,866 as

6. *The Chemical Industry: Facts Book*, 1955, p. 59.

7. U.S. Census data, in *Study of Monopoly Power*, Hearings before Subcommittee on Study of Monopoly Power, House Judiciary Committee, 81st Cong., 1st sess., 1949, Serial 14 (hereafter called Celler Hearings), Part 2-B, p. 1446.

TABLE 18

CHEMICALS: SALES AND CHIEF PRODUCTS OF FIFTEEN LARGEST COMPANIES, 1955

Firm	Sales[a]	Some Important Products
	(Millions)	
Fifteen leading companies	$7,594.1	
1. E. I. du Pont de Nemours & Co.	1,941.4	cellophane, dyes, explosives, paints, plastics, rayon, synthetic fibers
2. Union Carbide and Carbon Co.	1,187.5	alloys and metals, carbons, industrial gases, petrochemicals, plastics
3. Allied Chemical and Dye Corp.	628.5	acids, alkalies, ammonia, dyes, plastics
4. Olin Mathieson Chemical Corp.	560.5	cellophane, firearms and ammunition, industrial chemicals, pharmaceuticals
5. Monsanto Chemical Co.	522.3	dye intermediates, phosphates, plastics, synthetic fibers
6. Dow Chemical Co.	521.6	chlorine, industrial chemicals, magnesium, plastics
7. American Cyanamid Co.	451.1	dyes, industrial chemicals, pharmaceuticals, plastics
8. W. R. Grace & Co.[b]	427.1	banking, fertilizer, plastics, steamship transportation, sugar
9. Food Machinery and Chemical Co.[b]	264.6	farm and industrial chemicals, machinery
10. Koppers Co.[b]	230.3	gas and coke, tar products, wood preserving
11. Hercules Powder Co.	226.7	cellulose products, explosives, resins
12. Chas. Pfizer & Co.	163.8	organic chemicals, pharmaceuticals
13. Rohm & Haas Co.	161.6	plastics, resins
14. Merck & Co.	157.9	biologicals, farm and industrial chemicals, pharmaceuticals
15. Air Reduction Co.	149.2	industrial gases, welding equipment

Source: Annual reports of the companies.

a. Sales for some companies include other operating revenues.

b. Food Machinery and Chemical Co. and Koppers are not included in many lists of chemical companies; but their chemical sales (48 per cent of the former's total and 65 per cent of the latter's) are large enough and growing fast enough to warrant their inclusion here. Chemicals account for a smaller percentage of W. R. Grace's revenues.

against $10,829 for all manufacturing.[8] Only oil refining and tobacco ranked higher.

Distribution

The variety of products sold is perhaps greater in the chemical industry than in any other, and the industry's dynamic nature has

8. *Conference Board Business Record,* National Industrial Conference Board, New York, December 1954, p. 484.

prevented the freezing of its distribution patterns. However, the great bulk of sales is either direct to industrial users, usually on contract, or through wholesale branches of the manufacturers.[9] Many chemicals are produced as by-products but depend for sales on their own rate of demand, so that the carrying of large field inventories is necessary.[10] Jobbers and other distributors supply the needs of many of the smaller customers by buying in carload lots and reselling in smaller quantities.[11]

The chemical industry is by far the principal purchaser and user of its own products. However, it was reported in 1953 to be the only industry in the nation selling its products to all seventy-two industry groups into which the Department of Commerce classifies the economy.[12] Its course is thus tending to become representative of that of industry as a whole, aside from its very much greater rate of expansion.

Antitrust Suits

Since the Department of Justice had brought approximately eighty antitrust suits against firms in the chemical and allied products industries before 1951,[13] only those of special significance will be discussed.

The "Powder Trust"

In 1872 seven manufacturers of explosives organized the Gunpowder Trade Association, whose principal aim was to moderate the competition resulting from the excess capacity and surplus stocks created by the Civil War. Popularly known as the "powder trust," this association added members until it included 85 per cent of the industry in 1881 and 95 per cent by 1902. It fixed prices and apportioned markets among its members. Meanwhile the two largest producers, du Pont and Laflin & Rand, had been buying out the smaller members until by 1902 they themselves constituted the Association, along with their jointly and separately controlled subsidiaries. Du Pont, which had been a leading maker of explosives since its formation in 1802, now bought Laflin & Rand and proceeded to consolidate all its

9. *Statistical Abstract of the United States*, 1952, compare totals on pp. 774 and 879.

10. W. Cameron Caswell, "You Decide: Competitors or Partners," *Chemical Week*, November 1, 1952, p. 22.

11. *Chemical Week*, June 7, 1952, p. 38.

12. *The Chemical Industry: Facts Book*, 1953, p. 7.

13. See index under various headings from Ammonia to Vitamins in Commerce Clearing House, *The Federal Antitrust Laws with Summary of Cases Instituted by the United States, 1890–1951*, Chicago, 1952, pp. 385–403.

sixty-four acquisitions into its own corporate structure. High prices soon began to attract new firms into the industry, and some of them stayed despite du Pont's reversion in 1905 to a low-price policy.[14] In 1907 du Pont was producing from 64 to 74 per cent of the country's supply of each of five types of explosives and 100 per cent of the privately produced smokeless military powder.[15] Although the company's aim had been the elimination of competitors, its procedure of concentrating output in larger, more efficient plants did result in lower costs and lower prices.

In 1907 the Department of Justice filed a Sherman Act suit against du Pont, relying heavily on papers copied by one of the firm's employees who had left to become a competitor. Both the mergers and trade association activities were cited as offenses. In June 1911 the U.S. Circuit Court for Delaware sustained the government's contention.[16] The two parties next worked out a dissolution proposal which the Court accepted in 1912.[17] Hercules Powder Company and Atlas Powder Company were created to take over eleven and ten, respectively, of du Pont's forty-one plants. At the request of the Departments of War and the Navy, the two smokeless powder mills were left with du Pont. Du Pont was also required to furnish technical information for five years at reasonable cost to the new firms. Their securities were distributed among its stockholders, but 50 per cent of the stock which went to each of the twenty-seven individuals who had been trial defendants was stripped of voting power. A recent student considers it "certain" that these individuals still retained control of all three firms; [18] but, if so, this control gradually faded as time passed and new shareholders replaced old ones. In 1914 a jury found no cause for action in a treble damage suit which the government's original complainant and star witness brought against du Pont.[19]

14. Edward William Proctor, *Antitrust Policy and the Industrial Explosives Industry*, unpublished doctoral thesis, Harvard University, Cambridge, 1951, p. 86.

15. William S. Dutton, *Du Pont: One Hundred and Forty Years*, Scribner's, New York, 1949, p. 194.

16. *U.S. v. E. I. du Pont de Nemours & Co.*, 188 Fed. 127 (D. Del. 1911).

17. U.S. Department of Justice, *Decrees and Judgments in Federal Antitrust Cases*, 1918, pp. 193–206; *A History of the du Pont Company's Relations with the United States Government, 1820–1927*, E. I. du Pont de Nemours & Co., Wilmington, 1928, quoted in Norman Bursler, *The du Pont Industrial Group*, Association of American Law Schools, University of Pennsylvania Law School, Philadelphia, mimeographed, 1951, p. 9.

18. Proctor thesis, p. 320.

19. See *Buckeye Powder Co. v. E. I. du Pont de Nemours Powder Co.*, 196 Fed. 514 (D. N.J. 1912).

The Later Explosives Industry

In 1913 du Pont was left with about 32 per cent, and Hercules and Atlas with 12 per cent each, of dynamite capacity and the three respectively with 32, 11 and 10 per cent of black powder capacity.[20] Black powder, which had been the principal product, was becoming obsolete; by 1919 all but one of the six black powder plants assigned to Hercules in the decree had ceased operation. Dynamite capacity increased only from 520 to 580 million pounds between 1913 and 1950; but Hercules and Atlas increased their shares to 21 per cent each, while du Pont's share declined, to 23 per cent.[21] Each had made several acquisitions, and in 1921 the District Court, in approving the purchase of Aetna Explosives Company by Hercules, held that competition existed among the three successor companies. Their domestic dynamite *sales* were 73 per cent of the total in 1913, and 76 per cent in 1947, so their plants must have operated more continuously than those of other firms. The largest among their thirty or forty competitors was Olin Mathieson.

There have been writers who have contended that Hercules and Atlas are "tied very closely to the parent company by patent agreements and by mutual membership in cartels"; [22] that the court in 1912, by permitting as few as three firms to share the du Pont assets, missed a golden opportunity to create effective competition; [23] and even that this suit was "one of the outstanding farces of American judicial history." [24] A myth that the three companies are still united was bolstered by the fact that the Hercules and Atlas offices were in the same building, within a block of du Pont, until Atlas recently moved to a Wilmington suburb.

Although there is in fact competition in explosives, it can be characterized as "stabilized." Price cutting is frowned on; prices change rarely and are usually identical; and competition takes the form of rivalry in "technical service" offered by the hundreds of highly trained salesmen or service men sent out by the producers. One small com-

20. Proctor thesis, p. 313.

21. *Ibid.*, p. 468. Page 490, evidently using a different base, gives du Pont 30 per cent of capacity.

22. Joseph Borkin and Charles A. Welsh, *Germany's Master Plan*, Duell, Sloan & Pearce, New York, 1943, p. 87.

23. Proctor thesis, pp. 349, 506.

24. John K. Winkler, *The du Pont Dynasty*, Reynal and Hitchcock, New York, 1935, p. 167.

petitor reports that, as long as he keeps his share of sales below 3 per cent, he can get the technical help he needs from the big firms.[25] A good deal of the market is also pervaded by "reciprocity": "you buy my dynamite if you want me to buy your steel" or "you buy my coal if you want me to buy your dynamite" [26] — although the companies claim that here and in other chemical products "reciprocity" is a nuisance they would like to eliminate. Nevertheless, opinion in the industry is that the rivalry of the three firms has led to a much more rapid development of the arts of blasting than would have occurred if the three had stayed as one and not had large competitors to "shoot at." [27]

The 1943 Explosives Decree

In 1941 the Department of Justice began an investigation of the explosives industry. When a Norfolk grand jury refused to indict the six chief manufacturers of commercial explosives and blasting supplies, the Department took the extraordinary step of seeking an indictment in another jurisdiction. A Philadelphia grand jury obliged in June 1942. The charges were that the defendants had violated the Sherman Act by agreements (1) to sell at identical prices and discounts, (2) to establish a zone price system, (3) to maintain resale prices, and (4) to refrain since at least as early as 1938 from trying to sell to each other's "key" jobbers.[28] In February and March 1943 the defendants pleaded *nolo contendere* and paid fines. The explanation of one defendant is that the fines were trivial compared to the probable direct and indirect cost of defending the suit; and that there would be nothing lost by agreeing to refrain from practices in which it claimed never to have engaged.

The suspicion of an agreement is alleged to have been based on misinterpretation of remarks of salesmen, such as: "we always meet the X company's prices" or "Y is X's jobber and I don't [waste my time trying to] sell to him." The dynamite manufacturers thereafter told their salesmen: "Don't ever say 'the Wilmington companies' "; and "avoid talking with competing salesmen." One at least ceased collecting figures on the sales of its competitors and now relies on the

25. Proctor thesis, pp. 431–32.
26. *Ibid.*, pp. 406–09.
27. Compare *Wall Street Journal*, June 8, 1954, pp. 1, 7.
28. *U.S. v. E. I. du Pont de Nemours & Co.*, Cr. 9733 (E.D. Pa. 1942).

Bureau of Mines industry totals. There have been no significant changes in the methods of doing business, possibly because the government failed to insist on a strong enough decree [29] or perhaps because the practices for which the companies paid fines had not in fact seriously limited competition.

From Explosives into Chemicals

The government's antitrust suit of 1907 may have been one factor which prompted the fateful decision of the du Pont executives to branch out into other chemical manufactures beyond the field of explosives. It was safer to expand into some other field than the one which was under legal attack. Lammot du Pont called this a "very powerful influence." [30] The executive committee of du Pont had, however, decided in 1908 to anticipate possible government manufacture of its own powder by entering other lines which made use of the chief raw material, nitrocellulose.[31] The first step was taken in 1910 when du Pont acquired the Fabrikoid Company, manufacturer of artificial leather.[32] In World War I, du Pont made large war profits from the sale of explosives, and looked for a field of investment in which it could utilize its knowledge of chemistry. There was at this time an evident need to create a domestic dyestuffs industry, in order to relieve the nation's dependence on Germany for dyes, and du Pont entered this field. In 1918 it also purchased 23 per cent of the common stock of General Motors, and in 1920 another block. It continued to expand into such areas as paints and lacquers, rayon, cellophane, nitrogen, synthetic fibers and many others.

Hercules Powder Company, when it found itself after 1918 with plenty of cash but a suddenly reduced market for explosives, first selected the naval stores industry and then cellulose products as fields in which its chemists could employ their knowledge of nitrocellulose. Hercules, like du Pont, has become a diversified chemical company, also expanding but never passing 10 or 15 per cent of the giant company's size. Explosives now make up less than 15 per cent of its

29. View of Proctor thesis, p. 377.

30. Cited in William Haynes, *The American Chemical Industry: A History*, Vol. 3, "The World War I Period, 1912–1922," Van Nostrand, New York, 1945, p. 189, note *.

31. *U.S. v. E. I. du Pont de Nemours & Co.*, 126 F. Supp. 235, 265–66 (N.D. Ill. 1954).

32. E. I. du Pont de Nemours & Co., *Du Pont: The Autobiography of an American Enterprise*, Scribner's, New York, 1952, p. 62.

sales. Although explosives play a larger role in the Atlas Powder Company, this firm, too, has become a chemical company of broadening interests. It has deliberately spread its risks and opportunities into four other areas: industrial chemicals for the manufacture of products like cosmetics and detergents; activated carbons for many uses; industrial finishes for lacquers, enamels and the like; and plastic-coated laundry roll covers.[33]

Du Pont would surely have diversified after World War I even if no antitrust suit had been brought, since explosives no longer offered the expanding opportunities of the nineteenth century. However, the creation of two additional centers of research and enterprise in nitrocellulose chemistry is attributable to the 1912 decree.

Four Federal Trade Commission Orders

Orders were directed by the Federal Trade Commission against four branches of the industry as a result of developments in the 1930s. Trade association activities, including circulation of price lists, constituted much of the evidence. In January and July 1938 and May 1940, respectively, the Commission charged the nine principal manufacturers of liquid chlorine with price agreements and other understandings since 1931,[34] the four makers of flake calcium chloride with such restraints since November 1937,[35] and about thirty makers of agricultural insecticides and fungicides with restraints since 1934.[36] The first two groups accepted the Commission's statement of facts and its cease and desist order in December 1938. Most of the insecticide group did the same in July 1942, but six denied that they had been involved. The Second Circuit Court rejected their appeal, with Judge Thomas W. Swan pointing out that the courts may not substitute their own inference from the facts of a case if the one drawn by the Commission is "permissible." [37] The Commission did make one concession to the respondents, by limiting its order prohibiting cooperation in "any common course of action" to "any agreed or planned common course of action." [38]

33. *The Atlas Story*, booklet, Atlas Powder Co., Wilmington, 1951, pp. 12–18.
34. *Mathieson Alkali Works*, Docket 3317, 27 FTC 1413 (1938).
35. *Columbia Alkali Corp.*, Docket 3519, 27 FTC 1354 (1938).
36. *Agricultural Insecticide and Fungicide Ass'n.*, Docket 4145, 35 FTC 201 (1942).
37. *Phelps Dodge Refining Corp. v. FTC*, 139 F. 2d 393, 395 (2d Cir. 1943).
38. Docket 4145, 38 FTC 609 and 39 FTC 518 (1944).

The fourth case involved dry ice, sold to makers and distributors of foods and soft drinks. Since "economical distribution of solid carbon dioxide suggested a number of plants strategically located around the country, a factor seconded by the accompanying sale of CO_2 gas in heavy returnable cylinders," [39] Pure Carbonic, Inc. (an Air Reduction subsidiary), and Liquid Carbonic Corporation strove for national distribution by purchasing thirty-one competitors and contracting to market the output of thirty others. By 1940 only one third of the country's sales remained in the hands of small local firms. That these sometimes "lived dangerously" was illustrated by the experience of one in Los Angeles that reduced its price from $50 to $37.50 a ton in 1936. In September 1937 the two large producers simultaneously cut their Los Angeles price from $40 to $30, while selling at $55 in San Diego and San Francisco. The small firm closed its doors at the end of 1937, and in July 1938, again simultaneously, the big companies raised their Los Angeles price to $40.[40]

In March 1945 the Commission filed its complaint under Section 5 of the Federal Trade Commission Act and Section 2 of the Clayton Act as amended. In June 1948 respondents agreed to a cease and desist order on condition that the Clayton Act charge be withdrawn. This order forbade the purchase of competitors, contracts to market their output, price fixing, division of territories, discrimination among customers, and cutting prices in one area while maintaining them in another. According to a later statement of the Commission, the proceeding "gave relief" both to smaller producers and to those customers that had been discriminated against in price.[41]

The Department of Justice filed a civil suit the same month as the Commission's order against the same defendants, charging monopolization through control of patents and the primary product. Four years later a consent decree was issued in the Eastern New York District running in about the same terms as the order, but with a few added points such as appointment of a trustee to sell two Liquid Carbonic plants.[42] Since no bidders appeared within a year, the Court

39. Haynes, *The American Chemical Industry*, Vol. 5, "Decade of New Products, 1930–1939," 1954, p. 184.

40. *Pure Carbonic, Inc.*, Docket 5143, 44 FTC 1029, 1053 (1948).

41. FTC, *Monopolistic Practices and Small Business*, Staff Report for Subcommittee on Monopoly of Senate Small Business Committee, 1952, p. 55.

42. *U.S. v. Liquid Carbonic Corp.*, Civil 9179, Commerce Clearing House, *1952 Trade Cases*, No. 67248 (E.D. N.Y. 1952).

ordered the company to stop manufacturing at these plants. This novel order was reversed without an opinion by a 6–2 vote of the Supreme Court.[43] One plant, on Long Island, was later sold for real estate development, a result which no doubt helped other carbon dioxide producers but not consumers. Air Reduction, which had built four new plants, was reported in 1954 to account for over 50 per cent of the United States output of solid, liquid and gaseous carbon dioxide.[44]

The Borax Monopoly

One set of antitrust suits developed out of the exploitation of the mineral resources in the dry bed of Searles Lake, in southeastern California.[45] Part of the area was covered by 1912 mining claims which passed into the ownership of the American Potash and Chemical Corporation. When potash imports were cut off in World War I, development of these deposits became a matter of national interest, and in 1918 the Interior Department allowed ten lessees to try their luck. After the Armistice, all but the West End Chemical Company and the Burnham Chemical Company succumbed. The latter was not able to start selling borax, the product it first developed, until June 1928. But in that month the other producers of borax cut prices from $60 to $16 a ton. This forced Burnham to halt production, as its cost was $26 a ton, and soon to surrender its lease for inability to pay the rental.

The matter came into the courts in September 1944, when wartime seizure of the stock of the German-owned American Potash and Chemical Corporation had given the Department of Justice evidence of a price agreement between this company and Borax Consolidated, a British firm with a large California production through its subsidiary, Pacific Coast Borax Company. The government made this agreement, together with monopolization of the world supply of borax, grounds for criminal and civil proceedings. The defendants pleaded *nolo contendere* and paid fines. They also accepted a consent judgment which forbade price, output and market agreements, enjoined Borax Consolidated from acquiring any additional properties at Searles Lake,

43. *Ibid.*, 123 F. Supp. 653 (E.D. N.Y. 1954), reversed 350 U.S. 869 (1955).

44. Throop Wilder, "Air Reduction Co.," *Barron's*, August 23, 1954, p. 16.

45. This account is taken from the testimony of George B. Burnham, pp. 24–39, statements by Joseph W. Burns, attorney for American Potash and Chemical Corp., pp. 69–78, maps presented by Mr. Burnham, pp. 78–80, and a letter from Secretary of the Interior Oscar L. Chapman, pp. 80–85, in Celler Hearings, Part 5.

and required it to sell four mining claims with the improvements on them.[46] A coincident rise in the price of borax, however, yielded the producers several times the amount of the fines!

A further suit was filed against American Potash and Chemical under the antitrust provision of Section 27 of the Mineral Leasing Act of 1920. The result was another consent decree. Finally, treble damage suits filed by Burnham Chemical and another small firm failed because of the California statute of limitations.[47] This failure led to agitation for a statute of limitations of uniform and longer duration, or for reopening of such a case whenever a "discovery" like that of the Department of Justice in 1944 was made.

None of these suits disturbed the control of 97 per cent of the world's known supply of natural borax, which was then held as follows: Borax Consolidated, 55 per cent; American Potash and Chemical, 30 per cent; and West End Chemical Company, 12 per cent. Between its prewar peak year, 1937, and 1953 United States borax production doubled as a result of rising demand for its old uses as a flux in making glass and ceramics and the discovery of scores of new industrial and agricultural uses.[48] Borax Consolidated is reported to account for about two thirds of total production, American Potash and Chemical for about 20 per cent, and West End Chemical — now a division of the Stauffer Chemical Company — for nearly all the remainder.

Antitrust and the Fertilizer Industry

The antitrust experience of the fertilizer industry began in May 1906, when about sixty producers were indicted for allegedly restraining trade; but the indictment was abandoned as to the various defendants in July and September 1908.[49] The Department of Justice had better luck with its information filed against thirty-nine members of the industry, accounting for 85 per cent of its product, in December 1926. Thirty-seven of them conceded the illegality of agreeing to base

46. *U.S. v. Borax Consolidated Ltd.*, Cr. 28900–S and Civil 23690–G (N.D. Calif. 1944), Final Decree, *1944–1945 Trade Cases*, No. 57409 (1945).

47. *Burnham Chemical Co. v. Borax Consolidated, Ltd.*, 170 F. 2d 569 (9th Cir. 1948), certiorari denied 336 U.S. 924 (1949). See also *Suckow Borax Mines Consolidated, Inc. v. Borax Consolidated, Ltd.*, 81 F. Supp. 301 (N.D. Calif. 1948), 185 F. 2d 196 (9th Cir. 1950), certiorari denied 340 U.S. 943 (1951).

48. See *Wall Street Journal*, September 10, 1954, pp. 1, 6.

49. *U.S. v. Virginia-Carolina Chemical Co.*, 163 Fed. 66 (M.D. Tenn. 1908), *Decrees and Judgments*, pp. 689–91.

their selling prices on quotations at certain ports of import, plus freight from those ports, even when their shipments originated elsewhere. They pleaded *nolo contendere*, and paid fines which the Court made small in view of the severe losses the industry was at that time suffering.[50]

Under the National Recovery Administration, the industry adopted an open price system, which it asked the Federal Trade Commission in vain to approve as part of a proposed code of fair trade practices after NRA expired. Although the industry made no secret of how this system worked, since it considered the arrangement legal, it ran into an indictment under Section 1 of the Sherman Act in 1941. Ninety-nine fertilizer companies pleaded *nolo contendere* and paid fines aggregating $260,000.[51]

Some of the largest producers of mixed fertilizer own deposits of phosphate rock, which is the principal source of phosphorous and which they sell as rock or in treated or mixed form.[52] Their easy dominance of the world's export markets for phosphate rock was disturbed by the end of World War I and the simultaneous development of new deposits in Morocco. In 1919 rock producers took advantage of the Webb-Pomerene Act of 1918 to set up two export associations. These made agreements dividing markets with the French and other foreign producers, and this close cooperation on these export matters undoubtedly facilitated a similar cooperation, even if a tacit one, on domestic trade. Observers have noted that phosphate rock prices remained on the whole stable during the 1920s and 1930s, reflecting absence of price competition. This did not mean that large profits were being earned, however, since the industry lost money during most of these years of depressed farm purchasing power.

In 1944 the Federal Trade Commission recommended to the two Webb Act associations that they withdraw from quota agreements with foreign producers and abrogate all import restrictions and discriminations against nonmembers. The agreements and restrictions had been in abeyance since the beginning of World War II, and the associations made no objection to the Commission's requests. The Phosphate Export Association proceeded to dissolve in October 1945,

50. *U.S. v. American Agricultural Chemical Co.*, Cr. 9565 (D. Md. 1926); Arthur Robert Burns, *The Decline of Competition*, McGraw-Hill, New York, 1936, p. 297, note 4.

51. *U.S. v. National Fertilizer Ass'n., Inc.*, Cr. 1167 (M.D. N.C. 1941).

52. See FTC, *Report on the Fertilizer Industry*, 1950, pp. 54–84.

while the Florida Hard Rock Phosphate Export Association (which had only three members) continued to operate, but in obedience to the Commission's recommendations.

The Potash Cartel

Antitrust proceedings have been brought against suppliers of all three principal fertilizer materials. In potash, imports dominated the market until the late 1930s, and the first case was against the Franco-German cartel from which virtually the entire supply came.[53] The complaint was filed in April 1927, and in 1929 a petition by the French Ambassador denying American court jurisdiction over an instrumentality of the French Republic was rejected and a consent decree was signed. The solution found, and in fact already put into effect in May 1927, was the organization of a Dutch company through which the cartel could sell and which could "do exactly what the decree enjoined the parties from doing in the United States." [54]

Meanwhile the 128 domestic producers that had sprung up when imports were cut off during World War I had shrunk to one. This was the American Potash and Chemical Corporation, using brine from Searles Lake in California, and secretly controlled by the German cartel between 1929 and 1942. In 1928 extensive potash deposits were found at Carlsbad, New Mexico, and in 1931 and 1934 the United States Potash Company (British-controlled) and the Potash Company of America, respectively, began operation. In September 1938 these three producers formed the Potash Export Association for the purpose of negotiating with the potash cartel for an export quota in Europe. In view of the German control of one of the American concerns, its motivations were probably conflicting. However, the negotiation constituted a recognition of the practical facts of doing business in Europe:

> An attempt to break into the available foreign markets by price cutting would be undoubtedly met by the cartel with retaliatory price reductions in those markets with a view to making the realizations obtained by American plants so low as to be unprofitable.[55]

In September 1939, at the request of federal officials, exports to Europe were halted to avoid a shortage at home.

53. *U.S. v. Deutsche Kalisyndikat Gesellschaft,* Eq. 41–124 (S.D. N.Y. 1927).

54. FTC, *Fertilizer* Report, p. 97.

55. Willard L. Thorp and Ernest A. Tupper, *The Potash Industry: A Report Submitted to the Department of Justice by the Department of Commerce,* mimeographed, 1940, p. 72.

Antitrust Action in Domestic Potash and in Nitrogen

In 1939 the Antitrust Division opened a broad investigation of potash and nitrogen. An indictment was quickly secured against the domestic potash companies. When they protested to Assistant Attorney General Thurman Arnold, he arranged to place the indictment under seal, and then asked the Department of Commerce to make an impartial investigation of the facts. The principal issue was the method of price quotation. As long as the market had been dominated by imports, western producers competing in the cotton belt had to meet the port quotation. In 1940 imports had dwindled because of the war. The Department of Commerce report, therefore, recommended that the industry (1) add to its list of the forty seaports used to quote prices the two domestic producing points, Carlsbad, New Mexico, and Trona, California; (2) establish a more elaborate seasonal discount system to induce summer ordering and equal monthly shipments thereafter; and (3) permit any buyer, and not merely fertilizer manufacturers and farm cooperatives, to purchase direct in carload lots.[56]

The three American producers and the importers agreed to these recommendations and, the indictment having been dismissed, accepted a consent decree enjoining any collusion — existence of which they denied, however.[57] Consumers closer freightwise to Carlsbad and Trona than to the coast, who accounted for about a third of the purchases,[58] thus obtained a saving in freight which the Department of Justice estimated at more than $200,000, or approximately one half of one per cent of the delivered cost of all potash[59] and presumably 1½ per cent of their own purchases. As domestic production increased, this change in basing points would probably have occurred eventually under market pressure.

In the case of nitrogen-bearing materials, the Department of Justice secured five indictments in September 1939, charging conspiracy to control output, prices and foreign trade. Consent decrees in 1941 forbade such practices and enjoined the Barrett Company, a subsidiary of Allied Chemical and Dye that had been acting as selling

56. *Ibid.*, pp. 80–92.

57. *U.S. v. American Potash and Chemical Corp.*, Cr. 105–184 (S.D. N.Y. 1939), Civil 8–498 (1940), Final Decree, *1940–1943 Trade Cases*, No. 56040 (1940).

58. Samuel P. Hays, "Potash Prices and Competition," *Quarterly Journal of Economics*, November 1942, p. 55.

59. Calculated from Jules Backman, *The Economics of the Potash Industry*, American Potash Institute, Washington, 1946, pp. 6, 19.

agent for more than 55 per cent of the total domestic consumption of sulfate of ammonia (including imports), from handling over 35 per cent.[60]

In 1940 du Pont and Allied Chemical controlled 87 per cent of the synthetic nitrogen industry and five competitors the rest. Ten ammonia plants were built by the government during the war, almost trebling the industry's capacity. Since few producers had the requisite experience, du Pont became the chief single operator. After the war, plants were sold or leased to Lion Oil Company (acquired by Monsanto Chemical Company in 1955), Spencer Chemical Company, Mathieson Alkali Works, Phillips Petroleum Company and (for conversion to manufacture of alcohol) Commercial Solvents Corporation. By September 1946 the "big two" had only 54 per cent of privately owned capacity.[61] Synthetic nitrogen was, however, an exception: on the whole the Surplus Property Act was little applied to chemicals.[62] Between 1947 and 1956 nitrogen capacity increased almost fourfold, largely in the form of anhydrous ammonia,[63] and the share of Allied and du Pont was by this time less than one third.

The Titanium Pigment or "National Lead" Case

The manufacture of paint pigment out of the oxide of titanium — a metal theretofore almost unused — was developed independently in France, Norway and the United States. National Lead Company acquired the American patents, and in 1920 entered a cartel agreement with Titan Company A/S, holder of the Norwegian patents. Each made the other its exclusive licensee, with Titan reserving the right to sell in the Eastern Hemisphere and National Lead in North America, while both could sell in South America. Du Pont, whose early research in this field had been unsuccessful, became a producer in 1931 by purchasing the pigment subsidiary of Commercial Solvents, which held the United States rights to the French patents. In 1933 du Pont and National Lead cross-licensed their patents. On the

60. *U.S. v. Allied Chemical and Dye Corp.*, Civil 14–320 (S.D. N.Y. 1941); *U.S. v. Synthetic Nitrogen Products Corp.*, Civil 15–365 (S.D. N.Y. 1941); *U.S. v. Imperial Chemical Industries (New York), Ltd.*, Civil 17–282 (S.D. N.Y. 1941); FTC, *Fertilizer* Report, Appendix 9, pp. 173–76.

61. FTC, *Fertilizer* Report, pp. 25–26.

62. Edward L. Allen, *Economics of American Manufacturing*, Henry Holt, New York, 1952, p. 169.

63. *Business Week*, March 17, 1956, p. 90.

advice of its antitrust lawyers, du Pont did not enter a formal division of territory, but the same end was reached through its company policy of not selling in the Titan Company markets.

Between 1920 and 1944 United States production of pigments (measured by pure titanium content) increased from 100 tons to 133,000 tons. National Lead, which by this time had acquired its Norwegian partner, was the chief producer; du Pont was close behind; and subsidiaries of Glidden Company and American Cyanamid accounted for about 10 per cent of the total. When requested, licenses had been granted to these firms to avoid the taint of monopoly. Canadian, European and Japanese output had been 23,000 tons in 1938; these producers had patent agreements with the two dominant interests.

Criminal and civil suits against National Lead and du Pont were filed by the Department of Justice in June 1943 and June 1944, respectively.[64] Only the civil case was brought to trial. In July 1945 Judge Simon H. Rifkind of the Southern New York District ruled that this "domination of an entire industry" was in violation of Sections 1 and 2 of the Sherman Act.[65] His remedial decree ordered the defendants to cancel their agreements and forbade any new contracts aimed to divide markets, limit exports or imports, or bar a third party from any market. The defendants were to grant nonexclusive licenses to all comers under all their patents relating to titanium compounds, then in force or taken out within the next five years, at a uniform and reasonable royalty and along with all necessary technical information. Finally, National Lead was required to sell its stock in four small foreign titanium companies, which thus went out of American control. The sale in Germany was under hardship conditions. The proceeds in England had to be put, under existing regulations, into British government bonds.[66] This was hardly National Lead's preference, but the sum involved was small. The Antitrust Division's hope that the decree would increase the amount of imports and exports has been disappointed.

In June 1947 the Supreme Court rejected the companies' appeal by a 7–0 vote and the request of the government for royalty-free licenses

64. *U.S. v. National Lead Co.*, 63 F. Supp. 513 (S.D. N.Y. 1945); 332 U.S. 319 (1947).

65. 63 F. Supp., at 532.

66. Walter Adams, "Dissolution, Divorcement, Divestiture: The Pyrrhic Victories of Antitrust," *Indiana Law Journal*, Fall 1951, p. 23.

by a 4–3 vote. The Court held (through Justice Burton) that to give free access to patents to all who wished "would discourage rather than encourage competitive research." [67] Justice Douglas, for the minority, pointed out that "Each dollar of royalty adds a dollar to the costs of the new competitor and gives the established licensor another dollar with which to fight that competition." [68] Each opinion reasoned logically; what caused the majority and minority to disagree was a difference in view as to what consideration should control. National Lead itself shared the minority view. Having discovered during the lawsuit that du Pont's research was ahead of its own, it saw that it would be on the paying rather than the receiving end. Correspondingly, du Pont is reported by sources close to the case to have been privately pleased with the dissolution of the patent agreements and its resulting right to charge royalties, even though it had fought the case because of the divestiture issue.

The Development of Titanium

The decree in the *National Lead* case has been criticized for not requiring each defendant to dispose of one of its two plants and to grant its patents without a royalty charge. According to this view, effective competition in titanium was unlikely to develop in opposition to two dominant firms.[69] Fortunately, these fears were not fulfilled. In 1955 a student of the industry wrote:

> Entry of new firms into the pigment branch, which is continuing to date, suggests that the change in patent licensing policy introduced at that time has been a significant influence in easing the barriers to entry.[70]

By the same token the failure to order plant divestiture has not blocked entry. Thus the choice of remedies was probably a good one: indifference to the ownership of existing plants as long as research was free, and licensing to all, but not without compensation. It may be added

67. 332 U.S., at 359.

68. *Ibid.*, at 368.

69. George W. Stocking and Myron W. Watkins, *Monopoly and Free Enterprise*, Twentieth Century Fund, 1951, pp. 311–12; Adams, "Dissolution, Divorcement, Divestiture," pp. 13–15; Sergei S. Zlinkoff and Robert C. Barnard, "The Supreme Court and a Competitive Economy: 1946 Term (Trademarks, Patents and Antitrust Laws)," *Columbia Law Review*, September 1947, pp. 947–48.

70. Francis G. Masson, "Structure and Performance in the Titanium Industry," *Journal of Industrial Economics*, July 1955, p. 227.

that one dictum in Justice Burton's opinion, quoted from the District Court, to the effect that "this exchange between two corporations, who between them controlled the entire market, becomes an instrument of restraint," [71] implied that exclusive cross licensing of patents between the two leading companies in an industry may itself be illegal. This principle is regarded as "most important" by one commentator.[72]

In the years since the *National Lead* decision, there has been great progress, beyond its use in pigments, in this "wonder metal" — light, strong, and resistant to corrosion and heat. "It took aluminum fifty years, and iron centuries," one writer points out, "to cover the technological ground traversed by titanium in less than five years." [73] Several big metal and chemical concerns entered the field. At the end of 1955 it was guessed that sales of rolled and fabricated mill products in 1956 would double the $60 million of 1955.[74] Government assistance on a large scale shares the credit for this advance with laborious research into ways of separating the metal from the ore; but the various facets of the *National Lead* case were a further aid, or at least not a hindrance.

Patent Agreements in Plastics

One of the several instances of patent agreements between American and European chemical companies which were attacked by the Department of Justice during World War II related to acrylic resins. These are thermoplastic materials capable of being cast into flat sheets, or molded or extruded under pressure. Much of the pioneering work in this field was done by the famous German trust I.G. Farben, A.G., and still more by Röhm & Haas, A.G., of Darmstadt, Germany. Before World War I Otto Haas, the nonscientific partner, became an American citizen and founded Rohm & Haas in Philadelphia to exploit in the United States the scientific discoveries of Dr. Otto Röhm. Imperial Chemical Industries, Ltd. (ICI), also made discoveries in this field and licensed the American rights to du Pont.

71. 332 U.S., at 328, quoting 63 F. Supp., at 532.

72. Lawrence I. Wood, "Patent Pools," in Jerrold G. Van Cise and Charles Wesley Dunn, eds., *How to Comply with the Antitrust Laws*, Commerce Clearing House, Chicago, 1954, p. 263.

73. Edmund L. Van Deusen, "Better Alloys on the Way," *Fortune*, February 1955, p. 135.

74. *New York Times*, December 27, 1955, p. 36.

Rather naturally — especially since Dr. Röhm had a substantial ownership in the Philadelphia firm — agreements dividing world markets were made among these various companies. In the United States seven patent interferences between Rohm & Haas and du Pont had to be settled in July 1939 by a mutual licensing arrangement. On the whole Rohm & Haas set the terms in the soft, sticky acrylates and du Pont in the hard, tough methyl methacrylates.[75] Du Pont agreed, until war demand for this plastic to replace glass in airplanes ended this provision in 1941, to produce only half as much of its Lucite industrial molding powder (or "polymer") as Rohm & Haas produced of its identical Plexiglas. Rohm & Haas did not want to invite suicide by giving a free hand in its own specialty to its powerful rival. In addition, Lucite prices followed the leadership of Plexiglas.[76] On the combination unit of powder and liquid ("monomer") now offered for sale as a substitute for rubber in making dentures, du Pont limited Rohm & Haas to two distributors and itself fixed the selling price.

Government intervention began with the issuance of subpoenas by the Department of Justice in April 1941, continued through widely publicized hearings before the Senate Committee on Patents that year and the next, and led up to indictments of both corporations in August 1942. The methyl-methacrylate indictment — in which three dental supply houses were co-defendants — was suspended until after the war and then dismissed. That in acrylics was pushed to a trial in Newark, at which the two corporate defendants and eight officers were found not guilty in June 1945.[77] Rohm & Haas realized, however, that the Department of Justice would have a lesser burden of proof in the civil suit it was preparing, and agreed in November 1948 to a consent decree.[78] This required it to cancel its patent agreements with the German companies, to license without charge all its patents in the acrylic field, to refrain from any price or market agreements in domestic or international trade, and to charge all buyers of the same product the same price irrespective of end uses.

75. George W. Stocking and Myron W. Watkins, *Cartels or Competition?*, Twentieth Century Fund, 1948, pp. 79–80.

76. E. V. Huggins, legal adviser of Rohm & Haas, testimony in *Patents*, Hearings before Senate Patents Committee, 77th Cong., 2d sess. (hereafter cited as Bone Hearings), Part 2, p. 906.

77. *U.S. v. Rohm & Haas Co.*, Cr. 877–C and 878–C (D. N.J. 1942).

78. *Ibid.*, Civil 9068, Final Judgment, in *1948–1949 Trade Cases*, No. 62334 (E.D. Pa. 1948).

A representative of one of the two American firms involved in this episode sums it up this way: "We had won the criminal trial, but it did not leave us unaffected. Even without a consent decree, we would not have renewed those agreements when it became possible to do so after the war." A representative of the other firm takes the same general position: "We won the case but it is a healthier economy without the kind of agreement that obligations to foreign partners suggested and the state of the patent law permitted at that time."

In 1956, impressed by the fact that American consumption of methyl methacrylate had doubled since 1949, ICI and Hercules Powder Company announced the establishment of a jointly owned company that would become a third producer.[79]

Price Discrimination against Dentures

The aspect of this case which attracted perhaps the most attention was the price disparity between acrylic materials sold to industry and for dentures.[80] Before 1939 Rohm & Haas sold industrial molding powder in 400-pound drums at 85 cents a pound, and the dental-grade powder in small containers at about $3 a pound. When du Pont patented a process of mixing monomer and polymer for dentures, Rohm & Haas had to take a license. The monomer and polymer were now packed in one-ounce or one-pound foil packages and sold under vacuum in pound containers at $13. The companies explained or might have explained that this and the industrial powder were not identical; that the denture had to be refined and packaged; that bulk products for industrial use normally carry a lower price than fine products for human consumption (compare industrial alcohol and rye whiskey!); and that three quarters of the much publicized $50 or more eventually paid by the dentist went to the mixers, distributors, dental supply houses and dental laboratories. It remained true, however, that only the existing monopoly (based on patents) permitted such a price disparity to exist. This was proved by the fact that so-called "bootleggers" bought the molding powder, "cracked" it, and

79. *Journal of Commerce*, July 18, 1956, p. 8.

80. On this episode, see Wendell Berge, testimony in *Scientific and Technical Mobilization*, Hearings before ("Kilgore") Subcommittee of the Senate Military Affairs Committee, 78th Cong., 1st sess., 1943, Part 6, p. 729; *idem*, *Cartels: Challenge to a Free World*, Public Affairs Press, Washington, 1944, pp. 28–30; George W. Stocking and Myron W. Watkins, *Cartels in Action*, Twentieth Century Fund, 1946, pp. 402–03; Walter R. Hutchinson, Bone Hearings, Part 2, pp. 717–21; E. V. Huggins, *ibid.*, pp. 910–11.

undersold the established distributors. One of the latter even urged Rohm & Haas to prevent this ruse by adulterating the powder with arsenic or lead so as to disqualify it under the Pure Food and Drug Act.

The prices for both monomer and polymer are much lower today, but are still identical between the two companies since the products are identical.[81] Rohm & Haas has become less interested in sale for dentures, leaving du Pont nearly the whole market. Even this price has come down sharply in spite of du Pont's near-monopoly. But what du Pont sells at about $1 (per pound today, not per one-ounce or 30-gram unit) is resold by the processor (after coloring, grinding, etc.) at about $5, then by the dental supply dealer at about $7.50, by the dental laboratory at $20 or $25 (per denture in this case, not per pound) and by the dentist at $100 to $200. This progression carries no implication of profiteering, for the costs of distribution and of careful processing, shaping and placing must be paid for. It merely shows how insignificant the decline in price of the basic material from perhaps 90 to 6 cents per unit becomes when the patient pays his bill. This saving itself is probably due more to the reduction in cost from mass production and further technical development than to the breakup of the patent agreements, since the "duopoly" (two-company control) still exists.

In April 1951 the Department of Justice charged another denture monopoly, held by the one firm big enough that du Pont felt it had to sell it the monomer in 1939.[82] A consent decree in July 1952 prohibited this firm from combining with dental laboratories to fix resale prices of its special product to dentists.[83] According to one dental laboratory representative, the increasing competition of the many other trade names would have put an end to any effective price fixing of this sort with or without such a decree.

Construing the Webb-Pomerene Act

The Webb-Pomerene Act of 1918 was not construed by any court until more than thirty years after its passage. In 1919 the newly formed United States Alkali Export Association (called "Alkasso") filed the required registration statement with the Federal Trade Com-

81. Price change reported in *Chemical Week*, March 10, 1956, pp. 69–70.

82. Walter R. Hutchinson, Bone Hearings, Part 2, p. 720.

83. *U.S. v. Luxene, Inc.*, Civil 66–124 (S.D. N.Y. 1951), Final Judgment, *1952–1953 Trade Cases*, No. 67325 (1952).

mission. In March 1944 it became the "guinea pig" for the first test case under the act, when the Department of Justice filed a civil suit charging Alkasso, California Alkali Export Association ("Calkex"), their respective members, and their foreign partner ICI, with various restraints prohibited by the Webb Act.

Judge Samuel H. Kaufman, of the U.S. District Court in New York City, handed down a sweeping decision against the defendants in August 1949. The decision, which was not appealed, held in essence that the protection extended by the Webb Act to "an agreement made or act done in the course of export by such association" did not permit "cartel agreements," since these were not part of "the course of export trade." [84] Such agreements, the decision further held, necessarily restrained the trade of any domestic competitor that attempted to sell independently into the foreign markets involved. In short, the Webb Act was intended to promote competition between American export groups and foreign producers, and not to promote agreements between them. Among the defense arguments thus overruled were the plausible ones that (1) agreements without which American goods could not penetrate into certain markets actually promoted export trade, and (2) the hearings and debates that preceded the Webb Act's passage indicated an expectation that the export associations would enter into such agreements — the law having been, after all, intended to sanction actions which would otherwise have been illegal.

Specific restraints of trade were listed by Judge Kaufman as follows: (1) The reservation of the United States as exclusive Alkasso territory in the Association's agreements with ICI had the effect of preventing the import of alkalies, to the detriment of American consumers. (2) Exports of alkali were controlled by contracts with members (and some nonmembers) designating Alkasso as exclusive sales agent, and by contracts with domestic buyers forbidding them to resell abroad. No exports went to parts of the world reserved to ICI and the Belgian firm Solvay & Cie. (3) Alkasso was used as a device to stabilize the price of caustic soda in the United States, since in times of surplus the Association made a special effort to export more, granted higher export quotas to its members, or increased the amount in storage. Success was shown by the high degree of domestic price stability from 1931 to 1944, whereas export prices fluctuated frequently and sharply (indicating dumping of the surplus).

84. *U.S. v. U.S. Alkali Export Ass'n.*, 86 F. Supp. 59, 70 (S.D. N.Y. 1949).

These international agreements had already been brought to an end by World War II. In the postwar world ICI was no longer so dominant in South American markets, and the American exporters themselves were strong enough that they no longer needed the agreements. This situation accounts for the present opinion in the industry that the case had no practical effect whatever. It is true that the plan might have been revived had it not been for the court decision, but there are several other reasons, as the Federal Trade Commission has pointed out, which help account for its non-revival.[85]

The Attorney General's National Committee to Study the Antitrust Laws, in its 1955 report, approved both this and the Webb Act section of the subsequent and similar *Minnesota Mining and Manufacturing* case [86] as demonstrating judicial alertness to confine export trade associations within strict limits.[87] The present function of such associations is most often to aid small exporters lacking individual facilities in entering the export trade successfully. Few large American corporations need their help.

The du Pont–ICI Agreements

As early as 1897 du Pont began to make agreements with the Nobel Dynamite Trust in England for division of markets and after 1907 for the exchange of patents and technical information. When ICI was organized in 1926 to include the four principal British chemical producers, these agreements were widened.[88] Du Pont expected in this way to receive help from the more advanced chemical technology of Europe, and aid in placing its products on the world market through licensing companies that were already operating there — thus sparing itself the problems involved in building plants abroad.[89] The Department of Justice concluded later that the technical parts of the agreements were merely a smokescreen to hide the division of export markets, and it viewed the jointly owned subsidiaries in several countries as examples of restraint of trade. This interpretation may have been

85. FTC, *Report on International Cartels in the Alkali Industry*, 1950, p. 44.

86. *U.S. v. Minnesota Mining and Manufacturing Co.*, 92 F. Supp. 947 (D. Mass. 1950).

87. *Report of the Attorney General's National Committee to Study the Antitrust Laws*, 1955, p. 113.

88. "The 'Grand Alliance': du Pont and ICI," Stocking and Watkins, *Cartels in Action*, pp. 448–65.

89. Lawrence P. Lessing, "The World of du Pont," *Fortune*, October 1950, p. 93; Stanley Vance, *American Industries*, Prentice-Hall, New York, 1955, p. 267.

one-sided, but the statement of one of the parties in 1923 that the agreement was "a camouflage" intended "to cover all relationships between the two companies" [90] seems to have exaggerated only moderately the scope of the relation. Competitors, at least, take the view that some of the agreements could be justified, but that they went too far and were too exclusive.

In June 1948 du Pont, as part of unsuccessful negotiations to obtain a consent decree, canceled its agreements with ICI.[91] It was said to be motivated at this time by fear that if it lost the case all its patents covered by the agreements might be thrown open to use by all comers, without royalties.[92] The trial court, in September 1951,[93] found that the original division of territories had not been necessary in order to share the benefits of technology and found the setting up of jointly owned companies to be in restraint of trade. Judge Sylvester Ryan decided not to rely on du Pont's renunciation, but to confirm and strengthen it by a court order. In May 1952 he filed an Opinion on Remedies, and in July a Judgment, to the following effect:

1. Du Pont must discontinue its joint interests with ICI in Argentina, Brazil and Canada and cease to act in concert with ICI in world markets. Chile was not touched, partly because the Court recognized that no American trade with Chile in the products handled by the joint venture was feasible. Du Pont must make all reasonable efforts "to promote in the world markets the sale and distribution of chemical products manufactured by it" and report on such steps annually for five years to the Court.

2. Defendants must license freely certain patents "misused" by inclusion in the agreements, plus improvements patented up to July 1955, at reasonable royalties, and give technical information at reasonable fees in return for a pledge by the licensee to keep the information secret for fifteen years. The most important of the du Pont patents included were those in nylon and sodium.[94] Du Pont in turn was allowed reciprocal licensing on all related patents taken out by its

90. Quoted in Stocking and Watkins, *Cartels in Action*, p. 448.

91. Bursler, *The du Pont Industrial Group*, p. 93.

92. Lessing, "The World of du Pont," p. 160.

93. *U.S. v. Imperial Chemical Industries, Ltd.*, 100 F. Supp. 504 (S.D. N.Y. 1951), 105 F. Supp. 215 (1952).

94. Du Pont Co., Annual Report, 1952, p. 19.

licensees before July 1950. The Department of Justice opposed this last in vain, presenting the following argument:

> If du Pont, the greatest chemical company in the world, is to be the beneficiary of a reciprocal licensing program, then it will have gained more from the decree than if du Pont were to have a special immunity from the antitrust laws and were to be free to make any patent agreement that it desires.[95]

Results of the ICI Suit: International Relationships

A noteworthy feature of this decree was the intervention of an American court, under American law, in various commercial and legal relationships in foreign countries. One reaction was the issuance by a British court, at the request of the assignee of the nylon patents in Great Britain, British Nylon Spinners, Ltd. (a joint subsidiary of ICI and Courtauld's, Ltd.), of an injunction against the restoration to du Pont and then free licensing of the patents in that jurisdiction.[96] The injunction is still in effect. A second reaction was a protest by Canadian newspapers — which may have contributed its bit to the growing suspicion in Canada that it is in danger of United States domination — against an order from abroad that required either du Pont or ICI to sell its shares in Canadian Industries, Ltd.[97] The Canadian interests holding 17.4 per cent of that company's stock were not at first pleased by this threat to the balance of power position which they held between the two big foreign concerns. There was, in general, a considerable reaction in legal circles in several countries against the District Court's extension of American sovereignty in this case.

Nevertheless, in 1954 the Canadian concern was eventually separated with success into du Pont Company of Canada, Ltd., and Canadian Industries, Ltd.[98] The former took over the production of nylon and cellophane, and the latter the explosive, farm chemical, paint, plastic and polyethylene production. The Canadian interests

95. *Memorandum of the United States on Provisions in Tentative Draft of Proposed Final Judgment* (in *U.S. v. Imperial Chemical Industries, Ltd.*, S.D. N.Y. 1952), p. 7.

96. *British Nylon Spinners, Ltd. v. Imperial Chemical Industries, Ltd.*, English case, 1952, cited in George Nebolsine, "Trade or Commerce . . . With Foreign Nations," in Section of Antitrust Law, American Bar Association, Symposium, Chicago, 1955, p. 65.

97. Six newspapers are cited in *Journal of Commerce*, September 23, 1952, p. 17.

98. *New York Times*, February 23, 1954, p. 38; du Pont Co., Annual Report, 1954, pp. 18–19; *Business Week*, January 21, 1956, pp. 98–100.

accepted an 18 per cent representation in each. Neither company made the other's products; but very shortly du Pont began importing paints and building an automobile finishes and explosives plant, while Canadian Industries began to make terylene (ICI's name for Dacron, which it first developed), which would compete with du Pont's nylon. In the view of a Canadian close to one of the companies, "they are both playing for keeps, and I would expect to see the competitive trend develop." He points out also that (1) the chemical industry in Canada had grown to a point where the du Pont-ICI partnership could not in any event have continued much longer; (2) Canada now counts on benefits from competition between the two giants; and (3) the immediate reaction of resentment occurred only in legal and top business circles and has now been replaced by a greater feeling of tolerance for Judge Ryan's decision. It should be added that du Pont of Canada was soon selling nylon and cellophane in world markets in competition with American du Pont. Eighty-two per cent of the profits of that operation or any other would of course go to the Wilmington corporation. The bulk of the output of the two Canadian companies is still noncompetitive, however; and in this sense the effects of the decree are not yet important. The Canadian market, in any case, is too small to support many competitors in chemicals.

The Argentine and Brazilian ventures were similarly divided.[99] These sweeping results of the antitrust suit are certain to have a significant effect in discouraging future international agreements of the du Pont-ICI sort. Du Pont and ICI have no relations for the present (aside from those of buyer and seller) except as permission may be secured from the District Court.[100] It might be thought that this situation would discourage desirable exchange of technical knowledge; but such exchange is not frowned on by the decree except on the large scale that had been practiced in this instance and that some in the industry itself argue was so broad as to threaten the free market. The net effect of the decree should be to discourage restrictions on competition.

Perhaps the decision had a "reverse twist" in stimulating the American chemical industry to a greater interest in a protective tariff, since it was "now prevented by the antitrust laws from taking part in any international market-sharing agreements to protect its domestic

99. Du Pont Co., Annual Report, 1953, pp. 15–16.

100. See *Business Week*, December 3, 1955, p. 135.

sales." [101] However, the industry had always been interested in protection since its early days when free trade, especially in dyestuffs, would have meant its stifling through imports from Europe. Any intensification of its interest could also be explained by the reaction to a sharp cut in duties on ammonia, methanol, phenol and some other products in 1947 and to Germany's reappearance as an exporter. If barriers are raised against its products, ICI will have another cause for complaint. After many years of the du Pont alliance, during most of which the company believes it gave more than it received, it found the union dissolved just when it expected to reap greater benefits.

Results of the ICI Suit: American Patents

The freeing of nylon patents by Judge Ryan's decree of 1952 was the concluding step in what might be called a "campaign" by the Department of Justice against these particular patents. The opening step has been reported very briefly by former Assistant Attorney General Thurman Arnold:

> I will give you an example, and I do this without criticism, because in nylon the du Ponts immediately upon suggestion of the Antitrust Division stopped the practice. When nylon was first put out, they were going to control the price of nylon right down to the purchaser and control the quantities of nylon that each person put out.[102]

Du Pont declines to make any comment on this episode. Later, according to reports in the trade, the Department of Justice kept trying to secure the freeing of the nylon patents as one part of a consent decree with the du Pont Company. Their release was always refused, since du Pont had invested $45 million in nylon research and $197 million in production facilities.[103]

Finally, during the course of this antitrust suit, but before Judge Ryan's decision against the company in 1951, du Pont negotiated with Chemstrand Corporation, a subsidiary of Monsanto and the American Viscose Company set up in 1949, to license it to make nylon.[104] The license when concluded provided Chemstrand with full technical information. It is reported in the industry that such information is well

101. "Chemical Protection," *The Economist*, London, February 20, 1954, p. 537.
102. Bone Hearings, Part 2, p. 970.
103. 105 F. Supp., at 222.
104. Du Pont Co., Annual Report, 1950, p. 15.

paid for; and consulting engineers who had been charging fees for information on chemical processes complained against this new, government-ordered competition.[105] It is likely that du Pont lost potential profits in thus assisting its competitors, as well as in dedicating the name "nylon" to general use and resorting to "du Pont nylon" for its own product. One possible explanation is that the company deemed it wiser to invest its available funds in its own new fibers, Dacron and Orlon, than to concentrate on an attempt to keep 100 per cent of the nylon market.[106] By 1954 three more companies were preparing to make nylon.[107] Besides the basic nylon patents which Judge Ryan had ordered freed, but which expired in 1955, du Pont voluntarily gave the companies certain improvement patents with a much longer life.

ICI, like du Pont, offered its American patents to new licensees as a result of the decree, and prospective licensees had to consider whether they wanted to go into competition with du Pont on some of these products or enter the manufacture of others which du Pont (when it had exclusive rights) had found not worth making at all. Although hundreds of these patents were said to be "important," the only ones that aroused "widespread interest" were those on polyethylene, which ICI had discovered twenty years before.[108] Union Carbide had already joined du Pont as a producer under a special wartime arrangement, and between the summer of 1952 and the spring of 1953 four other large companies (one primarily a liquor producer, another a camera and film maker) had paid ICI's down payment and royalty in return for the polyethylene patents, a production manual and technical help. At least two more chemical giants entered later. The sudden spurt in production, which threatened to develop into overproduction within two or three years unless consumption expanded in line with the hopes of the optimists,[109] was thus in part the consequence of this antitrust case.

The Cellophane Case

Cellophane was a French invention, for which du Pont took out the North American patent rights and received the secret manufacturing

105. *New York Herald Tribune*, November 2, 1951, p. 31.

106. See Lessing, "The World of du Pont," p. 112.

107. Edmund L. Van Deusen, "You'd Hardly Know Allied Chemical," *Fortune*, October 1954, p. 166.

108. "The Polyethylene Gamble," *Fortune*, February 1954, p. 136.

109. *Ibid.*, p. 170.

information in 1923. Research by du Pont created a moistureproof variety in 1929 which made cellophane for the first time a desirable packaging material for food products, and which outsold ordinary cellophane by nearly 2 to 1 in 1932 and by nearly 10 to 1 in 1950.[110] In 1925 two former employees of La Cellophane, the French company, used their knowledge to found a rival firm. Their American venture, named the Sylvania Industrial Corporation, became du Pont's only competitor in 1930. It used the latter's patents without permission until sued for infringement in 1932, when it agreed to take out a license. The license gave Sylvania a quota, which was to increase from 20 per cent of total output in 1933 to 29 per cent in and after 1942.[111] In the market, however, it had succeeded by 1950 in winning only 23 per cent.[112] Meanwhile, it had been bought, in 1946, by American Viscose Company, of which it is now the Sylvania Division.

In November 1946 the du Pont basic patent on moistureproof cellophane expired, and thirteen months later the Department of Justice filed a suit charging monopoly and demanding divestiture of some of du Pont's eight factories. The suit brought quick results, for the company's executive committee had approved the building of another cellophane factory in 1947 but reversed itself at two meetings held in the three months after the complaint was filed.[113] The management now approached the nine firms that had previously asked it for licenses, offering them technical information and the use of du Pont's many remaining patents at a moderate fee if they would enter the industry. When Olin Industries, Inc., which was not one of the nine, came to du Pont and accepted such an agreement, a third producer was established. Du Pont has made it clear that this transaction originated in the fear that it might lose the antitrust suit and be faced with divestiture of its proposed new factory directly after its completion.[114]

Du Pont, however, successfully defended the antitrust suit, at a cost which rumor puts as high as $3 million. Chief Judge Paul Leahy of the U.S. District Court in Wilmington, after spending all of 1953 studying the record of the two-year trial, ruled that (1) du Pont had not illegally monopolized cellophane, and (2) a monopoly of cellophane

110. *U.S. v. E. I. du Pont de Nemours & Co.*, 118 F. Supp. 41, 123 (D. Del. 1953).

111. *Ibid.*, at 152.

112. *Ibid.*, at 123.

113. *Ibid.*, at 171.

114. Du Pont Co., Annual Report, 1949, p. 15.

would be meaningless in any event, since this product was in active competition with other flexible packaging materials.

On the charge of monopolization, he pointed out that in May 1952 du Pont had only 67.3 per cent of production capacity,[115] and, more important, that the company had not achieved this position by illegal means. First, its position rested on patents. That the government should concede the validity of du Pont's patents and yet sue it as a monopoly a year after the expiration of the chief patent seemed to Judge Leahy an attempt, without any precedent whatever, to use the Sherman Act to repeal the patent law.[116] Second, du Pont's "intense research activity, market development and expansion of productive capacity" were not illegal means of monopolization.[117] Third, the government's claim that du Pont had successfully kept out competitors by agreements or otherwise did not stand up in court.[118]

Judge Leahy's Economic Analysis

This opinion is most noteworthy as the first thorough study of intercommodity competition in the annals of the law. Judge Leahy was impressed with the concrete testimony of defense witnesses on this topic, and the fact that "not a single market witness was called by the government." [119] His opinion gave extensive details on the battle of du Pont to win acceptance for cellophane and the counterattacks of the other materials, with the varying fortunes of contenders in the meat, candy, bread, cigarette and other markets. In 1949 cellophane accounted for 23 per cent of the flexible packaging market, with du Pont accounting for 18 per cent — as against 31 per cent held by waxed paper, 21 per cent by vegetable parchment paper, greaseproof paper and the type of finished greaseproof paper called glassine, 12 per cent by sulphite paper, 9 per cent by aluminum foil, and 4 per cent by five other types of chemical film.[120] Since the trial record closed, intensified competition for cellophane has come from three of these plastic films: polyethylene, acetate and vinyl.[121]

115. 118 F. Supp., at 174.
116. *Ibid.*, at 213–14.
117. *Ibid.*, at 216.
118. *Ibid.*, at 126–29, 181, 210–11.
119. *Ibid.*, at 198.
120. Calculated from *ibid.*, at 111.
121. *Wall Street Journal*, March 26, 1954, pp. 1, 10.

Judge Leahy's conclusion that du Pont did not monopolize cellophane in the Sherman Act sense should not be taken to mean that the company did not possess monopoly power over cellophane in the sense in which economists use the word. An article by Stocking and Mueller has pointed out that du Pont's profits were far greater on cellophane than on other products, such as rayon, in which it faced competition.[122] Certainly the purpose of a product patent, such as du Pont possessed on moistureproof cellophane until late 1946, is to give its holder a monopoly profit and thus stimulate innovation. A patentee may, nevertheless, find his product competing against substitutes, as du Pont found with cellophane. The failure of other packaging materials to reduce their prices while cellophane was broadening its market through its own price cuts has been held to be inconsistent with the theory that the products were competing.[123] Perhaps these substitutes did not "compete" in this sense against cellophane, but the same facts show that cellophane competed against *them.*

Judge Leahy concluded his opinion with the following statement concerning the course and results of du Pont's whole cellophane venture:

> The record reflects not the dead hand of monopoly but rapidly declining prices, expanding production, intense competition stimulated by creative research, the development of new products and uses and other benefits of a free economy.[124]

The Supreme Court's Cellophane Opinion: Economic Issues

The District Court's decision was sustained in a 4–3 vote of the Supreme Court in June 1956. Although Justice Frankfurter's concurring opinion expressed a preference for avoiding "social and economic issues" until some other case "inescapably" required it,[125] both the majority and minority opinions paid considerable attention to economic factors. The article by Stocking and Mueller was cited twice by the majority and three times by the minority.

122. George W. Stocking and Willard F. Mueller, "The Cellophane Case and the New Competition," *American Economic Review,* March 1955, pp. 57–63. See comment by Joel B. Dirlam and Irwin M. Stelzer, "The Cellophane Labyrinth," *Antitrust Bulletin,* February–April 1956, pp. 633–51.

123. Stocking and Mueller, "The Cellophane Case and the New Competition," pp. 55–56. Compare 118 F. Supp., at 84.

124. 118 F. Supp., at 233.

125. *U.S. v. E. I. du Pont de Nemours & Co.,* 351 U.S. 377, 414 (1956).

The opinion of the Court, delivered by Justice Reed, was based on the position that the market under discussion was not the market for cellophane, but for flexible packaging.

> In considering what is the relevant market for determining the control of price and competition, no more definite rule can be declared than that commodities reasonably interchangeable by consumers for the same purposes make up that "part of the trade or commerce," monopolization of which may be illegal.[126]

Chief Justice Warren's dissenting opinion took direct issue:

> . . . the formula of "reasonable interchangeability," as applied by the majority, appears indistinguishable from the theory of "interindustry competition." The danger in it is that, as demonstrated in this case, it is "perfectly compatible with a fully monopolized economy." [127]

Carrying this thought further, a company that deliberately acquired a monopoly position in cellophane for the sake of exploiting those uses in which it met the least competition (such as cigarette wrapping), or that similarly monopolized any other commodity with close substitutes for some but not all uses, would under the majority's view have escaped the Sherman Act.

Where the minority's position was weakest was in its handling of du Pont's defense that, even if it held a monopoly, it was one protected by valid patents. The dissenters considered that the patents were tainted and showed no great merit, at least on the part of du Pont. The taint came from the concession made by du Pont in 1923, when it promised La Cellophane, in return for North American patent rights, not to sell elsewhere, and from du Pont's willingness in 1932 to give the infringer, Sylvania, a limited share of the market. The minority's position is a severe one, which allows no "rule of reason" in such cases. It assumes that du Pont should have refused to introduce cellophane into the United States altogether rather than accede to La Cellophane's timidity about licensing a giant American firm to compete in its own home market, and it assumes — and in fact stated explicitly — that a patentee faced with infringement should file suit and give the courts a chance to hold the patent invalid rather than permit a second firm to share, on a percentage basis, the "exclusive

126. *Ibid.*, at 395.

127. *Ibid.*, at 424, quoting Walter Adams, "The Rule of Reason: Workable Competition or Workable Monopoly," *Yale Law Journal*, January 1954, p. 364.

right" guaranteed to the patentee by the Constitution. As to the merits of the patent, the dissenters, disregarding Judge Leahy's finding that between 1924 and 1950 du Pont had spent $24.4 million on "cellophane technical activities expense," [128] declared that once du Pont possessed the basic cellophane process, "development of moistureproofing was relatively easy." [129] Since the patents could thus be ignored, the minority saw no excuse for du Pont's near-monopoly in cellophane, and accordingly laid down a broad generalization:

> If competition is at the core of the Sherman Act, we cannot agree that it was consistent with that Act for the enormously lucrative cellophane industry to have no more than two sellers from 1924 to 1951.[130]

Du Pont as an Antitrust Target

Few if any companies in any industry have been the object of as many antitrust suits as du Pont. Between 1939 and 1948 it was named as defendant or co-defendant in no less than nineteen.[131] Prior to these actions, the Federal Trade Commission made an inquiry in 1927 into du Pont's purchase, with $14 million of its cash reserves, of 1.6 per cent of the outstanding stock of the United States Steel Corporation. Du Pont announced that it had bought the stock solely as an investment and shortly sold its holdings.[132] Years later the Department of Justice asserted that du Pont had been seeking control of U.S. Steel, and this was again denied.[133] Certainly this 1.6 per cent of steel ownership did not give du Pont the influence it secured when it purchased 22.7 per cent of General Motors stock.

The nineteen antitrust suits after 1939 were, in summary, as follows:

1. In the first of these cases, du Pont was a defendant in two nitrogen indictments and a civil action, which eventuated in the consent decree in 1942 previously mentioned.

2. The company was also a defendant in separate suits filed in 1942 covering dyestuffs, explosives, sulfuric acid, chromic acid, formic acid

128. 118 F. Supp., at 74.
129. 351 U.S., at 426.
130. *Ibid.*
131. Bursler, *The du Pont Industrial Group*, pp. 16–19.
132. "U.S. Steel: IV," *Fortune*, June 1936, p. 170.
133. *Journal of Commerce*, November 21, 1952, p. 6.

and muriatic acid.[134] All of these were concluded by pleas of *nolo contendere*, "du Pont paying its fines without admission of guilt, to get on with its war work," according to one reporter.[135] According to one of the attorneys representing the defendants, some of the practices complained of had already been dropped, but, since the statute of limitations had not expired, the defendants could not plead this fact.

3. Du Pont was a defendant with Rohm & Haas in the plastic indictments of 1942, one of which was quashed while the other resulted in a verdict of not guilty.

4. Du Pont was co-defendant in the important *National Lead* and *ICI* cases. The first of these resulted in a plea of *nolo contendere* and fines on the criminal charge (in 1949), and in each case a civil decree was entered against the defendants.

5. Du Pont was at first a defendant, but was later dismissed, in the *Wisconsin Alumni Research Foundation* case, in which the government intervened in a private suit in 1944. This research body had filed suit for infringement of its patents on activation of vitamin D through irradiation with ultra-violet rays; but the court turned the tables, and in January 1946 the Foundation signed a consent judgment dedicating these patents to the public.[136]

6. Originally one of the defendants in the *hydraulic brake fluid* case brought in 1947, du Pont obtained a dismissal after it went out of this business in 1952.[137]

7. In 1947 and 1949 the government brought two important cases which eventually reached the Supreme Court. It charged du Pont with monopolization of the cellophane business (see above) and with unlawfully controlling General Motors Corporation through its stock ownership (see Chapter 8).

8. In July 1948 du Pont was one of nine corporations charged with price fixing in paints, lacquers and varnishes.[138] Most of the defendants pleaded *nolo contendere*, paying fines up to $5,000. The Glidden Com-

134. *U.S. v. Allied Chemical and Dye Corp.*, Cr. 753–C (D. N.J. 1942); *U.S. v. E. I. du Pont de Nemours & Co.*, Cr. 9733 (E.D. Pa. 1942); *U.S. v. Monsanto Chemical Co.*, Cr. 1265 (N.D. Ind. 1942); *U.S. v. E. I. du Pont de Nemours & Co.*, Cr. 1266, 1268 and 1269 (N.D. Ind. 1942).

135. Lessing, "The World of du Pont," p. 93.

136. *Wisconsin Alumni Research Foundation v. Douglas*, Civil 43C–704 (D. Ill. 1946), Final Judgment, *1946–1947 Trade Cases*, No. 57433.

137. *U.S. v. Bendix Aviation Corp.*, Civil 44–284 (S.D. N.Y. 1947).

138. *U.S. v. Sherwin-Williams Co.*, Cr. 12789, *U.S. v. E. I. du Pont de Nemours & Co.*, Cr. 12790 (W.D. Pa. 1948).

pany and du Pont stood trial and in December 1951 won a verdict of not guilty from a Pittsburgh jury, which perhaps concluded that this was an instance of exchange of price information rather than price fixing.

The president of Glidden stated that the defense had cost his firm $100,000; [139] but du Pont, at least, recouped its cost several times over. It was one of the corporations requesting an excess profits tax refund under Section 722 of the Internal Revenue law, on the ground that the base period for earnings, 1936–39, was unfair to it — chiefly because wartime nylon profits had no counterpart in the base years. The tax authorities were deducting from such refunds any "illegal" profits which antitrust cases "proved" to have been received in the base period, and the several pleas of *nolo contendere* that du Pont had made were thus costing it dear. The company's contest of the *paint and varnish* case, and the resulting decision, however, forced the government to relinquish one claim just as the net settlement was being finalized. Du Pont was not the only chemical manufacturer whose claim for a refund was thus being whittled down as a consequence of its *nolo* pleas.

The Reaction of du Pont

It is difficult to learn the effect of all of these lawsuits on du Pont, since the company is unwilling to discuss any aspect of the subject. The following suggestions are based in part on unconfirmed information:

1. One antitrust enforcement official states that du Pont, when antitrust proceedings against it were renewed after World War II, made a definite decision to fight every such suit to the limit. This policy, if policy it was, had paid off, by 1955, in several trial court victories. Du Pont had also defeated one known treble damage suit and settled another out of court.

2. According to the same source, the company also made a decision to avoid all legally doubtful or borderline activities which might give the government an excuse to bring it into the courts. Government officials are said, in fact, to have found examples of industry meetings attended by competitors which du Pont, for this reason, refused to attend.

3. Du Pont's announcement in 1949 that it had recently listed 4,000 patents, or two thirds of those it held, as available for licensing [140] may have been due in part to a desire to clear itself of the suspicion

139. *Wall Street Journal*, December 6, 1951, p. 18.

140. Du Pont Co., Annual Report, 1948, pp. 19–20.

of monopolistic interest. Two years later the number listed had reached 5,000 and was still growing.[141]

4. The most spectacular reaction of du Pont to the postwar antitrust attacks has been its policy of helping to get competitors into operation on the basis of its own patents and technical information. The chief examples have been in metallic sodium (licensed to National Distillers Products Corporation), nylon and cellophane. The question has been asked whether du Pont will want to compete vigorously against firms it has deliberately helped to set up, and whether the government's policy of inducing or harrying it to create competitors really promotes "the competition the antitrust laws were designed to nourish." [142] Observers of the chemical industry have as yet found no signs of a slackening in competitive efforts.

Opinions on the Antitrust Laws

Executives of leading chemical companies state — as do those in other industries — that they approve the antitrust laws in general,[143] and recognize their contribution to the maintenance of a competitive industry. Even some of the particular applications which have brought the companies into court are not condemned so far as the larger principles are concerned. It is pointed out, however, that some agreements now viewed as illegal either were necessary to receive the benefits of foreign technology or were at least believed to be legal under the law as interpreted at the time.

One executive, when asked in another connection to name the principal management problems in his firm, volunteered at once that one of the most important and difficult is to teach the operating officers what they can and cannot do under the antitrust laws. A recognized duty of legal departments is to advise executives of the effect on operating practice of antitrust interpretations by enforcement agencies or courts. As examples of practices abandoned as a result of such advice company representatives have mentioned: (1) discussion of prices with competitors; (2) meetings to discuss cost reduction in various types of munitions (explosives) plants; and (3) collection of figures from all possible sources on each individual competitor's pro-

141. *Ibid.*, 1950, p. 16.

142. Lessing, "The World of du Pont," p. 162.

143. Compare statement by Leland A. Doan, president of Dow Chemical Co., in "2. Free Trade . . . No! The Case Against Maximum Exchange of Goods," *Saturday Review*, January 23, 1954, p. 32.

duction. Few of these specific results are significant; but it *is* significant when an officer of one corporation declares:

> We objected to Thurman Arnold's and Wendell Berge's chemical suits when they brought them, and are not willing to agree even now that they were right on the merits; but we will admit that they inspired in the industry a real and salutary determination to avoid restraint of trade.

Competitive Status

Trend of Concentration

One attempt has been made to measure the long-time trend of concentration in this industry.[144] In 1901, 24.3 per cent of the value added by manufacture in the chemical and allied products industry group was produced in individual industries whose "concentration ratio" (share of the total in the hands of the four largest firms) was 50 per cent or over. In 1947, 33.7 per cent of the value added was so produced. By contrast, 32.9 per cent of all manufacturing value added was so produced in 1901 and 24.0 per cent in 1947. The fact that the chemical industry has entirely different components now than in 1901 weakens the force of this comparison.

Three efforts to measure the trend since 1935 seem on the whole to point to increasing concentration:

1. In *value added*, the concentration ratio increased in six of the subindustries between 1935 and 1947 (by an average of 6.1 percentage points) and decreased in three (by an average of 5.8 percentage points).[145]

2. In *sales*, du Pont had 6.8 per cent of the total for chemicals and allied products in 1935 and 8.4 per cent in 1955. The three largest firms had 14.9 per cent in 1935 and 16.3 in 1955.[146] The product lines of particular large companies are, of course, far from identical with those included in chemicals and allied products as a whole.

3. In *assets*, du Pont's share of the total assets reported by fifty-four large companies was 31.8 per cent in 1935 and 24.4 per cent at the

144. M. A. Adelman, "The Measurement of Industrial Concentration," *Review of Economics and Statistics*, November 1951, p. 291.

145. FTC, *Report on Changes in Concentration in Manufacturing, 1935 to 1947 and 1950*, 1954, pp. 141–42.

146. Company sales from Moody's *Industrials;* over-all estimates from U.S. Department of Commerce. The fourth and fifth companies in 1935 did not publish sales figures. See Table 18 for 1955 company figures.

TABLE 19

CHEMICALS: SHARES OF NINE LARGEST IN ASSETS OF FIFTY-FOUR LARGE FIRMS, 1935, 1945 AND 1954

(*Cumulative Per Cent*)

Firm	End of 1935	Firm	End of 1945	Firm	End of 1954
Fifty-four	100.0	Fifty-four	100.0	Fifty-one[a]	100.0
1. Du Pont	31.8	Du Pont	30.2	Du Pont	24.4
2. Allied	50.9	Union Carbide	44.2	Union Carbide	40.2
3. Union Carbide	67.0	Allied	56.9	Dow	49.0
4. General Aniline	70.4	Dow	61.7	Allied	57.7
5. American Cyanamid	73.3	American Cyanamid	66.4	American Cyanamid	63.9
6. Columbian Carbon	75.6	Hercules	69.9	Olin Mathieson	69.9
7. Hercules	77.5	Air Reduction	72.6	Monsanto	74.6
8. Air Reduction	79.4	Monsanto	75.1	General Aniline	76.5
9. Monsanto	81.1	General Aniline	77.5	Merck	78.4

Source: Moody's *Industrials* and letters. In choosing the 54 out of about 80 chemical corporations listed in Moody's for 1951 there were omitted: all foreign companies, all those known to have only a minority of their interests in chemicals (e.g., Eastman Kodak, Diamond Match, Pittsburgh Plate Glass, W. R. Grace), sulphur mining companies, and firms for which data were not given as far back as 1935 (except for nine, which answered a letter of inquiry).

a. Owing to mergers, the 54 firms had shrunk to 51 in 1954.

end of 1954, while the share of the three largest firms dropped from 67.0 to 49.0 per cent, that of the six largest from 75.6 to 69.9 and that of the nine largest from 81.1 to 78.4. (See Table 19.)

The increase in sales concentration and decrease in assets concentration become consistent on the assumption that the fifty-four large concerns whose assets were tabulated gained in comparison with the industry as a whole. It may also be noted that two of the nine largest concerns dropped out between 1935 and 1954, and five of the seven remaining showed a change in rank. Thus the relative position of firms in this industry is not rigid.

Economies of Size

Chemical manufacturing is an industry in which the economies of large size are important.[147] They may be classified under two broad headings: (1) ability to install the complicated automatic equipment

147. Edgar M. Queeny and Richard M. Lawrence, "The Chemical Industry," Chap. 14 in John George Glover and William Bouck Cornell, eds., *The Development of American Industries*, Prentice-Hall, New York, 3d edition, 1951, pp. 449, 451; Alfred E. Kahn, "The Chemical Industry," Chap. 6 in Walter Adams, ed., *The Structure of American Industry*, Macmillan, New York, revised edition, 1954, pp. 205–06.

which makes possible the most efficient processing of chemicals and recovery of by-products; and (2) ability to finance and utilize extensive research, to launch new products which may bring no return for years, and to reduce risks by diversifying output. The first of these economies is primarily a matter of plant size, the second of company size. The most sensational illustrations of the second point have been du Pont's huge investments — $43 million in dyestuffs, for example, and $27 million in both nylon and nitrogen fixation — before making a net profit.[148] Size, however, offers more than just the capital to finance new products. A big company can make more effective use of its research department because its technical staff is acquainted with a wider field of chemistry and can therefore recognize fruitful results more often.[149]

According to "raw" data of the 1947 Census of Manufactures, the share of business done by "small" manufacturers in various branches of chemicals ranged from zero in synthetic rubber to 80 per cent in animal oils, with the weighted average nearly 20 per cent. The definition of "small" is here related to the particular product — ranging from 50 or fewer employees in several fields to 2,300 in synthetic fibers. (See Table 20.)

A recent analysis of the position of the small chemical manufacturer, relying on these data and on interviews, concludes:

> Somewhat harassed but still going strong, the small chemical manufacturer speaks up. No Pollyanna, he knows he's battling for his economic existence, but he believes he can hold his own — and be the stronger for it.[150]

As examples of the small man's defenses against his big rivals, the following tactics are cited:

> To meet the lower prices of large production runs, he offers rapid service, products tailored to the customer's exact specifications. Where the large company promotes sales through heavy advertising, the small firm stresses personal contact and service. When his accounts turn into captive customers through competitive mergers, he relies on his flexibility, switches to a new product or a new customer.[151]

148. Crawford H. Greenewalt, president of du Pont, Celler Hearings, Part 2–A, pp. 545–46.

149. *Ibid.*, p. 548.

150. Nathan D. Froot, "The Small Manufacturer in the Chemical Industry: His Position, Problems and Future," *Chemical Week*, June 18, 1955, p. 39.

151. *Ibid.*, p. 42.

TABLE 20

CHEMICALS: SHARE OF SMALL MANUFACTURERS IN VARIOUS PRODUCTS, 1947

Product	Maximum Number of Employees of Company[a]	Per Cent of Production
Forty-one products	50–2,300	23.3[b]
Twelve lines with least participation		
Synthetic rubber	350	0
Carbon black	100	3.3
Linseed oil mills	100	5.0
Compressed and liquefied gases	50	6.2
Alkalies and chlorine	900	6.35
Synthetic fibers	2,300	7.1
Cyclic (coal-tar) crudes	75	7.35
Fatty acids	125	7.4
Salt	175	9.2
Fertilizers	125	9.3
Organic chemicals, n.e.c.	1,000	9.5
Inorganic color pigments	225	10.0
Twelve lines with most participation		
Essential oils	100	30.8
Paints and varnishes	100	31.0
Fertilizers (mixing only)	50	32.9
Chemical products, n.e.c.	75	37.2
Biological products	100	38.5
Insecticides and fungicides	100	38.6
Cleaning and polishing preparations	100	46.5
Whiting and fillers	50	49.7
Sulfonated oils and assists	50	54.5
Marine animal oils	100	59.0
Gum naval stores (steam-distilled)	50	64.0
Animal oils, n.e.c.	50	80.0

Source: U.S. Census Bureau, unpublished tabulation from 1947 Census of Manufactures data, reported in Nathan D. Froot, "The Small Manufacturer in the Chemical Industry: His Position, Problems and Future," *Chemical Week*, June 18, 1955, p. 38.

a. To illustrate the method used, a company with over 350 employees would not be called "small" in synthetic rubber production, regardless of the breakdown of its employment or output between synthetic rubber and other products.

b. Mean of all forty-one. The weighted average is "almost" 20 per cent (*ibid.*, p. 39).

n.e.c.: not elsewhere classified.

Interviews during the present study support the view that small manufacturers are optimistic about their place in the industry, and in some instances hope by a lucky find in their own research to become big in their turn.

TABLE 21

CHEMICALS: ROLE OF MERGERS
IN THE GROWTH OF SIX FIRMS FROM ORIGIN THROUGH 1948

Firm	Assets Added by: Acquisition[a]	Assets Added by: Internal Growth	Assets Added by: Acquisition	Assets Added by: Internal Growth
	(Millions)		*(Per Cent)*	
General Aniline and Film Corp.	$ 27.8	$ 16.8	62.3	37.7
Air Reduction Co.	40.0	45.8	46.6	53.4
Liquid Carbonic Corp.	18.8	23.9	44.0	56.0
National Cylinder Gas Co.	9.7	13.2	42.4	57.6
E. I. du Pont de Nemours & Co.	401.8	730.3	35.5	64.5[b]
Union Carbide and Carbon Corp.	162.8	347.9	31.9	68.1
68 firms in 21 other industries	4,524.4	19,162.1	19.1	80.1

Source: J. Fred Weston, *The Role of Mergers in the Growth of Large Firms*, University of California Press, Berkeley, 1953, pp. 143–44.

a. Original combinations — e.g., Union Carbide in 1917 — are not counted under acquisitions.

b. The president of du Pont attributed only 54 per cent of the company's expansion to internal growth (Crawford H. Greenewalt, in *Study of Monopoly Power*, Hearings before Subcommittee on Study of Monopoly Power, House Judiciary Committee, 81st Cong., 1st sess., 1949, Serial 14, Part 2-A, p. 549). Alfred E. Kahn criticizes this figure — and the criticism would apply to Table 21 also — as predicated on the assumption that firms merged into another would not have grown with the industry if they had remained independent ("The Chemical Industry," Chap. 6 in Walter Adams, ed., *The Structure of American Industry*, Macmillan, New York, revised edition, 1954, p. 206, note 13). Both sides of this issue can be defended.

Importance of Mergers in Chemicals

Mergers have played a greater role in swelling the big chemical concerns to their present size than in many other industries. They accounted for between 32 and 62 per cent of the growth, from their origin to 1948, of 6 chemical companies chosen for comparison by one writer, but for only 19 per cent of the growth of 68 companies in 21 other industries. (See Table 21.) Some chemical companies themselves originated in a merger. Notable instances were Union Carbide in 1917 and Allied Chemical in 1920, both intended to be strongly financed enterprises more capable of doing research and meeting European competition than the typical small firm of the young United States industry. In 1940–47 the 212 chemical mergers reported by the financial services exceeded the number in any other industry except food and beverages;[152] and in 1948–54 the 168 acquisitions (by 73 chemical

152. FTC, *Report on the Merger Movement: A Summary Report*, 1948, p. 18.

concerns) exceeded all except those in food and beverages, and non-electrical machinery.[153]

Any merger among the eight or ten biggest units would, in the industry's opinion, be impossible under the antitrust laws. Even medium-sized companies have steered clear of these laws by acquiring only firms whose share of their markets was not substantial. A situation like that in England, France, Germany or Italy, where ICI, Établissements Kuhlmann, I.G. Farben and Montecatini, respectively, have dominated the chemical industries,[154] is not in prospect here. Thus in the 1920s, when the various owners of the important General Chemical Company, Kalbfleisch Corporation, Grasselli Chemical Company and Merrimac Chemical Company decided to sell, they did not join in a single heavy-chemical combine, but each went in a separate direction: to Allied, American Cyanamid, du Pont and Monsanto, respectively.[155]

Motives for Mergers

One authority reports that the character of mergers in chemicals changed after World War I, in the following way:

> The earlier combinations in the chemical industry, as in other American industries, united direct competitors in order to alleviate the pains of excessive competition. . . . Since the war, however, monopolistic control over the sales markets (explicitly forbidden by the antitrust laws) has not been the primary purpose sought in mergers. The need of a more favorable position in respect to raw materials has inspired the vertical combination. Horizontal organizations have been prompted by a desire to broaden the sales opportunities through diversification.[156]

Analysis of the mergers between 1948 and 1954 — so far as the names of the firms involved and brief statements of their product lines permit analysis [157] — indicates that the motives mentioned hold good today.[158] The largest group appears to have involved diversification — like the

153. FTC, *Report on Corporate Mergers and Acquisitions*, 1955, p. 28.

154. Stocking and Watkins, *Cartels in Action*, pp. 406–18.

155. William Haynes, *Men, Money and Molecules*, Doubleday, Doran, New York, 1936, p. 108.

156. *Idem*, "American Chemical Mergers," *Industrial and Engineering Chemistry*, June 1932, pp. 708–09.

157. Mergers are listed in *Corporate and Bank Mergers*, Interim Report of Antitrust Subcommittee of House Judiciary Committee, 84th Cong., 1st sess., 1955, pp. 77–89.

158. See also Joseph V. Sherman, "Chemical Mergers," *Barron's*, December 6, 1954, p. 11.

two largest, those of Mathieson Chemical Corporation with E. R. Squibb & Sons in 1952 and with Olin Industries, Inc., in 1953 (one of the many mergers that went outside the chemical field). The next largest group appears to have combined diversification and the union of a very few competitive products — as in the big Merck & Co.–Sharpe & Dohme merger. Only a handful brought together clearly competitive products, like the Liquid Carbonic mergers, and even these instances involved chiefly firms doing business in different geographic markets.

One point emphasized by the industry today is that the safest way to branch out into a new line is to purchase an existing company, including its management and skilled chemists, just as one way to lose money is to enter a new line "cold" and expect the company's chemists to catch up with the accumulated knowledge of those already in the business. It is not surprising, therefore, that of the many offers by smaller companies to sell out to big companies each year — offers usually motivated by a desire to turn current profits into capital gains, or to prepare for retirement or eventual inheritance taxes — those are accepted most willingly where the product lines are closest, or where the management and scientists come to the buyer along with the physical assets.

One economy of size on which we have already quoted the president of du Pont appears again as a justification for this concern's many acquisitions between 1910 and 1944: "to get a diversified field in the chemical business against which to appraise the results of research." In response to the exclamation, "You seriously mean that, Mr. Greenewalt?" the president cited as an illustration the important discovery in 1923 of a fast-drying automobile finish. "Had we not been in the paint business and known nothing of it," he said, "there was a very poor chance that we would have developed Duco." [159]

Some mergers undoubtedly support the industry's view, as expressed by one correspondent, that the aim of mergers is "better to meet competition" by creating stronger units. Others have undoubtedly diminished competition between the merging firms, in some of their products if not in all. The net effect of any given merger manifests itself slowly; the net effect of chemical mergers as a whole is the "oligopoly" structure of the industry that exists today. Almost no big company other than Rohm & Haas has grown without the aid of mergers.

159. Crawford H. Greenewalt, Celler Hearings, Part 2–A, p. 585.

Policies on Vertical Integration

The chemical industry is not vertically integrated to any significant extent. It does not need to produce its own raw materials — coal, petroleum, natural gas, limestone and the rest. It shrinks from selling consumer products, both because of the entirely different market problems this would involve and because of reluctance to compete directly with its present customers. Du Pont is generally believed to sell only about 6 per cent of its total output in finished form; the rest, like nylon yarn or automobile finishes, goes into further manufacture or, like explosives, into mining or construction.

There are, however, stirrings in the direction of forward integration, and only a few companies (the Hercules Powder Company for one) still insist that it is unwise on principle. In the list of 1948–54 mergers there are several in which forward integration was involved — such as the purchase by Allied Chemical of two roofing companies to use its asphalt paints and cements.[160] One highly successful example of sale to the ultimate consumer is "all," the synthetic detergent which Monsanto developed into a best seller in its field. American Cyanamid, aside from the Lederle Laboratories division with its Aureomycin and other pharmaceuticals, has always been a producer of basic chemicals. Early in 1956 its purchase of the Formica Company, to which it had been supplying Melmac resins, signaled a new policy of moving at least in some degree closer to the consumer.[161]

Interlocking Directorates and Trade Associations

The Federal Trade Commission, having found only twelve cases of interlocking directorates between chemical firms, concluded that licensing of patents offered the companies a more effective means of regulating their relationships.[162] The twelve instances found were either based on a seller-customer relationship or on a "history of common ownership, sometimes direct and admitted, and sometimes of a tenuous character." [163] The seller-customer type included pairs like American Cyanamid and Bon Ami Company; the historic-connection type included pairs like Air Reduction and U.S. Industrial Chemicals,

160. *Corporate and Bank Mergers*, House Report, p. 86.

161. *Business Week*, February 11, 1956, pp. 54–58.

162. FTC, *Report on Interlocking Directorates*, 1951, pp. 329, 332.

163. *Ibid.*, p. 331.

Inc., 24 per cent of whose stock was owned by Air Reduction. The Commission's criticism of these interlocks ran as follows:

> The net incidence of such interlocks reduced competition to a greater or less degree. In the first type of case, buyer and seller removed themselves from the open market to engage in private bargaining; in the second, a community of interest existed and interlocking directorates which expressed it were likely to facilitate friendly cooperation rather than free and open competition.[164]

It is true that chemical companies, even without interlocking directors, often form long-term seller-customer relationships, and also that certain companies with separate corporate names are controlled by the same interests. These facts, of course, characterize other industries as well.

A list of "some trade organizations and professional societies concerned with chemical manufacturing and chemistry," as of April 1, 1955, runs to 137.[165] The Manufacturing Chemists Association is the principal trade association of the general chemical companies. In a very few cases, as we have noticed, trade associations in particular branches of the industry have been defendants in antitrust suits.

The "Gentlemanly Competition" Analysis

Several writers on the chemical industry have argued that its manner of competition is restrained and "gentlemanly." According to an article in *Fortune* in 1937:

> The alcohol sector of the industry has frequently been guilty of disorderly conduct, and alkali made by the Solvay process has got into some nasty brawls with electrolytic alkali. But by and large the chemical industry has regulated itself in a manner that would please even a Soviet Commissar.[166]

In 1946 George W. Stocking and Myron W. Watkins wrote:

> In general, the deportment of the principal manufacturers in the chemical trade is "ethical"; their attitude toward one another, "cooperative." This sector of industry is shot through with cartel arrangements — many of them loose and informal, most without official machinery for enforcement. But diverse and often nebulous as are these conventions, they weave the

164. *Ibid.*, p. 355.

165. *The Chemical Industry: Facts Book*, 1955, pp. 135–39.

166. "Chemical Industry: I," *Fortune*, December 1937, p. 157.

threads of many divergent interests into a business pattern resembling but slightly that of a free market.[167]

Alfred E. Kahn, in a study published in 1950 and revised in 1954, has presented the same point of view in terms of recognition of "spheres of interest" of each company into which others do not "trespass." [168] This is well expressed in the following statement:

> Mr. du Pont remarked that they are not producers of fertilizer as such but only produced ammonia which they sold to others for conversion into fertilizer; that they have had no experience whatever in the fertilizer end of the business and that that market seemed to be well taken care of by American Cyanamid, Allied, and others. The du Pont interest, for the present at least, centers mainly in a synthetic production of ammonia and its commercial use in the explosives and fertilizer industries.[169]

Kahn attributes this attitude primarily to the oligopoly structure of the industry and makes the following comment:

> Economic theory and experience alike suggest that this is a situation conducive to conservatism, with respect both to "excessive" investment, which may endanger satisfactory price and profit levels, and to price competition or similar "unfriendly" acts which might provoke retaliation. Negotiation and discretion are the better part of competitive valor, when the latter might precipitate a conflict in which all parties would suffer.[170]

The same writer has also summarized various formal methods by which the chemical companies cooperate with each other: (1) They form joint ventures to exploit fields of interest to both, like the combination of American Viscose and Monsanto (Chemstrand) to make nylon, or of Dow and du Pont (Midland Ammonia) to make synthetic ammonia. (2) They market new products through firms that are already established in the field, as U.S. Industrial Chemicals contracted to market the solvents and other by-product chemicals of Standard Oil of Indiana and the Texas Company. (3) They engage in patent pooling, as did du Pont with ICI and National Lead in the famous cases which came into the courts. (4) They buy chemicals from

167. Stocking and Watkins, *Cartels in Action*, p. 395.

168. Kahn, "The Chemical Industry," pp. 207–08, 213–14.

169. Standard Oil Company of N.J. memorandum in *Investigation of the National Defense Program*, Hearings before Special Senate ("Truman") Committee Investigating the National Defense Program, 77th Cong., 1st sess., Part 11, 1942, p. 4646.

170. Kahn, "The Chemical Industry," p. 211.

each other (frequently at preferential discounts), as du Pont buys industrial gases from Air Reduction and Union Carbide. (5) "They have frequently violated the antitrust laws," as evidenced since 1938 by five civil suits won by the government and thirty-three pleas of *nolo contendere*.[171]

The fact that the companies cooperate in these ways must be granted. This even includes the past violations of the antitrust laws — if one assumes (although the law does not assume) that a *nolo contendere* plea admits a violation, and provided one remembers that some cases involved practices which had previously been thought legal. The other four methods of formal cooperation constitute, in major part, attempts to: (1) spread the risk; (2) avoid setting up top-heavy systems of distribution; (3) share technology — and, it is true, sometimes divide international markets at the same time; and (4) buy products where they are cheapest. These policies are not peculiar to the chemical industry.

The Question of "Trespassing"

Granting that there is to some extent a "no trespass" attitude, this, too, is not necessarily abnormal. A substantial capital investment is needed to enter a given field of chemicals, and a corporation will naturally make this investment where it is most likely to yield a return. If a market is already adequately supplied by another company, such a return is unlikely. This is essentially an economic, rather than a "political" or an "administrative," consideration, and one which is central to the free enterprise system. It is a policy which is beneficial to the public, since consumers will be better served if producers fill the "gaps" than if they duplicate the work of others, and if they specialize in certain fields of applied chemistry than if they dabble in the whole field.

To whatever extent "no trespassing" existed when the authors quoted above wrote about "gentlemanly competition," it appears to be less prevalent today. In the words of one executive of a big company, "trespass is a current every day occurrence." This is supported by the executive of a small firm, who complains against the large ones that are using their financial resources to buy their way into new areas in which they have no previous experience.

171. *Ibid.*, pp. 215–17.

If "no trespassing" should in fact be found more prevalent in this industry than in others, the explanation would probably lie in the highly technical character of chemical operations. Profound knowledge is so essential to success that some companies confine their hiring for administrative positions substantially to men who have majored in chemistry or chemical engineering in college, while many executives have a doctor's degree in these subjects. Applied chemistry has become so vast a field that no one mind can comprehend more than a small portion of it, and no one company can operate in all of its divisions. Even the largest company would think it risky to plunge into an area in which some smaller company was much more experienced, unless it should happen to have found a new and superior process as a by-product of its regular research work.[172] Otherwise its waste effort might be tremendous before it could achieve an equal knowledge.

Forms of Competition

The real competition in the chemical industry goes beyond the manufacture of the same chemical from the same raw material by the same process — although this, too, exists, as in alkalies, chlorine and heavy acids. Competition is more characteristically found in the search for different raw materials and processes to make the same product, for different chemicals to perform the same function, for new chemicals to perform altogether new functions, and for new uses for established chemicals. To give a few illustrations out of thousands: by-product molasses from sugar making was the standard source of ethyl alcohol until petroleum's availability was discovered and quickly won for it the bulk of the market; acetic acid can be made from three different raw materials and by ten different processes; "glycerin, sorbitol, propylene and ethylene glycols, ethanol, methanol, isopropyl alcohol and pentaerythritol perform many of the same functions" [173] and are made by many different companies. A new product discovered by a company frequently displaces one of its own products. Thus sulfa discoveries by American Cyanamid forced it to scrap its investment in pneumonia serum, which had been an impressive discovery a few years earlier.

This is the famous "test-tube competition," or continual struggle of competing laboratories to find new products. In ten of the twelve

172. See *ibid.*, p. 213.

173. *The Chemical Industry: Facts Book,* 1955, p. 39.

years from 1942 through 1953 at least 350 new chemicals were introduced; in 1954, over 500.[174] In 1956, 50,000 new chemical compounds were said to be in process of creation, of which an unknown number would actually prove useful.[175] In 1948, 60 per cent of du Pont's sales were in products put into large-scale production since 1928.[176] In 1955 Dow was operating 59 pilot plants, of which 21 were experimenting with process improvement, 27 with products Dow had never made, and the remaining 11 with completely new products.[177] The effect of test-tube competition is expressed by a statement, which can be supported by examples, "that there are no 'gentlemen's agreements' protecting the position of the unprogressive chemical firm." [178]

Besides product competition — including, as in other industries, competition in improving the quality of a given product — chemical companies compete in the technical assistance they offer to customers. Their "technical sales service" departments are of great importance. The fact that the industry also recently led all manufacturing groups except beverages in percentage of the sales dollar spent for advertising [179] is certainly attributable to inclusion of "drugs and toiletries" among the industry's products; but there is a surprising amount of informative technical advertising in trade journals.

Price competition on identical products plays a relatively small role in the thinking of the companies. It is said that in a discussion of competition lasting several hours, the representative of one large company never mentioned the word "price." The effort of the industry to avoid competition in various trade practices was reflected, as one observer has pointed out, in the content of the National Recovery Administration codes of fair competition. These included

> prohibitions against concealed allowances, against excessive rebates on containers, against unearned discounts, free distribution services, espionage by competitors, enticement of employees, unjustified claims adjustments, contingent sales, dumping, and, of course, sales below cost.[180]

174. *Ibid.*, 1953, p. 16; 1955, p. 18.

175. Evan J. Crane, cited in *New York Times*, April 12, 1956, p. 37.

176. Crawford H. Greenewalt, Celler Hearings, Part 2–A, p. 547.

177. Standard & Poor's Corp., *Industry Surveys*, "Chemicals," Basic Analysis, September 15, 1955, p. C2–3.

178. Allen, *Economics of American Manufacturing*, p. 180.

179. *Business Week*, May 10, 1952, p. 46.

180. Theodore J. Kreps, *The Economics of the Sulfuric Acid Industry*, Stanford University Press, Stanford University (Calif.), 1938, p. 201.

TABLE 22

CHEMICALS: PRODUCT GROUPS OF NINE PRINCIPAL COMPANIES, 1955

Product Group	Du Pont	Union Carbide	Allied Chemical	Olin Mathieson	Monsanto	Dow	American Cyanamid	Hercules	Rohm & Haas	Number of Companies
1. Acids	x	x	x	x	x	x	x	x	x	9
2. Alkalies and chlorine	x		x	x	x	x	x			6
3. Anhydrous ammonia	x		x	x		x	x	x		6
4. Coal-tar intermediates	x	x	x	x	x	x	x			7
5. Dyes	x		x		x	x	x			5
6. Explosives	x			x	x		x	x		5
7. Fertilizers	x		x	x		x	x			5
8. Fluorine derivatives	x	x	x			x	x		x	6
9. Industrial gases (excluding ammonia)		x			x		x			3
10. Insecticides and fungicides	x	x	x	x	x	x	x	x	x	9
11. Petrochemicals	x	x	x	x	x	x	x	x	x	9
12. Plastics	x	x	x	x[a]	x	x	x	x	x	9
13. Pharmaceuticals and fine chemicals	x	x	x	x	x	x	x	x	x	9
14. Synthetic fibers	x	x	x		x	x				5
Number of product groups	13	9	12	10	11	12	13	7	6	

Source: Standard & Poor's Corp., *Industry Surveys*, "Chemicals," Basic Analysis, September 15, 1955, p. C2–5. The companies are listed in order of their 1955 sales.

a. Added on the basis of later information.

The same writer points out, however, that price fixing or other monopolistic efforts are not proof against new processes, products, types of equipment, and competitors.

Diversification

Chemical companies with broad research programs have inevitably pushed out of their original areas of interest when their research led into other fields. A remarkable degree of diversification has resulted. If one divides most chemicals into fourteen groups, du Pont and American Cyanamid were operating in 1955 in thirteen, Allied and Dow in twelve, and five of the other large general chemical companies in from six to eleven. All nine corporations produced acids, agricultural chemicals, petrochemicals, plastics and fine chemicals. The lowest concentration among the fourteen product lines was in industrial gases, produced by only three of the firms. (See Table 22). From 1952 to 1955 seven of the companies added between one and three lines.[181]

To illustrate how research may lead into many fields, the following are only a few of the products that can be derived from the same intermediate compounds out of coal tar: dyestuffs, perfumes, solvents, artificial flavors, explosives, lacquers, plastics, tanning materials.[182] When a chemical compound is separated in order to recombine one of its elements with something else, the other elements are left as by-products until some use is found for them by research, and the resulting new product may find its value in some entirely different industry.

Research thus often puts a company, whether or not it has any intention to trespass, into the spheres of other producers — both within and without the chemical industry. Du Pont, for example, has gone into film, competing with Eastman Kodak, and into paint, competing with Sherwin-Williams. The whole textile industry has been hard hit by the synthetic products emerging from chemical laboratories. In 1954 no fewer than twenty-five companies were doing research on such synthetic fibers, and the lament was heard in some quarters that it was easier to discover them than to market them.

The Position of du Pont

The degree of diversification of du Pont and the degree of concentration in its hands of certain product lines are shown by a breakdown of industry shipments in 1947 in the order of their dollar value. In what was then du Pont's chief line, organic chemicals, the company had 14.4 per cent of the total market; its highest position was in explosives, with 33.4 per cent, and its lowest in pharmaceuticals and toilet preparations, with 0.1 per cent. (See Table 23.) A signal example of the dynamic character of the chemical industry is the rise of du Pont's production of synthetic fibers from about $200 million in

181. Compare table in Standard & Poor's Corp., "Chemicals," Basic Analysis, May 1, 1952, p. C2–3.

182. Charles A. Welsh, *The Development of the Organic Chemical Industry: A Study in the Interrelationships of Technology, Industrial Organization and National Economic Policies*, abridgment of doctoral thesis, New York University, New York, 1944, printed by Edwards Brothers, Ann Arbor, 1947, p. 8.

TABLE 23

CHEMICALS: CONCENTRATION OF OUTPUT IN PRODUCT GROUPS, 1947

Product Line	Number of Companies	Value of Industry Shipments	Share of du Pont	Share of Four Largest Producers
		(Millions)	*(Per Cent)*	
Organic chemicals	188	$1,445	14.4	47.0
Paints and varnishes	1,154	1,249	7.8	27.3
Rubber industries, n.e.c.	733	953	.4	30.0
Pharmaceutical preparations	1,123	942	.1	28.0
Synthetic fibers	22	705	28.2	78.4
Inorganic chemicals, n.e.c.	242	673	11.7	32.1
Plastics products, n.e.c.	1,340	503	.9	22.2
Plastics materials	94	483	19.1	43.9
Photographic equipment	346	440	5.8	61.2
Chemical products, n.e.c.	1,135	393	4.4	12.7
Toilet preparations	692	372	.1	23.8
Inorganic color pigment	57	270	12.0	63.6
Cleaning and polishing preparations	1,018	262	3.1	23.5
Synthetic rubber	5	235	2.5	97.5
Medicinal chemicals	88	202	2.7	68.5
Primary zinc	14	191	3.8	53.3
Coated fabrics, except rubberized	106	157	9.8	33.9
Explosives	35	136	33.4	80.4
Insecticides and fungicides	146	73	5.0	37.4
Dental equipment and supplies	209	71	.7	39.6
X-ray and therapeutic apparatus	114	60	1.6	57.8
Whiting and fillers	66	19	.4	39.4

Source: Norman Bursler, *The du Pont Industrial Group*, Association of American Law Schools, University of Pennsylvania Law School, Philadelphia, mimeographed, 1951, pp. 35–36. The original sources are the industry totals in U.S. Census data, in *Study of Monopoly Power*, Hearings before Subcommittee on Study of Monopoly Power, House Judiciary Committee, 81st Cong., 1st sess., 1949, Serial 14, Part 2-B, pp. 1446–53; and du Pont figures from special tabulation prepared for du Pont and certified by the Census Bureau, in Trial Memorandum No. 1 for Defendants, in *U.S. v. Imperial Chemical Industries, Ltd.* (S.D. N.Y.), February 15, 1950, Appendix 3, Table 20, p. 158.

n.e.c.: not elsewhere classified.

1947 to possibly $500 or $550 million in 1955 — two thirds of current sales being in nylon and the rest in Dacron, Orlon and rayon. Du Pont was shifting out of rayon production in favor of the newer fibers.[183] A wave of price cuts in synthetic fibers near the end of 1955 was typical

183. Walter K. Gutman, "Du Pont," *Barron's*, November 21, 1955, p. 18.

of chemical product history, and reflected in this instance such factors as the expansion of du Pont's first nylon competitor, Chemstrand, the beginning of production by Allied, and the approaching production by American Enka Corporation.[184]

In only five of the twenty-two subindustries in Table 23 did du Pont ship a third as much as the total of the four largest producers. It seems to follow that du Pont could hardly have been the leader in many more than these five. Du Pont's size thus expresses itself in diversification and not necessarily in control over particular product lines. However, a successful research laboratory inevitably results in the monopoly of some products, and out of the thousand-odd synthetic organic chemicals which du Pont produced in 1947, it was the only producer of 274.[185]

Entry

New, small firms continually enter branches of the chemical industry where entry is possible. Experienced executives leave the established companies for the greater lure of profits than of salaries. The number of firms in "chemicals and allied products" increased from 8,839 in 1939 to 10,073 in 1947 and 11,421 in 1954. The 14 per cent gain from 1939 to 1947 compares with 39 per cent for all manufacturing, however.[186] Some idea of the number currently operating in various areas may be obtained from the following enumeration published in 1955: 18 in plastic materials, 21 in sulfuric acid, 17 in photochemicals, 17 in explosives, 41 in pigments, 52 in dyes, 54 in dye intermediates, 246 in antifreezes, and 1,200 in paints.[187] In only one case — explosives — can one clearly compare these figures with Table 23, and in this instance a sharp drop was registered between 1947 and 1955.

The formation out of hand of a big new chemical company would seem to be an impossibility; but in the mid-1950s W. R. Grace & Company was accomplishing it successfully through mergers. Limited-line chemical companies have often expanded greatly by developing fuller lines, and new entrants into limited lines have themselves created competition for existing firms. A recent complete newcomer was the Spencer Chemical Company, a war-born organization that

184. *Business Week*, December 3, 1955, p. 99.
185. Bursler, *The du Pont Industrial Group*, p. 38.
186. *Statistical Abstract of the United States*, 1950, p. 759.
187. *The Chemical Industry: Facts Book*, 1955, p. 39.

now operates in six of the product lines listed in Table 22; another is the Shea Chemical Corporation, which makes industrial phosphorous. These firms have entered fields which were traditionally dominated by very few companies.

The glamor of the chemical industry keeps enticing new competitors from outside. The leading rubber manufacturers were drawn in by the fact that synthetic rubber is derived from petrochemical compounds, and all of them now offer competition in the vinyl resin field, formerly dominated by Union Carbide, Dow, Monsanto and du Pont. Goodrich, taking the lead, formed its B. F. Goodrich Chemical Company in April 1945, and in 1948 opened a $6 million research center to carry on basic chemical research. Another important interloper is the Celanese Corporation, which pioneered in the production of chemicals from natural gases as early as 1925. Most important by far of these "outsiders" are the oil refiners, who are sharing the growing petrochemical industry with both rubber and chemical firms. Shell Oil Company's chemical subsidiary is the largest, with sales of $125 to $150 million annually. One oil man predicts that chemicals and petroleum will eventually become a single industry.[188]

Corporations that convert basic chemicals into end products like glass, film and paint were sometimes spurred by postwar shortages to begin making their own chemicals, and have continued to make them. Eastman Kodak, Pittsburgh Plate Glass and Sherwin-Williams are examples.[189] Chemical manufacture may also offer a use for by-products from regular operations of such firms which had previously been wasted.

Chemical Prices

Stability of chemical prices during business recessions has been remarked on by some writers; [190] but the rising trend of demand for these products in recent years must be recognized as a factor justifying a good deal of stability at such periods.

188. Chester F. Smith, vice president of Standard Oil Company of N.J., quoted in *Petroleum Refiner*, July 1955, p. 97.

189. "The Chemical Century," *Fortune*, March 1950, p. 70.

190. Richard Ruggles, "The Nature of Price Flexibility and the Determinants of Relative Price Changes in the Economy," paper in *Business Concentration and Price Policy*, a report of the Universities–National Bureau Committee for Economic Research, Princeton University Press, Princeton, 1955, p. 483; Clair Wilcox, *Competition and Monopoly in American Industry*, TNEC Monograph 21, 1941, p. 202.

There are various reasons why chemical prices are not always reduced quickly as supply increases. Joint costs combine with high overhead costs to suggest pricing conservatism.[191] Furthermore, the industry expands by making big jumps in capacity, then waiting for sales to catch up, then making another jump.[192] If each jump were followed by a sufficient price reduction to induce customers to buy all of the product (which is sometimes new and untried), the threat of losses might be sufficient to discourage the expansion entirely. One du Pont experience illustrates that price cuts are sometimes ineffective from the point of view of either producer or consumer. In the early 1930s the company put out a cheap methanol antifreeze, but in five years it had still not come out of the red. It then put out the methanol in slightly improved form, in sealed cans to prevent dilution, called it Zerone, raised the price, and in seven years increased "from nothing to top place." [193]

In spite of this frequent lack of close relationship between prices and amount sold, chemical prices have proved to be elastic over the long run. Increased volume of sales has led to sharp cuts in cost of production, to price declines and then to new and wide markets. Among the most striking examples are the 99 per cent declines in prices of drugs like cortisone and penicillin. (See Table 24.) This downward trend, noticeable in the chemical price average from 1899 to 1937,[194] has been offset since then by the general inflation of the whole price level. From 1939 to the first half of 1956 the Bureau of Labor Statistics wholesale price index for chemicals and allied products increased by approximately 90 per cent and the index of all wholesale prices other than farm products and foods rose by approximately 100 per cent.[195] Early in 1956 the press was reporting changes in chemical prices almost daily, some up and some down according to the supply and demand conditions for each product.

191. Stocking and Watkins, *Cartels in Action*, pp. 400–01; Kahn, "The Chemical Industry," pp. 211–12.

192. *Business Week*, March 17, 1956, p. 96.

193. Lessing, "The World of du Pont," p. 172.

194. G. Warren Nutter, "Secular Movements of Monopoly Prices in Manufacturing," paper presented to Conference on *Business Concentration and Price Policy*, Universities–National Bureau Committee for Economic Research, Princeton University, June 17–19, 1952, mimeographed, p. 2.

195. *Survey of Current Business*.

TABLE 24

CHEMICALS: DECLINES IN SPECIFIC PRICES TO 1955

Product	Unit	Early Date[a]	Early Price	Price, January 31, 1955	Percentage Decline
Acetone	lb.	1920	$ .23	$ .075	67.4
Ammonium sulfate	ton	1914	147.50	42.00	71.5
Aspirin	lb.	1920	1.04	.58	44.2
Borax	ton	1920	181.50	41.25	77.3
Cellophane	lb.	1924	4.56	.56–.81	87.5–82.2
Chlorine, liquid	lb.	1920	.09	.029	67.8
Cortisone	gram	1949	222.00	3.50	98.4
Furfural	lb.	1929	3.58	.12	96.6
Hydrazine	lb.	1944	82.00	1.60	98.0
Indigo dye	lb.	1917	2.06	.31	85.0
Iodine	lb.	1914	8.88	2.30	74.1
Penicillin	million units	1944	82.00	.075	99.9
Phthalic anhydride	lb.	1920	.66	.195	71.5
Rayon (150-denier viscose weaving yarn)	lb.	1920	6.60	.78	88.2
Sulfanilamide	lb.	1927	6.17	1.40	77.3
Synthetic vitamin A	million units	1949	.61	.12	80.3
Titanium metal	lb.	1948	5.25	4.00	23.8
Vitamin B_{12}	gram	1950	1,044.10	245.00	76.6

Source: The Chemical Industry: Facts Book, 1955, Manufacturing Chemists Ass'n., Washington, p. 20; percentage declines calculated for the present study.

a. The year 1920 so often appearing in this column was the peak year for general wholesale prices until after World War II.

Interindustry Competition

Instances of competition of chemical products with those of other industries are numerous, almost numberless: cellophane with other flexible packaging materials; synthetic with natural fibers; plastics with shell, bone and wood for buttons, with porcelain for insulators, with wood and metal for toys; and all the rest.

The experience of plastics, a newcomer in the chemical field whose output has been doubling every five years,[196] epitomizes that of the chemical industry in general. First, chemical manufactures crowd into

196. Joseph V. Sherman, "Plastics Progress," *Barron's*, May 16, 1955, p. 13.

the market at the expense of natural products (in the case of plastics, to replace ivory) and then competition grows increasingly intense among the chemicals themselves. The facts speak for themselves: in 1954, 25 per cent of our textiles, 59 per cent of our soap and detergents, 60 per cent of paints, 75 per cent of drugs and medicines and 99 per cent of dyes were synthetic.[197]

Performance of the Industry

The performance of the industry has been a remarkable one. The fact that physical productivity per man-hour in heavy chemicals is "probably" twice that in Britain[198] is typical of American-British contrasts. More significant has been the inflow of new products that the chemical producers have brought to the economy. In the words of *Fortune*, the prime characteristic of the chemical industry is "the extraordinary proliferation of its products."[199] To the materials offered by nature, chemistry has added tremendously. Its success in meeting the scarcity of raw materials is worth singling out. It has discovered how to use heretofore unworkable or wasted substances like low-grade ores or the sulfur which is eliminated from petroleum in the refining process; it has prolonged the life of existing materials by anti-rust and anti-pest discoveries; it has produced corrosion-proof metals and wear-proof fibers; and it increases the yield from land by means of fertilizers and pesticides.[200]

Not surprisingly, the industry spends more money on research than any other except electrical equipment and aircraft manufacturing. It spends, in fact, 20 per cent of the grand total.[201] Moreover, 93 per cent of its research expenditures are privately financed as against only 45 per cent for electrical equipment and 15 per cent for aircraft.[202] Recently (1954) American Cyanamid was spending 5.3 per cent of its sales receipts on research, a greater proportion than any other large

197. *The Chemical Industry: Facts Book*, 1955, p. 5.

198. Anglo-American Council on Productivity, *Heavy Chemicals*, London, 1953, p. 1.

199. *Fortune*, December 1937, p. 160.

200. "Investing for Tomorrow," by David L. Babson & Co., investment counsel, Boston, November 1953, p. 2.

201. *The Chemical Industry: Facts Book*, 1955, p. iii.

202. Bureau of Labor Statistics, U.S. Department of Labor, and Research and Development Board, U.S. Department of Defense, *Industrial Research and Development: A Preliminary Report*, January 1953.

chemical company. The largest outlay on research is, of course, du Pont's — $66 million in 1955.[203]

It has been argued in criticism that the chemical concerns have frequently delayed the introduction of new products or processes [204] and that many of these were actually discovered abroad, even if developed further here — cellophane, rayon, synthetic ammonia, Dacron and others.[205] These points are certainly true: in fact they are linked together. Many of the quantity limitations on new products and refusals to license them have been conditions imposed by their European originators in licensing them to the American producers. There are progressive chemical industries in both hemispheres, and the terms on which patented knowledge could be exchanged have had to be mutually acceptable. The speed of innovation in chemicals could theoretically have been faster, but by any practical standard it must be called fast — in this country as well as abroad.

The profits of the industry have been consistently above the average for manufacturing. This was so in three diverse periods: the prosperity of the 1920s, the depression of the 1930s and the renewed prosperity since 1945.[206] One explanation attributes this fact to the rapid rate of equipment obsolescence and the big investment needed for both capital equipment and research — two considerations tending to weaken the attraction that high profits would otherwise be likely to exert on prospective investors — with some assistance from reduction of labor costs through automatic processes.[207] But it is not surprising when an industry with such a high growth trend shows high profits.

Proposals for Reconstruction

The latest over-all evaluation by a university economist is that of Alfred E. Kahn. He grants "an impressive record of technical advance, expanding output, declining costs and prices," but points out that "in modern science it is difficult *not* to progress, whatever the system of organization" and stresses the agreements (leading off with that between du Pont and Rohm & Haas) which restricted introduction of

203. Standard & Poor's Corp., "Chemicals," September 15, 1955, p. C2–3.

204. Kahn, "The Chemical Industry," p. 226.

205. *Ibid.*, pp. 233–34.

206. *Ibid.*, p. 220, text and notes 31, 32.

207. T. S. Hodgins, director of Chemical and Rubber Division, Business and Defense Services Administration, Department of Commerce, press release, November 23, 1955, p. 16.

new products.[208] He appears to be presenting his own position when he writes:

> Others argue that such power, left in private hands, rendered in some degree irresponsible by the deficiency of competition, is inherently objectionable and susceptible to abuse, that the dangers of conservatism in pricing, investment, and output policies, resulting from the oligopolist's inevitable consideration of the effects of his action on the market, are too great to be permitted. . . .[209]

Kahn's most striking proposals are (1) compulsory licensing of patents; and (2) dissolution of the giant companies.[210] These are radical measures whose outcome cannot be predicted, since they have been applied only rarely and then usually on a small scale. If they are to be applied to chemicals, it should be only as part of a general revision of national patent and trust policy applied to all industry. The record of progress in chemicals is too outstanding to justify making it the first target of major reform.

SUMMARY

1. The largest chemical manufacturer has sales equal to about 10 per cent of the total for the *chemical and allied products industry* (excluding soap and oils), the four largest about 22 per cent, and the fifteen largest about 35 per cent. Within narrower product groups, concentration is necessarily higher, reaching up to 90 per cent in 1947 for the four main producers of cyclic (coal-tar) crudes.

2. The manufacture of *explosives* was controlled by a trade association after 1872, and in later decades du Pont acquired most of the industry through mergers. The antitrust dissolution of 1912 created the Hercules Powder and Atlas Powder companies as competitors. The explosives industry has progressed faster under competition. Although six producers pleaded *nolo contendere* to charges of collusion in 1943, such a plea is not necessarily an admission of guilt, and no significant change in practices has occurred. The highly important decision of du Pont to branch out from explosives into chemicals was perhaps partly motivated by the antitrust suit of 1907–12, but it was "in the cards" regardless. The fact that we have two additional chemical companies, Hercules and Atlas, is due to that suit.

208. Kahn, "The Chemical Industry," pp. 226–27.

209. *Ibid.*, pp. 231–32.

210. *Ibid.*, pp. 228–34.

3. Federal Trade Commission orders between 1938 and 1948 enjoined price fixing and monopolistic practices in *liquid chlorine, calcium chloride, insecticides and fungicides, and carbon dioxide.* In the last-named industry there was also a consent decree in 1952, which directed one defendant to sell two plants; but the position of the two national companies is unimpaired.

4. Department of Justice action, apparently intended to reduce the concentrated control of *borax* production by three companies, failed to achieve any significant result.

5. The antitrust agencies have intervened in the three principal *mixed fertilizer materials.* In phosphate rock, the producers abandoned in 1926 their system of quoting domestic rock solely on an f.o.b. port basis and in 1941 their open price system. In 1945 their two export associations agreed with the Federal Trade Commission not to renew their prewar division-of-market agreements with foreign producers. In potash, the Franco-German cartel met a 1927 antitrust suit by a change in form. Domestic producers agreed, in 1940, to quote f.o.b. their plants, thus saving nearby purchasers perhaps $200,000 in freight costs annually (although, if profits were not reduced, distant purchasers may in the end have lost correspondingly). In nitrogen, restraints of trade were enjoined in 1941, and the war plant disposal program reduced the share of the two largest producers from 87 to 54 per cent of capacity — a figure which is now much lower because of building by other producers.

6. The Supreme Court decision in 1947 that National Lead Company and du Pont monopolized the *titanium* pigments business led to a decree ordering them to license their patents to all comers. Fears that the failure to divest each company of one of its plants would make other firms hesitate to enter the industry were not realized. Other chemical and metal companies entering the titanium metal industry have leaned heavily on government assistance, but both the freeing of existing patents by the Court's decision and its reassertion that patent rights would not be confiscated may have contributed.

7. Although the du Pont–Rohm & Haas agreements which settled the patent dispute on *acrylic plastics* were apparently legal, since the firms were acquitted of conspiracy in 1945, Rohm & Haas foreswore restrictive agreements in a consent decree three years later. The decline in price of material for a denture from 90 to 6 cents, due probably less to the breakup of the agreement than to increasing scale of production, means little to the ultimate consumer who pays over $100.

8. In the *alkali* case of 1949, the Webb-Pomerene Act of 1918 was construed for the first time. District Judge Kaufman held that it did not give export trade associations the right to make international agreements which might stabilize prices in the United States, or might restrict imports or the

opportunity of nonmember American firms to export. Webb Act associations are now simply merchandising agencies.

9. The broad patent, process and market agreements between du Pont and *Imperial Chemical Industries, Ltd.*, were abandoned in 1948 as a result of antitrust action. The eventual court decree in 1952 directed du Pont to sever all relationships with ICI and to make the patents concerned available to all would-be licensees. Apart from some resentment in Britain and Canada at the interference by an American court in their business affairs, the result of the decree seems to have been satisfactory. The separation of the du Pont-ICI Canadian interests has been accomplished, and a few signs of competition between the two new companies are beginning to appear. The United States patents in question have been licensed to other producers insofar as a demand for them existed. Finally, the two practices of (1) broad and exclusive pooling of patents between two important companies and (2) division of export markets between them were once again condemned as they had been in the case of titanium.

10. The *cellophane* case is notable for the lengthy economic analysis of District Judge Leahy — later approved by the Supreme Court — which concluded that a monopoly of cellophane would not be illegal under the Sherman Act as long as this article competed with other flexible packaging materials. Thus the true market was the use, not the particular way of meeting the use. This doctrine is at the same time realistic in recognizing the importance of intercommodity competition and yet subject to abuse if taken literally, since it would permit deliberate monopolization of any product having close substitutes for most uses. Du Pont's monopoly in this case was due to its patents.

11. *Du Pont* has been the principal target of antitrust enforcement in the chemical industries, and perhaps in the whole of American industry. In many of the nineteen proceedings brought against it between 1939 and 1948, the company did not contest the case, but the eventual result of so many pinpricks is believed to have been its adoption of a twofold policy of fighting every case and avoiding all risks of law violation. As a result of these suits, du Pont adopted a more liberal policy of licensing its patents and even went out and found competitors to make cellophane, nylon and metallic sodium.

12. *Opinion of chemical executives* naturally objects to some of the Department of Justice proceedings, but accepts the fact that a competitive industry as required by the antitrust laws is healthier than one tied by the agreements which were once thought to be both legal and necessary to secure the benefits of European technology.

13. Whether measured over a fifty-year period or since 1935 only, the *trend of concentration* in the chemical industry appears to be upward.

14. The chemical industry is pre-eminently one in which there are great *advantages of size*, with special emphasis on automatic production methods

and on following out the results of successful research into new products not manufactured before. Small firms still hold an average of 20 or 25 per cent of chemical production, and are confident of their ability to maintain this position.

15. The chemical companies have grown much more by *mergers* and less by reinvestment of funds than American corporations in general. They believe that to enter a new line of products "cold" is less promising than to merge research resources with a company experienced in the field. Mergers for diversification are more frequent than those to unite directly competitive products. Without an antitrust law, the American situation might more nearly have approached that in Europe, where one huge company usually controls a much larger part of the industry. Vertical integration is not significant in this industry, but some tendencies toward it are appearing.

16. *Interlocking directorates* among chemical companies are usually found where there is a long-standing buyer-seller relationship or a history of common ownership or control.

17. In only a few cases have *trade associations* engaged in practices which brought them into a clash with the antitrust laws.

18. Several writers have commented on the "gentlemanly" *pattern of competition* in the chemical industry, with producers not "trespassing" on each other's fields. Trespassing, however, is apparently becoming more common. Where it does not exist, the explanation appears to lie in the highly technical character of chemical production and the heavy investment required. A company may not want to risk entering a line in which another firm has superior skill derived from its greater experience. Although this caution may reduce the number of sellers of specific products, it is likely to result in the most efficient use of skills and resources for over-all chemical production. Vigorous technological competition is responsible for the hundreds of new products introduced each year, as well as for new uses and reductions in cost of old products.

19. The consequence of expanding research is to give the big chemical companies a wide *diversification* of products within the bounds of the chemical industry. Thus du Pont is active in nearly every branch of the industry, with its participation in 1947 ranging from 0.1 per cent to 33 per cent of sales. Its size does not mean control of broad subindustries, but in hundreds of narrowly defined products it is often the only producer, being presumably in most instances the developer.

20. *Entry* into the industry on a large scale can be accomplished only with ample resources and by use of mergers, but on a small scale it is occurring all the time. Competition is strengthened by the entry of companies from the rubber, petroleum and other industries that produce chemical raw materials or employ some chemical processes.

21. Chemical *prices* are stable rather than flexible in the short run, but over the long run the prices of chemicals which have come into mass production and gained wide markets generally came down very sharply.

22. *Interindustry competition* is especially important in this industry, since chemicals must first fight their way into the market by displacing natural products.

23. The *record of the industry* in increased production, new products and long-run price reduction has been outstanding. The risks taken and success achieved have resulted in consistently high profits. The industry has earned the right not to be the first target of proposals to reform the patent system or dissolve large corporations.

In brief, the antitrust laws have made a moderate contribution to the amazing development of the chemical industry by breaking up the "powder trust," by stimulating the diversification of many companies in contrast to the monopolistic giants in European countries, and by breaking up the tight patent and market agreements which once seemed to be the price of access to European technology.

CHAPTER 5

Steel

Having replaced wood and iron in the late nineteenth century as the basic raw material for capital goods, steel now makes up all but a small fraction of the output of the "iron and steel industry." The United States produced 40 per cent of the world's steel in 1955, when this gigantic industry had 658,000 employees and sales of $13.9 billion.[1]

Stages in Steelmaking

The manufacture of iron and steel begins with the smelting of iron ore in blast furnaces. Nearly two thirds of the ore comes from the Lake Superior region, the rest from other states and from abroad. The smelting fuel used is coke, the carbon residue of "metallurgical" coal distilled in coke ovens by a process which also yields valuable by-product chemicals. Blasts of hot air are forced into the furnace, and as combustion takes place the gases are drawn off for cleaning and reuse, the impurities pour out as slag with the aid of a limestone flux, and about every six hours the furnace is tapped for its molten iron. Known at this stage as pig iron, the metal is carried in ladles to a nearby steel-making furnace, but 10 or 15 per cent of the total production is shipped to foundries to be made into iron castings or to distant steel furnaces for remelting.

Most steel is made in open hearth furnaces, into which varying amounts of scrap iron and steel are charged along with the pig iron. A flux is again introduced to take off the slag, and manganese or other minerals may be added. After eight or ten hours a "heat" of steel is

1. Calculated from American Iron and Steel Institute, *Steel Facts*, New York, February 1956, pp. 2, 8; April 1956, p. 3; June 1956, p. 2.

poured into molds to form either ingots or castings. By exact control of its chemical content, steel is given the strength and elasticity that distinguish it from iron — in particular, the open hearth removes the excess carbon absorbed from the coke in the blast furnace operation. A little steel is still made in old-fashioned Bessemer converters, which use only pig iron; and high-grade alloys like stainless steel, which contains chromium and usually nickel, are made in electric furnaces, whose charge is often 100 per cent scrap.

Ingots next go to a soaking pit for uniform heating, and then to the rolling mills, where they are given marketable shape. In semifinishing mills they are made into intermediate forms: blooms, slabs and billets. Four types of specialized finishing mills next turn these by hot rolling into (1) rails and structural shapes; (2) plate, sheet, strip and tin plate; (3) rods (from which wire is then drawn) and bars; or (4) pipes and tubes. Cold rolling sometimes follows to achieve a desired strength or finish.

Although rails and wire (as well as castings and forged specialties) are ready for use, most of these products are still "semifinished" from the consumer's standpoint and must be fabricated into end products. When steel companies enter fabrication, as they often do, they are stepping beyond the steelmaking function as such to compete with the metalworking industries which are their customers.

The American Iron and Steel Institute distinguishes six steelmaking districts. Their shares of total ingot capacity in 1956 were as follows: Pittsburgh-Youngstown, 35.4 per cent; Chicago, 21.7; Eastern, 21.4; Cleveland-Detroit, 10.1; Southern, 5.7; and Western, 5.6.[2] The nearby coking coal, plus water-rail access to Lake Superior iron ore, first created a great concentration of mills around Pittsburgh; but the industry has since spread into twenty-six other states.

The Integrated Companies

The great bulk of iron and steel output is in the hands of integrated companies that produce pig iron, ingots and rolled steel. On January 1, 1956, there were twenty-four, of which the fifteen largest had 89 per cent of the country's pig iron capacity, 86 per cent of its ingot capacity, and (in 1954) 84 per cent of its hot rolled steel capacity. The United States Steel Corporation had 30.6 per cent of ingot capacity,

2. Calculated from *ibid.*, February 1956, p. 2.

TABLE 25

STEEL: INGOT CAPACITY OF FIFTEEN LARGEST COMPANIES, JANUARY 1, 1956

Firm	Ingot Capacity	Share of Capacity
	(Thousand Tons)	*(Per Cent)*
Industry total	128,363	100.0
Fifteen largest companies	110,366	86.0[a]
1. U.S. Steel Corp.	39,215	30.6
2. Bethlehem Steel Corp.	20,000	15.6
3. Republic Steel Corp.	10,262	8.0
4. Jones & Laughlin Steel Corp.	6,166	4.8
5. National Steel Corp.	6,000	4.7
6. Youngstown Sheet and Tube Co.	5,750	4.5
7. Inland Steel Co.	5,200	4.1
8. Armco Steel Corp.	5,150	4.0
9. Colorado Fuel and Iron Corp.	2,514	2.0
10. Wheeling Steel Corp.	2,130	1.7
11. Ford Motor Co.	1,877	1.5
12. Sharon Steel Corp.	1,763	1.4
13. Kaiser Steel Corp.	1,536	1.2
14. Crucible Steel Company of America	1,423	1.1
15. McLouth Steel Corp.	1,380	1.1

Source: American Iron and Steel Institute, *Annual Capacities of Coke Ovens, Blast Furnaces and Steelmaking Furnaces as of January 1, 1956, by Companies, States and Districts (United States and Canada)*, New York.

a. The fifteen companies had 89.2 per cent of pig iron capacity. They had 83.7 per cent of hot rolling capacity in 1954 (*idem, Directory of Iron and Steel Works of the United States and Canada*, 1954).

Bethlehem Steel Corporation 15.6 per cent and Republic Steel Corporation 8.0 per cent. Five companies with capacities of 4 to 5 per cent brought the total of the eight largest firms to 76.2 per cent. (See Table 25.) Only U.S. Steel operates in all six districts.

The rest of the iron and steel industry, other than the integrated companies, may be classified as follows: [3] (1) 12 merchant pig iron producers, operating 24 blast furnaces, which sell to foundries and steelmaking companies; (2) 56 semi-integrated steel companies that purchase their pig iron; (3) 128 nonintegrated companies that buy crude and semifinished steel for rolling; and (4) about 3,000 gray iron, malleable iron and steel foundries. This omits various peripheral groups like the scrap brokers and the wrought iron manufacturers.

3. Numbers in this paragraph supplied by Professor Robert M. Weidenhammer of the University of Pittsburgh.

TABLE 26

STEEL: PRINCIPAL PRODUCTS SHIPPED, 1955

Product	Shipments	Some Important Markets
	(Million Tons)	
Total	84.7	
Sheets and strip	32.4	appliances, automobile bodies
Bars and tool steel	13.0	automobile parts, hardware, machinery
Pipe, tubing and oil country goods	9.8	gas, oil
Plates	6.8	railroad cars, storage tanks
Tin mill products	6.4	containers
Structural shapes and piling	5.1	bridges, heavy construction
Semifinished products	4.8	nonintegrated steel mills
Wire and wire products	4.3	agriculture, general manufacture
Rails and accessories	2.1	railroads

Source: American Iron and Steel Institute, *Steel Facts*, New York, April 1956, p. 7.

Steel Products and Distribution

Steel is not a single commodity, but is produced in tens of thousands of combinations of size, shape, chemical analysis and metallurgical properties.[4] "Carbon" or "tonnage" steels constitute the bulk of the output, "special" or "alloy" steels the rest. Products are currently classified by the American Iron and Steel Institute into eighteen classes. If seven of these are grouped as "sheets and strip" and four as "pipe, tubing and oil country goods," these two categories plus "bars and tool steel" account for two thirds of all shipments. (See Table 26.)

There is no complete classification of customers, but the principal user is the automotive industry, with 23 per cent of all domestic purchases in 1955; other major industry users are construction, oil and gas, containers, machinery and railroads.[5]

Steel is produced almost always to fill specific orders — from either users or distributors. About 80 per cent of sales are made direct to industrial users, and the rest to distributors. These, whether mill-owned or (as is usual) independent, are called warehouses. There are said to be about 30,000 direct-buying customers of steel companies, with manufacturers of machinery and equipment forming the largest group.[6]

4. See Bay E. Estes, Jr., "Steel," Chap. 13 of Richard M. Clewett, *Marketing Channels for Manufactured Products*, Irwin, Homewood (Ill.), 1954, p. 304.

5. *Steel Facts*, April 1956, p. 7.

6. *Basic Data Relating to Steel Prices*, Joint Committee on the Economic Report, 81st Cong., 2d sess., 1950, p. 4.

Steel is quoted in terms of a base price plus extras. The extras, for the particular size, shape, finish or quality ordered, are usually, as the name implies, additions to the price, but sometimes they are deductions. From April 1939 to April 1942 the percentage of sales of fifteen types of steel made at the base price ranged from 0 to 66, the mean being 16 per cent; while the charge for extras averaged (for eight types) 18 per cent.[7]

Antitrust Cases

The modern process of making steel was developed in the 1850s by William Kelly, Henry Bessemer and others. By the 1870s steelmaking had become a large-scale undertaking. Many firms were in competition, and the intermittent pools (price-fixing agreements) rarely lasted long.[8] Cutthroat competition during the depression of 1893–96 brought a reaction in 1898–1900 with an intensified merger movement. By 1900, twenty combinations, each with a capitalization of more than $10 million, had been formed.

The Biggest "Trust"

With a competition of giants threatening among the Carnegie Company, largest producer of basic steel, the Morgan-controlled Federal Steel Company and the W. H. Moore interests, J. P. Morgan & Company arranged an amalgamation of these three groups into the United States Steel Corporation, in February 1901. Included were the six largest and four more of the twenty combinations formed in the three preceding years, and 138 companies of all sizes. Capitalization was set at $1,403 million, of which the Commissioner of Corporations later rated 52 per cent as "water" — not backed by tangible assets.

Two major aims of the new cartel-like combination were to round out its facilities further and to avoid a renewal of cutthroat competition. The expansion policy resulted in purchase of seven companies between 1902 and 1908, lease or purchase of extensive iron ore lands, and construction after 1906 of the biggest steelworks in the world, at a place in Indiana which was named Gary after U.S. Steel's chairman.

7. "Labor Dept. Examines Consumers' Prices of Steel Products," U.S. Bureau of Labor Statistics study, by Kenneth H. Hunter, Willard Fazar and Fay Bean, reprinted in *Iron Age*, April 25, 1946, pp. 118–145H, at pp. 119 and 131.

8. Henry R. Seager and Charles A. Gulick, Jr., *Trust and Corporation Problems*, Harper, New York, 1929, p. 216.

The policy of cooperation found its most picturesque expression in the "Gary dinners" of steel executives, which began as an attempt to prevent a price collapse in the 1907 recession. After dinner Judge Gary made his "revivalist" appeals against price cutting, which are supposed to have had a moderate success in stabilizing prices.

These policies of expansion and cooperation heightened public suspicion of "the Corporation," as U.S. Steel was beginning to be called. Muckraking journalists attacked it; the American Federation of Labor denounced it; Democratic congressmen insinuated that only President Theodore Roosevelt's friendship with Judge Gary was preventing an antitrust suit. The President's advance approval of U.S. Steel's purchase in 1907 of the Tennessee Coal, Iron and Railroad Company on the ground that it would halt the Wall Street panic was denounced, and even years later was called the single administrative act which had most encouraged monopoly.[9] In 1911 a critical study by the United States Bureau of Corporations began to appear,[10] and the Stanley Committee of the House of Representatives conducted a sensational public investigation.[11] With the government's antitrust suits in oil and tobacco successfully concluded,[12] Attorney General George W. Wickersham filed a long-awaited dissolution suit against U.S. Steel in October 1911.

On the day the petition was filed, the Corporation's directors — perhaps influenced by the Stanley Committee hearings and expectation of an antitrust suit — voted to drop its controversial lease of the James J. Hill ore holdings in Minnesota. These holdings had been obtained at a rental so high that critics concluded the purpose could not have been mere commercial advantage, but must have been to keep the lands out of the hands of competitors.[13] However, even with the high price, the motive could have been a desire to be assured of iron ore under all future contingencies. These Hill properties now became "a major resource of several of the Corporation's competi-

9. Huston Thompson, "Highlights in the Evolution of the Federal Trade Commission," *George Washington Law Review*, January–February 1940, p. 258.

10. *Report of the Commissioner of Corporations on the Steel Industry*, Part 1, 1911; Part 2, 1912; Part 3, 1913.

11. Hearings before the House Committee on Investigation of the United States Steel Corporation (9 vols.), 62d Cong., 1st sess., 1911.

12. *Standard Oil Company of N.J. v. U.S.*, 221 U.S. 1 (1911); *U.S. v. American Tobacco Co.*, 221 U.S. 106 (1911).

13. *Report of the Commissioner of Corporations on the Steel Industry*, Part 1, pp. 322–23.

tors." [14] A definite result of the prospective suit was the abandonment at this time of the Gary dinners.

U.S. Steel Escapes Dissolution

The Department of Justice charged, and U.S. Steel denied, that the Corporation had (1) eliminated competition in 1901, (2) acquired competing companies thereafter, and (3) fixed prices with the remaining competitors. The shares of ore, coal, iron and steelmaking facilities controlled by the Corporation were placed in evidence. After trial, a four-judge District Court dismissed the suit in June 1915.[15] The government appealed to the Supreme Court, but requested postponement of the case in 1917 on the ground that dissolution of U.S. Steel would interfere with the nation's war effort.

When the Supreme Court spoke in 1920, four justices upheld the defendant and three the government, while two did not participate.[16] These two were Justice Brandeis, who had long before declared his opinion that the Corporation was in violation of the law, and Justice McReynolds, who as Attorney General had pushed the case between 1913 and 1915. Chance may thus have saved U.S. Steel from dissolution.

With Justice McKenna as its spokesman, the Court found that the Corporation had tried to achieve a monopoly but that it had not succeeded, since it did not possess more power than all of its competitors combined. The opinion took note that the Gary dinners had been dropped in the desire to conform to the law, and that both rivals and purchasers testified (without rebuttal by the government) to the existence of active competition. It emphasized the contrast between Judge Gary's fair attitude toward competitors and the oppressive tactics of the oil and tobacco combinations dissolved in 1911. It laid down a rule which was destined to prevail in antitrust decisions for twenty-five years to come: that "the law does not make mere size an offense or the existence of unexerted power an offense." [17] Finally, it held that the public interest would be damaged by dissolution, which, among other things, would reduce the steel industry's power to compete in the export market. From this opinion emerged the concept of a

14. "U.S. Steel: I," *Fortune*, March 1936, p. 158.
15. *U.S. v. U.S. Steel Corp.*, 223 Fed. 55 (D. N.J. 1915).
16. *Ibid.*, 251 U.S. 417 (1920).
17. *Ibid.*, at 451.

"good trust" — one that had abandoned its objectionable practices and no longer attempted to drive competitors out of business or to increase its domination of the industry.

Justice Day, dissenting, agreed that mere size of a corporation involved no conflict with the law provided it was attained by lawful means and natural growth. He believed, however, that U.S. Steel had been put together with an intent to monopolize, and that both its acquisitions and its cooperative practices showed continuing violations of the Sherman Act. He felt also that it had demonstrated its power to dominate the industry.

The Corporation's victory was a milestone in the development of the steel industry, though far from as important a one as the dissolution of Standard Oil in petroleum. Since mere size was no offense, other companies proceeded to expand actively through mergers. U.S. Steel had already ceased to expand for fear of losing the suit, and, realizing its narrow escape, slowed down its expansion for some time. It took over no companies by merger between 1908 and 1920, and not only ceased adding to its ore lands after 1912, but relinquished some of its properties.[18]

Pittsburgh Plus

Shortly after its Supreme Court victory over the Department of Justice, U.S. Steel was attacked by the Federal Trade Commission for its leadership in the "Pittsburgh Plus," or basing point, system of pricing. At that time most iron and steel products were quoted, no matter where delivered and no matter where manufactured, at the announced Pittsburgh price plus the railroad freight rate from Pittsburgh to the market.

The reasons for the spread of this system, which had begun to replace f.o.b. mill pricing after 1880, are in dispute. In part it was probably natural or noncollusive, since "outside" mills had to meet the price quoted from the principal center of manufacture if they wanted to make the sale, and were not obliged to cut below this price in order to find a market. On the other hand, the pools found that to quote prices as of the same city was a convenient method of arriving at identical prices, and Pittsburgh was naturally selected. The basing

18. John G. Munson, vice president of U.S. Steel Corp., in *Study of Monopoly Power*, Hearings before Subcommittee on Study of Monopoly Power, House Judiciary Committee, 81st Cong., 2d sess., 1950, Serial 14, Part 4A (hereafter called Celler Hearings), p. 675.

point system was finally established by U.S. Steel in 1903 and 1904. Two exceptions were rails, which were picked up by the buyer or by another railroad for its account at the point of manufacture, and pig iron, a product which did not travel far and which the big companies rarely sold. In 1909 complaints by customers of its Tennessee Coal and Iron company led the Corporation to make Birmingham a basing point for bars, but at a base price $3.00 per ton above Pittsburgh's — as against a former freight addition of about $15.00.

Some characteristics of this system may be seen in terms of three phrases: "freight absorption," "phantom freight" and "mill net price." (1) Since the price at a market was always the Pittsburgh price plus freight, any mill farther away from the market than Pittsburgh had to take the extra freight cost out of its profits — i.e., had to absorb freight. At this early period few outside mills were actually selling in territory closer to the Pittsburgh mills than to themselves. (2) Any outside mill located closer to its market than its Pittsburgh competitors could collect, as part of its delivered price, the equivalent of freight charges which had never actually been paid — i.e., phantom freight. On some sales Chicago mills had no freight at all to pay, and yet their sale price included the entire freight from Pittsburgh. (3) The net price obtained on each sale by one of these outside mills depended on whether it was absorbing freight, happened to have the same transportation cost to the customer as did Pittsburgh mills, or was receiving phantom freight. These differences in mill net prices were viewed as geographic price discrimination between the customers.

Abolition of Pittsburgh Plus

Opposition to Pittsburgh Plus emerged among customers that were closer to Chicago than to Pittsburgh, and for many years the *Chicago Tribune* ran the slogan "Abolish Pittsburgh Plus" just above its leading editorial every day. In 1909 and 1911 Chicago mills attempted to utilize some of their surplus capacity by making their city a separate basing point, but they soon went back to the higher profit they were accustomed to getting in the guise of phantom freight. The War Industries Board made Chicago a basing point in 1917, but rescinded the regulation in 1918. U.S. Steel "and one or two other steel producers" were suspected of inspiring this action,[19] but it should be

19. FTC, *The Basing Point Problem,* TNEC Monograph 42, 1941, p. 108.

noted that the Corporation had the largest mills in Chicago as well as in Pittsburgh.

Cancellation of the War Industries Board's ruling set off a new series of complaints. In January 1919 a "Western Association of Rolled Steel Consumers for the Abolition of Pittsburgh Plus" was established. Its attorney, after fruitless conferences with Judge Gary, went, with the latter's approval,[20] to the Federal Trade Commission. Other business associations, as well as cities in the West and South and thirty-two state governments, joined in the agitation. When railroad rates advanced 40 per cent in September 1920, the fight was intensified. The Federal Trade Commission, which had dismissed the matter by a 3–2 vote in July 1920, now reversed itself by the vote of a new member who replaced one of the majority. In April 1921 it filed a complaint against U.S. Steel, charging that Pittsburgh Plus violated Section 2 of the Clayton Act as price discrimination against western consumers and Section 5 of the Federal Trade Commission Act as an unfair method of competition. In July 1921 price cutting at Chicago caused the Corporation to make this a basing point for plates, shapes and bars.

After lengthy hearings, the Commission issued a cease and desist order in July 1924.[21] The order directed U.S. Steel to cease all quotations "upon any other basing point than that where the products are manufactured or from which they are shipped." Contrary to expectations, the Corporation did not contest the order, but promised to comply so far as practical. In September 1924 it made Chicago and several other cities basing points for various products. Although all base prices established were higher than at Pittsburgh, they were nevertheless lower, in some cases substantially lower, than the previous Pittsburgh quotation plus transportation charge.[22]

The Multiple Basing Point System

U.S. Steel considered it impractical to make all its mills basing points, and instead added to its list gradually as time went on. Its competitors, which should in the name of consistency have been cov-

20. Letter of Elbert H. Gary to FTC, July 7, 1919, quoted in Louis Marengo, *Basing Point Pricing in the Steel Industry*, unpublished doctoral thesis, Harvard University, Cambridge, 1950, p. 37.

21. *U.S. Steel Corp.*, Docket 760, 8 FTC 1 (1924).

22. Frank A. Fetter, *The Masquerade of Monopoly*, Harcourt, Brace, New York, 1931, pp. 159–60.

ered by the Commission's order, did the same. Thus in December 1927 Bethlehem made four of its eastern mills basing points for shapes, plates and bars; but again some of the base prices were above those at Pittsburgh. The surmise that this action was stimulated by a Federal Trade Commission investigation of acquisitions by Bethlehem in 1922 and 1923 which was pressed until 1927 and then put on the "suspense calendar" [23] would seem to have little basis. In 1933 the American Iron and Steel Institute directors, as the National Recovery Administration Code Authority, added pig iron to the list of basing point products. Pressure from the automobile companies caused the Code Authority to adopt "Commercial Resolution No. 21," which provided that a modest amount of freight would be absorbed on all sales to Detroit, although Detroit itself was not officially made a basing point. In 1934 the proportion of capacity actually located at basing points ranged for various products from 6.3 per cent (sheets) to 40.9 per cent (pig iron), with the median for seventeen products at 21.8.[24]

The biggest change occurred in June 1938, when U.S. Steel abolished the differentials of Chicago and Birmingham over Pittsburgh, and in retaliation the independents established some additional basing points of their own. U.S. Steel was now forced to absorb freight for the first time in many eastern markets.[25] Recent great increases in capacity outside Pittsburgh were perhaps responsible for these changes; [26] but one motive may have been to forestall criticism by the Temporary National Economic Committee, just established by Congress.[27]

By 1947 most producing cities were basing points for one product or another, as were some ports, and cities with important warehouses. All mills of U.S. Steel were basing points except a very few which shipped mostly to other mills for processing. For twenty-one products the median percentage of capacity located within fifteen miles of a basing point was 48.2.[28]

23. *Ibid.*, p. 163.

24. Carroll R. Daugherty, Melvin G. de Chazeau and Samuel S. Stratton, *The Economics of the Iron and Steel Industry*, McGraw-Hill, New York, 1937, Vol. 2, p. 710.

25. H. E. Alderfer and E. B. Michl, *Economics of American Industry*, McGraw-Hill, New York, 2d edition, 1950, p. 83.

26. Glenn McLaughlin, "The Abolition of Inter-Basing Point Differentials in the Steel Industry," *Pittsburgh Business Review*, Vol. 8, No. 9, p. 1, cited in Marengo thesis, p. 30.

27. Fritz Machlup, *The Basing-Point System*, Blakiston, Philadelphia, 1949, p. 70; John M. Clark, *The Social Control of Business*, McGraw-Hill, New York, 2d edition, 1939, p. 366.

28. Marengo thesis, p. 105.

The Federal Trade Commission may have expected a court defeat if it attempted 100 per cent enforcement of its 1924 steel order, since in 1925 the Supreme Court upheld a basing point system operating in the cement industry.[29] It was not until 1937 that the Commission felt safe in renewing its campaign in this area.

The Merger Movement in Steel

All of the twelve largest publicly held steel companies as of 1950, and two of the next four in size, came into being through the consolidation of separate companies.[30] A Federal Trade Commission study has shown that 6.9 per cent of the increase in assets of U.S. Steel between 1915 and 1945 resulted from mergers, as did 9.6 to 63.8 per cent (weighted average: 33.7) of the increase in assets of seven other companies. The merger movement accounted for 23.6 per cent of the increase in assets of these eight big companies combined; but reinvestment of profits and issues of securities accounted for 76.4 per cent. (See Table 27.) Mergers contributed also to a reduction in the relative power of the biggest corporation. In 1915 U.S. Steel had 37.7 per cent of the total assets of the eight largest firms; in 1945, if the only changes had been those due to mergers, it would have had only 30.8 per cent.

Of the thirty mergers which added $5 million or more in assets to the acquiring company, three were of producers of coal or iron ore, nine of fabricators or users of steel by-products, and eighteen of steel companies; the total capital increment obtained through the raw material producers was $22 million, through the fabricators $153 million, and through the steel companies $836 million. Some competition between steel companies themselves was eliminated in these cases; but the main objective appears to have been to acquire supplementary rather than competing production.[31] Thus Jones & Laughlin's acquisition of the $35 million (book value) Otis Steel Company in 1942 must have deprived some customers of a choice between suppliers, but it was primarily an effort to acquire strip production, in which Jones & Laughlin was weak.

29. *Cement Manufacturers Protective Ass'n. v. U.S.*, 268 U.S. 588 (1925).

30. SEC Commissioner Donald C. Cook, Celler Hearings, p. 423.

31. See Cecil Eaton Fraser and Georges F. Doriot, *Analyzing Our Industries*, McGraw-Hill, New York, 1932, pp. 241, 254–61.

TABLE 27

STEEL: IMPORTANCE OF ACQUISITIONS IN CAPITAL EXPANSION OF EIGHT COMPANIES, 1915–45

Firm	Acquisitions for Which Data Are Available	Undepreciated Additions to Net Assets: Total	Undepreciated Additions to Net Assets: Due to Acquisitions	Per Cent of Total Increment in Net Assets Due to Acquisitions
		(Millions)		
Eight companies	99	$4,502	$1,063	23.6
U.S. Steel Corp.	12	1,699	118	6.9
Bethlehem Steel Corp.	33	1,185	396	33.4
Republic Steel Corp.	13	496	316	63.8
Jones & Laughlin Steel Corp.[a]	13	257	40	15.7
Youngstown Sheet and Tube Co.	4	360	103	28.5
Inland Steel Co.[b]	13	206	20	9.6
American Rolling Mill Co.[c]	8	246	49	20.0
Colorado Fuel and Iron Corp.[d]	3	52	22	41.8

Source: FTC, *Report on the Merger Movement: A Summary Report*, 1948, p. 72.

a. 1923–45 only.
b. 1918–45 only.
c. Renamed Armco Steel Corp. in 1948.
d. 1936–45 only.

The Antitrust Agencies and Steel Mergers, 1922-35

The two antitrust agencies first took serious notice of the merger movement in steel in 1922,[32] when seven large companies proposed the formation of the "North American Steel Company," only slightly smaller than U.S. Steel, and the Senate requested both the Department of Justice and the Federal Trade Commission to report on its legality. The proposed merger meanwhile broke apart into two: one combining Midvale Steel and Ordnance Company with the smaller Republic and Inland companies; the other, Bethlehem and Lackawanna Steel Company. The Attorney General reported that neither merger would violate the Sherman or Clayton Act and that their result would be more effective competition with U.S. Steel, whose own recent approval by the Supreme Court he noted.[33]

The Federal Trade Commission, however, brought complaints against both groups, charging that the mergers would constitute unfair competition under Section 5 of the Federal Trade Commission

32. See history in FTC, *Relative Efficiency of Large, Medium-Sized and Small Business*, TNEC Monograph 13, 1941, pp. 214–97.

33. Opinion of Attorney General Charles M. Daugherty, reprinted in *ibid.*, pp. 255–66.

Act.[34] The Midvale-Republic-Inland combination was thereupon dropped by its promoters; but Bethlehem went ahead to acquire both Lackawanna and, in January 1923, Midvale itself. The Commission's complaint, revised to charge a Clayton Act violation, was suspended in 1927 when the Supreme Court held in the *Eastman Kodak* case that the Clayton Act gave the Commission no power to order divestiture of assets,[35] and later dismissed.

By these acquisitions Bethlehem increased its ingot capacity from 3.05 to 7.6 million gross tons, or to well over twice the size of the third and fourth ranking companies, Jones & Laughlin and Youngstown Sheet and Tube Company. When Bethlehem and Youngstown themselves tried to merge in 1930, minority stockholders in Youngstown blocked the move.

The first time a steel merger reached the courts was in 1935. Republic, whose ingot capacity had increased from 2.4 to 5.4 million tons by a merger in 1930, had now purchased the assets of the Corrigan, McKinney Steel Company. The Department of Justice contended that this union of the third and twelfth largest companies would "substantially lessen competition" and thus violate Section 7 of the Clayton Act. It was brought out at the trial that competition was eliminated between the two companies in several products, but that there would still be plenty of competition from other concerns, since Republic's 7.2 per cent of total ingot capacity would be increased only to 8.7. Judge Fred M. Raymond of the Northern Ohio District Court held that the merger's aim was to give Republic needed reserves of iron ore and coal, plus pig iron facilities. He ruled that mere lessening of competition did not necessarily condemn a merger, unless the government could show both that the lessening was substantial and that the public would thus be injured.[36]

The Antitrust Agencies and Postwar Steel Mergers

After World War II, mergers of steel companies to secure geographic and product diversification continued. The Department of Justice intervened at least three times. In 1947 it filed suit in the *Columbia Steel* case, discussed below. In the same year it declined to approve

34. *Midvale Steel and Ordnance Co.*, Docket 905, 5 FTC 487 (1922); *Bethlehem Steel Corp.*, Dockets 891, 5 FTC 488 (1923), and 962, 28 FTC 1732 (1939).

35. *Eastman Kodak Co. v. FTC,* 274 U.S. 619 (1927).

36. *U.S. v. Republic Steel Corp.*, 11 F. Supp. 117 (N.D. Ohio 1935).

purchase of a blast furnace property by Koppers Company and Hanna Coal and Ore Corporation because the purchase was a joint venture. Hanna sold its interest to Koppers and continued supplying the furnace with ore under a long-term contract.[37]

In 1954 the Department's objection stopped another proposed Bethlehem-Youngstown merger. These two companies were still, as they had been in 1930 when their merger was first proposed, "uniquely complementary." [38] Bethlehem sold mainly in the eastern and Pacific Coast districts, Youngstown in the Middle West; and Youngstown produced the seamless and electric-weld pipe and tubes which were the principal gap in Bethlehem's line. It is true that the two corporations did compete to some extent by selling identical products in the same markets. Thus Bethlehem supplied 10.7 per cent and Youngstown 2.3 per cent of Michigan's purchases of the products they both made, and the Department of Justice emphasized that to this extent competition would be removed.[39] A survey of the total industry situation, and of the plans for expansion in the Chicago area which the two companies had in mind and which could be much more easily financed by the consolidation than by Youngstown alone, leaves the impression that the competition suppressed might well have proved less than the additional competition created.[40] A single powerful nationwide company would certainly offer superior service to customers with scattered plants, as against possible damage to other customers who would lose one independent source of supply.

The real problems posed by the merger were of a social and political nature: if it were permitted, would not most other steel companies quickly seek the same advantages in transportation, allocation of raw materials and orders among plants, financing and the rest? Would this leave more than three or four steel concerns? Would not other industries follow? Would this be a healthy social situation even if it tended to reduce costs of production?

37. FTC, *Report on the Control of Iron Ore*, presented to Antitrust Subcommittee of House Judiciary Committee, 1952, pp. 75–76.

38. Arthur B. Homer, president of Bethlehem Steel Corp., in *A Study of the Antitrust Laws*, Hearings before Subcommittee on Antitrust and Monopoly, Senate Judiciary Committee, 84th Cong., 1st sess., 1955, Part 2, p. 494; and George McCuskey, vice president of Youngstown Sheet and Tube Co., *ibid.*, p. 498.

39. Arthur B. Homer, *ibid.*, p. 493.

40. See *ibid.*, pp. 490–92; C. H. H. Weikel, "Some Aspects of the Proposed Bethlehem-Youngstown Merger," *Michigan Business Review*, July 1955, pp. 29–31; John Chamberlain, "The Lost Merger," *Barron's*, October 11, 1954, pp. 23–24.

The Interlocking Director Proceeding

A companion suit to that against the Republic-Corrigan merger, based on the same investigation and filed on the same day in 1935, charged eight individuals with holding directorships in more than one steel company.[41] One interlock was between Republic Steel and the Delaware River Steel Corporation, which, despite its name, was a merchant blast furnace. Although Republic did not sell pig iron, the director found it simplest to resign from the Delaware board. The seven remaining interlocks were between Corrigan, McKinney (and holding companies that controlled it) and the Inland, Otis, Wheeling and Youngstown steel companies — and between Otis and Youngstown. When Corrigan, McKinney was absorbed by Republic (not one of the interlocking firms), the interlocks disappeared, and the suit was dropped. Despite the lack of a decision, the proceeding served until 1952 as the principal application of Section 8 of the Clayton Act.

Fifteen years later, a study of possible interlocking directorates in the steel industry revealed no situation which seemed to constitute a violation. The Celler Committee did discover a common director between the Alan Wood Steel Company and the Pittsburgh Steel Company;[42] but the Department of Justice had found in 1947 that the competition between these companies was "not such as to warrant further action."[43]

The Hepburn Act and Its Interpretation

The Hepburn Act of 1906, or "Commodities Clause" amendment to the Interstate Commerce Act, forbade any railroad to transport "any article or commodity, other than timber and the manufactured products thereof, manufactured, mined, or produced by it, or under its authority, or which it may own in whole or in part, or in which it may have any interest, direct or indirect" unless the railroad itself was to be the final user. The purpose of this clause, which has been enforced by the Antitrust Division, was to prevent discrimination by railroads in favor of their own commodities. The early cases that reached the Supreme Court were from the anthracite industry.[44]

41. *U.S. v. William G. Mather*, Civil 5153 (N.D. Ohio 1935), reprinted in Celler Hearings, Part 4-B (hereafter cited as Celler Exhibits), pp. 80–87.

42. Donald C. Cook, Celler Hearings, pp. 452–53.

43. Letter from Peyton Ford, Assistant to the Attorney General, *ibid.*, p. 463.

44. *U.S. v. Delaware & Hudson Co.*, 213 U.S. 366 (1909); *U.S. v. Reading Co.*, 253 U.S. 26 (1920); *U.S. v. Lehigh Valley Rr. Co.*, 254 U.S. 255 (1920).

The first important influence of the Commodities Clause in steel came in 1915 and 1916, when the Pennsylvania Railroad, as a result of federal indictment, sold its Pennsylvania Steel Company to Bethlehem.[45] This sale had no particular effect on competition and would almost certainly have occurred sooner or later even without the Hepburn Act, since a railroad's operations cannot be easily correlated with those of steel manufacture. Bethlehem gradually expanded the Sparrows Point, Maryland, plant — the slightly smaller of two thus obtained — from 672,000 tons of ingot capacity to 6,200,000 tons, making it its largest plant.

Some time later the government attacked U.S. Steel's ownership of all the stock of the Elgin, Joliet & Eastern Railway Company, which had come to it in 1901 as part of its original consolidation. Here a railroad company was owned by an industrial corporation, instead of the opposite relationship which the Hepburn Act had assumed. U.S. Steel shipped 60 per cent of the railroad's tonnage, had four representatives on its board of directors, and had itself approved the railroad's dividend declarations, capital expenditures and other important transactions. The Supreme Court, by a 6–3 decision in 1936, upheld the relationship, on Justice McReynolds' argument that "the mere power to control, the possibility of initiating unlawful conditions, is not enough, as clearly pointed out in *United States v. Delaware & Hudson Co.*" [46] Justice Stone, dissenting, felt that this decision reduced the Commodities Clause "to a cipher." [47]

In June 1943 a second suit was brought, at the request of the Interstate Commerce Commission, to test whether the "*E. J. & E.* rule" still held.[48] The Bethlehem Steel Corporation owned the stock of the South Buffalo Railway Company and had formerly controlled the railroad directly. A reorganization was effected in 1939 to comply with the *E. J. & E.* decision. Officers of the steel company ceased to advise the railroad, and previous rather than present employees of Bethlehem took over its operation. The Supreme Court voted 5 to 4 in 1948 that this separation was adequate. The majority was strongly influenced by the fact that in 1940 Congress rejected a proposal to reverse the *E. J. & E.* rule by statute. Justice Jackson also pointed out that it

45. ICC Commissioner Clyde B. Aitchison, Celler Hearings, p. 859.

46. *U.S. v. Elgin, Joliet & Eastern Ry. Co.*, 298 U.S. 492, 503 (1936).

47. *Ibid.*, at 512.

48. Arne C. Wiprud, Celler Hearings, p. 247.

would be impossible to find independent capital willing to invest in a "dependent facility wedged in between shippers, one of whom controls 70 per cent of its revenues, and the trunk-line railroads." [49] Justice Rutledge, speaking for the dissenters, wanted the *E. J. & E.* decision frankly overruled. He expressed one side of an important constitutional issue:

> This is another case where the Court saddles Congress with the load of correcting its own emasculation of a statute, by drawing from Congress' failure explicitly to overrule it the unjustified inference that Congress approves the mistake.[50]

Sequel of the Railroad Ownership Cases

As a result of these failures in court, no more complaints on this score have been lodged with the ICC, and all investigations undertaken by it have found relationships which conformed to these decisions. Further suits have been forestalled by the

> notable fact that the successive decisions of the Supreme Court have led carriers to make changes in their practices, and in their intercompany and intercorporate relations, designed to get them in the clear as against successful attack by civil process or criminal proceedings.[51]

There has been "an effort to remove some of the evils," according to one government attorney; for example, the steel-company-controlled railroads no longer discriminate in favor of their owners in spotting cars.[52] Representatives of the companies hold that they never did discriminate. Whatever the situation may have been previously, there is much less complaint against the operation of these railroads today. At the end of 1948 six of the ten largest steel companies owned tap line railroads.[53]

The Stainless Steel Patent Agreements

In November 1944 and January 1945 the Department of Justice brought criminal and civil proceedings against eighteen producers of

49. *U.S. v. South Buffalo Ry. Co.*, 333 U.S. 771, 784 (1948).
50. *Ibid.*, at 785–86.
51. Clyde B. Aitchison, Celler Hearings, p. 880.
52. Arne C. Wiprud, *ibid.*, p. 255.
53. Celler Exhibits, pp. 684–85.

stainless steel.[54] According to the charges, licensees of the Chemical Foundation (which had received the German patents seized in World War I) had persuaded it in 1934 to set prices at which they would sell stainless steel, and after 1937 they had followed published price lists of the Carpenter Steel Company (holder of improvement patents). Moreover, Krupp's American subsidiary had a list of fixed prices at which its six American licensees could sell. It was claimed that some of the manufacturers even offered to pay royalties on expired patents, so as to keep the agreement within the established legal rule [55] that a patentee could fix prices charged by his licensees. Periodic meetings to discuss prices were held at the Duquesne Club in Pittsburgh, the Biltmore Hotel in New York, and other places. Agreements were alleged to have been reached on all types of products made of stainless steel, and not merely on those which were patented.

In February 1945 the defendants pleaded *nolo contendere*, stating that a trial would require more time than their chief operating officers could spare during the war emergency.[56] In October 1948, after the *Line Material* and *Gypsum* decisions of the Supreme Court had removed much of the right of a patentee to control his licensees' prices,[57] the civil suit in stainless steel was settled by a consent decree. This directed the defendants not to fix prices, or exchange advance information when bidding on government contracts; and ordered the Carpenter company to issue licenses under any remaining patents to any applicant upon the payment of reasonable royalties. The patents, as it happens, were about to expire. A staff member of the Antitrust Division stated to the writer five years later that the consent decree of 1948 was being obeyed, and that the prevailing uniformity of prices was a natural result of competition rather than of price fixing.

Other Restrictive Agreements

Steel companies have been involved in very few restrictive agreements which have come into court under the antitrust laws. The list

54. *U.S. v. Allegheny Ludlum Steel Corp.*, Cr. 2793C (D. N.J. 1944), Civil 45–83 (D. N.J. 1945), reprinted in Celler Exhibits, pp. 504–27.

55. *U.S. v. General Electric Co.*, 272 U.S. 476 (1926).

56. Nathan L. Miller, general counsel of U.S. Steel Corp., Celler Hearings, pp. 606, 612–13.

57. *U.S. v. Line Material Co.*, 333 U.S. 287 (1948); *U.S. v. U.S. Gypsum Co.*, 333 U.S. 364 (1948).

which follows covers all or nearly all of these, except as treated elsewhere in the chapter, down to the year 1955.

1. Some steel companies were among the fifty defendants in a bolt, nut and rivet consent decree of March 1931.[58] This was one of several cases brought by Assistant Attorney General John Lord O'Brian which charged trade associations with controlling prices and terms of sale.

2. In June 1936 fourteen makers of tin plate agreed with the Federal Trade Commission to abandon a program of selling "stock plate" (consisting of "warming up sizes, overruns and seconds") for export only, and of mutilating any not exported into a form known as "waste waste" (scrap).[59]

3. In 1942 the Fourth Circuit Court of Appeals sustained a Federal Trade Commission order against tying clauses in the sale of wire and strapping, the latter consisting of strips or bands of steel. No distinction need be made here between these two articles, which are used to bind heavy materials. The three largest distributors — including a U.S. Steel subsidiary — also made machines which fastened the wire, and each refused to sell or lease these except to buyers of its own strapping. The respondent in this case did only 5 to 7 per cent of the total business in such wire. However, Judge John J. Parker emphasized not only that the three respondents together sold two thirds to three fourths of the wire handled by the twelve tying-machine manufacturers, but that the defendant's wire sales came to the "substantial" sum of $2 million a year. He foreshadowed the "quantitative substantiality" ruling of the Supreme Court in the *Standard Stations* case [60] when he declared that

> the substantiality of the lessening of competition is to be judged with reference to the effect of the trade practice upon the volume of business controlled by the person engaging in it, not with reference to the proportion which that business bears to the entire volume of such business throughout the country.[61]

4. Several steel companies, since they manufactured the basic material used to make rigid steel conduit (pipe which holds electrical wiring), cooperated with the sellers of this product in their basing

58. *U.S. v. Bolt, Nut and Rivet Manufacturers Ass'n.*, Eq. 58–383 (S.D. N.Y. 1931).

59. *American Sheet and Tin Plate Co.*, Docket 2741, 22 FTC 711 (1936).

60. *Standard Oil Company of Calif. v. U.S.*, 337 U.S. 293 (1949).

61. *Signode Steel Strapping Co. v. FTC*, 132 F. 2d 48, 54 (4th Cir. 1942).

point system. They thus became respondents in a Federal Trade Commission complaint in January 1941 and order in June 1944, a Seventh Circuit Court decision in 1948 sustaining the Commission, and a 4–4 Supreme Court split in 1949 which let the lower court decision stand.[62] This was the famous "conscious parallelism" case, which applied Section 5 of the Federal Trade Commission Act to require the companies to cease selling at uniform delivered prices in the knowledge that competitors also were doing so.

5. In June 1953 a group of corrugated metal culvert manufacturers and the mill supplying their steel signed a consent decree, agreeing not to establish quotas, divide sales territories or exclude others from the business.[63]

6. In January 1954 the Federal Trade Commission charged the largest scrap broker with acquiring competitors in violation of Section 7 of the Clayton Act and with making exclusive agreements to supply a number of iron and steel plants belonging both to large and small producers.[64]

7. In February 1955 the Commission secured a consent order directing three of the large steel companies and seventeen other makers of "rain goods" (parts for outside pipe, gutters, etc.) not to fix prices or terms of sale directly or indirectly.[65]

8. In April 1955 a similar consent order was directed against five manufacturers of steel drums, four of which were owned by integrated steel companies.[66] One of the respondents takes the position that the twenty independent drum manufacturers had similar or identical practices, but that the matter was not important enough to the steel companies to warrant a legal contest.

Steel on the West Coast

U.S. Steel and Bethlehem became the principal West Coast producers in 1930, when U.S. Steel purchased the Columbia Steel Corporation with two rolling mills in California and a blast furnace in

62. *Triangle Conduit and Cable Co. v. FTC*, 168 F. 2d 175 (7th Cir. 1948); *Clayton Mark & Co. v. FTC*, 336 U.S. 956 (1949).

63. *U.S. v. Republic Steel Corp.*, Civil 26043 (N.D. Ohio 1953), Consent decree, Commerce Clearing House, *1953 Trade Cases*, No. 67510.

64. *Luria Bros. & Co.*, FTC Docket 6156.

65. *Barnes Metal Products Co.*, FTC Docket 6225.

66. *U.S. Steel Corp.*, FTC Docket 6078.

Utah, while Bethlehem also acquired two rolling mill properties in California. Output in these states remained (and still remains) far below consumption. The chief West Coast supplier and the price leader there was Bethlehem, from its mills at Sparrows Point, Maryland. There was naturally much complaint on the West Coast about the high price of steel, but its basic cause was clearly the cost of transportation.

In 1945 an integrated steel mill at Geneva, Utah, which had cost the government nearly $200 million to build during the war and had been operated on contract by U.S. Steel, was put up for sale. The Corporation, finding that some members of the War Surplus Board opposed it as a buyer, decided not to bid but changed its mind when urged by state and civic groups in Utah and by the Surplus Property Administrator himself. Its bid of $47.5 million to the government, plus a pledge to spend $18.6 million in reconverting the facilities, secured the plant. The Attorney General, whose aides felt that this purchase would increase the availability of steel to West Coast customers, approved it over objections of the Federal Trade Commission. He noted that U.S. Steel had retired an equal amount of producing capacity in the East.

Earlier plans of U.S. Steel to build its own fabricating facilities for structural steel in California — matching those of Bethlehem, and dispensing with the necessity of shipping from its American Bridge Company plant at Chicago — had been postponed because of the war. In 1945 the president of Consolidated Steel Corporation, the largest independent fabricator and erector on the West Coast, offered to sell its facilities. With the fabrication business subject to cyclical fluctuations, he wanted to withdraw the stockholders' equity at a time when a favorable price could be realized. Learning that equivalent plants would cost $14 million to build, U.S. Steel was glad to have its subsidiary, Columbia Steel, make the purchase for $8.25 million. To its prewar motive there was now added the desire to find a peacetime outlet for the structural shapes and steel plates which were the chief items of production at the Geneva plant. In its opinion the open market was too small to take them.

The Columbia Steel Decision

The government brought suit in February 1947 to enjoin this merger. It argued (1) that it would give the Corporation 25 or 30 per cent of the fabricating facilities in eleven western and southwestern states which made up Consolidated's market, in addition to its existing 30 per cent of the ingot capacity there, and (2) that the independent steel producers that had previously sold to Consolidated would lose this market. In November 1947 the U.S. District Court in Delaware dismissed this suit, and in June 1948 the Supreme Court, by a 5–4 vote, sustained its ruling.[67]

The majority opinion, delivered by Justice Reed, reasoned as follows: (1) This was a case of normal vertical integration, permitted by law. (2) The competition between Consolidated and U.S. Steel on the West Coast had not been substantial, since the former did only light and medium structural fabrication and the latter heavy fabrication; Consolidated but not U.S. Steel manufactured plates; and Consolidated's pipe output was high-priced and not competitive with U.S. Steel's. (3) Other steel companies were not having much of their market foreclosed, since Consolidated used only 3 per cent of the rolled steel in the eleven states in which it operated. (4) Final consumers were not being subjected to a monopoly, since there were plenty of independent fabricators left, both those on the West Coast and firms that could ship in from the East. (5) U.S. Steel was not monopolizing the national market any more than the local, nor would this purchase permit it to do so.

The dissenting opinion of Justice Douglas has been widely quoted. "This is the most important antitrust case which has been before the Court in years," he declared.[68] "We have here the problem of bigness. Its lesson should by now have been burned into our memory by Brandeis"[69] (a reference to Justice Brandeis' published essays and dissenting opinions). Justice Douglas pointed out that U.S. Steel's purpose, to assure a market for Geneva's plates and shapes whenever demand fell off, amounted to a desire to avoid having to compete in the open market at such a time. Speaking of the disappearance of Consolidated as a competing fabricator, he refused to view either its $5 million of competitive purchases of steel or its 3 per cent of the western market as "immaterial." Although rejecting the national market as a criterion of monopoly, he stressed that U.S. Steel controlled a third of steel sales even on the national basis. He concluded:

67. *U.S. v. Columbia Steel Co.*, 74 F. Supp. 671 (D. Del. 1947), 334 U.S. 495 (1948).

68. *Ibid.*, at 534.

69. *Ibid.*, at 535.

"The least I can say is that a company that has that tremendous leverage on our economy is big enough." [70] This disappointment with the failure of the majority to put a curb on "bigness" may have been sharpened by the apparent contrast with the philosophy of the recently decided *Alcoa* and *American Tobacco* cases.[71]

Had the *Columbia* decision gone the other way, U.S. Steel planned to build its own West Coast fabricating plant. If Consolidated had then been forced out of business, the result would have been much the same as that of the merger, except for waste of capital. Quite likely, however, rising volume of business would have offered room for all.

Steel Abandons the Basing Point System

The most important antitrust decision affecting steel since 1920 was one in another industry. In 1937 the Federal Trade Commission began its campaign against the multiple basing point system in cement, and in April 1948 it won a Supreme Court ruling that this system constituted price discrimination under the Clayton Act, and collusive price fixing, hence unfair competition, under the Federal Trade Commission Act.[72] In June the Supreme Court denied a rehearing. U.S. Steel began selling on an f.o.b. mill basis in July, and in October it accepted after twenty-four years a final Federal Trade Commission order in the Pittsburgh Plus case.

Meanwhile the Commission had filed a complaint against steel's multiple basing point system in 1947, making the American Iron and Steel Institute and its eighty-five members defendants. In 1951 it negotiated an order by which the whole industry agreed not to pursue "any planned common course of action" in fixing prices or in applying "any system or formula which produces identical price quotations or prices or delivered costs." [73] There was no ban against "delivered pricing or freight absorption as such when innocently and independently pursued, regularly or otherwise, with the result of promoting competition." [74] The cooperative circulation of freight rate books and lists of uniform extra charges (like those issued under the NRA by the

70. *Ibid.*, at 540.

71. *U.S. v. Aluminum Company of America*, 145 F. 2d 416 (2d Cir. 1945); *U.S. v. American Tobacco Co.*, 328 U.S. 781 (1946).

72. *FTC v. Cement Institute*, 333 U.S. 683 (1948).

73. *American Iron and Steel Institute*, Docket 5508, 48 FTC 123, 152–53 (1951).

74. *Ibid.*, at 154.

American Iron and Steel Institute) was also forbidden. Customers were to be given the right to take their steel at the point of production if they wished. A very small fraction — certainly under 10 per cent — take advantage of this privilege today.

The summer of 1948 was an excellent time for steel to make this change — which was apparently inevitable even though the industry might have resisted legal attack on the ground that it had not employed the cooperative practices found in cement. Demand was so high that transportation costs could easily be passed on to consumers. Not only did customers not buying from the nearest mill thus lose the advantage of freight absorption, but base prices themselves were increased at the same time. It is not surprising that steel executives indicate satisfaction with the results of the decision. The words used by one in an interview are typical of the attitudes expressed by several:

> We now check carefully before we meet the price a customer tells us that a competitor is quoting. We are also careful in selecting customers, and customers are more insistent that we ship from the nearest mill. We are making sure that this mill is efficient for this product. Abandoning the old groove of always absorbing freight to meet the price has put us on our toes, and has reduced our costs in more ways than just by the saving of freight.

It was widely predicted that the abolition of the basing point system would cause a movement of steel mills closer to their markets in order not to lose customers who could no longer be reached by absorbing freight. Bethlehem's desire to acquire Youngstown and thus gain a Chicago mill has been used as an illustration.[75] U.S. Steel's construction of its Fairless plant on the Delaware River near Trenton has been attributed to the need of keeping eastern customers who were now being charged more than $7 a ton freight from Pittsburgh.[76]

Any such causal connection is hard to prove. *Iron Age* reported as early as May 1946 that plans for such an eastern mill were "about completed." [77] Moreover, freight absorption is not actually outlawed today, and U.S. Steel can still sell in the East from Pittsburgh. Finally,

75. *Business Week*, August 14, 1954, p. 25.

76. *Ibid.*; Gilbert Burck, "The Transformation of U.S. Steel," *Fortune*, January 1956, p. 200; Nathan Belfer, "Some Economic Effects of the New Morrisville, Pennsylvania, Steel Plant," *Current Economic Comment*, Bureau of Economic and Business Research, College of Commerce and Business Administration, University of Illinois, August 1953, pp. 46–48.

77. *Iron Age*, May 16, 1946, p. 94.

a plant on the Atlantic seaboard became almost a necessity when the Corporation announced in January 1950 its discovery of the huge Cerro Bolivar ore deposit in Venezuela. Raw materials remain predominant in determining the location of steel mills. Most, though not all, steel men dismiss the idea that abandonment of the basing point system has exerted any real influence yet on mill location.

The Impact on Customers

The attitude of customers was reflected in two polls taken by *Iron Age*.[78] Answering its questionnaire sent in June 1948 to firms with a net worth exceeding $125,000, 70 per cent of 881 metalworking companies opposed abandonment of basing points. Eighty per cent of those more than 500 miles from their source of supply felt this way, but so did 61 per cent of those within 50 miles — who would have lost little or no freight absorption. Ten months later, when the actual experience of increased delivered prices was added to the preference for established patterns, those wanting restoration of the basing point system increased to 87 per cent out of 1,846 answering. Although large customers and those in the western states had brought this average up, even small firms in the East showed 85 per cent opposed to f.o.b. pricing.

In view of these polls, it is not surprising that steel buyers joined with producers in demanding congressional action to legalize freight absorption. A bill which was passed after two years of agitation was vetoed by President Truman in June 1950. Meanwhile the movement for legislation was losing its momentum as it became clearer that freight absorption was probably still legal if unaccompanied by conspiracy.

The change to f.o.b. mill pricing in 1948 was only one of three developments that simultaneously affected steel users who were distant from their sources of supply. The most important was the shortage of steel resulting from the backlog of demand for civilian durable goods and for construction which accumulated during World War II. The third was the rise in freight rates after the war. Mills with more orders than they had steel to supply naturally sold first to their nearby customers, so as to reduce the amount of freight they had to absorb. A "large-scale swapping of customers" occurred, which reduced the

78. *Ibid.*, July 1, 1948, pp. 119–21; May 19, 1949, p. 141.

amount of cross hauling considerably.[79] Unfortunately some distant customers who were cut adrift could not find nearby mills to supply them, since to these mills they were "new" customers who had no "historical position" to give them a priority. In some cases distant mills refused to supply old customers even if they paid the full freight, since distant purchasers represented a market in which the mill did not expect to have any permanent interest. A real shortage emerged for a time in Texas and the Southwest, which had been benefiting especially from freight absorption. Some steel consumers who were buying from distant mills, and who after 1948 paid the full freight, suffered in competition with rivals who happened to buy from mills closer to them. Few fabricating plants had to shut down completely, however, for lack of a source of supply, and none at all as a consequence of the pricing change.[80]

Data showing the effect of these developments on steel users are sparse. It is of interest that some steel consumers in New England found their raw material cost raised by an average of 7 to 10 per cent, as a result of having to pay full freight from mills farther West than the base mills for their area.[81] A Senate committee that compared steel shipment figures for 1940 and 1947 found that, even before the institution of f.o.b. mill pricing, shipments to surplus production areas had increased by 44.2 per cent, those to deficit areas by only 3.3 per cent and those to nonproducing areas by 1.7 per cent.[82]

As a result of these pressures, some metalworking concerns made plans to build their new factories near surplus centers like Pittsburgh and Youngstown. Seven years later it was said that these two cities might soon cease, as a consequence, to be surplus locations.[83] Mills and customers agree that the latter must now exert greater care about their location and transportation arrangements than when they could count more surely on being supplied by distant mills.

79. "Basing Points: The Great Muddle," *Fortune*, September 1948, p. 78; Corwin D. Edwards, "Basing Point Decisions and Business Practices," *American Economic Review*, December 1948, p. 837.

80. Survey reported by Otis Brubaker, in *Competitive Absorption of Transportation Costs*, Hearings before a Subcommittee of the Senate Interstate and Foreign Commerce Committee, 81st Cong., 1st sess., 1949, p. 202.

81. Charles A. Bliss, "Some Field Notes on Freight Absorption," *Harvard Business Review*, November 1948, p. 659.

82. *Changes in Distribution of Steel, 1940 to 1947*, Senate Small Business Committee, S. Rept. 44, 81st Cong., 1st sess., 1949, p. 36.

83. Burck, "The Transformation of U.S. Steel," p. 200.

Freight Absorption Resumed

Since freight absorption was outlawed only when it formed part of a regular system, it is not surprising that it soon appeared again. In both 1949 and 1953 there were many reports of freight absorption stimulated by the current downturns in orders. At the end of September 1953 U.S. Steel announced a new formal policy: to sell f.o.b. mill or on a delivered basis according to the customer's wish and to absorb freight to meet lower delivered prices of competitors "when necessary and commercially desirable." [84] In October most other companies made similar announcements. For 1954 — a year in which operations were at a lower ratio to capacity than they had been since 1939 — *Iron Age* estimated that some freight absorption had become routine, and put its cost at $70 million, or $.75 to $1.00 per ton produced (between one half and one per cent of the total price). It was agreed, however, that mills were carefully checking to make certain they were meeting actual competition.[85] A private report from U.S. Steel at the end of 1955 indicated that it was absorbing freight on less than 10 per cent of its sales, and not at all on scarce products like plates and structural shapes.

A permanent situation of very little freight absorption might give U.S. Steel an advantage through its possession of plants in every district. It would certainly tend to give a greater hold in times of reduced demand and excess capacity to the mills located in areas where production is normally below consumption. This situation would not be endurable to the other mills. Judging from experience, they would hardly meet it by reducing their base prices sufficiently to extend their markets until all mills were operating at about the same rate of capacity. Systematic freight absorption would be more likely.

A recent analysis emphasizes a still more convincing reason why delivered prices will tend toward uniformity. A multi-plant concern that quotes different prices in a market depending on which of its mills is to make shipment is automatically asking its customers to buy from the lowest-priced mill and thus to dictate where production is to take place. But this will prevent it from achieving efficient operation by making its own allotment of orders to its mills.[86] This study sees

84. *New York Times*, October 1, 1953, p. 45.

85. Louis Marengo, "The Basing Point Decisions and the Steel Industry," *American Economic Review*, May 1955, p. 521.

86. Marvin J. Barloon, "Pricing Policy in the Steel Industry," *Business History Review*, September 1954, pp. 223–24.

an inevitable return to uniform delivered prices, perhaps through very small zones or some other pattern which will be distinguished from the basing point system in legal form and yet keep its substance.[87]

Steel is typical of, and prominent among, the "oligopoly" industries — those controlled by a few large firms. Its economic characteristics,[88] in briefest form, include: a durable, homogeneous product (even if thousands of forms are possible) made to specification; inelastic demand; high fixed costs and considerable economies of large-scale production; only a few sellers in each region; important markets which have no nearby mills; and high freight costs. In such an industry price cutting would quickly become cutthroat as each big concern tried to hold its own customers even if it could not cover fixed costs and if total demand failed to respond; buyers will not permit a difference in delivered prices to continue; and sellers farther from a market than rivals are bound to see the opportunity of entering it by accepting some of the cost of transportation. Experience to date indicates that in such circumstances it is hard to prevent a system of uniform or "matched" delivered prices from developing. A basing point system is a reflection rather than a cause of the danger to producers in — and hence the quiescence of — price competition.[89]

Effects of Universal Freight Equalization

The full effects of the abolition of the basing point system cannot be felt for many years. In forecasting these effects, we begin with the situation where all producing points are basing points, which is known also as universal freight equalization.

1. When shipping into territory closer to other mills, *a company gives up the power to select its own price.* Granted that competition will normally bring about a uniform price for a homogeneous product like most types of steel, it is still impossible to believe that the competitive system can work best in the long run if all companies automatically accept in advance (for all sales not in their own home territories) the selling prices set by others. This automatic acceptance is the very purpose of the basing point system, which is intended primarily to

87. *Ibid.*, pp. 233–34.

88. These have been listed by many writers — recently and in detail in George W. Stocking, *Basing Point Pricing and Regional Development*, University of North Carolina Press, Chapel Hill, 1954, Chap. 2, "The Economic Characteristics of the Iron and Steel Industry."

89. This is the "thesis" of the Marengo thesis (p. 1).

remove each seller's uncertainty as to what his competitors are charging in every market.[90] If each one used this knowledge to undercut such rival prices, and not merely to meet them, the system would be immediately destroyed.

2. The system *tends to discourage price changes, especially reductions.* Price changes are not frequent in the type of industry likely to use the basing point system, but the system discourages them still further. There are at least three reasons for this: (a) Since the sale price at every point in the country is known to all members of the industry, it is easier to enforce a price agreement by spotting any case of price cutting. (b) Price cutting is discouraged, even without a price agreement, since it is known that other producers will automatically meet the new price. (c) The competitive incentive to cut prices is weakened, because absorbing more freight to acquire a few new customers is likely to be preferred as against cutting the base price and thus giving the benefits to present customers as well.[91] The stable prices thus arrived at would be high enough to suit the producers, since a mill knows that, if it raises its price, the new price will become the official quotation for its territory, protected against undercutting.

3. The system *tends to increase costs.* This operates in three ways.

(a) As each mill tries to enlarge its sales by shipping its product farther, cross hauling arises. As one example, on the same day in April 1939, 108 tons of tin plate were started by rail from Sparrows Point (near Baltimore) to Wheeling, and 234 tons from Weirton (near Wheeling) to Baltimore.[92] Cross freight was said to be so important in the business setback of 1930 as to be "undoubtedly" a factor in causing Republic's expansion through merger.[93] It is impossible to measure the extent of unnecessary cross hauling, for several reasons. One is that difference in specifications may mean that an apparent cross haul of, say, sheets, wire or bars really involves different products. There is also some economy in placing a complete order with the one producer who alone can furnish some specific part of it, thus making it uneconomical to avoid cross hauling. When a multi-plant company makes the several products in a single order at separate mills, this problem is

90. *Ibid.*, p. 3.

91. J. M. Clark, "Imperfect Competition and Basing Point Problems," *American Economic Review*, June 1943, p. 290.

92. U.S. Board of Investigation and Research, *The Economics of Iron and Steel Transportation*, S. Doc. 80, 79th Cong., 1st sess., 1945, p. 83.

93. Fraser and Doriot, *Analyzing Our Industries*, p. 256.

compounded. A qualification of another sort is that freight absorption is especially tempting to a mill when its rate of operation is low, which is also a time when transportation agencies are themselves likely to have excess capacity. Thus they can carry extra freight without much additional cost.

Since the estimates which have been made are for freight absorption as a whole, they undoubtedly exaggerate the extent of *wasteful* cross hauling. In the second quarter of 1934,[94] and in February 1939 [95] — two periods in which ingot operations were at only 55 per cent of capacity, thus implying large current unused capacity — freight absorption was estimated at about 1.8 and 3.2 per cent, respectively, of delivered prices. The 1934 study was for mills in the Pittsburgh area. In the second quarter of 1948, a time of high production, U.S. Steel estimated its freight absorption at 75 cents a ton,[96] or about one per cent of price. Another company, whose mills were concentrated near Pittsburgh, from which freight absorption has been relatively high since 1938, estimated its own absorption at 1.2 per cent of price in 1938–40, 1.0 per cent in 1947, and 1.1 per cent in early 1955.[97] One may guess that *wasteful* cross hauling had been a good deal less than one per cent of price before 1948, and is even lower today. There may also be an offset on the credit side, in the form of greater pressure on costs at any given mill due to the competition coming in from the outside.

(b) The basing point system may increase sales costs, as producers strive to get and keep in touch with the additional customers in distant markets. "It is clearly wasteful to have the salesmen of ten or a dozen producers covering the same area when it could be adequately covered by a smaller number." [98] Here again there may be some offset due to the increased competition.

(c) The system is likely to increase cost also by inducing rail shipment when the purchaser might prefer waterway or truck transporta-

94. National Recovery Administration, *Report on the Operation of the Basing Point System in the Iron and Steel Industry*, November 30, 1934, cited in Marengo thesis, pp. 149–50.

95. John M. Blair and Arthur Reeside, *Price Discrimination in Steel*, TNEC Monograph 41, 1941, p. 39.

96. Letter of David F. Austin, vice president of U.S. Steel Corp., *Study of Pricing Methods*, Hearings before a Subcommittee of the Senate Interstate and Foreign Commerce Committee, 87th Cong., 2d sess., 1948, p. 1375.

97. Erle R. Lane, "Jones & Laughlin," *Barron's*, May 2, 1955, p. 22.

98. J. M. Clark, "Basing Point Methods of Price Quoting," *Canadian Journal of Economics and Political Science*, November 1938, p. 483; also George W. Stocking, "The Economics of Basing Point Pricing," *Law and Contemporary Problems*, Spring 1950, p. 174.

tion. One reason is that the buyer, having nothing to gain by asking for the cheaper method, as long as the price includes the full cost of shipping by rail, may stipulate the faster rail shipment when he does not require it. But this is not the real issue. Since the basing point system is fundamentally a method of letting all sellers know what their competitors are charging in every market, all must base their quotations on the same freight cost. For this purpose the rail cost is universally chosen. In steel, truck shipments were deliberately discouraged by crediting the purchaser with only 65 instead of 100 per cent of the rail rate when he took his order by truck. It is not surprising that, when the penalty was lifted in 1948, steel buyers turned "in droves" to the use of trucks and barges.[99] Even though some in the industry speak of this as merely a slight bulge in the long-term upward trend in trucking, it is clear that the basing point system encouraged shipment by rail.

Effects of a Partial Basing Point System

When some mills are not basing points, as has been true in the principal industries which have had to defend their systems in court, the foregoing disadvantages apply plus several others. For convenience, this case will be put in hypothetical terms, with Pittsburgh (P) assumed to be the basing point and Chicago (C) a district with high demand for steel and some production, but not itself a basing point.

1. *Non-basing point mills give up all independence in setting their selling prices*, even in the territory closest to home. The special importance of this is that a plant thus automatically takes the benefits of a superior location in the form of a higher mill net price and per unit profit and not in the form of a larger volume of business. If this automatic choice proved attractive, however, it might stimulate expansion, and thereby eventual competition and perhaps price competition, at C.

2. *Steel-using industries may not establish their operations near non-basing point mills even though this might otherwise be the best location*, since there is no saving in freight by doing so. Mislocation of their plants may thus result from a nonuniversal basing point system. Some steel executives agree that abolition of basing points will prove salutary in the end as steel-using firms establish themselves closer to mills.

Even under f.o.b. pricing, a steel user is likely to prefer to set up near P, where there is an excess supply of steel, rather than in a

99. *Iron Age*, August 5, 1948, p. 116; also *Business Week*, May 6, 1950, p. 23.

district like C where there are assumed to be many other fabricators but less steel. In other terms, those located at C may have to pay the mill there a premium, whether it is called a reward for its fortunate location under the f.o.b. system or is called phantom freight under the basing point system. However, under the f.o.b. system the mill at C might not always charge what the traffic would bear, but might let its customers have some of the advantages of its location; whereas under the basing point system it will (if it remains a non-base mill) automatically take all of the advantages in the form of phantom freight. To this extent there is a chance of lower prices to fabricators at C under the f.o.b. system and, conversely, an influence drawing them toward P under the basing point system. But it is hardly likely to be an important influence since, if the C mill under the f.o.b. mill system would want to cut prices and expand its market, the same mill under a basing point system might want to declare itself a basing point and do the same thing.

The importance of this matter of location of fabricating plants should not be exaggerated. With the exception of a very few products, among which steel fencing and oil field pipe are sometimes mentioned, the price of steel is likely to form so small a fraction of the price of the fabricator's final product [100] that the location of his plant will usually be determined by other considerations. He has his outbound freight to consider also.[101] Finally, there is no steel freight problem in locating fabricating plants for construction materials, since on these the "fabrication-in-transit" privilege allowed by the railroads makes it indifferent whether the plant is located near the source of supply or near the market.

3. The nonuniversal basing point system may create an *artificial influence on the location of plants* in the industry itself. Whether it causes them to locate near or away from basing points is, however, a matter of dispute.

There are several reasons why plants might be discouraged from locating at C. First, low freight costs might be assumed to have drawn fabricators toward P, thus influencing new mills in turn to locate near these customers. Second, the basing point system destroys one argument with which a new mill at C might appeal to prospective customers: "Buy from us and get your steel cheaper." Third, old mills decid-

100. Barloon, "Pricing Policy in the Steel Industry," p. 220.

101. Example mentioned by Tom J. Smith, Jr., Celler Hearings, p. 313.

ing to stay at P could count on a sort of crutch through the price at C being high enough to cover their freight costs to that city. The second and third reasons are weakened by the fact that the mill in C, if these arguments that being a non-base mill puts it at a disadvantage are valid, can meet them quite simply by declaring itself a base mill and cutting the price.[102] Although it can do this successfully only if its costs are low at that location, this merely brings the issue of location back to the basis of economic costs and away from that of pricing systems.[103]

Supporting the opposite view — that price quotations based on P will encourage mills to locate at C — is the fact that such a new mill can charge the prevailing price, offer local customers quicker delivery, and procure itself an extra profit equal to its saving on transportation. Under the rules of the basing point system, mills in P could not retaliate by underselling in C unless they reduced their base price and thereby gave all their customers the benefit of the reduction aimed at customers in C alone.

It is impossible to determine by an appeal to the facts which of these two viewpoints is correct. Certainly the steel industry did spread out under the pull of raw materials and markets during the basing point period — but it might have spread out faster under a free market system. For example, U.S. Steel's failure to expand its production at Birmingham in order to fill the needs of all markets best served by that low-cost center cannot be attributed to the basing point system alone, without reference to company policy.[104] Most authorities, it is true, support — either strongly [105] or moderately [106] — the position that the

102. Compare Arthur Smithies, "Aspects of the Basing Point System," *American Economic Review*, December 1942, pp. 722–23.

103. That the pricing system is not a dominant location factor is the conclusion of Walter Isard and William M. Capron, "The Future Locational Pattern of Iron and Steel Production in the United States," *Journal of Political Economy*, April 1949, at pp. 131–33.

104. See Stocking, *Basing Point Pricing and Regional Development*, pp. 110–11.

105. Machlup, *The Basing-Point System*, pp. 233–37; FTC, *Practices of the Steel Industry under the Code*, S. Doc. 159, 73d Cong., 2d sess., 1934, p. 43; Stocking, *Basing Point Pricing and Regional Development*, pp. 195–200; Frank A. Fetter, "Exit Basing Point Pricing," *American Economic Review*, December 1948, p. 826; Vernon A. Mund, in *Price Discrimination and Basing-Point Policy*, Hearings before a Subcommittee of the Senate Small Business Committee, 82d Cong., 1st sess., 1951, pp. 67–76; John M. Blair, *ibid.*, pp. 279–90; Walter Adams, "The Steel Industry," Chap. 4 in *idem*, ed., *The Structure of American Industry*, Macmillan, New York, revised edition, 1954, p. 180.

106. Arthur Robert Burns, *The Decline of Competition*, McGraw-Hill, New York, 1936, pp. 340–45, 362–63; Daugherty, de Chazeau and Stratton, *The Economics of the Iron and Steel Industry*, Vol. 1, pp. 542–44.

system discourages entry of new mills into deficit areas where they are needed to cater to local demand. Nevertheless, the issue is not resolved finally, either as to the direction or the importance of this influence.

Conclusion on the Basing Point System

It is undeniable that the system does intensify existing distortions. It tends to make prices even more rigid and uniform than they would otherwise be with a product like steel; it encourages cross hauling and discourages truck and waterway transportation more than a pattern of less certain freight absorption would do; and it adds an artificial element to the choice of location by customers — and perhaps by mills themselves. The weakening of these influences by the Supreme Court's 1948 decision is to be commended, even though the changes are not likely to be very important in practice.

Drastic results could not be achieved without more drastic action, but no perfect solutions have been worked out as yet. Some of the authorities on the economics of the basing point system have advocated uniform, compulsory f.o.b. mill pricing as the best practical alternative; [107] but this would be the equivalent of an agreement among the producers not to invade each other's home territories.[108] Others have suggested means of making pricing more individual and sporadic, so as to break the custom of "matching"; [109] but buyers themselves might suffer if the result proved to be quite disorderly. A recent writer, in advocating moderate steps toward removing some of the basing point system's price certainties, gives his opinion that if cutthroat competition resulted it would be more injurious than the basing point system itself.[110]

The Steel Industry's Attitude toward the Antitrust Laws

Executives of big and little steel companies say they are in favor of the antitrust laws, and a number emphasize that the Sherman Act has served as a desirable warning against price fixing. But complaints are

107. Fetter, *The Masquerade of Monopoly*, p. 411; Machlup, *The Basing-Point System*, p. 250; Vernon A. Mund, *Government and Business*, Harper, New York, 1950, p. 398.

108. Compare statements of Thurlow Gordon and Corwin D. Edwards, *Robinson-Patman Symposium*, 1947 edition, Commerce Clearing House, Chicago, p. 56.

109. Carl Kaysen, "Basing Point Pricing and Public Policy," *Quarterly Journal of Economics*, August 1949, pp. 313–14; Marengo, "The Basing Point Decisions and the Steel Industry," pp. 519–20.

110. Marengo thesis, p. 463.

made against the law. It is said to be too changeable: "Our lawyers are kept busy advising us as to changes and guessing what is coming next."

The Robinson-Patman Act's ban on price discrimination is said to prevent normal practices in meeting competition. For example, a steel company with nationwide distribution runs into competition from a local company that allows its distributor a larger discount. The national company cannot compete, for if it matched that discount it would be illegally discriminating against its customers elsewhere. A small company would not, of course, endorse this particular complaint, and some large concerns in other industries if not in steel have acted on the view that such meeting of competition "in good faith" would be legal.

Competitive Status

Trend of Concentration: U.S. Steel

The scattered ownership of the iron industry in its early history does not signify that competition was more pervasive then than today. The cost of transporting iron undoubtedly gave many of the 202 furnaces reported in the Census of 1830 something close to a monopoly in their neighborhood. Geographic concentration of production, wider markets, larger producing units and more competition emerged as railroads were built, coke replaced charcoal as fuel, and steel replaced iron. Consumption increased so fast that by 1880 there were as many as 735 companies, operating 697 blast furnaces and 382 steelworks and rolling mills.[111] The four largest companies held 7, 7, 6 and 5 per cent, respectively, of rolling mill capacity; and in 1892 the three largest held 14, 9 and 5 per cent.[112] By 1900 mergers had given to three big combinations approximately 18, 15 and 12 per cent of ingot capacity.[113]

In 1901 the share of the newly established U.S. Steel in blast furnace, ingot and rolling mill capacity was 33, 44 and 47 per cent, respectively. A few years later these figures had increased to 43 (1908), 52 (1907) and 51 per cent (1908).[114] However, many inactive or nearly obsolete mills must have been included in the industry total for ingot

111. H. B. McCoy, Celler Hearings, p. 102.

112. Willard L. Thorp and Grace W. Knott, "The History of Concentration in Seven Industries," Part 4 of Willard L. Thorp and William F. Crowder, eds., *The Structure of Industry*, TNEC Monograph 27, 1941, p. 258.

113. H. B. McCoy, Celler Hearings, p. 102.

114. TNEC Monograph 27, p. 258; U.S. Steel Corp., *Steel Serves the Nation*, New York, 1952, pp. 27–28.

TABLE 28

STEEL: RATE OF OPERATIONS, U.S. STEEL CORPORATION AND INDUSTRY, 1901–55

(5-Year Averages of Annual Ratios)

Period	U.S. Steel Output of Ingots and Castings as Per Cent of Industry Total	U.S. Steel Rate of Operations as Per Cent of Ingot Capacity	Industry Rate of Operations as Per Cent of Ingot Capacity
1901–05	62.9	86.2 [a]	55.0 [b]
1906–10	56.0	79.4	41.1 [c]
1911–15	52.5	79.6	68.6 [d]
1916–20	46.7	88.8	82.9
1921–25	46.2	72.4	62.8
1926–30	40.4	82.2	79.1
1931–35	35.1	31.4	35.5
1936–40	34.6	63.0	65.4
1941–45	34.4	93.9	94.3
1946–50	32.9	88.8	87.5
1951–55	31.7	89.7	89.1

Sources: American Iron and Steel Institute, *Annual Statistical Report*, 1947, p. 29; 1955, p. 51; and U.S. Steel Corp., annual reports. U.S. Steel's share of total before 1950 is in *Study of Monopoly Power*, Hearings before Subcommittee on Study of Monopoly Power, House Judiciary Committee, 81st Cong., 2d sess., 1950, Serial 14, Part 4-B, Exhibit S-298, p. 623 and also p. 651.

a. 1902–05 only.
b. 1904 only. The U.S. Steel figure was 72.8.
c. 1908 only. The U.S. Steel figure was 70.5.
d. 1914–15 only. The U.S. Steel figure was 73.8.

capacity, since the Corporation's share of ingot and castings *production* was no less than 65.7 per cent of the total in 1901. This share began declining at once, and has continued to do so, although since the early 1930s the rate of decline has leveled off. In 1951–55 it was just half as large as in 1901–05. (See Table 28.)

A comparison of rate of operations as a percentage of ingot capacity, for U.S. Steel and the industry as a whole (Table 28), shows the Corporation's rate considerably higher in all the years through 1930, lower through 1939, and closely parallel since 1940. The contrast in the 1930s has been explained in several ways: it is said, for example, that U.S. Steel holds more closely to its published prices than its rivals during a depression and loses correspondingly in sales; or that it is accustomed to establish its rate of production for its own policy reasons, whereupon other firms produce all they can sell. The former

TABLE 29

STEEL: SHARE OF LEADING COMPANIES IN STEEL INGOT CAPACITY, 1904–56

(*Per Cent*)

Firm	1904	1916	1928	1940	1948	1956
Largest firm	48.0	47.3	39.7	34.1	33.1	30.6
Next two	8.8	9.1	18.7	23.6	23.8	23.6
Next five	13.9	15.0	14.3	21.3	20.8	22.0
Largest eight	70.8	71.3	72.8	79.0	77.7	76.1

Sources: American Iron and Steel Institute, *Directory of Iron and Steel Works of the United States and Canada* for earlier years, and *Annual Capacities of Coke Ovens, Blast Furnaces and Steelmaking Furnaces as of January 1, 1956, by Companies, States and Districts* (*United States and Canada*), pp. 13–15. Figures are for the beginning of each year.

explanation seems plausible, whereas the latter finds no support in any other period than the 1930s.

Trend of Concentration: The "Big Three" and the "Big Eight"

Turning back to ingot capacity, we find that U.S. Steel's share has declined, while that of the other large companies has increased — largely as a result of mergers. The share of the top eight was five percentage points more in 1956 than in 1904. (See Table 29.) The second largest company of 1904 now ranks fourth; the fifth largest now ranks ninth; and the seventh largest ranks third. The third, fourth, sixth and eighth largest companies of 1904 were all absorbed in the expansion of Bethlehem Steel, which was at that time not even among the first ten.[115]

There was a good deal of concern just after World War II over the fact that most steel facilities built during the war belonged to the largest companies or, if government-built, had been operated by them. Between the end of 1939 and the end of 1944 the three largest producers increased their share of ingot capacity from 57.8 per cent to 58.8, and it was feared that these would be "enduring rather than merely temporary" gains.[116] The War Assets Administration intensi-

115. Gertrude G. Schroeder, *The Growth of Major Steel Companies, 1900–1950,* Johns Hopkins Press, Baltimore, 1952, p. 199.

116. *Economic Concentration and World War II,* Report of Smaller War Plants Corporation to Special Senate Committee to Study Problems of American Small Business, S. Doc. 206, 79th Cong., 2d sess., 1946, pp. 85–86. This report, which was prepared by John M. Blair, Harrison F. Houghton and Matthew Rose, was drawn on by the similar report, *United States versus Economic Concentration and Monopoly: An Investigation of the Effectiveness of the Government's Efforts to Combat Economic Concentration,* staff report to the Monopoly Subcommittee of the House Small Business Committee, 79th Cong., 2d sess., 1946, p. 111.

fied these fears when it disposed of its three integrated mills to their operators: U.S. Steel (Geneva plant), Republic (Chicago) and Armco (Houston). Nevertheless, after allowing for retirements of obsolete facilities, the share of the three largest producers in ingot capacity in 1948 was about one percentage point below the 1940 level, and in 1956 was still further down (Table 29).

Why U.S. Steel's Share of Output Declined

Many causes contributed to this decline in U.S. Steel's share of total production.

Deliberate purpose. "It is a traditional opinion in the industry, unquestionably true but no longer susceptible of proof," in the words of a steel executive, that during the last twenty years of his chairmanship Judge Gary, in order to forestall antitrust action, refrained from further acquisitions or large-scale construction. Gary has been quoted as remarking that even the most "trusted of radicals" could not call monopolistic a concern that thus confined itself.[117] U.S. Steel executives have been "advised" that this was his policy.[118] Self-restraint based on a desire to keep within the law could of itself explain a substantial part of the relative decline in capacity.

The "public institution" philosophy. The Corporation's original philosophy, that it was a public institution rather than just a money-making business and that its true aims should be to stabilize the industry and supply steel on terms fair to all parties, has not been completely abandoned even today. This concern for the general welfare meant that sales were lost to "less gentlemanly and more commercial competitors." [119] One expression of this philosophy was U.S. Steel's policy of always selling at openly announced prices, and under normal conditions at prices high enough to be fully profitable. Thus in good times rivals were able to expand by selling at a slightly lower price, and in bad times they could maintain their sales at the expense of the price leader by offering secret discounts.[120] The same "umbrella" for the benefit of smaller producers was set up by the Pittsburgh Plus system.

117. Ida M. Tarbell, *The Life of Elbert H. Gary*, Appleton-Century, New York, 1930, pp. 257–58.

118. Benjamin F. Fairless, president of U.S. Steel Corp., Celler Hearings, p. 488.

119. Burck, "The Transformation of U.S. Steel," p. 90.

120. See Burns, *The Decline of Competition*, pp. 85–87, on depression price shading.

Changes in the industry and handicaps of age. U.S. Steel's failure to expand aggressively after 1908 left it with the same locations and lines of product which it had then. Several technical and other changes took place in the next decades which tended to make this structure obsolete.

1. Demand has shifted from heavy products to light ones like sheet and strip. In 1905 rails and accessories, plates and structural shapes made up 50.9 per cent of all hot rolled products, in 1955 only 16.6 per cent.[121] U.S. Steel had its mills largely committed to the heavy products, and, although it did change over gradually, it was left with a big burden of more or less obsolete plant.[122] A few other producers have this problem also, and it is reported that one "nearly came a cropper" thereby.[123]

2. When new trends in costs and markets have suggested the wisdom of moving from obsolete locations and mills, U.S. Steel has found that the interlocked character of many of its operations, its heavy fixed investment, and personnel considerations have made it hard to move.[124] Thus its modern Irvin rolling mills built in the mid-1930s had to be constructed in the Pittsburgh district because of the coke ovens, blast furnaces and open hearth furnaces already there.[125]

3. A third consideration which has sometimes been mentioned is the increasing use of ferrous scrap to make steel. It is not only lower priced than the equivalent pig iron, as a general rule, but also permits greater flexibility. Thus a company with just two blast furnaces must reduce output 50 per cent (incurring heavy costs of closing and later reopening the furnace) or not at all. Companies without the heavy tax and maintenance costs of iron mines, which rely more on scrap from nearby industrial centers, have obtained a cost advantage.[126] This factor can perhaps be ignored, since U.S. Steel has enough blast furnaces to reduce output by degrees, and it does not consider its iron mines a burden.

121. American Iron and Steel Institute, *Annual Statistical Report*, 1924, p. 37; and *Steel Facts*, April 1956, p. 7. The 1905 figure included sheets, which were then unimportant, under plates.

122. Adams, "The Steel Industry," pp. 156–57; "U.S. Steel — Break It Up?", *Fortune*, April 1950, p. 157.

123. Lane, "Jones & Laughlin," p. 19.

124. Charles R. Walker, *Steeltown*, Harper, New York, 1950 (summarized in "The Case of the Contented Steelworkers," *Fortune*, May 1950, pp. 76–78).

125. Alderfer and Michl, *Economics of American Industry*, p. 66.

126. *Fortune*, March 1936, pp. 176, 178; also *ibid.*, April 1950, p. 157.

Deficiencies of management. Quite apart from the relatively noncommercial philosophy of the early Steel Corporation, it is clear that its management was frequently overcautious. The best-documented evidence of this is in the 240 reports submitted by Ford, Bacon & Davis, a firm of management engineers that conducted a survey of the company at the request of Chairman Myron C. Taylor between 1935 and 1938.[127]

1. *Market policy.* The engineers urged the company to charge more on sales of fabricated structures like the products of its American Bridge Company; sell less semifinished steel to others for rolling and instead sell finished products which would yield a higher profit, whose price could be better controlled, and for which it had unutilized capacity; expand further into manufacture of barrels, drums, boilers and the like as an alternative to an agreement among steel companies to cease buying up such fabricators and foreclosing this sales market; stop selling cement, a product not directly related to steel; sell fewer rails, a low-profit product; export fewer highly fabricated products and more heavy products with their lower labor component; and exploit the whole export market more.

2. *Management methods.* The engineers criticized U.S. Steel for lack of coordination and of a long-run planning office; lack of research into domestic and foreign markets; and failure to hold each subsidiary or the company as a whole up to a high standard of efficiency measured by profit, reliance on inadequate and antiquated cost accounting methods, and low production and cost standards compared to the rest of the industry.

3. *Unprogressiveness.* The engineers further charged the Corporation with slowness to adopt truck and water transport, possibly because of fear of antagonizing its railroad customers; possession of inefficient facilities; slowness to adopt technical developments such as continuous rolling, heat treating of sheets, manufacture of stainless steel and utilization of waste gases; and failure to allocate to its Tennessee Coal and Iron subsidiary, whose costs of assembling coal, ore and limestone were exceptionally low, more of the production of pipe for the Southwest, of other products for the West Coast, and of tin plate and semifinished steel for the Atlantic seaboard.

The significance of these and the other criticisms should not be exaggerated. Some of them referred to failure to take all profit oppor-

127. High points of these unpublished reports were mentioned at the Celler Hearings by Subcommittee Counsel Edward H. Levi, on pp. 524–26, 581, 589, 624–49; Congressman Emanuel Celler of New York, on p. 930; and George W. Stocking, on pp. 966–67.

tunities rather than to inefficiency. Others would have required that old customers be cut off ruthlessly, or were not wholly consistent, or were later proved unwise. The same engineers elsewhere spoke of U.S. Steel as being "equipped reasonably to meet present-day competition" in its "organization functioning and business procedures now in effect or shortly to be made effective." [128] By the very nature of their business, efficiency experts make critical reports to their clients. Nevertheless, it has been, and is, freely admitted within U.S. Steel itself that its management at the time left much to be desired.

U.S. Steel since the 1930s

The report of Ford, Bacon & Davis — many of whose recommendations were adopted [129] — was only one part of Taylor's program for improving the company's management. Other steps were compulsory retirement of executives at 70, reorganization of the sales department, buying of fabricating companies, expenditure of $350 million on modernizing and extending rolling mills and other facilities, establishment of a research department, and creation of a new corporate structure which gave the manufacturing subsidiaries more freedom. Between 1928 and 1938 plants were sold or shut down at no fewer than thirty-three locations.[130] *Fortune*, which published a series of articles critical of the company in 1936,[131] later referred to the 1930s as the period when it "was snapping out of its lethargy." [132] At the end of 1955 it devoted an article to the "extraordinary" performance of U.S. Steel,[133] which "stands today as an excellent example of how industrial progress occurs in the American economy." [134] Not only *Fortune* but others who had once sharply criticized the Corporation's efficiency concede that today it is probably "as efficient as any of its rivals." [135] The same opinion prevails among the great majority of the steel buyers interviewed in the course of this study.

128. Quoted by Roger Blough, later chairman of U.S. Steel Corp., *ibid.*, p. 644.

129. Benjamin F. Fairless, *ibid.*

130. Myron C. Taylor, "Ten Years of Steel," *Iron Age*, April 7, 1938, p. 70 D.

131. "The U.S. Steel Corporation," *Fortune*, March, April, May and June, 1936.

132. "Bethlehem Steel," *ibid.*, April 1941, p. 65.

133. Burck, "The Transformation of U.S. Steel," p. 94.

134. *Ibid.*, p. 204.

135. George W. Stocking, "The Rule of Reason, Workable Competition and Monopoly," *Yale Law Journal*, July 1955, p. 1136, note 106. Compare *idem*, Celler Hearings, pp. 961–90.

Some of its own executives grant that U.S. Steel's size prevents the company from moving as quickly as smaller producers, or giving the same personalized service to customers. It is still working to overcome inertia caused by size and to increase the flexibility of its operating divisions. It is, however, taking full advantage of the opportunities offered by size. Its industrial engineering, standard cost and foremanship programs are recognized by competitors as outstanding achievements, worthy of imitation. Its incentive compensation plan for executives is stimulating the profit motive as against the public service or any other motive.[136] At least one authority on steel industry research and technology [137] calls the Corporation the equal of any competitor in these areas today.

U.S. Steel began some time ago to expand again through acquisitions; and its policy today is to try to hold its full share of the market, no matter how much expansion this may require.[138] The rate of expansion involved at present may be more feasible than it would have been had the Corporation tried to retain two thirds of the country's basic steel production. U.S. Steel's position in a competitive economy is better from the company's own standpoint than if it controlled the bulk of the industry and had to make most of its decisions on a political basis.

The Question of Size

Although Bethlehem now has about half as much ingot capacity, "Big Steel" is still unique in size. It is the second largest coal producer in the country. Its Oliver Mining and Michigan Limestone divisions do not supply all of its consumption of iron and limestone, yet each is the biggest unit in its industry. It makes steel at about thirty-five locations, half of them operated by the Corporation in its own name and half by its American Steel and Wire, Columbia-Geneva Steel, National Tube, and Tennessee Coal and Iron divisions. It fabricates through the American Bridge, Consolidated Western Steel, Gerrard Steel Strapping, Oil Well Supply and United States Steel Products divisions, and United States Steel Homes, Inc. Its Universal Atlas Cement Company, originally set up to consume blast furnace slag, has the largest capacity in the cement industry. United States Steel Supply

136. Burck, "The Transformation of U.S. Steel," pp. 94–95.

137. Robert M. Weidenhammer.

138. See Benjamin F. Fairless, Celler Hearings, pp. 488–89.

Division has warehouses in thirteen cities; United States Steel Export Company has a world-wide business; and Union Supply Company recently operated 108 general retail stores in mill towns. There are also natural gas and dock subsidiaries. Finally, the corporation owns 4 trunk line and 11 tap line railroads and a fleet of ore-carrying ships.

Such size is obviously not essential to successful operation in the steel industry, but it does appear to be consistent with it. Enough direct causes explain the decline in U.S. Steel's share of industry output without resort to the hypothesis that size is inconsistent with efficiency. To coordinate so vast an operation, U.S. Steel relies on decentralization and operation through divisions in the same manner as giant corporations in other industries.

Even the smaller steel companies are of tremendous size, since the capital required for steel manufacture perhaps exceeds that for any other industry.[139] Companies ranking as low as seventh and eighth in the steel industry in 1955 ranked as high as forty-third and fiftieth in *Fortune's* list of the 500 largest manufacturing corporations of all sorts, whether measured by sales or assets. This situation may be in process of changing, at least in part, since recent technological developments may be giving smaller establishments a more important place in the industry.[140] For the present, however, size is still dominant.

Vertical Integration and Horizontal Combination

A question more at issue today than sheer size is that of the justification of vertical integration and horizontal combination of plants in the industry. The very earliest steel furnaces were not under the same ownership as iron smelters. The technical advantages of integration were proved by experience — for example, the efficiency of charging into steelmaking furnaces pig iron which is still molten; the recovery of coke oven and blast furnace gases; and better coordination between the steel furnace and steel rolling processes. There are also market advantages, such as ability to command a supply of pig iron in time of shortage instead of being outbid by a richer competitor or one whose end products may be in greater momentary demand. One British writer has defended the position that market strategy is the real motive

139. Alfred R. Oxenfeldt, *Industrial Pricing and Market Practices*, Prentice-Hall, New York, 1951, p. 491.

140. "The Limited Market Mill: Is It Steel's Best Bet?," *Business Week*, January 29, 1955, pp. 44–48.

for vertical integration.[141] This is denied by men in the industry; but whether true or not, none would call it practical today to separate the production of iron, crude steel and rolled products where they are joined. We shall discuss later the issues raised by entry into iron mining and fabrication.

Horizontal combination comes under sharper attack. A recent analyst sees only four advantages in it: (1) saving on administrative and selling costs; (2) product specialization in particular plants; (3) interplant competition; and (4) ability to finance research, new construction, and discovery of new raw material sources. He then cancels out these advantages with arguments that (1) the big companies have not shown any reduction in costs; (2) a one-plant company can specialize; (3) two profitable big firms, Inland and National, have almost no interplant competition; and (4) small companies have done well in research and in raising their own capital.[142]

Granting the strength of these arguments, the industry points to a differently phrased set of advantages from combination: (1) it gives security against a slump in sales in a particular region; (2) it makes it easier to serve the customer with a full line of products; and (3) it makes it possible to allocate orders to the particular plant which, by reason of location, temporary idleness or some other cause, can most efficiently make and ship the order.

In the long run, the merits of such arguments will be determined in the market by the relative success of the different types of companies. A small company can often, though not always, make a better rate of profit if other considerations, including managerial ability, are equal. But this is accompanied by a greater risk of loss and even of failure.

Profit Differences among Steel Companies

One possible test of relative efficiency is the rate of profit. A recent tabulation covering the years 1901–55 shows U.S. Steel's operating profit to have averaged 9.7 per cent of gross fixed assets as against a median figure for twelve integrated companies of 11.0 per cent. Its geographic and product diversification makes it natural for the Corporation to have ranked near the mid-point. Surprisingly, its relative

141. S. R. Dennison, "Vertical Integration in the Iron and Steel Industry," *Economic Journal*, June 1939, pp. 255–56.

142. Ward S. Bowman, Jr., "Toward Less Monopoly," *University of Pennsylvania Law Review*, March 1953, at pp. 600–11.

TABLE 30

STEEL: OPERATING PROFITS OF TWELVE COMPANIES AS PER CENT OF GROSS FIXED ASSETS, 1901–55

(Averages of Annual Rates)

Firm	1901–55	1901–10	1911–20	1921–30	1931–40	1941–50	1951–55
Median	11.0	14.1	19.5	6.3	2.7	14.0	16.5
Armco Steel Corp.	13.3	14.7	19.5	6.9	3.2	16.8	23.9
Bethlehem Steel Co.	10.1	8.9 [a]	16.6	4.7	2.9	13.2	17.8
Crucible Steel Co.	11.9	7.0	27.0	5.4	3.3	15.8	14.8
Inland Steel Co.	16.0	14.0 [b]	24.9	10.5	9.8	18.5	19.1
Jones & Laughlin Steel Corp.	6.5			8.8 [a]	–.1	9.8	9.4
National Steel Corp.	13.2				7.5	16.5	18.2
Pittsburgh Steel Co.	7.8		16.1	6.3	–.8	7.4	10.4
Republic Steel Corp.	10.1	9.7	16.5	4.1	1.7	14.7	18.6
Sharon Steel Corp.	18.0	50.1 [b]	27.8	3.3	2.4	23.8	26.8
U.S. Steel Corp.	9.7	14.2	16.9	6.7	.5	8.5	12.3
Wheeling Steel Corp.	7.6			4.5	3.4	10.9	15.1
Youngstown Sheet and Tube Co.	12.5	17.9	24.2	6.9	1.4	12.6	11.6

Sources: 1901–50 taken from five-year averages in Gertrude G. Schroeder, *The Growth of Major Steel Companies, 1900–1950,* Johns Hopkins Press, Baltimore, 1952, p. 175; 1951–55 from Moody's *Industrials.*

a. Covers only the second five years of the ten-year period.

b. Covers only the last three years of the ten-year period.

showing was better before 1930, when its management was comparatively unprogressive, than since. (See Table 30.) The explanation is probably that its operations were closer to capacity than those of its competitors, taken together, before the 1930s (see Table 28). Although this has been called "fortuitous," [143] it could have been due to J. P. Morgan's prudence in taking the most active plants into his combination or to the prudence of Judge Gary's management in the choice of new plants to acquire and old ones to keep running.

A weakness in comparison of profit figures arises from the unavoidable mixing of non-steel profits in the total. According to figures for 1941, 1948 and 1949, the average return on book investment was slightly higher for U.S. Steel's railroad subsidiaries and slightly lower for its shipping lines than for steelmaking, but twice as high for fabrication and three times as high for iron mining as for steelmaking. Steelmaking itself accounted for only 47 per cent of profits on this

143. Burck, "The Transformation of U.S. Steel," p. 95.

basis.[144] This is merely suggestive, since accounting methods cannot be the same in iron mining (with its arbitrary accounting for ore in the ground), transportation and steel. Nevertheless, one reason U.S. Steel holds "outside interests," especially in fabrication, is to stabilize its over-all earnings when steel profits are low.

Industry sources give several explanations of the lag of U.S. Steel's profits behind those of some of its rivals. A minor point they offer is that its accounting practices are conservative — as instanced by its charge against earnings in 1950, to fund its pension obligations, of enough money to have raised its return on capital by 2.3 per cent of investment.[145] It is also pointed out (by competitors and customers as well as by the Corporation itself) that U.S. Steel does not always try to maximize its profit, but makes it a rule of policy to take into consideration the effects of its actions on competitors, customers and the public. It attempts to operate on the basis of stable policies, and in boom times its profits are lower because it fails to boost prices, while in bad times its sales are lower because it fails to cut prices.

U.S. Steel's Product-Line Diversification

Some of U.S. Steel's principal competitors attribute its relatively low rate of profit to the fact that the Corporation makes and sells to nonintegrated concerns more semifinished steel than other companies do, and makes more heavy products relative to its total output. One such competitor states that the Corporation's willingness to supply all the lines of product needed by customers, while smaller firms (including his own) were concentrating on the more profitable lines, is one of the most significant reasons for the decline in U.S. Steel's share of the industry's output.

About a third of the customers interviewed in the course of this study concede, in spite of the interest of several in having the opposite believed to be true, that heavy and semifinished steel have as a rule been low-profit items. If U.S. Steel were to reduce its sales of these products, customers might carry their complaint to the government. As it is, its policy has been to restore a better balance among these prices gradually.[146]

144. Celler Exhibits, p. 666.

145. Frank D. Chutler, "U.S. Steel," *Barron's*, July 30, 1951, p. 19.

146. Compare *Business Week*, July 24, 1954, p. 27.

The breadth of the product lines of the larger companies is illustrated by figures for production capacity in fifteen rolled or drawn products. Only U.S. Steel produced all fifteen, and it had the largest capacity in all but two. Bethlehem had capacity in eleven product lines, and Republic, Jones & Laughlin and Youngstown in thirteen — though some of Youngstown's figures were negligible. The most profitable companies of the 1901–55 period, Inland, Armco and National, had capacity in only seven to ten lines and substantial capacity in six or seven at most. (See Table 31.) Profits can be enhanced by wise selection of products; but a defense can be made for the company that is willing to sell the less as well as the more profitable ones. The rapid improvement in U.S. Steel's profit margin in recent years is attributed by some observers in part to a growing appreciation by customers, and to the seasonal and cyclical stability, of its full line of rolled products.

Intercorporate Connections

Many people believe that the steel industry still works in harmony as it did or is reputed to have done in the period of the "Gary dinners." This view rests in part on facts about intercorporate connections brought out by various government studies. Thus in 1939 the National Resources Committee presented an argument based on interlocking directorships that four "interest groups" controlled nearly two thirds of total ingot capacity: (1) the "J. P. Morgan–First National Bank of New York group" with three representatives on the board of U.S. Steel; (2) the "Mellon interests" with interlocking directorates between Mellon banks, railroads, or coal or oil corporations and the Armco, Crucible and Jones & Laughlin companies; and (3) the "Cleveland group" of financiers, whose Cleveland-Cliffs Iron Company held 3 to 6 per cent of the common stock in Inland, Republic, Wheeling and Youngstown (with Republic holding 100,000 shares of Cleveland-Cliffs stock in its turn).[147] In 1951 the Federal Trade Commission found that this pattern still prevailed as of 1946 and added a fourth group (led by a Pittsburgh bank) that controlled five smaller steel companies. The Commission warned that "these interrelations stemming from these four groups encompass such a substantial share

147. Paul M. Sweezy, "Interest Groupings in the American Economy," Appendix 13, of Part 1, "Basic Characteristics," in National Resources Committee, *The Structure of the American Economy*, 1939, pp. 309, 312, 313.

TABLE 31

STEEL: ROLLING-MILL CAPACITY,
EIGHT LARGEST PRODUCERS, 1954

(Million Tons)

Product	U.S. Steel	Beth-lehem	Re-public	Jones & Laugh-lin	Na-tional	Youngs-town	In-land	Armco
Hot rolled sheets	6.99	4.59	2.02	1.93	4.43	1.93	1.90	1.98
Cold rolled sheets	2.79	2.46	1.65	1.13	2.97	1.04	.85	1.57
Pipes and tubing	3.95	.58	1.20	.80		1.33		.11
Merchant bars	3.34	2.07	3.25	.67	.06	.40	.44	.25
Plates	3.64	1.10	.03	.29		.09	.51	.64
Tin plate	2.87	.96	.30	.50	.94	.40	.36	
Wire rods	2.78	.81	.40	.26		.11		.32
Plain wire	2.25	.62	.35	.27		.07		.24
Skelp (for welded tubes)	1.18	.48	1.21	.44		.91		
Structural shapes (heavy)	2.35	2.10		.11	.20	.01	.27	.05
Hot rolled strip	.77		.40	.002	.38	.01	.02	
Billets for seamless tubes	2.29		.20	.42		.54	.01	
Cold finished bars	.06		.47			.09		
Cold rolled strip	.26		.22	.02	.18		.02	
Rails	1.01	.53					.14	

Source: American Iron and Steel Institute, *Summary of Annual Capacities of the Iron and Steel Industry as of January 1, 1954, by Products, Companies and States,* New York. Both products and companies are listed in order of total capacity.

of the steel industry and are so complicated that they may form a pattern of control over the industry." [148]

It is impossible for an outsider to judge whether or how far these relationships determine the actions of the companies and prevent their engaging in vigorous competition. None of the steel men or customers interviewed was willing to consider this charge seriously. Republic Steel's answer (to a congressional committee) is that it is "the head of our purchasing department who deals with Cleveland-Cliffs. As far as he is concerned, there is no stock ownership. We drive our bargains just as hard with them as we do with anyone else, and a few times, harder." [149] Another steel executive reacts with the comment that "we

148. FTC, *Report on Interlocking Directorates*, 1951, p. 145.

149. C. M. White, president of Republic Steel Corp., Celler Hearings, p. 232.

have more men on boards of Mellon banks than they have on our board, so maybe we control them rather than they control us."

Another study of these relationships was made by the Securities and Exchange Commission, whose spokesman emphasized that some directors of all of the sixteen largest steel companies except Bethlehem met on the boards of coal and coke, banking and other corporations. He added that one firm of certified public accountants audited the books of eight of the sixteen, another firm those of four, and a third those of two, while three law firms had represented three steel companies each in registrations of new securities.[150] The congressional committee that received these data felt that they suggested "more centralization of control than is characteristic of many other American industries." [151]

The Trade Association

The principal trade organization in the industry is the American Iron and Steel Institute. It does public relations work, publishes figures on capacity and production, and conducts research and technical conferences. As the Code Authority under NRA, it compiled uniform lists of deductions and extras, freight rate booklets, and the like. Its annual budget around 1950 was stated to be more than $2.5 million a year.[152]

The only connection which the Institute seems to have had with price policy except under NRA is through some past addresses at its annual national or regional meetings. These speeches are said to have "nearly always devoted a major part of their attention to the development and magnification of an instinctive dislike for price cutters." [153] Since 1940 there have been few if any such speeches, no doubt because of a greater appreciation of the antitrust problem as well as the stronger market for steel products.

Other Forms of Collaboration

Direct collaboration between steel companies on joint projects or in other ways is common. The ventures to develop new ore bodies in

150. Donald C. Cook, *ibid.*, pp. 449–55; also Celler Exhibits, pp. 395–488.

151. *The Iron and Steel Industry*, Report of Subcommittee on Study of Monopoly Power, House Judiciary Committee, 81st Cong., 2d sess., 1950, p. 81.

152. Oxenfeldt, *Industrial Pricing and Market Practices*, p. 535.

153. Thomas G. Gies, *The Effect of Trade Associations upon Competition*, unpublished doctoral thesis, University of Michigan, Ann Arbor, 1952, p. 246.

Canada and to exploit the low-grade, ore-bearing taconite of the Mesabi region in Minnesota are recent examples. The fact that investment in these projects will run into the hundreds of millions accounts for the desire thus to reduce the investment and risk undertaken by each company. Ore development, because of the exploratory risks and the fact that steelmakers always blend ore from several sources and therefore are not interested in exclusive ownership of small tracts, has often been carried on cooperatively.

Although the sums of money risked in research projects are smaller, here too steel companies may engage in joint ventures. In technology generally, there is a long practice of sharing knowledge "with a munificence unknown in any other industry." [154] Engineers go through each other's mills to learn the best current practice.

A good argument can be made that the necessity of good relations in these joint projects tends to keep competition in steel on a "gentlemanly" plane and to discourage cutthroat tactics.[155] Although the industry denies this and points to examples of competition between the cooperating companies, this does not meet the argument that really cutthroat tactics are prevented. The uncertain benefits of such competition would probably not outweigh the disadvantages of destroying the forms of collaboration under discussion.

Nature of Competition

Steel buyers choose among the possible suppliers of the products they want according to the following criteria:

1. Assured *quality* is essential in buying a product which becomes part of a machine, vehicle or building. Steel is, therefore, purchased on specifications, and not by brand name.

2. A nondiscriminatory *price* is essential when the buyer is not a final consumer, but resells his product in competition with others. The pressure of buyers has forced all steel mills to approximately the same level of quality and the same level of price. Sometimes a company has a special reputation in tool steel, stainless steel or some other specialty, and to this extent it draws a few extra buyers. Sometimes it undersells its competitors for a short time when market conditions seem to require it. But on the whole there is little variation in quality or price at any

154. Richard Austin Smith, "Bethlehem Steel and the Intruder," *Fortune*, March 1953, p. 104.

155. Barloon, "Pricing Policy in the Steel Industry," pp. 221–22.

one time. Those who assert that "competition within the steel industry basically centers around price" [156] probably refer primarily to the fact that customers will buy from any mill that either offers secret discounts or is close enough to offer a lower transportation charge.

3. *Location* determines many orders, since the heavy freight cost on steel relative to the value of the product will cause the buyer to patronize the nearest mill when possible, and since quick delivery is often desirable. Steel buyers, however, try to deal with more than one mill, so as not to become dependent on a single supplier — even when it may cost them an extra transportation charge to buy from the second.

4. Between mills whose quality, base price and location are about the same, the buyer will normally choose on the basis of three factors. He often wants a quick *delivery*, which, between mills at the same location, may dictate use of the one that is temporarily least occupied or is generally most flexible. He often wants to buy on "one shopping tour" the full *variety of products* he needs, with the required range of sizes, grades and finishes. These two factors are likely to work against each other, with the small steel company excelling in the first and the large one in the second. The third factor is *service* — primarily metallurgical advice to the buyer before the purchase, but also various forms of service afterward.

5. Aggressive selling, and *personal relations* between seller or salesman and buyer, are important here as in other industries. Buyers want to have permanent relations with their suppliers, both for smooth operation of their business and in order to be able, on occasion, to ask for special service (like a supply of steel in time of shortage). "Reciprocity," or the effort of steel mills to see that their own suppliers also buy steel from them, sometimes plays a role,[157] but its importance is impossible to determine. Finally, a buyer whose credit standing is not high may perforce be limited to one supplier.

Price Leadership

The history of price leadership on the part of U.S. Steel is an old one, and has been perhaps the most famous example of this phenomenon in the whole range of American industry. The Corporation's leadership has never been complete, it is true,[158] and today other com-

156. Standard & Poor's Corp., *Industry Surveys*, "Steel," Basic Analysis, June 28, 1956, p. S 78.

157. Smith, "Bethlehem Steel and the Intruder," p. 201.

158. Burns, *The Decline of Competition*, p. 77.

panies are said to lead the way more often than formerly.[159] U.S. Steel's leadership has sometimes merely reflected a price situation already brought about by its competitors without open announcement, and at times has proved abortive as its rivals failed to follow. The Corporation's changes are, nevertheless, still the most likely to stand. Others know that they are not bluffs or feints, that the announced prices can be trusted to be the real prices, and that they will cover one third of the market. A striking illustration of the Corporation's recognized leadership came early in 1956 when the chairman of another large concern remarked that although "independent" mills produced 69 per cent of the country's steel, they had only a "minority voice" in setting the price.[160]

People are sometimes puzzled by successive statements of U.S. Steel executives that they try to set the price with a sense of responsibility toward customers and competitors alike, and that they do not set the price but follow the currents of supply and demand. The explanation is that they do have some degree of power over price, regardless of disclaimers, but that they do not have enough power to escape the full impact of supply and demand.

A price increase is likely to occur when the traditional price leader, or another firm willing to act, decides that demand or cost has increased enough for competitors to be ready to follow it. Or else the firm reduces prices when costs have been cut, or when sales are falling off at current prices. Often the price leader finds its own sales declining because competitors are offering secret discounts, until it finally cuts its open price to match their secret prices — thereby gaining an undeserved reputation, for good or ill, of leading in the price reduction.

Price Discrimination

Prior to World War II, steel producers frequently gave large quantity discounts.[161] The principal beneficiaries were presumably the hundred users buying, as of 1934, 42 per cent of total output.[162] The first statistical tabulation of discounts was not made until after the

159. See Oxenfeldt, *Industrial Pricing and Market Practices*, p. 521; Burck, "The Transformation of U.S. Steel," pp. 200, 202.

160. Ernest T. Weir, chairman of National Steel Corp., quoted in *Wall Street Journal*, March 23, 1956, p. 22.

161. *Idem*, interview in *U.S. News & World Report*, September 10, 1954, p. 66.

162. *Fortune*, April 1936, p. 127.

Robinson-Patman Act of 1936 presumably limited discounts to those justified by differences in cost. If the average mill net price (for eight types of steel) received from buyers to whom 10 to 30 tons were shipped during February 1939 is taken as equal to 100, the price index for larger shipments (30–100, 100–300, 300–1,000, 1,000–3,000 and 3,000–10,000 tons) dropped off to 98.0, 94.6, 90.5, 93.1 and 90.0. In only one of the eight types — cold rolled strip, for which the automobile manufacturers were the biggest customers — was the contrast striking. Its biggest shipments went at a price only two thirds of that for 10 to 30 tons, and less than half that of 3 to 10 tons. (See Table 32.) In the absence of cost data, it is impossible to know whether or not these particular discounts violated the law. Moreover, there are too many statistical pitfalls in the interpretation of the figures to make them more than suggestive.

Eventually the principle of the Robinson-Patman Act fully prevailed, no doubt partly because of the rise in demand for steel which made it easier to resist requests for discounts. The steel mills now announce a policy of one open price, the same to all customers under like circumstances. Out of sixteen customers asked about this point in the present study, eight agreed that there is one open price for all and one doubted it, the other seven declaring themselves too small as buyers to know about terms for big purchasers. According to one steel executive, "The old-time price gouging by the automobile makers no longer occurs." This seems to be true, even though confirming statistics are not available. All industrial users and warehouses order in carload lots, and there is no extra discount for a larger order. Although an extra charge is made for a smaller order, several small orders for a standard product can sometimes be produced in one "heat" and carry the same price quotation as a large order. Mills refuse orders for less than five tons, and some even refuse orders for less than twenty. Any order may have extras tacked on for each added expense required: an order with particular specifications may, for example, require a change of rolls.

Price Uniformity

On the whole, prices as quoted by the various steel companies are uniform for standardized types of carbon steel. In the words of *Business Week:* "The really big-tonnage customers buy from numerous producers. Thus, no integrated carbon producer — from the largest to

TABLE 32

STEEL: PRICES IN RELATION TO QUANTITIES SHIPPED, FEBRUARY 1939

(*Price of Shipments of 10–30 Tons = 100*)

Tons Shipped	Relative Net Price, Average of Five to Eight Rolled or Drawn Products	Relative Net Price, Cold Rolled Strip, Separately
Under 3	117.3	132.2
3–10	112.2	138.7
10–30	100.0	100.0
30–100	98.0	88.4
100–300	94.6	88.0
300–1,000	90.5	67.6
1,000–3,000	93.1	..
3,000–10,000	90.0	..

Sources: Data collected from steel companies by Department of Justice, reported in John M. Blair and Arthur Reeside, *Price Discrimination in Steel,* TNEC Monograph 41, 1941, pp. 9–23. The figures are transcribed from this source to make the 10–30 group equal to 100, in recognition of the criticism that the two smallest classes consist largely of special types of steel and that the rounding off of orders to even tons might drastically affect the results below 10 tons. For this and other criticisms see John Scoville and Noel Sargent, eds., *Fact and Fancy in the T.N.E.C. Monographs,* National Association of Manufacturers, New York, 1942, pp. 772–76.

the smallest — can afford to be noncompetitive on price." [163] Out of eighteen customers questioned in the present study about this uniformity, eleven approved it while seven disapproved. Typical reasons in favor were that "it enables us to quote our customers and then buy from a number of sources," and that "we cannot expect price discrimination among customers to disappear as long as prices charged by sellers vary from each other." One authoritative study of the industry has stressed that small customers are especially anxious for uniformity in steel prices.[164]

There are two main types of departure from f.o.b. mill price uniformity among sellers in the steel industry today. One, which is permanent, consists of premiums received by companies on products in which they have a special reputation or by local companies selling in local markets protected by freight costs against competition from distant mills. The second, which is temporary, occurs either in boom times when certain companies (usually small) can charge premiums —

163. *Business Week,* November 5, 1955, p. 25.

164. Daugherty, de Chazeau and Stratton, *The Economics of the Iron and Steel Industry,* Vol. 1, pp. 563–65.

perhaps as a reward for a promise of rapid delivery — without losing customers to their competitors whose order books are already full, or in times of slump when they offer their steel at discounts.[165]

For many years rather complete uniformity prevailed in the extras charged for quantities, grades, qualities, etc., of steel products. On the whole, uniformity continues, although several authorities maintain the charges are now less uniform than formerly.

Identity of bids on government steel purchase contracts was made inevitable by the basing point system, under which there was always one delivered price at each place.[166] Even today, mills located at the same place often bid identically, for they merely bid their standard quotations, giving discounts neither to private buyers nor to the government. Nor do government regulations allow bargaining for a special price.[167] Steel companies are even less willing to give discounts to government than to private buyers, as these cuts cannot be kept secret from other customers.[168] As between mills located at different places, bids usually differ because of the freight factor.

The Question of Price Stability

After the 1898–1901 mergers, iron and steel prices became more stable. In the period 1902–22 as compared with 1880–1901 the number of price fluctuations decreased while fluctuations in output correspondingly increased.[169] A famous instance of rigid prices was that of standard rails, a product made by only a handful of companies (four at the present time). The quotation was unchanged at $28 from 1901 to 1916, and again at $43 from 1922 to 1932.[170]

Much attention was directed to the stability of published steel prices during the 1929–32 price drop. The composite finished-steel price index of the magazine *Steel* declined only 15 per cent as against a 23 per cent decline of the index for all commodities except farm products and foods. (See Table 33.) Steel and farm machinery were the two

165. Compare 1946–50 prices in Celler Exhibits, pp. 629–36.

166. Compare David F. Austin, Celler Hearings, pp. 589–99.

167. Kenneth H. Hunter, *ibid.*, p. 781.

168. Earl F. Reed, general counsel of National Steel Corp., in *Delivered Pricing and the Future of American Business*, U.S. Chamber of Commerce, Washington, 1948, p. 137.

169. Abraham Berglund, "The United States Steel Corporation and Price Stabilization" and "The United States Steel Corporation and Industrial Stabilization," *Quarterly Journal of Economics*, November 1923, pp. 1–30 and August 1924, pp. 607–30.

170. Burns, *The Decline of Competition*, pp. 205–06.

TABLE 33

STEEL: FINISHED STEEL AND GENERAL WHOLESALE PRICE INDEXES, 1929–55

	Composite Published Price of Finished Steel		Wholesale Price Index, All Commodities Except Farm Products and Foods	
Year	Annual Average Price, per 100 Lbs.	Percentage Change	Index	Percentage Change
			(1947–49 = 100)	
1929–55		+120.9		+78.6
1929	$2.54		65.5	
1932	2.15	− 15.4	50.2	−23.4
1941	2.65	+ 23.3	63.7	+26.9
1945	2.73	+ 3.0	71.3	+11.9
1948	3.91	+ 43.2	103.4	+45.0
1951	4.71	+ 20.5	115.9	+12.1
1955	5.61	+ 19.1	117.0	+ .9

Source: Indexes of magazine *Steel* and of U.S. Bureau of Labor Statistics, reported in *Survey of Current Business.*

industries that were most vehemently accused of hampering business recovery by failing to cut prices to meet the reduced purchasing power of their customers.

In defense against this charge, the U.S. Steel Corporation presented to the Temporary National Economic Committee in 1939 an economic analysis which has become a minor classic for the authority and clarity of its presentation.[171] The Corporation's explanation of the failure of steel prices to reflect declines in demand more directly may be summarized as follows:

1. Steel is used primarily in the manufacture of capital goods and consumer durable goods. The demand for both of these groups is subject to occasional sharp slumps.
2. The total demand for steel is inelastic — that is, a price reduction will do little to restore it once it has dropped. For example, a railroad with no prospect of good traffic will hardly buy locomotives just because their prices are reduced. Consumers who have stopped buying cars because their incomes have been cut or because they fear unemployment will hardly resume such buying if a 20 per cent reduction in steel prices

171. Exhibit 1410, presented by U.S. Steel Corp., TNEC Hearings, Part 26, 1940, pp. 13893–913.

is carried through to the automobile and brings its price down 2½ per cent.

3. Steel is so nearly uniform in quality among producers that a price cut by any one will draw customers from others.
4. There are so few important producers that each will feel this loss of customers and will have to meet the price cut at once.
5. Fixed costs are so high that general price cutting will have a serious effect on profits.

The validity of these points is hard to challenge, and critics of the analysis have either confined themselves to details or have boldly suggested that by breaking the industry into a large enough number of units price cutting could be stimulated regardless of demand or costs. The difficulty is that a moderate degree of dissolution would bring only moderate price cutting, whereas drastic dissolution (splitting the ownership of the steelworks in Gary, Indiana, for example) would seriously reduce the efficiency of production.

The Question of Secret Discounts

Despite the influences working against price cutting, something close to "cutthroat" competition did occur in 1911, 1921 and 1938,[172] and "price concessions were the most effective way of securing sales in the depressed 1930 decade." [173] Perhaps half the difference between the rates of decline of steel and other prices would be accounted for if these secret discounts were known. An authoritative price study was not made until the 1939–42 period. If each of seven types of steel is weighted equally, the average discount from published quotations appears to have been 4.8 per cent in the second quarter of 1939 when ingot production was at 51 per cent of capacity, as against only 0.3 per cent in the fourth quarter of 1941 when production was at 98 per cent.[174]

These discounts were probably not given to all customers, but only to those whose purchases were considered strategic and who themselves bargained.[175] It is not surprising, both in view of the recovery of

172. Marengo, "The Basing Point Decisions and the Steel Industry," p. 516.

173. Standard & Poor's Corp., "Steel," June 28, 1956, p. S 78.

174. Calculated from "Labor Dept. Examines Consumers' Prices of Steel Products," *Iron Age*, April 25, 1946, p. 118.

175. Kenneth H. Hunter, Celler Hearings, p. 772.

steel demand and the gradual triumph of the one-price-for-all principle, that less is now heard of such price concessions. Eleven out of thirteen customers questioned stated that price flexibility was less today than before World War II. Two explanations of the price stability in 1954 — a stability which "amazed" investment specialists — as given by a steel executive, are worth noting: the mills had learned from the 1930s the folly of indiscriminate price cutting, and they had adopted in the 1940s cost accounting systems which disclosed the loss involved in any given price cut.[176] Real price cutting in an industry like steel is not to be expected unless there is serious excess capacity, and even the drop to operation at 63 per cent of ingot capacity in the summer of 1954 hardly constituted such overcapacity as had existed during the 1930s.

Postwar Steel Prices and the Gray Market

The advance of steel prices has more than kept pace with that of other nonagricultural prices since the depression. Between 1932 and 1941 their recovery was at about the same rate; in World War II steel "held the price line" better; from 1945 to 1948 they advanced together; and since 1948 steel prices have continued up while general inflation has slowed down. In 1955 steel was 121 per cent above the 1929 level, while other prices were up only 79 per cent. (See Table 33.)

Steel prices, nevertheless, have increased less than supply and demand would have permitted. Since the mid-1930s, the demand of both the United States and the world has turned increasingly toward metal products, such as armaments and consumer durable goods, as against nondurable goods. Steel capacity did not rise correspondingly, for several reasons one of which was the bitter experience of losses in the depression. Under these conditions prices of steel could have gone well ahead of other prices as soon as the Office of Price Administration ceilings were removed.

Instead, the price of steel was deliberately held down. Shortages appeared, customers were rationed and a "gray market" sprang up — especially in 1947–48 and 1950–51. In other words, buyers wanted so much steel at the artificially low price that sellers limited their purchases to a percentage of their "historical position," whereupon some

176. William H. Lowe, treasurer of Inland Steel Co., *The Outlook for the Steel Industry and Its Implications for the Economy*, speech to Institute of Investment Banking at Wharton School of Finance and Commerce, University of Pennsylvania, Philadelphia, April 4, 1956, p. 14.

purchasers found it profitable to resell at advanced prices to those whose quotas, if any, were inadequate to their needs. Various distortions in the steel price structure developed, and public opinion was much exercised both by the shortages and the premium prices.[177]

A combination of reasons seems to explain why prices were not raised closer to the level justified by the current supply and demand situation:

1. Rapid price increases would increase profits so sharply that new capital would rush to enter the industry, only to prove redundant when demand turned down once again. Thus capital would be wasted, and both human and financial dislocation would occur.

2. They would draw criticism from the government and public opinion.

3. They would antagonize customers, who would consider themselves exploited for a temporary "killing" by the steel producers.[178] This was illustrated when customers turned to U.S. Steel late in 1920 and early in 1921 in resentment against higher prices exacted by the competitors during the inflation of 1919–20.[179] It is also illustrated by the resentment some customers still feel against Kaiser Steel Corporation's premium price established during the 1948 boom with the aim of paying off its Reconstruction Finance Corporation loan quickly.

4. They would bring demands for higher wages, and then, after a drop in sales had reduced prices again, the higher wage scale would remain as a rigid cost factor. Although wage demands come regularly, regardless of price changes, an increase in prices to the public to the extent permitted by buying pressure would doubtless augment such demands.

5. There may be a desire to contribute to the public welfare by preventing inflation. This desire would be mixed with motives 2 and 4, and runs up against the fact that inflation can in fact be prevented only through control of the money supply. The fate of U.S. Steel's refusal to raise either wages or prices in April 1948 is shown in a headline three months later: "Anti-Inflation Plan Fails; U.S. Steel Forced to Raise Wages,

177. *Steel Supply and Distribution Problems*, Interim Report of Senate Small Business Committee, 80th Cong., 2d sess., 1948; *Materials Shortages: Steel*, Hearings before Senate Small Business Committee, 82d Cong., 1st sess., Part 2, 1951; *Steel Gray Market*, Hearings before Subcommittee of Senate Small Business Committee, 82d Cong., 1st sess., 1952; *The Gray Market in Steel*, Report of Senate Small Business Committee, S. Rept. 1141, 82d Cong., 2d sess., 1952; "That Daffy Gray Market," *Fortune*, May 1948.

178. W. W. Sebald, president of Armco Steel Corp., interview in *U.S. News & World Report*, May 21, 1954, p. 65.

179. Marengo thesis, pp. 288, 336.

Prices. Increases Necessary to Cover Rise in Coal, Material and Freight Costs." [180] An earlier example of the same kind was the Corporation's refusal to raise prices in 1920.

Price Flexibility and the Public Interest

Whether the industry's "administered price" practices are in the public interest depends principally on the merit of the first point. The criticism made by many economists has been summed up by one of them in the following words:

> A relatively low prosperity price results, in effect, in a subsidization by the steel industry of steel using industries. It serves to violate the dictates of consumer demand as expressed in a competitive market, a market which should set a price conducive to an optimum allocation of resources.[181]
>
> Similar considerations apply in times of depression. If the object is to maintain profitable production, this cannot be done by allowing steel prices to remain artificially high, i.e., at a level relatively "out of line" with other, more competitive prices.[182]

Granting the validity of this argument as far as it goes, the accompanying problems would probably be greater under such a program of price flexibility than under the prevailing pattern of stability. If prices were actually to drop far enough in depression to keep unit sales from falling, a very much greater price cut would be required than might be needed for commodities for which demand fluctuates less. Such a deep price cut would quickly threaten the solvency of many steel companies, since their costs could not drop to anything like the same extent. Either the companies would be absorbed by their strongest rivals, under the rule used by the Department of Justice that a firm faced with bankruptcy may enter a merger which would otherwise be illegal; or they would shut down their plants. If the latter occurred, prices would have to jump equally high in the next period of prosperity to attract the needed capital, since no one would want to invest in equipment subject to such a serious danger of loss without the lure of tremendous (because temporary) profits. Alternatively, if the industry were highly competitive, it could not obtain such profits and

180. *Iron Age*, July 22, 1948, p. 121.
181. Adams, "The Steel Industry," p. 194.
182. *Ibid.*, p. 195.

would therefore suffer from insufficient capacity.[183] These patterns do not look attractive from the standpoint either of economical use of capital or of the public welfare generally.

The Postwar Wage-Price Spiral

More familiar than rationing and the gray market has been another postwar sequence of events in steel: the bargaining sessions between the United Steelworkers of America and the employers almost every year, punctuated by strikes about every third year; the increases in wages or fringe benefits or both, setting a "pattern" for other industries; and the ensuing price increases, spreading to articles made of steel. It is interesting that the price of steel, contrary to the assumptions of the antitrust laws, is thus determined by collective action under the pressure of circumstances — but with no need for the direct agreement among competitors which would constitute violation of the law.

The relevant figures, for U.S. Steel and Bethlehem before World War II and for nearly the whole industry thereafter, may be summarized briefly as follows: (1) Employment costs per hour and steel prices have both increased every year since at least 1945, and by 1955 were 200 and 112 per cent higher, respectively, than in 1940–41. (2) Owing to the rise both in selling prices and in productivity per man-hour, employment costs declined from more than 40 per cent of sales in 1945 and 1946, when output was hampered by reconversion and strikes, to a range of 32–37 per cent in the years since. (3) Net income per dollar of sales was low in 1945 compared to the 1920s or to 1940–41, showed no trend either way between 1946 and 1954, and then jumped in 1955 to about the average of U.S. Steel and Bethlehem in the 1920s. (4) Dividends have been held down since the war to between 2.4 and 3.3 per cent of sales (between 2.4 and 3.6 for U.S. Steel and Bethlehem), as against averages of 4.9, 4.9 and 3.7 per cent for the three prewar periods with which comparison is made. (See Table 34.)

Apparently the union's demands have given the steel producers an obvious occasion, and a defense required by the state of public opinion, for stepping up prices while the market was running strong. They have not charged all the traffic would bear — or there would be no gray markets — but as a result of the wage-price spiral they have come

183. Oxenfeldt, *Industrial Pricing and Market Practices*, p. 491. The case against unrestricted price competition in the heavy industries has been frequently presented by J. M. Clark, for example, in "Basing Point Methods of Price Quoting," at p. 486.

TABLE 34

STEEL: PRICE, HOURLY EARNINGS, AND RATIO TO SALES OF EMPLOYMENT COSTS, PROFIT AND DIVIDENDS, 1920–55

Year	Composite Published Price of Finished Steel	Employment Costs per Hour[a]	Ratio to Sales[b]		
			Employment Costs	Income	Dividends
	(Per 100 Lbs.)		*(Per Cent)*		
			U.S. Steel and Bethlehem		
1920–29	$2.73	$ .63	40.9	8.1	4.9
1930–39	2.44	.75	42.4	2.9	4.9
1940–41	2.65	.98	39.2	6.7	3.7
			48 to 53 Companies		
1945	2.73	1.37	41.0	3.1	2.4
1946	3.00	1.49	41.5	5.5	3.1
1947	3.42	1.63	36.9	6.2	2.8
1948	3.91	1.77	35.0	6.7	2.5
1949	4.21	1.89	35.2	7.2	3.0
1950	4.40	2.05	33.2	8.1	3.3
1951	4.71	2.25	32.5	5.8	2.6
1952	4.82	2.48	35.1	5.0	2.9
1953	5.13	2.64	34.2	5.6	2.5
1954	5.33	2.76	36.9	6.0	3.3
1955	5.61	2.94	33.7	7.9	3.2

Sources: Prices from *Survey of Current Business;* other 1920–41 data are simple averages for U.S. Steel and Bethlehem (annual reports); other 1945–55 data from American Iron and Steel Institute, *Annual Statistical Report*, 1955, pp. 12–13.

U.S. Steel and Bethlehem, being more integrated than the rest of the industry, have always had a higher ratio of employment costs to sales. Thus in 1952–55 the average of their two ratios ran 40.4, 39.0, 41.1 and 38.1, or at about the prewar prosperity levels.

a. These are averages of annual figures. Data for 1920–41 are hourly earnings; "fringe benefits" were not yet important in those years.

b. The ratios are for *totals* (of sales, employment costs, etc.) of each period.

closer to it. Most of the resulting profit has gone into improvement and increase of capital equipment at the high level of postwar construction costs — an increase the financial markets showed no inclination to finance. Between the end of 1945 and the end of 1955 the book value of the industry's capital stock and surplus increased from $3.6 to $7.9 billion, almost entirely through reinvestment of earnings. The rate of return on stockholders' equity (as of the beginning of each year) was 7.3, 11.1, 13.8, 11.6, 15.7, 12.5, 9.0, 11.6, 9.4 and 15.5 per cent, successively, in the years 1946–55.[184] According to a statement issued by U.S. Steel, even its 1955 return of 9 per cent on sales "would not reflect a proper relationship to the corporation's capital expenditure program." [185] The expanded demand for steel was not to be satisfied at prices which yielded only the same rewards to labor and capital as when demand had been less, relative to that for other goods.

The Issues of Diversification and Domination

The interests of some of the larger steel companies, especially U.S. Steel, in iron mining, railroads and fabrication have raised some discussion as to whether any of these have anti-competitive implications. In 1950 there was a rumor that suit would shortly be brought against U.S. Steel to force the separation of these outside interests; [186] but no action resulted. The Corporation has to meet occasional treble damage suits based on the idea that it has monopolistic power, but none has reached the published court reports.

Two opposing points of view on the position of U.S. Steel are illustrated by a congressional report which asserts that "the small companies live dangerously in the hands of Big Steel," [187] and a statement by an executive of a smaller company: "We can continue to compete with the Steel Corporation unless the government in some way interferes with us." [188] Apparently, fabricators "live dangerously" (when their suppliers compete with them), but the steel industry itself does not agree that *it* does so.

Control of Iron Ore

The extent to which U.S. Steel dominates the supply of high-grade iron ore from the Lake Superior region has been a subject of discussion for fifty years. Meanwhile its share has been declining. In 1910 it shipped 51 per cent of this material,[189] and in 1948 only 41 per cent.[190] Its Lake Superior mining subsidiary, Oliver Iron Mining Company

184. American Iron and Steel Institute, *Annual Statistical Reports*, especially 1955, pp. 12–15.

185. *Journal of Commerce*, August 3, 1956, p. 1.

186. David Lawrence, *New York Herald Tribune*, June 5, 1950, pp. 1, 4.

187. *December 1949 Steel Price Increases*, S. Rept. 1373, Joint Committee on the Economic Report, 81st Cong., 2d sess., 1950, p. 4.

188. Ernest T. Weir, quoted in *ibid.*, p. 52.

189. American Iron and Steel Institute, *Annual Statistical Report*, 1912, p. 151.

190. FTC, *Iron Ore* Report, p. 35.

(since 1952 called a "Division"), did not sell to outside steel producers before 1939, because, it was stated, there was little demand until then.[191] There was testimony before a congressional committee that no blast furnace had ever had to close for lack of iron ore.[192]

Since 1939 Oliver has sold to "12 or 14 purchasers," including eight of U.S. Steel's nine largest competitors.[193] In the 1945–49 period these sales were equal to only one fifth of its shipments to the Corporation's iron-making divisions.[194] These divisions received an allowance of 30 cents a ton for saving in selling costs, and in 1949 (its best year up to that time) Oliver itself earned $1.49 per ton produced. U.S. Steel's maximum net advantage (ignoring return on capital invested in ore properties) could thus be called $1.79, which was 25 per cent of the price of iron ore, or 2 per cent of the Corporation's total sales.[195] Cleveland-Cliffs, rather than Oliver, is considered to be the iron ore price leader.[196]

A recent student attributed U.S. Steel's decision to sell ore to its competitors to several motives: [197] (1) "First, ore hardships on the part of U.S. Steel's rivals might be expected eventually to lead to Congressional criticism and possible antitrust action against the Corporation." (2) The heavy taxes on ore in the ground make it desirable to mine and sell quickly [198] — an argument which implicitly denies the position that ownership of large raw material reserves is an advantage to a producer. (3) Royalty rates on ore leases were expected to be raised shortly, making it desirable to mine quickly — another argument of the same kind. (4) "Sale of ore to rivals, rather than proving a competitive disadvantage, might afford a subtle but most effective means of influencing rival steel firms' policies." In contrast to this fourth point, one firm that purchases a large part of its ore from Oliver Mining Division comments privately: "Would we have signed with the United Steelworkers in 1952, when U.S. Steel was still on strike, if we

191. Benjamin F. Fairless, Celler Hearings, p. 531.

192. Ernest T. Weir, *ibid.*, p. 812.

193. Benjamin F. Fairless, *ibid.*, p. 556; and Celler Exhibits, p. 13.

194. Calculated from Celler Exhibits, p. 496.

195. Calculated from *ibid.*, pp. 497–98, and U.S. Steel Corp., Annual Report, 1955, pp. 30–31.

196. *Business Week*, February 26, 1955, p. 32.

197. L. Gregory Hines, "Price Determination in the Lake Erie Iron Ore Market," *American Economic Review*, September 1951, p. 659.

198. Compare *Business Week*, September 11, 1954, p. 94.

were afraid of discrimination in the matter of ore?" No competitor approached in this study was willing to say that U.S. Steel exerts any domination through its sales of ore.

U.S. Steel itself reported in 1950 that it owned 51 per cent of the 1.4 billion gross tons of Lake Superior ore with more than 45 per cent iron content, 15 per cent of the 4.0 billion tons in the rest of the country, and 19 per cent of the 72.0 billion tons of low-grade Lake Superior ore.[199] Although it had a little over 80 per cent of the known, readily available, high-grade, open-pit reserves in the Lake Superior region,[200] the sum of all the figures indicates that its weighted average of total domestic iron ore reserves was still well below its share of pig iron capacity. In other words, its "domination" arising from control of iron ore is linked with the highest-grade ore only, and will shrink further as the industry relies increasingly on low-grade Lake Superior taconite ores, other domestic sources and imports from Canada and Venezuela.[201]

U.S. Steel's Transportation Facilities

U.S. Steel owns fifteen common carrier railroads, 13 per cent of whose total freight in 1949 was carried for outside shippers.[202] This ownership has drawn criticism along the following lines: (1) twenty independent mining companies "have no choice but to play ball with the Corporation" because they ship over its Duluth, Missabe & Iron Range Railroad; [203] and (2) these railroads charge unduly high rates, thus compelling U.S. Steel's competitors to pay it tribute.[204]

The two criticisms apply only within restricted limits. Perhaps a few of these independent mines had to ship via the Missabe line, but in 1948, 88 per cent of all independently mined Minnesota ore was shipped by other railroads and more could have been so shipped.[205] The rates on iron ore are under the jurisdiction of the Interstate Com-

199. Calculated from figures given by Benjamin F. Fairless, Celler Hearings, pp. 540–41, and in Celler Exhibits, p. 495.

200. FTC, *Iron Ore* Report, p. 88.

201. See William F. Boericke, "More Iron Ore," *Barron's*, January 23, 1956, p. 11.

202. Calculated from Celler Exhibits, p. 494.

203. Congressman John A. Blatnik of Minnesota, Celler Hearings, p. 899.

204. ICC Commissioner Joseph B. Eastman, statement in 1932, cited by Congressman Celler, *ibid.*, p. 867. This view is supported in Joel B. Dirlam and Alfred E. Kahn, *Fair Competition: The Law and Economics of Antitrust Policy*, Cornell University Press, Ithaca, 1954, p. 145.

205. Benjamin F. Fairless, Celler Hearings, p. 528.

merce Commission. More than one of U.S. Steel's ore-carrying railroads is very profitable; but to reduce ore rates in order to cut these profits would hurt railroads which, like the Great Northern, must make money on iron ore to keep their total operation profitable.[206] U.S. Steel points out that it is simply fortunate in having bought and improved well-located railroads many years ago.[207]

The same sort of criticism that was made of U.S. Steel's railroad holdings was directed at its ownership of the Isthmian Line of steamships. The line was set up in 1908 when U.S. Steel considered prevailing cargo rates too high, but eventually very little of the Corporation's water shipments were carried in its ships and continued ownership became unnecessary. If there was once a monopolistic or other advantage in owning the ships, their sale to the States Marine Corporation interests in March 1956 indicated that it had vanished.

Fabrication

Forward integration of steel companies into fabrication has caused much controversy. The construction and shipbuilding interests of Bethlehem and U.S. Steel always raised the question of competition with their own customers. U.S. Steel sold its shipbuilding facilities to the Navy in 1947, but it bought thirteen fabricating plants of all sorts, and Bethlehem fifteen, between 1930 and 1950.[208] In the manufacture of steel barrels and drums, 87 per cent of capacity had been taken over by steel companies before 1944;[209] and one of them states privately that it entered this field only in order to preserve its market, since customers were being rapidly bought by its competitors. The two principal purposes of entering fabrication have been to secure assured outlets and to take advantage of the customarily higher margin of profit there than in steelmaking.[210]

Fifteen out of seventeen steel fabricators asked about this trend during the course of the present study considered it a serious threat to their position, and four out of the five fabricators who made complaints at the Celler Hearings in 1950 wrote at the end of 1955 that

206. ICC Decision 29502, *Butler Bros. v. Great Northern Ry. Co.*, January 9, 1950, quoted as Celler Exhibit S-42, pp. 54–68, especially p. 65.

207. Benjamin F. Fairless, Celler Hearings, p. 579.

208. FTC Commissioner James M. Mead, *ibid.*, pp. 146–47.

209. *Iron Age*, September 21, 1944, p. 103.

210. Marengo thesis, p. 189.

they still felt the same way. These companies offer two principal objections to fabrication by steelmakers:

1. The steel company might sell its semifinished steel at a price so high as to keep independent fabricators on a very low margin of profits, while making up its own fabricating losses out of the high price of steel. Such a squeeze, even if unintentional, may come about whenever steel prices are affected by one set of causes and end products by another. Three of the seventeen fabricators questioned on their experience with the squeeze replied that they had felt it. On the other hand, an earlier student found some evidence that the integrated steel companies had as a rule tried to keep the margin high enough to permit buyers of semifinished steel to make a profit; [211] and the present writer was informed by more than one customer that squeezes have sometimes represented efforts to put underpriced semifinished steel into a more defensible relationship to prices of finished steel and fabricated products. This was the explanation offered by the integrated steel companies [212] to the charge that they had squeezed nonintegrated companies by raising semifinished steel prices in February 1948 and December 1949.[213] As it happens, the nonintegrated companies escaped the squeeze in February 1948 by raising their own selling prices, and ignored U.S. Steel's reduction in finished steel prices in May 1948 made as a gesture against inflation.[214] The squeeze argument was undermined by the chief witness on the February 1948 instance, when he elaborated as follows: "Well, they always put us in a squeeze. They are tough competition, and also the little fellows. I think the competition in this industry of ours is much more acute than most people realize. . . ." [215]

2. In times of tight supply, integrated producers may supply their own subsidiaries with steel at the expense of independent customers.[216]

211. *Ibid.*, pp. 120–22.

212. Statements by U.S. Steel, Bethlehem and Republic, in *Increases in Steel Prices*, Hearings before Joint Committee on the Economic Report, 80th Cong., 2d sess., 1948, pp. 9, 72, 73; Benjamin F. Fairless, Celler Hearings, pp. 592, 615.

213. FTC, *Monopolistic Practices and Small Business*, Staff Report for Subcommittee on Monopoly, Senate Small Business Committee, 1952, pp. 50–54; *The Iron and Steel Industry*, House Report, 1950, p. 54.

214. See price charts in Celler Exhibits, pp. 629–36.

215. H. G. Batcheller, chairman of Allegheny Ludlum Steel Corp., in *December 1949 Steel Price Increases*, Hearings before Joint Committee on the Economic Report, 81st Cong., 2d sess., 1950, p. 180.

216. Complaints by Tom J. Smith, Jr., Celler Hearings, p. 306; Robert K. Brown, *ibid.*, p. 341; J. Philip Murphy, *ibid.*, p. 347; Kenneth M. Keegan, *ibid.*, p. 356.

Thus a National Production Authority survey indicated that in June–August 1951 affiliated warehouses received 14.1 per cent of steel mill warehouse shipments as against only 9.9 per cent in the "easier" period January–September 1950.[217] Although the figures are not conclusive, most nonintegrated producers and fabricators who commented to the writer on this issue believed that an integrated firm will favor its own subsidiary as a matter of course. Several, however, specifically excepted U.S. Steel from any accusation of favoritism. The Corporation itself states that its American Bridge Division steadily lost ground to the independent members of the American Institute of Steel Construction from 1946 to 1955.

Whether integrated and independent firms can exist together on a mutually acceptable basis is a continuing issue. The investigations by Congress and the antitrust agencies are of some help — at least in the opinion of four out of the fifteen fabricators who commented on this point — in ensuring the independents fair treatment.

Entry

Between 1904 and 1956 the number of companies making pig iron or steel declined from about 500 [218] to 220. Thus during the 1930s the pressure of competition and financial losses, and the progress of integration and of technology, forced the majority of independent merchant blast furnaces (of which there were 83 in 1930 and 24 in 1956) and many independent hand rolling mills out of business. It is undeniable that today "because steel-making is so fantastically expensive, free entry is limited." [219] True, a number of nonintegrated firms have entered steelmaking since 1930; semi-integrated concerns were founded in 1937, 1941, 1944, 1946 and 1953; [220] and four integrated concerns (the McLouth, Kaiser and Detroit Steel corporations and the Lone Star Steel Company) have emerged since the beginning of World War II. Of these, only Kaiser was fully integrated from the start, having sprung into being under the influence of wartime needs. To establish a completely integrated enterprise today, from iron and coal mines to rolling mills, might require something approaching the half

217. FTC, *The Distribution of Steel Consumption, 1949–1950*, Report to Subcommittee on Monopoly, Senate Small Business Committee, 1952, p. 12.

218. *The Iron and Steel Industry*, House Report, 1950, p. 46.

219. "Steel Catches Up," *Fortune*, March 1951, p. 127.

220. Compare Oxenfeldt, *Industrial Pricing and Market Practices*, p. 536.

billion dollars U.S. Steel is reported to have spent on its Delaware River mill and subsidiary properties in ore, shipping and the rest.

The difficulty of entry is explained first by the huge investment required. But the country does possess much capital available for investment. Why has this gone to a greater extent into chemicals and petroleum than into steel? The only answer, in logic, must be that other industries have, and that steel has not, offered enough profits in relation to the risks of the industry.[221] This situation is reflected in the level of steel earnings, which in the thirty-year period 1925–54 were only once (in 1953) in the top half of a list of forty-one to forty-five industries tabulated; the average thirty-year position was tenth from the bottom.[222]

Interindustry Competition

Even steel, basic product that it is, competes actively in many uses with other commodities. A few random examples cited recently include cooking utensils, where the Census of 1947 showed steel to have 42 per cent of the market, aluminum 47 per cent, glassware 9 per cent and other metals 6 per cent; farm roofing, where galvanized steel sheets compete with asphalt, asbestos, wood shingles, aluminum sheets, slate, tile and tar paper; containers, where tin plate competes with glass, paper, plastics and fibreboard; and office furniture, where steel competes actively with wood.[223]

These uses (especially containers) are important to the profits of the steel companies. For the bulk of consumption, however, there is little chance of substitution as long as cost relationships stay anywhere near their present levels. Steel executives feel that most of the market is safe from substitution until revolutionary new materials or methods are developed.

Performance of the Industry

Although the performance of the steel industry has drawn much criticism at various times, the consensus of informed comment in recent years appears to be favorable. In 1950 the Director of the Office of Domestic Commerce in the Department of Commerce spoke of "a

221. *Fortune*, March 1951, p. 128; Marvin J. Barloon, "The Question of Steel Capacity," *Harvard Business Review*, March 1949, pp. 229–31.

222. From First National City Bank of New York figures on rate of return as per cent of net worth, as tabulated in *Steel Facts*, August 1955, p. 1.

223. The first three examples are those of David F. Austin, Celler Hearings, pp. 697–98.

steady pace of technological progress in the iron and steel industry in spite of certain facts which make research more difficult than in many other industries."[224] In 1953 the United Nations Economic Commission for Europe called the technical progress of the American industry a shining example to Europe.[225] In 1956 *Fortune* showed charts of value added and output per man-hour, and summarized as follows:

> To many semi-informed people, steelmaking, like railroading, is one of the nation's most stuffy and inefficient industries. The charts on these pages do not measure the steel industry's stuffiness, but they do show that it has scored a remarkable efficiency record. Its productivity, indeed, has risen fourfold in fifty years, or nearly twice as fast as that of the economy. The charts also show that U.S. Steel Corp., no longer a model of unprogressiveness, has over the years done nearly as well as the industry average, and in 1955 surpassed it.[226]

A striking example of the improvement in performance is given by the change in labor conditions, from the 84-hour week at 30 cents an hour (for common labor in Pittsburgh) in 1922 to the 40-hour week and minimum wage of $1.69 an hour in 1955. The United Steelworkers of America has been the primary agent in raising wages since 1936, but all its efforts would have been futile without the rise in productivity of the industry to back it up. In fact, the rise in common labor rates from 15 cents an hour in 1900 to 47 cents an hour in 1935 would imply that, union or no union, rising productivity will raise wages.[227]

The Question of Steel Capacity

There have been shifting tides of opinion over the decades regarding the question of expanding steel capacity. In the 1930s the industry was criticized for overexpansion during the late 1920s, with the presumed result of helping to cause a national "boom and bust"; and some industry representatives appear to concede today that overbuilding did occur.[228] The heavy fixed costs incurred by the expansion were a major cause of losses in the 1930s.

224. H. B. McCoy, *ibid.*, p. 110.

225. *New York Times*, May 5, 1953, p. 19.

226. Burck, "The Transformation of U.S. Steel," p. 94.

227. Figures from *Steel Facts*, April 1956 Supplement, p. 3.

228. Thomas Dimond, "This New Round of Steel Expansion," *Harvard Business Review*, May–June 1956, at pp. 85, 93. See TNEC Monograph 42, p. 3, for attribution of excess capacity to the basing point system.

Early in World War II the government pressed for a big expansion; but it had to finance most of the 7-million-ton increase in the 1942–44 period. The gray markets of the late 1940s led to further criticism of the industry for not expanding its capacity enough to fill the current demand, which had to be rationed.[229] Again the industry was afraid of overcapacity when demand should drop. When the Korean War broke out, with the help of accelerated amortization provisions of the income tax law, it did launch a big program which carried ingot capacity up by 25 million tons in the five years 1950–54.

Most of the new, expensively constructed facilities proved to have such low operating costs that they made money even during the recession in demand of 1953–54. By the summer of 1955 the industry was fully convinced, and its leaders vied with one another in optimistic statements and announcements of expansion plans. The new program was to add another 15 million tons to ingot capacity within four years.

It would be easy to say that government economists are quicker than industry to see the need for expansion — and it cannot be denied that their prodding was helpful — but the public was showing little faith and giving little help to steel in raising new capital. Even at the end of 1955, after steel common stock prices had quadrupled, the market value of the capital of the eight largest producers was only $96 per ton of steelmaking capacity as against an average construction cost of $180 per ton for capacity installed during 1951–54 and an estimated $300 per ton for new, fully integrated capacity.[230] It was evident that steel companies must rely largely on reinvestment of earnings to finance expansion, and this necessity was bound to be a strong influence toward higher prices.

SUMMARY

1. *Concentration* in steelmaking is high, with United States Steel possessing 30 per cent, Bethlehem 15 per cent, Republic 8 per cent, and the eight largest integrated companies 76 per cent of ingot-producing capacity.

2. The 1911 *dissolution suit against U.S. Steel* charged the largest of the "trusts" with monopolization through the initial merger, later acquisitions, and cooperation with its rivals. An early consequence was the abandonment of industry meetings to discuss prices. In 1920 a 4–3 majority of the Supreme Court rejected the government's case, establishing the rule that mere size is

229. See Louis Bean, Celler Hearings, pp. 785–801.

230. Dimond, "This New Round of Steel Expansion," p. 91.

not an offense against the law when not accompanied by predatory tactics. This rule encouraged competitors to expand by merger, while U.S. Steel, cognizant of its narrow escape, refrained from doing so.

3. The *Pittsburgh Plus* system of quoting steel prices in all markets on the basis of the Pittsburgh quotation plus freight from Pittsburgh had an origin which was probably in part natural and in part collusive. It caused steel companies not at Pittsburgh to pay the freight on some shipments ("freight absorption"), receive a price on others which included the equivalent of transportation cost never incurred ("phantom freight"), and receive varying "mill net prices" on sales to different localities. In 1924 the Federal Trade Commission directed U.S. Steel not to base the price of any product on a shipping point other than its own. Additional basing points were gradually established thereafter, creating a "multiple basing point system."

4. *Mergers* have been an important means of growth for the larger steel companies, especially Bethlehem and Republic. Their main objective has been to acquire supplementary lines of production rather than to eliminate competition. The Federal Trade Commission blocked a Republic-Inland merger, but not Bethlehem's Lackawanna and Midvale mergers. In 1935 a suit against Republic's merger with Corrigan, McKinney was dismissed because the competition eliminated was not significant. In 1954 a proposed Bethlehem-Youngstown merger (blocked by the Department of Justice) raised the issue whether combinations of giant companies should be permitted even in cases where the firms fitted each other very well in location and products.

5. A 1935 suit to break up several *interlocking directorates* was dropped when the interlocks disappeared. This suit did serve as a warning for the future. A 1950 study revealed no instance of an illegal interlock in steel.

6. The Hepburn Act of 1906 caused the Pennsylvania Railroad to sell its steelmaking subsidiary to Bethlehem, but it would probably have sold it soon in any case. The act failed to achieve separation from steel companies of their *railroad subsidiaries*, but the former complaints against such relationships are rarely heard.

7. There have been relatively few *cases of restrictive agreements* in the steel industry. In 1945, fourteen producers of stainless steel pleaded *nolo contendere* to charges of using patent licenses to fix prices on both stainless steel and other products — a practice which many had thought permissible. Steel companies were among those involved in cases directed against the bolt and nut, tin plate, steel strapping, rigid steel conduit, metal culvert, rain goods and metal drum industries.

8. The *Columbia Steel decision* of 1948, in which a 5–4 Supreme Court majority approved U.S. Steel's purchase of a Pacific Coast fabricator, implied that even the biggest producer may absorb smaller ones so long as the

companies do not compete directly to a significant extent and other companies do not have a significant market foreclosed.

9. The *abolition of the basing point system* finally came with the *Cement Institute* decision in 1948. Steel companies began selling on an f.o.b. mill basis, thus adding to their profits by ceasing to absorb freight. The Federal Trade Commission consent order which they accepted in 1951 forbade only common action in pricing or use of a price formula; and in recessions since 1948 or when trying to hold distant markets steel companies have again absorbed freight. The effect of f.o.b. mill pricing on location of mills has probably been very minor, and has been hard to distinguish from the effects of the postwar steel shortage and the rise in railroad rates. An eventual return to a greater degree of freight absorption is not unlikely in an industry like steel — with its few producers, high fixed costs, homogeneous product, heavy transport costs, and necessity of seeking distant customers.

10. A summary of the *effects of the basing point system* may help to indicate the eventual results of its abolition. Under a system where all producing points are basing points: (1) a company forfeits the power to select its price outside its own territory; (2) stable prices are likely to prevail because price agreements are easy to enforce, because lower prices are discouraged by knowledge that they will be met by competitors, and because firms tend to compete by absorbing more freight rather than by reducing prices; and (3) there are wastes due to cross hauling and to discouragement of barge and truck transportation. When some mills are not basing points, as was the case in steel, the above disadvantages apply plus others: (1) non-basing point mills never set their own prices, but instead automatically take the benefits of their location in higher mill net prices rather than in expanding their markets; (2) mislocation of fabricating plants may result from the lack of a freight advantage in establishing them near a non-basing point mill; and (3) it is possible that steel mills may be wrongly located because an artificial element is introduced into decisions. Whatever effects emerge in the long run from abolition of the system should be salutary, but they are not likely to be important since the fundamental characteristics of the steel industry make for stable prices and some cross hauling in any case, and since natural factors are dominant in choosing plant locations.

11. The *trend of concentration* shows an increase up to 1901, and thereafter a decline in U.S. Steel's share but an increase in that of its seven chief competitors. U.S. Steel's output of ingots and castings averaged 62.9 per cent of the total in 1901–05 and only 31.7 per cent in 1951–55. Despite wartime acquisitions by the three largest companies, their share of ingot capacity declined slightly between 1940 and 1948.

12. There are several *reasons for the decline of U.S. Steel's share* of output. First, the company deliberately followed a conservative expansion policy to

avoid bringing on another antitrust suit or public criticism. Second, its concept of itself as a public institution rather than merely a profit-seeking corporation made it vulnerable to the tactics of its rivals. Third, changes in technology, demand and locational advantage hurt it more than its rivals, just because it was the oldest large producer. Fourth, the management in the 1920s was overcautious and lacked initiative in many of its policies. Its former cautious policies did not make for active competition then, but the industry structure is healthier today as a result of the fact that the largest concern is not so dominant as before.

13. *U.S. Steel today* is modern and efficient. Its size reduces its flexibility, but affords cost advantages in other directions. Management changes since the late 1930s include, among others, acquisition of fabricating companies, modernization of plants, expansion of research and decentralization of authority. The corporation has adopted the policy of maintaining its present share of the industry's output.

14. Concentration in steel is fostered by the huge investment required, and by the advantages of *vertical integration and horizontal combination.* Vertical integration has both technical and market advantages. Combination offers security against regional slumps, and assists in reaching local markets and in making a full line of products.

15. *Rates of profit* for twelve large companies from 1901 to 1955 show U.S. Steel earning a rate below the average. Opinion in the industry attributes this in large part to its special commitment in unprofitable heavy products and semifinished steel.

16. *Indirect interlocking directorates,* which link steel companies through other corporations and banks, have led the National Resources Committee, the Federal Trade Commission and the Securities and Exchange Commission to suspect that the industry is controlled by a few financial "interest groups." No further concrete evidence has been developed to illustrate the practical effect.

17. The principal *trade association* in steel has technical and statistical functions, and has given industry leaders a forum in which to denounce cutthroat price cutting.

18. *Collaboration* among steel companies in the exploration for new sources of ore and in research projects is a factor working against cutthroat competition among them.

19. *Competition in steel* rarely takes the form of price or quality variation. Mill location, ability to deliver quickly a wide range of products, service and personal relations are frequently the factors which win customers.

20. *Price leadership* has been normal, and U.S. Steel has clearly been the leader. Its price announcements have sometimes merely followed changes made privately without formal announcement by one of its competitors.

21. *Price discrimination* existed in the 1930s, when the big buyers received large discounts. The Robinson-Patman Act and the revival of a seller's market changed this situation. Steel producers, so far as is known, now sell at an open price which is the same for all direct mill buyers.

22. *Price uniformity* among sellers is normal in steel, except when one seller has a special reputation in certain products, or its market is protected by transportation costs. Some firms may charge premiums in boom times; and more may offer rebates in depressed times. Many customers (but not the government when it acts as a buyer) prefer such uniformity.

23. *Price stability* was more characteristic of steel after the establishment of U.S. Steel than before. In the 1929–32 recession, the price decline was moderate, owing to the inelastic demand which made it seem pointless to cut prices, the fact that a price cut in this homogeneous product of few sellers would force immediate retaliation, and the high fixed costs making general price cutting dangerous to financial stability. The true price reduction was greater than it appeared, because of secret discounts to large buyers. After World War II prices were kept below the level which would have equalized supply and demand, from fear of stimulating overinvestment and public criticism. Rationing and a "gray market" resulted. A strong argument can be made for price stability, as against wide swings in steel prices which might lead alternately to underinvestment and overinvestment.

24. Since World War II the annual *wage-price spiral* has very much reduced the likelihood of individual-firm initiative in steel pricing. The price increases which have followed wage increases have thus won a justification in the public eye which might not have been granted to increases based solely on the rise in steel demand. They have enabled the industry to raise funds for the expansion of capacity which the public wants but has been unwilling to finance through the security markets.

25. *Control of iron ore* is no longer a serious competitive issue. U.S. Steel's chief mining subsidiary began selling ore to other steel companies in 1939. With the gradual exhaustion of the high-grade deposits in the Lake Superior region, U.S. Steel's ownership of domestic iron ore reserves is tending to decline below its share of blast furnace capacity.

26. *Ownership of railroads by U.S. Steel* has been criticized, in part because some independent mining firms must use them, with the result that money these companies pay in freight rates benefits their big competitor. However, the Interstate Commerce Commission fixes rates on iron ore.

27. *Forward integration into fabrication* by steel companies creates dangers for customers. These may be squeezed because the integrated companies both set the prices for the semifinished products bought by the independents and sell the finished products in competition with them. The independent fabricators may also suffer when supplies are short if integrated companies supply their

own fabricating subsidiaries first. This supply squeeze has been more of a practical danger than the price squeeze in recent years.

28. There has been only a minor degree of *entry* of new firms into integrated steelmaking for many years, while many of the small independent blast furnaces and the semi-integrated or nonintegrated steel companies have shut down or sold out. It appears that the level of profits, which has been below the average of most industries except in a few peak years, has not appealed sufficiently to investors to stimulate any large-scale entry into this industry.

29. *Interindustry competition* is only peripheral. Steel in automotive, construction, machinery, railway and other uses cannot be replaced under present-day techniques and costs.

30. Big gains in technology, productivity and labor conditions are examples of an *improving performance* by the industry. The industry was slow to expand its capacity in recent war emergencies, fearing a subsequent decline in demand, and capital losses; but it has now adopted a program of expansion.

In brief, the antitrust laws have contributed to the decline in U.S. Steel's former domination; have made for a freer market by abolishing the basing point system even though the nature of the product still makes for a great deal of uniformity in delivered prices except at times of peak demand; have assisted in the elimination of price discrimination; and help to safeguard fabricators against unfair competition; but they do not, nor would it necessarily be desirable if they could, create unrestricted price competition in steel.

CHAPTER 6

Paper

Since 60 per cent of the world's paper is consumed in the United States, it is not surprising that "paper and allied products" ranks fifth or sixth among industries in this country in value added by manufacture. Sales in 1955 were estimated at $10.0 billion, against only $5.8 billion as recently as 1947; number of employees at 453,000, against 391,000.[1]

Pulp and Paper Manufacture

Paper can be made from all cellulose fibers, but in 1955 wood pulp comprised 68 per cent of the materials used, waste paper (used especially for boxboard) 28 per cent, and such sources as rags and straw 4 per cent.[2] Seventeen per cent of wood pulp came from hardwood trees, the rest from pine, spruce and other softwoods.[3]

By simply forcing logs against a grindstone, "groundwood" pulp, which constitutes 80 per cent of newsprint, can be made; but more often the non-cellulose elements are cooked away chemically by whatever method best fits the kind of wood being pulped and the kind of paper to be produced. The chief method was once the acid or "sulphite" process; but the "sulphate" process, which produces "kraft" (strong) pulp, now predominates.

The pulp flows by pipe to an adjacent paper mill or is shipped in sheets to a distant one. After being "prepared" by washing, mixing and other steps, it is pumped to the paper machine. This is actually

1. U.S. Department of Commerce, *Pulp, Paper and Board*, Industry Report, March 1956, p. 4.

2. *Ibid.*, pp. 11–12.

3. U.S. Census Bureau, *Facts for Industry*, Series M 14A, "Pulp, Paper and Board, Summary for 1955."

a series of machines, perhaps a city block long, over which the pulp flows while the water is forced out and the fibers matted together. "Finishing" may include processes like coating and supercalendering (pressure rolling), and culminates in cutting to size, inspecting and packing.

Pulp mills are usually located near forests, while paper mills may or may not be adjacent to a pulp mill. Most mills are in the northeastern and north central states. The South has been catching up rapidly with new large plants since the sulphate treatment of southern pines was perfected.

A final step for some paper is to "convert" it into finished products. Bags are frequently made at the paper mill. Paperboard (thick, relatively inflexible paper) is either made into boxes at a "combined" plant or sold by an "independent" paperboard mill to any one of hundreds of converting firms. Some book paper has "off-the-machine coating" applied to it by the converter. All told, there are several thousand independent converters, most of them operating near large cities. Big paper makers do much of their own converting.

Pulp and Paper Companies

"Integrated" companies are those that produce both pulp and paper. In 1948 they numbered 102, and their 179 paper mills used four fifths of the nation's total supply of pulp. The 583 independent paper mills, owned by 425 companies, bought their pulp from the surplus output of integrated companies, from a handful of "market pulp" mills, and from Canada and Scandinavia.[4] Today there are somewhat fewer nonintegrated and market pulp mills.

The International Paper Company is the largest unit in the industry, with 21 pulp and paper mills and 31 converting factories. In 1955 it accounted for 8 per cent of the industry's sales. Crown Zellerbach Corporation, with 9 mills and 14 converting plants, is dominant on the Pacific Coast and is rumored to be vying for first place.[5] The four largest producers had 17 per cent of 1955 sales, and the fifteen largest 34 per cent. (See Table 35.) This degree of concentration, comparable to that in the chemical industry, is less than the average in American manufacturing.

4. Louis T. Stevenson, "The Pulp and Paper Industry," Chap. 6 of John George Glover and William Bouck Cornell, *The Development of American Industries*, Prentice-Hall, New York, 3d edition, 1951, p. 533.

5. *Journal of Commerce*, March 29, 1956, p. 1.

TABLE 35

PAPER: SALES OF FIFTEEN LARGEST COMPANIES, 1955

Firm	Amount	Per Cent of Total Production
	(Millions)	
Industry total	$9,996	100.0
Fifteen leading companies	3,389.0	33.9
1. International Paper Co.	796.4	8.0
2. Crown Zellerbach Corp.	414.1 [a]	4.1
3. St. Regis Paper Co.	257.1	2.6
4. Scott Paper Co.	246.7	2.5
5. Kimberly-Clark Corp.	242.1 [b, c]	2.4
6. Container Corp. of America	215.6	2.2
7. West Virginia Pulp and Paper Co.	181.0 [c]	1.8
8. Robert Gair Co.	160.2	1.6
9. Mead Corp.	150.5	1.5
10. Champion Paper and Fiber Co.	149.7	1.5
11. Rayonier, Inc. [d]	142.5	1.4
12. Marathon Corp.	141.7 [c]	1.4
13. Union Bag and Paper Corp.	123.0	1.2
14. National Container Corp.	95.3	1.0
15. Minnesota and Ontario Paper Co.	73.1	.7

Sources: Moody's *Industrials;* total sales from U.S. Department of Commerce, *Pulp, Paper and Board*, Industry Report, March 1956, p. 4.

a. Sales include those for Gaylord Container Corp., taken over by Crown Zellerbach on November 30.

b. Sales include those for International Cellucotton Co., taken over by Kimberly-Clark on September 30.

c. Year ending January 31, 1956.

d. Rayonier is principally a pulp producer, and most of its pulp is the "dissolving" type sold to make rayon and other non-paper products.

In particular sectors of the industry there is a fairly high concentration, since most companies specialize in a few product lines. For example, in 1947 the four largest producers of "pulp goods, pressed and molded" sold 85.5 per cent of the total of these goods, the four largest wallpaper producers 48.7 per cent of that product, and so on to lower figures.[6]

Products and Their Distribution

The uses of paper are expanding rapidly, and between 1945 and 1955 United States production increased by 70 per cent. In 1955

6. U.S. Census data, in *Study of Monopoly Power*, Hearings before Subcommittee on Study of Monopoly Power, House Judiciary Committee, 81st Cong., 2d sess., 1950, Serial 14, Part 2-B, pp. 1446–53.

TABLE 36

PAPER: PRINCIPAL TYPES MANUFACTURED, 1945 AND 1955

(*Thousand Tons*)

Type	1945	1955
Total United States production	17,371	30,140
Paperboard	7,907	13,865
Book, printing and similar papers	2,137	3,919
Coarse paper	2,403	3,682
Building paper and building board	1,778	3,197
Sanitary and tissue paper	981	1,568
Fine paper (chiefly writing paper)	1,001	1,463
Newsprint	725	1,459
Special industrial paper (tag stock, etc.)	327	604
Wet machine board (shoe board, etc.)	112	183
Newsprint, Canadian production	3,592	6,191

Sources: U.S. Department of Commerce, *Pulp, Paper and Board*, Industry Report, March 1955, p. 18; March 1956, p. 20; U.S. Census Bureau, *Facts for Industry*, Series M 14D, "Paper and Board Production, 1955 and 1954 (Preliminary Report)."

paperboard accounted for 46 per cent of tonnage produced. Newsprint came next if Canadian production (80 per cent of which goes to the United States) is included. These together with three other categories — book and printing paper, coarse (kraft) paper for such uses as wrapping and bags, and building paper and board — accounted for the great bulk of the North American output. (See Table 36.)

Newsprint is often classed with printing and writing stock as "cultural" paper, the other types as "mechanical" paper. Over 75 per cent of the newsprint consumed in the United States is bought on long-term contracts by large newspapers, and most of the rest goes to printing firms or jobbers either on contract or spot market transactions.[7] Small newspapers, and publishers of cheap books and magazines, usually buy from these.

Altogether, there are more than 5,000 individual paper products. Dealers generally handle the products of a number of competing suppliers. Each has his schedule of price differentials for sizes, colors, trimming, finishes, etc. — lists which are often uniform for any one type of paper.

Most book paper is finished by the manufacturer and sold to large users, such as printers and magazine and book publishers, or to paper

7. On paper distribution, see John A. Guthrie, *The Economics of Pulp and Paper*, State College of Washington Press, Pullman, 1950, pp. 90–92.

merchants. Paper merchants handle the bulk of writing paper; a good deal goes through converters who make particular types of envelopes, stationery and the like from the raw paper stock; and the rest is sold direct by manufacturers to large users. Kimberly-Clark Corporation, Scott Paper Company and other producers of sanitary and tissue paper sell heavily to wholesale grocers, chain stores and supermarkets. Wrapping paper goes direct to industrial users or is handled by paper wholesalers or by "super jobbers" who buy from the mills and supply the smaller wholesale merchants. Paper bags are usually sold by integrated mills and independent bag converters to jobbers or to industrial consumers. Most paperboard is sold by the integrated mill to the consumer, or goes to manufacturers of shipping containers and folding boxes. The rest is distributed by merchants to bookbinders and printers.

Antitrust Suits

Antitrust proceedings in paper, including those against distributors, have been mostly concerned with price fixing and other cooperative trade practices. Few of them have been other than routine actions.

Pooling Associations of 1900–1915

The first suits were against so-called "pooling associations." Fourteen (later twenty-three) wrapping paper and newsprint mills in the Lake states (Minnesota, Wisconsin and Michigan) organized the General Paper Company in 1900 as a common selling agent—attempting thus to match the International Paper Company, a big "trust" that emerged in the Northeast in 1898.[8] Each mill was represented on General's board of directors, which was given power to regulate output, fix prices and conditions of sale, and levy penalties on mills exceeding their quotas. After congressional hearings on the high price of paper, the Department of Justice, which had investigated International and decided against action, filed a suit against this rival group in December 1904. Eighteen months later the defendants accepted a consent decree dissolving General Paper; [9] but they organized almost

8. See Ethan Ellis, in *Study of Monopoly Power*, Hearings before Subcommittee on Study of Monopoly Power, House Judiciary Committee, 81st Cong., 2d sess., 1950, Serial 14, Part 6A (hereafter cited as Celler Hearings), p. 198.

9. *U.S. v. General Paper Co.*, Civil 813 (D. Minn. 1904), Department of Justice, *Decrees and Judgments in Federal Antitrust Cases*, 1918, pp. 75–79.

immediately into the Fibre and Manila Association. In 1908 the members pleaded guilty to a charge of price fixing,[10] and in 1909 the association was enjoined in a civil suit.[11]

The correspondence of John H. Parks, manager of the association, shows that it was not easy to keep the members from slashing prices, quite apart from any intervention by the law.[12] A veteran of this type of work, however, claims the "Parks pools" were moderately successful in limiting the amount of price cutting.

Some of these firms later merged with the Union Bag and Paper Company (which had not been a defendant). Possibly this move was stimulated in part by the law's refusal to let them unify their operations as International Paper could do for its mills.

In 1910 thirty-three paperboard companies were convicted and fined in the New York federal courts for fixing prices.[13] Of nineteen more indicted in the following year, twelve were cleared and seven pleaded *nolo contendere* in 1915.[14] On the other hand, juries acquitted Arizona stationery firms of price-fixing charges in 1908,[15] and wallpaper manufacturers and jobbers in 1915.[16]

The Newsprint Investigation of 1916

Many years of intermittent bickering (through bargaining, propaganda and lobbying) between the organized newsprint manufacturers and the newspapers finally resulted in an appeal of the latter to the antitrust laws in 1916.[17] They were prompted to act when:

> Wartime prosperity induced an advertising boom in 1916 which put an intolerable strain on the existing supplies of newsprint, and prices skyrocketed. This was particularly galling to the country papers which bought their small supplies on the "spot" or open market . . .[18]

10. *U.S. v. John H. Parks*, Indictment (S.D. N.Y. 1908), *Decrees and Judgments*, pp. 733–34.
11. *U.S. v. Allen Bros. Co.*, Eq. 4–49 (S.D. N.Y. 1909).
12. Myron W. Watkins, *Industrial Combinations and Public Policy*, Houghton Mifflin, Boston, 1927, p. 198.
13. *U.S. v. Albia Box and Paper Co.*, Indictment (S.D. N.Y. 1909), *Decrees and Judgments*, pp. 736–38.
14. *U.S. v. William C. Geer*, Indictment (S.D. N.Y. 1911), *ibid.*, p. 758.
15. *U.S. v. Corbett Stationery Co.*, Cr. c-1925 (D. Ariz. 1907), *ibid.*, pp. 718–19.
16. *U.S. v. J. B. Pearce*, Cr. 3480 (N.D. Ohio 1911), *ibid.*, pp. 777–78.
17. Ethan Ellis, *Print Paper Pendulum*, Rutgers University Press, New Brunswick, 1951, Chap. 6.
18. *Idem*, Celler Hearings, p. 199.

These newspapers induced the Senate to pass a resolution in April 1916 directing the Federal Trade Commission to study the rise in prices. The Commission's investigators found in the correspondence files of the manufacturers a number of evidences of collusive action.[19] Customers were voluntarily surrendered to new mills that were being built. Mills booked to capacity helped would-be customers to find other sources of supply. An effort had been made in 1915, before the sharp rise in demand, to prevent one or more firms from expanding their facilities. One agreement was intended to help small producers keep their profitable spot business, while the big producers stayed with their lower-priced contracts. Granting the illegality of some of these activities, they were not intended to hurt small competitors and they probably did little to boost prices. The history and character of the newsprint market made it clear that prices on the spot market were likely to jump whenever demand increased rapidly as in 1916.

In January 1917 the Commission turned its findings over to the Department of Justice. A grand jury was summoned, and in April 1917 it indicted for restraint of trade under the Sherman Act seven leading newsprint executives, forty-five corporations (the fifteen Canadian producers being exempt from attack), and the News Print Manufacturers Association. In November 1917 all pleaded *nolo contendere*, except one whose attorney insisted on a trial, at which the judge directed a verdict of acquittal after hearing the government's evidence. On the day the *nolo* pleas were entered, the leading manufacturers of both Canada and the United States signed an agreement with the Attorney General, acting as "trustee" for United States newspapers, by which they accepted the dissolution of their association and the imposition of price ceilings.[20]

Difficulties of Price Regulation

The history of these ceilings illustrated the difficulty of regulating specific prices during a general inflation.[21] Roll newsprint in carload

19. See FTC, *News-Print Paper Industry*, S. Doc. 49, 65th Cong., 1st sess., 1917, pp. 127–31.

20. *U.S. v. George H. Mead*, Eq. 14–384 and Cr. 9–371 (S.D. N.Y. 1917), *Decrees and Judgments*, pp. 637–44, 860; documents reprinted in Celler Hearings, Part 6-B, *Newsprint Exhibits* (hereafter cited as Celler Exhibits), pp. 82–93.

21. Figures from FTC, *News-Print Paper Industry*, p. 51, and E. O. Merchant, "The Government and the News-Print Paper Manufacturers," *Quarterly Journal of Economics*, February 1918, pp. 238–56, and "The Government and the Newsprint Paper Manufacturers," *ibid.*, February 1920, pp. 313–28.

lots averaged $47 or less per ton at destination in 1915. By the end of 1916 some open market prices were $100 or more, the quotations being now f.o.b. mill (i.e., buyers were paying the freight). In March 1917 the Federal Trade Commissioners, serving in their individual capacities as arbitrators, arranged for a $50 price; but the companies, upon their indictment, withdrew their cooperation and during 1917 charged moderately higher prices. In November they accepted the Attorney General's proposed $60 a ton, effective in January 1918. The following revisions were made in 1918, each retroactive by several months: $62 in June, set by the Federal Trade Commission; $70 in September, set by the Second Circuit Court of Appeals, to which an appeal had been taken by consent of all parties; and first $72.65 and then $75 in October, in a supplemental ruling by the Commission.

Although newsprint prices were thus put under control, other basic industrial commodities were controlled by wartime authority without an appeal to the antitrust laws. When newsprint ceilings expired three months after the Armistice, prices quickly reached new heights. The new capital thus attracted led to overproduction in the 1920s and to a long depression in the industry. The entire new investment went into Canada. Only two of the forty-five defendants of 1917 still make newsprint in this country. In fact, a former newsprint producer contends that one effect of the whole case was to cause certain manufacturers to make plans "immediately" to shift their machines to other sorts of paper. If this is so, the antitrust action would have boomeranged against the newspapers had it succeeded in controlling prices over a longer period, and thus discouraged entry of new capital.

John A. Guthrie, in a study of the economics of the paper industry, states that this episode caused the newsprint industry to switch from price fixing to an attempt "to moderate or restrict price competition by employing price leadership" — with International Paper as the price leader east of the Rockies, and Crown Zellerbach west. According to this authority, "by the use of price leadership, some price competition has been avoided. However, the effect on prices or profits has probably been slight."[22]

The Book Paper Investigation of 1916

In September 1916 another Senate resolution asked the Federal Trade Commission to investigate book paper, for which contract prices

22. Guthrie, *The Economics of Pulp and Paper*, p. 112.

had risen since early 1915 by 65 per cent for coated, 66 per cent for supercalendered, and 85 per cent for machine-finished grades. Most spot prices had risen even more.[23] The Commission reported its "Conclusions" the next summer as follows:

> The foregoing findings of fact support the conclusion that the advance in the prices of book paper in 1916 was excessive and not justified either by the increase in cost or by the changes in conditions of supply and demand. The advance was brought about in part by the activities of the members and secretary of the bureau of statistics.[24]

Even though members had encouraged each other to "make up somewhat" for past losses by raising prices,[25] the true cause of the sudden rise was certainly found in supply and demand. In the body of the Commission's own report we read:

> During 1916 the book-paper mills were run at high speed, some of them exceeding their rated capacity, but although production increased almost 20 per cent, this was not sufficient to take care of the demands of both domestic and foreign buyers, so that stocks declined about 50 per cent. The rising prices and declining stocks caused a panic among buyers, which resulted in considerable hoarding of paper.
>
> In refusing to accept the orders of new customers, jobbers generally stated that they could not get more than enough paper to supply their regular customers. The result was that jobbers could and did charge any price they wished, and as a consequence their profits increased enormously.
>
> Most of the book-paper manufacturers were making good profits in 1915, their assertions to the contrary notwithstanding. They were not contented with maintaining those profits, however, but sought to exact the maximum profits obtainable as a result of panic conditions among buyers.[26]

There is nothing surprising in a desire to "exact the maximum profits," or in the fact that a rise in demand pushes prices up in an industry which has as many as forty regular manufacturers,[27] plus those making book paper as a sideline, plus jobbers, instead of concentrated control and administered prices.

In November 1917 the Commission ordered the Bureau of Statistics of the Book Paper Manufacturers Association dissolved. Its twenty-

23. FTC, *Book-Paper Industry*, S. Doc. 79, 65th Cong., 1st sess., 1917, p. 11.

24. *Ibid.*, p. 17.

25. *Ibid.*, p. 101.

26. *Ibid.*, pp. 38, 62 and 82.

27. *Ibid.*, p. 14.

three members, representing about 75 per cent of the industry's tonnage, did not contest the order.[28] Prices ceased to rise — but, as with newsprint, wartime controls could have halted the advance without antitrust action.

Price Fixing as an Unfair Practice

The first reported antitrust court decision in paper originated in an order issued by the Federal Trade Commission in 1923 against the Pacific Coast jobbers. They were organized in local associations in Seattle-Tacoma, Spokane, Portland, San Francisco and Los Angeles; in larger Northwest and California associations; and finally in the Pacific States Paper Trade Association. They handled 75 per cent of the Coast wholesale business, exclusive of newsprint in large rolls sold to contract buyers. Their methods of operation to which the Commission took exception included (1) inducing manufacturers not to sell direct to retailers, large users or brokers; (2) adoption by each local association of a uniform price list, to be definitely applied to sales within its state (including those calling for direct shipment to the retailer by a mill in another state), and to be carried by salesmen interviewing retailers in other states but with no obligation to use them; and (3) discussion of intrastate prices and discounts at meetings.[29]

On appeal to the Circuit Court, the Commission's order was reversed in 1925 as to the price lists and direct mill shipments, on the ground that interstate commerce was not involved.[30] In 1927, the Supreme Court unanimously reinstated the full order.[31] Justice Butler pointed out that mill shipments across state lines constituted interstate commerce no matter where the sales transaction occurred, and that a uniform price list carried by salesmen and enforced as to intrastate transactions was not unlikely to be followed on interstate sales also. If so, an illegal conspiracy existed. Ten years later a $10,000 fine (about $300 apiece) was imposed on more than thirty companies for violating the decree.[32] This was the first time a violation of a Federal Trade Commission anti-monopoly order had been penalized.[33]

28. *Bureau of Statistics of the Book Paper Mfrs.*, Docket 17, 1 FTC 38 (1917).
29. *Pacific States Paper Trade Ass'n.*, Docket 934, 7 FTC 155 (1923).
30. *Pacific States Paper Trade Ass'n. v. FTC*, 4 F. 2d 457 (9th Cir. 1925).
31. *FTC v. Pacific States Paper Trade Ass'n.*, 273 U.S. 52 (1927).
32. *Ibid.*, 88 F. 2d 1009 (9th Cir. 1937).
33. Earl W. Kintner, "Post-Hearing Procedures and Compliance," in Section of Antitrust Law, American Bar Ass'n., Proceedings of Spring Meeting, Chicago, 1954, p. 201.

The 1927 case was the first test in the courts of the Commission's practice (dating from the book paper order of 1917) of treating price and output agreements as unfair competition under Section 5 of the Federal Trade Commission Act. The respondents did not protest this interpretation, although in one sense it was rather strained since, the higher the collusive price, the easier rather than harder it becomes for competitors. The doctrine was approved tacitly by the Supreme Court, and in many subsequent cases has been explicitly sustained.[34]

In this period the Department of Justice secured three consent decrees.[35] In 1921 the members of the Corrugated Paper Manufacturers Association foreswore price fixing. In the same year some producers of white glazed paper abandoned a common selling agency and "other means calculated to control the trade," and in 1930 makers of watermarked paper did likewise.

In 1928 Zellerbach Corporation, which controlled a newsprint mill among other holdings, acquired the stock of Crown Willamette Paper Corporation, which owned two such mills. Since the resulting Crown Zellerbach Corporation controlled 80 per cent of Pacific Coast newsprint production, the Federal Trade Commission in 1933 charged violation of Section 7 of the Clayton Act. Its complaint was dismissed [36] after the Supreme Court decision that an original violation could be purged by the formal dissolution of the purchased corporation prior to Commission action, even though the assets were simply absorbed by the acquiring company.[37] Nevertheless, the respondent considered this proceeding as "a warning to us to be careful about expansion in newsprint." [38]

Sequel to the NRA

In 1939 the government opened a drive against cooperative practices which had (1) long existed in the industry, (2) taken definite

34. See Myron W. Watkins, *Public Regulation of Competitive Practices*, National Industrial Conference Board, New York, 3d edition, 1940, pp. 229–33.

35. *U.S. v. Corrugated Paper Manufacturers Ass'n.*, Eq. 20–329 (S.D. N.Y. 1921); *U.S. v. American Coated Paper Co.*, Eq. 21–33 (S.D. N.Y. 1921); *U.S. v. Alden Paper Co.*, Eq. 1312 (N.D. N.Y. 1928, 1930).

36. *Crown Zellerbach Corp.*, Docket 2135, 20 FTC 489 (1935); documents reprinted in Celler Exhibits, pp. 1173–76.

37. *Arrow-Hart & Hegeman Electric Co. v. FTC*, 291 U.S. 587 (1934).

38. J. D. Zellerbach, president of Crown Zellerbach Corp., Celler Hearings, p. 984.

shape under the many National Recovery Administration paper and paper product codes which "materially" restricted competition,[39] and (3) continued after NRA expired in 1935.[40] Quoting prices on a uniform zone basis, open price filing, and standard lists of discounts and trade differentials were typical of these practices.

First came an indictment of the Pacific Coast newsprint producers in 1939, under both the Sherman Act and the Wilson Tariff Act, on charges of jointly fixing prices, jobbers' commissions, and terms and conditions of sale since 1935.[41] In May 1941 the Canadian defendants were discharged; the three American companies pleaded *nolo contendere*. A representative of one of these companies concedes only that it had agreed to a uniform differential charge on a type of newsprint whose sales constituted 2 per cent of the total.

In April 1939, as in 1917, the Federal Trade Commission charged the book paper industry with unfair competition by means of a conspiracy to eliminate competition.[42] The trade association in book paper, formed in 1933 under NRA with 45 members and 80 per cent of total output, had exchanged sales and price information, held meetings at which members agreed on trade policies and identical schedules of discounts and finishing differentials, and sponsored a geographic pricing system. Nearly all defendants listed identical prices in Zone 1, 20 cents more in Zone 2, 40 cents more in Zone 3, and 60 cents more in Zone 4, to all customers. A cease and desist order was issued in 1945, and in June 1948 the Seventh Circuit Court held that there was enough evidence to support the Commission's findings of fact. In announcing the verdict Judge Minton used language suggestive of the later "conscious parallelism" doctrine: [43]

> . . . a uniform participation by competitors in a particular system of doing business, where each is aware of the others' acts and where the effect is to restrain commerce, is sufficient to establish an unlawful conspiracy.[44]

39. Guthrie, *The Economics of Pulp and Paper*, p. 113.

40. *Idem*, "Price Regulation in the Paper Industry," *Quarterly Journal of Economics*, February 1946, pp. 203–10.

41. *U.S. v. Crown Zellerbach Corp.*, Cr. 26680–S (N.D. Calif. 1939); documents reprinted in Celler Exhibits, pp. 93–102, 1187.

42. *Allied Paper Mills*, Docket 3760, 40 FTC 696 (1945).

43. Sumner S. Kittelle and George P. Lamb, "The Implied Conspiracy Doctrine and Delivered Pricing," *Law and Contemporary Problems*, Spring 1950, p. 250.

44. *Allied Paper Mills v. FTC*, 168 F. 2d 600, 607 (7th Cir. 1948).

Significance of the Second Book Paper Case

An economic consultant of the defendants expresses doubt that there was effective price fixing, since prices were in fact cut, in spite of an inelastic demand. Guthrie, who reviewed the full evidence, concluded that, although some book paper mills did at times discuss prices and "probably agreed upon certain changes," this practice was "not general or widespread." He found that price changes were initiated by several different firms and were followed because of competitive pressure. Uniform differentials and trade customs and price zones had been adhered to for reasons of convenience rather than to suppress competition.[45]

Representatives of the defendants are still willing to argue the case. They point to the acknowledged fact that on 15 per cent of sales, representing about 25 per cent of tonnage, prices were "off-list"[46] — to which one might reply that price fixing may occur even if it is not altogether successful. They maintain that the individual lists of differentials which they filed along with their certificates of compliance to the Commission's order still showed the same uniformity as before — owing in both cases to competition. An officer of the one company that was cleared by the Court says the rest were no more guilty than this company: "I know of no collusion before and I know of none since."

It should not be surprising that the writer found opinion unanimous in the paper industry that these lists of differentials for particular grades, sizes, colors or finishes are a mere convenience, appreciated most of all by buyers who do not have to look up, reflect upon, and negotiate separately regarding separate charges for each seller. Nor did anyone admit that the Federal Trade Commission's actions or its victories had any real effect on these trade customs, except for the inconvenience of preparing separate lists, nearly all of which turn out to be approximately uniform. The greater assurance against price agreements which results when separate companies put out separate lists, as contrasted with meetings to adopt a uniform list, is the justification for these suits and for this inconvenience.

Quota Plans

In 1939 and 1940 the Department of Justice filed criminal and civil proceedings against members of the Kraft Paper Association, who pro-

45. Guthrie, "Price Regulation in the Paper Industry," p. 209.
46. 168 F. 2d, at 606–07.

duced 90 per cent of this product, and a civil suit against Stevenson, Jordan & Harrison, engineering and management consultants. This firm was at that time sponsoring over twenty cooperative industry programs, designed to prevent cutthroat competition by distributing the available business among competitors through quotas. Consent decrees in September 1940 enjoined the kraft paper quotas, the gathering of statistics "for the purpose of establishing such quotas," and "promoting, advocating, advising or recommending" any sort of agreement which interfered with independent action by firms in setting prices.[47]

A defense can be made for such plans: when demand is low but will recover soon, it is wasteful to allow price competition, for it will merely drive out of business weaker firms whose equipment and labor force will be needed when demand recovers. But the dangers are obvious, and in some cases the plan will keep in business a firm that ought to go out whether or not demand recovers. Moreover, such plans prevent the industry itself from contributing (admittedly at a cost to itself) to general recovery. On the whole, the abolition of quota plans by government action is preferable to waiting for their natural disappearance when demand recovers.

Members of the National Paperboard Association, also comprising 90 per cent of the industry, had contracted with F. G. Becker Corporation in 1934 to operate a similar quota plan. The corporation's fee was a certain sum per ton of paperboard produced and a larger sum per ton produced in excess of quotas or of the average running time of the industry. When the case was brought before a grand jury in 1939, the illegal features of the plan were dropped. Another Justice Department investigation in 1942, and a Federal Trade Commission investigation in 1945, uncovered no evidence of continuing illegality.[48] Much of the industry is reported to have disapproved of the quota plans.

In February 1942 a consent decree halted a boycott by which some Detroit waste paper wholesalers, with whom the local labor union had cooperated, were trying to force retailers to deal only with them.[49]

47. *U.S. v. Kraft Paper Ass'n.*, Cr. 105–336a (S.D. N.Y. 1939), Civil 10–329, Complaint and Consent Decree (S.D. N.Y. 1940); and *U.S. v. Stevenson, Jordan & Harrison*, Civil 10–213, Complaint and Consent Decree (S.D. N.Y. 1940). The quotations are from these two decrees, respectively.

48. *National Paperboard Ass'n.*, Docket 5359, 42 FTC 461 (1946).

49. *U.S. v. Wholesale Waste Paper Co.*, Cr. 25959, Civil 3234 (E.D. Mich. 1942).

The Tag Manufacturers' Victory

The Federal Trade Commission charged in 1941 that the price filing plan in the tag manufacturing industry had the purpose and effect of restricting competition and therefore constituted an unfair trade practice. Thirty-one companies, controlling 95 per cent of the business, exchanged their published price lists plus all off-list sales (without customers' names). The agent for this exchange also served as Executive Director of the Tag Manufacturers Institute, formed in 1933 under NRA.

The Commission's cease and desist order of 1947 [50] was vacated in 1949 by the First Circuit Court, which found no proof in the record that such price uniformity as existed was due to agreement.[51] Moreover, Judge Calvert Magruder's opinion emphasized that 25 per cent of the cases represented off-list prices and added that buyers were allowed access to the data. One jobber had in fact subscribed to the sheets; but most buyers did not purchase in large enough quantities to make this worth while.[52]

In the opinion of a law review commentator on the decision, exchange of such intimate information about prices "exceeds the legitimate needs of business." [53] Although a strong case can be made for the public benefits of price publicity, the details of the reporting in this instance seem to have been slanted toward the discouragement of price cutting (even if only 75 per cent of sales conformed to list prices) rather than toward general price publicity.[54]

The *Tag* case is considered a support of the price-filing power of trade associations; but it is not a very firm one. The dividing line is narrow between this case and the *Allied Mills* case of a year earlier, when another Circuit Court found more convincing evidence of collusion.

Continuance of the Antitrust Drive

Four additional proceedings were brought against the paper industry in 1941 and 1942.

50. *Tag Manufacturers Institute*, Docket 4496, 43 FTC 499 (1947).

51. *Tag Manufacturers Institute v. FTC*, 174 F. 2d 452 (1st Cir. 1949).

52. George W. Stocking, "The Rule of Reason, Workable Competition, and the Legality of Trade Association Activities," *University of Chicago Law Review*, Summer 1954, pp. 609–10.

53. James W. Wilson, in *Texas Law Review*, November 1949, p. 283.

54. Stocking, "The Rule of Reason, Workable Competition, and the Legality of Trade Association Activities," pp. 590–610.

In December 1941 the Federal Trade Commission issued an uncontested order against the manufacturer of cheap, flexible, "bogus" paper, its three distributors, and six firms that cut this material into paper linings ("stays") for purses. It appears that they had dealt exclusively with each other, and that the Stay Die Cutters Association had been formed in October 1933 to assist in allocating customers and in other doubtful practices.[55]

The Commission issued another complaint in 1941, and an order in April 1944, against eight firms that had formed the National Crepe Paper Association in July 1933 to implement an NRA fair practice code.[56] Two industry informants today say that the association's activities "were on the borderline" and that they "were known by the members to be legally risky, but considered worth the risk." These recollections are supported by the fact that two members withdrew in November 1939, one giving as a reason fear of antitrust involvement. In sustaining the Commission's order, in July 1946, the Seventh Circuit Court put special weight on the zone system which was set up in 1933 and which included the plants of all eight companies within a single zone, within which quotations were identical.[57] The Wisconsin firms thus implicitly bound themselves to accept phantom freight rather than sell to Chicago customers at less than their Massachusetts competitors. The Court felt that at least this type of zone system was proof of conspiracy.[58] An aftermath of the case was dissolution of the association and cessation of the promotional work on which it had spent 90 per cent of its budget. One defendant company reports that, discouraged, it "just discontinued making the item entirely"; but the other seven are still in business, and have 31 (presumably smaller) competitors as against only 25 in 1946.[59]

In January 1942, 138 companies and individuals in the waxed paper industry were indicted for fixing prices, agreeing on identical methods of manufacture and distribution and on kinds and quantities to be

55. *Newton Paper Co.*, Docket 4559, 34 FTC 418 (1941).

56. *National Crepe Paper Association of America*, Docket 4606, 38 FTC 282 (1944); George W. Stocking and Myron W. Watkins, *Monopoly and Free Enterprise*, Twentieth Century Fund, 1951, pp. 245–49.

57. *Fort Howard Paper Co. v. FTC*, 156 F. 2d 899 (7th Cir. 1946).

58. Bueford G. Herbert, "Delivered Pricing as Conspiracy and as Discrimination: The Legal Status," *Law and Contemporary Problems*, Spring 1950, p. 202.

59. *Thomas' Register of American Manufacturers*, 1946, Vol. 2, p. 10471; 1956, Vol. 2, p. 4767.

sold, circulating "codes of fair competition," and zoning.[60] All but 32 pleaded *nolo contendere* later that year and paid fines averaging $1,150 apiece. An industry representative today admits that the law was violated. The Federal Trade Commission also filed a complaint against this group of manufacturers in 1944, but decided two years later that the Department of Justice had settled the matter.[61]

In 1942 the Commission charged the Liquid Tight Paper Container Association with violating Section 5 of the Federal Trade Commission Act. The respondents did not contest the charge, and in 1945 an order was issued against their zone pricing system, the classification of each customer as jobber or consumer, and the fixing of uniform prices and terms of sale.[62] No important change occurred in policies or practices through this order. These containers are standardized; no manufacturer has been able to establish a brand preference in the minds of buyers, and uniformity of prices is still found.

Since the Office of Price Administration continued the price zones and differentials used by the paper industry, a sort of government sanction was lent during World War II to practices which the Department of Justice and Federal Trade Commission had been, supposedly with success, attacking.[63]

Suits in 1946 and 1948: Principally against Jobbers

Postwar proceedings through 1955 have followed much the same lines as earlier cases.

In 1946 Crown Zellerbach's jobbing subsidiary was charged under Section 2(f) of the Clayton Act with knowingly receiving lower prices from paper producers than competing jobbers received, and with receiving information about their prices.[64] The case was dismissed in February 1955 on the precedent of the Supreme Court's *Automatic Canteen* ruling[65] that, to make a case against a buyer, it must be proved that he knew that the seller could not justify the low price to him on a cost basis.[66]

60. *U.S. v. American Waxed Paper Ass'n.*, Cr. 9319 (E.D. Pa. 1942).

61. *American Waxed Paper Ass'n.*, Docket 5149, 42 FTC 450 (1946); Celler Exhibits, pp. 1177–83.

62. *Liquid Tight Paper Container Ass'n.*, Docket 4675, 40 FTC 630 (1945).

63. Guthrie, "Price Regulation in the Paper Industry," pp. 210–11.

64. *Crown Zellerbach Corp. v. FTC*, 156 F. 2d 927 (9th Cir. 1946); documents reprinted in Celler Exhibits, pp. 1183–86.

65. *Automatic Canteen Company of America v. FTC*, 346 U.S. 61 (1953).

66. *New York Times*, February 22, 1955, p. 26.

In 1948 eight wallpaper manufacturers were indicted for price fixing, and in 1949 a group of wholesalers were indicted for price fixing and "retarding more desirable lines of wall paper." [67] The wholesalers pleaded *nolo contendere* in June 1949, and the manufacturers in September 1950. The latter maintain that the sole reason for their plea was that trial costs would have been greater per defendant than the $5,000 fine.

In 1948 also, the Federal Trade Commission began an investigation of the use by fine paper and coarse paper jobbers, respectively, of a Blue Book and a Brown Book to list grade differentials and suggested resale prices. Most of the twenty-two jobbers' associations thereupon dropped these books, but a member of the fine paper industry reports that other (unspecified) methods of cooperative action to achieve the same goals were informally adopted.[68] In the Commission's order of October 1954, which "was not fully contested" by the respondents, all such cooperative activity was outlawed.[69] In a concurring opinion Commissioner Lowell B. Mason referred to the fact that the Blue Book was devised to cooperate with the NRA and a Yellow Book (predecessor of the Brown Book) to cooperate with the OPA: ". . . part of the time the wholesalers engaged in concerted or uniform action, they would have gone to jail if they hadn't, and part of the time they would go to jail if they did." [70]

Suits since 1950: Jobbers, Retailers and Manufacturers

In May 1950 four Northern California jobbers were indicted for fixing prices on "chipboard, cardboard and bristols." [71] A year later they were found not guilty by the jury. One ground for this verdict may have been the feeling that simultaneous withdrawal of discounts to large customers, which was cited by the government as evidence of price fixing, could reasonably have been due to supply shortage caused by a strike. Another 1950 suit developed from the action of an officer of

67. *U.S. v. Wall Paper Institute*, Cr. 14705, Civil 8621 (E.D. Pa. 1948); *U.S. v. National Wall Paper Wholesalers Ass'n.*, Cr. 14–954 (E.D. Pa. 1949).

68. Memorandum prepared for the writer in 1953 by a person connected with the fine paper industry (hereafter cited as Fine Paper Memorandum).

69. *National Paper Trade Association of the United States*, FTC Docket 5592 (1954).

70. *New York Times*, October 15, 1954, p. 33.

71. *U.S. v. Blake, Moffitt & Towne*, Civil 29749, Cr. 32606 (N.D. Calif. 1950); documents reprinted in Celler Exhibits, pp. 1188–92.

Dixie Paper Cup Company in leaving to set up a competing business. When sued for patent infringement, he charged Dixie with monopoly. Both suits were dropped.

In 1952 the Department of Justice found that about eighty stationery stores in southern California, Arizona and Nevada were using identical price lists supplied by their trade association. This plan was intended to halt price cutting started by certain big chain stores that had a buying advantage. In January 1954 a consent decree was secured.[72] A salesman who visits the defendants reports that they are now relying on their own self-control not to let the lower prices of the chains induce general price cutting.

In June 1953 the Federal Trade Commission charged another trade association and six members with such familiar offenses as setting uniform differentials for grades, colors and sizes, and using a zoning system.[73] A cease and desist order was accepted six months later.

In February 1954 the Commission charged that Crown Zellerbach's acquisition of St. Helens Pulp and Paper Company in June 1953 had deprived many West Coast paper jobbers and converters of their alternative source of supply, especially for coarse paper.[74] This was the Commission's second proceeding under the 1950 Celler-Kefauver amendment to Section 7 of the Clayton Act, the first having been against Pillsbury Mills.

In May 1955 two firms in the paper towel business were charged with division of customers. One means was said to be by attaching a special device to towel cabinets so the jobbers of either defendant would not be able to sell to customers of the other.[75] In July the Federal Trade Commission began action against another merger, that of Union Bag and Paper Company with Hankins Container Corporation, a competitor in the field of corrugated boxes and sheets.[76] In December the Commission charged twenty-one manufacturers of multi-wall bags with price fixing.[77]

72. *U.S. v. Stationers Association of So. Calif.*, Civil 14777C (S.D. Calif. 1952); Department of Justice press release, January 15, 1954.

73. *Blotting Paper Manufacturing Ass'n.*, FTC Docket 6107 (1953).

74. Docket 6180, FTC News Summary, May 23, 1955.

75. *U.S. v. Crown Zellerbach Corp.*, Civil 55 C 115; Department of Justice press release, May 18, 1955.

76. *Union Bag and Paper Co.*, FTC Docket 6391 (1955).

77. *St. Regis Paper Co.*, FTC Docket 6476 (1955).

Canadian Developments, 1902–49

With great softwood forests, Canada was destined to become the center of North American newsprint manufacture. The impetus was given to its rapid rise when three Canadian provinces placed embargoes on the export of pulpwood in 1902, 1910 and 1911 and when the United States tariff on newsprint was removed in 1911. By 1926 Canadian output outstripped that in the United States, and today it is four times as large, despite development of the industry in the southern states in recent decades.

Since Canada is a seller of newsprint, attempts to stabilize prices have been favored, not opposed, by Canadian government authorities.[78] Prices were under pressure from the mid-1920s, partly as a result of industry expansion encouraged by the government to develop forest resources and give employment. A pool selling scheme was attempted by three companies in 1927, but failed the next year. In 1928 the provincial governments of Quebec and Ontario encouraged the Newsprint Institute of Canada in an attempt to restrict production. The members cut their output to 80 and then to 70 per cent of capacity; and the provincial authorities used threats of retaliation to compel the International Paper Company to raise its price on a contract with the Hearst newspapers. International refused to restrict its output, and the Institute was dissolved in 1930. In 1933 International itself was active in another pooling scheme to prevent cutthroat price cutting, but this failed in 1934. In 1935 the provincial governments were directing mills to share orders according to capacity, and in 1936 Quebec passed a Forest Resources Act, which allowed the government to increase stumpage dues (royalties) on companies that acted "against the public interest" (i.e., cut prices). In 1938, the price having fallen below $40 a ton while the cost was above $50, Stevenson, Jordan & Harrison managed a quota plan with the blessing of the provincial governments. After the period of wartime control, individual responsibility came back, but in 1949 the Quebec and Ontario governments were again warning against price cutting.

78. FTC, *Newsprint Paper Industry*, S. Doc. 214, 71st Cong., special sess., 1930, pp. 85–90, 100–03; *Newsprint*, Report of Subcommittee on Study of Monopoly Power, House Judiciary Committee, H. Rept. 505, Part 1, Union Calendar 145, 82d Cong., 1st sess., 1951, pp. 83–85, 91–93; John A. Guthrie, *The Newsprint Paper Industry*, Harvard Economic Studies No. 68, Harvard University Press, Cambridge, 1941, pp. 94–100, 108–14; John H. Hinman, president of International Paper Co., Celler Hearings, p. 647.

The United States Department of Justice, as part of a grand jury investigation of newsprint, issued subpoenas in March 1947 to officers of a great many Canadian pulp and paper companies that exported to the United States. They were directed, on penalty of contempt of court, to bring their business records to New York City. The Province of Ontario thereupon passed the Business Records Protection Act, making it a crime to take corporate records out of the province on such a demand.[79] Companies in other provinces than Ontario took the hint.

Recent Canadian Developments

The Canadian fine paper industry, which provides primarily for home consumption, has fared differently at the hands of its government — to the surprise and distress of newsprint companies that were in the fine paper business as well. In November 1952, the Combines Commissioner issued a report accusing virtually the entire $50 million industry of fixing prices, and restricting competition by "loyalty discounts" which tied customers to specific mills. The Minister of Justice announced in April 1953 that the combine, which had lasted for seventeen years, would be prosecuted.[80] It, and the coarse paper industry as well, were later found guilty.

The Canadian government tried a new approach to newsprint in May 1952, when it let the mills raise export prices, but not Canadian prices, by $10 a ton. Nine months later home prices were allowed to rise. When, in October 1955, the Canadian producers announced the next price increase, legislation was introduced by the Quebec Premier providing that Quebec newspapers must receive preferential prices from newsprint producers in the province.[81] Another novelty on this occasion was a Department of Justice request that American producers come to Washington for individual conferences so as to "prevent any joint efforts" to increase the price.[82] After eight Canadian firms had raised prices, the first United States firm to follow was one that had recently counted thirty-five newspapers among its owners.[83] By year-end the price settled at $130 a ton (New York City basis) as against the

79. Documents in Celler Hearings, pp. 205–06; Celler Exhibits, pp. 80–82, 102–09, 135–36.

80. *New York Times*, April 8, 1953, p. 43.

81. *Business Week*, January 14, 1956, p. 134.

82. Department of Justice press release, October 21, 1955; *New York Times*, October 25, 1955, p. 45.

83. See *Newsprint*, House Report, p. 39.

previous $126. Collusion was hardly needed in a supply-demand situation such that spot market prices were running over $180 a ton.[84]

Other Antitrust Influences in Newsprint

Twenty-two congressional investigations of newsprint took place between 1904 and 1951. The importance of good relations with newspapers is no doubt one explanation of this interest of congressmen in searching (as the 1904 congressional committee expressed it) for "information relative to causes of high prices of paper used for newspapers."[85] One book publisher recently complained that he could not seem to get the same sympathy in Washington for his own higher cost of paper.

It has been argued that these investigations have deterred capital from entering the industry and thus bringing down prices.[86] If there is any truth in this at all, other causes must have been more significant. One deterrent may have been that profits were not high enough[87] or, specifically, that each period of high newsprint prices and profits before World War II was followed by a collapse. Newsprint capacity began a steady expansion in 1946, though it has not kept pace with demand under the stimulus of a boom in newspaper advertising. Between 1946 and 1955 Canadian output increased by 37 per cent, the smaller United States output by 90 per cent. Some companies have preferred to expand in other types of paper, which they contend are more profitable and less sensitive to attack.

The claim has also been made that the newsprint industry moved to Canada to escape the antitrust laws. As compared to the attraction of virgin forests and removal of the tariff barrier, the antitrust laws could hardly have played an important role. Their influence might possibly have been more important if the laws had been applied more severely, as some have desired.

One minor example of antitrust influence was disclosed in 1951. Under stress of the Korean emergency, the National Production Authority's Printing and Publishing Division secured a Justice Department ruling that agreements among newspapers to abolish the un-

84. *Business Week*, February 11, 1956, p. 126.

85. *Supplies for a Free Press: A Preliminary Report on Newsprint*, Subcommittee on Newsprint, Senate Small Business Committee, Committee Print, 82d Cong., 1st sess., 1951, p. 1.

86. *Business Week*, July 7, 1951, p. 146; Robert L. Smith, Celler Hearings, pp. 586–87; J. D. Zellerbach, *ibid.*, p. 982.

87. *Newsprint*, House Report, p. 51.

limited privilege of newsdealers to return unsold copies would not be prosecuted. It was alleged that lack of such an agreement had caused a waste of 3 per cent of the country's supply of newsprint in the form of copies which were returned unsold.[88] On a similar matter, some newspapers complain that the antitrust laws block any agreement (which would hardly be practical in any case) to limit advertising space proportionately (e.g., by reducing each full page to a quarter, each quarter page to a sixteenth).

Opinions on the Antitrust Laws

Opinion in the paper industry seems on the whole sincerely to favor the Sherman Act. A trade association officer says:

> Prices are never mentioned at our meetings; if it were not for the antitrust laws, they would certainly be discussed frequently.

An executive in the fine paper business says:

> Except for the antitrust laws, we might long ago have attempted to drive our one competitor out of business and monopolize the ______ branch of the industry; this might be fun for a while, but it would not be healthy, even for us.

An economist formerly engaged in the industry argues that the function of the Sherman Act is to prevent price-fixing agreements and the dislocation which would occur with the inevitable collapse of any such agreements.[89] Expressing agreement with this in principle, one executive admits that his company may have been legally in the wrong when it was an antitrust defendant, but he does not concede that the actions ever damaged the public interest.

A slightly different opinion runs as follows:

> In an industry so widely scattered as paper, price fixing agreements cannot succeed. What need is there to apply the Sherman Act, therefore? Far too often the Act is used to attack useful forms of cooperation.

Approving this statement, another paper executive terms a "nuisance" the repeated charges of price fixing, which can have no concrete result because uniform prices or differentials are business necessities; but he strongly endorses the anti-monopoly section of the Sherman Act.

88. *Newsweek,* October 15, 1951, pp. 58–59.

89. Louis Tillotson Stevenson, *The Background and Economics of American Paper Making,* Harper, New York, 1940, p. 225.

Competitive Status

Trend of Concentration

Several brief comparisons of earlier and recent concentration in the paper industry can be made.

In 1913 and 1928, respectively, the five largest newsprint producers had 49.1 and 48.3 per cent of North American production, and in 1951 the five largest had 46.0 per cent of estimated capacity. Four of these leading producers were in the United States in 1913 but only one in 1951, and this one had some operations in Canada. The 49.1 per cent of the five particular companies that were largest in 1913 had dropped to 44.2 in 1928, and to 35.2 (in terms of capacity) in 1951. Most of this decline could be attributed to International Paper's share alone. During this period International shifted its United States mills to other products. (See Table 37.)

TABLE 37

PAPER: PRODUCTION AND CAPACITY OF LARGEST NORTH AMERICAN NEWSPRINT COMPANIES, 1913, 1928 AND 1951

(*Per Cent of North American Totals*)

Firm (Successor Firm Indented)	Production 1913	Production 1928	Capacity 1951
Five largest producers as of 1913	49.1	44.2	35.2
Five largest in each year	49.1	48.3	46.0
International Paper Co.	24.3 [a]	13.1 [b]	12.1 [c]
Great Northern Paper Co.	9.1 [a]	8.2 [a]	5.6 [a]
Spanish River Pulp and Paper Mills	6.6 [c]		
Abitibi Power and Paper Co.		10.8 [c]	10.8 [c]
Crown Willamette Paper Co.	5.2 [a]		
Crown Zellerbach Paper Co.		7.2 [b]	4.3 [b]
Minnesota and Ontario Power Co.	3.9 [a]		
Minnesota and Ontario Paper Co.		4.9 [b]	2.4 [c]
Laurentide Co., Ltd.	3.8 [c]		
Canada Power and Paper Corp.		8.3 [c]	
Consolidated Paper Corp., Ltd.			10.8 [c]
Price Bros., Ltd.	1.6 [c]	6.3 [c]	6.7 [c]

Sources: Calculated from FTC, *News-Print Paper Industry*, S. Doc. 49, 65th Cong., 1st sess., 1917, p. 32; FTC, *Newsprint Paper Industry*, S. Doc. 214, 71st Cong., special sess., 1930, pp. 18–22; *Newsprint*, Report of Subcommittee on Study of Monopoly Power, House Judiciary Committee, H. Rept. 505, Part 1, Union Calendar 145, 82d Cong., 1st sess., 1951, pp. 41, 43.

a. Mills in the United States.

b. Mills in Canada and in the United States. Pacific Mills, Ltd., controlled by Crown Zellerbach, did not report for 1928; its production is here estimated as 60,000–63,000 tons.

c. Mills in Canada.

TABLE 38

PAPER: TREND OF CONCENTRATION IN SALES, 1945, 1950 AND 1955[a]

(Per Cent of Dollar Sales)

Firms	1945	1950	1955
Largest firm	6.3	7.1	8.0
Largest four	12.6	14.1	17.1
Largest ten	20.1	22.6	28.1
Largest ten as of 1945	20.1	22.1	25.3

Sources: Calculated from total sales given in U.S. Department of Commerce, *Pulp, Paper and Board*, Industry Report, March 1956, p. 4, and company sales for 1945 from FTC, *Report on Interlocking Directorates*, 1951, p. 486, and for 1950 and 1955 from Moody's *Industrials.* Since sales of Great Northern Paper Co. and Oxford Paper Co., which ranked 8th and 15th by assets in 1945, were not published at that time, the present comparison stops at ten companies, and excludes Great Northern.

a. Figures are for calendar years or for fiscal years ending in the years named (with the exception of Kimberly-Clark, for 1950, for which the only year available is 1950–51).

In wrapping paper, International Paper and Crown Zellerbach together accounted for 21.5 per cent of total capacity in 1931.[90] In 1955 their combined production was 790,000 tons out of 3,682,000, or 21.7 per cent.[91]

The concentration ratio, or share of the four largest companies measured by value of product, increased in pulp mills, paper bags, paperboard boxes and wallpaper between 1935 and 1947, and decreased in envelopes. The mean ratio for these five subindustries was 29.3 per cent in 1935 and 33.8 per cent in 1947.[92]

Figures on total sales of paper and allied products show what seems to be a steady increase in the share of the ten largest companies, from the 20.1 per cent of 1945 to the 28.1 per cent of 1955. (See Table 38.) Only two of the ten largest firms in 1945 were no longer on the list in 1955: one had dropped to thirteenth place and the other had been acquired by the second largest producer. These figures seem to prove increasing net concentration in the industry, despite the decline in the newsprint branch.

90. Cecil Eaton Fraser and Georges F. Doriot, *Analyzing Our Industries*, McGraw-Hill, New York, 1932, p. 331.

91. International Paper Co., Annual Report, 1955, p. 6; Crown Zellerbach Corp., Annual Report, 1955, p. 5; *Pulp, Paper and Board*, March 1956, p. 18.

92. FTC, *Report on Changes in Concentration in Manufacturing, 1935 to 1947 and 1950*, 1954, p. 141.

How Concentrated Is the Industry?

Whatever the recent trend, the paper industry as a whole still cannot be called exceptionally concentrated. Out of 452 branches of manufacture tabulated for 1947,[93] "paper and board mills" ranked 396 from the top in terms of the concentration ratio. Pulp mills ranked 292, and the converting of paper products 397. Although these broad categories showed a low concentration, the average for nine specialties was 231, compared to 226.5 for all industries tabulated.

The latest edition of Lockwood's trade directory lists 874 products, from abrasive paper and absorbent paper down to writing paper and yarn.[94] There was an average of 15 companies making each product; but this average is influenced by such large competing groups as the 675 firms making paper boxes and the 181 making bags. In 292 products there were 3 manufacturers or fewer, and about a third of these products (activated carbon pads, aprons, art paper and others) were made by only one.

For most products, therefore, the consumer is dependent in the first instance on a mere handful of suppliers, even though for the important ones (such as bags and boxes) he has a much wider choice. He is much better protected, however, than the bare figures would indicate, since machinery can often be shifted from making one type of paper to making another, if relative prices so suggest. This is the process known as "grade shifting." A study by the NRA Code Authority for 1934 showed that 53 per cent of paper machines could be adjusted to make some other kind of paper, with a range for the various types from 19 per cent for machines designed to make tissue paper to 74 per cent for those making writing paper.[95]

The Early Combinations

An interesting chapter in the history of the paper industry is the formation of combines in the late nineteenth and early twentieth centuries, and their failure to hold a position of dominance.[96]

93. U.S. Census data, in *Study of Monopoly Power*, House Hearings, Part 2-B, pp. 1446–53.

94. *Lockwood's Directory of Paper and Allied Trades*, Lockwood Trade Journal Co., New York, 1956, pp. 561–788.

95. Peter J. Clarke, *Monopoly and Competition in the American Paper Industry*, unpublished doctoral thesis, Graduate School of Business Administration, New York University, New York, 1941, p. 93a.

96. Watkins, *Industrial Combinations and Public Policy*, pp. 180–93; Clarke thesis, pp. 134–55.

The beginnings of combination came in 1869, when the Union Bag Machine Company of Pennsylvania acquired various patents which enabled it to make the first successful paper bags. In 1875 it took the name Union Bag and Paper Company. Its original 90 per cent share of the market dropped sharply when the company, by restricting output in order to raise prices, began to attract competitors. Its timber supply became exhausted, it had to import pulp, and it was not really successful until after 1936, when it opened an efficient integrated mill in Georgia.

The American Strawboard Company, organized in 1889, soon acquired or leased mills with 85 or 90 per cent of the total output of paperboard, which was then made of straw. New companies sprang up for the purpose of selling out to the combine. In 1897, 1901 and 1903 the combine and the remaining independents formed a common selling agency, but each time the emergence of new competition put an end to the agency. Meanwhile, wood pulp largely replaced straw, and the American Strawboard Company's share of the shrinking straw division fell to one third by 1919. In August 1920 control of the corporation, which still had eight plants, was purchased by another firm; but just two years later it went into receivership and out of production.[97]

After the wallpaper manufacturers had tried a profit-pooling experiment which collapsed in 1888, firms controlling 60 per cent of the industry combined in 1892 into the National Wall Paper Company. After this in turn failed, 98 per cent of the industry established the Continental Wall Paper Company as a common selling agent in 1898. The new combine was liquidated in 1900, as the market proved that individual design and taste were too important in wallpaper for satisfactory unified operation. Long afterward, the Supreme Court declared that Continental had been a trust in violation of the Sherman Act.[98] It was a 5–4 decision, with Justice Harlan's majority opinion declaring that Continental was entitled to no assistance in collecting payment for goods sold to a jobber at trust-dictated prices and under a resale price maintenance agreement, while the dissent of Justice Holmes argued that even a trust should be allowed to collect its debts.

The United Paper Company, organized in 1892, was called the "Tissue Paper Trust." It raised prices, whereupon other mills turned to making tissue, and the merger was dissolved in 1899.

97. Poor's *Industrials*, 1923, Vol. 2, p. 1902; 1924, Vol. 2, p. 911.

98. *Continental Wall Paper Co. v. Louis Voight & Sons Co.*, 212 U.S. 227 (1909).

Paper "Trusts" in the 1898–1902 Merger Movement

In 1898 "fear of bankruptcy and ruin, as competition among the manufacturers had gone beyond all reasonable bounds,"[99] led sixteen paper mills and a number of pulp mills to unite as the International Paper Company. International had capacity to produce two thirds of the newsprint made in North America and an unstated percentage of the coarse paper, which made up 10 per cent of the combination's output.[100] By 1911 the newsprint proportion was down to about 30 per cent. Commentators attribute this decline to the many deteriorating mills, in dwindling forests, which International had taken over;[101] but the umbrella of high costs and prices that invited new mills to compete, and "mossback management" made complacent by the feeling of having a near-monopoly, played a part also.[102] The International Paper Company joined the newsprint migration to Canada in 1920, and by 1940 had closed down or converted to other products or to production of electric power all eighteen of its newsprint locations in the United States.[103] Today the corporation is the recognized leader in several branches of production and in the pulp and paper industry as a whole.

In 1899 the American Writing Paper Company consolidated twenty-six separate producers; but its policy of reducing output opened the way to new firms, some of them founded by its own defecting officers.[104] Between 1899 and 1952, during which time it underwent two reorganizations, the company's share of the market dropped from about 75 per cent to less than 5 per cent. It is now successful, but is no longer the biggest producer in its branch of the industry.

The last of these early combinations was the United Boxboard and Paper Company, created in 1902 to consolidate both the paper and straw divisions of the paperboard industry. For a time the combine held the majority of the stock of American Strawboard Company. In 1908, however, it failed and was forced to reorganize. Under the name United Boxboard Company, it failed again in 1912, and in 1917 was reorganized as the United Paper Board Company. It is now the

99. A trade journal of that day, quoted by Ethan Ellis, Celler Hearings, p. 198.

100. John H. Hinman, *ibid.*, p. 600.

101. "International Paper & Power," *Fortune*, December 1937, p. 134.

102. "Paper Heavyweight," *Forbes Magazine*, January 11, 1951, p. 14.

103. *Newsprint*, House Report, p. 32.

104. Stevenson, *The Background and Economics of American Paper Making*, p. 168.

United Board and Carton Company, and its sales are well under one per cent of the total for that industry.

Recent Mergers

In recent decades promotors have no longer had hope — either practically or legally — of obtaining a monopoly in any branch of the paper industry. Modern consolidations are usually designed to round out a corporation's position horizontally by acquiring a broader product range or wider markets, vertically by getting an assured supply of timber or pulp or an assured market, or geographically.[105] An example of the product range is provided by one big company whose book paper salesmen found themselves handicapped in selling to merchants by having no writing paper to offer; it met this difficulty by acquiring a firm that produced the full line (four grades of sulphite bond) of this product.

The big acquisitions by Crown Zellerbach and Scott Paper illustrate three current types of merger.[106] In June 1953 the former acquired St. Helens Pulp and Paper Company, a competitor on the West Coast (whose effectiveness, however, was declining owing to lack of modern equipment and methods) with a capital about 6 per cent of its own, and Canadian Western Lumber Company, Ltd., a firm three times as large as St. Helens. Not discouraged by a Federal Trade Commission complaint issued in 1954 against the St. Helens merger, Crown Zellerbach took over in 1955 Gaylord Container Corporation, one of the fifteen largest producers, which made many of Crown Zellerbach's own products but sold east of the Rockies. Thus it came into competition with the International Paper Company in the latter's markets.

Scott Paper Company increased its net assets 62 per cent in November 1951 by acquiring Soundview Pulp Company and 47 per cent in September and October 1954 by acquiring a small firm, Detroit Sulphite Pulp and Paper Company and a large one, Hollingsworth & Whitney Company.[107] Soundview was the largest remaining market mill selling bleached sulphite pulp. As a result of Scott's increased use of Soundview's output the latter's pulp sales dropped from $26.0 million in 1951 to $17.7, $15.7, $11.5 and $10.6 million in succeeding

105. See *Journal of Commerce*, May 10, 1955, p. 9.

106. See merger list in *Corporate and Bank Mergers*, Interim Report of Antitrust Subcommittee, House Judiciary Committee, 84th Cong., 1st sess., 1955, pp. 70–75.

107. Some of the figures in this paragraph were supplied by Scott Paper Co.

years. Detroit Sulphite was not a competitor, but had been selling over half its unconverted paper to Scott. Hollingsworth & Whitney's eighty or ninety types of specialty paper hardly duplicated those made by Scott in a single item.[108]

A special type of vertical integration occurs when newspapers buy an interest in newsprint mills.[109] All but the four biggest of the ten producers in the United States are believed to be partly owned by newspapers, some of the largest of which also have Canadian interests. This gives the newspaper valuable protection against scarcity of newsprint when demand is high, and the producer valuable assurance of a market when general demand is low.[110] The loan of money to several newspapers by International Paper Company in 1928, in return for contracts to buy paper, was a similar step; but this policy was soon changed, and the loans repaid.[111]

Advantages of Integration

Two technical advantages of integration in paper are most often mentioned: (1) When a pulp mill and a paper mill are adjacent, there is no need to dry the pulp, ship it (in sheets), and wet it again. On the other hand, some types of paper are made from dry pulp, and many integrated companies do not have their pulp and paper facilities adjacent. (2) The integrated company can regulate the quality of pulp precisely to its needs for the types of paper it is planning to make. Even integrated companies, however, must usually buy from outside their own organization some of the special types of pulp they need.

These two advantages and others arising from technology can only partially explain the trend toward pulp-paper integration which, between 1940 and 1953, reduced from 24 to 16 the percentage of United States pulp output (including dissolving pulp for nonpaper uses) that was offered on the market.[112] In addition, there is the desire of pulp mills to be assured of a market if demand should fall off and of paper mills to be assured of raw material if supply should become tight. It is this kind of consideration which accounts for the further integration

108. *Lockwood's Directory*, 1952, pp. 114, 156, 261. Waxed paper is the only apparent exception. Scott Paper Company states that there were no competing products at all.

109. *Newsprint*, House Report, pp. 47–48.

110. Guthrie, *The Newsprint Paper Industry*, p. 105.

111. Archibald R. Graustein, former president of International Paper Co., Celler Hearings, p. 553.

112. U.S. Pulp Producers Ass'n., *Wood Pulp Statistics*, New York, 1954, pp. 43–45.

from paper mill into converting. The "stepped-up merger drive" noted late in 1955 was intended, according to the paper companies, to "cushion the shock of a more competitive market" caused by declining demand, both through diversification and through ability to carry the product at least through the converting stage.[113] Although this would not assure sale to ultimate consumers, the paper companies seem to prefer the one uncertainty of the consumer's preference to the double uncertainty of the converter's plus the consumer's. Early in 1956 the drive toward complete integration, especially in kraft paper and paperboard, was said to be "more intense than ever." [114] Several large companies were seeking what the industry considered the three essentials for an assured future and for expansion: diversification, integration and adequate size to support an extensive research program.[115]

Diversification

A tabulation of the product groups that were made in 1954 by the ten producers whose sales were largest in 1955 shows a range from three groups, manufactured by Container Corporation, Robert Gair and Scott, to ten, made by International. The number of producers of each group ranged from ten for "paper specialties" through eight for paperboard and seven for magazine or book paper down to three for newsprint and one for lumber. (See Table 39.)

The product spread of these companies is undoubtedly greater today, owing to continuing mergers and entry into new lines generally.

Three Types of Small Company

The nonintegrated paper mill, the converter and the general paper merchant are the important types of small paper company. Nonintegrated paper mills in 1951 accounted for the following percentages of total United States output of various types of paper: wet machine board, 96; absorbent, 59; paperboard, 47; tissue, 45; fine, 40; building, 29 (or a little less); book, 25; sanitary, 23; special industrial, 19; coarse, 11; and for a very small but unknown amount of newsprint and other printing papers. The over-all average for the several types was 29 per cent.[116]

113. *Journal of Commerce*, November 21, 1955, p. 1.
114. *Ibid.*, March 21, 1956, p. 1.
115. *Ibid.*, March 29, 1956, p. 3.
116. *Pulp, Paper and Board*, March 1953, p. 54.

TABLE 39

PAPER: PRODUCT GROUPS OF TEN PRINCIPAL COMPANIES, 1954

Product Group	Number of Companies	International	Crown Zellerbach [a]	St. Regis	Scott	Kimberly-Clark	Container Corp.	West Va.	Robert Gair	Mead	Champion
Number of product groups		10	6	7	3	5	3	8	3	6	5
1. Wood pulp	5	x		x	x					x	x
2. Newsprint	3	x	x							x	
3. Bag or wrapping	4	x	x	x				x			
4. Paperboard	8	x	x	x			x	x	x	x	x
5. Fiber or corrugated board	4	x					x	x	x		
6. Rotogravure	4	x		x		x		x			
7. Magazine or book	7	x	x	x		x		x		x	x
8. Bond or ledger	6	x		x		x		x		x	x
9. Tissue or absorbent	4	x	x		x	x					
10. Paper specialties	10	x	x	x	x	x	x	x	x	x	x
11. Lumber	1							x			

Source: Standard & Poor's Corp., *Industry Surveys*, "Paper," Basic Analysis, May 6, 1954, p. P1–9. The companies are listed here in the order of their 1955 sales. The source gives data for 13 other United States companies, which averaged 3 product groups apiece.

a. Product groups 1 and 5 were added by the Gaylord Container merger of 1955.

The nonintegrated companies have some protection in the fact that a natural division of labor obtains between the large mills capable of handling big orders on a mass production basis, and the smaller ones with the flexibility to make the higher-priced specialty items and to give quick service on small orders. When pulp is in surplus supply, the nonintegrated mills have a competitive advantage because they buy rather than make it. In times of scarcity they must pay high prices or go without, while the integrated companies continue on an even keel. How well the nonintegrated firms would survive under the conditions being created by the current merger movement was an open question in early 1956.

Converters are apparently increasing in number. In 1939 the Census reported 2,433 converting establishments; in 1947, 3,212; in 1954, 4,017.[117] The number of firms has probably increased less rapidly, since in recent years integrated companies have been assuring their markets by acquiring their converter customers.

One independent converter described his position to the writer in the following terms:

> We can compete with the integrated mills by bringing out new lines (i.e., different patterns) every so often, and as long as the final consumer accepts these there is no danger that the giant mills with their low costs of mass production can sweep the market. We have the advantage of knowing our localities and our customers. Moreover, our chain store customers deliberately divide their purchases among all suppliers who can meet delivery and quality specifications, and we get our share by making regular calls. Few if any paper mills convert stationery any more, and our biggest integrated supplier recently gave up converting even scratch pads, finding that it could not meet the costs of its converter customers.

The third type of small firm, the general paper merchant, has almost held its own in share of sales, although not clearly in numbers. Between 1947 and 1954 the estimated annual sales of paper and its products by wholesale merchants increased from $1,828 to $2,681 million, but this was a reduction from 31.5 to 30.7 per cent of manufacturers' sales.[118] *Lockwood's Directory* listed approximately 2,150 merchants for 1939, 2,830 for 1947 and 2,280 for 1955. In some geographic areas, mer-

117. Calculated from *Statistical Abstract of the United States*, 1948, p. 839; 1950, p. 763; and advance reports of 1954 *Census of Manufactures*.

118. *Pulp, Paper and Board*, March 1955, pp. 12–13.

TABLE 40

PAPER: NUMBER OF FIRMS AND MILLS, 1929–55

Year	Firms	Paper Mills	Pulp Mills
1929	619	834	293
1939	528	727	246
1945	517	741	242
1946	559	744	241
1947	560	758	241
1948	570	768	245
1949	565	764	255
1950	572	767	259
1951	530	769	278
1952	492	768	303
1953	483	772	299
1954	486	773	321
1955	495	788	326

Source: "Statistical Table of Mills," *Lockwood's Directory of Paper and Allied Trades*, Lockwood's Trade Journal Co., New York, various editions. Number of paper mills in 1946 is the sum of figures for each state.

chants are complaining of an increasing trend to direct selling, by which mills are able to bypass them.[119]

Entry

Entry into the pulp and paper industry does not proceed rapidly. The number of *concerns* listed in *Lockwood's Directory* declined from 619 in 1929 to 528 in 1939, then, after recovering to 572 in 1950, dropped off again and was 495 in 1955. The number of paper and pulp *mills* also declined from 1929 to 1939, but has increased almost steadily since World War II. It is clear, therefore, that the decline in number of concerns in recent years has been due to mergers, not to complete closing down of companies. Between 1945 and 1955 there was a net gain in number of mills in operation: 47 for paper, 84 for pulp. (See Table 40.) Industry sources report, however, that the majority of these mills, and especially those with the larger capacities, were built by firms already in the industry rather than by those newly entering.

Entry is plainly difficult. Besides the sheer outlay of money, there is the problem of finding a suitable location. Most of the easily accessible

119. "Are Mills Forcing Jobbers Out of Business?", *Paper Trade Journal*, May 21, 1956, p. 39.

TABLE 41

PAPER: RATE OF RETURN ON NET WORTH OF PULP AND PAPER MILLS, 1939–54

(*Per Cent*)

Year	Industry	Integrated Mills	Non-integrated Paper Mills	Market Pulp Mills
1939–42	7.5	7.4	7.2	9.9
1943–46	7.6	7.3	8.4	8.4
1947	18.1	17.0	19.9	28.7
1948	15.8	16.3	6.2	24.5
1949	11.6	12.2	6.0	10.9
1950	15.2	15.0	13.6	20.5
1951	13.3	13.4	9.6	16.3
1952	10.9	10.9	7.1	14.5
1953	10.8	10.8	8.4	13.8
1954	11.0	10.9	9.3	13.5

Source: American Paper and Pulp Ass'n., *A Capital and Income Survey of the United States Pulp and Paper Industry, 1939–1954*, New York, 1955, pp. 9–12. Rate of return is after income tax.

sites for an integrated plant are already occupied. Only in converting, where the capital requirements are much smaller, is entry still active.

Profits by Type and Size of Company

According to the American Paper and Pulp Association tabulation of earnings as a percentage of net worth, the whole industry was highly profitable in 1947. However, in 1948 and all subsequent years, the nonintegrated mills have lagged behind the integrated companies. The market pulp mills have been more profitable than either type of paper mill, except in 1949, a year of relatively poor business. (See Table 41.) The high price of pulp, which increased 243 per cent between 1939 and the end of 1955 (owing mainly to a sharp rise during 1939–47) as compared with an increase of only 120 per cent for paper,[120] contributed to these profits, and thus to the trend toward integration through purchase of market pulp mills by paper companies.

If companies are classified according to size (as measured by sales), the same type of trend in return on net worth since 1947 appears. In that year the five producers with sales of $91 million or more earned

120. Wholesale price indexes of wood pulp, and paper exclusive of paperboard, from U.S. Bureau of Labor Statistics, *Monthly Labor Review*.

TABLE 42

PAPER: RATE OF RETURN ON NET WORTH OF LARGER COMPANIES, 1947 AND 1954

	1947			1954		
Rank of Firms in Sales	Group Sales	Lowest Sales	Mean Profit Rate	Group Sales	Lowest Sales	Mean Profit Rate
	(Millions)		*(Per Cent)*	*(Millions)*		*(Per Cent)*
Industry total	$5,368.1		22.1	$8,492.0		9.9
1–5	899.7	$91.0	20.1	1,597.7	$186.6	15.1
6–10	346.7	57.3	33.1	704.4	116.4	11.2
11–15	240.0	43.4	35.1	466.4	75.6	12.1
16–20	164.0	28.5	31.6	303.1	54.2	7.4
21–25	129.7	24.7	24.8	237.1	44.6	9.5
26–30	112.3	20.4	27.6	207.0	38.5	10.6
31–35	85.7	15.5	23.9	146.2	25.1	13.2
36–40	69.7	13.3	45.3	105.9	20.5	10.9
All smaller firms	3,320.4		21.2	4,724.2		7.3

Sources: Total profit from FTC–SEC, *Quarterly Financial Report for Manufacturing Corporations;* company data from Moody's *Industrials.* The companies are ranked in their order in 1947 and 1954, respectively, so the identities of those in parallel groups are not necessarily the same. The "mean profit rate" (after income tax) is the mean of the percentage returns on net worth of the five firms in each group: thus in 1954 International earned 16.54 per cent, Crown Zellerbach 14.58, Scott 15.56, St. Regis 12.08, and Container Corporation 16.51, and the average was 15.1.

20.1 per cent on net worth, the next seven groups of five producers (with sales running down to $13.3 million) earned between 24.8 and 45.3 per cent, and all smaller firms combined earned 21.2 per cent. In 1954 the profits were much lower, but the return of the top five producers had slipped only to 15.1 per cent, while the next seven groups of five had dropped to between 7.4 and 13.2 per cent, and all smaller firms to 7.3 per cent. The increase in sales between 1947 and 1954 was 84 per cent for the forty largest producers and only 42 per cent for the rest of the industry, so the decline in the profits of the smaller firms may be largely due to failure of their sales to keep pace. (See Table 42.)

Intercorporate Connections

A number of interlocking directorates were found by the Federal Trade Commission for 1946 among companies with slightly different types of product, but some of these had disappeared by 1949.[121] Indirect interlocks of the type indicated for International and the Con-

121. FTC, *Report on Interlocking Directorates*, 1951, pp. 422–25.

tainer Corporation of America were common: the board of "Colgate-Palmolive-Peet Co. provided the meeting ground." [122]

From its evidence the Commission concluded that "the multiplicity of the interlocking relations is so great — particularly when viewed in the light of other interlocking arrangements such as jointly owned affiliates, long-term contracts and patent license agreements — as to indicate the existence of a community of interest having serious competitive implications." [123] A recent member of the Securities and Exchange Commission also believed that "International is the center of an elaborate network of newsprint company interrelations . . . Virtually the entire newsprint industry, with the exception of Crown Zellerbach and Blandin, thus seems to be interrelated." [124] There was, however, no evidence of concrete cooperative practices, and one executive protested that his company could not dictate what men other corporations might select as directors.[125] Another informs the writer that the most prominent "interlocking director" of his own corporation, J. M. Hancock, was on so many boards that he rarely attended the meetings of this one, which finally discussed with him whether he ought to resign.

Another form of intercorporate connection is the jointly owned subsidiary, of which there are several examples in pulp and paper. Scott Paper Company is active in this field also. The Federal Trade Commission noted its joint ownership with Mead Corporation of a pulp producer.[126] Mead and Scott had then and still have one interlocking director,[127] but the two concerns do not make competing types of paper. In 1956 the Bowater-Scott Corporation, created by Scott and Bowater Paper Corporation, Ltd., to make and sell household paper products in Britain, was expected to be the first of many such "marriages." [128]

Trade Associations

The American Paper and Pulp Association is the over-all trade association of this industry. In 1956 it had fifteen "divisional" units —

122. *Ibid.*, p. 422, note 12.
123. *Ibid.*, pp. 432–33.
124. Donald C. Cook, Celler Hearings, p. 412.
125. John H. Hinman, Celler Exhibits, p. 501.
126. FTC, *Interlocking Directorates*, p. 420, note 1.
127. *Poor's Register of Executives and Directors*, Standard & Poor's Corp., New York, 1956.
128. *New York Times*, February 27, 1956, p. 29.

from the Blotting Paper to the Writing Paper Association — and two more which were "affiliated." There are also a good many independent organizations, like the National Paperboard Association. The pulp industry has separate associations for importers, integrated companies, market pulp mills, and pulp consumers (nonintegrated mills).

A recent congressional investigation found evidences of discussions within some pulp associations, touching on prices and other legally sensitive topics.[129] Trade associations in paper have sometimes tried to achieve uniformity in discounts, differentials, and methods of quoting prices, and several have accepted antitrust decrees or Federal Trade Commission orders. One association secretary, with much experience in the paper field, maintains that most of the antitrust investigations to which associations have been subjected have given them a clean bill of health. The paper executive who mentioned in a recent letter that he dislikes furnishing price data to his competitors wants associations to refrain from involvement in any way with prices. The Newsprint Association of Canada, in accordance with the different political climate there on this product, takes more positive cooperative action.[130]

A team of experts sent over by the Organization for European Economic Cooperation has listed constructive services of these associations under several headings — economic, public relations, labor relations, and technical — and has urged the European industry to adopt similar methods:

> The most important activity is undoubtedly statistical research . . . trade promotion may eventually be considered just as important as statistical research work . . . "Cost accounting" . . . is of enormous assistance to manufacturers . . . Standardization and Simplification . . . bring about substantial savings in production, transportation and storage costs . . . The Technical Association of the Pulp and Paper Industry . . . is one whose name has become synonymous with the technical progress of the industry . . . "Cooperation" is not incompatible with "individualism" . . .[131]

129. *Pulp*, Report of Subcommittee on Study of Monopoly Power, House Judiciary Committee, 82d Cong., 2d sess., 1952, H. Rept. 595, Part 2, pp. 26–43.

130. *Newsprint*, House Report, p. 106.

131. *The Pulp and Paper Industry in the USA: A Report by a Mission of European Experts*, Organization for European Economic Cooperation, Paris, 1951 (hereafter cited as OEEC Mission Report), pp. 83–84, 85, 138–40, 144, 153–64, 328–48.

Economic Characteristics of the Industry

The manufacture of pulp and paper is marked by high fixed costs and slow turnover of capital.[132] A paper executive estimates that a new integrated plant, with its own power supply, would cost up to $60,000 per employed worker. Mills must be placed where there is a good power supply and source of water, and pulp mills must have cheap access to pulpwood. Mills and machines are massive as well as highly specialized, and it is impractical to move them once they are built. Huge inventories of pulpwood or of pulp must be carried, and if these are stored too long there is a heavy financial cost as well as risk of spoilage. For these reasons there is a considerable cost difference between intermittent and continuous operation (168 hours a week, except for an annual shutdown for repairs).

Important factors relating to the market are the wide diversity of paper products and the great distance from points of production to those of consumption. The lack of sales response to a change in price is especially significant. For a factory using paper boxes or a store buying rolls of wrapping paper, the cost of these items is so small a fraction of total cost that it can almost be ignored. Newsprint and book paper form a larger part of the total cost of the end product, but even here demand is relatively inelastic since paper is treated as an unavoidable cost. The sales of paper rise and fall with the business cycle, but more gently. Even in depressions the demand for food cartons, advertising space in newspapers, or sanitary paper is only moderately reduced. Thus between 1929 and 1932 paper and paperboard production decreased from 81.3 per cent of capacity to 58.3, while steel ingot output was falling from 88.5 per cent of capacity to 19.5. In the postwar period the stability of both has improved: the decline between 1948 and 1949 was from 93.6 to 82.6 per cent for paper and from 94.1 to 81.1 per cent for steel.[133] The stock market has recognized this improvement in both industries, especially in paper. The fifteen-fold price advance in paper stocks between 1935–39 and 1956 outstripped even that of aluminum and rubber stocks, their nearest rivals.[134] In-

132. See statement by George Olmsted, Jr., president of S. D. Warren Co., in *Study of Pricing Methods*, Hearings before a Subcommittee of the Senate Interstate and Foreign Commerce Committee, 80th Cong., 2d sess., 1948, pp. 1012–13, also pp. 1020–22; and Guthrie, *The Economics of Pulp and Paper*, pp. 109–11, 181–82.

133. American Paper and Pulp Ass'n., *The Statistics of Paper*, New York, 1954, p. 53; American Iron and Steel Institute, *Annual Statistical Report*, New York, 1953, p. 37.

134. Standard & Poor's Corp., *The Outlook*, June 25, 1956, p. 737.

vestors believe increasingly that all of these industries will show both growth and stability.

The high fixed cost puts pressure on the mills to secure enough orders to keep operating, and this leads to price cutting[135] — which, however, is usually fruitless because it fails to increase total sales. In industries of this character, formal or informal restraints on competition designed to prevent its excesses are likely to develop. For example, the statistical services of the trade associations indicate to producers periods when overproduction may lead to price cutting, with the result that firms individually limit their output.[136]

In spite of such self-restraint, one writer who has compared price movements in book paper, writing paper, kraft, newsprint and paperboard from 1914 through 1944 has judged them to be as competitive as those in other manufactured goods, whether measured by number of changes or their amplitude.[137] By contrast with European conditions, competition in paper appears "keen," although it is not "cutthroat."[138]

Competition in Fine Paper

Some distinction may be drawn between tonnage grades of paper like newsprint, kraft and paperboard, and more individualized grades like book, writing and household-use paper, which may be grouped under a very general title of *fine paper* (though the term is usually reserved for certain specific types within this group). In many of the items of this second group there is a good deal of product differentiation. In these instances it would take more than a small price difference to make the average customer change his supplier. Service, credit policies, advertising, basic quality, and contrasts in finishes and appearance are among the factors which determine from which mill customers will buy.[139] The mill brand is especially important in those papers for which dependable product tests have not been developed. Sometimes reciprocity plays a role. "You buy my paper if you want me to buy your chemicals."

135. Standard & Poor's Corp., *Industry Surveys*, "Paper," Basic Analysis, June 2, 1955, p. P1–3.

136. OEEC Mission Report, p. 135.

137. Guthrie, "Price Regulation in the Paper Industry," pp. 214–15.

138. OEEC Mission Report, pp. 134–35.

139. George Olmsted, Jr., in *Study of Pricing Methods*, Senate Hearings, p. 1023; Roy I. Arroll, *Competition in the Fine Paper Industry*, unpublished master's thesis, New York University, New York, 1953.

Quite commonly a purchaser will spread his orders among the two or three nearest mills, to avoid dependence on any single supplier and yet keep transportation cost as low as possible. One exceptional buyer that shows no such fear, but believes that quality, efficiency and, above all, security can best be obtained from a single supplier, is the United States Treasury. It contracts for the entire paper money stock from a single producer, making the latter a "monopolist."

In many sorts of book, magazine or sanitary paper, the branded products of different sellers are recognized to be close enough in quality to make it useless for one to demand higher prices than another. Price lists for these articles are uniform.[140] One producer of these papers emphasizes this in a recent letter with the remark: "To say that customers tend to buy on the basis of quality seems to me more wishful than practical." He adds that for most of his products not only price, but salesman–purchasing agent relationships, service and credit rank ahead of quality.

Fair trade contracts requiring resale at a stipulated price are regularly used in only a few of the branded and specialty papers.[141] On the other hand: "Many manufacturers, while not interfering with the freedom of prices, 'suggest' retail prices, and usually paper merchants are guided by these suggestions." [142] It is well understood, however, that merchants may "skip columns" if forced to by market conditions; they may, for example, pay at the lower four-carton price for one carton. Retailers in turn may demand this privilege from jobbers.[143]

Tonnage Grades of Paper

In the large-volume or tonnage grades of paper — newsprint, kraft and paperboard — branding is much less important. The products of the different mills are usually equivalent in quality. Mills are more often tempted than in the case of fine paper to cut prices in order to enlarge their orders, and this has led to occasional price wars in various branches of the industry for many decades. The mills have naturally tried to avoid price competition. We have already discussed some of these attempts which have tangled with the law; but it is the opinion of experts in the industry that most such agreements would not have

140. Fine Paper Memorandum.

141. *Ibid.*

142. OEEC Mission Report, p. 135.

143. Fine Paper Memorandum.

lasted in any event. Grade shifting is likely to disrupt them, for a profitable situation in one branch of the paper industry will quickly draw competitors from other branches who are not bound by the agreement.[144] The feeling both in the industry and among outside students [145] that price-fixing attempts will prove fruitless draws strong support from this fact.

All of this means that prices are more likely to differ among the branded products than among the tonnage products. Although this might seem to indicate the presence of greater price competition among the former, it is evidence, instead, that consumers are not buying on a price basis but may prefer a higher-priced brand on its merits regardless of price. Customers may consider the various brands of book or writing paper so different as to warrant different prices, but they look upon newsprint as a single product.

Prices in Newsprint

The newsprint industry, which has been subjected to such frequent public investigations, has been discussed enough to permit a more extended analysis. Newsprint is on the whole a tonnage, undifferentiated product — even though a few publishers express a preference for particular makes or the service given by particular suppliers.[146]

In 1954 there were 38 mills in Canada and 14 in the United States. Twenty-eight of the mills were owned by the ten companies that had two or more plants.[147] The great bulk of the tonnage goes to perhaps 200 newspapers on long-term contracts (their average length is about five years), and the price is the same to every buyer of carload lots — whether he buys one carload or a hundred.[148] Mills must meet competitors' prices, and the result is both uniformity and stability of price. The 10,000 or so small daily and weekly papers that buy through distributors necessarily pay a higher price.

144. Stevenson, *The Background and Economics of American Paper-Making*, p. 150; Stanley Vance, *American Industries*, Prentice-Hall, New York, 1955, p. 355.

145. Letter from Edward H. Levi, who was general counsel for the Celler subcommittee.

146. William F. Canfield, Celler Hearings, p. 158; contrast J. D. Zellerbach, *ibid.*, p. 927.

147. Thomas D. Durrance, "More Newsprint," *Barron's*, January 5, 1955, p. 3.

148. Albin R. Caspar, vice president of Great Northern Paper Co., in *Problems of American Small Business*, Hearings before Special Senate Committee to Study Problems of American Small Business, 80th Cong., 1st sess., 1947, Part 2, "Investigation of Newsprint Shortages and Other Factors Affecting Survival of Smaller Independent Newspapers: II," pp. 290–93; William L. Hurlbut, vice president of International Paper Co., *ibid.*, pp. 299–300.

Even in newsprint, significant price variations among the sellers have sometimes occurred. Guthrie found in 1950 that these were greatest from 1919 to 1922, 1938 to 1940, and 1947 to 1949. Since these were periods in which the demand was generally very good, all producers could have charged the highest price if their motive had been simply to maximize profits.[149]

During the 1920s International Paper, the largest producer, was usually the price leader, but in the 1930s and again after World War II other companies frequently took over the leadership.[150] Thus, in 1948, an announcement by Crown Zellerbach led at once to a similar change by all but three of the North American mills; and in 1955 the St. Lawrence Corporation was the leader. The newsprint companies consider price leadership inevitable, and they have relied in their talks with the Department of Justice on the precedents which hold that leadership without actual agreement is not unlawful.

Interlocking Contracts in Newsprint

Another established practice is the "interlocking contract," which provides that the seller's price will be the average of the prices charged by certain other specified producers. The Minnesota and Ontario Paper Company was using the following clause in 1950:

> The price per ton . . . shall . . . be the average of the contract price then currently quoted for the destination by International Paper Company, Consolidated Paper Corporation, and Abitibi Power & Paper Co., Limited . . .[151]

Price Brothers' contracts also named International, Consolidated and Abitibi; Bowater Paper Company named Price Brothers, Consolidated and International; Consolidated named International; and Great Northern, while not naming the other companies on whose quotations its price would be based, said its price would not exceed that of any "substantial tonnage" sold by another producer. Great Northern has in fact customarily undersold its rivals by a very small amount [152] — a tradition which it would understandably like to break.

149. Guthrie, *The Economics of Pulp and Paper*, pp. 117, 174.

150. FTC, *Newsprint Paper Industry*, 1930, p. 81; John A. Guthrie, Celler Hearings, pp. 218, 222; Richard C. Doane, vice-president of International Paper Co., *ibid.*, p. 673.

151. Celler Exhibits, p. 110.

152. *Wall Street Journal*, December 22, 1954, p. 18; Albin R. Caspar, Celler Hearings, p. 806.

Although these contracts have looked suspicious to government investigators, they originated in the desire of newsprint users for assurance against being charged more by one seller on long-term contracts than they would have had to pay to other suppliers.[153] It was reported in 1950 that some of the mills were trying to escape the contracts in order to exploit the currently tight market situation by charging more than the mills whose prices they had contracted to follow.[154]

Are Newsprint Prices Set by Collusion?

A congressional committee on newsprint reported in 1951 that "the evidence adduced was overwhelmingly convincing that newsprint prices were set by collusive agreement between the mills." [155] The evidence cited consisted of one reference to an economic monograph (Guthrie's), six to exhibits filed with the Celler Committee, and thirty-one to testimony given before it. The reference to Guthrie's book runs as follows:

> As a result of these characteristics, the price and production policies of manufacturers have occasionally been directed toward reducing price competition and preventing the accumulation of excess supplies. Various methods have been used to achieve these objectives. Most important of them have been price leadership, open-price filing, uniform plans, and collusive or concerted action among producers and trade associations. These attempts have probably been made most frequently by newsprint manufacturers, but producers of other types of paper have also tried at times to moderate price competition. Not all branches of the industry have pursued this policy, and those that have frequently did so for a relatively short time. For the most part, attempts to restrict price competition have proved unsuccessful, because of the vigorous opposition shown by consumers and federal anti-trust agencies and also because of inherent characteristics of the industry which make difficult the successful restriction of price movements.[156]

These comments of an authority on the paper industry indicate his belief that the mills have tried to control prices, but without success.

153. R. A. McDonald, executive vice president of Crown Zellerbach Corp., Celler Hearings, p. 923; *Business Week*, November 5, 1955, p. 80.

154. John A. Guthrie, Celler Hearings, pp. 222–23.

155. *Supplies for a Free Press*, Senate Report, p. 12.

156. Guthrie, *The Economics of Pulp and Paper*, p. 182.

The six references to the Celler Committee's exhibits comprised the *nolo contendere* pleas in the *Pacific Coast newsprint* case concluded in 1941 (discussed below), two documents in the *paper jobber* case brought in 1950 and later dismissed,[157] two references by Scandinavian representatives to "discussions" (and a possible "decision") [158] — and one which might be convincing were it not unsigned and unverifiable. This was a report by a Scandinavian representative on his trip to Canada in 1938, referring to meetings to agree on export prices to the United States as an accepted practice — a practice whose mention in "one of the economic journals" appeared to the companies to have been quite "unnecessary." [159]

Evidence of Price Discussions

Most of the thirty-one references to the Celler Hearings fall into the following categories: (1) repetitions of statements in the Exhibits; (2) statements by Guthrie, whose view is better summarized in the passage from his book quoted above; (3) references to the special 1915–16 situation studied by the Federal Trade Commission in 1917; (4) arrangements among companies with corporate affiliations; (5) interlocking price contracts; and (6) buyer testimony, which must necessarily be taken with a grain of salt. The most persuasive piece of evidence introduced at the Hearings was a memorandum from a company's files which showed that at a meeting in October 1937 representatives of several West Coast producers (American and Canadian) made what seemed to be pledges as to prices they were going to charge.[160] This memorandum was the chief piece of evidence used in a Department of Justice indictment to which the American companies pleaded *nolo contendere* [161] — explaining their actions in terms of habits of cooperation started under the NRA but not known about or endorsed in 1937 by the chief executives of the companies.[162]

Even though most of this evidence is unconvincing, enough does remain to permit the conclusion that Canadian producers (sometimes

157. *U.S. v. Blake, Moffitt & Towne*, Celler Exhibits, pp. 1188–92.

158. Letters, *ibid.*, pp. 927, 987.

159. *Newsprint*, House Report, p. 79; unsigned, *Report on Orientation Trip to U.S.A. and Canada, September–October, 1938*, by a "Scannews" representative, Celler Exhibits, pp. 231–32.

160. *Newsprint*, House Report, pp. 82–83; Celler Hearings, pp. 1001–04; Celler Exhibits, pp. 714–15.

161. *U.S. v. Crown Zellerbach Corp.*, Celler Exhibits, p. 1187.

162. J. D. Zellerbach and Philip S. Ehrlich, Celler Hearings, pp. 1005–07.

with cooperation from the United States), encouraged by provincial government officials and secure against Sherman Act prosecution, have engaged in price discussions and tried to reach price agreements. That they have not always been successful is proved by the price wars which have occurred at times of excess capacity.[163] One executive of a company operating in Canada describes the situation as follows:

> Whenever the price has dropped, and especially in the depression when we wanted to shut down some of our mills and cut our losses, the various Canadian governments have put pressure on us both to keep them open and to keep up export prices. No country is going to let the impact of depression abroad hurt its employment or even its foreign exchange position if it can help it. So far as my company was concerned, we never entered price discussions except under government pressure.

Market Factors in Setting Newsprint Prices

A Department of Commerce study analyzes the newsprint market as one characterized by a monopolistic situation on both sides, with price stability and uniformity the object of both manufacturers and newspapers:

> Price decisions emanating from the newsprint market are surrounded by a high degree of competitive restraint partly because the principal manufacturer-sellers and publisher-buyers are cognizant of each others' power to influence prices.[164]

One interesting evidence that newsprint prices are "administered," instead of following the fluctuations of demand and supply closely, is the fact that throughout the post-World War II boom in newsprint — in which the chief factor was a tremendous rise in advertising — prices were held well below what the market would have justified. Thus in 1950 publishers were willing to pay $150 a ton for imported newsprint because the supply of North American newsprint at the official price of approximately $100 was inadequate.[165] In July 1952 newsprint produced in the United States was selling on contract at $10 a ton below

163. Clarence D. Long, Jr., "News Print: Costs and Competition," *Harvard Business Review*, Spring 1940, pp. 382–83.

164. Edward Margolin and William P. McLendon, *Transportation Factors in the Marketing of Newsprint*, U.S. Department of Commerce, Transportation Series No. 2, 1952, pp. 93–94.

165. John A. Guthrie, Celler Hearings, p. 243; James Donaldson, *ibid.*, pp. 845–49.

the price charged by the Canadians, and 90 per cent of it was selling on contract at anywhere from $10 to $94 below the individual ceiling prices set for the companies by the Office of Price Stabilization.[166] In 1956 the contract rate was still below what the mills could have obtained had they wished, since "gray market" prices were $200 per ton or more as against an established quotation of $130.[167]

Among the reasons for this conservative pricing policy are (1) fear of antagonizing customers by seeming to exploit them in each period of shortage and some fear of antagonizing congressional opinion, (2) a feeling that a stable price through booms and depressions is healthier than a get-rich-quick policy followed by one of unrestricted price slashing, and (3) fear of attracting more mills into the industry. The third point is not wholly convincing, since anyone considering entry would be well aware of the basically strong demand situation; but failure to reflect the demand in high published prices may, nevertheless, have a psychological effect. On the whole, the industry goal has been a satisfactory long-run level of profits rather than the greatest immediate profit.[168]

Zone Pricing in Paper

A zone pricing system has prevailed in many paper products. In fine paper, for instance, there are four zones used by all the companies, with the same step-up of delivered prices by 20 cents a hundredweight for each zone from east to west that was an issue in the second *book paper* case.[169] One authority states that in several kinds of paper some companies have established their own zones since World War II, which do not coincide with those of competitors as had been customary before. On the other hand, an industry member reports that his branch of the industry has an agreement not to absorb freight beyond $1.00 per ton.

In newsprint, prices were f.o.b. pressroom, with freight paid by the seller, until 1916; from 1917 to 1928 they were f.o.b. mill; finally the zone system came into being by action of the International Paper Company in 1928.[170] International's apparent motives were to meet

166. *Business Week*, July 19, 1952, p. 173.

167. *Wall Street Journal*, April 23, 1956, p. 24.

168. Guthrie, *The Economics of Pulp and Paper*, p. 174; *Newsprint*, House Report, pp. 86–89.

169. 40 FTC, at 705.

170. John A. Guthrie, Celler Hearings, p. 226.

Canadian competition by absorbing freight to buyers nearer Canada and to keep customers' goodwill by offering a uniform delivered price from all of the company's mills with no freight charge tacked on.[171] These zones were later modified and were imitated by most of International's competitors.

Under the National Recovery Administration, a map with ten zones was agreed upon by the industry.[172] The Office of Price Administration adopted the paper price zones during World War II.[173] The general rule today, subject to very minor exceptions, is that the price of newsprint is the same to all buyers of carload quantities within each zone, no matter from which company or which mill of a given company the paper is bought.[174]

Guthrie explains zone pricing in terms of both competition and convenience in quoting prices, although he grants that an auxiliary reason might be "to limit price competition and facilitate the detection of price cutting." [175] Some small newspaper owners consider the uniform price of the zone system one of their valuable protections against lower prices to their larger rivals.[176]

The high overhead costs in paper making, especially in newsprint, are part of the background of zone pricing.[177] The companies have attempted in this way to keep their mills in steady operation by selling at the same price as competitors who might be closer to a given customer. A Department of Commerce study found that the system has had the useful consequence of stimulating the utilization of capacity by letting distant mills reach the market on a price parity with others,[178] but has had the uneconomic consequence of causing some cross hauling.[179] This study concluded that the system "may have" discouraged the building of new mills in the South, since prospective customers tended to be satisfied with their previous distant suppliers because the

171. Margolin and McLendon, *Transportation Factors in the Marketing of Newsprint*, pp. 95–96; Ethan Ellis, Celler Hearings, p. 202; John H. Hinman, *ibid.*, p. 644.

172. John A. Guthrie, *ibid.*, p. 226.

173. Margolin and McLendon, *Transportation Factors in the Marketing of Newsprint*, p. 97.

174. Frank M. Jepson, Celler Hearings, p. 524.

175. John A. Guthrie, *ibid.*, p. 227, also p. 229; *idem*, *The Economics of Pulp and Paper*, p. 107.

176. Charles E. Moreau, in *Study of Pricing Methods*, Senate Hearings, pp. 1159–60.

177. Guthrie, *The Economics of Pulp and Paper*, p. 108.

178. Margolin and McLendon, *Transportation Factors in the Marketing of Newsprint*, pp. 97–98.

179. *Ibid.*, p. 110.

latter absorbed part of the transportation cost.[180] However, the study noted that southern mills earned a specially large profit because of their phantom freight,[181] and one must suppose that this encouraged capital to enter the business.

Such a formal pricing system tends sometimes to be associated with a cooperative spirit among the producers. One producer of fine paper located at a distance from an important market says that, when freight rates go up, he can count on competitors there to cooperate in setting a new zone price which will allow him a margin of profit.[182] Another, in a recent letter, takes the view that "zones should be set by free competition, not by cooperative methods," but expects uniform differentials to evolve in any event as a matter of convenience.

Interindustry Competition

Although there are no direct substitutes for paper in its "cultural" uses (newsprint, printing and writing stock), printing itself must compete with other media of communication and entertainment such as motion pictures, radio and television. Publishers have been unable to escape the impact of this competition, but paper makers have found new markets in the so-called "mechanical" uses of paper, which now take three quarters of United States output and two thirds of North American output.

Intercommodity competition is strong in these mechanical uses. Typical of the advance of paper is the increasing use of multi-wall sacks, which appeared in their modern form in 1931 and were reported in 1954 to be used for 400 different products. They packaged 75 per cent of the nation's bakery flour as compared to 10 per cent a decade earlier, and 25 per cent of animal formula feed as compared to 3 per cent in 1949, to give only two examples.[183]

The various substitute products — composition building materials, which compete with building paper; glass bottles, which compete with milk containers; plastic cups, which compete with paper cups; and all the rest — are fighting back. Early in 1956, when the kraft paper producers were considering their current price increase, there was a division of opinion:

180. *Ibid.*, p. 105.
181. *Ibid.*, p. 107.
182. Fine Paper Memorandum.
183. Wilber E. Higbee, "St. Regis Paper," *Barron's*, September 27, 1954, p. 19.

> Some analysts feel that, with paper basic to the economy, and with its increased use as part of the "merchandising revolution" which emphasizes self-service in retailing, consumers can only look at a price rise and "grin and bear it." This view is not shared by all industry circles, however. Some paper companies are aware of important inroads into the packaging market being made by producers of plastic film, most of whom are marketing their products aggressively, to say the least.[184]

A future threat to one paper company is the "long-range project" of du Pont to develop nylon currency which would outlast paper money by five times.[185]

A few of the paper companies also produce one or more of the substitute products. A trend toward this type of diversification appears to be under way.

Record of the Industry

The paper industry has measured up to high standards of performance in its expansion of production and improvement of methods, as well as in opening up new uses for its products. Since 1914 the per capita output of paper and paperboard in the United States has increased more than threefold,[186] in spite of the migration of newsprint to Canada. All customers interviewed in the course of this study expressed admiration for the industry's efficiency.

The active and productive research of the individual companies and of their Institute of Paper Chemistry at Appleton, Wisconsin, is supplemented by that of federal and state agencies, universities, and chemical firms selling to the pulp and paper mills.[187] A backhanded kind of encouragement from government comes through laws against polluting streams with waste sulphite liquor. The Sulphite Pulp Manufacturers Research League had spent $1.5 million through 1955 in searching for ways (some of them useful, others merely harmless) of disposing of this liquid; while its member mills in Wisconsin and Michigan had spent over $11 million in pollution control.[188]

184. *Journal of Commerce*, March 6, 1956, p. 6.

185. *Newsweek*, June 4, 1956, p. 80.

186. *Statistical Abstract of the United States*, 1955, pp. 13, 719.

187. OEEC Mission Report, pp. 69–76.

188. Sulphite Pulp Manufacturers Research League, Appleton, Wis., Reports, 1951–55, and correspondence. Compare Maurice Lloyd Branch, *The Paper Industry in the Lake States Region, 1834–1947*, unpublished doctoral thesis, University of Wisconsin, Madison, 1954, pp. 143, 148; *Wall Street Journal*, August 16, 1954, pp. 1, 7; *Business Week*, November 29, 1954, pp. 70, 75.

Profits in the industry have as a rule been good, but not out of line with those in other industries. In 1954 and 1955, when the paper industry was operating at record levels, seventy-six corporations averaged a return of 12.4 and 13.8 per cent, respectively, on their net book assets, as compared with the 12.3 and 15.0 per cent earned in these years by 1,765 manufacturing companies of all sorts.[189] The return on mills built at recent high construction costs is much lower than that on prewar capacity.

Conservation and the Sherman Act

Price competition in the paper industry has sometimes led to overcutting of forests.[190] High-cost mills, unable to make money any other way, may exploit their best timber, thus leaving isolated and poorer stands which it might never pay to cut. Under normal price conditions it might have paid to cut both at the same time. In general, according to timber men, practices are the most wasteful and destructive when prices are low.

Amendment of the Sherman Act has been suggested as one means of preventing price cutting and thus encouraging conservation. Attacking wasteful practices directly by prohibitions, penalties, or rewards for proper management (along the lines of the soil conservation payments now made to farmers) would be less drastic than attempting, by amending the antitrust laws to permit price agreements, to make companies so profitable that they would not be tempted to resort to wasteful practices. On the other hand, any antitrust dissolution of the largest companies would do damage to the policy of "sustained yield" which most of them have adopted. No big enterprise "can tie up a huge capital investment in bricks, mortar and machinery without being concerned that it shall, for a long time to come, have timber economically accessible." [191] A recent development — again possible only for large companies — is intensive utilization of the same forest tract for both lumber and paper production.

The contribution of the large pulp and paper producers to conservation is illustrated by a recent United States Forest Service study. After noting that 1952 was the first year studied in which timber growth was

189. First National City Bank of New York, Monthly Letter, April 1956, p. 43.

190. Guthrie, "Price Regulation in the Paper Industry," pp. 215–18; *idem*, Celler Hearings, p. 238.

191. "Crown Zellerbach's Second Growth," *Fortune*, January 1954, p. 154.

greater than drain, it tabulated the percentage of recently cut lands qualifying for the "upper productivity class" as follows: pulp industry, 84; national forests, 81; lumber industry, 73; farms and other private owners, 46.[192]

SUMMARY

1. The paper and pulp industry has only a *moderate degree of concentration*, with the largest company having 8 per cent of total sales in 1955, the four largest companies 17 per cent, and the fifteen largest 34 per cent. The industry ranked 396 out of 452 in percentage of shipments accounted for by four producers in 1947. In particular branches concentration was naturally much higher.

2. Between 1904 and 1911 the Department of Justice dissolved *pools* among the wrapping paper and paperboard companies. The formation of mergers by other firms in 1898, and later mergers by some of the defendants in these cases, illustrated the legal principle that, although firms might not legally suppress competition by agreement, they could do so by merger.

3. The Federal Trade Commission's *newsprint and book paper investigations in 1917*, and the Department of Justice's accompanying newsprint prosecution, resulted in dissolution of two trade associations that had been indiscreet in encouraging some forms of collusion. However, the price increases which had caused these investigations were due to natural market conditions emerging from the war. The temporary restraint put on prices by these proceedings merely took the place of the wartime government price fixing applied to other commodities.

4. The most significant antitrust case of the 1920s from a legal standpoint was the Federal Trade Commission order against the *Pacific States Paper Trade Association*, or West Coast jobbers. The Supreme Court, in sustaining this order in 1927, accepted without comment, and thus in fact established, the important principle that price fixing constitutes unfair competition as outlawed by the Federal Trade Commission Act.

5. The major attack on the paper industry under the antitrust laws came in 1939–42. Cooperative plans or actions which had been encouraged by the *National Recovery Administration* were enjoined by the antitrust authorities in six or eight branches of the industry. Several such plans attempted to establish uniform lists of differentials for grades and sizes of paper, to make prices known to all sellers, and to use uniform zone systems of pricing. The zones and lists of differentials were developed gradually for the convenience of producers

192. U.S. Forest Service, *Timber Resource Review*, 1955, cited in American Paper and Pulp Ass'n., *Monthly Statistical Summary*, New York, October 1955, p. 2.

and consumers, and they have continued in use by individual action of the companies. It was, nevertheless, healthy to enjoin agreements to use them.

6. In only one of these 1939–42 cases, the prosecution of the *tag manufacturers' price filing plan*, were the companies sustained on appeal to the courts. On the assumption that this decision holds today, producers may exchange through their association full information on price lists and on completed sales away from list — as long as they are not bound to follow their lists, do not disclose buyers' names, and always make the data available to buyers.

7. The most important *postwar suits* in paper are those which are seeking to halt the merger movement, but the order against use of a "Blue Book" and "Brown Book" which listed grade differentials and resale prices for jobbers abolished one type of cooperative activity.

8. Provincial authorities in *Canada* have frequently influenced the newsprint producers to avoid price cutting; but the Canadian fine and coarse paper industries, which sell for home consumption rather than export, have been made defendants in anti-combine proceedings by the Dominion government.

9. The argument that repeated *congressional investigations* of newsprint have deterred capital from entering this industry or have contributed to its migration to Canada has little if any merit.

10. Professed *opinion in the industry* favors the antitrust laws, as constituting a desirable barrier against attempts to monopolize or to fix prices — which, as experience has shown, would fail in any event, frequently because of "grade shifting" by which competitors divert machines to making the higher-priced papers. This is probably a sincere viewpoint — the more so, perhaps, because some of those who hold it have themselves participated in such attempts and learned by experience.

11. The *trend of concentration* in the paper and pulp industry is evidently upward. Since 1945 at least, there has been a steady increase in the share of total sales controlled by the ten largest companies; and only minor changes have occurred in the make-up of this group. Newsprint may be an exception: the five largest companies in 1951 had a smaller share of capacity than the five largest in 1913 or 1928 had of output.

12. *Early combinations* with monopolistic intent were formed in paper bags, paperboard, wallpaper, tissue paper, newsprint and writing paper; but without exception they soon lost their market dominance to competitors. Although the wallpaper combination was condemned by the Supreme Court long after it had vanished, no antitrust suits were brought against these combinations, and it would appear from their history that none was necessary.

13. *Recent mergers* in paper have been designed to achieve vertical integration or product or geographic diversification rather than monopoly. The advantages of vertical integration are partly technical, in the coordination of

pulp and paper production, but chiefly strategic, in assurance of raw materials and markets. The other large producers are striving to emulate International Paper's diversified position in nearly all the important product lines.

14. *Nonintegrated mills and converters* presumably account for a decreasing share of the industry's sales, but many of them are successful because of their ability to make specialty products at low overhead costs. The number of independent concerns in basic paper manufacture declined by 20 per cent between 1929 and 1955. The number of converting establishments, on the other hand, increased by more than 60 per cent between 1939 and 1954, and the number of converting firms probably somewhat less owing to mergers. In 1955 and 1956 the continuing merger movement threw some doubt on the future of the nonintegrated companies.

15. In the years since 1947 *profits of the big integrated companies* have been higher than those of the smaller and nonintegrated paper producers, but market pulp mills have made good profits throughout.

16. *Intercorporate connections* in the industry include a few interlocking directorates among companies making different types of paper, some jointly owned subsidiaries, and various indirect connections of doubtful significance.

17. *Trade associations* in the industry conduct the usual activities, and foreign observers consider their influence highly constructive. A number of these organizations have engaged in activities intended to limit or control competition; but frequently these have been merely attempts to codify industry practices.

18. The *economic characteristics* of the pulp and paper industry, including considerable immobility and heavy investment per employee or per unit of output, as well as inelastic demand for many of its products, create a danger of cutthroat price competition in order to keep plants in operation when demand declines. These facts encourage either restraint of competition or at least self-restraint by the producers.

19. *Competition* in some types of fine paper is as much in quality and service as in price, but in others merchants will buy wherever the price is lowest. Instead of formal resale price maintenance, there are informally "suggested" resale prices. In coarse paper and paperboard the absence of product differentiation makes any price difference so appealing to customers as to discourage such differences altogether. If price agreements or demand conditions should put the price of a given type of paper unduly high, "grade shifting" of machinery previously used for other types is likely to bring it back into line.

20. In *newsprint*, the "interlocking contracts" by which some mills tie their prices directly to those of other mills are an open expression of the price leadership which is an accepted custom in the industry. They originated in customer demand, and they are not the equivalent of an outright price agreement. The Canadian producers (many of them controlled by United States

capital), who account for the bulk of North American output, have attempted at times to fix export prices, but this has been done, sometimes at least, with the encouragement or at the demand of provincial government officials. These attempts have been unsuccessful when unwarranted by market conditions. Newsprint capacity increased more slowly than demand after 1945. The producers held prices below what they could have charged, in an effort to avoid public criticism and a "boom and bust" cycle.

21. The *zone system of pricing* became common in paper as a matter of convenience and as an attempt by distant mills to remain in competition with mills closer to the market. It may be useful also as a means of keeping watch on competitors' prices. A government study reached mixed conclusions on the economic merits of zone pricing and its effects on expansion of the industry.

22. There are no *substitutes* for paper in its cultural uses — writing and printing — but two thirds of the industry's product goes into mechanical uses, in many of which there is severe competition with glass, plastics, textiles and other products.

23. The *record of the industry*, in expanding production in line with rising demand for its product, is a good one; and it has vastly improved its previously unsatisfactory conservation record. Excessive price competition, or dissolution of the large companies, would make the task of conservation harder.

In brief, much of the antitrust enforcement in this industry has been directed against uniform methods of price quoting; though these arose chiefly for convenience, the rule against formal agreements on such methods is a good one; and the antitrust laws have also served as a desirable restraint on the attempts, formerly more common than now but probably fruitless at any time, to make binding price agreements or monopolize branches of the industry.

CHAPTER 7

Bituminous Coal

In the United States the word "coal" is now almost synonymous with bituminous or soft coal, since the output of Pennsylvania anthracite, or hard coal, has dwindled to a mere 5 per cent of the total. In both number of employees (210,000 in 1955) and value of output ($2.3 billion),[1] bituminous coal far outranks all other branches of mining.

Coal Mining and Coal Labor

Fully three fourths of the coal supply comes from underground mines, the rest from surface or "strip" operations in which the soil, rock and coal are lifted by power shovels. The "room-and-pillar" method is usual underground. The miners hollow out "rooms" whose roof-supporting pillars of coal are later removed one by one. Successive operations include cutting into the room wall; drilling and blasting; loading on cars; transportation to the mine mouth; washing the coal and sorting it on screens in a building called the "tipple"; and loading it into freight cars, trucks or barges. Machines are used for about 95 per cent of underground cutting and 85 per cent of loading; and 60 per cent of all coal is mechanically cleaned.[2]

A recent estimate places total bituminous reserves at nearly 2 trillion tons, which, with current methods and rates of recovery, would last almost two thousand years.[3] Two thirds of the reserves lie west of

1. Calculated from U.S. Bureau of Mines, *Mineral Industry Surveys*, Weekly Coal Report 2009, March 16, 1956, p. 14.

2. National Coal Ass'n., *Bituminous Coal Trends*, Washington, 1956, p. 74; U.S. Bureau of Mines, Weekly Coal Report 2009, p. 14.

3. Calculated from *Bituminous Coal Trends*, 1956, pp. 142–43, 147.

the Mississippi, and two thirds of these, in turn, consist of subbituminous coal and still lower-grade lignite. Seventy-five per cent of 1955 production, however, was supplied by the Appalachian coal field, extending from Pennsylvania and Ohio to Alabama. Thirty per cent came from West Virginia alone. A second great field, which underlies Illinois, Indiana and western Kentucky, supplied another 19 per cent.[4]

The ownership of coal mines is scattered, but coal mine employees have in recent years been represented by a single union. The United Mine Workers of America holds sway over all unionized mines except a few poorer ones in Illinois held by the tiny Progressive Miners of America. In 1954, according to the union's records, 85 per cent of bituminous coal employees were members. And nonunion firms, found mainly in the smaller strip operations, cannot ignore the union's policies. Mining is a well-paid occupation in terms of hourly wages, but the worker faces serious layoff and unemployment hazards. Wages and the 40-cent-per-ton contribution to the union's Welfare Fund make up about half the cost of production.

Small Producers and Large Consumers

There is a relatively low degree of concentration in bituminous coal compared with that in most industries. In 1955 there were 7,500 to 8,000 mines recorded by the United States Bureau of Mines, and this number did not include "wagon mines" or "snowbirds" which yield less than 1,000 tons a year and often operate only in winter. The largest single company, with its twenty-four mines, accounted in 1955 for only 6.0 per cent of the output, the four largest for 18.3 per cent, and the fifteen largest for 35.0 per cent. In each instance firms acquired during 1955 are included in the totals. (See Table 43.) A merger of the first and seventh companies announced in 1956 would (on a 1955 output basis) raise these percentages to 7.8, 20.1 and 36.0.

Four of the fifteen largest firms are steel companies mining coal for their own use. Such "captive" mines accounted in 1955 for 18 per cent of the coal produced, including 58 per cent of that used by the steel industry and 7 per cent of that used by utilities.[5]

The principal markets for bituminous coal have changed considerably over the years. Today the electric utilities take 30 per cent of

4. Calculated from U.S. Bureau of Mines, Weekly Coal Report 2009, p. 10.

5. Captive output in *Coal Production in the United States*, 1955, pamphlet compiled by Keystone Coal Buyers Manual, McGraw-Hill, New York, p. 4.

TABLE 43

BITUMINOUS COAL: OUTPUT OF FIFTEEN LARGEST COMPANIES, 1955

Firm	Output	Per Cent of Total
	(*Thousand Tons*)	
Industry total	470,000	100.0
Total, fifteen firms	164,297	35.0
1. Pittsburgh Consolidation Coal Co.	28,001	6.0
2. U.S. Steel Corp.	25,159	5.4
3. Peabody Coal Co.	19,054	4.1
4. Island Creek Coal Co.	13,749	2.9
5. Bethlehem Steel Corp.	9,886	2.1
6. Eastern Gas and Fuel Associates	9,307	2.0
7. Pocahontas Fuel Co.	8,464	1.8
8. Pittston Co.	8,058	1.7
9. Truax-Traer Coal Co.	7,662	1.6
10. West Kentucky Coal Co.	7,493	1.6
11. Freeman Coal Mining Corp.	6,423	1.4
12. Republic Steel Corp.	5,499	1.2
13. North American Coal Corp.	5,331	1.1
14. Jones & Laughlin Steel Corp.	5,313	1.1
15. Berwind-White Coal Mining Co.	4,896	1.0

Source: Coal Production in the United States, 1955, pamphlet compiled by Keystone Coal Buyers Manual, McGraw-Hill, New York, pp. 8–11. Figures include tonnages of companies that were merged with Peabody, Island Creek, Pocahontas and West Kentucky on or before January 1, 1956.

TABLE 44

BITUMINOUS COAL: PRINCIPAL CONSUMING OUTLETS, 1935 AND 1955

(*Million Tons*)

Market	1935	1955	Change
Total	366.1	474.5	+108.4
Electric utilities	30.9	140.5	+109.6
Coke plants and steel mills	62.3	112.6	+ 50.3
Miscellaneous manufacturing	100.5	100.6	+ .1
Retail deliveries	84.0	53.8	− 30.2
Exports and bunker (ship) use	11.3	51.7	+ 40.3
Railroads (Class I)	77.1	15.5	− 61.6

Sources: U.S. Bureau of Mines, *Mineral Industry Surveys,* Weekly Coal Report 2009, March 16, 1956, pp. 13–14; 1935 exports from National Coal Ass'n., *Bituminous Coal Annual,* 1953, Washington, p. 88.

production, steel mills and their associated coke plants 24 per cent, and miscellaneous manufacturing industries 21 per cent, with retail deliveries, exports and railroads accounting for the remaining 25 per cent. Most of the 108-million-ton increase in sales between 1935 and 1955 was accounted for by the shift of utilities to coal and their expanding rate of activity. Coke ovens and export trade made up for sharp drops in retail deliveries and railroad use. (See Table 44.)

Much of the coal is thus bought by large users — such as steel, utility and chemical companies — whose bargaining power is presumably superior to that of the typically small mine operators.

Types and Distribution of Coal

As a result of their different geological histories, the various coal beds of the country differ considerably. Large buyers carefully analyze the various coals with regard to their undesirable components ("moisture" or water, "ash" or mineral impurity, and sulfur), their combustible fixed carbon, and their "volatile matter" or gases (which reduce burning quality but are valuable in themselves if properly treated).[6] On the basis of its use, coal is classified as domestic, coking (metallurgical) and steam (industrial). As to size, coal is graded into such classes as lump or block, egg, nut and stoker. The finer residue after sorting out the other sizes is called "slack" or "screenings"; and "mine run" is any coal sold without screening. Slack, little in demand when boilers were fired by hand, is now sought by industrial establishments, and many mines crush larger sizes down to fine slack.

In 1953, 73 per cent of coal was transported entirely by rail, 10 per cent by truck, 8 per cent by water, 6 per cent by truck and then rail, while 3 per cent was burned locally.[7] The freight cost averages nearly 40 per cent of the wholesale price of the coal at destination.[8]

Three principal marketing channels are traversed by coal.[9] (1) Many larger companies and some small ones sell direct to industrial

6. See Waldo E. Fisher and others, *Report of the Committee on Prices in the Bituminous Coal Industry*, prepared for the Conference on Price Research, National Bureau of Economic Research, New York, 1938, pp. 6–7, also pp. 10–11.

7. W. H. Young, R. L. Anderson and E. M. Hall, *Coal — Bituminous and Lignite*, advance preprint from U.S. Bureau of Mines, *Minerals Yearbook*, 1953, p. 106.

8. Thomas C. Campbell, *The Bituminous Coal Freight-Rate Structure — An Economic Appraisal*, West Virginia University Business and Economic Studies, Vol. 3, No. 3, Morgantown, June 1954, p. 8.

9. Allan Sherman and Allen B. MacMurphy, *Facts about Coal*, U.S. Bureau of Mines, 1950, p. 24.

users and others. (2) A number of producers market through sales agents or brokers operating on commission, who take over the entire selling responsibility. (3) Other coal is sold by the mines to wholesalers, also known as distributors, who resell either to retailers or industrial firms and rarely take physical possession of the coal themselves. Much of the coal going to large buyers is sold under contracts running for a year or longer, with the price tied to the principal mine costs by an escalator clause.

Prices, whether on the "spot" market or on contract, depend on the grade of coal, size specifications, particular use planned, washing and sorting required, length of contract, quantity bought, time of year, transportation costs, bargaining position of the parties, and of course on market competition. There are literally thousands of quotations for coal at any one time.

Antitrust Suits and Legislation

Of chief interest in the relation of the bituminous coal industry to the antitrust laws is its temporary exemption in the 1930s through special legislation; but the industry's experience with the Sherman Act goes back to the year 1890.

Early Applications of the Sherman Act

The first three antitrust proceedings in coal involved price fixing. In the first attempt to test the Sherman Act in any industry, a civil suit was brought in 1890 against mines and dealers in Kentucky and Tennessee. Their Nashville Coal Exchange had declared its intention to "treat all parties in a fair and equitable manner"; but in fact the producers made an agreement, enforced by fines, to sell only to their associated dealers. The price was to be 13 cents a bushel, with any increase divided 50–50. The Circuit Court refused to grant an injunction without a hearing, on the ground that "the act is new, and this is a most important application of it"; but after the hearing it condemned the scheme as unfair to Nashville consumers.[10]

In 1896 members of the Salt Lake Coal Exchange were found guilty of fixing prices and denying their special prices to other dealers.

10. *U.S. v. Jellico Mountain Coal and Coke Co.*, 43 Fed. 898, 899 (N.D. Tenn. 1890), 46 Fed. 432 (1891), Department of Justice, *Decrees and Judgments in Federal Antitrust Cases*, 1918, p. 1.

The conviction was upset when Utah's admission to the union removed federal court jurisdiction.[11]

Retail and wholesale members of the Coal Dealers Association of California were charged in a civil suit in 1897 with regulating shipments into San Francisco and fixing prices to consumers.[12] Although there were nonmembers from whom consumers could buy, and prices had fallen since the association began to operate, and although dishonest methods in the trade had made regulation seem necessary, the government won an injunction.

In 1895 a West Virginia statute compelled the Chesapeake & Ohio Railway to cease acting as sales agent for coal mined along its lines, and in 1899 a successor agency, which regulated the output of fourteen West Virginia producers according to market demand, was enjoined as being in restraint of trade. The defense that the agency helped these mines penetrate more distant markets was overruled as irrelevant.[13]

Sherman Act Cases from 1909 to 1921

Besides two charges of price fixing that were not proved,[14] the 1909–21 period witnessed three unusual episodes. The *Lake Shore* case enjoined cooperative division of coal traffic among a number of railroads running through Ohio.[15] One of the joint ventures had involved development of three mining properties with the help of two railroads that guaranteed their bonds in return for the coal traffic they were to originate. This type of rail-mine relationship has not reappeared.

In 1912–14, a time of low coal sales and drastic price cuts, about a hundred companies producing West Virginia "smokeless" coal tried a program of common sales agencies, price discussions and price announcements at trade association meetings, and agreements not to change prices without notifying the other companies. In 1916, by which time prices were rapidly advancing, the Department of Justice secured indictments for these earlier activities in the New York federal

11. *F. H. Moore v. U.S.*, 85 Fed. 465 (8th Cir. 1898), *Decrees and Judgments*, pp. 683–84.

12. *U.S. v. Coal Dealers Association of Calif.*, 85 Fed. 252 (N.D. Calif. 1898), *Decrees and Judgments*, pp. 49–53.

13. *U.S. v. Chesapeake & Ohio Fuel Co.*, 105 Fed. 93 (S.D. Ohio 1900), 115 Fed. 610 (6th Cir. 1902), *Decrees and Judgments*, pp. 55–56.

14. *Union Pacific Coal Co. v. U.S.*, 173 Fed. 737 (8th Cir. 1909); *U.S. v. W. Hamilton Smith*, Cr. 37630 (D. Colo. 1921).

15. *U.S. v. Lake Shore & Michigan Southern Ry. Co.*, 203 Fed. 295 (S.D. Ohio 1912), *Decrees and Judgments*, pp. 289–309.

court. The defendants offered to plead *nolo contendere*, but the government hoped to win a verdict and perhaps a jail sentence. This hope failed when an Alabama judge who was assigned to preside charged the jury that agreement on reasonable prices was not unlawful. The defendants proved that competition had been severe, that they had not succeeded in controlling prices and that the advance in 1916 was due to wartime demand. The jury acquitted them, and no appeal against the judge's individualistic interpretation of the Sherman Act was legally possible.[16]

A singular episode occurred in October 1920, when the National Coal Association, at a special meeting called as a result of a telegram from the Attorney General, who was pursuing coal "profiteers" in the courts, voted to report to United States attorneys those operators who might charge unreasonably high prices. Thus the members of a benevolent conspiracy to fix prices (downward) were to complain against those who set their own prices (upward).[17]

The Coronado Damage Suit

In 1914 and 1916 the government attempted to apply the Sherman Act to certain activities of the United Mine Workers of America, or of the union and operators working together, but without success.[18] A celebrated private suit at last won a partial legal victory over the union as a result of strike violence in 1914. Strikers had dynamited mines and set fire to tipples and coal cars of the Bache-Denman Coal Company mines in Arkansas, of which the Coronado Coal Company was one. Operations ceased, and receivers for the mines brought suit for treble damages under the Sherman Act. The case was tried twice and went twice to the Supreme Court, with Chief Justice Taft delivering both opinions for a unanimous tribunal. The first time, the question was whether a union could be made a defendant in such a suit. The Court held that it could, since Section 7 of the Sherman Act applied to "associations." [19] Three years later, in 1925, speaking on the immediate question at issue, the Court ruled that the purpose of the

16. *U.S. v. Aileen Coal Co., U.S. v. Algoma Coal and Coke Co., U.S. v. Baker-Whiteley Coal Co.: Decrees and Judgments*, pp. 853–57 (1917).

17. Annual Report of the Attorney General, 1920, pp. 48–50.

18. *U.S. v. John P. White*, Cr. 1287 and 2948, *Decrees and Judgments*, p. 804 (1914), 808 (1916); *U.S. v. Frank J. Hayes*, Cr. 2947 and 2948, *ibid.*, p. 809 (1916); *U.S. v. George M. Jones*, Cr. 1652 (D. Ind. 1921).

19. *United Mine Workers of America v. Coronado Coal Co.*, 259 U.S. 344 (1922).

strike and the violence was to halt shipments of nonunion coal into other states in competition with union coal, and thus involved direct restraint of trade.[20] Two years later the Coronado plaintiffs — seeing little hope of collecting damages from the union's District 21, on which sole responsibility had been placed — settled out of court for $27,500, the expected cost of a third trial.[21] This was thirteen years after the suit had been filed.

The expectation that the Coronado decisions would have far-reaching significance was not fulfilled. The decline of the United Mine Workers in the 1920s was not due to damage suits or fear of them; and its resurgence after 1933 proceeded without such fear. In fact, the exemption of the national union from liability "has been quoted in favor of unions in practically every suit for damages involving strikes." [22]

In recent years coal operators have at times sued union locals (sometimes under state antitrust laws) for destruction of property or interference with shipment of coal, but they have only rarely gained court victories or settlements. Such suits are always dropped as part of the bargaining for new collective agreements, and these agreements now regularly include a clause prohibiting them.

Coal as a Sick Industry

Coal did not share in the national prosperity of 1922–29. In the only years for which complete profit data are available, the industry suffered a net loss. The number of mines declined by more than a third, prices fell, and in no year of the 1920s was the average miner employed more than 220 days. (See Table 45.) The industry had a reputation in the 1920s of being the worst conducted in the United States.[23] It underwent nineteen investigations or hearings by Congress or by specially created commissions between 1913 and 1935.[24] In the most important of these the United States Coal Commission recommended, in 1923, an excess profits tax and regulation of output by a new division of the Interstate Commerce Commission.

20. *Coronado Coal Co. v. United Mine Workers of America*, 268 U.S. 295 (1925).

21. See Edward Berman, *Labor and the Sherman Act*, Harper, New York, 1930, pp. 119–30; Charles O. Gregory, *Labor and the Law*, Norton, New York, 1946, pp. 211–19.

22. Letter from Harrison Combs, counsel for the UMWA.

23. Isador Lubin, "The Coal Industry," *Encyclopaedia of the Social Sciences*, Vol. 3, p. 595.

24. *Carter v. Carter Coal Co.*, 298 U.S. 238, 331 (1936).

TABLE 45

BITUMINOUS COAL: NUMBER OF MINES, PRODUCTION, PRICES, DAYS WORKED AND PROFIT, 1915–55

(Mines Producing 1,000 Tons or More)

Year	Number	Production	Average Value per Ton at Mine	Average Number of Days Worked in Year	Profit or Loss after Federal Taxes (All Corporations)
		(Million Tons)			*(Millions)*
1915	5,502	443	$1.13	203	
1916	5,726	503	1.32	230	
1917	6,939	552	2.26	243	$133
1918	8,319	579	2.58	249	83
1919	8,994	466	2.49	195	49
1920	8,921	569	3.75	220	173
1921	8,038	416	2.89	149	18
1922	9,299	422	3.02	142	
1923	9,331	565	2.68	179	
1924	7,586	484	2.20	171	
1925	7,144	520	2.04	195	−27
1926	7,177	573	2.06	215	
1927	7,011	518	1.99	191	
1928	6,450	501	1.86	203	−28
1929	6,057	535	1.78	219	−16
1930	5,891	468	1.70	187	−45
1931	5,642	382	1.54	160	−49
1932	5,427	310	1.31	146	−52
1933	5,555	334	1.34	167	−49
1934	6,258	359	1.75	178	−11
1935	6,315	372	1.77	179	−18
1936	6,875	439	1.76	199	− 7
1937	6,548	446	1.94	193	− 4
1938	5,777	349	1.95	162	−28
1939	5,820	395	1.84	178	− 9
1940	6,324	461	1.91	202	8
1941	6,822	514	2.19	216	24
1942	6,972	583	2.36	246	34
1943	6,620	590	2.69	264	47
1944	6,928	620	2.92	278	44
1945	7,033	578	3.06	261	36
1946	7,333	534	3.44	214	51
1947	8,700	631	4.16	234	168
1948	9,079	600	4.99	217	197
1949	8,559	438	4.88	157	54

(Continued on following page)

TABLE 45 (*Continued*)

Year	Number	Production	Average Value per Ton at Mine	Average Number of Days Worked in Year	Profit or Loss after Federal Taxes (All Corporations)
		(*Million Tons*)			(*Millions*)
1950	9,429	516	4.84	183	94
1951	8,009	534	4.92	203	57
1952	7,275	467	4.90	186	33 (or 49 [a])
1953	6,671	457	4.92	191	28 [a]
1954	6,130	392	4.51	185	13 [a]
1955	7,756	470	4.83	217	41 [a]

Sources: National Coal Ass'n., *Bituminous Coal Data*, 1954, Washington, pp. 2–3 and (for profit data from U.S. Bureau of Internal Revenue, *Statistics of Income*) p. 73; 1954 and 1955 figures from U.S. Bureau of Mines.

a. Profit of 24 coal companies in 1952–53 and 21 companies in 1954–55 (First National City Bank of New York, Monthly Letter, April issues).

The economic problems of the coal industry have been made clear by a number of writers,[25] and need not be analyzed in detail here. Some of the salient points may be listed briefly.

1. *Entry is easy*, owing to the many coal deposits and the reasonable capital requirements, plus the willingness of railroads to supply cars to a new customer. As a result, any sharp price increase — like the 100 per cent advance between 1915 and 1917 or the 46 per cent advance between 1939 and 1943, both of which carried much further in the next years — may lead to an equally sharp increase in the number of mines. Each world war and the immediate postwar boom drew in three or four thousand new commercial mines, in addition to wagon mines and snowbirds. It may take three years for a mine to reach full operation, whereupon a downturn in demand may leave old and new mines—some of the latter too small for efficiency—with excess capacity. Thus between 1915–17 and 1920–22 the average annual output per mine decreased from 83,000 to 54,000 tons, and between 1938–40 and 1948–50 it decreased from 67,000 to 57,000 tons (Table 45).

2. "*Exit*" *is difficult*, in the sense that a mine once opened may continue in operation for a long time even without making a real profit. One reason is that much of the invested capital cannot be withdrawn.

25. An influential early critique was Walton H. Hamilton and Helen R. Wright, *The Case of Bituminous Coal*, Macmillan, New York, 1925. The most recent is Jacob Schmookler, "The Bituminous Coal Industry," Chap. 3 in Walter Adams, ed., *The Structure of American Industry*, Macmillan, New York, revised edition, 1954.

Another is that temporary closing of a mine may result in flooding by underground water, unless pumping is continued on the normal scale. Moreover, there is always the hope of making money at the seasonal peak of demand. Overcapacity is therefore hard to eliminate.

3. In the early 1920s *demand ceased to advance*, because of competition from oil and natural gas and advances in the combustion efficiency of coal. This fact was not noticed at first, for strikes and other shortages kept prices high and invited more mines into the industry.

4. While prices dropped after 1920, wages per hour or per ton were not cut, as a result of the "no backward step" principle announced by John L. Lewis, who had been elected president of the United Mine Workers in that year. High labor costs gave a further impetus to *opening of nonunion mines in the South*, which was already in progress because of the widespread occurrence of coal seams and the availability of surplus manpower on the farms. Northern mines were closing in larger numbers than the figures suggest. It is not surprising that the union (more than the operators) supported bills introduced in Congress in 1928 and 1932 to set up commission control of the industry with federal licensing to discourage new mines.[26]

The Depression and the Sales Agency Plan

The industry's sickness became critical in the general depression which followed 1929, and by 1931 output had dropped to the lowest level since 1909. Following an emergency meeting of the governors of seven Appalachian states, the governor of West Virginia appealed to the National Coal Association to produce a plan for the industry.[27] The plan which emerged in the last three months of 1931 was to establish exclusive sales agencies to represent the mines in each of eighteen coal-producing regions, with the broad purpose of halting cutthroat competition.

The first agency established was Appalachian Coals, Inc., with 137 members in eastern Kentucky, eastern Tennessee, southwest Virginia and the southern part of West Virginia. Despite its name, the agency represented only the "southern high-volatile field" within the larger Appalachian field. It was to fix minimum prices for sales by all its

26. Ellery B. Gordon and William Y. Webb, "Price Fixing in the Bituminous Coal Industry," Part 3 of Donald H. Wallace, ed., *Economics Standards of Government Price Control*, TNEC Monograph 32, 1941, pp. 255–56.

27. Glen Lawhon Parker, *The Coal Industry: A Study in Social Control*, American Council on Public Affairs, Washington, 1940, p. 163.

members (its first price list carried 3,500 quotations), but was obligated to move all the coal its members cared to produce, at the best price obtainable. It had the right to allocate orders among its members. It planned also to establish standard grades of coal and improve methods of distribution in various ways — notably, by elimination of unfair practices like "pyramiding," that is, the simultaneous offer of coal through several agents with the incidental consequence of creating a fictitious oversupply. When the agency did the actual selling, it was to receive a commission of 10 per cent from the members, but when the member did his own selling (as was to become the prevailing practice [28]) the commission was to be 2 per cent.

Appalachian Coals opened an office early in 1932, but suspended operations at once when the Department of Justice expressed doubt of its legality. Colonel (later General) William J. Donovan, who had retired in 1929 as Chief of the Antitrust Division of the Department of Justice, defended the agency against his successor's suit brought in July 1932. A three-judge federal court, in an opinion by Circuit Judge John J. Parker, enjoined its operation as being in restraint of trade.[29] In March 1933, however, the injunction was lifted by the Supreme Court.[30]

The Supreme Court's Appalachian Coals Decision

In this notable Supreme Court decision, Chief Justice Hughes spoke for all his colleagues except Justice McReynolds, who dissented without opinion. After analyzing the facts as to the industry and the agency, the Court's opinion reached three conclusions:

1. The defendants were sincerely trying to alleviate a severe crisis of unemployment, low wages and bankruptcy; and consumers as well as producers are injured by such phenomena in an industry.

2. Coal reserves were so widely scattered, transportation so easily available, and mines therefore so easy to open, that monopolistic price fixing was not feasible. True, prices would be raised to higher levels by the sales agency, but "the fact that the correction of abuses may tend to stabilize a business, or to produce fairer price levels, does not

28. Rondal C. Blankenship, *Appalachian Coals, Incorporated: A Bituminous Coal Producers' Marketing Agency*, unpublished master's thesis, West Virginia University, Morgantown, 1949, p. 28.

29. *U.S. v. Appalachian Coals, Inc.*, 1 F. Supp. 339 (W.D. Va. 1932).

30. *Appalachian Coals, Inc., v. U.S.*, 288 U.S. 344 (1933).

mean that the abuses should go uncorrected or that cooperative endeavor to correct them necessarily constitutes an unreasonable restraint of trade." [31] Moreover, the defendants included only 52 per cent of the producers and 74 per cent of the output in their southern high-volatile territory, or 12 per cent of total output east of the Mississippi.

The promoters of the plan had in fact tried to include at least 70 per cent of regional production so that the agency would not be ineffective, but less than 80 per cent so as to escape a charge of monopoly. Evidently the 74 per cent achieved was just right for them. More important in saving the plan legally — but also in making it ineffective as to its main purpose — was the fact that southern high-volatile coal competed in its markets with coal from other areas.

3. The defendants had understood that a merger would not be illegal, but had preferred to keep their independence (except in selling) by forming an agency instead. Contrary to a series of past decisions,[32] this Court did not feel that a merger was necessarily the right approach and cooperation wrong, or that elimination of competition among the defendants themselves would condemn their plan.

There was a strong string tied to the decision. Although it dismissed the injunction, the Supreme Court directed the District Court to retain jurisdiction in case the sales agency should in practice unduly restrain trade. Meanwhile the Department of Justice itself remained unconvinced, and it continued to look on sales agencies with suspicion.

The Supreme Court's decision came as a surprise: it is said that nine out of ten lawyers had advised the promoters that their plan was illegal.[33] At first it seemed that the antitrust law had been drastically modified. But the *Socony-Vacuum* decision of 1940 [34] was to make it clear [35] that the earlier condemnation of cooperative activity which had the consequence of fixing prices [36] still held good. Thus only the fact that the Appalachian group "must still meet effective competition

31. *Ibid.*, at 374.

32. Milton Handler, *A Study of the Construction and Enforcement of the Antitrust Laws*, TNEC Monograph 38, 1941, p. 85.

33. Parker, *The Coal Industry*, p. 196; "Coal at a Profit: Island Creek," *Fortune*, March 1938, p. 176.

34. *U.S. v. Socony-Vacuum Oil Co.*, 310 U.S. 150 (1940).

35. See *U.S. v. Aluminum Company of America*, 148 F. 2d 416, 427 (2d Cir. 1945).

36. *U.S. v. Trenton Potteries Co.*, 273 U.S. 392 (1927).

in a fair market and neither seeks nor is able to effect a domination of prices,"[37] together with the notorious distress in coal, won the case.

Coal and the NRA

As soon as Appalachian Coals won its right to exist, it increased the price of slack from 40 cents a ton to 70 cents, and that of better grades by 25 or 30 per cent. Within four months slack was up 162 per cent from the bottom.[38] In these same months, however, there was a revival of confidence and of the speculative spirit in the whole economy, and many commodity prices jumped sharply in the spring of 1933 without the benefit of cooperation. At first the agency's sales lagged behind those of the rest of the coal industry because of its sharp price increases and the fact that it charged a premium of 15 cents a ton, but the loss in sales was soon made up.[39]

Before other districts could create effective sales agencies, the National Recovery Administration emerged as the new hope of this as well as other industries. Appalachian Coals helped formulate the industry's code of fair competition, which became effective in September 1933. The code's chief provision was a declaration that selling below a "fair market price" was an unfair practice. This code occupied more of the administrative attention of NRA than any other. Its effectiveness was limited by the operators' insistence on decentralization and their reluctance to concede power to the government. The five Divisional Code Authorities were largely autonomous. Eventually production quotas and minimum prices were established by districts, and they are said by those concerned to have had some influence.

A much more significant effect of NRA was in the protection given to unionization by the act's Section 7a. John L. Lewis was influential in preventing this section from being struck out of the law. A whirlwind organizing campaign followed, and in April 1934 the United Mine Workers secured a collective agreement which included southern mines for the first time and raised wages while reducing the work day from 8 hours to 7 hours. The NRA permitted a rise in prices in

37. 288 U.S., at 374, cited in *Report of the Attorney General's National Committee to Study the Antitrust Laws*, 1955, p. 23.

38. *Fortune*, March 1938, p. 176.

39. *Ibid.;* Parker, *The Coal Industry*, p. 171.

order to cover the cost increase — which the operators also met by stepping up the rate of mechanization.[40]

During the NRA period one antitrust action was brought. The Federal Trade Commission enjoined a coal dealers' association from boycotting producers and wholesalers who sold to depression-born "irregular" or snowbird coal dealers not permanently engaged in the business and lacking adequate storage facilities. The defense that these activities were in harmony with the code was overruled by the Eighth Circuit Court of Appeals.[41]

The Two "Guffey Acts"

Legislation applying the principles of the NRA specifically to bituminous coal was already under discussion when NRA expired. The Guffey-Snyder "Bituminous Coal Conservation Act," passed in 1935 under pressure from the United Mine Workers, contained no reference to conservation measures, but set up procedures for fixing prices and for recognition of unions and wage agreements. The act was enjoined at once by suits filed to test its constitutionality, which were decided by the Supreme Court in May 1936.[42] The Court declared, with Justice Sutherland as spokesman, that regulation of labor conditions in production went beyond the powers of Congress, even though the product was later sold in interstate commerce. Without passing on the price-fixing part of the statute, the opinion ruled it inseparable from the labor-regulating part, since the two were intended to operate together for the common purpose of stabilizing the industry.

Chief Justice Hughes, who wrote a concurring opinion, stated that he would have deferred to the statute's declaration that its provisions were separable and would have ruled out only the labor provisions. Justice Cardozo, speaking for a three-man minority, declined to comment on the labor provisions as long as the case could be settled on a narrower basis: that the coal companies should pay their tax, accept the price-fixing provisions as valid, and sue later if and when a schedule of wages and hours was imposed upon them against their will. Had the Court majority taken this view that "the complainants have

40. Waldo E. Fisher, *Economic Consequences of the Seven-Hour Day and Wage Changes in the Bituminous Coal Industry*, Wharton School of Finance and Commerce Industrial Research Study No. 32, University of Pennsylvania Press, Philadelphia, 1939, pp. 94–100.

41. *FTC v. Wallace*, 75 F. 2d 733 (8th Cir. 1935).

42. *Carter v. Carter Coal Co.*, 298 U.S. 238 (1936).

been crying before they are really hurt,"[43] the machinery of the act would have been put laboriously into operation and then invalidated after a second series of suits. As it was, the problem was thrown back to Congress at once.

In its next session, Congress passed the Guffey-Vinson "Bituminous Coal Act" of 1937, which merely renewed the price section of the other statute. The primary aim of this section, as understood by supporters of both laws, was to enable operators to pay good wages.[44] The constitutionality of the new law was affirmed by the Supreme Court in 1940 in a case brought by an Arkansas company which objected, among other things, to having its coal classified as bituminous.[45] Justice Douglas rested his opinion on the fact that the constitutional power to regulate interstate commerce must include the power to set prices directly or through an administrative agency (although not by giving the industry self-regulatory powers). He pointed out that none of the three opinions in the previous *Carter* case had denied this. Justice McReynolds alone of the two remaining members of the 1936 majority dissented.

Bituminous Coal under Federal Regulation

It is claimed that the 1937 act eventually brought in no less than 16,000 operators as code members, under the whip of a 19½ per cent tax on sales of nonmembers. Captive mines were exempted by court decision,[46] over the objections of the National Bituminous Coal Commission. This body was set up with seven members, two of whom were to be former operators and two former miners. Activities under its auspices were exempt from the antitrust laws. The law forbade thirteen specific unfair practices, such as misrepresentation and discrimination. It approved sales agencies in principle. It contained no restrictions on either production or new investment. An interesting innovation was a "Consumers' Counsel," who was independent of the Commission. Although one investigation has found that the Counsel made useful studies and filed needed protests,[47] creation of such an office without

43. *Ibid.*, at 341, dissent of Justice Cardozo.

44. TNEC Monograph 32, p. 271.

45. *Sunshine Anthracite Coal Co. v. Adkins*, 310 U.S. 381 (1940).

46. *Consolidated Indiana Coal Co. v. National Bituminous Coal Commission*, 103 F. 2d 124 (7th Cir. 1939).

47. Waldo E. Fisher and Charles M. James, *Minimum Price Fixing in the Bituminous Coal Industry*, Conference on Price Research Study No. 5, National Bureau of Economic Research, Princeton University Press, Princeton, 1955, pp. 341–42.

positive power hardly takes away the sting to consumers of a law designed to raise prices. The Counsel's view, difficult to apply in practice, was that prices should be just equal to "cost." He feared that lower prices "would wreck the industry," but felt that higher ones would exploit the consumer.[48]

In December 1937 the business recession then in progress induced the Commission to make its first price schedules effective without delay; but omission of the prescribed formal procedure caused them to be enjoined by the courts. A long series of public hearings now began. Before these had been completed, new legislation abolished the Commission and transferred its functions, on July 1, 1939, to a Bituminous Coal Division at the Interior Department, thus eliminating the potential majority control by special interests which many had criticized.[49] By October 1, 1940, all the preparatory steps had been completed, and the minimum price schedules went into effect.

Upon its expiration in April 1941 the law was extended, partly because it had had an effective life of only half a year. In August 1943 it was allowed to expire. Revival of demand for coal had made price floors superfluous, and there was now a "Solid Fuels Administration for War." The schedules of minimum prices had already been used by the Office of Price Administration in May 1942 as the basis of price ceilings — a purpose opposite to that originally intended.

Procedure in Fixing Prices

The procedure laid down by the statute for fixing minimum price schedules is significant for its very length and complexity: [50]

1. Each producer was to report every spot order and contract and all cost data to one of the 22 (originally 23) district statistical bureaus set up by the Bituminous Coal Commission. Each of 22 district boards (containing from two to sixteen operators and one union representative) was then to calculate the weighted average cost of production plus "reasonable costs of selling" per ton in 1936, with an adjustment for any

48. Consumers' Counsel report, quoted in Ralph Hillis Baker, *The National Bituminous Coal Commission: Administration of the Bituminous Coal Act, 1937–1941*, Johns Hopkins University Studies in Historical and Political Science, Series 59, No. 3, Johns Hopkins Press, Baltimore, 1941, p. 252.

49. Fisher and James, *Minimum Price Fixing in the Bituminous Coal Industry*, p. 340; Baker, *The National Bituminous Coal Commission*, p. 125.

50. Section 4, Part II, of Public Law 48, 75th Cong., 1st sess., reprinted in Fisher and James, *Minimum Price Fixing in the Bituminous Coal Industry*, pp. 492–97.

later change in important cost elements. The Commission was to approve or modify these costs and convert them into averages for 9 (originally 10) "minimum price areas" into which the districts were combined.

2. Each district board was to recommend f.o.b. mine prices for its district for all kinds, qualities and sizes of coal. These prices should not only (a) be "equal as nearly as may be" to the weighted average costs, but should also (b) "reflect, as nearly as possible, the relative market value of the various kinds, qualities and sizes," (c) be "just and equitable as between producers," and (d) "have due regard to the interests of the consuming public." The boards were also to propose marketing regulations.

3. The Commission itself was to approve, disapprove or modify these proposals.

4. The district boards were to "coordinate in common consuming market areas" these prices and regulations, or, if they could not agree (as was actually to happen), the Commission was to do it. Such prices were to be (a) equitable between districts; (b) equal "as nearly as possible" to "relative market values"; (c) related to "values as to uses, seasonal demand, transportation methods and charges" and the competition of other fuels; (d) consistent with "existing fair competitive opportunities"; and, at the same time, (e) such as to make the average return for the minimum price area equal to the weighted average cost as found under step 1.

5. The Commission was to approve or modify these "coordinated" prices, after holding hearings if any single producer, any state or local government, or the Consumers' Counsel expressed dissatisfaction. Revision was required whenever costs in any minimum price area changed by 2 cents a ton (i.e., by approximately half of one per cent).

Inconsistent Criteria and Cumbersome Procedure

It would have called for a magician to obey all of these injunctions at once — to find a price high enough to cover cost in a period of low sales and yet low enough to compete with oil and gas; to follow "relative market value" and yet lift up to average cost the price of those coals which had suffered from price cutting; or to do justice to producers and yet give "due regard" to consumers.

It might be argued that such inconsistencies could be ironed out in a more carefully drawn statute; but this is not so. The pressures of the market bring about a practical adjustment between the quotations at different places, between the prices of competing commodities, between those of different brands of coal, and between gains of producers and consumers. This practical adjustment is one that permits the maximum transactions to occur, but this is its only claim to justice or equity. There is no way to express in a statute or regulation any wholly just and equitable reconciliation of the conflicting claims of producers and consumers. Nor is there any reason to believe that the drafters of the statute were unaware of the inconsistencies that they were handing over to the new agency. Its staff needed all the "competence, persistence and public service" attributed to it by its historians.[51]

The greatest single complexity in the price fixing resulted from the "coordination" of prices in common consuming markets. The Coal Commission and its successor agency, the Bituminous Coal Division, compiled and indexed over one million freight rates for coal, from each point of origin to each point of destination named in the freight rate structure.[52] It consolidated the points of destination into "only" 157, later 193, common consuming markets. The magician's trick of fitting average f.o.b. mine prices to cost and yet making destination prices equal was solved by subtracting from the destination price the freight from each mine that shipped into the market. A mine would thereby receive a separate permissible f.o.b. price on identical coal for each market into which it shipped. For example, the "Ocean" mine of the Pittsburgh Coal Company in Allegheny County had a table of 120 minimum prices (at least half of which duplicated others, however), to provide for sale of fifteen sizes and qualities into eight markets which had their own freight rate structures. The widest percentage range of the f.o.b. prices allowed to this mine for any one grade was from $1.65 to $2.05 a ton.[53]

Insofar as this procedure fulfilled its purpose, it put prices up but without forcing any mine out of any of its previous markets. If a mine had a high freight rate to a market, it was allowed a low f.o.b. price to offset it. "Existing fair competitive opportunities" were thus maintained, and by the same token mines were discouraged from trying to win new markets.[54]

51. *Ibid.*, p. 402.

52. *Ibid.*, p. 380.

53. *Ibid.*, p. 188.

54. Eugene V. Rostow, "Bituminous Coal and the Public Interest," *Yale Law Journal*, February 1941, p. 578.

Besides the inconsistencies and freezing of marketing patterns, the most obvious feature of this procedure was its cumbersomeness. This, commentators have pointed out, is inherent in regulating so complex an industry as coal.[55] Any price fixing by government must rely on lengthy hearings and detailed regulations if the legal rights of the persons involved are to be protected.[56] One review of the act found its "most serious defect" to be "the unresponsive lag between changes in market conditions and the adjustment of prices to meet them, which seems to be imposed by the cumbersome procedural provisions of the act." [57] Another review contrasted the $20 million cost of the whole price-fixing procedure with the $3 million deficit (before income taxes) reported by the industry to the Treasury the year before the act was passed, and concluded that a judiciously distributed subsidy might have done more good.[58] Long after the act had expired, coal operators recalled as a nightmare the ultimate rigid structure of 400,000 prices which the Bituminous Coal Division created.

Effect on Prices

The actual effect on prices was slight, since the price floors were in effect only for two months in the winter of 1937–38 and during the period after October 1940. The national average of the mine-run wholesale price showed a temporary 3 per cent increase in January 1938 (a time when most large consumers were out of the market [59]) and a permanent 3 per cent increase (from almost exactly the same level as in 1937–38) in October 1940.[60] These advances no doubt reflect the establishment of the price floors.

Coal executives agree today that, although the price floors may have helped marginal companies to a slight extent, prices continued throughout to be determined basically by market forces. This became quite clear as early as the spring of 1941, when spot prices were above the official minima for nearly all quotations. In May of that year rising demand caused published prices to start a steady, month-by-

55. Baker, *The National Bituminous Coal Commission*, p. 324.

56. Leverett S. Lyon and Victor Abramson, *Government and Economic Life*, Brookings Institution, Washington, 1940, Vol. 2, p. 981.

57. TNEC Monograph 32, p. 316.

58. Rostow, "Bituminous Coal and the Public Interest," p. 576.

59. Frank G. Smith, "The Attempted Stabilization of the Bituminous Coal Industry," *Harvard Business Review*, Winter 1939, p. 188.

60. *Survey of Current Business.*

month advance which continued until the over-all price freeze of 1943.

With so many mines and so many prices, a vast enforcement problem loomed in 1941. The best hope of securing compliance was through voluntary cooperation,[61] but cooperation could hardly be expected in an industry whose tendency to engage in cutthroat competition had made such a law necessary in the first place. Violation complaints came in at the rate of 114 a month during that year, and from October 1940 through August 1943, 394 violation orders were issued or penalties imposed. Many complaints could not be acted on because of a shortage of compliance attorneys.[62] Yet the temptation to violate was relatively weak in these months because of the rising trend of market prices. One hesitates to guess how many compliance attorneys might have been needed in a period of price cutting such as the Coal Act envisaged.

Doubtful Economic Principles

Basic economic criticisms have been made of the central principle that minimum prices should approximate the weighted average cost of the mines in each district. As contrasted with the operation of a free market, this would have the following results:

1. The costs used would be, at best, those of the year before, whereas in the free market sale prices are influenced by current and future estimated costs. In actuality, the 1940 prices rested on "costs of 1936 as adjusted to the actual costs of 1937, and with regard to certain known tax and other changes effective since then." [63] The act was thus "backward-looking"; it did not work to encourage efficiency, but to preserve past relationships.[64] A strong expression of this criticism is the statement in *Fortune:* "By underwriting present mining costs, a new Guffey Act would destroy the urgent need to throw out old-fashioned mining methods." [65]

2. The price-fixing procedure would have held to its cost principle at times when the free market would depart from costs. It would mean declining prices in times of rising demand, because at such times over-

61. TNEC Monograph 32, p. 313.

62. Fisher and James, *Minimum Price Fixing in the Bituminous Coal Industry*, pp. 293–95.

63. TNEC Monograph 32, p. 318.

64. Donald H. Wallace, "A Critical Review of Some Instances of Government Price Control," Part 4 of TNEC Monograph 32, pp. 465–66.

65. "Continuous Coal Mining," *Fortune*, June 1950, p. 127.

head costs are lower per unit, and it would mean rising prices when demand was slumping, because at lower levels of operation overhead costs would be higher. This would intensify any rise in demand by putting prices down, and intensify any slump by putting them up. This paradox would be heightened by the influence on consumption of the higher prices at which the statute aimed. If sales of coal were to fall off, mines would operate at less than capacity, and the rise in their overhead costs would logically call for still higher prices and a further fall in sales.[66]

3. With regard to the varying effects of the price floor on different classes of producers, the hope was held that inefficient mines, unable to make a profit at the weighted average cost of the industry, would be forced out of business. Their elimination would cause the average cost (which would now be that of the remaining producers) to decline, thus forcing out a new layer of inefficient companies. Those who had faith in the machinery of price fixing believed it would prove to be less violent and more gradual than the ruthless process of competition.[67] However, it would not have removed the two most important obstacles to the smooth working of the elimination process in coal: (1) the "hanging on" of mines hoping for a revival of demand, and (2) sale of a bankrupt company at a price which would give the successor low capital costs with which to begin operations. The reasoning on this elimination of the inefficient is purely hypothetical in any case, with little relation to what could or would have been done in coal.[68] The intention, after all, was to hold prices up, not to force them down.

Later Views on the Act

The second Guffey Act, despite the number of years it was in operation, was thus unable to get its price floors into effect in time to show what they would have accomplished in a period of downward pressures on the market. An over-all judgment must therefore be based largely on theoretical considerations.[69]

66. TNEC Monograph 32, pp. 317 (Gordon and Webb), 467 (Wallace); Fisher and James, *Minimum Price Fixing in the Bituminous Coal Industry*, pp. 337–38.

67. Smith, "The Attempted Stabilization of the Bituminous Coal Industry," p. 188; Norman H. Leonard, "The Bituminous Coal Industry," Chap. 2 in Walter Adams, ed., *The Structure of American Industry*, Macmillan, New York, 1950, pp. 54–55, 56–57.

68. Fisher and James, *Minimum Price Fixing in the Bituminous Coal Industry*, pp. 406–07.

69. Compare Rostow, "Bituminous Coal and the Public Interest," pp. 543–94, Walton H. Hamilton, "Coal and the Economy — a Demurrer," pp. 595–612, and Rostow, "Joinder in Demurrer," pp. 613–20, in *Yale Law Journal*, February 1942.

After careful study of the 1937–43 experience, Waldo E. Fisher and Charles M. James concluded that minimum price fixing would, on balance, (1) give consumers better coal and more security from strikes as offsets to the higher prices they would pay, (2) give workers better pay and shorter hours, and (3) give investors better profits — but at the same time would (4) increase the industry's overcapacity and reduce demand.[70] Their final conclusion, therefore, was adverse: price fixing might prove to be "curing the symptoms while weakening the patient's ability to rally from his fundamental disease." [71]

The whole experience has also served frequently as a case study for textbooks on the relation of government to business, which generally have arrived at adverse judgments.[72] One commentator believes that the chief practical effect of the NRA and the two control laws was to create an atmosphere among mine operators favorable to the acceptance of collective bargaining.[73]

Interviews and correspondence with twelve mine operators during the present study disclosed only two who felt that their companies, which had favored the stabilization experiment of the 1930s, would favor it again if the same conditions reappeared. There was a third who advocated, in place of price fixing, a production control program of the type enjoyed by burley tobacco raisers. If coal demand were to collapse again, however, some of the hostile opinions might well change. Thus a poll of operators taken by *Coal Age* in January 1941 still showed 73.8 per cent favoring extension of the act.[74] It is said by one authority that high-cost producers were the ones that on the whole favored extension.[75] Another possibility which has been suggested is that a renewed decline in the union's membership might finally threaten so to weaken its bargaining ability that it would demand a new cartelization of the industry.[76]

70. Fisher and James, *Minimum Price Fixing in the Bituminous Coal Industry*, p. 440.

71. *Ibid.*, p. 444.

72. Compare Melvin Anshen and Francis D. Wormuth, *Private Enterprise and Public Policy*, Macmillan, New York, 1954, p. 694; Clair Wilcox, *Public Policies toward Business*, Irwin, Homewood (Ill.), 1955, pp. 470–71.

73. Schmookler, "The Bituminous Coal Industry," p. 103.

74. Baker, *The National Bituminous Coal Commission*, p. 318.

75. *Ibid.*, p. 294.

76. Morton S. Baratz, *The Union and the Coal Industry*, Yale University Press, New Haven, 1955, p. 143.

Early in 1950, at a time of low demand, Senator Harley M. Kilgore of West Virginia introduced a bill to revive price fixing by commission, but sales picked up and the matter was forgotten.[77]

Later History of the Sales Agencies

The NRA, the Coal Commission and the Bituminous Coal Division had successively taken over the stabilizing function for which the coal sales agencies were originally planned. During the life of NRA, a handful of agencies (such as Northern Coals, Inc., and Hocking Coals, Inc.) were in operation but had little influence. Under the first Guffey Act the agencies did little, although Alabama Coals made a futile effort to win some sort of official endorsement. By 1936 Appalachian Coals itself was handling only 52 per cent of the output of its district as against 74 per cent formerly, and by then or a little later had declined from 147 members to 80 and from 250 separate mines to 150.[78] The Coal Act of 1937 approved sales agencies provided they obeyed the Commission's regulations and did not "unreasonably restrict the supply of coal," charge more than "fair and reasonable prices" or "operate against the public interest." Although sixteen agencies asked for such approval, which was freely given, little seems to have been accomplished in practice. In 1939 only three, accounting for 20 per cent of the country's production, were in actual operation, and these three had shown a great decline in membership since 1937.[79] They were handicapped by the fact that, with government in control, they had lost their "ability to move independently and shift prices rapidly to cope with the pace of competition."[80] In July 1941 the Bituminous Coal Division itself initiated new regulations curbing sales agency powers further, but the regulations moved through the proper channels too slowly ever to reach final approval.[81]

When the Division's life terminated in August 1943, the agencies consulted the Department of Justice concerning their status. Assistant Attorney General Tom Clark replied that it "might not be objectionable" for one agency to stabilize the price of the coal its members

77. *Business Week*, April 15, 1950, pp. 114–15.

78. Parker, *The Coal Industry*, p. 172.

79. TNEC Monograph 32, p. 323; Lyon and Abramson, *Government and Economic Life*, pp. 980–81.

80. *Fortune*, March 1938, p. 176.

81. Howard W. Vesey, "Marketing Agencies for Producers of Natural Resource Products," *Mining Congress Journal*, November 1944, p. 34.

produced, but that the same action by each of the existing fourteen agencies would result in a stable and uniform price for the industry as a whole, and thus violate the Sherman Act.[82] From this point of view, the Supreme Court in 1933 had said little more than this: "If your agency gets past the practical obstacles and controls its members as well as a merger could do, it may stabilize their selling prices — provided it controls so little of the industry that it has no significant influence. It must choose between being ineffective with regard to price cutting and being illegal." Nevertheless, as General Donovan pointed out twenty-two years after his Supreme Court victory, "the wide area of permissible action presents a blueprint that few industries in this country possess." [83]

Appalachian Coals Today

All the other sales agencies had vanished by the end of 1943, but Appalachian Coals continues in operation today. Its members do their own selling, although at a basic price set at monthly meetings plus or minus established differentials for particular coals. The agency is said to have improved the classification of coals, conducted some cooperative advertising, checked certain trade practices like pyramiding and selling coal on consignment, and offered information, engineering and expert marketing services to its members, most of whom are small producers.[84]

Its spokesmen claim that Appalachian Coals has secured for its members at least 25 cents a ton more on 600 million tons of coal sold in twenty-one years.[85] This is chiefly attributed to the greater confidence buyers have in the product its members offer. If this gain had been achieved for the whole industry, it would have doubled total industry profits in a "fair" year like 1951 (see Table 45). Nine mine operators questioned about the present role of Appalachian Coals felt that it serves a useful function and could be a model for other districts. As to any possible antitrust aspects, they agreed (regretfully)

82. Letter of Assistant Attorney General Tom Clark to president of Appalachian Coals, Inc., August 21, 1943, quoted in *ibid.*, p. 35.

83. William J. Donovan, in "Mass Power for Better Marketing: 21 Years of ACI Experience," *Coal Age*, April 1955, p. 57.

84. See R. E. Howe, "The Coal Marketing Agency," *Journal of Marketing*, July 1945, pp. 35–41.

85. James D. Francis, president of Powellton Coal Co., in *Coal Age*, April 1955, p. 54.

that agencies can do little to prevent price cutting even in their own territories, much less over a broader area.

The Union's Three-Day Week Experiment

After 1938, demand for coal increased rapidly, and by 1947 and 1948 both production and profits were at an all-time high. Then suddenly demand slipped off again, at first because of a revival of European coal production in 1948. The United Mine Workers, at its convention that October, discussed possible action to reduce output and stabilize prices. It is reported that John L. Lewis originally planned a joint union-management board that would fix the weekly output justified by current demand at prevailing prices and assign to each mine its corresponding quota. This would have been similar to the anthracite control plan operating in Pennsylvania since 1940, but it could not be arranged. Many operators feared both union domination and the Sherman Act, and the captive mines that could use their entire production each week were adamant in their opposition.

In 1949 the union chief took the initiative himself. When the miners' contract expired in June, he did not negotiate a renewal, but simply announced a three-day week for union members — Monday, Tuesday and Wednesday for all mines east of the Mississippi. Thereby he automatically reduced the output of these mines from early July to mid-September 1949, and again (after an intervening strike) from the beginning of December until early in the following March. The formal three-day week was then dropped.

The short work week might possibly have been held illegal under the Sherman Act had it been tested in the courts, but the antitrust authorities took no action. A member of the President's Council of Economic Advisers warned that this failure to act might become a precedent opening the antitrust laws to violation with impunity in other industries.[86] The General Counsel of the National Labor Relations Board charged that the edict was an unfair labor practice, but the Board itself held that in the absence of a contract the union had the right to set the working week. Some observers felt that employers could normally be counted on to resist union actions which seemed illegal, but wondered if they would do so if they benefited from them.

86. John D. Clark, in *Study of Monopoly Power,* Hearings before Subcommittee on Study of Monopoly Power, House Judiciary Committee, 81st Cong., 1st sess., 1949, Serial 14, Part 1, p. 112.

Indeed, some of the employers who denounced the three-day week are said to have admitted their own preference for a shorter work week as against large-scale layoffs, much as they disliked having the union impose the action on them.[87]

Critics of the Union's Plan

The wisdom of the three-day week was debated at length in Senate Hearings entitled: *To Protect Trade and Commerce against Unreasonable Restraints by Labor Organizations.*[88] Critics argued that this weekly opening and shutting of mines resulted in waste of coal and greater hazards, an increase in accidents and electrical breakdowns, and a higher overhead cost per ton of coal.[89] The plan, both by dramatizing the union's power and by hampering a regular schedule of operations, was said to reduce the possibility of raising new capital or borrowing from the banks, and indeed to lessen management's own interest in installing technological improvements.[90]

An important aspect of the scheme was its varying impact on different sorts of companies. Those whose sales had dropped off anyhow liked the plan, although few if any would have let this be known publicly. The largest and most efficient companies, which had sold on long-term contracts and scheduled their work with the expectation of being the last to close down, stated openly their dislike of the plan. Although their production in 1949 dropped less than that of smaller companies,[91] they might have been hurt had the plan lasted long enough. In fact, some of them believed the union was trying to force a redistribution of sales between strong and weak companies by preventing the former from fulfilling their contracts, and were worried lest this succeed on its next trial. Captive mines also, many of which operate efficiently and regularly over a full working week, might have

87. Compare "Coal vs. the People," *Fortune*, October 1949, p. 71; *U.S. News & World Report*, April 14, 1950, pp. 43–45.

88. Hearings before a Subcommittee of the Senate Judiciary Committee, 81st Cong., 2d sess., 1950.

89. Sources of the criticisms are, respectively, Report of Senate Banking and Currency Committee, cited in memorandum by Gustav Peck, *ibid.*, p. 14; Earl B. Maize, safety director of National Coal Ass'n., *ibid.*, pp. 308–09; and John A. Wolfe, president of South Chicago Coal and Dock Co., *ibid.*, p. 86.

90. George H. Love, in *The Economic Power of Labor Organizations*, Hearings before a Subcommittee of the Senate Banking and Currency Committee, 81st Cong., 1st sess., 1950, p. 15.

91. Calculated from National Coal Ass'n., *Bituminous Coal Annual*, 1953, Washington, p. 57.

been forced to buy coal (an outcome which, according to rumor, was among the union's purposes [92]). In brief, the three-day week put a premium on inefficiency by refusing to let a mine that could sell more coal produce it.

In the contract negotiations of 1952 and 1953 the union president showed his imagination again in suggesting new plans, but none was pushed to a conclusion.[93] One was a time-and-a-half penalty wage rate to go into effect on the fourth day's work within a week, followed by double time on the fifth day. Another was a large wage increase for mines making the most money, a small increase for those making less, and none at all for the marginal mines — at least until, with labor costs thus held down, they graduated into the profit-making class. The union evidently traded its control scheme for a wage increase.[94]

The Antitrust Laws and Coal Today

In an industry with so many operating units, price-fixing combinations are likely to recur from time to time. Coal wholesalers or dealers were sued under the Sherman Act in 1944, 1946, 1948 and 1953.[95] As of 1956, the defendants had been cleared by a jury in the first case and had pleaded *nolo contendere* and paid fines in the second and third.

There are two points of view in the industry on the antitrust laws as a whole. The more common one can be expressed as follows: "They have no influence, and I have no complaint against them." The other is that they do harm by throwing legal doubts on the mergers and effective cooperative marketing that would help set the industry on its feet.

Competitive Status

Trend of Concentration

Figures on the share of bituminous coal output accounted for by the 300 largest companies in years past are given by one writer as follows: 71 per cent in 1895, 67 per cent in 1905, 57 per cent in 1920 (when so

92. *New York Times*, August 26, 1952, p. 22.

93. *Ibid.*, September 16, 1952, pp. 1, 20; *Business Week*, September 13, 1952, p. 158; July 4, 1953, pp. 104–05; October 17, 1953, p. 173.

94. Charles Killingsworth, public member of the U.S. Wage Stabilization Board, quoted in Baratz, *The Union and the Coal Industry*, p. 141, note 13.

95. *U.S. v. Spokane Fuel Dealers Credit Ass'n.*, 55 F. Supp. 387 (E.D. Wash. 1944); *U.S. v. MacLeod Bureau*, Cr. 17512 (D. Mass. 1946); *U.S. v. Greater Kansas City Retail Coal Merchants Ass'n.*, Cr. 17328 (W.D. Mo. 1948); *U.S. v. Akin-Denison Co.*, Cr. 53–96–F (D. Mass. 1953).

TABLE 46

BITUMINOUS COAL: PERCENTAGE SHARE OF LARGEST COMPANIES IN TOTAL OUTPUT, 1941–55

Year	Largest Company	Ten Largest Companies	Twenty-five Largest Companies
1941	5.6	21.4	33.4
1946	4.6	20.3	31.3
1951	5.3	24.1	37.0
1955	6.0	29.1	43.4

Sources: National Coal Ass'n., *Bituminous Coal Annual*, 1953, Washington, p. 57; *Coal Production in the United States*, 1955, pamphlet compiled by Keystone Coal Buyers Manual, McGraw-Hill, New York, pp. 8–11. Figures for 1955 include tonnages of smaller firms acquired by merger on or before January 1, 1956.

many small mines were operating in the postwar boom), and 67 per cent again in 1930.[96] In 1950 and 1955 the 300 largest companies had 61 and 72 per cent of total output, respectively, and the 300 largest "groups" ("based on apparent operating affiliations") had 76 and 81 per cent.[97] A trend toward concentration is clearly evident only for the most recent period.

A sharp step-up in the size of mines (as distinguished from companies) has been observable since World War II, owing to the increasing economies offered by mechanization.[98] In 1945 the fifty largest mines accounted for 6.7 per cent of total output and in 1955 for 18.9 per cent. Fifteen of the 1955 group had been opened in 1946 or later.[99]

The share of the largest single producer (United States Steel Corporation before 1951 and Pittsburgh Consolidation Coal Company since) increased from 5.6 to 6.0 per cent between 1941 and 1955. With the acquisition of Pocahontas Fuel Company in 1956 adding a low-volatile business to its high-volatile one, Pittsburgh Consolidation appeared likely to expand its share to 7.8 per cent if mine outputs remained proportionate. Between 1941 and 1955 the share of the ten largest firms increased from 21.4 to 29.1 per cent, and that of the twenty-five largest from 33.4 to 43.4 per cent. (See Table 46.) Announcements of consolidations of several companies in 1955 and early

96. Parker, *The Coal Industry*, p. 12.

97. Calculated from *Coal Production in the United States*, 1950, page facing p. 2; 1955, p.5.

98. *Journal of Commerce*, May 20, 1955, p. 1. See also "Mechanisation in Coal Mines," *The Economist*, London, July 24, 1954, pp. 284–85.

99. *Coal Age*, April 1956, p. 67.

1956 made it appear that a real merger movement was coming into full swing in the bituminous coal industry.

The Pittsburgh Consolidation Coal Merger

Since its formation in November 1945 the Pittsburgh Consolidation Coal Company has been the unquestioned leader of the industry. Over the period 1915–45 the Pittsburgh Coal Company, a "Mellon enterprise," had mined 100 million tons of high-grade coal at a net loss of $7.5 million.[100] Between 1925 and 1940 its loss, plus that of another big producer, the Consolidation Coal Company, is reported to have amounted to $100 million — or one third of the industry's total loss.[101] M. A. Hanna Company (manager of iron, coal and Great Lakes shipping operations, with big investment interests in the steel industry) combined the two properties with the intention of achieving the size and resources necessary to introduce modern methods of management in the coal industry.

Pittsburgh Consolidation exemplifies the advantages of size for planning, modernization, distribution and research. In the corporation's own opinion, they would be likely to apply to other mergers as well, such as those which built the Peabody Coal Company and the Island Creek Coal Company to their present size.

Planning. Unprofitable properties were sold, and carefully selected strip coal land and underground reserves were bought. Some observers consider ability to close down high-cost mines one of the chief advantages of merging, and in this connection the saving in transportation by shipping to a market from the nearest mine is a factor.

Modernization. The corporation increased man-day output sharply through mechanization (including the stepping up of machine loading from 34 per cent to almost 100 per cent), and through greater emphasis on strip mining (accompanied by development of more powerful equipment for this operation). Its financial resources enabled it to take a leading part in the industry-wide mechanization movement.

Distribution. The corporation was able to offer a greater variety of coals, to emphasize sale to big customers on long-term contracts, to conduct a scientific study of markets, and to command the financial resources necessary to reduce the temptation to and danger from competitive price cutting.

100. *Business Week,* June 9, 1956, p. 142.

101. "Coal: The 'Pitt Consol' Adventure," *Fortune,* July 1947, p. 101.

Research. Pittsburgh Consolidation launched the first big research and development program of any single coal company. The need for large financial resources to take on the associated risks may be deduced from its admission in 1950 that it had "made a few false starts here and there" in its modernization program, and that up to date it had "gained little except information" from its research and development program.[102] Thus its cooperative experiment with Standard Oil of New Jersey in making gasoline from coal was abandoned after costing several million dollars.[103] By 1955, however, other aspects of its research were beginning to pay off.[104]

Size and Profits

The available statistics are consistent with the thesis that large size in this industry tends to be associated with profitability. Between 1946 and 1952 Pittsburgh Consolidation earned after income tax an annual average of 49 cents on each ton of coal it produced or sold on behalf of others, whereas the coal industry as a whole earned only an estimated 36 cents on its production.[105] Part of this difference may, it is true, have been due to the better coal seams of the big company. Since 1952 these figures have not been published for the industry as a whole, but Pittsburgh Consolidation's profits have continued high.

A tabulation of bituminous coal and lignite corporations, ranked according to size of assets, shows for 1947, a prosperous year, and 1949, a depressed year, an almost consistent upward progression by asset class in the percentage of companies reporting a net income. The progression in net income as a percentage of sales for 1947, 1949 and 1952 is not quite so consistent, but shows the same general trend. (See Table 47.)

Using similar evidence, the consulting economist of the National Coal Association concluded the summary of his pamphlet entitled *More Capital Equipment: Coal's Foremost Economic Need* with the suggestion: ". . . smaller companies should consider combining their resources, since larger corporations have, in general, been more profit-

102. Pittsburgh Consolidation Coal Co., *Annual Report and 5-Year Review*, 1950, pp. 8, 12.

103. *Business Week*, January 7, 1950, p. 26.

104. Pittsburgh Consolidation Coal Co., *Annual Report and Ten-Year Review*, 1955, pp. 7–8.

105. *Ibid.*, pp. 12–13; industry profits for both corporations and private firms from *Survey of Current Business*, National Income editions.

TABLE 47

BITUMINOUS COAL: CORPORATION PROFITS, 1947–52

Lower Limit of Asset Class	Per Cent with Net Income		Net Income as Per Cent of Gross Income		
	1947	1949	1947	1949	1952
(Millions)					
$ 0	54	32	.7	−5.7	−7.1
50	73	40	4.8	−4.0	− .1
100	86	55	8.0	.3	−1.1
250	88	67	10.0	2.1	− .2
500	96	71	11.4	3.7	.6
1,000	95	80	12.0	5.8	3.2
5,000	96	84	14.3	8.4	3.6
10,000	97	94	9.8	6.2	3.8
50,000	—	—	—	—	a
100,000	100	100	25.9	10.5	6.6

Source: Calculated from U.S. Bureau of Internal Revenue, *Statistics of Income* (Part 2), 1947, pp. 264–65; 1949, pp. 222–23; 1952, p. 78. The same general relationships would be shown if the table were expanded to include 1946, 1948, 1950 and 1951.

a. Less than 0.05.

able." [106] Finally, the chief of the United Mine Workers is reported to hold the opinion that "These great combines now being formed in the industry are able to save enormous sums of money. That is modern operation." [107]

Obstacles to Mergers

Some advantages obtainable through mergers in other industries are likely to be missing in coal. It is inherently difficult to manage a corporation whose places of production are scattered and isolated. The attempt to manage many mines has been found to present difficulties like those in centralized management of many firms. Coal cannot economically be shipped as far as more finished products, in view of its high ratio of weight to value, and therefore a corporation with many mines has to operate them with reference to their several markets, on a decentralized basis. A smaller firm, through its greater flexibility, is often able to compete successfully in its particular market.

Many in the industry consider the antitrust laws a major obstacle to mergers. The Pittsburgh-Consolidation merger did receive a "railroad

106. Donald R. G. Cowan, *More Capital Equipment: Coal's Foremost Economic Need*, National Coal Ass'n., Washington, 1948, p. 3.

107. *Journal of Commerce*, October 9, 1956, p. 4.

release" from the Department of Justice — a written statement that the Department saw no reason for intervention and that if such reason did emerge, it would not resort to criminal action. The fact that in every market area each of the two companies had competitors, with whom competition would continue active after the merger, undoubtedly played a major part in securing this negative sort of approval.

The nonlegal obstacles to mergers in coal (quite apart from the question of efficiency) must be accounted far more important than the legal ones. Some of the basic obstacles which are often cited are: [108] (1) the wide distribution of coal lands and of their ownership, and the difficulty in valuing the coal reserves to be merged; (2) the ease of opening a new mine (at least before the present trend toward extreme mechanization), which has made it seem easier to expand in this way than by merging; (3) the bad reputation of the industry as a "prince and pauper," more often the latter, with the consequent difficulty of securing financing; and (4) the fact that the principal stockholders of small coal companies are often working officers as well and do not want to render their own positions superfluous by merging. Illustrative of a changing point of view of the financial world toward coal and coal mergers is the announcement of a large Boston investment company in 1956 that it had put $16.5 million into a half dozen coal enterprises.[109]

Questioning of ten mine operators regarding mergers brought the following comments: one found little value in them; nine saw advantages, and two of these felt that mergers were absolutely necessary to save the industry. Four of the nine emphasized the reduction of price cutting, five the need for large capital to finance research and improvements; several cited both reasons or others in addition. The obstacles were not considered insuperable, although two saw the antitrust laws as offering an obstacle and four mentioned that company executives would fear loss of their positions.

Forms of Collaboration in the Coal Industry

An industry with many small firms presumably needs more cooperation among its members than one in which each company is large enough to be self-sufficient in many ways. In coal, however, inter-

108. See Parker, *The Coal Industry*, pp. 9–11.
109. *Business Week*, June 9, 1956, p. 143.

change of price, cost and statistical information is minor. Personal contacts among executives of the kind that make for harmony of action in other industries are, or have been until recently, few.

In at least one producing district the operators have frequent meetings to discuss market conditions and exchange sales forecasts and statistics, but these are private because of fear of the Sherman Act. The meetings are considered to have two advantages: first, avoidance of price cutting due to ignorance; and, second, development of mutual acquaintanceship and therefore easement of suspicions typical among executives of an industry composed of many small companies. As long as such meetings continue to be suspect under the law, they are not likely to become widespread or effective. The same problem of illegality applies even more clearly to those incidents — which are said to occur sometimes — in which sellers submit identical bids by agreement or divide up bids secretly on an agreed basis.

There are district trade associations, federated in the National Coal Association, which functions in such fields as public relations, market promotion, safety, engineering and traffic. The Association also sponsors Bituminous Coal Research, Inc., an institution supported by more than three hundred coal, railroad and mining equipment companies which conducts research projects in the improvement of mining efficiency and utilization of coal.

There are a handful of other trade organizations of various sorts. One is the American Coal Sales Association, whose executive vice president, W. W. Bayfield, maintains the industry has suffered from the absence of a "hard hitting, industry-wide, sales promotional program." He adds (in a letter):

> I think you will find that architects, design engineers, as well as many consulting engineers, are on the whole poorly informed on modern coal-burning equipment, coal-handling, and ash-handling techniques.

Price Competition

The character of competition in coal is influenced by the buyer's search for the particular types which will serve his purpose; but, when acceptable quality is found, price becomes a dominating influence. Buyers of metallurgical coal state their specifications and compare the offerings of the producers who can meet them. Buyers of steam coal pay close attention to the price per million btu's. Retailers buy on the basis of established quality and compare the prices and reputations of the producers' agents or distributors offering such quality. With the changing characteristics of demand for coal — away from house heating and small industry use, for instance, and toward use by utilities and steel plants — an increasing percentage is being sold on long-term contracts. Thus price cutting is probably becoming less significant than in the past.

Excess capacity, small size of firms, and the nature of the product have been the principal influences making for price competition.

The excess capacity from which the industry usually suffers as a result of ease of entry induces price cutting in an effort to attain full-time operation. The very mechanization of the industry has tended to increase its overcapacity and to stimulate price cutting to keep the machines busy. Idle capacity is usually measured by contrasting the average number of days worked with a theoretical 280-day year.[110] On this basis, operations averaged only 70 per cent of capacity in the five years 1951–55 (Table 45).

Firms are too small for any one of them to feel that its own price policy will have a significant influence on the market. Each hopes that its price cut will move its own product, but not stimulate immediate and widespread retaliation. It is already noticeable that the larger coal companies are less active price cutters than the smaller ones. The individualism and independence typical of coal operators may also promote price cutting.

Coal by its nature lends itself to price cutting, for coal buyers are chiefly industrial firms that are interested only in the energy-producing quality of the fuel per dollar of price. Advertising does little good, and brand preferences are only spasmodic.[111] Competition centers accordingly on price:

> In coal the marginal producer sets the price, and the rest of the industry follows. In coal the concept of competition has been the I'll-sell-it-to-you-cheaper-than-he-will attitude of a bargain basement in bad times.[112]

110. Compare Fisher and James, *Minimum Price Fixing in the Bituminous Coal Industry*, p. 445.

111. See John P. Miller, "The Pricing of Bituminous Coal: Some International Comparisons," Chap. 5 of C. J. Friedrich and Edward S. Mason, eds., *Public Policy*, Vol. 1, Yearbook of the Graduate School of Public Administration, Harvard University, Harvard University Press, Cambridge, 1940, p. 146.

112. "Coal," *Fortune*, March 1947, p. 87.

The demand for coal has generally been held to be inelastic in the short run, since an industrial establishment buying coal for power or a household buying it for heat will hardly stop buying because the price rises or step up its use very much if the price falls. Moreover, because of the heavy transportation cost, a cut in coal prices at the mine will mean a smaller cut to the ultimate consumer and give him correspondingly little encouragement to increase his consumption. In the long run, however, demand has proved elastic, as shown by increased substitution of oil and gas; and even short-run elasticity is appearing as industrial plants are becoming equipped to burn whatever fuel is cheaper.

It is against these competitive market forces that both the big companies and the union are contending, apparently with increasing success.

The Influence of the Union

Since its revival of strength in 1933 under the protection given its organizing campaign by the National Industrial Recovery Act, the United Mine Workers of America has been one of the most powerful influences in the industry. In twenty of the past twenty-two years hourly earnings of production workers in bituminous coal showed a gain, and in most years the gain was directly due to union action — although two forces that are more fundamental must be kept in mind: the necessity of paying good wages to induce men to work in the mines, and the fact that only increased labor productivity in terms of quantity and dollar output permitted the payment of increased wages. The union, unlike many in other industries, has not opposed technological progress, and has been quite conscious of the fact that higher wages would compel mechanization. In a certain sense, by demanding higher wages the union may be said to have worked toward reduction of employment and of its own membership.

Between 1933 and 1955 hourly earnings increased more than fivefold and average annual pay more than sixfold. (See Table 48.) These rates of increase were well above those in almost every other industry, and at the end of 1955 the only reporting industry with higher hourly earnings was building construction, with a rate of $2.73 as against $2.67 for bituminous coal.[113]

113. *Survey of Current Business*, March 1956, p. S–15.

TABLE 48

BITUMINOUS COAL: LABOR STATISTICS, 1929–55

Year	Hourly Earnings	Full-Time Annual Earnings	Output per Man-Day	Value per Ton, f.o.b. Mine	Labor Cost: Per Ton	Labor Cost: As Per Cent of Price	Employment	Total Compensation of Employees
			(Tons)				*(Thousands)*	*(Millions)*
1929	$ .68	$1,293	4.85	$1.78	$1.12	63	503	$ 618
1933	.50	748	4.78	1.34	.84	62	419	284
1937	.86	1,170	4.69	1.94	1.28	66	492	573
1941	.99	1,500	5.20	2.19	1.35	62	457	712
1945	1.24	2,629	5.78	3.06	1.95	64	383	1,056
1949	1.94	2,930	6.43	4.88	2.71	56	434	1,277
1953	2.48	4,202	8.17	4.92	2.89	59	293	1,403
1955	2.56	4,555	10.32	4.83	2.44	50	210	1,187

Sources: Hourly and annual earnings and compensation of employees from *Survey of Current Business* (including National Income editions); output, value and employment from National Coal Ass'n., *Bituminous Coal Data*, 1954, Washington, pp. 2–3, and U.S. Bureau of Mines, *Mineral Industry Surveys*, Weekly Coal Report 2009, March 16, 1956, p. 14; labor cost derived from data on output and on union contract rules as to hours paid for, Welfare Fund payments and vacation pay in National Coal Ass'n., *Bituminous Coal Trends*, Washington, 1956, pp. 72 and 114–19.

These rapid gains by labor were offset by a doubling of tons produced per man-day of work, and by an increase in the average f.o.b. mine price from $1.34 in 1933 to $4.83 in 1955. As a result of these changes, the share of labor cost in the mine price of coal decreased rather than increased, from the 62–66 per cent of 1929, 1933, 1937, 1941 and 1945 — and, indeed, the 65 per cent of 1900.[114] In 1949 labor cost was 56 per cent; in 1953, 59 per cent; in 1955, only 50 per cent (Table 48).

This decrease in relative labor cost did not result in as much of a net gain to employers as might be supposed. It was accomplished entirely through mechanization and increased reliance on stripping, and a capital cost had to be incurred to buy machines. To the extent that machine makers charged all that the market would bear, that is, the full value of their products in terms of labor cost saved, there would be little relief from the mine operator's rising costs, but competition among, and promotional pricing by, machine manufacturers evi-

114. Annual reports of West Virginia Chief Mine Inspector, 1898–1900, Part 3, p. 276, cited in William McKinley Merrill, *Economics of the Southern Smokeless Coals*, unpublished doctoral thesis, University of Illinois, Urbana, 1953, p. 128.

dently permitted a substantial part of the gain to be held by the coal companies. The annual deficits of 1928–39 were turned into profits in every year from 1940 on (Table 45).

Problems Faced by the Union

The advances of the past two decades have not been pure gain from the union's point of view.

First, the process of mechanization has reduced the number of workers required: thus employment has declined by 50 per cent since 1933. Total compensation of employees has accordingly increased less rapidly than pay per employee, and, in fact, declined 15 per cent between 1953 and 1955, as Table 48 shows. John L. Lewis has held to the philosophy: "Better half a million men at good wages and high standards than a million in poverty and degradation." [115] The redundant workers moved in three directions: some left the industry, some became unemployed, and some retired on pensions provided by the union's Welfare Fund—which is built up by the employer's contribution of 40 cents per ton of coal mined and in 1956 was supporting one ex-miner for every three on the payroll.

Second, the union must fight continually against the temptation of the small mines and their employees to contract on a nonunion basis, thereby permitting the operator to reduce his labor cost enough to undercut established prices and the worker to earn a larger annual (although a smaller daily) income. Between 1948 and 1954 many mines went nonunion in this way, although some of them came back to the union with the upturn of coal demand in 1955.

Operators' Opinions of the Union

The ten operators consulted in this study expressed three types of attitude toward the union. Two operators held that it had greatly benefited the industry by setting a floor under wages and thus removing one channel of cutthroat competition, and said they hoped for complete unionization of the industry. Several of the others agreed that the absence of any wildcat strikes after 1952 was of great benefit to the industry — for example, in permitting it to offer customers (originally public utilities, but now steel mills and sometimes even

115. *Coal Age*, June 1953, p. 72.

foreign buyers) long-term contracts. Four operators conceded that a floor under wages was desirable, whether set by the union or by government, but declared that the union had damaged the industry's position by setting it too high. The four others condemned the union's high-wage policy outright for its effect on production costs — although they granted that the higher labor costs had produced an offset in the form of a stimulus to mechanization.

The real difficulty, according to two of these operators, is that coal could not afford even this much of a dollar increase in labor costs. In other words, the price increase, which was one reason the ratio of labor cost to price declined, also helped turn customers to oil and gas. Both of these fuels have a lower labor factor, and their labor cost has increased more slowly. It may be said more generally that the same power which stabilizes an industry against price cutting is quite likely by that very fact to render it less effective in its competition with other industries.

The union itself vigorously denies that it has increased labor costs, pointing to the stimulus its wage demands gave to mechanization, and argues that "the resurgence of coal in the electric industry, etc., is the best answer to this old saw about the UMWA pricing coal out of the market: it just isn't true." [116]

Competition with Other Fuels

One of the most intense forms of interindustry competition is that among the various sources of energy — water power, oil, natural gas and coal. In many instances, particularly for heating, one fuel may be preferred because of convenience, regardless of price. Thus coal is always at a disadvantage as against natural gas once the latter reaches a market. In other instances, price is the key to use of a fuel. A large buyer of steam coal who is purchasing heat units on a delivered basis is likely to switch to oil or gas if their price per million btu's is lower. A typical modern power plant is built to permit quick transfer between powdered coal and fuel oil, and frequently natural gas as well. The fact that residual fuel oil is a by-product of oil refining which will be produced no matter how far its price may decline gives it a tremendous advantage in the competition with coal. One battle, therefore, in which all coal producers and workers are united is the fight

116. Letter from Justin McCarthy, editor of the *United Mine Workers' Journal.*

in Washington (alongside the domestic crude oil producers) against fuel oil imports.

In 1900, 1910 and again in 1920 the share of bituminous coal in the total energy market was approximately 70 per cent, while anthracite was already losing its place in the market to petroleum. In 1930, 1940, 1950 and 1955, however, bituminous coal accounted for only 55, 48, 39 and 32 per cent, respectively — the losses being in favor of both petroleum and natural gas.[117] That price may have had some influence even as to heating is indicated by a comparison of retail prices and consumption for heating purposes of these three fuels in 1935–39 and 1950. The price of coal advanced the most, and its consumption the least. (See Table 49.)

TABLE 49

BITUMINOUS COAL: PERCENTAGE CHANGE IN RETAIL PRICES AND HEATING CONSUMPTION COMPARED WITH THAT OF NATURAL GAS AND FUEL OIL, 1935–39 TO 1950

Fuel	Retail Price	Consumption for Heating
Bituminous coal	+100.2	+ 11.5
No. 2 distillate fuel oil	+ 80.7	+101.9
Natural gas	− 15.4	+255.2

Source: Figures from Waldo E. Fisher and Charles M. James, *Minimum Price Fixing in the Bituminous Coal Industry*, Conference on Price Research Study No. 5, National Bureau of Economic Research, Princeton University Press, Princeton, pp. 415–16.

In particular markets we find that coal has lost out in space heating, locomotives, ships' bunkers, and power plants on tidewater or in the natural gas areas; it is holding its own or gaining in other public utilities and fighting for the market in other industries; and it has kept for itself the coke market.[118] The coal industry puts great faith in continued sales to the rapidly expanding electric power industry. Through research on steam turbines it hopes to win back the locomotive market from diesel fuel.[119] Eventually, as oil and natural gas slip off from peak production or as rising demand forces up the price of these competitors, the industry is confident that sales will radically increase.

117. *Bituminous Coal Trends*, 1956, p. 27.
118. W. Harvey Young of the U.S. Bureau of Mines.
119. *Coal Age*, February 1956, p. 57.

Performance of the Industry

Norman H. Leonard, writing in 1950, summarized the defects of the industry's performance as follows:

> (1) Consumers have been plagued with periodic shortages and with erratically fluctuating prices which make production planning and marketing extremely difficult. (2) Workers have faced seasonal and cyclical unemployment, unsanitary and dangerous working conditions, and low annual wages. (3) Operators have experienced long periods of deficit operation. . . . The outstanding waste is incurred by leaving coal in the seams. In American commercial pits approximately 35 per cent of the coal is lost in this manner, compared to 5 to 10 per cent in Western European mines before World War II.[120]

In weighing the first of these criticisms, it should be noted that the levels of output and prices are not criticized, but rather their undue fluctuation. In recent years this defect has not been present. Collective bargaining without the aid of strikes now seems to have become the rule, and output fluctuations are responses to changes in consumer demand. The stability of prices from 1948 through 1955, with a maximum range of 3.5 per cent between the high and low average price, would be considered remarkable in almost any industry. The increase in output per man-hour, which in recent years was running at twice the rate of American industry as a whole,[121] is also worthy of notice from the consumer's point of view — although it is obvious that much of the credit for this achievement must go to another industry, the manufacture of mining machinery.

As to the worker's situation, its radical improvement in recent years has been one reason why consumers have had to pay higher prices. In 1929, bituminous miners employed full time earned 16 per cent less than the average manufacturing worker; in 1955 they earned 5 per cent more.[122] The advance in safety conditions has also been impressive: in 1926–30 there were 1.95 fatal accidents per million man-hours of work; in 1951–55, only 0.94.[123] As a result workmen's compensation rates in important mining states have declined.

120. Leonard, "The Bituminous Coal Industry," pp. 38, 40–41.
121. *Bituminous Coal Annual*, 1953, p. 19.
122. *Survey of Current Business*, National Income edition.
123. *Bituminous Coal Trends*, 1956, p. 126.

A serious weakness in the performance of the industry is its inability to offer steady employment. This may be attributed to a number of factors, such as the lack of alternative opportunities in some of the isolated mine areas and the economic and psychological difficulties of moving to areas where more stable employment can be found; the fact that mines that cannot sell their coal do not close permanently and release their labor force, but close temporarily or work on short time, illustrating again the ease of entry and difficulty of exit; and possibly the high hourly wage whose deceptive allure helps dissuade the redundant miner from leaving the industry.

The operating deficits of the companies have been reduced since 1940, but the industry is still not a markedly profitable one. It might even be defended on this ground — that is, it has performed its services for a relatively low reward. However, society has suffered a real loss in the investment of capital in so many mines which have later been abandoned. Improvement of the profit ratio may prove to be one achievement of the present-day combination movement.

Conservation

The regrettable practice of leaving so large a percentage of coal in the ground is explained by geology and economics — and is no different from the practice in oil and natural gas. Because the cost of mining out coal seams has been higher than that of opening new veins, producers have sometimes abandoned as much as 50 per cent of the coal. Now that it is becoming harder to find new, rich veins, and more expensive to open new mines, the recovery ratio is improving.[124] In modern auger mining, bits go 200 feet into the ground and get coal that would not have been reached by old methods. Ways are being found also to mine thin seams effectively.

The large producers are making rapid progress in conservation methods of various sorts, just as they are in other aspects of progressive modern management. It is the smallest operators who are least able to mine all the coal — as well as least able to reclaim land abandoned after strip operations. Those especially who mine coal on a royalty basis use the quickest and cheapest methods. Where private economic motives to conserve coal are weak, government action is needed if it is decided that conservation should be awarded a higher priority.[125]

124. Yale Brozen, "Determinants of the Direction of Technological Change," *American Economic Review*, May 1953, pp. 300–01.

125. Fisher and James, *Minimum Price Fixing in the Bituminous Coal Industry*, p. 437.

Conservation can, however, be advanced by greater prosperity in the industry. The following comments from a 1939 report of one government agency are still valid today:

> Little progress in the reduction of waste may be expected if production must be pursued under conditions of prolonged loss and bankruptcy. It is inevitable that harassed enterprise will seek a way out by ruthless exploitation or by building its own defense mechanism of control.[126]

Other defects in the performance of the industry, such as the intermittent character of employment, are in part attributable to its failure to achieve a stable prosperity. This in turn is the combined result of unstable demand and the peculiar conditions of the industry, especially those governing entry and exit. If one rejects governmental regulation designed to maintain prices and to control entry, and also governmental intervention to protect coal against oil and natural gas, then the industry's prosperity depends on the absence of such fluctuations in general business as have occurred in recent decades, particularly in association with wars.

Although the conservation record is much better in Europe, which is forced to conserve by reason of its poorer seams and limited resources, the productivity record is much better in the United States, which must economize on its costly labor. A recent estimate placed Poland, with 1.91 tons produced per man-day, ahead of Germany, England and France, compared with 10.32 tons for the United States.[127]

The record in both conservation and productivity is determined by the economic conditions of the industry. It is embarrassing, nevertheless, when an American industry is told that its annual expenditure of $17 million on research is less than half the research bill of a single chemical company (which is studying coal as one project),[128] or when it is told that European countries are ahead of it in coal research and that 209 named projects call for immediate attention.[129] One avenue to catching up may be through the merger movement with its access to adequate capital and management resources.

126. National Resources Committee, *Energy Resources and National Policy*, 1939, p. 111.

127. *Bituminous Coal Trends*, 1956, p. 107.

128. J. G. Davidson, vice president of Union Carbide and Carbon Corp., cited in *Journal of Commerce*, June 14, 1956, p. 4.

129. U.S. Bureau of Mines report, cited in *Business Week*, June 9, 1956, p. 90.

SUMMARY

1. The bituminous coal industry is one with a *low degree of concentration*, for the largest company, according to advance estimates, would have less than 8 per cent of total output in 1956, and the four largest companies only 20 per cent. There were 7,500 to 8,000 mines in 1955.

2. In an industry with so many small units in both production and distribution, it is not surprising that a number of *scattered price-fixing agreements* and other attempts to restrain competition have been uncovered since the Sherman Act was passed. These have been mostly among distributors.

3. The Supreme Court's *Coronado decisions* of 1922 and 1925 opened the way for levying treble damages against a district of the United Mine Workers for destruction of property during a strike, on the ground that its actions were aimed to restrain the flow of interstate commerce in nonunion coal and thus violated the Sherman Act. Although this seemed likely at the time to create a precedent for union liability, it proved impossible to carry the case to conclusion, and no important suit of this nature has ever been brought successfully.

4. The intense competition resulting from the overcapacity created by World War I and from the decline in demand during the 1920s and early 1930s spurred part of the coal industry to seek a solution through cooperative sales agencies. *Appalachian Coals*, the first of these, was approved by the Supreme Court in 1933 on the grounds that an industry in such distress required special measures and that this agency controlled in any event only a small fraction of total output. This second proviso meant that marketing agencies could not successfully stabilize the industry; but they could hardly have done so regardless of the outcome of this case unless they clearly violated the Sherman Act by joint action. Although several agencies sprang up, most were ineffective. Appalachian Coals is the only one in existence today, and its work relates to efficient marketing by its members rather than to control of competition.

5. The National Recovery Administration and the *National Bituminous Coal Commission* (along with the Coal Division of the Interior Department, successor to the Commission) attempted to halt price cutting in the industry through a system of government-fixed minimum prices. By the time the Coal Division finally had its price schedules ready, however, demand was rising sufficiently to lift spot prices above the price floors. Although the experiment thus failed to receive a thorough trial, it could hardly have achieved success in any event. The price-setting principles and procedure used had at least the following defects: (1) serious delays required by the necessity of allowing "due process" and avoiding injustice to any interest; (2) a cumbersome machinery

and price structure arising from the attempt of a government agency to fix the prices of so many types and sizes of coal mined at so many locations and shipped to so many markets; (3) a tendency to discourage competition, since the drafters and administrators of the statute tried to avoid injury to the established market positions of firms; (4) reliance on costs of a past period, in contrast to the reliance on anticipated costs and demand which actuates a free market; and (5) a perverse influence on prices, boosting them when overhead costs were high due to declining demand and depressing them when demand was rising. If the act had achieved its purpose, it would have improved the economic position of both workers and investors — but only by increasing the fundamental difficulty of overcapacity in relation to demand.

6. In 1949 the *United Mine Workers* made an attempt to prevent overproduction in the industry by requiring that no mine operate more than three days a week. This was an inefficient way of accomplishing the goal of stabilization, since it kept high-cost mines alive and raised the costs of efficient mines by forcing them to shut down when they could be operating successfully. Although the three-day week seemed to offer the industry a means of controlling output without violating the antitrust laws, its union sponsorship and the discriminatory effect against more efficient mines made it unacceptable. Nor have similar proposals of the union been accepted since then. The union has, however, had a very important and complex influence on the competitive condition of the industry. It has tended to prevent the wage cutting which once encouraged price cutting. On the other hand, the increase in labor cost of production which it fostered forced up prices steadily from 1933 to 1948 and thus tended to reduce the market for coal and total coal mine employment. Since 1948 mechanization and resort to strip mining have caused labor costs to decline, while selling prices have ceased to advance.

7. Although bituminous coal has its regular *trade association activity*, some forms of intercorporate collaboration are less common here than in other industries, because of the multitude of small companies.

8. *Competitive price cutting* in coal goes back, on the supply side, to ease of entry. The industry consists of several thousand small operators without the domination by a few large companies which is found in most American industries of its size, and excess capacity has developed after periods of high demand such as World Wars I and II. Also, the physical impossibility of transferring capital out of coal mining means that "exit" is slow and that excess capacity continues for some years. An industry of so many small firms, with excess capacity, whose industrial consumers are indifferent to branding, naturally resorts to price cutting.

9. On the demand side, coal has suffered seriously from the *competition of other fuels*. Oil and natural gas have been aided by their physical convenience in use and by lower labor costs. If coal companies were larger or more co-

operative, they might be better able to conduct the individual or cooperative research which would give the industry a better chance in this competition. Coal operators are confident of a coming expansion in demand as oil and natural gas become harder to find and more expensive.

10. *Mergers* lifted the share of the ten largest producers in total output from 21 to 29 per cent between 1941 and 1955, but have not carried concentration in coal as far as in other industries. This is due, among other things, to the fact that coal is so widely scattered; it cannot be mined at just a few locations with all the advantages of concentration of facilities and management. Nevertheless, one of the best hopes for the industry lies in more mergers, which should discourage cutthroat price competition, make it possible to finance technical and product research and greater use of cost-cutting machinery, and in general permit the use of modern management methods. The antitrust law is probably not a serious obstacle to mergers.

11. *The performance of the industry* is a mixed one. Fluctuations in output and prices, formerly wide, have been much reduced in recent years, except as output must necessarily fluctuate in response to changes in demand. The advance in the position of the employed worker has been remarkable as the industry has moved toward a more stabilized situation with a much smaller, but better-rewarded, labor force. Although this advance has been due directly to union action, it would have been impossible without the remarkable gains in productivity achieved with the aid of the mining machine industry. The conservation record is improving as it becomes more difficult to find new deposits. Conservation could always be increased with adequate motivation, but higher prices to the consumer would be one cost.

In brief, the economic conditions of the coal industry and its competition with other fuels more easily obtained from nature have made it a "sick industry" except during spurts in demand; exemption from the antitrust laws during the 1930s proved no remedy for its problems; but merger into more efficient units may now (within the limits possible in an industry whose production sites are necessarily scattered and isolated) combine with a rising trend of demand to create a better future.

CHAPTER 8

Automobiles

Of all manufacturing industries in 1954 "motor vehicles and parts" ranked first in value added by manufacture, with $6.1 billion; its employment in 1955, as estimated by the Department of Labor, averaged 921,000. This chapter will touch on most branches of the industry, but with primary emphasis on passenger cars. Certain branches, however, such as the manufacture of glass, tires and trailers, are too important as separate industries to be included in this discussion.

Parts Making and Assembly

The production of automobiles or trucks consists of two broad stages — the making of component parts, and their assembly into the finished product. There are thousands of manufacturers of parts and only a few assemblers, some of whom also produce many of their own parts. The assemblers contract in advance for the parts they purchase, usually specifying what proportion of the forthcoming model's consumption will be awarded to each supplier.

The process of manufacturing a passenger car includes several substages as well: (1) A new model must be designed and engineered, and specifications written for each part. (2) The special-purpose machine tools and accompanying dies to make the various components must be manufactured, unless they are on hand from preceding years. (3) The parts are then made — a step called "machining," since such processes as boring, milling, pressing and stamping are applied to the rolled metal, rough castings and forgings which form the raw material. (4) Next comes the "subassembly" of components into major units such as engine, chassis and body. (5) Final assembly combines these and smaller units, such as cushions and headlights, into the finished car.

Although the motor vehicle industry grew up around Detroit, and still has its headquarters there, Michigan accounts for only about half of total employment and value added, and a third of the final assembly of passenger cars. The largest manufacturers have been scattering new assembling plants around the country since as early as 1909, to obtain lower shipping and labor costs and to facilitate quick delivery.

The Assemblers and Parts Makers

The industry is centered in the handful of companies that assemble passenger cars. General Motors Corporation accounted for 50.8 per cent of new car registrations in 1955, Ford Motor Company for 27.6 per cent and Chrysler Corporation for 16.8 per cent. Studebaker-Packard Corporation and American Motors Corporation were the only "independents" that survived into 1956. Gross income from all products ranged from $441 million, for American Motors, to $12,443 million, for General Motors. (See Table 50.)

In trucks the picture is not far different. In 1955 the Chevrolet and GMC Truck and Coach divisions of General Motors accounted for 43.3 per cent of new commercial car registrations, while Ford had 30.9 per cent, the Dodge Division of Chrysler 6.9 per cent, and International Harvester Company 10.5 per cent. The Willys Jeeps accounted for 2.8 per cent, and White Motor Company, Mack Trucks and Studebaker-Packard made most of the remaining commercial cars.[1]

Diversification of product is characteristic of the larger automotive companies. General Motors makes electrical appliances, locomotives, road-building machinery, and aircraft and marine engines. Ford is one of the large producers of farm machinery, and International Harvester is the largest. Chrysler makes air conditioning, industrial engines and other products; American Motors manufactures the Kelvinator and Leonard appliances. All motor companies have been important defense producers during times of war and preparation for war.

Parts manufacturers also have tried to escape complete dependence on the fluctuating automotive market by diversifying into machinery, aviation equipment and other lines. At least ten parts makers had gross sales of over $150 million in 1955, and all of these had outside

1. *Automotive News*, 1956 Almanac Issue, April 30, 1956, p. 32.

TABLE 50

AUTOMOBILES: DEALERS, NEW CAR REGISTRATIONS, AND GROSS INCOME OF PASSENGER CAR MAKERS, 1955

Firm and Car	Dealers (1956)	Per Cent of Total New Car Registrations	Gross Income
			(Millions)
Total	41,167 [a]	100.0	$21,991.1
General Motors Corp.		50.8	$12,443.3
Chevrolet	7,596	22.9	
Buick	3,582	10.3	
Oldsmobile	3,861	8.2	
Pontiac	3,978	7.4	
Cadillac	1,736	2.0	
Ford Motor Co.		27.6	5,594.0
Ford	7,009	21.9	
Mercury	3,046	5.2	
Lincoln	1,449	.5	
Continental	653	[b]	
Chrysler Corp.		16.8	3,470.5
Plymouth	8,957	9.0	
Dodge	3,768	4.0	
Chrysler	2,986	2.2	
De Soto	2,610	1.6	
Studebaker-Packard Corp.		2.1	482.2
Studebaker	2,548	1.3	
Packard	1,986	.7	
American Motors Corp.		1.9	441.1
Nash	1,584	1.3	
Hudson	1,309	.6	
Kaiser Motors Corp., sport cars and imports		.8 [c]	

Source: Automotive News, 1956 Almanac Issue, April 30, 1956, pp. 32, 91, 96.

a. Total excludes 17,491 dual franchises.

b. Under .05 per cent.

c. Kaiser stopped producing about the middle of 1955.

interests. (See Table 51.) According to a recent estimate there are about 400 parts companies, and 2,000 others that make components for these parts.[2] For particular accessories the number of companies ranges on up from 16 for wheels, 21 for transmissions and 27 for bumpers.[3] Ford and General Motors, both of which make many

2. *Business Week*, May 19, 1956, p. 64.

3. *Automotive News*, 1956 Almanac Issue, April 30, 1956, p. 91.

TABLE 51

AUTOMOBILES: SALES OF LARGEST PARTS MANUFACTURERS, 1955

Firm	Total Sales	Automotive Sales (Estimated)	Some Leading Parts Made	Some Other Markets
	(Millions)	*(Per Cent)*		
Bendix Aviation Corp.	$567.2	20	diversified	aircraft, appliances
Borg-Warner Corp.	552.2	43	diversified	aircraft, appliances
Budd Co.	316.6	80	body units	farm equipment, railroads
Electric Auto-Lite Co.	296.0	96	electrical parts	defense
Thompson Products, Inc.	286.2	35	pistons, pumps, valves	aircraft, electronic
Rockwell Spring and Axle Co.	271.9	a	axles, bumpers, springs	farm equipment, materials handling equipment
A. O. Smith Corp.	237.1	33	frames	oil and gas, utilities
Eaton Manufacturing Co.	218.1	75	engine parts, truck axles	farm equipment, machine tools
Timken Roller Bearing Co.	196.1	a	roller bearings	machinery, railroad
Dana Corp.	186.6	90	clutches, frames, transmissions	aircraft, general manufacturing

Sources: Moody's *Industrials* and Standard & Poor's Corp., *Industry Surveys*, "Auto Parts," Current Analysis, January 5, 1956, pp. A3–4 to A3–7. Tire and glass manufacturers are not included.

a. No estimate available.

of their own parts, buy goods or services from approximately 20,000 companies each.[4]

Distribution of Motor Vehicles

In the early years of the industry, manufacturers sometimes sold their cars through their own branch houses; but this tied up the manufacturer's cash in inventories, and the sales effort was often inadequate.[5] Today, therefore, independent dealers are universally em-

4. Lewis D. Crusoe, executive vice president of Ford Motor Co., in *A Study of Monopoly Power*, Hearings before Subcommittee on Antitrust and Monopoly, Senate Judiciary Committee, 84th Cong., 1st sess., 1955 (hereafter called Kilgore Hearings), Part 2, p. 652; Harlow H. Curtice, president of General Motors, *ibid.*, Part 8, p. 4045.

5. See questionnaire reported by Ralph C. Epstein in *The Automobile Industry: Its Economic and Commercial Development*, A. W. Shaw Co., Chicago, 1928, pp. 133–35.

ployed to distribute passenger cars, the number ranging down from about 9,000 for Plymouth (Table 50). Except in some of the smaller communities, a dealer sells the cars of one producer only, and in most cases only one of its makes. Even Plymouth, now handled as a second car by nearly all Chrysler Corporation dealers, may eventually be set up under separate dealerships.[6]

The manufacturer sells the automobile outright to the dealer, always for cash, at the retail list price less the dealer's so-called "commission" of 24 or 25 per cent. The dealer himself must usually accept a secondhand car in trade for the new car, and perhaps another and older used car when he sells the first; for both of these he must in turn find buyers. He can legally charge either more or less than the list price, but in practice he cuts or increases prices by adjusting the trade-in allowance. Installment buying is quite common. In 1955, 60 per cent of new passenger cars and 61 per cent of used passenger cars were purchased on time.[7]

Trucks are distributed either through passenger car dealers, truck dealers or branch houses of the manufacturers. Independent dealers are less interested in handling them for several reasons — the many special models, the small volume of sales in any one district, the number sold direct to business concerns and the greater need for technical knowledge.

Antitrust Suits

In view of the number of firms engaged in the parts and accessory business, it is not surprising that the majority of motor vehicle antitrust cases have been in this area.

Collusive Agreements

The three earliest cases began during World War I. In 1917 an association of accessory makers and jobbers was charged with monopoly and restraint of trade, only to be cleared later by a jury.[8] The Automobile Bumper Association was dissolved in that year for controlling the bumper trade through patent licenses.[9] Later, in 1923, the

6. *Automotive News*, August 29, 1955, p. 1.

7. Automobile Manufacturers Ass'n., *Automobile Facts and Figures*, 1956, p. 17.

8. *U.S. v. William M. Webster*, Indictment (S.D. N.Y. 1917).

9. *U.S. v. Grant F. Discher*, Eq. 14–393 (S.D. N.Y. 1917), U.S. Department of Justice, *Decrees and Judgments in Federal Antitrust Cases*, 1918, pp. 645–48.

same charge was made against eleven bumper makers,[10] but the case was dismissed in 1927 after the Supreme Court's *General Electric* decision upholding a similar plan.[11] In 1918, on court order, the largest horn producer agreed to stop imposing resale price maintenance on its jobbers.[12]

The remaining collusion proceedings have been brought since 1947. Seven have so far been completed.

1. In August 1947 members of the Brake Lining Manufacturers Association were charged with selling at identical prices, classifying customers, and agreeing on discounts and terms of sale.[13] In September 1948 fines were paid, and the Association was dissolved.

2. In December 1948 the government charged a conspiracy to fix uniform prices and resale prices on Chrysler parts in the state of Washington.[14] Two years later five defendants pleaded *nolo contendere* and paid fines, stating that the Korean crisis prevented their taking time to fight the case. The judge of the District Court is reported to have considered the case unimportant.[15]

3. In February 1950 the Department of Justice charged a conspiracy among battery manufacturers, battery retailers, scrap metal companies and a lead smelter to monopolize the salvage of lead from used batteries, and claimed that this would destroy the livelihood of battery rebuilders. In December 1953 and May 1954 all but four of the defendants pleaded *nolo contendere* and paid small fines.[16] The defendants explain their scrap salvage activity as an attempt, which failed in practice because of the scattered nature of the business, to relieve the lead shortage by an organized, nationwide plan of collecting used batteries; sources of supply of the few battery rebuilders in the country were not to be touched. If that explanation is accepted, any organized plan to rationalize a business of this type is subject to antitrust attack by local operators who cannot be included, and perhaps even by newcomers.

10. *U.S. v. American Chain Co.*, Eq. 27–27 (S.D. N.Y. 1923).

11. *U.S. v. General Electric Co.*, 272 U.S. 476 (1926).

12. *U.S. v. Klaxon Horn Co.*, Eq. 2005 (D. N.J. 1918).

13. *U.S. v. Brake Lining Manufacturers Ass'n.*, Cr. 126–205, 126–206, 126–207 (S.D. N.Y. 1947).

14. *U.S. v. Chrysler Association Parts Wholesalers*, 180 F. 2d 557 (9th Cir. 1950). The case against the named defendant was later dismissed.

15. *Automotive News*, February 5, 1951, p. 6.

16. Department of Justice press release, May 12, 1954.

4. Another 1950 suit, filed in June, was that against the National Automotive Parts Association, a group that has been described as "unique and difficult to classify." [17] Organized in 1925, it consisted recently of 24 wholesalers operating 39 warehouses, who select jointly as the "NAPA line" particular brands of automotive parts. Members may carry other brands; these, in fact, amount to nearly half of their total turnover. When the suit was brought, sales were $80 million annually, principally to "secondary jobbers" who resell to retail outlets. The virtue of the plan is its emphasis on the selected NAPA brands, which members can offer to jobbers as a full line of quality products.

In 1954 a consent decree forbade exclusive arrangements with parts manufacturers, as well as allocation of territories, price fixing and uniform policies of customer selection among the members.[18] No significant change in the group's operations ensued. Contracts binding parts makers to sell exclusively to NAPA were dropped, but the grant to NAPA of exclusive use of brand names was permitted and continued.[19] Agreements to handle only NAPA parts were banned, but inspection of the organization's catalogue shows that members have chosen individually to handle only one NAPA brand in each type of accessory. Otherwise, there would have been a loss in merchandising efficiency through dilution of the planned market cultivation.[20]

5. In June 1951 the three principal wheel manufacturers were charged with monopolizing the replacement market by sharing patents and using common distributors and price lists.[21] By a consent decree in July 1955, the companies agreed to license at reasonable royalties, to all except vehicle manufacturers, existing patents and those to be taken out within five years, unless based on inventions by company employees or consultants; to cease publishing composite price lists; and not to agree upon common distributors.[22] Because of their mastery of the complex manufacturing techniques, the patent

17. Charles N. Davisson, *The Marketing of Automotive Parts*, Bureau of Business Research, School of Business Administration, University of Michigan, Ann Arbor, 1955, p. 897.

18. *U.S. v. National Automotive Parts Ass'n.*, Civil 9559 (E.D. Mich. 1950); Department of Justice press release, May 6, 1954; *Automotive News*, May 10, 1954, pp. 2, 63.

19. National Automotive Parts Association Bulletin, Detroit, May 6, 1954.

20. Davisson, *The Marketing of Automotive Parts*, p. 901.

21. *U.S. v. Kelsey-Hayes Wheel Co.*, Civil 10–655 (E.D. Mich. 1951).

22. Department of Justice press release, July 1, 1955.

licensing is not expected to weaken their position.[23] Price lists are still identical, although no longer composite. Distributors are still the same for all, although no longer "agreed upon." An injunction against common distributors would have amounted to a requirement of exclusive dealing.

6. Another complaint in June 1951 was filed against the two principal makers of induction-hardened crankshafts, whose patent agreements were alleged to be "suppressing the commercial development of inductive heat treatment as a means of hardening metal products." [24] By an unusual consent decree, in April 1956, the companies acquired in part a public utility status — agreeing to harden or manufacture crankshafts for anyone, within the limits of their capacity and without discrimination.

7. In February 1953 Trico Products Corporation, which had developed the vacuum-operated windshield wiper, signed a Federal Trade Commission consent order not to fix its customers' resale prices.[25] The firm was promptly served with treble damage suits by two small competitors who alleged that it had used a tying clause.[26]

Tying Clauses

In several cases the use of tying clauses in arrangements with distributors has been the principal offense charged.

1. A manufacturer of pneumatic tire accessories was charged in 1918 with resale price fixing. In 1922 a consent decree canceled its licensing agreement — especially the stipulation that customers buy from it all their requirements of such accessories.[27]

2. The Pick Manufacturing Company, a hubcap maker, filed a damage suit against General Motors in 1935, citing a clause in the latter's dealer franchises which forbade dealers to "sell, offer for sale, or use" in repair of General Motors cars "any part or parts not manufactured by or authorized by" General Motors. The Seventh Circuit Court, in upholding the U.S. District Court's decision for the defendant, found

23. Compare Standard & Poor's Corp., *Industry Surveys*, "Auto Parts," Basic Analysis, July 21, 1955, p. A3-4.

24. *U.S. v. Ohio Crankshaft Co.*, Civil 28299 (N.D. Ohio 1951), Consent decree (1956).

25. *Trico Products Corp.*, Docket 6050, 49 FTC 1033 (1953).

26. *Automotive News*, April 6, 1953, p. 51.

27. *U.S. v. A. Schrader's Son*, 264 Fed. 175 (N.D. Ohio 1919), 252 U.S. 85 (1920), Eq. 1116 (E.D. N.Y. 1922).

"an exception to the applicability of the Clayton Act," since the defendant was merely protecting its own reputation by insisting on repair parts of whose quality it felt assured and which would not cause user dissatisfaction with the car itself.[28] The opinion, by Judge Lindley, noted also that the sale of replacement parts by independent firms had been increasing "substantially." [29]

Although the Supreme Court affirmed this decision in October 1936 by a 6–0 vote, refusing to revise without clear proof of error a ruling on which both District and Circuit Courts agreed,[30] its 1947 opinion in the *International Salt* case [31] was to provide for a different solution. Here it established the rule that a large company might not require that its *own* product be used in such a case, but only a product of the desired *quality*.

3. Trouble arose briefly in the carburetor business in the 1930s.[32] A good deal of the replacement market and over 90 per cent of the original equipment market were held by Carter Carburetor Company and Bendix Products Corporation. When some officials of Bendix resigned in 1934 to form the Chandler-Groves Company, Carter, fearing loss of its trained service outlets to the aggressive new firm, warned that preferential discounts would be discontinued to outlets that accepted a second line of carburetors — especially any line "introduced since 1934." The Federal Trade Commission issued a cease and desist order against Carter in April 1938 and was upheld by the Eighth Circuit Court in June 1940. The opinion, by Judge Woodbrough, found that many dealers, knowing that the cars which carried this new carburetor as original equipment had not been operating long enough to call for replacements, either "ceased to deal in Chandler-Groves products" or "kept such stock out of sight, and ceased to promote the sale thereof." [33] The defense that Carter had advanced the industry's welfare through research, engineering, advertising and instruction to service station mechanics was overruled as irrelevant.

According to its successor firm, Chandler-Groves' main problem had been, not to fight the tying agreements, but to persuade car manu-

28. *Pick Manufacturing Co. v. General Motors Corp.*, 80 F. 2d 641, 643 (7th Cir. 1935).

29. *Ibid.*, at 644.

30. *Ibid.*, 299 U.S. 3 (1936).

31. *International Salt Co. v. U.S.*, 332 U.S. 392 (1947).

32. *Business Week*, December 25, 1937, pp. 20–21.

33. *Carter Carburetor Corp. v. FTC*, 112 F. 2d 722, 728, 729 (8th Cir. 1940).

facturers that it could offer adequate replacement parts in the field. The Court's decision might well have been helpful if it had come earlier, but in 1938 Chandler-Groves had withdrawn from the business. The company does not, however, attribute this failure to unfair competition.

4. Not satisfied with the outcome of the *Pick* case, the Federal Trade Commission filed an exclusive dealing complaint against General Motors in June 1937. Franchises were then being renewed only after annual conferences with officers, including those in charge of parts distribution, and dealers felt pressure to handle only General Motors parts if they expected renewal. Contrary to the holding of the courts in the *Pick* case, the Commission found that sales of independent jobbers had been declining. It pointed out that for some parts, such as spark plugs, General Motors was insisting that those in its own packages be used, and not the identical plugs which it had sold to independent jobbers. Some other parts in which exclusive dealing was required had nothing to do with mechanical operation of the car. In neither of these two instances could the respondent truly claim risk of consumer dissatisfaction with the car through use of the product of independents.

In November 1941 the Commission issued a cease and desist order,[34] and in August 1942 General Motors withdrew an appeal to the courts.[35] It abandoned its formal insistence on use of General Motors parts, but there is no consensus as to the practical effects. In 1954 another change in the corporation's discount and distribution pattern brought on a seven-month investigation by the Commission, from which no charges had resulted by the end of 1955.[36] Ford's parts program was under investigation at the same time by the Antitrust Division.[37]

5. In 1946 the Timken-Detroit Axle Company (renamed Rockwell Spring and Axle Company in 1954) accepted a consent decree directing it to permit truck and bus manufacturers to use its vital patent on multi-wheel construction without having to buy its unpatented products as well.[38]

34. *General Motors Corp.*, Docket 3152, 34 FTC 58 (1941).

35. FTC, *Statutes and Decisions*, 1939–1943, pp. 506–07.

36. Louis H. Bridenstine, General Motors attorney, Kilgore Hearings, Part 8, pp. 3888–89; also Donald P. MacDonald, FTC attorney, *ibid.*, Part 6, pp. 2761–62.

37. Stanley N. Barnes, Assistant Attorney General, Kilgore Hearings, Part 1, p. 302.

38. *U.S. v. Timken-Detroit Axle Co.*, Civil 5642 (E.D. Mich. 1946).

6. Seven manufacturers of brakes were charged in December 1947 with, among other things, compelling customers to buy unpatented along with patented parts of braking systems. One defendant signed a consent decree a year later, and the rest nearly six years later (in October 1953), agreeing to license at reasonable royalties all their patents and any taken out within five years. They also forswore price fixing, division of markets and similar practices.[39]

Advertising of Prices

Until 1936 automobiles were advertised without inclusion of either the federal excise tax, costs of preparing the car for delivery, or spare tires and bumpers. In 1932 and 1933 the Sales Managers' Committee of the Automobile Manufacturers Association had nearly reached agreement to include these essential items in prices as advertised, but this was blocked by the opposition of one of the General Motors car divisions. Within a few weeks of an investigation by the Federal Trade Commission late in 1936, this change was finally effectuated.[40]

In July 1937 the Commission followed up this work by issuing complaints on the matter against General Motors and Ford. There followed in 1941 orders directing that all advertising material naming, or showing a picture of, a particular model must give the full price inclusive of "any equipment or accessories illustrated or described in the advertisement as necessary for said automobile's operation or customarily included as standard equipment" as well as all charges for "advertising, handling, delivery or for any similar or like purposes." [41]

Integration into Installment Finance

The first Department of Justice suit against automobile manufacturers, in 1937, arose out of the situation in installment financing of passenger car sales. The several hundred sales finance companies made loans to dealers secured by their own or their customers' notes. Three quarters of the wholesale credit (to finance purchases by dealers) and two thirds of the retail credit were in 1937 in the hands of three large

39. *U.S. v. Bendix Aviation Corp.*, Civil 44–284, Consent decrees, Commerce Clearing House, *1948–1949 Trade Cases*, No. 62349, *1952–1953 Trade Cases*, Nos. 67583, 67591 and 67601 (S.D. N.Y. 1948, 1953).

40. FTC, *Report on Motor Vehicle Industry*, H. Doc. 468, 76th Cong., 1st sess., 1939, pp. 49–51; Donald P. MacDonald, Kilgore Hearings, Part 6, pp. 2762, 2787.

41. *General Motors Corp.*, Docket 3173, 32 FTC 807, 824 (1941); also *Ford Motor Co.*, Docket 3174, 33 FTC 1541 (1941). A later order against exaggerating the merits of a "fog lamp" was *General Motors Corp.*, Docket 4724, 44 FTC 436 (1948).

"factory-related" or "national" companies.[42] In 1919 General Motors had established General Motors Acceptance Corporation (GMAC) to handle financing of its products. In 1928 Ford, observing the advantages gained by General Motors, followed suit by acquiring part ownership of the Universal Credit Company. In 1933, however, Commercial Investment Trust Corporation (CIT) bought Ford's shares and in 1938 all of the stock of Universal. Chrysler, in 1934, purchased stock in Commercial Credit Company, which had financed sale of its cars since 1925.

There were several motives for this association with sales finance firms. General Motors may have wanted to expand its earnings in the finance business thereby, but this motive could not be attributed to Ford except between 1928 and 1933 or to Chrysler before 1934, and it was probably not a compelling reason. More important was the manufacturer's interest in promoting retail sales of his cars by making their financing easy. With a great many finance companies in the business, it seemed desirable to keep financing costs low by using a single efficient company as far as possible. The ready access of these factory-related companies to manufacturers and dealers gave them a low "acquisition cost" for the paper they financed — unfairly low in the view of independents, although it could also be considered simply an advantage of this form of integration.

The battle was mainly over retail financing, which is much more profitable than wholesale financing. Early installment notes were "recourse" notes, that is, in case of default the finance company could have recourse to the dealer to make good. In 1925 GMAC opened a drive to increase its sales by setting up a "repossession loss reserve" from which to reimburse the dealer if he had a loss on his guaranty. Losses were expected to be much lower than the amount provided, with the dealers receiving the difference as a profit. GMAC's business shot upward, both as a result of this plan and because of intensified pressure by General Motors on dealers to patronize GMAC.[43] The other national companies hastily set up their own reserves, which protected varying percentages of the dealer's guaranty.[44]

42. Wilbur C. Plummer and Ralph A. Young, *Sales Finance Companies and Their Credit Practices*, National Bureau of Economic Research, New York, 1940, p. 264.

43. Russell Hardy, "Another View on the Origin of Dealer Participation in Automobile Finance Charges," *Indiana Law Journal*, Spring 1955, p. 312.

44. *Business Week*, December 25, 1937, p. 21.

The little companies competed by accepting dealers' retail paper on a "nonrecourse" basis and by paying the dealer a rebate equivalent to the reserve. There was often a premium over the straight cash price of a car plus finance charges — the dealer's "pack," which generally escaped the customer's notice. The national companies competed in kind by giving dealers a "kickback" through periodic payments from the loss reserve whether losses were incurred or not.[45] The dealer came to regard this as his "legitimate commission," and in times of low car demand it was often his only profit.[46] The whole setup illustrates the basic fact that competition in the finance business is for the dealer's rather than the customer's favor.

The "6% Plan"

In the autumn of 1935 GMAC launched another round in the competitive battle when it announced its simplified "6% Plan" — i.e., one half per cent monthly interest on the sum of the original unpaid balance plus retail insurance premium. This not only reduced the current rate by about 25 per cent for cars sold on twelve installments (which was then a frequent payment plan), but enabled the buyer to see that there was no pack at his expense and, correspondingly, to detect whether any other finance plan of a competitor contained a pack. In the words of the Federal Trade Commission:

> . . . the so-called 6-per cent plan as advertised not only constituted a substantial reduction in the rates of finance charge but also was a clever competitive device both for increasing the volume of sales of General Motors products and for obtaining finance business for General Motors Acceptance Corporation.[47]

The GMAC plan forced the other big finance companies, in order to compete successfully, to follow suit. The Federal Trade Commission felt that the plan "constituted one step in what is possibly a vicious circle,"[48] by which the big manufacturers and their affiliated finance companies could get the better of independent finance companies.

45. See pp. 47 and 50–51 in "Installment Selling: The Real Situation," *ibid.*, November 13, 1937.

46. "C. . . . . I. . . . . T. . . . ," *Fortune*, September 1947, p. 174.

47. FTC 1939 Report, p. 973.

48. *Ibid.*, p. 943. See also Plummer and Young, *Sales Finance Companies and Their Credit Practices*, p. 268.

Other critics added that the car buyer would not necessarily gain by a reduction in charges if this squeezed the dealer so much as to make him squeeze the buyer in turn (probably by giving him a smaller trade-in allowance on a used car).

In 1936 the Commission filed complaints against the big companies using the "6% Plan." It charged that the name and advertising of the plan concealed the fact that the rate was 6 per cent on the original unpaid balance rather than on the current unpaid balance (for which it was nearly 12 per cent in the case of twelve-month contracts). Commercial Credit dropped the title, but General Motors and Ford fought the case. The Commission issued its order in December 1939, and in August 1940 was upheld against General Motors by the Second Circuit Court of Appeals.[49] According to Judge Augustus N. Hand's opinion, the title "6% Plan" might mislead the "ignorant" and the "careless." An appeal by the Ford Motor Company was dismissed by the Sixth Circuit Court on the same grounds.[50] The name was therefore dropped, but the plan continued in effect, and the standard rate on new cars is the same today.[51] On used cars the rate is likely to be 50 or 100 per cent higher, since costs and losses are greater.

The Department of Justice Action

In the same year, 1936, the American Finance Conference, representing (as it still does) more than 350 local and regional companies, accused the big manufacturers of aiding their "related" finance companies by advertising their finance plans and by having their own employees help solicit business. It claimed that they were coercing dealers to patronize these concerns by such methods as refusing to allow independent finance companies to check on cars at the factory, delaying car deliveries to dealers who patronized independents, and threatening to cancel franchises of such dealers.[52]

After an investigation by the Department of Justice, a federal grand jury was convened at Milwaukee, but it was dismissed indignantly by

49. *General Motors Corp. v. FTC*, 114 F. 2d 33 (2d Cir. 1940), certiorari denied 312 U.S. 682 (1941).

50. *Ford Motor Co. v. FTC*, 120 F. 2d 175 (6th Cir. 1941).

51. Clyde William Phelps, *Financing the Installment Purchases of the American Family*, Studies in Consumer Credit No. 3, Commercial Credit Co., Baltimore, 1954, pp. 41–42; Standard & Poor's Corp., *Industry Surveys*, "Finance and Small Loan Companies," Basic Analysis, April 28, 1955, p. F1–7.

52. Plummer and Young, *Sales Finance Companies and Their Credit Practices*, pp. 270–71.

Judge Geiger in December 1937 when he found that the Department was simultaneously negotiating for a consent decree — a practice it has since dropped. A second jury, at South Bend, indicted the three big motor companies and the big finance companies in May 1938 for conspiring to restrain trade in automobile financing. Effects of the investigation appeared early in 1938 when Chrysler sold its stock in Commercial Credit and Ford reaffirmed an old — but evidently not fully effective — policy of leaving its dealers free to choose their own financing connection.[53]

In November negotiations with Ford, Chrysler, CIT and Commercial Credit were completed, and a consent decree became effective in March 1939.[54] The defendants, while denying any violation of the antitrust laws, agreed that dealers were to be free to deal with any finance company they wished. They agreed to the imposition of certain restraints on activities which might suggest that the manufacturer was favoring a particular finance company. They retained the right to give certain types of assistance to any finance companies that would register with the Court under a prescribed procedure and agree to live up to certain rules of good conduct such as limiting fees, delivering policies upon payment of premiums, and not misusing the right of attaching wages. This part of the decree had little effect, since, until 1950 at least, no such plan or criteria were filed with the Court by Ford or Chrysler; hence no finance company had registered.[55]

The GMAC Settlement

The position of General Motors differed in that it owned its financing company outright. This made its stakes greater and weakened the claim of conspiracy (with an outside company). It refused to negotiate a consent decree, and four associated corporations and seventeen officers were tried in South Bend. The government produced as witnesses forty-eight General Motors dealers (and presented evidence on twenty-seven more) who had been urged to patronize GMAC or, in some instances, threatened with loss of their franchises if they did not do so. The defense brought forward ninety-nine dealers who had not

53. FTC 1939 Report, pp. 284–86, 614.

54. *U.S. v. Ford Motor Co.*, Civil 8 (N.D. Ind. 1938); *U.S. v. Chrysler Corp.*, Civil 9 (N.D. Ind. 1938).

55. Phillip W. Haberman and Harold F. Birnbaum, "The Auto-Finance Consent Decree: An Epilogue," *Washington University Law Quarterly*, Winter 1950, p. 47.

been so urged or threatened and who either did not patronize GMAC or, in a few instances, used other sources of finance as well.[56] The defense testimony was barred on the ground that there was already enough evidence to support a charge of conspiracy. The outcome was that the corporations were found guilty in November 1939 of violating Section 1 of the Sherman Act, and were fined, while the officers—who had personally ordered the acts in question—were found not guilty. In 1941 the Seventh Circuit Court affirmed the conviction, and the Supreme Court denied a review.[57]

Meanwhile the government had filed a civil action in Chicago in October 1940, citing both the Sherman and Clayton Act, to achieve the dissolution of the connection between General Motors and its sales finance affiliate. Approximately 400 depositions were taken, and, after delays due to World War II and other causes, a consent decree became effective in November 1952.[58] The idea of divorcement was dropped, but General Motors agreed that its dealers should be free to deal, or encourage their customers to deal, with independent finance companies, and that it would not recommend the use of GMAC by name (except for mentioning it in institutional advertising).

The Ford and Chrysler decrees had provided that they could be terminated if General Motors should win its case. On the sixth extension of the decree requested by the Department of Justice, in 1946, Ford and CIT objected. The Supreme Court in 1942 had voted 4 to 2 that Chrysler had not proved the terms of the decree put it at a competitive disadvantage, Justice Byrnes delivering the opinion.[59] In November 1948 the Court voted 4 to 3 that certain restraints in the Ford decree, including the provision which severed affiliation between manufacturer and finance company, should be suspended unless or until they were imposed on General Motors.[60] The new majority, for which Justice Frankfurter spoke, was made up of the two dissenting justices of 1942 and two newcomers to the Court. The parties to the Ford and Chrysler decrees did not want to be bound by restrictions which did not bind their competitors, but the manufacturers have not again affiliated with finance companies.

56. See Brief for Appellants, August 29, 1940, pp. 108–21, in *U.S. v. General Motors Corp.*, No. 7146 (7th Cir. 1940).

57. *Ibid.*, 121 F. 2d 376 (7th Cir. 1941), 314 U.S. 618 (1941).

58. *Ibid.*, *1952–1953 Trade Cases*, No. 67323 (N.D. Ill. 1952).

59. *U.S. v. Chrysler Corp.*, 315 U.S. 556 (1942).

60. *Ford Motor Co. v. U.S.*, 335 U.S. 303 (1948).

Consequences of the Decrees

These decrees are, in theory, excellent. They have given dealers the right to choose their own wholesale and retail financing connections. They have thus assured banks, as well as independent finance companies, the right to compete with the big finance companies. On the other hand, they preserve the right of "free speech" of the automobile companies and they have not forcibly dissolved corporate structures.

In practice, it was reported in 1948 that "the automotive trade is firmly convinced that the consent decree caused no substantial decline in the proportion of Ford cars financed by CIT or of Chrysler cars financed by CCC." [61] It is generally held in the trade that the total business of each of the national finance companies depends primarily on the sales of the particular manufacturer with which it does its principal business. One representative of the smaller competitors, however, has an "impression" that some of these may have gained slightly as a result of the consent decrees.[62]

The available figures show a decrease in the share of automobile retail installment paper held by the national companies, from 45.4 per cent at the end of 1939 (when the Federal Reserve series originated) to 35.1 per cent at the end of 1954. The share of all smaller finance companies increased from 13.4 to 18.4 per cent — despite a loss in sales by independent car producers, with whom they did much business. In 1954 Associates Investment Company had risen to third place as a purchaser of automobile and truck paper.[63] It is true that GMAC increased its share of total installment business for all durable goods from 9.2 to 10.8 per cent, but this was apparently because automobile paper increased in proportion to the total (from 33 to 46 per cent). Commercial banks had increased their share of automobile loans from 27.7 to 37.0 per cent by 1954, after touching a higher figure in 1948. Bank paper turns over faster than finance company paper, since more of it is direct-customer paper rather than discounted dealer notes: hence the 37.0 per cent understates the importance of the banks. (See Table 52.) Before concluding from the figures that the

61. *Business Week*, November 20, 1948, p. 20.

62. Thomas W. Rogers, executive vice president of American Finance Conference, Kilgore Hearings, Part 7, pp. 3153–54.

63. Annual reports of companies to depositaries or shareholders, cited by *idem*, at p. 3136.

TABLE 52

AUTOMOBILES: RETAIL INSTALLMENT CREDIT OUTSTANDING, 1939 AND 1954

(End of Year)

Firm	Amount 1939	Amount 1954	Per Cent 1939	Per Cent 1954
	(Millions)			
Estimated automobile credit	$1,497	$10,396	100.0	100.0
Sales finance companies	878	5,563	58.7	53.5
C.I.T. Financial Corp.[a]	182	885	12.2	8.5
Commercial Credit Co.	97	442	6.5	4.3
General Motors Acceptance Corp.	399[b]	2,327	26.7	22.4
Others[c]	200	1,909	13.4	18.4
Commercial banks	415	3,843	27.7	37.0
Other financial institutions[d]	81	596	5.4	5.7
Automobile dealers	123	394	8.2	3.8
Total retail installment credit	4,503	22,467	100.0	100.0
Sales finance companies	1,197	6,421	26.6	28.6
C.I.T. Financial Corp.[a, e]	182	885	4.0	3.9
Commercial Credit Co.	134	548	3.0	2.4
General Motors Acceptance Corp.	415	2,424	9.2	10.8
Others[c]	466	2,564	10.3	11.4
Commercial banks	1,079	8,633	24.0	38.4
Other financial institutions[d]	789	3,881	17.5	17.3
Retail outlets	1,438	3,532	31.9	15.7

Sources: Company figures from Moody's *Banks, Insurance, Real Estate, Investment Trusts*, 1939, pp. 1233, 1247, 1474; and 1955, pp. 914, 1181, 1186; Commercial Credit Co. 1954 automobile figure from Standard & Poor's Corp., *Industry Surveys*, "Finance and Small Loan Companies," Basic Analysis, April 28, 1955, p. F1-10; total figures from *Federal Reserve Bulletin*, September 1955, pp. 1024–25.

a. Renamed from Commercial Investment Trust in 1945.

b. In 1954, 96 per cent of GMAC's volume of receivables purchased was in automotive vehicles (Morgan Stanley & Co., Debenture prospectus for GMAC, New York, August 17, 1955, p. 2). It is assumed in this table that the same percentage applies to 1939; this figure consists, therefore, of total GMAC installment credit multiplied by 96 per cent.

c. Obtained by subtracting figures for named companies from totals.

d. Industrial banks, credit unions, small-loan companies, etc.

e. For lack of published nonautomobile credit totals for CIT, the automobile figure is used here again.

decrees have definitely reduced the share of the big finance companies, one must bear in mind that many other factors have influenced the trends.

Several dealers brought treble damage actions against their factories on the ground that their franchises had been canceled for not urging customers to patronize the factory-related finance companies. Most of the actions were dismissed, but one or two were settled by the defendants. General Motors made no settlement, and fought the only case brought to trial until the plaintiff gave up for lack of means to carry it further. Since the jury's verdict for the plaintiff in this case was overruled by the Circuit Court and the Supreme Court, which directed a retrial, there has been no real decision on the merits.[64]

The Position of GMAC

The principal complaint made in the installment finance field today is that of the independent sales finance companies against GMAC. Competitors do not feel that they will have a fair chance for the business of the General Motors dealers until GMAC and General Motors are separated.[65] The same opinion was evidently held by the staff of the Antitrust and Monopoly (Kilgore) Subcommittee of the Senate Judiciary Committee, which made a study of the problem in 1955.[66]

Figures presented by the trade association of smaller finance companies for the period 1948–54, which GMAC accepts as accurate, show that GMAC's share of automobile installment credit extended by all finance companies increased from 18.6 per cent in 1948 to 34.0 per cent in 1954. The reason for this increase, according to GMAC, is that much of the 1948 credit was on used cars, which were customarily disposed of by General Motors dealers (to whom alone GMAC made loans) as soon as received.[67] Thus its 1948 figure was at an all-time low, while in 1940 and 1941 its share was as high as in 1954. If the figures are translated into installment credit extended on automobiles by all types of lenders, the result is about the same: an increase in GMAC's share from 1948 to 1954 which raised it back to the 1940 level. Figures on this broader basis for the 1929–39 decade as a whole show a decline

64. *Emich Motors Corp. v. General Motors Corp.*, 181 F. 2d 70 (7th Cir. 1950), 340 U.S. 558 (1951).

65. Compare complaints of other finance companies, Kilgore Hearings, Part 7, pp. 3076, 3099, 3103, 3119, 3139.

66. *A Study of the Antitrust Laws*, Staff Report of Subcommittee on Antitrust and Monopoly, Senate Judiciary Committee, 84th Cong., 2d sess., 1956, p. 76. The subcommittee was under the chairmanship of Senator Harley M. Kilgore of West Virginia and later of Senator Joseph C. O'Mahoney of Wyoming.

67. Charles G. Stradella, president of GMAC, Kilgore Hearings, Part 8, p. 4019.

in GMAC's share since that time. Because the percentage of new cars made by General Motors showed an upward trend during these years, GMAC's "penetration" of its own market—General Motors dealers—advanced more slowly after 1948 than its penetration of the total market. (See Table 53.) Apparently, the rising trend in GMAC's share of the market since 1948 is not necessarily a portent of monopoly. In 1955 total automobile credit expanded approximately 40 per cent, and so did GMAC's business.

Although many General Motors dealers finance through independent sales finance companies or banks, it is certainly true that many use GMAC for fear of antagonizing the automotive company. Since the finance business is in no sense a public utility, General Motors' possession of a financing affiliate, but without any tying clause which requires dealers to use its services, cannot lead to an antitrust decree ordering separation except under some new antitrust interpretation.

To complete the picture it should be added that many local finance companies are merely a front for the dealer himself. It is at least as difficult for an independent finance company to enter in these cases as to enter in competition with GMAC. If the ultimate purchaser demands financing by another firm, as a condition for buying a car, he can presumably get it in either case.

Fair Practice Rules in Installment Finance

The American Automobile Association, the Better Business Bureaus and the Federal Trade Commission have been active in trying to stamp out the abuses of installment financing.[68] After 1943 the Commission began to treat as "unfair competition" various practices of "skip tracers" (firms that locate delinquent installment debtors who have skipped out), such as pestering friends of the debtor or telling them that the debtor will receive an unexpected legacy if he returns.

As it extended this work, the Commission met opposition from automobile dealers and finance companies that claimed there was sufficient state regulatory legislation already, and that the Commission should not regulate them since it could not regulate their principal competitors, the commercial banks. Despite these arguments, the Commission held hearings in September 1949 on five proposed fair trade practice

68. Reavis Cox, *The Economics of Installment Buying*, Ronald Press, New York, 1948, pp. 135, 320.

TABLE 53

AUTOMOBILES: PER CENT OF INSTALLMENT CREDIT EXTENDED BY GENERAL MOTORS ACCEPTANCE CORPORATION, 1929–54

	Per Cent of Credit Extended by Sales Finance Companies		Per Cent of Credit Extended by All Lenders	
Year	All Automobile Credit	New General Motors Cars	All Automobile Credit	New General Motors Cars
1929–39, average	a	a	23.6	59.3
1940	33.6	70.7	18.7	39.4
1941	31.4	66.4	a	a
1948	18.6	45.8	8.4	20.7
1949	25.6	59.7	13.1	30.5
1950	27.1	59.7	13.8	30.4
1951	26.1	61.0	13.3	31.1
1952	26.0	62.4	12.7	30.5
1953	31.7	70.3	15.8	35.0
1954	34.0	67.1	17.6	34.7

Sources: 1929–41 from Charles G. Stradella, in *A Study of the Antitrust Laws*, Hearings before Subcommittee on Antitrust and Monopoly, Senate Judiciary Committee, 84th Cong., 1st sess., 1955, Part 8, p. 4019; 1948–54 finance company figures from Thomas W. Rogers, *ibid.*, Part 7, p. 3137. Second and fourth columns obtained by dividing first and third columns by the percentage of all new cars made by General Motors — thus, with GMAC confining itself almost exclusively to new General Motors cars, its 33.6 per cent of all automobile credit extended to sales finance companies in 1940 would be 70.7 per cent of the credit on its own new cars, since General Motors made 47.5 per cent of all new cars that year. This calculation makes the assumption that the average price of General Motors cars sold on time was the same as that of the average for all cars sold on time. It assumes also that used cars available for financing by General Motors dealers increased in proportion to their new car sales.

a. Not available.

rules, which were issued in February 1951 and made effective in July.[69] They required the seller of a car to itemize to the buyer the price of the car, the trade-in allowance, the cost of insurance, the finance charge and other relevant factors in the transaction. The primary purpose was to show the purchaser the amount, over and above the stated finance charge, the dealer might be receiving in the form of a pack. Other provisions of the trade practice rules prohibited blank lines in contracts to be filled in later by the seller, any misrepresentation by the seller, and any requirement that the buyer must use a specific insurance company if the effect might be substantially to lessen competition.

69. FTC, *Trade Practice Rules Relating to the Retail Installment Sale and Financing of Motor Vehicles*, 1951; Phelps, *Financing the Installment Purchases of the American Family*, pp. 92–93; Bureau of National Affairs *Letter to Executives*, Washington, July 9, 1951.

These rules may well have a good moral effect, even though their legal application is limited by the fact that this is an intrastate transaction (between dealer and purchaser) rather than an interstate one. For this reason, it is possible that the regulatory statutes in a few of the larger states will be more effective; the content of these statutes is not very different.

The Yellow Cab Case

Antitrust action in the automotive industry was stepped up after World War II. One of the first cases reached the Supreme Court twice and established an important legal precedent. The Checker Cab Manufacturing Corporation, founded in 1922 to build cabs for a group of Chicago driver-owners, within three or four years after 1929 bought control of a number of cab companies so as to acquire customers. It eventually lost its holdings in several cities, and many "Checker" cabs are owned by other companies. But in 1946 it was still important in four cities: its Parmelee Transportation Corporation, Checker Taxi Company and Yellow Cab Company held 86 per cent of Chicago cab licenses; other "Yellow" companies owned 58 per cent of the licensed cabs in Minneapolis and 100 per cent in Pittsburgh; and its National Transportation Company owned 15 per cent in New York. In July 1946 the Department of Justice charged monopolization of these "captive markets" by the manufacturing company and monopolization of transportation between Chicago railroad stations.

When the U.S. District Court in Illinois ruled that a manufacturing company may lawfully monopolize the business of supplying its own subsidiaries, and that the Sherman Act does not encompass restraints arising from the regulatory activities of local governments (over taxi operation in this case),[70] the government took an appeal to the Supreme Court. In 1947 this body, with one dissent and one Justice not sitting, remanded the case for trial. The opinion, by Justice Murphy, pointed out that Section 2 of the Sherman Act forbade monopolization of "any part" of interstate commerce, and ruled that "interstate purchases of replacements of some 5,000 licensed taxicabs in four cities" was "an appreciable amount of commerce under any standard." [71] The opinion also held that the Sherman Act applied to

70. *U.S. v. Yellow Cab Co.*, 69 F. Supp. 170 (N.D. Ill. 1946).
71. *Ibid.*, 332 U.S. 218, 225–26 (1947).

the failure of the jointly owned Checker, Yellow and Parmelee firms to bid against each other for contracts to carry passengers between Chicago railroad stations.

This Supreme Court decision has become famous for the principle that a parent and subsidiary corporation may conspire to monopolize.[72] Since the units of an integrated firm necessarily deal with each other rather than in the open market,[73] this decision would imply that a vertical integration of any "appreciable" size can be made secure against the law only by complete corporate consolidation. Justice Murphy's opinion contributed also to the clarification of — or, as some think, the confusion concerning — what is meant by a "market," and a "part" of commerce, subject to illegal monopolization.[74]

The trial court now heard the case and found for the defendants, emphasizing that the government had not proved intent to monopolize.[75] In a 5–2 Supreme Court decision in 1949, Justice Jackson, for the majority, held that "the government's evidence fell short of its allegations — a not uncommon form of litigation casualty, from which the government is no more immune than others." [76] Dissenting, Justice Black emphasized that the local cab companies had not been allowed to buy cabs from outside manufacturers even when these vehicles were cheaper.

Although Checker won its case, it has not had the easy life of a monopolist. It has never built more than 10,000 vehicles in a single year; Chrysler alone has been selling several times as many taxicabs; Ford and General Motors have entered the field; and Checker has lost money in four of the ten years since 1946. In 1955 Checker was planning to introduce a new model, carefully designed to combine comfort and maneuverability, which it hoped would win back much of its lost market.[77] Developments thus proved that Checker would never be able to make money unless it sold in quantity beyond its captive market, in competition with others.

72. *Report of the Attorney General's National Committee to Study the Antitrust Laws*, 1955, pp. 31–32.

73. M. A. Adelman, "Effective Competition and the Antitrust Laws," *Harvard Law Review*, September 1948, pp. 1316–17.

74. *Report of the Attorney General's National Committee to Study the Antitrust Laws*, pp. 47–48.

75. *U.S. v. Yellow Cab Co.*, 80 F. Supp. 936 (N.D. Ill. 1948).

76. *Ibid.*, 338 U.S. 338, 341 (1949).

77. *Business Week*, October 15, 1955, pp. 150–54; Dana L. Thomas, "New Move by Checker," *Barron's*, March 5, 1956, pp. 5–6.

The Timken "Cartel"

A famous international antitrust suit concerned a corporation usually classified in the automobile accessory industry, although its sales in this field are probably well below half of its business. In 1909 the Timken Roller Bearing Company, established at Canton, Ohio, in 1905, made arrangements to sell its tapered roller bearings in Europe, a market solidly committed to ball bearings. Metropolitan Vickers, Ltd., took a license to make and sell the product through the British firm Timken, Ltd., which was set up as a subsidiary of Wolseley Motors (one of the Vickers units). In 1927 Michael Dewar, manager of Timken, Ltd., persuaded Timken Company that sales in Europe could be pushed better by a firm that was not occupied with other products and that, as a competitor, was not suspect to other automobile producers.

Dewar now received 52 per cent of Timken Limited's stock and Timken Company 48 per cent. The American firm agreed to continue giving assistance to Timken Limited, to keep a representative on its board of directors, and to leave to it the British and Continental markets. In 1929 the French tariff made it necessary to set up Société Anonyme Française Timken to serve the French Empire. After some Timken Limited shares were publicly offered, Timken Company kept 30 per cent of its stock, Dewar 23 per cent and the British public 47 per cent. Timken Company and Dewar each owned 50 per cent of the French firm's stock.

After World War II the Department of Justice brought actions against the principal bearing manufacturers in the United States, naming their foreign affiliates as co-conspirators. In September 1947 General Motors and five other makers of ball bearings pleaded *nolo contendere* to charges of agreeing on noncompetitive prices and discriminatory differentials in price, and paid fines.[78] In September 1950 SKF Industries, controlled by the big Swedish producer Aktiebolaget Svenska Kullagerfabriken, signed a consent decree agreeing to establish its own trademark for export purposes and "to use its best efforts" to export in competition with its parent company.[79] Report has it that this unusual demand was accepted because the president of SKF

78. *U.S. v. General Motors Corp.*, Cr. 18895 (N.D. Ohio 1946).

79. *U.S. v. SKF Industries, Inc.*, Civil 9862, Consent decree, *1950–1951 Trade Cases*, No. 62708.

Industries needed clearance for a government post. The one case in this group which was litigated was that against the Timken "cartel."

The Timken Case in the Courts

In March 1949 Judge Emerich B. Freed of the U.S. District Court in Ohio ruled that the American, British and French roller bearing companies had smothered competition among themselves through their exclusive trading areas and by fixing the prices on products sold by one company in another's area for replacement purposes, and that they had restrained United States imports and exports.[80] He enjoined performance of the exclusive patent and trademark agreements among the three firms, and of any agreements dividing world markets or fixing prices in the United States, and ordered Timken Company to sell its stock in the others. In December 1950, while the appeal to the Supreme Court was pending, Dewar died, and Timken Company exerted its contractual right to buy his stock, thereby becoming owner of a majority of the stock of Timken Limited. The Supreme Court refused to dismiss the case on this ground, and in June 1951 accepted the basic reasoning of the lower court by a 5–2 vote.[81]

Justices Jackson and Frankfurter filed dissenting opinions which insisted that a rule of reason must be applied to international cases. The former defended Timken Company's division of export markets:

> Since many foreign governments prohibit or handicap American corporations from owning plants, entering into contracts, or engaging in business directly, this seems the only practical way of waging competition in those areas.[82]

To this Justice Black, for the majority, replied that the attempt to surmount such handicaps to trade did not give anyone the right to violate the law.

District Judge Freed's decree against Timken was softened in an important respect by the Supreme Court. Chief Justice Vinson and Justice Reed parted company with the other members of the majority, Justices Black, Douglas and Minton, on the proposal that Timken be required to sell its foreign holdings outright. This remedy (which had

80. *U.S. v. Timken Roller Bearing Co.*, 83 F. Supp. 284 (N.D. Ohio 1949).
81. *Timken Roller Bearing Co. v. U.S.*, 341 U.S. 593 (1951).
82. *Ibid.*, at 607.

been applied to a much smaller degree in the *National Lead* case [83]) they considered unduly harsh. Thus the illogical middle ground was chosen as against the two wings of the Court that urged, respectively, that this was a cartel which must be broken up and that it was a sensible business arrangement.

Significance of the Timken Case

A few commentators have regretted that the Court did not break up the "cartel" regardless of hardship.[84] Other writers point out that the decision does not outlaw division of markets with foreign subsidiaries that are wholly owned.[85] However, Timken Company owned all of Société Timken by 1951, and had in fact created this firm which the courts thought should be its competitor. Even the outlawing of market division with partially owned affiliates ignores what local partners can contribute to foreign ventures by American corporations. They have local know-how, political and other connections, and their own profit motive. Certainly such partners will refuse to accept the dual role of partners and competitors. It may not lead to the highest efficiency to require a management team in Canton to contain among its members experts in European manufacturing and marketing problems, or to force it to deny its European partners a share in the business. Some commentators, however, have seen in the refusal to order stock divestiture a sign that the Supreme Court may in future cases take into account the special circumstances of foreign trade.[86]

The Supreme Court's decision may be criticized on more fundamental grounds. It directed Timken Company, majority stockholder in Timken Limited, to compete with the latter even if this meant loss to the minority stockholders in that firm. The clash with accepted principles of corporation law is evident; but in practice Timken Limited is more experienced and aggressive in the markets in which it sells, so that the minority stockholders have as yet no complaint. The decision also directed two firms to compete with each other while

83. *U.S. v. National Lead Co.*, 332 U.S. 319 (1947).

84. Walter Adams, "Dissolution, Divorcement, Divestiture: The Pyrrhic Victories of Antitrust," *Indiana Law Journal*, Fall 1951, p. 24.

85. Donald E. Claudy, "Sherman Anti-Trust Law: Applicability to Foreign Commerce," *Cornell Law Quarterly*, Summer 1952, p. 830; *Report of the Attorney General's National Committee to Study the Antitrust Laws*, pp. 88–90.

86. S. Chesterfield Oppenheim, "Foreign Commerce under the Sherman Act — Points and Implications of the Timken Case," *Trademark Reporter*, January 1952, pp. 10–11.

using the same trademark. Here again there is a clash with accepted legal principles — this time those of trademark law; but in practice the big railroad, automobile and manufacturing customers would not be deceived by this peculiar trademark situation.

The chief practical consequence of the decree has been the setting up of additional representation in various parts of the world where the three Timken concerns formerly sold through a single agent.[87] Thus a South American distributor would formerly have carried British, French and American tapered bearings as replacements for the corresponding makes of automobile. He can still carry British and French bearings, since Timken Limited still manages Société Timken, but a separate dealer must handle the American article. This involves duplication — and expense for Timken Company. In industrialized countries, where original equipment calling for bearings is manufactured, actual competition between the local representatives and hence the British and American companies does occur. But it is hard to evaluate competition between an American firm and its foreign subsidiaries most or all of whose profit it receives. In Great Britain and France, national protectionist policy prevents this competition, and American bearings are allowed to enter only for necessary replacement or when the British and French firms cannot fill an order.

There is active competition, meanwhile, between tapered and ball bearings. General Motors makes and sells both. A recent estimate puts the world's export market in bearings at about $110 million, with Timken Company accounting for perhaps $4 million out of the United States total of $28 million.[88]

The Spark Plug Cases

Upon passage of the Robinson-Patman Act in 1936, the Federal Trade Commission opened an investigation of price discrimination in the spark plug industry. The proceeding was broadened after the *Morton Salt* decision of the Supreme Court [89] ruled that the Commission might find any difference in price to constitute discrimination, subject to rebuttal by the respondent. In 1939 formal complaints were filed against the A.C. Spark Plug Division of General Motors and the Champion Spark Plug Company, and in 1947 and 1948 revised com-

87. *Business Week*, November 5, 1955, pp. 62–64.

88. *Ibid.*, p. 63.

89. *FTC v. Morton Salt Co.*, 334 U.S. 37 (1948).

plaints were coupled with one against Electric Auto-Lite Company. These three units accounted for about 80 per cent of the replacement spark plug sales (about forty competitors shared the rest), and practically all of the original equipment business. The charges were exclusive dealing, resale price maintenance and price discrimination. Thus Champion sold to Ford for original equipment at 6 cents and for replacement at 22 cents, to big oil companies at 23.5 cents, and to wholesalers at 26.1 cents. The Commission's order, in July 1953,[90] rejected the recommendations of its trial examiner that a lower price for original equipment than for replacement purposes be prohibited, and dismissed the charges of resale price maintenance, but enjoined (1) different prices to buyers in competition with each other and (2) all arrangements for exclusive dealing.

Critics of this case have pointed to two possible dangers which such a ruling might create.[91] First, denial of special discounts to firms, like the oil companies in this case, that give special promotional aids or perform additional marketing functions may discourage improvements in marketing. Second, prohibition of exclusive dealing might eliminate its special virtue of stimulating intense selling effort. These are long-range rather than immediate worries. Two years after the spark plug order one small competitor reported that exclusive dealing and special prices to favored customers still prevailed — in part, apparently, because news of the order never reached all buyers of spark plugs.[92] Another small competitor maintains that his own situation has been alleviated by the Commission's order.

Recent Automotive Parts Discrimination Cases

In 1949 the Commission began a series of actions against the quantity discount schedules of small automotive parts manufacturers. By the end of 1955 fourteen such proceedings had resulted in five preliminary or final cease and desist orders, four of which had been appealed to the courts.[93] The discount schedules — which are still in

90. Dockets 3977, 5620, 5624.

91. Harry L. Hansen and Marcell N. Smith, "The Champion Case: What Is Competition?," *Harvard Business Review*, May 1951, pp. 89–103.

92. Alfred R. Brenholts, president of Stitt Ignition Co., Kilgore Hearings, Part 3, pp. 1275–89.

93. Harold T. Halfpenny, counsel of National Standard Parts Ass'n., *ibid.*, p. 1253. The cases include FTC Dockets 5722, 5723, 5770, 5913, 6052: *Whitaker Cable Corp.*, *Moog Industries, Inc.*, *E. Edelmann & Co.*, *P. & D. Manufacturing Co.*, *P. Sorensen Manufacturing Co.*

force pending appeal — typically varied the discount with the amount purchased by each customer within the month. For example, 27 per cent of one firm's jobber customers, buying 63 per cent of its output, received the 20 per cent discount; 13 per cent of the jobbers, buying 10 per cent, received the 15 per cent discount; and so forth.[94] The jobbers frequently organized in "buying groups" to get the discounts, but with shipment made to the individual jobbers.

In a thorough study of the parts industry, financed by the industry but conducted by impartial researchers, its type of pricing was denominated "competitive-functional pricing" and by contrast "cost pricing" was shown to be unrealistic and noncompetitive.[95] Whatever the merits of this contrast, the Clayton Act required cost pricing.

Several points of considerable interest in the interpretation of the law emerged in these cases:

1. A price discrimination violates the law even if the recipient followed the suggested resale prices, and thus did not take business away from competing jobbers through price cuts. It can be assumed that the money saved by the larger buyer gave him a wider margin of profit and enabled him to conduct sales promotion of any kind more effectively. This remains true even though all the competing jobbers called as witnesses — who bought in smaller quantities because their business was smaller, or because they did not want to carry a large inventory, or because they wanted several sources of supply [96] — denied they had been hurt by the discounts.[97] The Commission pointed out that if these witnesses considered the 2 per cent cash discount important to them, as they all declared, they must have been hurt by the larger quantity discounts given to competitors, even if they did not realize it.

2. Price differentials cannot be justified on the ground that they are made in good faith to meet equally low prices of competitors if in fact they are part of a nationwide pricing system formulated to meet competition generally and not designed to meet a particular competitor's prices. A spokesman for the respondents hinted that it was General Motors and its wholesaling subsidiary United Motors Service Division against which they were competing.[98]

94. *P. & D. Manufacturing Co.*

95. Davisson, *The Marketing of Automotive Parts*, pp. 38–42, 951–54.

96. Compare *ibid.*, p. 434.

97. *Moog Industries, Inc.*, Dissenting Opinion of Commissioner Mason.

98. Harold T. Halfpenny, Kilgore Hearings, Part 6, p. 2828; see also Davisson, *The Marketing of Automotive Parts*, p. 35.

3. Similarly, the fact that other firms may still be giving illegal discounts does not permit a respondent to plead that it will lose its customers if it obeys the law. Its proper protection will come from Commission action against these competitors.

4. The fact that a respondent does less than one per cent of the business in its line does not enable it to escape on the ground that its actions have no substantial effect on competition, if in fact its dollar volume is substantial — e.g., $1.6 million.

The Big Suit against du Pont

In June 1949 the Department of Justice filed in Chicago one of the most important suits in the history of the antitrust laws. It demanded termination of ownership relations between E. I. du Pont de Nemours and Company and the du Pont family, on the one side, and General Motors and United States Rubber Company, on the other. By outlawing what it held to be control of the largest automobile company by the largest chemical company, the government expected both to restore a free market in the articles which these companies purchased and sold between each other, and to break up what it called "the largest combination of manufacturing enterprises in the United States." [99]

The corporate relationships as described in the government's complaint may be summarized as follows:

1. About two thirds of the stock in Christiana Securities Company was owned by members of the du Pont family and by the personal holding company of some of them, Delaware Realty and Investment Corporation.

2. Christiana owned 27 per cent, Delaware 3 per cent, and members of the du Pont family 7½ per cent, of du Pont stock, thus permitting control at stockholders' meetings since the remaining stock was scattered among 82,000 owners.

3. The du Pont Company had used part of its World War I munitions profits to purchase, chiefly in 1918 and 1920, about 23 per cent of General Motors common stock, or 20 million shares out of the 88 million outstanding in 1949. This was enough to control the corporation's Board of Directors.

99. *U.S. v. E. I. du Pont de Nemours and Co.*, Civil 49–C–1071 (N.D. Ill. 1949), paragraph 18.

4. This control was further secured by the fact that du Pont officers or directors had always formed a majority of the Finance Committee of General Motors and its Bonus and Salary Committee, which reviewed the recommendations of the corporation's president as to the bonus payment to each participating executive. Thus, it was declared, "General Motors executives have responded readily to the influence and desires of the du Pont Company." [100]

5. In the late 1920s several members of the du Pont family purchased about 17 per cent of the outstanding stock of U.S. Rubber, thereby acquiring the same practical control of this corporation's policies. This control was strengthened by installation of another executive bonus system.

Alleged Conspiracy in Chemicals, Motor Vehicles and Tires

The chief injuries to competition resulting, according to the government, were these:

1. Du Pont agreed to give General Motors the benefits of any automotive discoveries it might make, while General Motors would turn over chemical discoveries to du Pont. Thus General Motors and, later, the Ethyl Corporation (half owned by General Motors and half by Standard Oil Company of New Jersey) gave du Pont the contract to make tetraethyl lead in plants which they had built; and General Motors gave du Pont 51 per cent of the stock of Kinetic Chemicals, Inc., which held the rights to Freon, a nontoxic and nonflammable refrigerant discovered by General Motors, and sold some of its own best products exclusively to General Motors.

2. General Motors bought from du Pont 75 to 80 per cent of its lacquers, paints, varnishes, thinners, antifreeze, coated fabrics and artificial leather. U.S. Rubber and du Pont bought from each other all but "limited amounts" of the products which they could supply. Du Pont bought from General Motors "substantially all" of the cars and trucks it used. Finally, U.S. Rubber supplied 55 to 75 per cent of the tires used by the various divisions of General Motors. In each case the market was foreclosed from competitive suppliers.

3. General Motors received at various times special discounts on its purchases — for example, a secret rebate ranging from 7½ to 15 per cent from du Pont, and discounts from U.S. Rubber ranging from 1½ to 10 per cent.

100. *Ibid.*, paragraph 55.

4. The corporations had refrained from expanding into each other's fields. Thus General Motors had rejected a proposal to make tires.

5. Du Pont had secured lists of General Motors' suppliers, to use loss of this trade as a threat to make them purchase all chemical components from du Pont.

Consequences of the Conspiracy

The government argued that this presumed conspiracy had serious practical consequences.

1. As a result of the "assured availability of a substantial and non-competitive market for any product usable by General Motors which du Pont might contemplate manufacturing," [101] du Pont entered upon a "subsidized and protected expansion program" which made it the largest chemical company in the country.[102]

2. The discounts received from the other two companies "contributed substantially to the enhancement of the size, power, and market control of General Motors." [103]

3. "Availability of the guaranteed noncompetitive General Motors' market for a tremendous quantity of tires and tubes has enabled United States Rubber to advance from a position of financial distress to one of profit and power." [104]

4. While these three corporate giants were expanding through "intercompany subsidization," [105] independent firms were suffering from inability to compete on sales to the three, from having to buy du Pont chemicals if they sold to General Motors, and from the higher prices charged by these three corporations in trying to make up their losses on sales to each other.

Relief Asked by the Government

The Department of Justice, claiming violations of Sections 1 and 2 of the Sherman Act and Section 7 of the Clayton Act, demanded the following sweeping relief: (1) that du Pont and the other stockholding corporations, Christiana and Delaware, each "be required promptly to dispose by sale of all of its holdings of such stock in General Motors,

101. *Ibid.*, paragraph 84.
102. *Ibid.*, paragraph 105.
103. *Ibid.*, paragraph 133.
104. *Ibid.*, paragraph 132.
105. *Ibid.*, paragraph 134.

and promptly thereafter to pay to its stockholders in cash dividends the entire proceeds of such sale"; [106] (2) that members of the du Pont family be required to sell their stock in General Motors and U.S. Rubber; (3) that General Motors and U.S. Rubber be given one-year options to buy these stockholdings; (4) that du Pont be required to sell its half interest in Ethyl Corporation, and that General Motors and du Pont be required to sell their shares in Kinetic Chemicals; (5) that U.S. Rubber and General Motors be required to drop as directors any person who had ever been an officer, director or employee of du Pont; (6) that all of these prohibitions and injunctions be made perpetual; and (7) "that each and every contract between du Pont, General Motors, United States Rubber, or any of them relating to the sale of goods, the grant of licenses or agreements to license under patents or applications for patents, or agreements providing for the exchange of knowhow and information, be cancelled." [107]

In connection with the fourth demand, General Motors had already begun in 1948 negotiations to sell its remaining 49 per cent share in Kinetic Chemicals to du Pont. This sale was completed in 1949 with the government's approval. A monopoly of certain chemicals was thus considered less dangerous in the hands of one company than in the hands of two.

Victory of du Pont

Preparation and trial of the case, and writing of the opinion, required five years. In December 1954, Judge Walter J. LaBuy of the U.S. District Court in Northern Illinois held for the defendants on all counts. His conclusions of fact may be summarized as follows:

1. The original stock purchase had been "essentially an investment" and not an effort to control the companies and thus restrain trade.[108]

2. The record of the relations of du Pont and General Motors "shows consultation and conference, but not domination," [109] and the bonus system was installed in General Motors as a good management method and not as a mechanism of control. On the General Motors Policy Committee, created in 1937, there were only three (perhaps

106. *Ibid.*, "Prayer," paragraph 3, also 5.
107. *Ibid.*, paragraph 22.
108. *U.S. v. E. I. du Pont de Nemours & Co.*, 126 F. Supp. 235, 242 (N.D. Ill. 1954).
109. *Ibid.*, at 251.

two) du Pont representatives out of nine members. In fact, the Court found that for three decades du Pont had not had "practical or working control of General Motors." [110]

3. Instead of buying all of its chemicals from du Pont and its tires from U.S. Rubber at the behest of du Pont, General Motors had bought purely with an eye to its own interests. Although du Pont officials made many efforts to capitalize on the stock relationship to make sales to General Motors and had some early successes,[111] the evidence was convincing that "General Motors trade could only be secured on a competitive basis." [112] Thus Goodyear and Goodrich (not Firestone, which had close relations with Ford) were asked for quotations on tires before the contract was made with U.S. Rubber because of its much lower figure, and the price secrecy merely followed the custom in that trade. Judge LaBuy also found some of the government's estimates of product buying among the three companies exaggerated.

4. Du Pont influence did not prevent General Motors from using its chemical discoveries in whatever way it might see fit; and no conspiracy is implied by intelligent collaboration on the application of technical research — for instance, by having an experienced chemical company like du Pont handle dangerous manufacturing processes in this field.

The Court did not have to rule on whether or not domination of a big company in one industry by one in another is legal, since it held that such domination did not exist in this case. The purchase of another company's stock or assets with the effect of substantially lessening competition is, therefore, not protected in any way by the decision.

This decisive defeat for the Department of Justice in the Chicago District Court, following upon defeats in a case against du Pont in Wilmington on charges of monopolizing cellophane and in a case in New York against seventeen important investment bankers, seemed to some observers to mark 1954 as a significant year in setting limits on antitrust enforcement. The drive against giant business launched in the 1940s had been sharply checked, for a time at least.

110. *Ibid.*, at 254.

111. Example in Plaintiff's Pre-trial Brief, October 15, 1952, p. 41.

112. 126 F. Supp., at 243.

Implications of the du Pont Case

The government appealed the General Motors part of the case, though not the U.S. Rubber part, to the Supreme Court. Even if the Court should later order du Pont to dispose of its shares in General Motors on the ground that the situation constituted a threatening concentration of power, some of the issues raised by the District Court trial and decision will continue to be important. Four of the issues will be discussed briefly.

The du Pont group had in fact purchased a sufficient interest in General Motors and U.S. Rubber to permit it to exert an important influence on some of their management policies, even if not (as Judge LaBuy decided) on their purchasing policies. It is the opinion of investment experts, backed up by the statements in the government's complaint, that the du Pont influence helped to improve the performance of both companies. Gradually General Motors became more independent, and long before the 1949 suit the du Pont group was apparently exerting only moderately greater influence than other large stockholders. The decision indicated that such an investment, if proved to be beneficial by the growth to large size of the corporation whose shares were bought, would not by that very outcome also prove to have been unlawful.

The suit highlighted the desirability of clarifying the income tax position of a corporation that, after such a successful investment, is required by a court to distribute such shares and step out of the picture. The government's demand in this case, that du Pont sell its stock in General Motors and distribute the proceeds as a cash dividend to its own stockholders, would have called for a punitive tax, by (a) imposing a capital gains tax on the company itself, (b) imposing on the individual shareholders a tax at the personal income tax rates, and (c) pushing these shareholders into a temporary high bracket for the year of this dividend. If one uses the figures in the complaint as to the ownership of General Motors stock by the du Pont family and their holding companies, and assumes that the 186 members of the family who were made defendants and the other 82,000 du Pont stockholders as of 1949 had an average income between $20,000 and $25,000 (as did the median receiver of dividends subject to income tax [113]), the corporate plus individual tax payable would have taken a full two

113. Calculated from *Statistical Abstract of the United States*, 1952, pp. 321–23.

thirds of the total gain on the General Motors stock between its purchase and 1949 — which gain was almost its total value by that time.[114] The milder remedy of a "spinoff" of the stock to du Pont shareholders — which the government did not believe would create a real separation — would have relieved the corporation of tax but still taken close to half the proceeds in individual income tax. Had it not been for the tax threat and the stigma attached to defeat in an antitrust suit, the defendants in this case — according to widespread rumor [115] — would have been willing to dispose of these investments.

A constructive aspect of the decision was the refusal of Judge LaBuy to declare the patent and research agreements in this case illegal. It would have been a backward step to forbid an automobile company to license a chemical company — experienced as such a company is in technology, quality control and accident prevention — to make a chemical product which the automobile company might discover. This would be especially important with chemicals as dangerous as those used in making tetraethyl lead and Freon.

A debatable point is the Court's refusal to condemn under the Sherman or Clayton Act the contracts by which one company agreed to purchase a large part of its requirements of a given product (such as tires or lacquer) from another company at a discount. The complaint itself conceded the value of these contracts — in cutting the costs of one firm by giving it an assured market, and reducing the price paid by the other — but wanted them abolished as giving an advantage over competitors. The economic good in generally preventing two firms from making a mutual agreement which reduces the costs of one and the price paid by the other is dubious, but it should be healthy to discourage such contracts among corporations with mutual stockholdings. Such stockholdings are too likely to be used to foreclose a market from competition. Judge LaBuy's decision can be justified on the ground that evidence at the trial proved that General Motors had successfully resisted the attempts of some du Pont officers to keep it as a captive market. A court which had to pass on the legality of a newly executed stock purchase would have no reason to expect such resistance, and might reasonably rule that only sale of the stock would assure a fair chance for competitive products.

114. An estimate that taxes would take 50 per cent of du Pont's capital gain is made in Lawrence P. Lessing, "The World of du Pont," *Fortune*, October 1953, p. 160.

115. Compare *Business Week*, April 11, 1953, pp. 60–64.

Competitive Status

Disappearance of Automotive Producers

Since 1896, when the Duryea Motor Wagon Company produced thirteen gasoline cars, the automotive industry has yielded fabulous profits to successful participants, but the number of failures has far exceeded the number of successes. The complete list of 1,119 producers before 1926 included mostly "paper" firms,[116] but an impressive number, according to Ralph C. Epstein's researches, did produce cars commercially between 1903 and 1926. Twelve were in operation in 1902; 169 more had entered before 1926; and yet only 44 were in existence in the later year. The average annual rate of failure had been 8.1 per cent, or nine times the failure rate of all manufacturing and trading firms.[117]

Nor did the process of disappearance come to an end in 1926, for by 1954 only six companies were left and by 1956 only five. A few had vanished by merger — some only when they were close to bankruptcy — and one or two by withdrawal from car production, but most of the industry's "exits" represented outright failures. Disappearance of nine in prosperous 1928 furnishes one indication that these failures have been due to the intensity of competition within the industry itself. (See Table 54.)

As for the makes of passenger cars, there are said to have been 2,726 sold in the history of the industry.[118] Many must have vanished almost as soon as they made their appearance.

The "Big Three"

The first very successful producer of gasoline automobiles was the Olds Motor Works, whose Oldsmobile is estimated to have comprised one quarter to one third of the passenger cars turned out from 1900 to 1904. In 1905 Cadillac led with 16 per cent; then the Ford Motor Company took over the leadership for three years; and in 1909 and 1910 the newly organized General Motors Corporation was temporarily in first place. From 1911 through 1926 the famous Model T kept Ford continuously in top position.

116. Donald A. Moore, "The Automobile Industry," Chap. 8 in Walter Adams, ed., *The Structure of American Industry*, Macmillan, New York, revised edition, 1954, p. 278.

117. Epstein, *The Automobile Industry*, pp. 176–77.

118. Lewis D. Crusoe, Kilgore Hearings, Part 2, p. 673.

TABLE 54

AUTOMOBILES: PRODUCTION OF PASSENGER CARS AND NUMBER OF PRODUCERS, 1903–55

Year	Number of Producers (Start of Year)	Number of Cars Produced	Per Cent of Total New Car Output or Registrations			
			General Motors[a]	Ford[b]	Chrysler	"Independents"
		(Thousands)				
1903	12	11		15.1		
1904	24	22		7.6		
1905	35	24		6.6		
1906	38	33		26.3		
1907	43	43		34.6		
1908	44	64		16.1		
1909	52	124	25.0	14.3		
1910	69	181	21.7	17.7		
1911	52	199	17.9	35.0		
1912	53	356	13.8	47.8		
1913	57	462	10.1	43.9		
1914	70	548	9.8	56.2		
1915	71	896	8.5	56.0		
1916	75	1,526	8.7	48.2		
1917	74	1,746	19.6	35.6		
1918	76	943	26.2	46.2		
1919	71	1,652	21.8	49.7		
1920	77	1,906	18.1	22.0		
1921	84	1,468	13.9	61.6		
1922	88	2,274	19.5	51.6		
1923	83	3,625	21.3	47.8		
1924	70	3,186	17.7	50.2		
1925	57	3,735	20.0	42.4	9.1	28.5
1926	49	3,692	27.2	35.2	10.7	26.9
1927	44, 29[c]	2,937	42.5	15.2	10.6	31.7
1928	24	3,775	41.3	15.5	10.6	32.6
1929	15	4,455	32.7	33.9	8.7	24.7
1930	16	2,787	34.5	40.3	8.5	16.7
1931	16	1,948	43.3	27.9	12.0	16.8
1932	16	1,104	41.5	23.9	17.4	17.2
1933	16	1,561	43.3	21.0	25.8	9.9
1934	16	2,161	39.8	28.2	22.9	9.1
1935	13	3,274	38.3	30.2	22.9	8.6
1936	13	3,679	43.1	22.4	25.0	9.5
1937	12	3,929	40.6	22.7	25.4	11.3
1938	10	2,020	44.8	20.5	25.0	9.7
1939	10	2,889	43.7	21.4	24.2	10.7
1940	10	3,717	47.5	18.9	23.7	9.9
1941	8	3,780	47.3	18.8	24.2	9.7

(Continued on facing page)

TABLE 54 *(Continued)*

Year	Number of Producers (Start of Year)	Number of Cars Produced	Per Cent of Total New Car Output or Registrations: General Motors[a]	Ford[b]	Chrysler	"Independents"
		(Thousands)				
1946[d]	8	2,149	37.8	22.0	25.7	14.5
1947	10	3,558	41.9	21.1	21.8	15.2
1948	10	3,909	40.6	18.8	21.5	19.1
1949	10	5,119	42.9	21.3	21.4	14.4
1950	10	6,666	45.4	24.0	17.6	13.0
1951	10	5,338	42.8	22.2	21.8	13.2
1952	10	4,321	41.7	22.8	21.3	14.2
1953	9	6,117	45.1	25.2	20.3	9.4
1954	6	5,559	50.7	30.8	12.9	5.6
1955	6	7,942	50.8	27.6	16.8	4.8

Sources: Number of companies through 1927 from Ralph C. Epstein, *The Automobile Industry: Its Economic and Commercial Development*, A. W. Shaw Co., Chicago, 1928, p. 176; number since 1928 derived from list of cars produced in *Automobile News*, 1956 Almanac Issue, April 30, 1956, p. 75; number of cars produced from Automobile Manufacturers Ass'n., *Automobile Facts and Figures*, 1956, p. 3; General Motors output before 1925 from Florence Heiman, *The Relation of Theory to Economic History in the Automobile Industry*, unpublished master's thesis, New York University, New York, 1948, p. 26; Ford output before 1925 from company archives as tabulated in *Wall Street Journal*, November 7, 1955, p. 14; other registration percentages, 1925–28, from Paul H. Banner, *Competition in the Automobile Industry*, unpublished doctoral thesis, Harvard University, Cambridge, 1953, p. 53; General Motors, Ford and Chrysler registrations, 1929–55, from Standard & Poor's Corp., *Industry Surveys*, "Autos," Basic Analysis, June 7, 1956, p. A 109, independents being obtained by subtraction. The original source for these percentages is usually annual statistical issues of the trade journal, *Automotive Industries*.

a. Through 1924, total new car output. b. Through 1922, total new car output.

c. Start of new series. Since the new source shows only 29 instead of 44 producers in 1927, it is evidently less exhaustive, and the interpretation of "producing company" probably differs.

d. In the war period 1942–45, only 293,000 passenger cars were manufactured.

In those early years Henry Ford and his engineers perfected the characteristic feature of automobile production, the assembly line, which was the key to large-volume, low-cost production of cars. At the same time Ford introduced his famous policy of pricing below cost in order to stimulate sales to the point where his volume would be great enough to bring average cost again below price. Ford's output leaped year by year: in 1921 it was 61.6 per cent of the industry total, the highest figure any company has reached (Table 54). In 1924 the official price of a Ford runabout was only $260, "the lowest-priced automobile that Ford or anyone else had ever built" [119] — even if the consumer paid more in practice because of accessories [120] — but sales had already leveled off.

General Motors was formed by William C. Durant in 1908 to bring together his Buick — then the second-ranking car — the Oldsmobile and two cars which were later dropped. The Oakland and Cadillac were added in 1909. By 1910 twenty-six companies of all sorts had been combined. The Chevrolet Motor Company — also built up by Durant, independently — merged with General Motors in 1917. The Pontiac car, launched in 1926, soon absorbed the Oakland and completed General Motors' present line. Although General Motors originated in and grew by mergers, its advance after 1917 was due to success in production and selling much more than to its further acquisition of parts makers. In 1927, when it was no longer making acquisitions, it passed the Ford Motor Company, which in its fourth year of declining sales had been obliged to close down to modernize its car. Ford's new Model A took back the lead in 1929 and 1930, but General Motors then resumed first place and has held it ever since, with its share of the total market ranging from 38 to 51 per cent. From 1936 through 1949 Ford ranked behind the Chrysler Corporation, which had taken over from the declining Maxwell Motor Company in 1923, had bought the successful producer, Dodge Brothers, in 1928, and from then on grew by its own merits rather than by further mergers. In 1950 Ford recovered second place.

The trend toward concentration in the industry is best seen in the decline of the so-called "independents," whose share of the market dwindled from 24 per cent and over in the late 1920s to 5 per cent in 1955, and whose number has fallen to two.

Concentration in Truck Manufacture

The history of truck makers is similar, although the rate of disappearance has been lower. For the thirty-year period 1926–55, *Automotive News* lists eighty makes of trucks produced by almost as many companies, plus an unstated number of "miscellaneous" makes whose output was never more than 4 per cent of the total. In 1926 Ford had 52 per cent of the total output, General Motors 15 per cent, Graham-

119. E. D. Kennedy, *The Automobile Industry: The Coming of Age of Capitalism's Favorite Child*, Reynal & Hitchcock, New York, 1941, p. 166.

120. E. Steward Freeman, letter to *Business Week*, July 14, 1956, p. 10.

TABLE 55

AUTOMOBILES: PERCENTAGE DISTRIBUTION OF NEW TRUCK REGISTRATIONS, BY MAKE, 1926–55

Make of Truck	1926	1937	1948	1955
All makes	100.0	100.0	100.0	100.0
Ford	51.7	30.6	21.8	30.9
Chevrolet and GMC (General Motors)	15.1	36.7	36.4	43.3
Graham	6.4	—	—	—
Dodge (Chrysler Corp. since 1928)	6.3	12.6[a]	11.1	6.9
International	3.7	12.3	12.1	10.5
Reo	3.5	.7	1.0	.3
White	2.3	1.0	1.1	1.5
Mack	2.3	.9	.9	1.1
Diamond T	.4	1.3	1.0	.4
Willys	—	.2	7.4	2.8
Studebaker	—	.8	4.9	1.1
Others	8.3	2.9	2.3	1.2
Number of makes listed	24	19	43	12
Number of trucks made (*thousands*)	387.3	618.2	1,035.2	957.0

Source: Calculated from *Automotive News*, 1956 Almanac Issue, April 30, 1956, p. 77.
a. Including Plymouth.

Paige and Dodge 6 per cent each, and International Harvester 4 per cent. General Motors with its two makes, Chevrolet and GMC, passed Ford in 1933, and has held its lead. In 1955 its production was 43 per cent, Ford's 31 per cent, International's 10 per cent, Dodge's 7 per cent. Studebaker and Willys had been added to the important makers in the 1930s, and four other small makers had continued to produce throughout the thirty years. The remaining transitory and tiny producers made 8 per cent of the total in 1926, 4 per cent in 1937, 2 per cent in 1948 and 1 per cent in 1955. They numbered (exclusive of those in the "miscellaneous" category, which were individually too small to mention) 14 in 1926, 8 in 1937, 32 in 1948, and one in 1955. (See Table 55.)

The same firms are dominant in trucks as in passenger cars, with the one major addition of International Harvester in heavy trucks. However, the small producers have held on better in trucks (including the Willys Jeep) than in passenger cars. Heavy trucks are often custom built, leaving no scope for mass production. The truck business in general lacks some of the features which hurt the small producer in the passenger car field — for example, the necessity of financing frequent model changes and supporting as large a dealer organization.

Reasons for Survival

The automobile industry is almost the best example in American manufacturing of an industry in which large size is essential to success. It is on the whole the economy of size, rather than the process of merger, which has reduced the number of passenger car assemblers to five. In fact, the need for enlarging the capital base to make production more efficient has been behind every merger.[121] The Ford company attained its size by the manufacturing genius and farsighted price policy of its founder, and its huge resources based on continuous reinvestment of profits enabled it to avoid shipwreck when the founder lost his magic touch. General Motors attained size at the start by merger; then its diversification as planned by Durant, plus the investment of du Pont money and the installation of a new management under Alfred P. Sloan, Jr., enabled it to weather the difficulties caused by Durant's overexpansion after World War I. Chrysler Corporation expanded both through its merger with Dodge, which gave it needed facilities, dealers and executives, and through the engineering and styling genius of Walter P. Chrysler — one of whose achievements was to launch the low-priced Plymouth in 1928 as a successful rival of Ford and Chevrolet.[122] Again, the wealth and size of the company were necessary to enable it to survive the failure of the unduly advanced "Airflow" model of 1934 and the much more serious reluctance to restyle its cars in 1951.

These examples serve to illustrate the opinion of an authority on the early history of the industry that "the elusive and imponderable qualities of personality have been the most effective causes of conspicuous success in the automobile industry." [123] They may also demonstrate that when managers, "having become accustomed to methods and tactics which they themselves have developed," ignore "methods later devised by newer and bolder minds," [124] large capital plus product diversification may be necessary to save a company.

Economies of Size

The advantages of size in automobile manufacturing have been effectively summarized by Donald A. Moore, in his chapter in Walter

121. Paul H. Banner, *Competition in the Automobile Industry*, unpublished doctoral thesis, Harvard University, Cambridge, 1953, Chap. 5, "Mergers."

122. See *Chrysler Corporation: The Story of an American Company*, Chrysler Corp., 1955.

123. Lawrence H. Seltzer, *A Financial History of the American Automobile Industry*, Houghton Mifflin, Boston, 1928, p. 66.

124. Epstein, *The Automobile Industry*, pp. 210–11.

Adams' collection of studies, *The Structure of American Industry*.[125] These advantages fall into six categories.

First and foremost, large size permits the most effective use of the *tools of mass production* developed by the industry. For example, the cost of the expensive machine tools to stamp out parts from strip steel would be prohibitive unless spread over many units.

A closely allied point is the need for large *resources to finance new models*. Without an occasional "face lifting," any car loses its attraction for the public, and its sales eventually decline; but tools, dies and other requirements for a new model are tremendously expensive. If the new model proves to be a "bust," the producer may have to live on working capital for a year. It is of decisive importance that $25 million spent on tools and dies for two years' use may cost $10 per Chevrolet made, but $250 per Hudson.

An advantage of great importance is the ability to finance the *technical and market research*, *engineering*, *advertising*, *styling* and other central office services which a big company can offer to its manufacturing plants. It is here that General Motors, most of whose individual parts factories and assembly plants are no bigger than those of other companies, has had a pre-eminent advantage. A recent estimate puts the corporation's annual research and development expenditures at $250 million.[126] The profitable discoveries of its research department in fuels, chemicals and engines are illustrative. These are regularly made available to competitors, but the finder has a head start, royalties and a valuable reputation as an innovator. The opening in May 1956 of General Motors' Technical Research Center, near Detroit, built at a cost of perhaps $150 million, was expected to be followed soon by an equally costly Ford Center.[127] This whole advantage may also be put in terms of ability to hire the necessary high-priced talent in several fields. The big motor companies call themselves "pools of talent."

Only a big company can support the widespread *dealer organization* that makes it possible to tap demand wherever it may arise and at the same time gives car owners confidence that, wherever they may be driving, reliable repair service and replacement parts will be available. This knowledge helps support the level of used-car prices of a manufacturer's model, and this in turn makes the new cars more salable.

125. Moore, "The Automobile Industry," pp. 294–300.

126. Francis Bello, "How Strong Is G.M. Research?," *Fortune*, June 1956, p. 188.

127. *Ibid.*, pp. 139–40.

A dealer organization does not, however, rank first in importance, since experience has shown that what promises to be a popular car will attract all dealers that a producer can use.

A company with a *diversified product line* of high- and low-priced models can capitalize on the particular price class which wins public favor in a given year or period, and protect itself against failure of a model by reason of an engineering or styling mistake. Such diversification offers economies which might not at first be apparent, since it is possible to standardize many of the parts of the different cars — even in some instances the bodies. Thus the Cadillac and two of the Buick cars use the same body, two other Buicks and the Oldsmobile a second, and the Chevrolet and Pontiac a third. Diversification is especially important in times of depressed business, when a company with several cars can still achieve economies of mass production by this use of parts which the maker of one car cannot achieve.[128] Diversification into nonautomotive lines serves somewhat the same function, and its absence is considered a weak point in a company's structure.[129]

Size yields a net advantage in *purchasing*. The price of steel is the same to all buyers above a minimum quantity, but in a time of shortage the large customer (unless there is government allocation) may get his steel before the small one.[130] There is said to be little or no difference in price to manufacturing buyers of standard parts.[131] But a large company has greater freedom of choice between buying parts and making its own, and can hold that alternative before a supplier in order to obtain better terms on quantities large enough or specifications different enough to satisfy Section 2 of the Clayton Act.[132]

Increasing Advantages of Size

The advantages of size have been increasing in recent years. One factor is the invention of more complicated machinery, culminating in "automation." While it is forecast that small producers will be able to

128. Banner thesis, p. 85.

129. *Wall Street Journal*, May 19, 1955, p. 16.

130. George W. Mason, then president of American Motors Corp., cited in *Business Week*, February 6, 1954, p. 56.

131. James J. Nance, president of Studebaker-Packard Corp., in *Automobile Marketing Practices*, Hearings before a Subcommittee of the Senate Interstate and Foreign Commerce Committee, 84th Cong., 2d sess., 1956, Part 1, p. 380.

132. Compare L. L. Dodge, director of planning and budgets of Dana Corp., Kilgore Hearings, Part 7, pp. 2972, 2974, 2981.

use this extreme form of substitution of automatically controlled machinery for labor, the big manufacturers can nevertheless use it most effectively. Another factor is the increased importance of style, which gives the mass producer an advantage through "sheer impact of product volume," since "familiarity helps shape styling preferences." [133] The frequency of model changes is increasing; moreover, the cost of tooling for a new model is said to have advanced 200 per cent between the immediate postwar years and 1955, as against an advance of only 35 per cent in wages.[134] Increased emphasis on research and product improvement plays into the hands of the big companies. This is reflected in the increased complexity of the car itself: a Ford, for example, has over 10,000 parts today as compared to about 5,000 in the days of the Model T.[135] Some believe that the vogue of long-distance vacation trips has shown car owners the desirability of a widespread network of repair and service facilities. Certainly the failure of so many companies over the years has pointed up the danger of buying a car which may become an "orphan" through discontinuance of its manufacture.

A survey of the ratio of earnings before income taxes to gross income of all the passenger car producers that published figures throughout the whole period from 1935 through 1953, omitting the war and reconversion period 1942–46, discloses that General Motors had the highest ratio in each of the fourteen years, and Chrysler the second highest except from 1947 through 1951, when it ranked behind Nash-Kelvinator and, in 1948 only, behind Packard as well. A comparison for the whole period, and for two three-year periods before and after World War II, shows a strong tendency for profits to vary with size. (See Table 56.) Ford was an exception in the twenty-year period 1927–46; though no figures were published, the company is believed to have lost money on net balance or earned very little at best during those years. The explanation appears to be, not its size, but the obsolete management methods during Henry Ford's old age. Since 1949 the Ford company, second largest in size, has consistently had the second highest profit ratio.

The price trends since 1941 seem to illustrate this growing advantage of size. According to a tabulation by General Motors, its list price

133. George Romney, president of American Motors Corp., *ibid.*, Part 1, p. 455.

134. James J. Nance, *ibid.*, Part 2, p. 862.

135. Lewis D. Crusoe, *ibid.*, pp. 651–52.

TABLE 56

AUTOMOBILES: PERCENTAGE RETURN ON SALES OF AUTOMOBILE MAKERS, 1935–53

(Ratio of Earnings before Income Taxes to Gross Income)

Firm [a]	Median [b]	Mean [c]	
		1939–41	1950–52
General Motors Corp.	17.5	18.2	21.3
Ford Motor Co.	—	—	14.5
Chrysler Corp.	8.4	8.0	9.0
Studebaker Corp.	5.0	4.2	5.9
Nash-Kelvinator Corp.	6.6	3.0	9.4
Willys-Overland Motors, Inc.	3.4	−6.8	5.5
Packard Motor Car Co.	4.4	1.9	5.3
Hudson Motor Car Co.	3.2	.3	4.8

Source: Moody's *Industrials.*

a. Firms are listed in order of their 1952 gross income.

b. War and reconversion period 1942–46 omitted.

c. The prewar years used in this comparison begin with the revival of demand in 1939, and the postwar period ends before mergers began to combine the firms listed.

for four-door sedans (model not otherwise specified) advanced 122 per cent between the model years 1941 and 1956, while Ford's price advanced 133 per cent, Chrysler's 136 per cent, and that of "all others" 143 per cent. (See Table 57.) Although a difference of $25 or $50 in the price of two cars of different names and somewhat different characteristics is not decisive in the market, it may swing to the big seller a few buyers whom his small competitor might need badly.

"The Closure of Entry"

The contrast in the passenger car industry is impressive between the early period, when new companies entered every year, and the present time, with no existing competitor that has entered since 1923. The author of an article on "the closure of entry" [136] in this industry attributes the ease of entry down to the 1920s to rapidly expanding sales, techniques which called for relatively little capital, etc. As of 1952 he found a "plateau" in the long-run trend of demand for cars (a hypothesis which was apparently weakened in 1955), a need for both plant and firm size to be much larger than formerly in order to

136. Harold G. Vatter, "The Closure of Entry in the American Automobile Industry," *Oxford Economic Papers* (New Series), Clarendon Press, Oxford (England), October 1952, pp. 213–34.

TABLE 57

AUTOMOBILES: INDEXES OF PASSENGER CAR LIST PRICES, 1947–56

(1941 = 100)

Model Year[a]	General Motors	Ford	Chrysler	"Independents"
1947	150	151	153	160
1950	182	187	193	205
1953	207	209	229	228
1956	222	233	236	243

Source: Years selected from statement by Harlow H. Curtice on "The Development and Growth of General Motors," in *A Study of the Antitrust Laws*, Hearings before Subcommittee on Antitrust and Monopoly, Senate Judiciary Committee, 84th Cong., 1st sess., 1955, Part 7, p. 3516; or Part 8, p. 4484.

a. Prices are "at about the beginning of the year" for all four-door sedans. The source gives all intervening years except 1943, 1944 and 1945.

minimize costs, and, as the years pass, increasing difficulty for a new firm in winning popularity as against the established and well-known makes of car.

Proof of the present difficulty or impossibility of entry is to be found in the postwar experience. In 1948, in hopes of riding the postwar boom, at least twenty motor companies were incorporated, but not one ever produced in volume.[137] Most, it is true, planned to make midget or other special types of cars.[138] Henry J. Kaiser, however, had entered the industry in 1945 with huge capital available from three sources: the other Kaiser enterprises, which were eventually to pour in $70 million according to one estimate; [139] $53 million in stock sold to the public on the basis of the Kaiser name; and government aid in the form of favorable plant lease terms plus a loan of $44 million from the Reconstruction Finance Corporation in 1949. He also had Graham-Paige — the shell, with some equipment, of a former producing company.

The Kaiser-Frazer Corporation had to spend $40 million in acquiring steel by barter and otherwise, owing to the postwar shortage.[140] In some other respects the new company was even aided by established

137. *Business Week*, February 6, 1954, p. 55.

138. Banner thesis, p. 29.

139. William B. Harris, "Last Stand of the Auto Independents?," *Fortune*, December 1954, p. 206.

140. Edgar F. Kaiser, president of Kaiser Motors Corp., Kilgore Hearings, Part 2, p. 537.

companies.[141] As long as the shortage of cars created a market for every unit produced, Kaiser-Frazer did well, but when the market turned down, its sales dropped sharply. The difficulty has been attributed by industry members to two basic causes. Competitors usually cite high costs of production due to inexperience and lack of the most effective facilities, together with inability to match the high-priced production talent, and hence the quality of product, of existing companies. Some stress the difficulty of building up a first-rate dealer organization, which was all the more necessary for a new, unestablished car that some customers might fear to buy lest it soon be orphaned. All of these problems might have been solved in time, with sufficient (if fantastically large) capital.[142] In 1953 the company, newly named Kaiser Motors Corporation, sought a solution in merger with Willys-Overland Motors, an independent that was still making money; but in 1955 it had to retreat to manufacture of the Willys Jeep. In 1956 it became a unit in the new Kaiser Industries Corporation.

Such "entry" as still exists in passenger cars seems likely to be through new cars produced by established companies, or through changes in the character of established cars without change of name.[143] The Nash company's Rambler, unveiled in 1950, has been the only successful new car introduced since the Plymouth in 1928. Although the continual freshening of the industry by the entry of new firms has vanished, the present companies give the consumer a choice of product almost as wide as in the time when there were many more sellers, but when each had far fewer models.[144]

Last Stand of the Auto Independents?

Between 1946 and 1952 the seven independents, favored by the government in allocations of scarce materials and benefited in some cases by well-styled models, accounted for 13 to 19 per cent of the passenger car market. By the summer of 1953 consumers had satisfied their first postwar needs and could afford once again to pick and choose. The share of the independents now decreased rapidly, by reason of the increasing disadvantages of relatively small size — but

141. See "Kaiser-Frazer: 'The Roughest Thing We Ever Tackled'," *Fortune*, July 1951, p. 157.

142. Banner thesis, p. 32.

143. Vatter, "The Closure of Entry in the American Automobile Industry," p. 229.

144. Banner thesis, p. 44.

perhaps also because their managements proved less resilient than those of the "big three." [145]

Crosley Motors dropped out of the race, and in 1953 and 1954 the six others merged into three companies. The Department of Justice and the Federal Trade Commission gave their approval to the combinations in hopes that larger companies could put up a stronger competitive battle. But the formula on which independents had often prospered — avoiding direct price competition with the "big three" by offering cars with features which the latter considered too radical for the mass market — seemed to have failed.[146] The big producers had found the secret of putting into their products as much difference in style as the public seemed to want, and at the same time their research departments were now developing new mechanical features whose appearance in the mass-produced cars compelled their acceptance by the independents.[147] In 1956 American Motors was optimistic that its small Rambler would carry it over the top as a car for the economy-minded or a second car for the family. Studebaker-Packard, however, escaped the probability of failure only by negotiating with the big Curtiss-Wright Corporation to take a three-year management contract, and again the aim of keeping out of competition with the "big three" and finding the niches to fill in was stressed.[148]

In no other industry — not even in integrated steel manufacture — would corporations with a quarter of a billion in assets be in danger of inability to compete. Among the top 350 industrial corporations in 1955 the only two to lose money were Studebaker-Packard and American Motors, which ranked seventy-fifth and eighty-first in sales. In size called for, the automobile industry appears to be unique.

The Diversification of General Motors

Of the twenty industries examined in this book, only shoe machinery shows a greater concentration of production in a single company than passenger cars. In the first postwar years General Motors' share of production ran at about 42 per cent, though it was larger in 1950 when Chrysler was hampered by a one-hundred-day strike. The corporation

145. James J. Nance, Kilgore Hearings, Part 2, pp. 860, 869.

146. Harris, "Last Stand of the Auto Independents?," p. 114.

147. *Ibid.*, p. 211.

148. Roy T. Hurley, president of Curtiss-Wright Corp., cited in *Automotive News*, August 13, 1956, p. 50.

hoped to step this up to the 48 per cent which it had almost reached in 1940 and 1941,[149] or to resume its "historic position." [150] In fact, it found itself selling more than 50 per cent in 1954 and 1955, while its Chevrolet held the Number 1 position against the challenge of Ford. In 1956 General Motors was doing fully as well, but it still had no guarantee that the public would go on preferring the style and mechanical features of its models to those of its two big competitors, or even that the public would not again favor cars made by some smaller firm.

Although the bulk of General Motors' gross income comes from cars and trucks, and 84 per cent of its 1955 domestic employment was in automotive work of all sorts,[151] it has become important or dominant in several other fields. Its standard procedure has been to purchase a small company in some type of manufacturing to which it believes its skills are adapted, and then to put its resources to work there.

One field it has entered in this way is electrical refrigeration. In 1918 Durant purchased a small and unprofitable refrigerator company, hoping to develop a product for General Motors dealers to handle during the wartime automobile shutdown.[152] Over a period of several years of research General Motors developed the Frigidaire, which pioneered the mass use of electrical refrigeration and won 50 per cent of the market. As new competitors entered, this share dropped to less than 20 per cent in 1951 and, after a recovery, to less than 30 per cent in 1954, while the Frigidaire Division began producing a full line of appliances so as to stay competitive.

General Motors purchased control of the Yellow Cab Manufacturing Company in 1925, and in 1943 acquired the minority interest and changed the name to GMC Truck and Coach Division. Besides its production of taxicabs (discontinued in 1939) and trucks, this unit gradually became the principal producer of motor buses. Its share of this business was 24 per cent in 1924–31, 34 per cent in 1932–41, 38 per cent in 1942–51, and 66, 73, 78 and over 80 per cent, respectively, in 1952, 1953, 1954 and January–August 1955.[153] In 1952 and 1953

149. *Business Week*, February 13, 1954, p. 68.

150. General Motors Corp., Annual Report, 1952, p. 8.

151. *New York Times*, December 11, 1955, Sec. E, p. 11.

152. Roger M. Kyes, vice president of General Motors, Kilgore Hearings, Part 8, pp. 3939–44.

153. Statement of General Motors, *ibid.*, Part 6, p. 2628; see also Part 8, pp. 4312–13.

eight competitors dropped out of business,[154] one of those remaining being the Flxible Company, headed by a member of the General Motors board of directors who was also its largest individual stockholder. Meanwhile GMC Truck and Coach Division was becoming interested in the designing of lightweight trains.

In 1929 General Motors entered the aircraft engine field by purchasing, for $592,000, the Allison Engineering Company, a firm with a small building in Indianapolis.[155] General Motors had invested $4 million in unprofitable research before its liquid-cooled aircraft engine found wide use in World War II. In 1953 it allocated $75 million to research and development in air transport, according to an announcement of December 1955.[156]

In 1930 the corporation purchased a small firm that was making diesel engines and another that was designing and servicing gasoline engines for railroad branch lines.[157] By a large expenditure of research money, it used these organizations to develop the diesel locomotive. In the past twenty years this product of General Motors research has virtually ended the manufacture of steam locomotives. Although the corporation's Electro-Motive Division has licensed the firms that formerly made steam locomotives, its own share of diesel production has been around 60 per cent, and rose to 75 per cent in 1954.[158]

Purchase of the Euclid Road Machinery Company in 1953 promised similar developments in that industry.

Decentralization, Efficiency and Size

The widely publicized decentralization of the General Motors organization is one of the principal reasons for its success.[159] Its methods have been copied both within and outside the industry. The executives of each division are given wide authority — for example, to purchase either from other divisions of the corporation or from outside, depending on the terms offered — and are compensated in part according to division profits. Apart from foreign holdings, there were recently thirty-nine divisions, including five making passenger cars and

154. *Business Week*, July 14, 1956, p. 25.
155. Kilgore Hearings, Part 8, pp. 4292–93.
156. *Journal of Commerce*, December 20, 1955, p. 1.
157. Kilgore Hearings, Part 8, pp. 4297–98.
158. *Ibid.*, p. 3964.
159. Peter Drucker, *Concept of the Corporation*, John Day, New York, 1946.

separate divisions for many kinds of parts and accessories, such as spark plugs, radios and bearings. Thirty-two of the divisions do defense work in addition to their production of civilian goods.[160]

A minor reason for the corporation's success may be its willingness to dispose of properties which are no longer sufficiently profitable, or, as General Motors puts it, to which it can no longer make a contribution. It has sold interests in leather, glass and chemicals and in the Hertz Drivurself Company, for example.[161]

What was probably an unexpected, and possibly a resented, criticism came in July 1956, when the American Institute of Management announced that General Motors was one of the seventeen most efficient firms among the 413 it rated as excellent in management, but was also simply too big.[162] This represents a social point of view, on which opinion will differ, rather than an economic one. The automobile industry, the national economy and General Motors have all grown to unprecedented size. Ford had a larger share of the passenger car output in the early 1920s than General Motors thirty years later. Between 1929 and 1955 sales of automotive dealers increased by about 450 per cent, sales of General Motors by 706 per cent, and the gross national product by 274 per cent.[163] It could be said either that General Motors grew too fast or that it (and to a lesser degree, the rest of the automobile industry) lifted the rate of growth of the economy as a whole.

Does General Motors Fear to Compete Too Hard?

There is a widely held belief that General Motors restrains its expansion in the automobile field to avoid becoming an illegal monopoly under the Sherman Act. The corporation denies this, pointing out that no organization — especially one with an executive bonus plan — can keep its morale if such restraint is imposed.[164] On the contrary, its aim is said to be "an ever expanding G.M. in an ever expanding U.S. economy"; [165] and the corporation's president holds

160. Kilgore Hearings, Part 7, pp. 3481–91.

161. Louis C. Goad, executive vice president of General Motors, *ibid.*, pp. 3658–59.

162. *Journal of Commerce*, July 26, 1956, p. 2.

163. *Automobile Facts and Figures*, 1956, p. 10; General Motors annual reports.

164. *Business Week*, February 13, 1954, pp. 68–72.

165. Robert Sheehan, "How Harlow Curtice Earns His $750,000," *Fortune*, February 1956, p. 215.

that a 51 per cent share of sales "means we're losing almost five out of every ten deals." [166]

A more plausible form of this belief is that General Motors refrains from price cutting lest it ruin its competitors.[167] The corporation denies this also, arguing that price cutting just is not the most effective way of selling cars.[168] As a matter of fact, we have seen (Table 57) that General Motors has been keeping its prices below its competitors'. In 1955, for example, three Chevrolet models which could be matched precisely against Ford and Plymouth models were brought out at $22 to $61 less. General Motors declared in that year that it was setting prices to meet competition and if possible to make 15 to 20 per cent on capital investment after taxes.[169]

The most defensible argument is that a desire to escape the charge of becoming too large in car and truck production accounts for the corporation's expansion into nonautomotive fields. Even as to this, other explanations are possible — for example, the corporation might rationally have expected greater profits from entering a different field than from struggling against the terrific opposition for a few more points in the motor car field. The strength of this opposition should not be overlooked because more attention is given in these pages to General Motors. Ford and Chrysler as well possess the efficiencies of size and by their comebacks from serious slumps have proved their resiliency and flexibility.

General Motors and the Antitrust Agencies

Since early 1954 the antitrust agencies have given much of their attention to General Motors.[170] The then chairman of the Federal Trade Commission made clear early in 1955 that he wished there were some way under the law to break up the corporation.[171] The Antitrust Division investigated General Motors' domination of the locomotive indus-

166. *Ibid.*, p. 135.

167. Questions by Senator J. William Fulbright of Arkansas, *Stock Market Study*, Hearings before Senate Banking and Currency Committee, 84th Cong., 1st sess., 1955, pp. 829–30.

168. Harlow H. Curtice, *ibid.*

169. Albert Bradley, executive vice president of General Motors, Kilgore Hearings, Part 7, pp. 3585–87.

170. *Wall Street Journal*, April 15, 1954, pp. 1, 12; *Automotive News*, May 3, 1954, p. 1; *Business Week*, May 8, 1954, pp. 30–31.

171. *Automotive News*, January 10, 1955, p. 2; *Wall Street Journal*, March 21, 1955, p. 9.

try, but decided against suing. In 1955 it prepared a suit charging General Motors with monopolizing the bus market, and finally announced it in July 1956 on a television interview of the Attorney General. It thus risked the charge by political opponents that it had an eye on the national election and was trying to show that the presence of a former General Motors president and two dealers in the Cabinet had not made the administration pro-General Motors or pro-big business. The government's petition and the corporation's reply indicated that the issue would revolve around whether this domination of bus manufacturing had been achieved through unfair practices or through efficiency.

An interesting innovation in this bus suit was one part of the relief which the Antitrust Division asked. It would have been senseless to request the breakup of the Truck and Coach Division, a manufacturing business with a single plant; and to transfer it to a new owner would not have ended the monopoly. The government urged merely that General Motors not be allowed to sell more than half the requirements of each of four big users.[172] An incidental advantage — from the antitrust rather than the bus rider's point of view — might have been a rise in the cost of producing General Motors buses as a result of idle capacity, and hence perhaps a further loss in sales.

Meanwhile Assistant Attorney General Stanley N. Barnes conducted a war of words against General Motors. In one statement he suggested that it might be made the object of a "crash program" by the Antitrust Division and urged voluntary divestiture of two of its five passenger car divisions. Stockholders who did not expect an increase in the number of competing firms to produce greater profits must, in his opinion, believe in monopoly.[173] He had, however, approved the merger of independents in 1954 on the ground that they would "economize by eliminating duplicating facilities, secure better dealer representation and sell more complete lines of cars" [174] — a principle according to which the divestiture by General Motors would reduce efficiency. Even the nonautomotive units, whose separation is all that is asked by the Senator who conducted the 1955 hearings on General Motors (but who himself, like half of all drivers, "prefers G.M. cars

172. *Business Week*, July 14, 1956, p. 26.

173. *New York Times*, March 9, 1956, p. 32.

174. Kilgore Hearings, Part 1, p. 298.

actually" [175]), draw aid from the central organization.[176] Their separation would either reduce quality or increase costs.

The size and diversification of General Motors offer wide scope for charges of restraint of trade and monopoly. The undue influence which the company might obtain from its production of essential parts for sale to its competitors has been discussed, but one competitor denies that influence has been brought to bear.[177] Another broad charge is that its diversification gives the corporation power to cut prices in any one of its many markets and thus to ruin competitors and gain a monopoly there.[178] Although General Motors would hardly attempt a maneuver so obviously illegal under the Sherman Act, there is considerable truth in the view that "GM is in the position of a clean-fighting, but hammer-fisted, heavyweight matched against a middleweight. Unless the big fellow pulls his punches, he is sure to give his opponent a bad beating." [179] Fortunately for the consumer, the "beating" is likely to be first of all in technology and cost of production.

Two Patent Associations

The patent history of the industry has been marked by two well-known episodes. From 1903 to 1911 almost all motor vehicle manufacturers paid royalties for the use of the broad and vague Selden patents, which since 1895 had claimed to cover every essential feature of the gasoline-driven automobile. Henry Ford, who refused to pay, secured in 1911 a court decision that the patent applied only to the two-cycle engine, then nearly obsolete.[180]

Anxious to avoid further litigation, all producers except Ford and Packard agreed in 1915 to license patents to each other without charge. Long afterward, the Temporary National Economic Committee, although otherwise critical of prevailing patent practices,[181] presented this pool as the best example of efficient operation of the

175. Senator Joseph C. O'Mahoney of Wyoming, *New York Times*, March 11, 1956, p. 48.

176. Alfred P. Sloan, Jr., chairman of General Motors, Kilgore Hearings, Part 7, pp. 3545–46.

177. James J. Nance, *ibid.*, Part 2, p. 871.

178. T. K. Quinn, *ibid.*, Part 6, pp. 2323–24.

179. "Giant Motors," *The Economist* (London), July 14, 1956, p. 129.

180. *Columbia Motor Car Co. v. A. C. Duerr & Co.*, 184 Fed. 893 (2d Cir. 1911).

181. *Final Report and Recommendations of the Temporary National Economic Committee*, S. Doc. 35, 77th Cong., 1st sess., 1941, pp. 36–37.

patent system. Several facts concerning the pool's very limited use shed doubt on this judgment. Packard officials knew of no patents included in the agreement which were important enough to use.[182] A General Motors attorney reported that since 1925 the pool had meant little to his company.[183] Patents on body shapes and other designs had never been included; nor had "revolutionary patents," for which it was believed protection was necessary if companies were to do the required research. At the time of the 1925 and 1930 renewals, it was decided to include only existing, not future, patents; and in 1935 it was agreed to include no patents taken out since 1930, lest research by the larger companies be discouraged.[184] By 1955 only patents taken out before 1940 were included [185] — which would mean only patents with less than two years to run.

Regardless of legal arrangements, automotive patents constituted 18.3 per cent of all patents issued from 1899 to 1955, and 18.4 per cent of those issued during 1953–55.[186] One producer reported in 1955 that its competitors were usually willing to license their patents at reasonable royalties and sometimes without royalty.[187] If all patents were licensed, and without royalty in every case, the patent pool would be perfect and all-embracing — in fact, the patent law itself could be abandoned as needless.

Interlocking Directorates

In its 1951 report on interlocking directorates, the Federal Trade Commission found two principal types of interlock (as of 1946) among automobile manufacturers.[188]

Ties with parts manufacturers were one. Chrysler had eight directors who were also directors of parts manufacturing firms, General Motors seven, Studebaker four, Nash four, Ford three and Packard three. This type of relationship seemed to the Commission inimical to the maintenance of free entry and competition in the parts industries.

182. Alvan Macauley and Milton Tibbets, TNEC Hearings, Part 2, p. 310.

183. James McEvoy, *ibid.*, pp. 362–63.

184. Alfred Reeves, *ibid.*, pp. 290–91, 296–97.

185. L. L. Colbert, president of Chrysler Corp., Kilgore Hearings, Part 1, p. 343.

186. *Automobile Facts and Figures*, 1956, p. 67.

187. W. T. Gossett, vice president and general counsel of Ford Motor Co., Kilgore Hearings, Part 2, p. 659.

188. FTC, *Report on Interlocking Directorates*, 1951, pp. 308–28.

Certainly it reflected in many cases buying and selling relationships among the firms concerned. Yet the contractual relations often existed prior to the common directorships.

Interlocks with banks were found. Several leading banks had directors who were also on the boards of automobile and parts companies. The Commission felt that the banking influence would tend to reduce the intensity of competition; but this untoward effect has apparently not emerged in practice.

Trade Associations

The trade association of the car and truck makers is the Automobile Manufacturers Association, successor to organizations dating from 1900. Its purposes are to correct abuses, spread information, and improve public and industry relations. The Ford Motor Company did not join until 1956. This association, after an exhaustive investigation by the Federal Trade Commission in the late 1930s, was cleared of any implication in "price agreements or other cooperative activities that appear to be contrary to the antitrust acts." [189]

Local automobile dealers' associations, which exist throughout the country, have as their chief purpose the promotion of favorable legislation, but have also given much attention to abuses arising out of transactions in used cars.[190] The National Automobile Dealers Association represents about three fourths of all dealers. Finally, parts manufacturers have a number of trade associations.[191]

Motives in Car Buying

The purchaser of an automobile has to weigh a number of qualities, some of them conflicting, in making a choice. Principally he considers appearance, style and comfort; mechanical power — ease of control, smoothness, pickup, speed; maneuverability (which may mean small size and/or high power), safety and dependability; original price and probable trade-in value; economy of operation (especially as to gasoline consumption); and expectation of good dealer service.[192] A few

189. FTC 1939 Report, p. 1065.

190. *Ibid.*, pp. 313–14.

191. List in *Automotive News*, 1956 Almanac issue, April 30, 1955, p. 197.

192. A General Motors "Consumer Survey" lists almost the identical qualities, except the last (cited in Charles N. Davisson, "Automobiles," Chap. 4 of Richard M. Clewett, ed., *Marketing Channels for Manufactured Products*, Irwin, Homewood (Ill.), 1954, pp. 90–91).

buyers are seeking only a prestige name — Cadillac being the best, although not the only, example — but such a name must rest on possession of most of the qualities just mentioned.

Henry Ford once dominated the market by offering a dependable cheap car. By the 1920s, when high per capita real income made price a less essential consideration, the automobile had become so universal that the public no longer looked upon it merely as a means of transport.[193] The prestige value of having a car as good as the next man's, or better if possible, had become important; a new automobile, as one writer puts it, now served as "a means of acquiring distinction and of expressing one's personality." [194] To obtain such qualities as comfort, style and power, consumers were now willing to pay both a higher purchase price and higher costs of operation.

Since it is physically impossible to combine all desired qualities in one vehicle, the essence of success in manufacture is to discover which qualities interest consumers most in their current mood. After World War II, until the great backlog of demand was met, the dominant need was transportation as such. During this brief spell all automobile makers flourished and Kaiser-Frazer was able to break in. When it was over, automobile makers had to guess what turn demand would take next. Chrysler, true to a long tradition of good engineering, placed its bet on safety, dependability and convenience of operation, combined with conservative styling.[195] The new Ford management guessed differently, dropped the last vestiges of the Ford stress on "cheap transportation," and offered models with flashier style and greater comfort and mechanical power. For the 1955 models (planned in 1953), Chrysler, having lost sales, was forced to take the chance of antagonizing its conservative customers by swinging into line with the prevailing emphasis on "sleekness" and "tailored steel." Its recovery in sales proved the correctness of this decision.

The automotive companies have thus learned by experience what consumer polls and talks with dealers have also taught them [196] — that in the consumer's present scale of values, comfort, style and appear-

193. Mark Adams, "The Automobile — A Luxury Becomes a Necessity," Chap. 2 in Walton Hamilton and Associates, *Price and Price Policies*, McGraw-Hill, New York, 1938, pp. 42–43; "A New Kind of Car Market," *Fortune*, September 1953, p. 224.

194. Moore, "The Automobile Industry," p. 310.

195. William B. Harris, "Chrysler Takes the Bumps," *Fortune*, April 1954, p. 127.

196. *New York Herald Tribune*, March 30, 1952, Section 2, p. 4.

ance count first. In the words of the sales manager of the Chevrolet, the car with the most units on the highways today, "styling is the one thing that makes people buy." [197] The exact degree to which the manufacturers must follow public taste rather than mold it by advertising is a point in dispute. The president of General Motors claims that advertising can do a good deal to mold taste — and proves his sincerity by being the biggest purchaser of advertising space in all American industry — but he points to examples of well-advertised cars which failed in the market because the public did not like their appearance.[198]

Nature of Competition

Under these conditions, competition among passenger car makers usually takes three forms: (1) innovations in design and style and in mechanical improvements — "for engineering creativity today ranks second only to styling in persuading the public to buy a car"; [199] (2) massive sales campaigns, and advertising which in 1955 amounted to $100 million for General Motors and $70 million for its dealers [200] — a total of $47 per new car registered; and (3) efforts to reduce costs of production in order to keep selling prices down.

The third point is important because, regardless of other buying motives, many or most consumers will make their choice on the basis of price when the features of two cars are similar. On the whole, the manufacturer who can change his new models enough to attract the consumers who are looking for something new, stylish and superior to the old, yet not so much as to run ahead of public taste or to make the change-over costs prohibitive, has the best chance of financial success.

Competition in the passenger car industry is vigorous enough, as we have seen, to threaten extinction to many of the competitors. According to the recent head of the Antitrust Division, "there is competition in the automobile industry in just about everything except price." [201]

197. William E. Fish, quoted in *Business Week*, October 30, 1954, p. 45. See also *Automotive News*, November 1, 1954, p. 46; and Herbert Brean, " '54 Car: 3 Years Old at Birth," *Life*, January 18, 1954, p. 80.

198. Harlow H. Curtice, Kilgore Hearings, Part 7, p. 3673.

199. Raymond J. Brady, "Under the Hood," *Barron's*, April 16, 1956, p. 3.

200. Frederick G. Donner, vice president of General Motors, Kilgore Hearings, Part 7, p. 3671; Frederick J. Bell, executive vice president of National Automobile Dealers Ass'n., *ibid.*, p. 3177.

201. Stanley N. Barnes, Kilgore Hearings, Part 1, p. 21.

With vigorous price competition, the mortality rate in the industry would undoubtedly have been stepped up.[202] The suggestion of price cutting which the Senate investigating committee's staff made to General Motors [203] therefore came as a surprise. A very moderate degree of price competition does exist in certain senses — for example, in the price differences noted in Table 57, or when a maker brings out a new and cheaper model of one of his standard cars, or in those rare instances when he pays dealers a bonus for each car sold and thus encourages them to cut prices.[204]

Price Competition at the Dealer Level

It is the dealer who nearly always bears the brunt of price competition. Only rarely does he offer his cars at less than the manufacturer's list price (suggested retail price); instead, he offers a larger trade-in allowance. Trade-ins have been taken on about 80 per cent of new-car transactions and 50 per cent of used-car transactions since 1953.[205] In a weak market the dealer's profit on the new car is substantially reduced by his loss on the used car. When the market is strong the dealer not only offers less than its resale value for the trade-in, but sometimes charges for accessories which might otherwise be included in the purchase price of the new car.

A trick always available but most often used when demand is low is to name a fictitiously high list price to the purchaser in order to be able to entice him with a higher trade-in allowance. When the term "pack" is used today, it generally refers to this boost in the list price. The object in most cases is to let the customer make his down payment — typically one third of the price — with little or no cash but rather by using his trade-in. There is a danger to the dealer or the finance company when the purchaser has so little cash investment in the car and so large a debt still owing as to lack the incentive to keep up his payments.

The dealer's operations are made difficult in that he is forced to carry almost the full burden of price competition during a model year because both manufacturer and consumer frown on changes in the list

202. Donald A. Moore, *ibid.*, Part 6, p. 2309.

203. *A Study of the Antitrust Laws*, Staff Report of Senate Judiciary Subcommittee, p. 8.

204. *Wall Street Journal*, July 14, 1955, p. 1.

205. *Automobile Facts and Figures*, 1956, p. 18.

price. As a result, he has gained, unfairly in many cases, a reputation as a trickster and a deceptive advertiser, reflected in thousands of complaints to Better Business Bureaus.[206]

Manufacturer Prices

No real evidence has ever been brought forward to justify the opinion sometimes voiced by car buyers that automobile companies "get together and fix their prices in advance." Nor is there any one price leader, partly because the company making the first announcement for a new model year may find, when competitors announce their prices, that they are underselling it or, if they have shown greater confidence in the market and named higher quotations, that it is "giving away money." In rare instances the leader, finding itself far out of line, hastily readjusts its price list. Identity of prices between cars of the same price range almost never occurs; there is at least a few dollars' difference. The announced prices, in any case, are merely the suggested list prices; the price at which the car changes hands from manufacturer to dealer is usually 24 or 25 per cent lower.

General Motors' pricing method as described today is the same as it was thirty years ago. The management estimates the cost of producing a reasonable or "standard" number of cars, ignoring the chance of a specially good or bad year, and sets a "standard" price which would yield a "standard" return on its investment.[207] This price is likely to be a "hope figure." [208] The final decision must set the price at a point which the company guesses will enable it to dispose of a given volume of cars it hopes to sell, taking account of competitors' policies and prices. If the prospective costs and prices do not leave a margin of profit, the company may eliminate some of the features it planned to offer. More often it looks on quality as a selling weapon which permits a higher price to be charged. Expressed another way, the system is to set the price first, deduct the desired profit, then tell the engineer-

206. *Automotive News*, March 28, 1955, pp. 1, 4.

207. Albert Bradley, Kilgore Hearings, Part 7, p. 3583. Compare Donaldson Brown, "Pricing Policy in Relation to Financial Control," *Management and Administration*, February 1924, pp. 195–98, March 1924, pp. 283–86, April 1924, pp. 417–22, partly reprinted in Jules Backman, ed., *Price Practices and Price Policies*, Ronald Press, New York, 1953, pp. 359–65; also two articles by Homer B. Vanderblue in the *Harvard Business Review*: "Pricing Policies in the Automobile Industry," Summer 1939, pp. 385–401, and "Pricing Policies in the Automobile Industry: Incidence of Demand," Autumn 1939, pp. 64–81.

208. Vanderblue, "Pricing Policies in the Automobile Industry," p. 398.

ing department to plan the best possible product within the cost allowed.[209]

Once fixed, the price cannot easily be changed during the model year. If it turns out that a higher price could be obtained, the manufacturer will be handing dealers an inventory profit on their unsold stocks if he announces an increase, besides courting public criticism. If he cuts the price because sales are unsatisfactory, he risks antagonizing customers who bought at the original price.[210] On rare occasions the case is so desperate that a price cut must nevertheless be made, or an unbalanced supply-demand situation in the other direction will permit an increase.

Price Flexibility

Over the course of a business cycle, the flexibility of the manufacturer's quoted price is limited. A theoretical argument can be made that sharp reductions in time of depression will cause demand to pick up again; [211] but the manufacturers fear that such action will merely cause a postponement of buying as the consumer waits for further cuts.[212] This position receives support from statistical studies published in recent years which show the controlling importance of factors other than price.[213] In a recent Department of Commerce analysis,[214] four "basic demand factors" were listed, not necessarily in the order of their importance: (1) number of households, (2) real income per household and current direction of change in real income, (3) average age at which cars are scrapped, and (4) price of automobiles in relation to other prices. There were three factors of less, but "considerable," significance: (5) credit terms, (6) geographic shifts in population, and

209. Banner thesis, p. 90; J. W. Scoville, in "Methods of Control in the Automobile Industry," *Mechanical Engineering*, July 1937, p. 493, cited in *ibid.*, p. 115; Lewis D. Crusoe, Kilgore Hearings, Part 2, p. 675.

210. Cecil Eaton Fraser and Georges F. Doriot, *Analyzing Our Industries*, McGraw-Hill, New York, 1932, p. 37; Vanderblue, "Pricing Policies in the Automobile Industry," p. 64, note 2.

211. Wilford I. King, "Can Production of Automobiles Be Stabilized by Making Their Prices Flexible?," *Journal of the American Statistical Association*, December 1939, p. 651.

212. Vanderblue, "Pricing Policies in the Automobile Industry," pp. 66–67.

213. Charles F. Roos and Victor von Szeliski, "Factors Governing Changes in Domestic Automobile Demand," in *The Dynamics of Automobile Demand*, General Motors Corp., New York, 1939.

214. L. Jay Atkinson, "Consumer Markets for Durable Goods," *Survey of Current Business*, April 1952, pp. 19–21.

(7) mechanical improvements in automobiles. Price is thus only one out of seven determinants of demand.

It is difficult or impossible to measure price flexibility in automobiles statistically, because of the concealed price changes at the dealer level. Between 1907 and 1917, when the average wholesale price of a passenger car was declining from $2,131 to $604,[215] there was clear long-run flexibility. The figures are not comparable to an index of prices for a particular car, since they reflect mainly a shift in buying from the higher-priced to the lower-priced makes. But this shift itself represents a kind of price flexibility, for it means that enough models were offered to the public to make effective its desire for the lower-priced ones.

Since 1933, when the average wholesale price of all cars reached its all-time low of $485, the price has moved up with the general price level. As with other commodities, rising taxes — said to be $700 on a high-priced Chrysler today as against little more than $100 in 1924 [216] — are among the factors that have made it hard to "hold the price line." The manufacturers found that sales responded better if they made improvements or changes in their product than if they kept its price down, and acted accordingly. The car of today is entirely different from the car of 1933, whereas a package of sugar (as of many other standardized commodities) remains the same as it was then. The fact that sugar and automobile prices have risen comparably is, therefore, deceptive — though it should be said on behalf of sugar that it is not as susceptible as automobiles to economies of scale.

Price Classes

Competition in passenger cars is closest among makes in the same "price class," even though a good salesman can sometimes interest a buyer in a higher class than he originally had in mind. Luxury cars compete; medium-priced cars compete; low-priced cars compete; and models at the lower edge of one group compete with those at the top edge of a lower group. Finally, many buyers let the amount of difference in price decide whether they will purchase a new car or a late-model used car.

Each manufacturer tries to offer cars in several classes, so as to tap the pocketbooks of various types of buyer. The broad range of General

215. Calculated from *Automobile Facts and Figures*, 1956, p. 3.

216. L. L. Colbert, Kilgore Hearings, Part 1, p. 347.

Motors cars is one of that producer's strategic advantages, which Ford in 1956 was preparing to emulate. Furthermore, General Motors and Chrysler sell more than one car within some of the classes, partly because the technical development of the cars started from different points but wound up at the same point, and partly to stimulate initiative and effort by creating "intracompany competition." The divisions of a company that compete in this way, such as the Oldsmobile, Buick and Pontiac, regard each other as real competitors. Independents admit that lack of a well-balanced offering is a weakness.[217]

"As anyone with eyes can see, cars have come to look more and more alike," [218] and the concept of price classes has lost its clarity and precision in recent years.[219] In 1930 the Cadillac sold at four times the average price of all cars; in 1955 at less than twice the average.[220] The spreading practice of making several series of a particular car — for example, the Rambler's De Luxe, Super and Custom, representing ascending order of value — and the custom of offering various types of optional equipment have created a situation in which there was no price gap of more than 3 per cent between price classes of 1955-model four-door sedans below the $3,000 mark. (See Table 58.) Nevertheless, the concept of classes is still useful, for all customers know in which broad class — luxury, medium-priced or low-priced — a car belongs.

Those who feel that the antitrust laws should be applied more rigorously to the automobile industry frequently contend that each car should be made by a separate corporation. This demand takes no account of the production economies or market advantages that wide market coverage can offer, or of the difficulty a company with only one car would have in maintaining a stable market as tastes change. If Cadillac were split off from General Motors, the chances are that it would soon have to add a lower-priced model or run into these difficulties.[221] The present situation might thus eventually be recreated, but with a higher all-around cost due to the increased number of companies.

217. James J. Nance, Kilgore Hearings, Part 2, pp. 863–64.

218. *Fortune*, September 1953, p. 220.

219. *Automotive News*, December 28, 1953, pp. 1, 10; April 4, 1955, pp. 1, 7.

220. William H. Whyte, Jr., "The Cadillac Phenomenon," *Fortune*, February 1955, p. 107.

221. Banner thesis, p. 88.

TABLE 58

AUTOMOBILES: ARBITRARY PRICE CLASSES OF FOUR-DOOR SEDANS, 1955 MODELS[a]

Price Class	General Motors	Chrysler	Ford	Studebaker-Packard	American Motors
$1,695–$1,993	Chevrolet (3)	Plymouth (3)	Ford	Studebaker (4)	Hudson (2) Rambler (3)
$2,014–$2,196	Pontiac	Dodge		Studebaker (2)	Hudson Nash
$2,256–$2,498	Buick Oldsmobile Pontiac (3)	De Soto	Mercury	Studebaker (2)	Nash (2) Hudson (2)
$2,503–$2,876	Oldsmobile (2) Buick (2)	Chrysler De Soto		Packard (2)	Nash Hudson (2)
$3,344–$3,977	Buick Cadillac	Chrysler	Lincoln (2)	Packard (2)	
$4,483–$4,728	Cadillac	Imperial			

Source: Classified from data in *Automotive News*, December 20, 1954, p. 20, after omitting Kaiser and Willys.

a. Cars with V-8 engines are not included when there are alternatives.

Note: Within each price class cars are arranged by increasing order of price (based on highest-priced series within the class). Number of series offered in the price class, when greater than one, is given in parentheses.

Why Is There No "Economy Car"?

The industry is often criticized for not having produced a really cheap car, at a much lower price than the present low-priced models, easily maneuverable and with low gasoline consumption.[222] The time may come when someone will show that it can be done. Up to the present, no manufacturer that has attempted to produce "stripped" cars, offering little beyond transport, has been able to build up the volume of sales necessary to make a profit. The failure of the Ford Model T to hold its place after 1924, when the price reached an all-time low, is one instance. Later the public was to show no interest in "austerity models" offered by several producers in turn. The little American Austin lasted only a few years, and as an import from Britain it has never had a large sale. General Motors considered making a cheap car in 1945, but concluded that "when you reduce the

222. Consumers' Union, *Consumer Reports*, Mt. Vernon (N.Y.), May 1955, p. 246.

size of a car you take value out faster than you can reduce cost." [223] In 1955 and 1956 the imported Volkswagen began to make a stir, but the Chevrolet and Ford were still outselling it and other small foreign cars several times over. The principal market for small foreign makes was as a family "second car."

In social terms, the failure of a light, cheap car to take hold in the United States may reflect the fact that an automobile is, as one writer puts it, "an item of conspicuous consumption, prestige, and comfort for people at all levels." [224] In practical terms, a buyer who wants a low original price can satisfy his needs with a secondhand car. The two presidents of American Motors, George Mason and his successor, George Romney, have pushed their Rambler and imported Metropolitan with the argument that a large car, even if bought second hand, costs too much to operate. It is true that a person who wants low gasoline consumption per mile cannot do as well as he could in Britain, but in that country taxes make gasoline much more expensive and fuel consumption therefore a more important consideration. The relatively slow sales of Chrysler's short-wheel-base Plymouth of the early 1950s revealed that maneuverability was not of first importance to American buyers. Some of these factors may change quickly, particularly as roads become more congested.

Automobile Makers and Parts Suppliers

The first small automobile factories were merely assemblers of purchased parts, but as early as 1905 larger plants were making their own components [225] and advertising this fact as a proof of controlled quality. As total car production expanded, the economies of specialized manufacture of parts for sale to several assemblers emerged clearly, and soon the advertising message began to mention that the car used Continental engines, Timken-Detroit axles, Hyatt roller bearings, and so forth.[226] The ratio of cost of materials to value of product, which is higher when more parts are bought outside, increased steadily from 38 per cent at the time of the Census of 1899, to 44 per cent in 1904, 56 per cent in 1909, 58 per cent in 1914 and 66 per cent in 1919. After a

223. View of President Harlow H. Curtice, as reported in *Business Week,* March 21, 1953, p. 107.

224. Moore, "The Automobile Industry," p. 275.

225. 1905 Census, Part 4, p. 275.

226. Epstein, *The Automobile Industry*, p. 51.

pause in the 1920s, it picked up again to 67, 70, 75 and 77 per cent in 1931, 1933, 1935 and 1937.[227] The year 1937 may have been close to the high point for the parts industry; but since then the Census has ceased to give the total figures.

The Ford Motor Company moved during its Model T period (1909–1927) in the opposite direction. Having at first made very few parts,[228] it tried later to make many or most of them — to the point where the company was considered a prime example of *over*diversification.[229] At the same time the vehicle makers, and Ford in particular, gained the reputation of bargaining sharply with suppliers.[230] Some of these policies have been modified by experience. Thus Ford sold its rubber plantation in Brazil, ceased to make batteries, and in fact makes fewer parts than General Motors. Its postwar management is said to have required that all contracts show a fair profit to the vendor [231] — a policy announced by General Motors as well.[232]

But the assemblers make their own parts when it appears more economical to do so. They also try to keep their parts factories operating regularly, an effort which leads to "tapered integration" — that is, giving out fewer parts orders proportionately in years when automobile sales are expected to be low and thus imposing greater fluctuations on their suppliers.[233] Knowing by experience the dangers of depending on a single source of supply, and of having to shut down assembly for lack of some one vital part, they usually have at least two sources for essential parts. They also reserve "shop rights" to manufacture given parts themselves in case a strike ties up the supplier.

The position of the parts industry is unquestionably precarious. Having experienced some notorious "squeezes" in the past, its members try to avoid dependence on a single customer; but the concentration of automobile and truck manufacture has gone so far that this is often unavoidable. The parts manufacturer may therefore have to

227. U.S. *Census of Manufactures*, 1929, Vol. 2, p. 1223, and 1937, Vol. 1, p. 1203.

228. Seltzer, *A Financial History of the American Automobile Industry*, pp. 100–01.

229. See Gilbert Burck, "The Urge to Diversify," *Fortune*, September 1955, p. 206.

230. Fraser and Doriot, *Analyzing Our Industries*, p. 50.

231. William B. Harris, "Ford's Fight for First," *Fortune*, September 1954, p. 195.

232. Louis C. Goad, Kilgore Hearings, Part 7, p. 3651.

233. See Moore, "The Automobile Industry," pp. 298–99; Standard & Poor's Corp., "Auto Parts," July 21, 1955, p. A3–3; Davisson, *The Marketing of Automotive Parts*, pp. 709–10.

operate on a narrow margin of profit, but even this is naturally preferred to having to seek new customers outside the automotive industry if the automobile manufacturer should decide to make its own parts.

The Current Trend toward Integration

A renewed trend toward integration is in progress today. The big automobile manufacturers obviously agree with Alfred P. Sloan, Jr., the renowned elder statesman of General Motors, that "it is much more efficient to make the part yourself, under your own supervision, because you can bring together the [two] engineering staffs." [234] Although postwar figures on the share of dollar sales originating in outside purchases show no particular trend for General Motors, the Ford share decreased from about 61 to 57 per cent between 1947–48 and 1955 and the Chrysler share from 65 to 60 per cent. The figures are not conclusive, since they are subject to ups and downs as a result of inventory changes (like the dips in 1950 and 1952) and since they include purchases of basic materials like iron and steel and of transportation and other services as well — none of which involve the parts industry. Nevertheless, a trend is apparent. (See Table 59.) The high 73.1 per cent of Studebaker's sales paid for materials and services, shown by its report for 1953, indicates one of that producer's weaknesses.

In terms of sales of parts for new cars in 1955, estimated at perhaps $2.5 billion,[235] the shift since 1947 (confined to Ford and Chrysler) would represent a sales loss of probably more than $250 million. An important current example of the trend is the new Ford glass factory, intended to make half its glass and replace purchases from the Pittsburgh Plate Glass Company. A different kind of integration, which did not reduce the market of independent parts manufacturers as such, was Chrysler's December 1953 purchase of the Briggs Manufacturing Company, maker of its Plymouth bodies. Chrysler then leased to Studebaker-Packard the Briggs unit which had been making Packard bodies.[236]

The threat of further integration is great enough that leaders of the parts industry consider themselves on notice to better their customers

234. Alfred P. Sloan, Jr., Kilgore Hearings, Part 7, p. 3526.

235. A "responsible guess," *Journal of Commerce*, January 10, 1956, p. 32.

236. James J. Nance, Kilgore Hearings, Part 2, p. 870.

TABLE 59

AUTOMOBILES: PURCHASES OF MATERIALS AND SERVICES AS PER CENT OF SALES, GENERAL MOTORS, FORD AND CHRYSLER, 1946–55

	General Motors [a]			
Year	A	B	Ford [a]	Chrysler
1946	46.2	b	57.4	67.9
1947	49.6	b	61.2	65.5
1948	48.0	50.2	61.6	64.9
1949	48.4	50.3	60.3	63.6
1950	46.5	46.8	58.0	62.8
1951	49.7	49.4	57.9	67.0
1952	48.2	48.4	55.3	61.2
1953	52.5	52.7	59.2	65.8
1954	50.5	51.1	57.3	62.8
1955	48.6	48.5	57.0	60.2

Sources: Annual reports of General Motors Corp. and Chrysler Corp.; Ford Motor Co., stock prospectus, January 17, 1956, pp. 4–5 and 12, and 1955 Annual Report.

a. The first General Motors column and the Ford column were calculated by dividing sales into "cost of sales" minus "payrolls." The 1948–55 General Motors comparisons make it appear that this formula is close to the formula used by the companies: gross income divided into materials and services bought.

b. Not available.

in development of new products or efficiency of production.[237] Nearly fifty firms are said to have disappeared in 1955 alone,[238] and Motor Products Company — whose total sales had been $83 million — announced that it would abandon its automotive business (window frames, ventilators and the like) after the 1956 season. Many more parts companies are merely adding nonautomotive outlets as they can, some of them showing a lower proportion of automotive sales each year.

The Department of Justice has intervened on at least two recent occasions to halt mergers in the parts industries — both of them proposed acquisitions by Thompson Products.[239] However, a table of mergers in which 121 "significant" automotive parts companies participated from 1950 through 1953 filled twenty inches of newspaper

237. Parts company executive quoted by Norris Willatt, "Skid in Auto Parts," *Barron's*, July 5, 1954, p. 6; Standard & Poor's Corp., "Auto Parts," July 21, 1955, p. A3–2 to A3–3; *Business Week*, October 23, 1954, p. 78.

238. *Journal of Commerce*, January 10, 1956, p. 32.

239. Thompson Products Co., Annual Report, 1950, p. 7; Burck, "The Urge to Diversify," p. 208.

space, and in 1953 three of the forty-one largest firms in the industry disappeared through merger.[240]

The Battle for the Replacement Market

The independent parts industry must compete with its customers, the automobile assemblers, not only in the original equipment market but in the replacement market as well. The statistics on this market vary widely. According to estimates by the Automobile Manufacturers Association based on federal excise tax receipts, the wholesale value of replacement parts and accessories sold in the domestic market averaged $444 million in 1935–40, reached $2,451 million in 1948 and decreased to $1,805 million in 1955.[241] The increase to 1948 was undoubtedly due to a rise in both volume and prices. The decrease to 1955 was perhaps due in part to improved durability of the parts manufactured,[242] but another reason was undoubtedly that the average car in 1948 was a prewar make and hence much older than the average car in 1955.

According to a representative of the independent parts makers, their sales before the war were 75 to 80 per cent of the total and in 1955 perhaps as little as 40 per cent.[243] If so, only the increased size of the market would have saved many of the independents from extinction. General Motors estimated its own share of the market in 1954 at 22.9 per cent, and hoped to expand it.[244] It gave no prewar figures. In the absence of dollar figures, and of any figures on Ford and Chrysler sales, it is impossible to make any positive statement about the trend in parts sales; but it may be noted that General Motors did not deny directly that its share of the replacement market had increased.

The Federal Trade Commission found in 1939 that franchises either prohibited dealers in new cars from recommending competing parts, allowed them to sell such parts only if the customer specially requested them, or went so far as to forbid the handling of those parts not made or authorized by the manufacturer.[245] The Commission was already proceeding against General Motors on this issue and in 1941 secured

240. *Journal of Commerce*, January 4, 1954, pp. 1, 3.
241. *Automobile Facts and Figures*, 1956, p. 9.
242. Standard & Poor's Corp., "Auto Parts," July 21, 1955, p. A3–6.
243. Harold T. Halfpenny, Kilgore Hearings, Part 6, p. 2838.
244. Sherrod E. Skinner, vice president of General Motors, *ibid.*, Part 8, p. 3868.
245. FTC 1939 Report, p. 134.

an order which the corporation accepted.[246] Perhaps as a result of the Commission's work, franchise provisions now merely require the dealer to use "genuine" parts — defined as parts, no matter by whom made, which were used in the original equipment. Ford adopted this principle in 1949.[247] Dealers must stock an adequate inventory of "genuine" parts,[248] and the larger the inventory, the less likely they are to see a profit in handling other parts as well. However, "unbiased surveys" were reported to show in 1952 that dealers buy at least half their "fast-moving" parts from jobbers.[249]

These agreements put strong pressure on parts makers to get their parts used as original equipment, and as a result they are likely to quote "favorable" prices for this.[250] Assemblers are alleged to have taken advantage of these low prices to buy more parts than were needed for original equipment so as to sell the rest at low prices in competition with the independent's parts in the replacement market.[251] If true, this would mean that the parts manufacturers were giving a price discrimination which the vehicle manufacturers were then using to lessen competition.

Developments in 1954 and 1955

Early in 1954 one authority declared it "incorrect to state" that vehicle manufacturers dominated the replacement market sufficiently to control the over-all price level, whatever their influence might be in particular items.[252] At the same time General Motors enlarged its drive to sell more replacement parts by setting up its dealers as wholesalers of parts made by its various accessory-manufacturing divisions. To compensate its wholesale outlets for the increased competition, it let them in turn handle parts made by its car divisions which had previously been handled only by the dealers; [253] but this particular change was abandoned as a failure two years later.[254] The independent parts

246. *General Motors Corp.*, Docket 3152, 34 FTC 58 (1941).
247. W. T. Gossett, Kilgore Hearings, Part 2, p. 668.
248. Davisson, *The Marketing of Automotive Parts*, p. 701.
249. *Automotive News*, April 14, 1952, p. 8.
250. Davisson, *The Marketing of Automotive Parts*, p. 669.
251. Harold T. Halfpenny, Kilgore Hearings, Part 3, p. 1245.
252. Davisson, *The Marketing of Automotive Parts*, p. 742.
253. *Business Week*, April 3, 1954, pp. 160–61.
254. *Automotive News*, June 18, 1956, pp. 1, 6.

manufacturers and the wholesalers handling their products, much disturbed by the new competition from General Motors dealers, saw no real hope except in prohibiting vehicle manufacturers from entering the replacement market.[255]

The independents had complained for many years against advertising by vehicle manufacturers which urged purchasers to insist on "genuine" parts — that is, those made at their own factories or by others to their specifications. In 1955, at the request of the Federal Trade Commission, General Motors abandoned the practice of showing photographs of two identical parts with a warning to the reader to buy the "genuine" one.[256] But it continued to use the theme, and in December 1955 was served by the Commission with a complaint calling such advertising false and misleading.[257] The outcome of the case would affect the similar advertising of Chrysler, Ford and Studebaker-Packard as well. The independent parts manufacturers hoped for some relief through this case,[258] but the auto makers might merely shift to the line: "Buy for best performance parts made at our factory or under our inspection."

Grievances of Franchised Dealers

The all-time peak in production and profits reached by the big automobile manufacturers in 1955 was accompanied by increasing resentment on the part of the dealers who were distributing the millions of cars. A similar resentment had come to the fore in March 1938, when dealer representatives induced Congress to vote for an investigation of "the policies employed . . . in selling motor vehicles" and the methods by which manufacturers maintained "their control or monopoly." [259] As a result, the Federal Trade Commission published the most thorough report on manufacture and distribution of automobiles yet made. Although the Commission believed that its investigation had reduced the pressure on dealers,[260] the persistence of four principal "unfair practices" which it felt should "be abated" [261] shows that no permanent change occurred.

255. Harold T. Halfpenny, Kilgore Hearings, Part 6, pp. 2833–34.
256. Thomas H. Keating, vice president of General Motors, *ibid.*, Part 7, p. 3830.
257. *General Motors Corp.*, FTC Docket 6477 (1955).
258. Harold T. Halfpenny, Kilgore Hearings, Part 3, p. 1244.
259. FTC 1939 Report, p. 1.
260. *Ibid.*, p. 212.
261. *Ibid.*, p. 1076.

One-sided contracts without security for the dealer. After some dealers had won lawsuits against their factories in the early days of the industry, on charges of unfair or arbitrary treatment, the lawyers for the manufacturers redrew their franchises to avoid liability in every way possible.[262] The result was a document characterized as one-sided by many court decisions — but treated, nevertheless, as a free contract with which the courts could not interfere. This view was concisely stated by Judge John J. Parker of the Fourth Circuit in 1933:

> While there is a natural impulse to be impatient with a form of contract which places the comparatively helpless dealer at the mercy of the manufacturer, we cannot make contracts for parties or protect them from the provisions of contracts which they have made for themselves. Dealers doubtless accept these one-sided contracts because they think that the right to deal in the product of the manufacturer, even on his terms, is valuable to them . . .[263]

As late as 1952 the courts reaffirmed that a manufacturer might cancel a dealer's franchise with or without "just cause." [264] General Motors used ninety-day nonrenewal notices on annual contracts and Ford ninety-day termination notices on continuous contracts; but each gave advance warnings along with suggestions as to how the dealer could improve his business.[265] The best protection dealers had against cancellation was the fact that a change of dealers costs the manufacturer money; a former Ford dealer reported in 1952 that few Ford dealers feared cancellation.[266] Until that time, at least, it appears that most terminations by manufacturers were for dealer malpractices.[267] This evidently ceased to be true, for General Motors terminations for all causes doubled between 1951 and 1954, and at least some of the "voluntary" resignations were apparently of the "quit before you're

262. Charles M. Hewitt, Jr., Kilgore Hearings, Part 7, p. 3205.

263. *Ford Motor Co. v. Kirkmyer Motor Co.*, 65 F. 2d 1001, 1006 (4th Cir. 1933).

264. *Biever Motor Car Co. v. Chrysler Corp.*, 108 F. Supp. 948 (D. Conn. 1952), affirmed 195 F. 2d 758 (2d Cir. 1952), certiorari denied 345 U.S. 942 (1952).

265. See statement by Henry Ford II, president of Ford Motor Co., *Automotive News*, March 19, 1956, p. 79.

266. William L. Haeberle, *A Study of the Relations between an Automotive Manufacturer and Its Franchised Dealers*, unpublished doctoral thesis, Indiana University School of Business, Bloomington, 1952, pp. 47, 129.

267. Adolph A. Berle, Jr., *The 20th Century Capitalist Revolution*, Harcourt, Brace, New York, 1954, p. 80.

fired" type.[268] The reason for this stepping up of terminations was the dealers' inability to sell enough cars to suit their factories.[269]

Sacrifice of capital. The most humanly distressing aspect of this problem has been the loss of capital to the dealer whose franchise has been terminated. The premises usually have little value for other purposes, and if the new dealer is not interested in buying them at a fair value, the canceled dealer may find himself losing at once both his livelihood and his savings. When a $250,000–$300,000 investment is made useless, it is hardly compensated by the factory's willingness to pay half of any obligated rental for one year, plus $8,678.60 for parts, signs and tools.[270] In another instance, as reported to the National Automobile Dealers Association, the manufacturer was so anxious for all its dealers to have adequate working capital that it refused to let its new dealer pay as much as he was willing to offer for the canceled dealer's premises.

Dictation to dealers. The Federal Trade Commission in 1938 found that dealers greatly resented factory interference in their management, and expenses which the manufacturer imposed upon them. Examples cited were uniform accounting systems to fit the needs of the manufacturer; dictation as to type of premises used and size of sales staff; and levying on dealers the major cost of cooperative advertising campaigns.[271] The complaints of 1955 were similar or identical.[272]

Forcing. The most serious issue has been the insistence of factories that dealers sell more cars than they feel they can profitably handle. Similar to this "forcing" of cars is the insistence that dealers handle factory-made replacement parts instead of those made by independent parts companies, that they take cars with accessories the factory finds convenient to supply rather than those the dealers think their customers want, and that they pay for special tools, advertising signs and other items whether wanted or not. Such forcing is often instigated by the manufacturer's local representatives, but headquarters in Detroit can hardly escape responsibility if the local representative does the

268. Edgar H. Zimmer, former General Motors dealer, *ibid.*, Part 7, p. 3400.

269. Compare *Automotive News*, October 25, 1954, p. 1; August 15, 1955, p. 1.

270. Ed Travis, former General Motors dealer, Kilgore Hearings, Part 7, pp. 3238, 3258; William F. Hufstader, vice president of General Motors, *ibid.*, pp. 3724–25.

271. FTC 1939 Report, Chaps. 3–9.

272. Summary by Charles M. Hewitt, Jr., Kilgore Hearings, Part 7, pp. 3217–18. See also *idem*, *Automobile Franchise Agreements*, Irwin, Homewood (Ill.), 1956.

same thing repeatedly. There is also suspicion that Detroit approves of some of the forcing as long as it is not written down "in black and white" for investigators to see.[273] As long ago as 1925 high executives in the industry disapproved of forcing,[274] but the practice has, if anything, accelerated. There will always be a temptation to force, since an automobile producer must get its cars distributed if it is to stay in competition.

Most dealers were philosophical about the problem as long as their primary difficulty was to get cars rather than to dispose of them. Since the postwar seller's market ended in 1953, however, it has become very real. The factories established high production schedules, shipped out the cars, and insisted that they be sold by offering higher trade-ins, by increasing advertising and sales forces, or by any other method that dealers could devise. This amounted to putting the burden on dealers to sell whatever number of cars the factories chose to make. Independent automobile manufacturers, who were obvious victims of this "blitz," urged dealers to stand firm against such pressure.[275] Dealer quotas were usually figured as the same percentage of sales within the car's price class locally that the car was selling nationally. For an increasing number this proved impossible, and more and more notices went out from manufacturers terminating the franchises of dealers who had not met their quotas. In 1955 Ford canceled 28 dealers, Chrysler 37, and General Motors 118 in ten months (or annual rates close to 0.4, 0.4 and 0.8 per cent).[276]

Bootlegging of Automobiles

In this crisis an old problem, which had never previously reached the critical point, re-emerged to plague the franchised dealers. Many of them sold their excess inventory at wholesale to so-called bootleggers — unfranchised dealers who stored cars on an open lot and sold them at well below the factory list price. This was a volume operation, with both the dealer who supplied the cars and the one who sold them making only a small profit per unit. Although some factory representa-

273. Don B. Robbins, former General Motors dealer, *ibid.*, p. 3392.

274. FTC 1939 Report, pp. 174–75.

275. Paul G. Hoffman, chairman of Studebaker-Packard Corp., *NADA Magazine*, December 1954, p. 43.

276. Henry Ford II, president of Ford Motor Co., *Automobile Marketing Practices*, Senate Hearings, p. 978; C. L. Jacobson, vice president of Chrysler Corp., *ibid.*, p. 454; General Motors exhibit, Kilgore Hearings, Part 8, pp. 4381–82.

tives may have urged franchised dealers to bootleg their cars,[277] and although the whole process was one which proved necessary to dispose of the huge production of 1955, the manufacturers frowned on it. A contract provision forbidding dealers to resell except to final users or other franchised dealers was dropped in 1949 after the *Standard Stations* decision against exclusive contracts covering a substantial share of the market.[278] When the Antitrust Division was asked to clear such a clause in 1954, it took the position that bootlegging might be just "a healthy form of price competition." [279] General Motors then agreed to buy back at cost price cars its dealers were unable to sell, but it was not expected that many dealers would risk a black mark at the factory by taking advantage of this offer.

One cause of bootlegging has been "phantom freight." Cars were traditionally priced f.o.b. Detroit regardless of their place of assembly. A dealer in a city where there was a branch assembly plant might thus pay $100 freight on a car on which there was no outbound freight charge at all (although the plant still had its inbound freight on parts, which averaged almost half the freight on the finished car [280]). One form of evasion was the sale of excess cars by dealers in or near Detroit to firms that would secure drivers to take them, for perhaps $25, to unauthorized dealers in distant states, where they were sold at cut prices.[281] The manufacturers finally became convinced that they should make some concession to dealer opinion on this issue, although they still believed they had every right to the financial advantage that resulted from setting up branch plants near consumer markets. In two steps, one in November 1954 and the second in February 1956, they announced a variety of reductions in freight charges for areas far from Detroit, at the same time raising base prices enough to keep the average mill net price about the same. Although dealers applauded the freight reduction aspect of these moves, some informed observers worried lest the West and South ultimately suffer from discouragement to the setting up of branch plants there.[282] The change was also a blow to

277. Sumpter T. Priddy, Jr., former General Motors dealer, Kilgore Hearings, Part 7, p. 3383.

278. *Standard Oil Company of Calif. v. U.S.*, 337 U.S. 293 (1949).

279. Stanley N. Barnes, Kilgore Hearings, Part 1, p. 305.

280. ICC figures, in *Automobile Marketing Practices*, Senate Hearings, Part 1, p. 133.

281. Stacy Rowell, president of National Independent Automobile Dealers Ass'n., *ibid.*, pp. 936–37.

282. John O. Munn, *Automotive News*, April 2, 1956, p. 3.

the independent manufacturers, who had no branch assembly plants and yet had to meet the prices announced by Ford and General Motors in the South and West,[283] and even to Chrysler, 85 per cent of whose cars were assembled in the Detroit area.

While dealers felt that phantom freight led to bootlegging, some others suspected that "territorial security" had the same effect. Under this plan a dealer who sold a car to a resident of another dealer's territory had to pay the latter a penalty ranging from $25 to $75. Ford stopped enforcing this clause in the 1920s and joined its competitors in formally dropping it after the *Standard Stations* decision.

In September 1955 Senator A. S. Mike Monroney of Oklahoma, as chairman of the Subcommittee on Automobile Marketing Practices of the Senate Committee on Interstate and Foreign Commerce, sent a questionnaire, chiefly on bootlegging and related subjects, to all dealers whose names he could find. By the time his report on this subject was prepared, 19,113 returns had been received.[284] Surprisingly, "the most typical of prosperous, local entrepreneurs and by reputation the most contentedly conservative" [285] voted by 13,749 to 1,991 (with the rest not answering this question) in favor of "congressional study or federal legislation" on their problems. Legislation permitting manufacturers to cancel franchises of dealers selling to bootleggers was favored by 14,185 to 3,411, abolition of phantom freight by 14,891 to 984, and territorial security by 8,693 to 7,766.

The bills introduced in Congress to accede to the dealers' wishes on these three specific issues were, however, pigeonholed. No doubt opposition of the Department of Justice and the Federal Trade Commission was a determining factor.

Remedies for Dealers' Problems

Measures to meet the problems of dealers may be grouped under the headings self-help, legislation and manufacturer policies.

283. William H. McGaughey, vice president, and John G. Staiger, assistant comptroller, American Motors Corp., in *Automobile Marketing Legislation*, Hearings before a Subcommittee of the House Interstate and Foreign Commerce Committee, 84th Cong., Committee Print, 1956, pp. 288–96, and Charles L. Jacobson, *ibid.*, pp. 316–19.

284. *The Automobile Marketing Practices Study*, Report of Subcommittee on Automobile Marketing Practices of Senate Interstate and Foreign Commerce Committee, 84th Cong., 2d sess., 1956, pp. 4–7.

285. Hubert W. Kelley, Jr., "Mutiny of the Car Dealers," *Harper's Magazine*, August 1956, p. 69.

Dealer self-help. In 1938 the Federal Trade Commission found "a steady growth in activities and plans to prevent overallowances on trade-ins." [286] This was sometimes done through "appraisal bureaus," but most of these had vanished out of inability to secure dealer co-operation, fear of antitrust action, or because manufacturers or the public had learned of their existence.[287] In 1955 the Department of Justice learned that similar activities were continuing. It was especially interested in the fact that local dealer associations were agreeing upon uniform "packs" to put on prices of new cars and upon uniform charges for accessories. As long as "the vastly more powerful manufacturer is free to set the price at which it will sell to all dealers," the Department hesitated to prosecute local dealer price fixing, but it finally issued a warning that if this continued criminal action might be undertaken.[288]

State legislation. Self-help merges into legislation when dealer pressure secures passage of favorable laws. In 1938 the Federal Trade Commission found twenty-one states which required dealers to be licensed (probably in part so as to protect established dealers), and one or two of them threatening to revoke licenses of those giving "excessive" trade-in allowances.[289] It found thirteen states regulating "import" of used cars, and fifteen prohibiting sales of goods below cost in terms broad enough to include automobiles.[290] In 1956 sixteen states required manufacturers selling in the state to take out licenses, and forbade certain practices deemed oppressive to dealers.[291] No license, however, has been revoked.[292] In Wisconsin dealers can ask the Motor Vehicle Department to deny a license to a new competitor if existing facilities are "adequate."[293] The Department has final discretion. In most states dealer and industry opinion holds that laws intended to aid dealers — particularly laws designed to restrict price cutting — are not likely to be effective.[294]

286. FTC 1939 Report, p. 365.
287. *Ibid.*, Chap. 11.
288. Stanley N. Barnes, Kilgore Hearings, Part 1, pp. 305–06.
289. FTC 1939 Report, pp. 400–07.
290. *Ibid.*, pp. 368–69.
291. *Automotive News*, December 27, 1954, p. 3, March 5, 1956, p. 6.
292. *Ibid.*, May 23, 1955, pp. 1, 50.
293. *Ibid.*, August 29, 1955, p. 3.
294. *Ibid.*, January 31, 1955, p. 3.

Several states have passed legislation to protect dealers directly against pressure by their factories. In November 1955 a Wisconsin statute of twenty years earlier, prohibiting cancellation of franchises without "cause," was held to be constitutional by a 4–3 vote of the state's Supreme Court, which declared it applicable to the claim of a widow whose husband's franchise had been terminated "without considering the dealer's equities" upon his death.[295] New York adopted a similar statute in April 1956. In Rhode Island termination of franchises may be appealed to a state board. In August 1956 a three-judge federal court ruled unconstitutional a stringent Colorado statute passed the previous year.[296] Among other things, this had forbidden cancellation of a franchise without a court order, inducing a dealer to share in cooperative advertising campaigns, and shipping a vehicle to a dealer otherwise than in the manner he desired. The court was especially incensed at the attempt to outlaw "inducing." The state put up the defense, in vain, that the plaintiff, General Motors, had no right to sue since its whole dealer franchise constituted unlawful exclusive dealing.

Federal legislation. About thirty bills, some of which, according to one observer, "would have done the industry and consumers irreparable harm,"[297] were introduced into the second session of the Eighty-fourth Congress to help the dealers. The only law to emerge was the Automobile Dealer Franchise Act, approved on August 8, 1956. This short statute was enacted "to supplement the antitrust laws" but in no way to "repeal, modify, or supersede" them. It simply gave dealers the right to recover damages if factories did not "act in good faith in performing or complying with any of the terms or provisions of the franchise, or in terminating, canceling or not renewing the franchise," and defined good faith as fair and equitable action without coercion or intimidation. The local influence of automobile dealers made a negative vote seem imprudent, and in the Senate only one member, Senator Potter of Michigan, risked it. President Eisenhower, in signing the bill, hinted that it might be unconstitutional, and asked the Department of Justice to report to Congress alternative ways of meeting the problem.

295. *Kuhl Motor Co. v. Ford Motor Co.*, discussed in *ibid.*, November 14, 1955, pp. 4, 8.

296. *General Motors Corp. v. Blevins*, 144 F. Supp. 381 (D. Colo. 1956).

297. Kelley, "Mutiny of the Car Dealers," p. 74.

It was by no means clear that the statute would help dealers. The report of the House Judiciary Committee pointed out that it would not interfere with the manufacturer's right to terminate a franchise if the dealer was not giving "adequate representation" and that it would not legalize in any way steps to control bootlegging.[298]

Factory policies. Manufacturers have sought in the past to develop efficient and satisfied dealers by such methods as capital loans to promising candidates, training programs, and establishment of councils to represent dealers handling various makes. Although constructive as far as they went, these actions did not meet the problems of forcing and cancellations. Another approach is the board of review, consisting of top officers of a company, to hear appeals by its dealers against cancellation. Although this was hailed as at least a start toward "due process of law," [299] the General Motors board decided only 6 out of 37 appeals in favor of the dealers from 1938 to 1953, and none out of 16 in 1954 and 1955.[300] According to dealers, the top executives, "in their massive endeavors, have lost the human touch." [301]

The findings of the Senate investigations in 1955, headed, respectively, by Senators Monroney and O'Mahoney (the latter as part of Senator Kilgore's investigation), were a surprise to the manufacturers. Their own investigations among their dealers now confirmed the fact that some of their policies had been shortsighted and that their dealers were in a state of hot resentment.[302] Suddenly General Motors announced at the O'Mahoney hearings that it had telegraphed all its dealers extending franchise terms from one to five years, thus automatically postponing the dreaded "recontracting day" for all and wiping out all outstanding notices of nonrenewal.[303] General Motors announced to the trade eighteen major changes in its franchise. These included factory responsibility for the full cost of warranty payments on new cars, permission to pass on a dealership for a year's trial to a son or son-in-law or any other qualified person actively in the business, group insurance running up to $100,000 per dealer, a larger factory

298. Commerce Clearing House, *Trade Regulation Reports*, No. 54, August 10, 1956, Part 1, p. 9.

299. Berle, *The 20th Century Capitalist Revolution*, pp. 80–81.

300. General Motors exhibit, Kilgore Hearings, Part 8, pp. 4382–83.

301. Frederick J. Bell, *ibid.*, Part 7, p. 3162.

302. Kelley, "Mutiny of the Car Dealers," p. 74.

303. Harlow H. Curtice, Kilgore Hearings, Part 7, p. 3700.

share in the cooperative advertising, and greater weight to local conditions in judging whether a dealer was making a "satisfactory penetration" of his potential market.[304] At the same time dealers around the country found that the practice of forcing cars on them was in abeyance.[305] As other manufacturers followed General Motors in establishing new contractual relations with their dealers or announcing their intention to do so,[306] it was clear that the dealer's position was rapidly improving. The change could be credited primarily to the Senate investigations and to the willingness of state legislatures and Congress to intervene.

The Dealer's Economic Position

The human issues aside, dealers have, on the whole, enjoyed great prosperity in most years since World War II. Between 1929 and 1948 the average annual sales of new-car dealers increased from $148,000 to $363,000,[307] and between 1948 and 1955 sales approximately doubled.[308] A statement by a Northern California dealers' convention is revealing:

> There is an increasing and probably warranted feeling among dealers, most of whom have done well, that they should retire and conserve what they have, and that there will no longer be an adequate profit for them because of bootlegging.[309]

The National Automobile Dealers Association has published rates of return on sales since 1950, profit per new car sold since 1953, and rates of return on investment since 1954. These rates are given before the corporate income tax, applicable to the many incorporated dealers. The return in 1950 was apparently very high, and the steady 1950–54 decline left a strong impression on dealers. In the words of the O'Mahoney subcommittee's staff: "Since standards of profits and of living are to some extent based upon experience, dealers with memo-

304. *Business Week*, March 3, 1956, pp. 104–11.

305. *Wall Street Journal*, January 31, 1956, pp. 1, 9.

306. George Romney, *Automobile Marketing Practices*, Hearings, Part 1, p. 17; *Automotive News*, August 20, 1956, pp. 1, 58.

307. *Statistical Abstract of the United States*, 1955, p. 858.

308. *Automobile Facts and Figures*, 1956, pp. 10, 68.

309. Statement of San Francisco Motor Car Dealers Ass'n. and Northern Calif. Motor Car Dealers Ass'n., *Automobile Marketing Practices*, Hearings, p. 483.

ries of lush postwar years are restive today."[310] In 1935, 1936 and 1937 samples of 285, 325 and 361 dealers, respectively, had earned (before income tax) 10.3, 18.3 and 15.7 per cent on their investment — not far from the levels since 1950.[311]

General Motors has disclosed figures on investment and profits of its dealers for 1940 and 1955, plus partial figures for 1953 and 1954; Ford has disclosed figures for 1954 and 1955. Although there are differences in the accounting methods used, since NADA would want to show low profits and General Motors and Ford high profits for the dealers covered, the apparent fact that General Motors and Ford dealers made more money than others in 1953, 1954 and 1955 is not at all surprising. On the whole, such figures as General Motors and Ford have reported (Table 60) make little change in the broad picture.

Returns on Sales and on Net Worth

When General Motors compared the rate of return *on net worth* in 1953 and 1954 with the rates for eleven other important forms of retail selling, in each year the General Motors dealers ranked first.[312] On its side, NADA offered figures which showed that, in return *on sales*, dealers reporting to it ranked at the bottom of forty types of retailers, and that their return ranged between about 5 per cent and 30 per cent of that of the General Motors Corporation in the 1949–55 period.[313] Although many dealers argue that their net worth is undervalued by factory methods of accounting,[314] return on sales is probably a less revealing figure than return on net worth in judging this situation. Thus grocery stores were next lowest to franchised dealers in return on sales, but this is a reflection of the rapidity of turnover of capital in groceries (and automobiles) rather than an indication that these lines of business are doing badly. So also in contrasting the returns on sales of General Motors itself and its dealers, it must be noted that dealers turn over their capital three times as fast as the corporation.

It is clear, then, that most dealers have done well financially since World War II, with the usual individual exceptions and with many

310. *A Study of the Antitrust Laws*, Staff Report of Senate Judiciary Committee, p. 77.

311. FTC 1939 Report, p. 827.

312. Kilgore Hearings, Part 7, pp. 3503–04, or Part 8, p. 4470.

313. *Ibid.*, Part 7, pp. 3180–81.

314. Senator A. S. Mike Monroney, *Automobile Marketing Practices*, Senate Hearings, Part 2, pp. 1481–82.

TABLE 60

AUTOMOBILES: PROFITS OF FRANCHISED DEALERS, 1940 AND 1950–55

Item	1940	1950	1951	1952	1953	1954	Jan.–Sept. 1955	1955
				All Reporting Dealers				
Total sales (*billions*)		$27.38	$26.28	$26.39	$31.50	$29.96		$36.27
Profit before taxes per new car or truck sold [a]					$100	$29		$80
Total profit before taxes (*millions*)[b]		$1,725	$1,288	$950	$693	$180		$617
Rate of return before taxes on sales (*per cent*)[a]		6.3	4.9	3.6	2.2	0.6	2.6	1.7
Rate of return before taxes on investment (*per cent*)[c]		34.5	25.8	19.0	13.9	8.2 [a]		11.1[a]
				All General Motors Dealers				
Investment (*millions*)	$249						$2,200	
Total sales (*millions*)	$3,106						$13,490	
Profit before taxes (*millions*)	$72						$414	
Rate of return before taxes on sales (*per cent*)	2.31				2.25 [d]	1.39 [d]	3.07	
Rate of return after reported taxes on net worth (*per cent*)					14.40	9.04		13.81
				All Ford Dealers				
Rate of return after taxes on sales (*per cent*)						1.43		1.73
Rate of return after taxes on net worth (*per cent*)						11.27		16.28

Sources: Total sales from Automobile Manufacturers Ass'n., *Automobile Facts and Figures*, 1956, p. 10, with 1950 adjusted to new basis; National Automobile Dealers Association figures from *Journal of Commerce*, December 6, 1955, p. 4; *Automotive News*, 1956 Almanac Issue, April 30, 1956, p. 96; Frederick M. Sutter, first vice president of NADA, in *Automobile Dealer Franchises*, Hearings before Antitrust Subcommittee, House Judiciary Committee, 84th Cong., 2d sess., Serial 26, 1956, p. 589; and *A Study of the Antitrust Laws*, Hearings before Subcommittee on Antitrust and Monopoly, Senate Judiciary Committee, 84th Cong., 1st sess., 1955, Part 7, p. 3187; General Motors figures from "The Development and Growth of General Motors," statement by Harlow H. Curtice, *ibid.*, Part 8, pp. 4468–71, and Robert A. Bicks of the Antitrust Division, in *Automobile Dealer Franchises*, House Hearings, p. 249; Ford figures by Lewis D. Crusoe, *Automobile Marketing Practices*, Hearings before Subcommittee of Senate Interstate and Foreign Commerce Committee, 84th Cong., 2d sess., 1956, Part 1, p. 1046. Rates of return on net worth as reported by General Motors and Ford are not for actual dealer capital, but for minimum capital as recommended by the factories, according to officials of NADA, in *Automobile Dealer Franchises*, House Hearings, p. 589.

a. As reported by the National Automobile Dealers Association.

b. Derived from total sales and return on sales.

c. 1950–53 capital is assumed to be the $5 billion estimated for 1956 (*The Automobile Marketing Practices Study*, Report of Subcommittee on Automobile Marketing Practices of Senate Interstate and Foreign Commerce Committee, 84th Cong., 2d sess., 1956, p. 1).

d. Rate of return after reported taxes.

exceptions among the representatives of car producers whose own sales have decreased. The problem for the automobile producers is not so much one of seeing that their dealers are well enough rewarded to stay in business as one of conveying a sense of justice, both in their general policies and in their treatment of individual cases. A special difficulty for the dealer is that, even though "most manufacturers need additional dealers, and are actively seeking them," [315] there are too few manufacturers for most dealers to move easily from one to another. This fact might suggest the dissolution of the big producers, so that dealers might have the benefit of the competition between makes which consumers already enjoy. To avoid such remedies, it behooves the manufacturers to pursue as constructive human relations policies with their dealers as they do with their employees.

Dealers versus Supermarkets

A background threat to the position of franchised dealers is the possibility that exclusive dealing in the distribution of automobiles might be abolished, either by court action or as a result of economic factors. For the moment neither threat is imminent. The right of manufacturers to insist on exclusive dealing was sustained in court in 1954, in a suit against Hudson by a canceled dealer whose performance had been unsatisfactory in part because he handled Willys and Packard cars as well.[316] This outcome was presumably welcome to most dealers, since, if the courts denied manufacturers the right to insist on exclusive dealing, "supermarket" dealers handling any or all makes of cars might soon invade the local brand monopolies of the franchised dealers even more than they already have (under the guise of bootleggers). Meanwhile suits by used-car dealers to force manufacturers to sell them new cars have been floundering in the courts.[317]

The economic threat, that exclusive dealers might be replaced by supermarket dealers, seemed in 1956 to be momentarily checked. In 1955 many dealers felt that their pattern of business was "disintegrating" [318] under bootleg and supermarket competition; [319] but in 1956

315. James J. Nance, *ibid.*, Part 1, p. 394.

316. *Hudson Sales Corp. v. Waldrip*, 211 F. 2d 268 (5th Cir. 1954), certiorari denied 348 U.S. 821 (1954).

317. *Business Week*, March 19, 1955, p. 68.

318. *Ibid.*, February 19, 1955, p. 56.

319. *Ibid.*, October 1, 1955, pp. 104–10.

many supermarkets appeared to be in trouble from lack of a sure source of supply and inability to obtain state licenses.[320] There are eminent marketing experts who predict that volume selling will be the future pattern and that automobile dealers must adjust to it or give way to the new volume outlets,[321] but from the consumer's point of view, a means of distribution which gives him reliable conditioning of new cars, and service thereafter, may be as important as one which stresses volume. A good argument can be made for letting the open market decide this issue, without intervention by the government except for outlawing of all deceptive practices and without arbitrary requirements adopted by mere majority vote of the industry.

Interindustry Competition

Plenty of evidence of the competitive impact of automobiles on other industries is to be found in the competition of passenger cars and buses with railway passenger service and municipal streetcar systems, and in the battle of truck against rail transportation of freight. Up to the present, the automotive industry has held the upper hand.

Performance of the Industry

The achievements of the automobile industry require no elaboration. The automobile has speeded up transportation and travel, released farmers from social isolation, made suburban living popular, created such giant subsidiary industries as gasoline and tire production, taught other industries how to revive demand by offering new models, and transformed American life in innumerable other ways. The Federal Trade Commission, which rarely goes out of its way to commend industries it investigates, said in 1939: "Consumer benefits from competition in the automobile manufacturing industry have probably been more substantial than in any other large industry studied by the Commission." [322]

In answering questions posed by Edward S. Mason as to industrial performance,[323] Donald A. Moore quoted this statement and gave a

320. John O. Munn, *Automotive News*, August 20, 1956, p. 3.

321. Charles Franklin Phillips, cited in Kelley, "Mutiny of the Car Dealers," p. 71.

322. FTC 1939 Report, p. 1074.

323. Edward S. Mason, "The Current Status of the Monopoly Problem in the United States," *Harvard Law Review*, June 1949, pp. 1281–82; Moore, "The Automobile Industry," pp. 321–23.

net balance of praise to the industry. His main points were five: (1) The industry is engaged in effective competition in processes and products. (2) Cost reductions, although not passed on to consumers in the form of lower prices, are in fact passed on as product improvements. (3) If investment is in any way excessive in relation to demand, it is because of cyclical and seasonal fluctuations in demand. (4) Although the profits of some manufacturers have been high, the industry on the average has not taken an exceptional rate of return in reward for its efforts. (5) Selling expenditures are large, but service and product improvement is continuous.

Criticisms of automobile design have been heard increasingly in recent years — for example, that too much power is being put into cars for safety; that cars are too long for convenient garaging or parking; that the way in which fenders are built makes access to the wheels difficult and minor repairs expensive; and that the emphasis on repeated style changes, even apart from its threat to the survival of small companies, involves great economic waste. These criticisms cannot be ignored. In testifying as to safety, automobile executives have pointed out that the number of accidents per mile traveled has been reduced 55 per cent in thirteen years.[324] They also point out that in a year (1956) when Ford stressed safety and Chevrolet stressed power and performance, the latter was running sharply ahead in sales. To most criticisms, they are able to say that they are following consumer wishes; but manufacturer advertising is a powerful factor in shaping demand.

Some of the virtues and weaknesses of the industry came to the fore in the terrific burst of passenger car production in 1955, when nearly 8 million cars were produced as against less than 5.6 million in 1954. On the positive side, this was the most dynamic element in lifting the economy as a whole from a mild recessionary level to an all-time peak. On the negative side, 750,000 of the cars remained unsold at the end of the year; competition in sales became so intense as to lead to the "mutiny of the car dealers"; a fairly uniform rate of production was replaced by a boom and decline; and a vast increase in consumer credit was required which inevitably resulted in a period of quiet business while consumers were paying off their borrowings. Whatever the final judgment may be on the automobile industry's big year, it is clear that it resulted from vigorous competition.

324. Lewis D. Crusoe, Kilgore Hearings, Part 2, p. 655.

SUMMARY

1. *Three big automotive manufacturers,* General Motors, Ford and Chrysler, are the strongest powers in the largest manufacturing industry, "motor vehicles and parts." In 1955 they produced 95 per cent of all passenger cars and, together with International Harvester, 90 per cent of commercial cars. General Motors alone produced 51 per cent of passenger cars and 43 per cent of trucks.

2. Few if any of the particular antitrust suits against alleged *agreements among makers of and dealers in parts* have been of real importance. Presumably the mere existence of the Sherman Act has had a deterrent effect here as elsewhere in the economy.

3. Perhaps the principal *suits against tying clauses* have been one in the carburetor business, which, since the company had gone out of business, came too late to have any real effect, and one which enjoined General Motors in 1941 from requiring its dealers to use only replacement parts made in its own factories. This order is presumably being obeyed, but its practical consequences are not clear.

4. *Advertising* of car prices and cars, as well as of credit terms, was rendered more realistic in the 1930s, partly through efforts of the Federal Trade Commission.

5. Rivalry between the independent *sales finance companies* and the three large "factory related" finance companies has led to extensive litigation. The Federal Trade Commission required General Motors Acceptance Corporation to drop the title of its "6% Plan" of installment financing as misleading to the ignorant or careless; but the plan itself was widely adopted and had a correspondingly large influence in reducing charges to car buyers. Consent decrees were signed by Ford and Chrysler in 1939, and by General Motors in 1952 as a sequel to its 1939 conviction of restraint of trade. The decrees provided that these producers' dealers should be free to use any source of financing they pleased, or to recommend any source to their customers — a desirable step in giving dealers greater freedom of action and creating fair competition among finance companies and between finance companies and other institutions. Although industry opinion doubts that there has been any practical effect, statistics show that between 1939 and 1954 the share of the big companies in automobile retail installment notes outstanding dropped from 45 to 35 per cent, and this may be in part a result of the decrees. General Motors still gets a considerable advantage from its ownership of a finance company, but the increase in its business since the low point of 1948 has not yet carried its proportion of the total back to the high level at which it stood in the decade of the 1930s. Finally, the Federal Trade Commission has estab-

lished fair practice rules for automobile loan contracts, which are a good deal like the statutes in a number of states and may have some moral influence.

6. In the so-called *Yellow Cab case* of 1947, the Supreme Court ruled that Checker Cab Manufacturing Corporation was monopolizing the market of the taxicab firms it owned. Although this ruling threatened the legal position of vertical integrations short of complete consolidation, Checker went on to win its own case. The later difficulties of the company indicate that its prosperity depended on selling outside its "captive markets," so that the integration attacked was not a passkey to success.

7. In the *Timken case* of 1951, the Supreme Court ruled that a corporation violates the Sherman Act if it owns foreign companies jointly with local nationals, licenses them to make its product, and agrees that various national markets shall be reserved to each. It is too soon to know how far the doctrine that a corporation must compete against a unit it controls, to the possible detriment of minority stockholders, will be carried. In practice a very modest amount of competition — and duplication — has been created abroad in this product (tapered roller bearings).

8. After 1948 the Federal Trade Commission launched a campaign against *price discrimination* in the parts industry. The degree to which small producers of spark plugs have been aided by the orders against their three large competitors is in dispute. In other discrimination cases (in which the respondents are small firms, and discount schedules are still in force pending appeal to the courts), the principle is being applied that price cuts to some customers unjustified by costs violate the Clayton Act by giving their recipients an advantage, even if they in turn do not cut resale prices.

9. One of the most important of all antitrust suits was brought in 1949 to compel disposal of the *du Pont stockholdings in General Motors and United States Rubber*. The government charged that the du Pont family had used its influence on the boards of directors of these corporations to keep General Motors and U.S. Rubber from competing with each other or with the du Pont Company, and to require the three corporations to supply each other with chemical products, trucks and tires in transactions closed off from competition. The District Judge ruled in December 1954 that the evidence showed that the operations of the companies were determined independently, and in particular that purchases by General Motors had been made by its own officers for the corporation's best interests as they saw them. In other words, the potential danger that du Pont's stock purchase in General Motors would foreclose an important market to du Pont's competitors had not been realized in practice. The suit highlighted the need of legislation to permit a corporation which had made a successful investment in another company and later wanted to or was compelled by a court to "spin off" the stock to its own shareholders to do so without imposing on them a prohibitive tax penalty.

10. The *trend toward concentration* in the manufacture of passenger cars has gradually eliminated all but five of the 180 or more companies that have made cars commercially since about 1900. Unless firms were able to gain enough original success to graduate into the large-size classification, they have had little hope of continuing in existence. Such early success has depended on the genius of the management in combining effective engineering with an understanding of consumer tastes. The number of makes of trucks has also decreased — by half since 1926.

11. The *advantages of size* in passenger car manufacture are as great as, or greater than, in any other manufacturing industry. They include the ability to make use of expensive, cost-cutting machinery; to finance the introduction of new models at appropriate intervals; to finance costly research, styling and other services; to finance a widespread dealer organization which will give the public convenient points for both purchase and service of cars; to offer a diversified line of cars, and perhaps other products, and thus avoid disaster if any one model fails; and to bargain with the parts industry successfully and make parts if this promises to be more profitable. Profits per dollar of sales are positively correlated with size in automotive manufacturing, and the relative advantage of large size seems to be increasing.

12. Before the 1920s, growth of the industry favored the *entry* of new firms; but the rate of failure was correspondingly high. Today entry is apparently closed as a result of the much greater capital required both to manufacture cars and to gain a reputation equal to that of producers long in the field. Innovation is thus likely to come more successfully from established companies than from newcomers. Fortunately, the few remaining companies, by offering a variety of cars, give the consumer almost as wide a choice as he ever had. The number of "independent" car producers was reduced to two after mergers, approved by the Department of Justice, brought together Nash and Hudson, and Studebaker and Packard.

13. The size of *General Motors*, unique in all of industry, has made it a special subject of antitrust interest. Perhaps as an alternative to striving for a still larger share of the passenger car market, perhaps as the most direct route to larger profits, it has expanded successfully into other fields — electrical refrigeration, motor buses, aircraft engines, diesel locomotives and road machinery. The popular view that General Motors refrains from more aggressive competition for fear of ruining its rivals and becoming an illegal monopoly is not justified. It is true, however, that if the corporation engaged in vigorous price competition (which, as experience has taught it, would not pay in any case) these results would probably follow. Much study by the Antitrust Division has resulted in only one suit: against General Motors' bus manufacturing division, whose share of this market had increased over a thirty-year period from 24 to more than 80 per cent. As the economy has grown, General

Motors has been a prime mover in its growth — and Ford, Chrysler and the rest of the industry next only to the automotive giant.

14. The automobile manufacturers' *patent licensing* agreement, which allows all members to use patents without paying royalties, has received much praise; but exclusion of basic patents from the beginning and of all recent patents in the current plan indicates a recognition of the need of the profit motive to stimulate research.

15. *Interlocking directorates* that tie certain car manufacturers to supply firms are probably the outgrowth of close commercial relationships which already existed.

16. *Trade association activity* is of the normal, legitimate kind, with the possible exception of occasional efforts of local dealers' associations to control trade-in allowances on used cars, and these have had little success.

17. The *nature of competition* in the industry is determined by the buying motives of consumers. Greatest success in recent years has attended the companies that have been able to make their new models appear stylish and otherwise superior, and yet keep their costs of production down. No producer can ever be sure that its new cars will prove popular.

18. *Price competition* is important among dealers, operating through the fluctuations of trade-in allowances on used cars. Among manufacturers it appears only rarely during a model season, partly because a price cut will anger customers who have just paid more. Nevertheless, in setting his price each manufacturer must consider what other producers are charging or likely to charge. Experience has taught the factories that price is only one of many factors determining the sale of cars and that more money is to be made by product and style improvement than by price competition. Except in the early period, when costs and prices dropped as the industry achieved the economies of mass production, prices have moved with the general price level; yet over the decades the total value offered in a passenger car has increased.

19. The industry offers its cars in various *price classes*, permitting the consumer to suit his purchase to his purse, with used cars available for those with the least buying power. If producers were denied the right to manufacture in several price classes, competition would be hamstrung and costs increased.

20. Critics of the industry have long argued that it should produce a light "*economy car*"; but experience suggests that the consumer (aware of the bargains he can command in more substantial models in the used-car market) will not pay enough for such a car to enable its producer to make money. If traffic congestion increases or saving on gasoline becomes more important to motorists, light cars may yet win a substantial share of the market.

21. The *independent parts manufacturers* live a precarious business existence. Their original equipment sales are cut down wherever manufacturers decide to make more of their own parts — a trend which is in progress today as Ford

and Chrysler seek to reach the position of General Motors, only half of whose sales receipts are spent for materials and services. Parts makers have sought to protect themselves by improving efficiency, diversifying into production for other industries, and merging. In the replacement market, they must compete with the vehicle manufacturers. In the absence of official statistics and reports, it is impossible to state with certainty what the trends are in the battle for this market or how far exclusive dealing is being practiced. The Federal Trade Commission has in progress a suit assailing the use by General Motors of the phrase "genuine parts" to exclude parts made by competitors, but it will be hard to prevent buyers from regarding the manufacturer's own parts as superior.

22. In 1938 the Federal Trade Commission found a number of *grievances of new-car dealers* against manufacturers — for example, one-sided contracts (recognized as such by many court opinions which nevertheless enforced them because the parties had entered into them voluntarily) with little protection against sudden cancellation; loss of much of a dealer's capital investment upon termination of the franchise; interference with a dealer's operations and levying on him the major share of cooperative advertising costs; and forcing on dealers parts, equipment and, especially, cars in amounts greater than they wanted. In 1955 these grievances were more acute than ever, having been sharpened by cancellation of about 200 franchises (out of some 40,000). In addition, dealers felt their pattern of business imperiled by the "bootlegging" of new cars through "supermarket" operators who sold them at cut prices — a practice they quite reasonably attributed in part to overproduction at the factories, forcing of unwanted cars on franchised dealers, and the custom of charging freight from Detroit on cars assembled at branch plants.

23. *Remedies sought by dealers* have been of several sorts: agreements among themselves to prevent various types of price cutting, which agreements are vulnerable under the antitrust laws; state and federal legislation, the constitutionality and scope of which have not yet been fully defined; and a change in policies on the part of their factories. As a result of the Senate investigations and other developments in 1955, the manufacturers liberalized franchises in the dealers' favor. Forcing of cars seemed not to be a real problem in 1956, bootlegging was on the decline, and a great deal of the "phantom freight" had been abolished by the manufacturers.

24. *Dealer profits* have been at a high level since World War II, except in the year 1954 and except for representatives of factories whose cars were not selling well. Nevertheless, the declining profit trend since the peak around the year 1950 has naturally made dealers restive. The problem of the successful manufacturers is less that of insuring a fair return for their representatives than that of arriving at relations with their dealers, as a group and as individuals, which will appear equitable to them.

25. The automobile industry has participated vigorously in *interindustry competition*, with railroads and streetcar systems on the receiving end.

26. The *performance* of the industry has been outstanding and has had an immense effect on the American economy. Many critics are pointing out that it is marred in recent years by a competitive race to build cars which appeal more to the consumer's vanity than to his good sense. Although consumers have shown in the market place that they consider the changes improvements, they are responding in part to industry advertising.

In brief, the antitrust laws have perhaps had a modest effect in protecting small firms in such areas as sales finance and parts manufacture, and in diverting the expansion of General Motors into nonautomotive fields; and congressional antitrust investigations have brought considerable benefit to dealers since 1955; but on the whole the industry is one in which the antitrust laws have not had a strong direct impact, and in which large investment and concentration of output have contributed to outstanding economic performance.

CHAPTER 9

Cotton Textiles

Cotton manufacture is one of the oldest of the large American industries, being generally considered to date from 1790. In recent years it has been gradually merging into a more broadly defined "textile" industry. Not only are cotton and synthetic cloth now often produced by the same company in different mills, and sometimes even alternately in the same mill as prices may dictate, but finished goods consist increasingly of blends. Cotton, however, still constitutes two thirds by weight of all textile fibers consumed. The 1954 Census attributed to the cotton broad woven fabrics industry shipments of $2.8 billion and employment of 296,000. Many or most of the 204,000 workers engaged in four other Census categories — narrow fabrics, thread, yarn, finishing (except wool) — also worked on cotton. The value of cotton textile shipments, excluding duplications, is somewhere in the neighborhood of $3.5 billion.

Stages in the Industry

The successive steps through which cotton moves from bale to store counter may be summarized as follows:

The fibers are cleaned and straightened by "carding" (plus combing if "fine" cloth is being made), then spun into yarn or into thread. At the time of the 1954 Census 357 mills shipped "sales yarn" to weavers, knitters, twine makers and others. Most yarn, however, is spun and woven at the same establishment — in other words, at one of the 582 broad woven fabric mills. There were also 97 thread mills and 513 narrow fabric mills. The industry was once centered largely in New England, but nearly 90 per cent of active spindles are now in the southeastern states.

Some cloth mills do their own selling; others are represented by agents called "selling houses." These may handle the entire output of a number of mills. In return for a 2 to 5 per cent commission, they find customers, guarantee their credit, sometimes help finance the mills, indicate what kinds of cloth they should produce, or even plan their production schedules. In recent years, the ownership of many selling houses and mills has been combined. Textile "factors" are another important source of working capital to cotton mills. Finally, cloth brokers are employed in some transactions. Distribution is heavily concentrated in New York City, where (until a recent movement to the midtown garment district) Worth Street has denoted cloth market as Wall Street signifies financial market.

A substantial amount of cloth goes in unfinished form ("gray" or "greige" goods) to makers of industrial products. The rest must be "finished," usually by bleaching, dyeing or printing. Some cloth is dyed in the yarn; some is finished directly after weaving in the same or an associated plant; the rest goes to independent finishing companies. There were 726 finishing establishments in 1954. Nearly two thirds of these were in the Middle Atlantic states, but here too the South is gaining rapidly. These mills do not take title to the cloth, but receive their instructions from its owner — either the weaving mill, a large manufacturer or distributor of cotton goods, or a specialized middleman known as a "converter." Converters handle about half the cloth which requires finishing: they buy it, have it finished according to their own design and style, and find a market. In 1948, 90 per cent of the 1,151 converters were in New York City; more handled synthetic than cotton goods and many handled both; and 6 per cent were affiliated with their own finishing plants.[1]

Finally, buyers of finished cloth include (1) manufacturers of apparel and household furnishings (known in the trade as "cutters" or "cutters-up"), (2) makers of certain industrial products for which the cloth must be finished, (3 wholesalers, and (4) large retailing organizations that buy cotton goods or articles direct instead of through wholesalers.

Relatively Low Concentration

It follows from the large number of textile producers that concentration in the industry is likely to be low. This remains true even when

1. National Credit Office, Inc., Market Planning Service, *The Converting Industry*, leaflet, New York, January 5, 1950.

the larger units are grouped into "interests" on the basis of intercorporate relationships and of stock control in one firm held by managing officers in another. Under the supervision of Solomon Barkin, research director of the Textile Workers Union of America, data were recently prepared for the forty-three largest companies and "interests." Comparison of these estimates of 1955 employment with an estimate for the industry total (exclusive in each case of knitting interests and synthetic fiber and yarn manufacture) indicates that the largest concern accounted for nearly 5 per cent of total employment, the four largest for 13 per cent, and the fifteen largest for 29 per cent. Plants owned by the fifteen largest numbered about 300. (See Table 61.)

These are necessarily very rough estimates. Furthermore, the individual companies' activities are by no means confined to cotton textiles or even to the textile industry. All firms in the list make some cotton goods; but several of them do substantial rayon and synthetic weaving. The largest, Burlington Industries, is reported to have less than a fourth of its capacity in cotton goods; [2] Textron has nearly half its sales outside of textiles; [3] while sales and employment of United Merchants and Manufacturers are swollen by apparel manufacture and the distribution of "Robert Hall" clothes through this firm's more than 200 retail stores.

Sales of these fifteen companies, based on published figures of thirteen and very rough estimates obtained from the industry for the other two, amounted to perhaps $2.8 billion in 1955, or 35 per cent of the textile industry total, which an industry source estimates at roughly $8 billion (Table 61). The same factors that apply to employment make this estimate very inexact.

The four largest companies in cotton broad woven fabrics in 1947 made shipments of approximately $430 million, or 13.1 per cent of the total. This would place the industry near the bottom of the list in terms of concentration, ranking 412 out of 452 tabulated by the Census Bureau. Cotton yarn ranked 411, finishing 409, and narrow fabrics 385.[4] Among individual cotton products — denim, duck, colored yarn or any other — the concentration ratio is, of course, higher

2. Dero A. Saunders, "Burlington Weaves a New Pattern," *Fortune*, December 1954, p. 162.

3. *America's Textile Reporter*, February 23, 1956, p. 24.

4. U.S. Census data, in *Study of Monopoly Power*, Hearings before Subcommittee on Study of Monopoly Power, House Judiciary Committee, 81st Cong., 1st sess., 1949, Serial 14, Part 2–B, p. 1452.

TABLE 61

COTTON TEXTILES: EMPLOYMENT, SALES AND PLANTS OF FIFTEEN LARGE "INTEREST GROUPS," 1955

Firm	Employment	Sales	Number of Plants
		(Millions)	
Industry total (estimate for textile industry as a whole)	770,000	$8,000	2,748
Fifteen "interest groups" or companies	222,200	2,800 [a]	302
Burlington Industries, Inc.	36,000	515.2	65
J. P. Stevens & Co.	25,000	321.1	37
Cannon Mills Co. interests	22,000	196.7	17
Deering, Milliken & Co.	17,200	200 [a]	26
Cone Mills Corp.	15,000	163.6	20
Abney-Erwin interests	13,900	59.9 [a]	25
West Point Manufacturing Co. interests	12,600	128.6	16
Berkshire Hathaway, Inc., interests	12,200	65.5	16
Springs Cotton Mills	12,000	100 [a]	8
M. Lowenstein & Sons, Inc.	10,700	228.2	11
Dan River Mills	10,000	91.7	1
Pepperell Manufacturing Co.	9,300	84.7	8
Textron, Inc., interests	9,200	189.2	21
United Merchants and Manufacturers, Inc.	9,200	392.2	20
Lester Martin interests	7,900	60.7 [c]	11

Sources: Classification of companies, and estimates for their employment and plants from Research Department, Textile Workers Union of America, constituting a revision as of November 1955 of the similar table for June 1955 inserted in *A Study of the Antitrust Laws*, Hearings before Subcommittee on Antitrust and Monopoly, Senate Judiciary Committee, 84th Cong., 1st sess., 1955, Part 2, p. 787; company sales of all products from Moody's *Industrials;* total employment from *Survey of Current Business*, March 1956, p. S–12 (excludes knitting); total sales estimated by an industry source, which notes it "may be a billion or two off, partly depending on what one includes"; total plants from the 1954 *Census of Manufactures*, for cotton and rayon broad woven fabrics, narrow woven fabrics, thread, yarn and finishing (except wool).

a. Dollar sales are for the named or principal company in each group and not for the associated "interests." Deering, Milliken and Springs sales are rough estimates received from industry sources.

b. Erwin Mills only.

c. Bates Manufacturing Co. only.

than for the industry as a whole; the same is true, however, for comparable industries such as paper or chemicals.

Products and Uses

Broad woven fabrics, the chief products of cotton manufacture, are divided by the Census into eight groups. Print cloth and sheeting, each

TABLE 62

COTTON TEXTILES: TYPES OF BROAD WOVEN FABRIC AND SOME END PRODUCTS, 1955

Type of Goods	Per Cent of Total Broad Woven Fabric Production	Some Important Uses
Print cloth	38.9	dresses, shirts, underwear, tobacco cloth
Sheetings and allied fabrics	25.5	sheets, bags, upholstery, pillowcases
Fine fabrics	13.4	dresses, shirts, pajamas
Colored yarn fabrics	7.1	work clothes, bedticking
Toweling	4.9	towels, bath mats
Napped fabrics	2.4	flannels, blankets
Duck and allied fabrics	2.4	tents, belting
Other	5.4	upholstery, bandages, drapery

Source: Figures from U.S. Census Bureau, *Facts for Industry*, Series M15A, "Cotton Broad Woven Goods."

of which is the base for hundreds of end products of all sorts, accounted for 39 and 25 per cent of the total, respectively, in 1955. Fine fabrics made up 13 per cent, and five other groups the remaining 22 per cent. (See Table 62.) Print cloth and sheeting are standardized gray goods, in which there is wide and active competition.

In 1954 apparel took 42 per cent of the raw cotton whose final use could be determined (men's and boys' wear 25 per cent, women's 10 per cent and children's 7 per cent); nonapparel household uses 35 per cent; and industry 23 per cent. The top six industrial uses — automotive, bags, industrial thread, insulation, cordage, and machinery belts — accounted for about 12 per cent of the total.[5]

So broad is this demand that consumption of cotton is strongly affected by national income and industrial production. The arrival of other fibers has had the effect of expanding the total market rather than reducing the quantity of cotton used. Nevertheless, the rate of buying of cotton for many uses fluctuates widely. Among the reasons for this are fashion changes; new blends and technical discoveries in the fiber field; habits of inventory building and reduction; and fluctuations in the raw cotton market due to weather, insect pests and government policies.

5. U.S. Department of Agriculture data tabulated in National Cotton Council, Inc., *Cotton Counts Its Customers*, Memphis, April 1955, pp. 5–16.

Antitrust Cases and the NRA Code

There has been very little antitrust action in the cotton textile industry. This is undoubtedly due to the atomistic character of the industry and the absence of corporations of dominating size.

The "Thread Trust," Labels and Book Cloth

In 1898 the English Sewing Cotton Company took over the ownership of fourteen United States mills, which it consolidated as the American Thread Company.[6] Eventually it concentrated production in a few of the most efficient ones. J. & P. Coats, Ltd., a still larger British organization allied with the English Sewing Cotton Company through stockholdings, had its own American subsidiary. The two together were estimated to control two thirds of United States thread production. Much more of the thread manufactured in those years went to home consumers than today.

In the antitrust drive under President Taft, American Thread and the English Sewing Cotton Company were sued, and in 1914 they accepted a consent decree. They agreed to cancel all stock or other connections with J. & P. Coats and not to engage in various sorts of monopolistic practices.[7] The two firms are still the largest producers of thread, especially household thread, with sixteen mills between them.[8] The four principal manufacturers accounted for 65.3 per cent of the shipments of this product in 1947.[9]

In 1917 the Woven Label Manufacturers Association was dissolved by a consent decree. Its rules had governed the entire trade in labels, tabs and similar articles.[10]

Another consent decree, in 1918, dissolved a price-fixing combination among corporations that manufactured 90 per cent of the country's production of the cloth used for binding books.[11] In 1951 the same

6. Melvin T. Copeland, *The Cotton Manufacturing Industry of the United States*, Harvard University Press, Cambridge, 1912, pp. 169–70.

7 *U.S. v. American Thread Co.*, Eq. 312 (D. N.J. 1913), Department of Justice, *Decrees and Judgments in Federal Antitrust Cases*, 1918, pp. 449–56.

8. Solomon Barkin, research director of Textile Workers of America, in *A Study of the Antitrust Laws*, Hearings before Subcommittee on Antitrust and Monopoly, Senate Judiciary Committee, 84th Cong., 1st sess., 1955, Part 2, pp. 768, 787.

9. U.S. Census data, in *Study of Monopoly Power*, House Hearings, p. 1447.

10. *U.S. v. Adolph C. Kluge*, Eq. 14–343 (S.D. N.Y. 1917), *Decrees and Judgments*, pp. 631–34.

11. *U.S. v. Interlaken Mills*, Civil 15–19 (S.D. N.Y. 1918).

segment of the industry, consisting chiefly of new firms, was again the subject of antitrust charges — this time by the Federal Trade Commission. First under the auspices of the Institute of Book Cloth and Impregnated Fabrics Manufacturers, organized during the National Recovery Administration in 1933, and then informally for nine years after the Institute's disappearance in 1941, the firms had engaged in various cooperative practices. These included discussion and fixing of prices and terms of sale, and elimination of quantity discounts and free delivery points. Four companies accepted an order against such practices in June 1953, while the case against four others (including E. I. du Pont de Nemours & Company) was dismissed.[12]

Commission Converters, Airplane Cloth and Twine

A more unusual case occurred in 1928. Converters handling 75 per cent of the shirting cloth were found to be instigating a boycott to eliminate competing trade channels. One of these channels was direct sale by mills to shirt manufacturers, who then proceeded to make their own deal with finishing mills. In this case, "the big six" — certain large shirt manufacturers whose right thus to finish their own cloth had been sanctified by long custom — were excepted from the hostility of the converters. The second channel was through two new firms, called "commission converters," which arranged the finishing of the shirting cloth for a commission from shirt manufacturers. Unlike regular converters, these firms took no title to the cloth.

The regular converters feared a threat to the independence of their branch of the industry if these procedures should spread. Their reaction took the form of threats not to deal with mills, selling houses, brokers, finishing mills and most shirt makers if they used these channels. They tried also to make an arrangement with the newly organized and short-lived Association of Cotton Cloth Brokers along the line: "You sell only to us and we'll buy only from you." The Department of Justice secured a consent decree in which the converters, and the others that had been cooperating, forswore these practices.[13] Commission converters are still employed by some of the larger organizations, principally retail establishments,[14] but they are

12. *Sayles Finishing Plants, Inc.*, Docket 5878, 49 FTC 1427 (1953).

13. *U.S. v. E. O. Barnard & Co.*, Eq. 46–131 (S.D. N.Y. 1928).

14. John L. Severance, "Textiles," Chap. 14 of Richard M. Clewett, ed., *Marketing Channels for Manufactured Products*, Irwin, Homewood (Ill.), 1954, p. 331.

so unimportant that some leaders in the textile industry are not even aware of their existence.

In 1940 four corporations that made practically all of one small product, airplane fabric (balloon cloth), pleaded *nolo contendere* and paid fines on charges of price fixing.[15] Three of the mills making this product have since closed, and four have switched to other cotton or rayon fabrics. Airplane cloth is now made by four entirely different firms.[16]

A recent case was brought by the Federal Trade Commission in March 1949 against a number of manufacturers and some wholesalers of twine. Two years later nine of the respondents accepted an order directing them to cease fixing prices and terms of sale in various cotton wrapping and other twines.[17]

Efforts to Control Working Hours

The northern and southern branches of the spinning and weaving industry long had separate trade associations. In 1926, while retaining these associations, they organized another: the Cotton Textile Institute. The Institute had several purposes: it obtained the 1933 award of the American Trade Association Executives for its work in cost accounting, statistics, finding new uses for cotton, and other activities. But its chief single aim was to limit hours of operation of the mills to the number necessary to meet the current demand.[18]

Many mills, chiefly in the South, were maintaining a second and perhaps a third shift each day in an attempt to reduce unit overhead costs. The Institute at first attacked this cause of overcapacity and cutthroat competition by exhorting its members to keep their hours of operation down. Visits to Washington on behalf of a group of print cloth mills brought no assurance that the Department of Justice would not prosecute any direct curtailment plan. Nevertheless, the industry representatives did find sympathy for their difficulties both at the Justice and Commerce Departments. Thus emboldened, they carried out a temporary curtailment plan in 1928.

15. *U.S. v. Wellington-Sears Co.*, Cr. 108–163 (S.D. N.Y. 1940).

16. *Davison's Textile Blue Book*, Davison Publishing Co., Ridgewood (N.J.), 1941, p. 1137; 1954, p. 1330.

17. *Bibb Manufacturing Co.*, Docket 5838, 47 FTC 1126 (1951), and earlier Docket 5644, 47 FTC 1588, dismissed.

18. Among sources for the following account are a memorandum prepared for the writer by one of the participants, and Cotton Textile Institute, Annual Reports, 1931 and 1932.

Again, in January 1930, three fourths of the industry indicated approval of an Institute recommendation to limit operations to a day shift of 55 hours plus a night shift of 50 hours. In March 1931, 80 per cent of the mills agreed to abandon the practice, then under public criticism, of employing women and children at night. The resulting decrease in operations seems to have been approximately offset by continued lengthening of the hours of nonconforming mills, some of which may even have interpreted the plan as an endorsement of the two-shift schedule as against the single shift. Average number of hours of operation per active spindle dropped from 3,191 in the two years 1928–29 to 3,025 in 1931–32 [19] — a reduction of only 5 per cent in spite of the depression. In all these plans, the Institute itself took no steps to secure compliance beyond urging the mills to follow orthodox business practices and to produce for the purpose of filling orders rather than swelling inventories.

Cotton Textiles and the NRA

As the depression deepened, cotton textile leaders were among those who became interested in a change in national antitrust policy which would permit industries plagued by overcapacity and cutthroat competition to put a floor under prices or a ceiling on production. Experience had seemed to show that without governmental compulsion the whole of an industry could not be persuaded to cooperate.

When the National Industrial Recovery Act was passed in June 1933, leaders of the cotton textile industry had their code of fair competition ready in advance, and it became Code No. 1. It approved collective bargaining, limited hours of work to 40 a week with a proviso against reduction in weekly pay, limited mill operations to two shifts of 40 hours each, provided for the collection of statistics and accounting data, and prohibited installation of new machinery without permission of the National Recovery Administrator. The Institute itself became the Code Authority.

Much emphasis was put during the code period on halting wage cutting and the lengthening of the work week, since the absence of any controls had led some southern mills by this time to cut prices to the point where adequate funds for replacement of plant were threatened. Another key provision was that which limited mills to 80 hours a week. Operations of some southern mills were thus reduced in 1933

19. Calculated from *Survey of Current Business*, 1936 Supplement, p. 142.

just when a flood of new orders was causing New England mills to increase their schedules to two shifts. Between January–May and July–November of that year hours operated per active spindle dropped by 4 per cent in the South and increased by 7 per cent in New England.[20] The year 1933 as a whole showed profits which, although not big, were at least the best since 1927. In 1934 demand dropped off again, and the continuance of hours operated per active spindle within a fraction of one per cent of the 1932 figure showed that the industry's psychology had not basically changed. Both the President's Committee on Industrial Analysis and perhaps the only independent economist who reviewed this phase of the NRA concluded that the machine-hour limitation in cotton textiles was not effective in stabilizing the industry — in fact, probably contributed to its fluctuations.[21]

The Later 1930s

With the expiration of NRA in May 1935, all conformity to the 80-hour limitation ceased, and hours worked per active spindle increased rapidly. Fortunately for the industry, demand for cotton goods was to advance to new peaks in the early 1940s.

The machine-hour limitation had some surprising consequences, nevertheless. With the 40-hour shift once established, it proved impossible to lengthen it again. As demand increased, therefore, it was not met by lengthening the two shifts to 50 hours each, but by adding once more the socially undesirable "graveyard" third shift. This increased total machine-hours far more than two 50-hour shifts would have done, and caused the NRA's aim of improving social conditions to boomerang. On the other hand, the adoption of the five-day week and its spread into other industries was stimulated by the 40-hour pattern thus established, since this fitted better into a five-day than a six-day week.

There were two more limitation episodes. Effective July 1, 1938, 97½ per cent (evidently 78 out of 80) of mills in the "Print Cloth Group" that had been operating a third shift agreed to eliminate it, thereby relieving an unwieldy inventory situation.[22] Print cloth mills

20. Charles F. Roos, *NRA Economic Planning*, Cowles Commission for Research in Economics, Monograph No. 2, Principia Press, Bloomington (Ind.), 1937, p. 368.

21. *Ibid.*, pp. 369–70; *The National Recovery Administration: Report of the President's Committee of Industrial Analysis*, 1937, pp. 177–78.

22. *American Wool and Cotton Reporter*, July 7, 1938, p. 36.

with over 95 per cent of the looms agreed in 1939 to reduce July–September output to 75 per cent of normal, to sell no goods not currently produced, and to publicize the plan but keep its termination secret whenever this might occur. Although curtailment ceased on September 8, after war broke out in Europe, the Department of Justice brought a criminal suit in January 1940 against the managing committee, whose five members pleaded *nolo contendere* and paid fines of $100 each.[23]

General Influence of the Antitrust Law

Expressed opinion in the industry today is almost uniformly to the effect that the antitrust laws have no influence on its operations. Judging by the small number of suits this may well be true. One converter, however, took the position in an interview that it is fortunate the various branches of the industry are protected against conspiracies within some other related branch. The industry has not again been in quite as serious a situation as it was during the 1930s. Hence any possible effect of the antitrust laws in deterring production control agreements has hardly come under discussion. Some mill owners say their industry is too individualistic today to permit such agreements.

One possible qualification to the industry's view as to the lack of any antitrust influence may be noted in connection with the rising export of Japanese textiles to the United States. With their industry a principal victim of Japan's effort to support herself again through foreign trade, some manufacturers blamed the antitrust enforcement agencies for denying them permission to negotiate with Japanese interests on establishment of quotas.[24] Although the cloth is made partly from southern cotton, and the volume of United States cotton textile and apparel exports in 1955 still exceeded imports by a ratio of two to one, imports from Japan were in that year the one issue about which almost any member of the industry was willing and eager to talk to an outsider. Each branch of the industry feared that the Japanese drive would shift from blouses, ginghams or velveteens to its own specialty and earnestly hoped that the Japanese cotton industry would at least diversify its product line. At the beginning of 1956 the Japanese government adopted a "voluntary" quota for the export to the United States of the particular cotton goods most in dispute, hoping thus to forestall action by the American government.

23. *U.S. v. Joseph E. Sirrine*, Cr. 8019 (W.D. S.C. 1940).
24. *America's Textile Reporter*, February 23, 1956, p. 66.

Competitive Status

A "Sick Industry," 1924-40

During the prosperity of the 1920s cotton textiles became known as a "sick industry," along with bituminous coal and a few other patients. The industry's good profits in previous decades had been tempting new capital to enter — especially during World War I — in the North as well as in the faster-growing South. Spindles in place (for which more data are available than for looms) reached their peak in 1925. This represented a substantial overcapacity, in view of the "remarkable discovery" of the southern mills that they could cut unit overhead costs by running two or three shifts instead of one.[25] Between 1923 and 1936 the average weekly hours operated by each active spindle increased from 55 to 75, boosting effective capacity by one third.[26] Prices fell under the pressure of this oversupply. Mill margins, or the difference between raw cotton and cloth prices, declined by about 25 per cent between 1925–26 and 1930–31 and were still at the 1930–31 level nine years later.

In 1923 earnings were still excellent; but between 1924 and 1940 there were seven years of net loss (exclusive of any correction for inventory losses or profits) in cotton manufacturing as a whole — whatever the earnings in individual specialties may have been. Average annual profit of leading producers from 1925 through 1939 was 1.1 per cent on net worth, as against 7.2 per cent for a sample of companies from many manufacturing industries.[27] The unprofitability of the industry was not due to a drop in the demand for cotton goods, since the absolute use of cotton was unchanged between 1923–27 and 1935–39. (See Table 63.)

Causes of the Sickness

Economic analysts have generally attributed the prewar troubles of the cotton textile industry to its structure, which is closer to "pure" competition than that of any other manufacturing industry. Such

25. See Roger Milliken, *Teamwork: The South's Secret Weapon*, Spartanburg (S.C.) Chamber of Commerce, pamphlet, 1955, p. 2.

26. Lloyd G. Reynolds, "Cutthroat Competition," *American Economic Review*, December 1940, p. 740.

27. National City Bank of New York, Monthly Letter, April issues.

TABLE 63

COTTON TEXTILES: SPINDLES, MATERIAL CONSUMED, MARGINS AND PROFITS, 1923–40

Year Ending July 31	Spindles in Place[a] New England	Spindles in Place[a] South	Cotton Consumption	Mill Margin on 17 Constructions	Net Income before Taxes of All Cotton Manufacturing Corporations, Calendar Year
	(Millions)		*(Thousand Bales)*	*(Cents per Pound)*	*(Millions)*
1923	18.9	16.5	6,666	b	$103.9
1924	18.6	17.2	5,681	b	−39.8
1925	18.3	17.6	6,193	b	b
1926	17.9	17.9	6,456	16.0	−30.8
1927	16.9	18.2	7,190	15.4	75.8
1928	15.5	18.5	6,834	14.2	10.6
1929	14.5	18.8	7,091	13.6	22.0
1930	13.5	19.1	6,106	13.2	−91.5
1931	12.2	19.1	5,263	12.2	−63.6
1932	11.4	19.1	4,866	9.4	−53.7
1933	10.8	19.1	6,137	10.1	31.8
1934	10.6	19.3	5,700	14.0	8.4
1935	9.7	19.3	5,361	11.8	−10.3
1936	8.1	19.0	6,351	12.6	37.5
1937	7.2	18.9	7,950	16.6	40.5
1938	6.8	18.8	5,748	12.2	− 4.3
1939	6.1	18.3	6,858	10.4	37.3
1940	5.9	18.1	7,784	12.7	71.3

Source: Jules Backman and M. R. Gainsbrugh, *Economics of the Cotton Textile Industry,* National Industrial Conference Board, New York, 1946, pp. 172, 174, 199 and 204.

a. In 1923 there were 2.0 million other spindles, chiefly in the Middle Atlantic states; in 1940 there were 700,000.

b. Not available.

"purity" has two aspects: (1) Since most gray cloth is standardized, and no firm can assure itself of a market on the reputation of its particular product, competition has tended to center on price. (2) There are so many sellers in relation to the size of the total market, because of the relatively small amount of capital needed for entry, that a mill that cuts prices need not fear retaliation.

Contributing factors included the absence of important patents, the impossibility of controlling the supply of raw material, and the ease with which some machinery could be transferred from one product to another more profitable one. One serious imperfection in competition was the fact that the mills often had so little knowledge of their market that they would produce merely to keep their machines and labor occupied, and then find the output unsalable except at a loss.[28] Some critics have argued also that selling houses, since they were compensated according to volume, were tempted to cut prices whenever demand fell off.[29] The selling houses with which this was discussed entered a denial, at least as to conditions today.

Another factor which combined with this general competitive situation in accounting for the industry's difficulties was the continuing new investment in the South — involving a 10 per cent addition to spindles between 1925 and 1935 (Table 63). Lower wages and fringe benefits, and fewer restrictions on output laid down by unions or by regional custom or legislation, were the South's most important advantages.[30] Lower fuel costs, lower taxes, and certain other considerations played a role also. More broadly, the textile industry was acting as "the spearhead of industrialization" in the South at the expense of New England, just as it has done in Asia at the expense of Britain.[31] Losses in New England were heavy, and have seemed likely to remain so until only such operations are left in that region as can compete with the South.

Cotton Manufacture since 1940

The industry achieved a marked turn for the better after 1940, both because much excess capacity had been squeezed out through closing of mills and scrapping of equipment and because of the general business recovery. Spindles in place declined a full third from their 1925 peak to 1940, as Table 63 shows — and this despite a small increase in

28. See "The Bolt in Cotton Textiles," *Fortune*, July 1947, p. 62; Claudius T. Murchison, "Vertical Integration in the Cotton Textile Industry," Chap. 8 of Nugent Wedding, *Vertical Integration in Marketing*, Bulletin 74, Bureau of Economic and Business Research, College of Commerce and Business Administration, University of Illinois, Urbana, 1952, p. 123.

29. Melvin T. Copeland and Edmund P. Learned, *Merchandising of Cotton Textiles: Methods and Organization*, Graduate School of Business Administration, Harvard University, Boston, 1933, p. 64; E. B. Alderfer and H. E. Michl, *Economics of American Industry*, McGraw-Hill, New York, 2d edition, 1950, p. 378.

30. See James A. Morris, "Cotton and Wool Textiles — Case Studies in Industrial Migration," *Journal of Industrial Economics*, November 1953, p. 70.

31. W. S. and E. S. Woytinsky, *World Population and Production*, Twentieth Century Fund, 1953, p. 1051.

the South. The industry's sickness had slowly and painfully brought its own remedy. As demand increased after 1940, mills modernized their equipment instead of adding to it; [32] and the number of spindles in place continued to decline slowly, from a national total of 24.7 million in 1939–40 to about 22 million in 1955.

In 1947, with price ceilings and the excess profits tax both removed, cotton manufacture had blossomed out briefly as perhaps the most profitable industry in the country. Expansion of output was accomplished by putting machines on a 24-hour basis whenever possible. Although the postwar recovery wilted when demand declined in late 1948, and the "two-year textile cycle" was in operation again, the general position of the industry remained much better than in the 1920s. After June 1950 (at least into 1956) no month has seen less than 98 per cent of broad woven fabric looms operating on two shifts, or less than 79 per cent on three shifts.[33] Recessions in activity are handled by a reduction in days worked per week. In mid-1955, "excess" spindle capacity was estimated at a mere 3 per cent, and investment experts were counting on "more consistently profitable operations in future years." [34]

Size of Mills and Efficiency

The increasing size and rising productivity of cotton mills as the industry developed is indicated by increases, between 1870 and 1914, of 242 per cent in spindles per mill but of 112 per cent in employees per mill. Since 1914, spindles per mill have declined, but productivity has continued its increase.[35]

Figures on the relation of size to efficiency are few and inconclusive. Office of Price Administration data covering 28 carded yarn mills, 19 combed yarn mills and 24 print cloth mills give net operating profit as a percentage of sales for 1936, 1939, 1941 and 1944. For carded yarn and print cloth, the group of mills with lowest sales (as of 1936) had a lower rate of profit in each year; for combed yarn this group had a

32. John W. Murray, Part 2, "Textile Manufacture," in Chap. 7, "The Modern Textile Industry," in John George Glover and William Bouck Cornell, eds., *The Development of American Industries*, Prentice-Hall, New York, 3d edition, 1951, p. 172.

33. *Cotton Textile Hi-Lights*, private publication of American Cotton Manufacturers Institute, Charlotte, April 1956, p. 5.

34. H. William Knodel, "The Textile Renaissance," *Analysts Journal*, August 1955, p. 3.

35. Jules Backman and M. R. Gainsbrugh, *Economics of the Cotton Textile Industry*, National Industrial Conference Board, New York, 1946, pp. 168, 188.

TABLE 64

COTTON TEXTILES: NET OPERATING PROFIT AS PER CENT OF SALES FOR LARGE AND SMALL MILLS, 1936–44

	Carded Yarn		Combed Yarn		Print Cloth	
Year	12 Large Mills	16 Small Mills	9 Large Mills	10 Small Mills	12 Large Mills	12 Small Mills
1936	4.4	3.0	7.2	7.9	7.3	7.0
1939	4.8	3.0	5.9	7.0	3.9	.9
1941	14.7	12.3	14.4	16.9	20.0	18.9
1944	8.5	6.8	6.4	7.0	12.2	11.2

Source: Office of Price Administration data reported in *Study of Agricultural and Economic Problems of the Cotton Belt*, Hearings before Special Subcommittee on Cotton of House Agriculture Committee, 80th Cong., 1st sess., 1947, Exhibit 3, "Cotton-Goods Production and Distribution: Techniques, Costs, and Margins," pp. 131, 132, 146. The dividing lines between "large" and "small" were based on sales in 1936: $500,000 for carded yarn, $1 million for combed yarn, and $1.5 million for print cloth.

higher rate in each year. (See Table 64.) Opinion in the industry, so far as the writer could ascertain, holds that large mills are usually technologically more efficient.

Trend of Concentration

Turning from size of mills to size of firms, we find that between 1860 and 1937 the four largest producers (a group of firms whose composition was not constant) possessed between 8 and 12 per cent of the assets of the cotton textile industry. In 1947 their share had risen to 19.6 per cent. Similarly, between 1937 and 1955 the share of total spindles owned by the four largest companies had increased from 4.9 to 16.8 per cent. (See Table 65.) Even these recent figures are low by comparison with other industries. In the median manufacturing industry among 452 tabulated from the Census of 1947, the four largest producers accounted for 36.5 per cent of the value of shipments.[36]

Of the four largest firms in 1920, none remained a leader by 1937. Two had dropped considerably in their share of the market and had been absorbed by other firms, while the other two had been liquidated outright. One of the four largest as of 1955 had appeared in the group for the first time in 1930 (referring only to the years listed in Table 65), and was out of it temporarily in 1937. Two more appeared in 1947,

36. U.S. Census data, in *Study of Monopoly Power*, House Hearings, pp. 1446–53.

TABLE 65

COTTON TEXTILES: PER CENT OF TOTAL SPINDLES AND ASSETS HELD BY FOUR LARGEST COMPANIES, 1860–1955

Year	Spindles	Assets (or Capitalization)
1860		10.0 [a]
1899		8.7 [a]
1920	6.3	8.0 [a]
1930	8.5	11.0 [a]
1937	4.9	12.1 [a]
1947	10.7	19.6 [b]
1955	16.8	—

Sources: 1860–1937 from Willard L. Thorp and Walter F. Crowder, in *The Structure of Industry*, TNEC Monograph 27, 1941, pp. 252–56; 1920 spindles figure and 1947 from Jesse W. Markham, "Integration in the Textile Industry," *Harvard Business Review*, January 1950, p. 86; 1955 derived from spindle data received from Research Department, Textile Workers Union of America (the union, however, calculates 1955 as 19.2 per cent of active cotton spindles, which it uses instead of spindles in place).

a. Capitalization used to measure assets.

b. "Estimated; not strictly comparable to data for previous years" (Markham, p. 86).

and the fourth in 1955. Some firms have disappeared from the list of largest companies as a result of commercial decline, some merely through failure to expand by merger as rapidly as other concerns.

History of Integration and Mergers

One form of integration which developed to its present stage in the nineteenth century was the union of spinning and weaving in the same company. Weaving mills, contrary to the prevailing British practice, purchase very little of their yarn in the open market.

Before the 1920s examples either of integration forward from the weaving process or of horizontal combination among cotton mills were rare. Sometimes a combination would raise prices and thus cause other mills to adapt their machinery to its product.[37] The Mount Vernon–Woodberry Cotton Duck Company combined seven firms and fourteen mills in 1899 and by 1905 (under the name Consolidated Cotton Duck Company) had acquired 90 per cent of all duck production for making sails; but manufacturers of other kinds of duck shifted their machines to making sail duck as soon as the price policies of the

37. Cecil Eaton Fraser and Georges F. Doriot, *Analyzing Our Industries*, McGraw-Hill, New York, 1932, p. 132.

combine made this profitable.[38] The firm failed in 1910, was reorganized in 1915 as the Mt. Vernon–Woodberry (today simply Mt. Vernon) Mills, Inc., and became prosperous but without monopolistic aims.

Enduring combinations included Cannon Mills Company, which merged twelve plants and their selling houses to become the leader in both toweling and bed sheets; Deering Milliken, a selling house that bought several southern mills and a New York printing works; and the Cone Export and Commission Company, called the "plaid trust" after it began selling for thirty-eight of the forty-four southern plaid mills in 1891 and went on to merge many of them (taking the name Cone Mills Corporation in 1948).[39]

In the late 1920s the pace of mergers was stepped up. Berkshire Fine Spinning Associates (now Berkshire Hathaway, Inc.) combined five companies, and Pacific Mills took over its selling house. United Merchants and Manufacturers formed a complete vertical structure by absorbing selling houses, converters, finishers, manufacturers of end products, and even retail stores. Nevertheless, by 1930, only 10 per cent of cotton textile firms were fully integrated through selling and converting, and only 43 per cent acted as their own selling agents.[40] Some writers on the industry were now urging integration as the answer to its major problems.[41]

Mergers since 1930

Between 1930 and 1939, 492 acquisitions of textile (not merely cotton) mills by other mills were recorded (only 26 per cent were cases of vertical integration); from 1940 through 1948 there were 486 more (42 per cent were vertical).[42] By 1947, 33 per cent of cotton textile firms listed in *Moody's Manual* operated in all stages of the industry and 73 per cent, accounting for about 75 per cent of broad goods sales, acted as their own selling agents.[43] In 1952, about two thirds of all finished piece goods were estimated by one authority to be produced

38. Copeland, *The Cotton Manufacturing Industry*, pp. 164–66.

39. "Cone Mills: Old King Denim," *Fortune*, January 1953, p. 87.

40. Jesse W. Markham, "Integration in the Textile Industry," *Harvard Business Review*, January 1950, p. 82.

41. Copeland and Learned, *Merchandising of Cotton Textiles*, p. 83; Claudius T. Murchison, *King Cotton Is Sick*, University of North Carolina Press, Chapel Hill, 1930, pp. 146, 161.

42. Calculated from Markham, "Integration in the Textile Industry," p. 78.

43. *Ibid.*, pp. 82, 84.

by companies integrated into converting and finishing.[44] Other estimates run a good deal lower than this.

As one example: in the Carolinas, which have over half the country's spindles, the proportion owned by firms that had at least some degree of integration in their production processes beyond the mere combination of spinning and weaving, and in addition marketed their products at least partially through their own selling organizations, increased from 11 per cent in 1939 to 24 in 1946, to 40 in 1950.[45]

After 1953 the pace of the merger movement was stepped up again. In 1954 about 80 mergers were reported and in 1955, 160.[46] When, in July and August 1954, Burlington acquired Pacific Mills and Goodall-Sanford, while Textron acquired American Woolen Company and Robbins Mills, the industry seemed to be "changing its structure so fast that you [could] watch it happening."[47] At the same time M. Lowenstein bought the well-known sheet maker, Wamsutta Mills, and late in 1955 purchased the cotton goods units of Pacific Mills — thus, it is rumored, obtaining 54 per cent of all printing machines for percale (one type of fine cloth).[48] Between 1945 and 1955 both Lowenstein and Burlington increased their assets ninefold, chiefly through mergers.

Temporary and Permanent Advantages of Integration

Among the motives for integration which distinguish the textile industry from others, several temporary ones arising out of World War II gave a strong stimulus to the mergers of the 1940s.[49] When, under Office of Price Administration price ceilings, separate markups were allowed converters and finishers, integration made it possible to obtain such markups. The shortage of gray goods caused firms with large marketing organizations to integrate backward in order to assure their supply; and the shortage of fabrics caused some mills to combine

44. Murchison, "Vertical Integration in the Cotton Textile Industry," p. 117.

45. Calculated from Robert H. Cole, *Marketing Aspects of Vertical Integration in the Textile Industry, with Particular Reference to the Carolina Textile Industry*, unpublished doctoral thesis, University of North Carolina, Chapel Hill, 1952, pp. 73–75.

46. *America's Textile Reporter*, May 17, 1956, p. 59.

47. *Business Week*, July 31, 1954, p. 58.

48. *America's Textile Reporter*, December 22, 1955, p. 24.

49. Stanley J. Goodman, "Make It Pay: The Government-Industry Tussle over Consumer Goods," *Harper's Magazine*, September 1946, pp. 203–12; FTC, *Report on the Merger Movement: A Summary Report*, 1948, p. 55.

in order to obtain a full line. Shortage of machinery sometimes made it much easier for firms to grow by merger than by internal expansion.

Some wartime mergers proved uneconomic and had to be liquidated, but permanent motives were also at work. These include, as in all industries, the tax motivation. Either an unprofitable company is bought in order to gain its income tax credit, or a closely held company is offered for sale so that its owners may turn their accumulated profits into a capital gain taxable at lower rates than regular income, or the owners sell to put their estates in shape. Aside from taxes, the economic motives may be summarized under three broad headings.

Vertical integration. The chaos that plagued the nonintegrated industry in the 1920s and 1930s was in itself enough to cause some firms to desire integration. It was seen that integrated firms could guarantee the quality of their product and command consumer recognition, whereas otherwise the gray goods were completely buried in the "great inland sea" of the cloth market and so hidden in the finished product that the consumer would not know who made them.[50] The example of successful branding and advertising by the makers of bed sheets — Cannon, Pepperell and Wamsutta — was increasingly admired, and the premium price their branded products commanded was envied. It can be said that the ultimate objective of uniting mills, selling houses and converting was to create a stable market through brand promotion.[51] The converter, in turn, often wanted to escape from his complete dependence on the violent fluctuations of the finished goods markets. The broad principle aimed at by all participants in the integration movement was to coordinate all stages of production, avoid misdirection of production at the earlier stages, and achieve greater stability.[52]

Diversification. In recent years the movement has been dominated less by vertical integration than by mergers uniting mills that produce different kinds of fiber — cotton, woolen and synthetics (including rayon). The largest consolidations have interests in all fibers; and the smaller ones are seeking to match them. Such diversification has had a double purpose: to cope with the fluctuations in popularity between

50. Murchison, "Vertical Integration in the Cotton Textile Industry," p. 119.

51. Hiram S. Davis, George W. Taylor, C. Canby Balderston and Anne Bezanson, *Vertical Integration in the Textile Industries*, Industrial Research Department, Wharton School of Finance and Commerce, University of Pennsylvania, and Textile Foundation, Washington, 1938, pp. 11–12.

52. *Ibid.*, p. 2.

the fibers, and to be able to produce the blends of fibers which are becoming the rule rather than the exception in many end products. The president of Burlington has expressed this motivation as follows:

> Thus Burlington woke up, seven or eight years ago, to realize that if it was to survive as a major company in the fierce competition which was beginning, it must achieve a diversification of primary materials and products so that it could develop the proper blends and at the same time average out the inescapable ups and downs and the inevitable variations of consumer preferences and caprices.[53]

If diversification is justified in any industry, these reasons make it so in textiles.

Combination. The third major group of advantages sought through integration is that resulting from sheer combination of large amounts of capital. The bigger the company — assuming efficiency is the same — the easier it is to raise new funds when needed, either from banks or from the investing public. With capital, a company can install modern methods. According to one trade organ:

> Those big fellows represent good merchandising, sound financing, expert fabrication and good styling. They install new, effective machinery, provide good mill management, and a general all-around service to the great consuming public, as opposed to the small mill operations by small men, a lot of nepotism, and run-out family relationship.[54]

The integrated companies have begun to employ their resources in research and advertising, recognized as among the most effective tools of successful companies in other industries [55] but scarcely used until recently in textiles — a fact which some observers call the "key to world textile ills." [56] Between 1940 and 1945 the ratio of research expenditures to sales receipts among a sample of six cotton manufacturers increased by seventy times (from .0017 to .12 per cent).[57] The Institute of Textile Technology near Charlottesville was founded by some of the large companies in 1944, to train textile engineers and

53. J. Spencer Love, *A Study of the Antitrust Laws*, Senate Hearings, p. 740.

54. *America's Textile Reporter*, March 15, 1956, p. 22.

55. Compare heading in Paul A. Samuelson, *Economics: An Introductory Analysis*, McGraw-Hill, New York, 2d edition, 1951, p. 523: "Monopolies Maintained by Constant Research and Advertising."

56. *Journal of Commerce*, December 29, 1952, p. 10.

57. Backman and Gainsbrugh, *Economics of the Cotton Textile Industry*, p. 207.

conduct research.[58] Prior to World War II the only important textile advertising, that of retail stores, put its stress on low prices.[59] By 1953 Cannon Mills and Burlington were each spending over a million dollars a year on advertising; and some industry men felt that these amounts should be trebled or quadrupled and then matched by other companies. In their view, "underpromotion" was and is the industry's major difficulty.[60]

Criticism of the Mergers

One of the most outspoken critics of the mergers is Solomon Barkin, research director of the United Textile Workers. The evolution of his thinking on the subject is indicated by two of his articles, published seven years apart. In 1949 he wrote:

> These large mills have . . . been at the head of the mill modernization movement. Their mills are among the most modern. Their costs are among the lowest. Their technical efficiency tends to be high. Moreover, they have led in the application of modern managerial techniques to the textile industry.[61]

Although he went on to point out that many mistakes had been made in the application of techniques from other industries, and that mill managements were "learning the hard way," his position on net balance appeared favorable.

After seven more years of observation, his view had changed. Although conceding that the integrations were "able to average out the experiences of different products and markets," he found "only the most modest contributions":

> They have not provided new leadership needed by the industry in the form of a whole host of new products or even offered substantial support for research, either of a fundamental or immediate nature.[62]

He found much else to criticize, including the recent practice of acquiring mills that had a tax-loss credit and then closing them down.

58. *Wall Street Journal*, March 13, 1952, p. 1.

59. Reavis Cox, *The Marketing of Textiles*, Textile Foundation, Washington, 1938, p. 326.

60. *America's Textile Reporter*, March 8, 1956, pp. 36, 40.

61. Solomon Barkin, "The Regional Significance of the Integration Movement in the Southern Textile Industry," *Southern Economic Journal*, April 1949, p. 410.

62. *Idem*, "New Industrial Giants in the Textile Industry," *Analysts Journal*, February 1956, p. 5.

On this point there was agreement from the staff of a congressional committee [63] and from a study group commissioned by the governors of the six New England states.[64]

With regard to the mill closings, the prevailing opinion in the industry (so far as the writer has been able to ascertain) is that New England mills that were losing money were doomed to close in any event — as in the case of the Goodall-Sanford mill in Maine, closed by Burlington, which the previous management had started to liquidate.[65] There is less agreement on the success of the integrations as a whole; but most observers believe they have made more contributions than the union economist will concede. They grant, however, that these are mere beginnings, and that it is too soon to determine the ultimate place of the combinations. Static consumer demand creates obstacles greater than those faced by big firms in many other industries.

Persistence of Smaller Firms

Opinion in the industry supports the view that the small enterprise will continue to hold a significant place. Many feel that, in competition with the individual converter, the integrated mill is likely to suffer from lack of flexibility.[66] It may lose heavily if it guesses wrong on styles with a big production program in progress; and it may do better, therefore, to confine its production to staples. The integrated mill cannot, like the independent, buy distress lots of goods for short runs in the finishing mills. Moreover, if it develops a new and popular product, small firms may copy the product without permission and also without the expense of development.[67]

When a short production run is in question, there is likely to be truth in the optimistic remark that "a good little company can beat a good big company any day, provided both produce the same type of fabric." [68] There is some tendency, therefore, toward a division of labor, with the converter taking the high-style items on short runs and the integrated mills the less stylized and larger quantity lots. One of

63. *The Merger Movement in the Textile Industry,* A Staff Report to Subcommittee No. 5, House Judiciary Committee, 84th Cong., 1st sess., 1955, pp. 32–35.

64. Seymour E. Harris, *New England Textiles and the New England Economy: Report to the Conference of New England Governors,* Boston, February 1956, p. 7.

65. J. Spencer Love, *A Study of the Antitrust Laws,* Senate Hearings, p. 751.

66. Interviews in *America's Textile Reporter,* March 17, 1955, p. 33.

67. J. Spencer Love, *A Study of the Antitrust Laws,* Senate Hearings, p. 739.

68. Saunders, "Burlington Weaves a New Pattern," p. 154.

the largest enterprises recently sold its consumer goods units and retreated to the gray cloth market.[69] Diversification is accepted by all as desirable; but the degree to which vertical integration should be pushed is still very much in dispute.[70]

A notable development of the last sixty years has been the rising importance of the converter, largely as a result of the increased importance of fashion and the consequent need for flexibility in operations. In 1900 there were 85 converters; in 1925, 300; and by 1948, 1,151, including those in synthetics.[71] The share of business done by independent converters has shrunk somewhat since 1940 as mills have established converting departments; but a few of the largest integrations have resumed their converter contacts after attempting to dispense with them.

The ability of most mills to hold their own in this industry in spite of its uneven history is illustrated by the list of cotton mills published annually; the number was slightly larger in 1954 than in 1934.[72]

Competition in Particular Types of Fabric

Thomas M. Stanback, Jr., tabulated from *Davison's Textile Blue Book* for 1947 the number of single-plant and multi-plant firms manufacturing ten important constructions, or types, of cotton cloth. The number of firms ranged from 12 in denims to 92 in sheetings. There were 278 one-plant firms competing with 41 multi-plant mills, and the latter operated 304 plants in these ten fabrics. (See Table 66.)

Although there are many companies making each of these constructions, there might not be enough to constitute "pure" competition except to the extent that firms can adapt their machinery to make another fabric if the price of one gets out of line. The fact that more than half of the mills listed were owned by multi-plant companies was in contrast to the state of the industry twenty years earlier, and the trend has undoubtedly gone much further since 1947.

Stanback found that the only major branches of the industry in which one firm was outstanding in size were fine goods (the present Berkshire Hathaway, Inc.), toweling (Cannon Mills), and both denims

69. *Business Week*, February 14, 1953, p. 64.

70. See twenty-two interviews reported in Cole thesis, pp. 130–90.

71. National Credit Office, *The Converting Industry*.

72. *Davison's Textile Blue Book*, 1934, pp. 1222–52; 1954, pp. 1330–62.

TABLE 66

COTTON TEXTILES: NUMBER OF FIRMS AND MILLS IN EACH TYPE OF FABRIC, 1947

Construction	Number of Multi-plant Firms	Number of Mills Operated by Multi-plant Firms [a]	Number of One-Plant Firms
Total	41 [b]	304	278
Ducks and awning stripes	22	35	30
Osnaburgs [c]	14	16	22
Sheetings (except bed sheetings)	35	59	57
Drills	22	27	25
Plain print cloths	36	67	33
Flannels	16	21	12
Denims	6	8	6
Fine goods	18	37	59
Towels and towelings	15	21	34
Bed sheetings	13	13	0

Source: Davison's Textile Blue Book, 1947, Davison Publishing Co., Ridgewood (N.J.), tabulated in Thomas M. Stanback, Jr., *Short Run Instability in the Cotton Broad Woven Goods Industry, 1946–1951*, unpublished doctoral thesis, Duke University, Durham, 1954, pp. 300–19.

a. Only a few of these multi-plant firms have more than one plant in any single type of cloth named.

b. Calculated by the writer.

c. A rough, strong cloth which goes into such uses as overalls.

and flannels (Cone Mills).[73] If branch of the industry is more narrowly defined, many more branches are dominated by only two or three firms. The research department of the Textile Workers Union supplies a list which includes such products as absorbent cotton (Johnson & Johnson, Kendall Mills) and bedspreads and counterpanes (Bates Manufacturing Company, Cannon Mills).

Interlocking Directorates

The Federal Trade Commission study of interlocking directorates found that of the 85 textile companies among the 1,000 largest manufacturing corporations in 1946, 39 had interlocking directors. In most cases the interlocked companies made different products (e.g., cotton goods and wool carpets, or cotton goods of a different character), but

73. Thomas M. Stanback, Jr., *Short Run Instability in the Cotton Broad Woven Goods Industry, 1946–1951*, unpublished doctoral thesis, Duke University, Durham, 1954, p. 39.

in some instances their production overlapped. "Such interlocks," the Commission concluded, "could hardly fail to have some effect on competition." [74] A great many indirect interlocks also existed, linking two or more textile mills or their factors or selling agents with the same retail outlets, banks, insurance corporations, suppliers (both machine makers and chemical companies), and the like.[75]

If one may judge by the history of the industry, it does not appear that any reduction of competition resulting from these relationships could have been serious. The competition suppressed when two companies making competing products are acquired by the same controlling group is usually minor, the record in cotton textiles shows, compared with what remains.

Trade Associations

A book on the history of cotton manufacture, published in 1912, referred to three trade associations — two in the South and one in Boston — that sometimes made an "attempt" to secure a reduction in output by their members when demand declined.[76] We have noticed the activity of the Cotton Textile Institute in the late 1920s and early 1930s in attempting to achieve the same goal. Reavis Cox, writing in 1938, referred to the existence of more than 300 trade associations in the textile industry as a whole, and found that their principal function was to try to establish rules of convenience and good conduct for their branches of the industry. He felt that their activities were considerably restricted by the danger of being "haled before some public body on charges of unlawful behavior" — the reference evidently being to the antitrust laws.[77]

Another writer, in 1954, mentions the existence of many product, functional and local associations and related groups that are active in public relations, statistical work, and standardization of terms and trade practices. In his view, they have "refrained from active participation in the formulation of price or production policies, and have avoided extensive conflict with the antitrust laws." [78]

74. FTC, *Report on Interlocking Directorates*, 1951, pp. 390, 393.

75. *Ibid.*, pp. 412–13.

76. Copeland, *The Cotton Manufacturing Industry*, pp. 157–58.

77. Cox, *The Marketing of Textiles*, p. 342.

78. Archibald M. McIsaac, "The Cotton Textile Industry," Chap. 2 in Walter Adams, ed., *The Structure of American Industry*, Macmillan, New York, revised edition, 1954, p. 54.

Has Price Behavior Changed?

If the merger movement in textiles has significantly affected competition, the effect should be noticeable in the industry's price behavior. For decades, price competition had been more important in cotton manufacturing than in most other American industries, with changes in demand reflected quickly in corresponding price changes. This has been emphasized by most writers on the economics of the industry in the past.

The probable effect on price competition of the recent merger movement has been discussed by several writers. William Kessler, in 1951, believed that "either because of a realization of past errors or because of the growth of large units in the industry and the high costs of producing for inventory," a decline in demand had resulted in 1949 and 1951, contrary to prewar practice, in a sharp curtailment of production.[79] C. T. Murchison, writing in 1952, felt that it was too soon to measure the contribution of vertical integration, but that this form of organization should work in the direction of price stability; [80] and in 1955 he was still of the same opinion. Archibald McIsaac, in 1954, classified the industry as "monopolistically competitive (in terms of the theoretical classification of market forms), with a low degree of monopoly power, rather than as purely competitive." [81] Solomon Barkin, in 1956, held that "recent improvements in market prices" had shown the "potential capacity" of the mergers for price control.[82]

The argument that the big companies will do less price cutting relies partly on the likelihood that they will be less often short of cash and will thus be able to contract output until a decline in demand has spent its force. Integration has also given the mills a greater knowledge of market conditions, so that they learn sooner of any slackening in demand. Previously the knowledge filtered through converters, brokers and selling houses, and did not reach the mills until overproduction was well under way. It is also said that large firms are more likely to feel a sense of responsibility for the market as a whole, and thus will try to restrain upward as well as downward price movements.[83]

79. William C. Kessler, "An Outline History of the Textile Industry in the United States," p. 39, in E. C. Bancroft, W. H. Crook and William C. Kessler, *Textiles: A Dynamic Industry*, Colgate University, Hamilton (N.Y.), 1951, mimeographed.

80. Murchison, "Vertical Integration in the Cotton Textile Industry," p. 124.

81. McIsaac, "The Cotton Textile Industry," pp. 64–65.

82. Barkin, "New Industrial Giants in the Textile Industry," p. 3.

83. Stanback thesis, pp. 196–97.

Price Variations before and since World War II

Stanback has noted that, for every one of eleven fabrics, price changes were less frequent in 1947–51 than in 1936–41, before the degree of integration was as great. (See Table 67.) He puts much less emphasis on this change than on the continuing, and inherent, instability in the competitive gray goods markets, which comprise about half of all cloth sales. This "spills over" into and thus strongly affects, through buyer substitution and shifting of machinery by producers, the "monopolistically competitive" finished goods markets.[84]

A study by Irwin M. Stelzer compares the number and size of price changes in the periods 1923–29, 1934–40 and 1946–52. The frequency of price changes was practically invariable for print cloth, but declined slightly for sheetings and substantially for denims, while the size of the changes increased for two of the three. (See Table 68.) He concluded that demand shifts are not reflected in price as quickly as before and therefore cause a greater jump when they do become effective.

Stelzer also found that in both the prewar and postwar cycles prices and output changed by about the same percentage, but the fact that prices were first to move in the one prewar downturn in which its turning-point was different from that for output, whereas output moved first on the postwar downturn, led him to conclude that mills now have greater control over their prices. The fact that prices and mill margins were falling during the year 1928, while mills were stepping up their production in an attempt to maintain their profits, seemed to him a characteristic reaction under pure competition. (See Table 69.)

Evidence of Continuing Price Competition

To check these suggestions that prices may have been stabilized by the merger movement, a statistical analysis was made for the present study. The extent to which the average price of seventeen constructions of unfinished cloth, and the mill margins on the same constructions, declined during the short (usually two-year) downward cycles in mill production was tabulated for the period since first publication of these prices and margins. The results were as follows:

In the prewar period, cloth prices declined further than production three out of six times and mill margins four out of six. In the postwar

84. *Ibid.*, pp. 138, 183–86, 187, 209.

TABLE 67

COTTON TEXTILES: FREQUENCY OF PRICE CHANGES, 1936–41 AND 1947–51

(Per Cent of Months in Which Price Changed)

Construction	1936–41	1947–51
Average of 17 unfinished goods [a]		77.2
Average of 6 unfinished goods	90.8 [b]	75.8 [b]
Print cloth	99	98
Sheeting	96	93
Twill	96	75
Osnaburg	93	76
Drill	93	63
Duck	68	50
Average of 9 finished goods [a]		47.7
Average of 5 finished goods	60.0 [b]	35.0 [b]
Bed ticking	76	44
Denim	69	32
Flannel	65	41
Gingham	51	34
Toweling	39	24

Source: U.S. Bureau of Labor Statistics price quotations tabulated in Thomas M. Stanback, Jr., *Short Run Instability in the Cotton Broad Woven Goods Industry, 1946–1951*, unpublished doctoral thesis, Duke University, Durham, 1954, pp. 73–75, 90–91.

a. These groups include products for which 1936–41 figures are not available.

b. The difference between price variability of finished and gray goods increased in 1947–51, but this is probably not significant. Stanback, in fact, presents the figures differently and interprets the trend as being the opposite (p. 92).

TABLE 68

COTTON TEXTILES: FREQUENCY AND AMOUNT OF PRICE CHANGES, 1923–52

	Print Cloth		Sheetings		Denim	
Years	Number of Changes	Average Percentage Change	Number of Changes	Average Percentage Change	Number of Changes	Average Percentage Change
1923–29	76	3.6	69	3.4	58	2.8
1934–40	75	4.2	70	4.1	53	3.2
1946–52	74	5.5	58	4.0	28	3.7

Source: Number of changes calculated from figures in Irwin M. Stelzer, *The Cotton Textile Industry*, unpublished doctoral thesis, Cornell University, Ithaca, 1954, pp. 116–19. His original source was the *Survey of Current Business* and correspondence with the Department of Commerce. Changes are between monthly averages, and therefore understate the actual numbers of changes. The average percentage change was obtained by the present writer by dividing the average change in each period by the average price for that period.

TABLE 69

COTTON TEXTILES: CYCLICAL CHANGES IN PRICE AND PRODUCTION, 1927–51

(*Per Cent*)

Cycle Periods	First to Move	Production	Unfinished Cloth Prices, 17 Constructions
Prewar			
Jan.–Mar. 1929 to Apr.–June 1932	Price	− 46	
Oct.–Dec. 1927 to Jan.–Mar. 1933			− 60
Apr.–June 1932 to Jan.–Mar. 1937	Output	+107	
Jan.–Mar. 1933 to Jan.–Mar. 1937			+127
Jan.–Mar. 1937 to Apr.–June 1938	Neither	− 40	
Jan.–Mar. 1937 to Apr.–June 1939			− 40
Apr.–June 1938 to Apr.–June 1942	Output	+128	
Apr.–June 1939 to Apr.–June 1942			+112
Postwar			
Jan.–Mar. 1947 to Apr.–June 1949	Output	− 33	
Oct.–Dec. 1947 to Apr.–June 1949			− 36
Apr.–June 1949 to Jan.–Mar. 1951	Neither	+ 36	
Apr.–June 1949 to Jan.–Mar. 1951			+ 37

Source: Survey of Current Business, as used by Irwin M. Stelzer, in *The Cotton Textile Industry*, unpublished doctoral thesis, Cornell University, Ithaca, 1954, p. 123. Production is measured by mill consumption of cotton.

period, prices declined further than production two out of three times, and margins all three times.

In the four out of six prewar downward production cycles in which the price of raw cotton also declined, cloth prices declined less than cotton prices in two cycles and more in two cycles. In the postwar period cloth prices declined more than twice as much as cotton prices on both occasions that cotton prices declined.

These figures tend to rebut the hypothesis that the integration movement since World War II has given the mills greater power to control downward movements of gray goods prices. (See Table 70.)

Further Comments on Cotton Textile Prices

On net balance, the evidence in the several tables supports the position that the signs of diminution of price competition in the gray goods market as a result of the merger movement are not yet convincing. This is also the opinion of most of the industry executives who

TABLE 70

COTTON TEXTILES: PRICE CHANGES DURING DOWNWARD CYCLES IN COTTON CONSUMPTION, 1925–54

(*Per Cent*)

Downward Cycle Periods [a]	Mill Consumption of Cotton	Price of Raw Cotton, Wholesale Middling	Unfinished Cloth Prices, 17 Constructions	Mill Margin, 17 Constructions	Ratio of Drop of Cloth Prices to Drop in Cotton Consumption	Ratio of Drop of Mill Margins to Drop in Cotton Consumption	Ratio of Drop of Cloth Prices to Drop of Raw Cotton Price
Prewar							
Dec. 1925 to July 1926	−12.9	−13.1	−16.4	−23.6	127	183	125
June 1927 to July 1928	−21.3	+ 5.3	+ 2.5	−19.6		92	
May 1929 to Aug. 1930	−39.8	−45.1	−28.0	−10.4	70	26	62
July 1931 to July 1932	−24.4	−41.2	−34.6	−32.8	142	134	84
June 1933 to June 1935	−34.0	+52.0	− 6.2	−42.4	18	125	
June 1937 to Apr. 1938	−30.1	−35.3	−36.3	−37.3	121	124	103
Postwar							
Feb. 1948 to June 1949	−35.3	− 9.1	−39.6	−56.8	112	161	436
Feb. 1951 to June 1952	−27.7	−14.5	−32.2	−50.2	116	182	222
Mar. 1953 to June 1954	−19.6	+ 2.0	− 9.3	−22.6	47	115	

Sources: Cotton consumption from *Survey of Current Business;* prices from U.S. Department of Agriculture, *Prices of Cotton Cloth and Raw Cotton and Mill Margins for Certain Constructions of Unfinished Cloth, 1925–52*, February 1953, p. 10, and annual supplements since.

a. The prewar months are those selected by Bert G. Hickman, in *Cyclical Fluctuations in the Cotton Textile Industry*, unpublished doctoral thesis, University of California at Berkeley, 1951, pp. 104–05, as cited in Thomas M. Stanback, Jr., *Short Run Instability in the Cotton Broad Woven Goods Industry, 1946–1951*, unpublished doctoral thesis, Duke University, Durham, 1954, p. 9. The postwar months named are the mid-months of the quarters which mark peaks and troughs of cycles in cotton consumption by mills, but the figures given are monthly averages for the quarter (for both prewar and postwar periods). The price and margin figures are the highest or lowest, depending on whether it is a peak or a trough in production, of any month in the same quarter. For both prewar and postwar cycles, the choices here differ slightly from those used in Table 69. The 1946–47 downturn is omitted because price movements in late 1946 were distorted by the expiration of wartime price ceilings.

were interviewed on the subject. Remarks from these quarters of the kind that used to be heard in the 1930s still recur: "Mill margins have all but disappeared"; [85] and "We all thought when the mills got into stronger hands that prices would be more stable. The opposite is true now." [86] A letter from a fabric buyer for a large chain is typical: "This is an industry where competition is savage, and the current mergers are not of sufficient scope to interfere with the operation of a free market."

Comments sixteen years apart by two research organizations that have analyzed the industry are both appropriate today. According to a committee of academic and industry authorities that studied textile prices in the late 1930s:

> . . . within the bounds of the textile industries may be found examples of virtually every kind of price mentioned in modern economic literature, including all shades of competitive and non-competitive prices, and of so-called flexible and inflexible prices.[87]

An investment advisory service reflects the consensus of informed opinion:

> As a result of the merger movement, the industry is considerably less disorganized than in former years, but competition remains extremely keen and the tendency to overproduce whenever demand improves is likely to continue.[88]

Interindustry Competition

In few if any areas of consumption is interindustry competition stronger than in textiles. Consumers always had a choice of cotton and wool for some sorts of clothing and household uses; but a keener competition was introduced by the rayon industry in the 1920s and by the chemical industry with its synthetic fibers in the 1940s. In 1923 cotton comprised 86.1 per cent of total textile consumption by weight (exclusive of jute, an important competitor in the bag field), wool 11.7 per

85. *America's Textile Reporter*, July 22, 1954, p. 13.

86. *Ibid.*, March 17, 1955, p. 33.

87. Stephen J. Kennedy, Chairman, and Hiram S. Davis, Arthur R. Burns, Alfred Cahen and James G. Torrens, *Textile Markets: Their Structure in Relation to Price Research*, Report of the Committee on Textile Price Research to the Conference on Price Research, National Bureau of Economic Research Price Studies No. 2, New York, 1939, p. xii.

88. Standard & Poor's Corp., *Industry Surveys*, "Textiles and Apparel," Basic Analysis, June 30, 1955, p. T2–10.

TABLE 71

COTTON TEXTILES: SHARE OF TOTAL TEXTILE CONSUMPTION, 1923–55

Year	Total, Per Capita [a]	Cotton	Wool	Silk	Rayon and Acetate	Other Synthetic Fibers
	(Pounds)			*(Per Cent)*		
1923	32.6	86.1	11.7	1.3	0.9	—
1927	34.8	87.2	8.6	1.8	2.4	—
1931	26.0	82.9	9.7	2.4	5.0	—
1935	27.6	78.8	11.9	1.8	7.4	—
1939	34.8	80.1	8.8	1.0	10.1	—
1943	48.4	79.9	9.6	—	9.9	0.6
1946	46.0	74.2	11.4	0.1	13.5	0.8
1947	44.5	72.8	11.0	—	15.4	0.8
1948	43.6	69.8	11.0	0.1	18.0	1.1
1949	36.4	70.6	9.4	0.1	18.3	1.7
1950	45.0	68.5	9.5	0.1	19.8	2.1
1951	44.3	71.1	7.3	0.1	18.7	2.9
1952	40.9	69.5	7.5	0.1	19.0	3.9
1953	40.7	69.2	7.7	0.1	18.7	4.3
1954	37.0	68.7	6.5	0.1	19.2	5.5
1955	40.4	65.7	6.4	0.1	21.3	6.5

Sources: Percentages calculated from U.S. Department of Agriculture data tabulated in *Textile Organon*, March 1956, p. 42; column 1 from *Cotton Textile Hi-Lights*, private publication of American Cotton Manufacturers Institute, Charlotte, April 1956, p. 24.

a. The 1922–24 average was 30.2 pounds. This column includes about 0.1 pounds of flax per capita each year.

cent, silk 1.3 per cent, and rayon 0.9 per cent. After various fluctuations, cotton's share in 1955 was only 65.7 per cent, that of wool 6.4 per cent, silk 0.1 per cent, rayon (including acetate) 21.3 per cent, and other synthetic fibers 6.5 per cent. (See Table 71.)

A subcommittee of the House of Representatives Committee on Agriculture, in 1947, attributed "nearly all" the decrease in cotton consumption since 1939 to the inroads of rayon, made possible by an aggressive research program which improved its quality, lowered the cost of production and therefore the price, and adapted it to various new uses.[89] A few years later the share of rayon (and acetate) in textile

89. *Study of Agricultural and Economic Problems of the Cotton Belt*, Hearings before Special Subcommittee on Cotton of House Agriculture Committee, 80th Cong., 1st sess., 1947, Project 4, pp. 267–73, cited in Jesse W. Markham, *Competition in the Rayon Industry*, Harvard University Press, Cambridge, 1952, pp. 167–68. See also Cyril O'Donnell, "Recent Trends in the Demand for American Cotton," *Journal of Business of the University of Chicago*, January 1945, Supplement.

markets had been stabilized, and profits were suffering from over-expansion due to false expectations of a continuing increase. Du Pont's nylon, Dacron and Orlon were the new fast movers. Cotton was making a very good comeback through effective styling, aggressive promotion, and such technical improvements as a new resistance to creasing and shrinking. By this time the cutters were accustomed to experimenting with and employing blends of the fibers in various end uses to which they were best suited, and the producers of each fiber had to be on their toes to hold their own. Other competitors in the same broad market are plastics (for table linen, automobile seat covers, window shades and other uses), paper (for bags) and glass fibers.

The improvement of synthetic fibers has helped cotton manufacturing in one respect — by making it possible for mills to fabricate synthetics or cotton or blends of both on the same machines. Some firms even weave rayon cloth one year and cotton cloth the next, depending on the market.[90] Moreover, the addition of synthetic fibers has undoubtedly increased the over-all sale of textiles. Total fiber consumption increased by 87 per cent between 1922–24 and 1952–54, and per capita consumption by 31 per cent. The rise in dollar value of textiles sold to the consumer has, however, lagged far behind other goods in recent years. The share of total consumer expenditures going for "clothing and accessories except footwear," which was 9.5 per cent in 1929 and 10.4 per cent in 1946 (when wardrobes were being replenished after World War II), declined every year thereafter without exception, to a new low of 6.6 per cent in 1955.[91] The battle of textiles against other forms of expenditure was no less grueling than that of cotton against other textiles.

Performance of the Industry

The cotton textile industry led the industrial revolution in England in the eighteenth century, earning a bad reputation because of child labor and long hours of work along with a good one for abundance of output. It dropped out of the list of "glamor" industries — such as railroads, mining, electricity, automobiles, petroleum and chemicals — which successively carried on the industrial revolution in the nineteenth and twentieth centuries. One authority declared in 1936 that

90. Markham, *Competition in the Rayon Industry*, p. 34, note 155, and p. 166.

91. *Survey of Current Business*, National Income editions.

there had been no important technological development in cotton textiles between 1900 and the late 1920s.[92] It seemed as though the original rapid advance had left the industry less scope for improvement.[93]

Man-hour output did increase by 77 per cent between 1921 and 1944;[94] but this rise was a good deal slower than the rate in most other manufacturing industries. The high profits earned from 1941 to 1948 enabled the large firms to step up such progress and to modernize their machinery and finishing processes.[95] Air conditioning, electronic controls, automatic winders, mechanical conveyors, high-speed looms and spindles and combers, and other devices were installed. In 1950 American yarn output per spindle was more than seven times that of the United Kingdom.[96] In 1955 textile machinery purchases were four and a half times the dollar value of 1929 and three times that of 1941.[97]

A recent writer concludes that "the relative lack of technical advance in the cotton textile industry is due to the industry's market structure"; but that "the present situation in cotton textiles — large firms with funds for research, and the competition of smaller but vigorous competitors to keep them alert and forward looking — may perhaps turn out to be the most conducive to rapid advance." [98]

Although the industry has not been in the loss column since before World War II, its earnings are still low. In 1953 and 1954 the return on net book assets of thirty-five cotton manufacturing companies was only 6.9 and 3.6 per cent, respectively, as against 12.7 and 12.4 per cent for 1,778 manufacturing corporations.[99] The low level of wages in the industry compared to those paid elsewhere in manufacturing is evidently related to this low level of profits as well as to the general wage level in the South. If wages in that region had not been relatively low initially, the industry's function of bringing industrialization

92. Stephen Jay Kennedy, *Profits and Losses in Textiles*, Harper, New York, 1936, p. 161.

93. Stanley Vance, *American Industries*, Prentice-Hall, New York, 1955, p. 438.

94. Backman and Gainsbrugh, *Economics of the Cotton Textile Industry*, p. 188.

95. Wilfrid H. Crook, Introduction, p. 1, in Bancroft, Crook and Kessler, *Textiles: A Dynamic Industry*.

96. Edward L. Allen, *Economics of American Manufacturing*, Henry Holt, New York, 1952, p. 375.

97. Index published monthly in *Textile World*.

98. Irwin M. Stelzer, "Technological Progress and Market Structure," *Southern Economic Journal*, July 1956, pp. 72, 73.

99. First National City Bank of New York, Monthly Letter, April 1955, p. 40. In 1955 the classification "Cotton textiles" was dropped in this source in favor of "Textile products."

to the South and thus pushing up the whole wage level there could not have been accomplished.

Finally, it may be assumed that the low level of profits is of some benefit to the consumer in assuring relatively low consumer prices.

SUMMARY

1. The cotton textile industry is one characterized by a *relatively low degree of concentration.* The fifteen largest producers, several of which make other textiles as well, account for only about 30 or 35 per cent of employees or sales.

2. *Antitrust suits* in any branch of the industry have been few and unimportant. The most important was probably the first, which in 1914 directed the two leading thread manufacturers to cancel agreements with each other. These two companies are still the principal producers. In labels in 1917, book cloth in 1918 and 1953, airplane fabric and print cloth in 1940, and twine in 1951, companies accepted consent decrees or pleaded *nolo contendere* to charges of restraining trade. In the more important shirting cloth branch of the industry, a group of converters and some others agreed in 1928 not to pursue their attempt to boycott finishing operations which bypassed them; but this type of operation has remained insignificant.

3. An interesting episode was the effort of the Cotton Textile Institute after 1926, and especially under the National Recovery Administration, to prevent spasmodic overproduction by putting a ceiling on the *hours of machine operation.* These attempts to prevent cutthroat competition, which was driving down both prices and wages, failed. This was partly because the permitted two shifts of 40 hours each were nevertheless enough, if spread throughout the industry, to support an excessive output. The final straw was the withdrawal of legal protection to this plan when the National Recovery Administration disappeared, as a result of which print cloth executives were prosecuted for their brief curtailment in 1939. Today the machine-hour average is far above what it was at that time; but the demand is much higher also.

4. The *reasons for cutthroat competition,* which prevailed in the industry from 1924 through 1939, were: (a) ease of entry, due to relatively low capital requirements and to the frequently standardized product; (b) the resulting large number of firms in relation to the size of the market, and overcapacity following each period of high demand, with a corresponding willingness to cut prices without regard to the effect on rivals; (c) ignorance by mills of conditions in the ultimate market and lack of communication through the layers of intermediary firms; (d) the shift from New England to the lower labor costs of the South, which resulted in duplication of capacity; and (e) spread of two- and three-shift operations, which added to effective capacity.

5. The industry achieved a *considerable improvement after 1940*, for two fundamental reasons. The long years of price competition had at last brought their own remedy in the form of elimination of enough capacity from the industry to make it possible for the remaining companies to earn money. Secondly, demand recovered sharply with the revival of national business activity, and during and since World War II has run, despite fluctuations, far above earlier levels.

6. Although large mills have *economies of scale* in the manufacture of unfinished cloth, the relative efficiency of different sizes of firms at different levels of the industry is still being determined in the market place.

7. There has been a recent sharp *trend toward greater concentration*. Between 1937 and 1955 the share of the four largest firms in total spindles increased from 5 to about 17 per cent.

8. The *merger movement* in textiles had its beginnings before World War I, progressed in the 1920s and 1930s under the impact of the intense competition of that period, but became especially significant during and after World War II, reaching its peak in 1954 and 1955. Mergers have offered the advantages of (a) integration closer to the ultimate market; (b) diversification among the various textiles; and (c) enough capital to adopt modern management methods, including research and advertising.

9. Despite the advantages of the integrated companies, *converters and other smaller firms* have offsetting advantages, which many feel will permit them to retain their place in the industry.

10. *Concentration in particular fabrics* is naturally much greater than in the industry as a whole, and many of them are dominated by two or three producers. However, in 1947 there were between 12 and 92 firms in each of ten important lines of product.

11. Although *interlocking directorates* and financial relationships connect many textile firms, these are rarely firms that make the same types of cloth. Even when they are, the amount of competition thus prevented is only a small part of the total in existence.

12. There were attempts by earlier *trade associations* to prevent overproduction, but such organizations today are not known to function in the area of price or production policies.

13. The effects of the merger movement on *price behavior* are not clear. It was expected to make gray goods prices less responsive to movements in demand, and some of the available statistics give support to this view. Other data contradict it, however, and one cannot conclude that any real change has occurred in the competitiveness of most markets for unfinished cloth.

14. *Competition with substitutes* such as other textile fibers, plastics and paper is of increasing importance for the cotton industry. It has not prevented the consumption of cotton from reaching new high levels as part of the general

growth of the textile industry; but in dollar terms textiles have lagged in the growth of the economy.

15. The *performance* of the industry in this century has not been "glamorous" like the record of automobiles or chemicals, and both profits and wages have been low. These low labor costs, however, are in part a reflection of low wage rates in the South. Entry by the cotton textile industry in that region paved the way for other industries such as chemicals and paper. Presumably the consumer has benefited from the low profits.

In brief, the antitrust laws have had little influence on the cotton textile industry in view of its structure of many small firms; this same structure made it for a long time a "sick industry," but it improved after 1940 by discarding machinery and because of revived demand; and there is a good chance, though far from a certainty, that the integration movement will transform it into an industry like others in the United States today — progressive and profitable.